NATIONAL GEOGRAPHIC KiDS

INFOPEDIA 2017

A mountain gorilla mother watches toddlers play in a bamboo forest in Parc National des Volcans, Rwanda.

NATIONAL GEOGRAPHIC
KiDS

INFOPEDIA 2017

NATIONAL GEOGRAPHIC
WASHINGTON, D.C.

NATIONAL GEOGRAPHIC KiDS

Welcome to the *National Geographic Kids Infopedia 2017!*

If you love adventures, fun, puzzles and games, this is the book for you!

Infopedia 2017 is bursting with all the fun stories and fascinating facts that you'll find each month in *National Geographic Kids* magazine—from amazing animals and extreme adventures to prehistoric monsters, spectacular space, wild weather, marvellous maps and incredible inventions.

Get ready to explore your world with exciting chapters including Wonders of Nature, Super Science, Going Green, Awesome Adventures and Culture Connection. Plus, there's a bumper fun-and-games section that's packed with riddles, jokes and comics.

Crammed with cool photographs and facts, the *National Geographic Kids Infopedia 2017* is the perfect read for kids who want to know about everything—and more. So what are you waiting for? Get ready to explore!

Tim Herbert
Editor, *National Geographic Kids* magazine

If you enjoy the *Infopedia 2017*, look out for *National Geographic Kids* magazine—it's jam-packed with adventure and fun every month!!

To subscribe for the special price of just £30 for 12 issues*, go to www.ngkids.co.uk or call 0844 322 1213** and quote the reference NGKINFO17.

*Regular price £39.60 for 12 issues.
**Call charged at standard rate from a BT landline.

Contents

Your World 2017

8

Amazing Animals

18

Going Green

80

Culture Connection

96

Awesome Adventure

122

Fun and Games

142

Super Science

162

Wonders of Nature

198

History Happens

222

Geography Rocks

254

The results are in!
Who Stepped Up to the
Plate to Fight Food Waste
in 2016? See page 89.

Want to become part of the
2017 Almanac Newsmaker Challenge?
Go to page 105 to find out more.

BepiColombo, a European Space Agency mission to check out the planet Mercury in collaboration with the Japanese space agency, JAXA, is scheduled to launch in early 2017. Composed of two orbiters and a carrier spacecraft, it is scheduled to reach Mercury in 2024.

SCIENTISTS IN DISGUISE

For these animal researchers, playing dress-up is part of the job.

A t China's Wolong National Nature Reserve, a pair of large pandas gently tend to a tiny cub, first easing it onto a scale and then checking its temperature as a part of a physical examination. But look closely and you'll see that those aren't giant pandas examining their young—they're actually humans wearing fuzzy costumes. It's a funny scene, for sure, but these researchers are working to collect valuable data while minimizing the animal's stress and human attachment.

WILD PLAY

At this Chinese center in particular, where pandas are bred in captivity with the hopes of returning them to the wild, experts wear the costumes to help the animals acclimate to life on their own. The less obvious human interaction, they believe, the better equipped the cub will be to survive in the wild. And scientists don't stop at the costume: Researchers also sprinkle themselves with panda poop and pee to mask their human scent.

OTHER CLEVER COSTUMES

But it's not just panda people who play dress up. In Wyoming, U.S.A., a pair of scientists once donned moose suits created by a Star Wars designer to track the animal's interaction with natural predators, while employees at a whooping crane center in Wisconsin, U.S.A., use bird-shaped hand puppets to feed hatchlings. While these methods may seem fun for the humans involved, they are a necessary step to help the animals.

Battling DROUGHT

CALIFORNIA, U.S.A., is suffering its worst drought on record. And experts have come up with some clever and creative approaches to battle this devastating dry spell. One such solution? Turning the Los Angeles Reservoir into a giant ball pit. By filling the reservoir with millions of "shade balls"— four-inch (10-cm) black plastic spheres that provide shade to the water, reducing evaporation—experts expect to conserve up to 300 million gallons (1.1 billion L) of water each year. Meanwhile, other places in California are doing their part to save water. Dodger Stadium in Los Angeles has turned to low-flush toilets, while Exposition Park has removed some of its lush green lawns in favor of drought-tolerant plants and reduced watering times. Important steps in saving water—and, hopefully, securing the future of the state.

Meet Sparklemuffin
and Skeletorus

These two spiders are sure to make you squeal ... with delight. Recently discovered in Australia, these two tiny peacock spiders—a species named for the "fan" on the male's abdomen that looks similar to the brightly colored bird's plumage—have unusual, bold markings. But that's not all that makes these spiders stand out: They dance, too! To get a female's attention, male peacock spiders perform a mesmerizing mating display, doing everything from a one-legged leg boogie to an elaborate tail wiggle. So even if you're afraid of arachnids, you have to admit that these crawlers are more cool than creepy.

SKELETORUS

SPARKLEMUFFIN

LETTUCE IN SPACE

Traveling in outer space and craving a salad? No problem! NASA has revealed that it has been able to grow lettuce in the harsh, microgravity environment of space. In fact, astronauts recently munched on leaves of red romaine—the first food to be both harvested and consumed by NASA astronauts on the International Space Station. But this experiment (nicknamed "Veggie" by NASA) isn't just about getting astronauts to eat healthier. It's a push towards creating a more sustainable spacecraft, so that astronauts onboard can have access to fresh food. That's especially essential on lengthy deep space trips, like the planned mission to Mars set for some time in the 2030s.

Edible CUPS

YOU CAN EAT THIS CUP!

Why toss that cup away when you can eat it? To combat the worldwide issue of excess waste (the typical person in a developed country produces about 2.6 pounds [1.2 kg] of garbage a day), companies are coming up with eco-friendly edible cups and tableware. With flavors like vanilla bean and tart cherry, Loliware cups are made from seaweed, organic sweeteners, and flavors from fruit and vegetables. Or, you can sip milk in a crunchy cookie mug, which doubles as a sweet treat once you're down to the last drop. In Japan, one company sells edible dishes made of shrimp, salt, and potato starch that it hopes will be served at the 2020 Olympic Games in Tokyo. Soon you just may be able to clean your plate—and eat it, too.

New Human Ancestor
DISCOVERED

LEE BERGER
EXAMINES
A JAWBONE.

What began as an adventurous caving trip in the Rising Star cave near Johannesburg, South Africa, turned into a major archaeological discovery for a pair of spelunkers. In the cave, their eyes locked on what looked like human bones in the sediment below. They quickly snapped pictures and sent them to Lee Berger, a paleoanthropologist and a National Geographic Explorer who had been doing research in the area. Sensing that the cavers' sighting was significant, Berger launched an excavation that required a team of "underground astronauts"—highly qualified scientists small enough to slide through supernarrow passageways in order to reach the thousands of bones more than 100 feet (30.5 m) below.

The harrowing recovery process was worth it: Berger's squad eventually unearthed *Homo naledi*, a previously unidentified species of early humans. The discovery of these ancient fossils has been applauded around the world as it potentially gets us one step closer to truly understanding the beginnings of humankind.

Kermit's Twin

DIANE'S
BARE-
HEARTED
GLASS
FROG

Kermit the Frog has a double! Scientists recently discovered a real-life frog that resembles the famous character from the Muppets. Found in eastern Costa Rica's forests, the one-inch (2.5-cm)-long amphibian is named Diane's bare-hearted glass frog. Like other glass frogs, it has see-through skin covering its belly. The amphibian's back is lime-green, which helps the frog blend into its environment. And rather than croaking, this hopper whistles. Because of the frog's Kermit-like looks, it's winning many human fans. That makes it a little bit easier to be green!

13

DOG SCREEN TIME

Sure, your dog is smart. But your pup may be more perceptive than you even realize—especially when it comes to watching TV. A recent study shows that most dogs can recognize onscreen images of other dogs as they would in real life and actually pay attention to whatever they're watching. This discovery is even linked to programs and channels made just for canines. (DOGTV, for example, shows images of pooches playing in grassy fields or shots of dogs surfing in southern California, U.S.A.) So is it OK to let your pet park it in front of the TV? Experts say that a little screen time here and there is OK—but a walk outside is still the best type of doggie entertainment, paws down.

HOT MOVIES in 2017*

STAR WARS

TOY STORY 4

DESPICABLE ME 3

- **Star Wars: Episode VIII**
- **Despicable Me 3**
- **LEGO Batman Movie**
- **Toy Story 4**
- **The Croods 2**
- **Get Smurfy**

*Release dates and titles are subject to change.

Camera Ball

The Throwable Panoramic Ball Camera really gets the big picture. The ball's surface is embedded with 36 tiny cameras that snap simultaneously to create a 360-degree panoramic image. Chuck the ball into the air and the cameras automatically capture what's happening in all directions. Upload the images to your smartphone, tablet, or computer, and a software program weaves all the photos together to make one big image. Small and lightweight, it's tough enough to survive a drop if you don't catch it on the way down. Heads up!

THE BALL TOOK THIS PHOTO!

Cat's Meow
What kind of tunes are music to your cat's ears?

Turns out it's not calming classical—rather, it's the sound of other cats. Scientists from the University of Wisconsin-Madison say that while cats typically ignore music made for humans, they become more at ease while listening to rhythms imitating purrs and the suckling sounds of kittens nursing. One musician has even recorded an album where he layered such sounds with melodies from a cello, creating soothing songs that are made for both feline and human listening pleasure. The ideal end result? That these tunes can help calm skittish shelter cats or anxious kitties left home alone. Scaredy cats, no more.

BACKYARD BEATS

Better known by his stage name, DJ Ecotone, Ben Mirin is a sound artist and DJ who travels the world composing music from the sounds of nature—a career that includes hosting the Web show *Wild Beats* on National Geographic Kids, and being named the 2016 Artist in Residence at the Wildlife Conservation Society and New York's Bronx Zoo. From squawks to moos and even his own voice, he really gets the animal world rocking. Why all the noise? Ben wants to make music that inspires conservation and engages people with the natural world. Now that's something to tune in to!

15

Cool Events in 2017

International Tiger Day

Sport your stripes today as you show love—and raise awareness—for these beloved (and endangered) big cats.

July 29

Inauguration Day

The new AMERICAN PRESIDENT is sworn in on the steps of the U.S. Capitol building.

January 20

Gilroy Garlic Festival

Taking place in Gilroy, California, U.S.A., it's one of the world's largest (and smelliest!) food festivals. Why not try the garlic ice cream?

Late July

World Puppetry Day

Talk to the hand! Puppets get their time to shine today as we celebrate the mastery of this art form.

March 21

Amazon Day

Make some noise! Honor the Amazon—the world's largest rain forest—today.

September 5

Star Wars Day

May the *fourth* be with you! Celebrate all things from a galaxy far, far away today.

May 4

World Teacher Day

Honor the COOLEST PERSON in school today.

October 5

Yorkshire Pudding Boat Race

In this wacky race, held in North Yorkshire, UK, competitors paddle across a pond in—you guessed it—GIANT YORKSHIRE PUDS!

Usually in June

Punkin Chunkin World Championships

Using catapults, air cannons, and more, competitors in Delaware, U.S.A., attempt to launch their pumpkins THE FARTHEST.

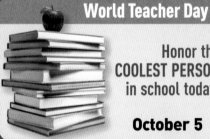

Early November

3

PYGMY SEAHORSE

Among seahorses, it's the males who carry the pair's eggs in a kangaroo-like pouch. When the babies hatch, they gallop out of the pouch in a wild herd of mini seahorses, with the smallest species only half an inch (1.5 cm) tall.

4

DIK-DIK

One of the smallest ungulates (animals with toed hooves, such as buffalo and deer), the dik-dik is a tiny antelope. It lives in parts of Africa with dense cover, where it's easy to find food, keep cool, and hide from predators such as lions and leopards.

5

WALLY THE BUNNY

Wally, an English Angora rabbit, is quite the funny bunny! With adorably giant ears and fur trimmed like a poodle, this famous rabbit has an Instagram account with more than 206,000 followers.

6

WHITE TERN

A white tern's mother balances her eggs on a tree branch or ledge, so these tropical birds are placed in a precarious perch as soon as they're born. Luckily, their strong feet help to keep a grip on things.

7

PATRICK THE WOMBAT

If wombats could talk, Patrick would have plenty of tales to tell! At over 30 years old and 79 pounds (36 kg), Patrick is believed to be the oldest and largest wombat living in captivity.

8

AMERICAN ALLIGATOR

Born at 6 to 8 inches (15 to 20 cm) long, a male baby alligator can grow to be about 11 feet (3.5 m) long and can weigh half a ton (453 kg).

9

STRIPED SKUNK

A wild skunk's ability to hit a target with its stinky spray doesn't come easy. Young skunks practice their moves by picking a target, stomping their feet, threatening with their tails, and letting out little toots.

10

SAND CAT

This rare, fluffy-faced feline lives wild in parts of Africa and Asia. Its soft coat provides camouflage and keeps it warm at night and cool during the day. A great sense of hearing helps this cat hunt for gerbils, reptiles, and insects.

11

KINKAJOU

The kinkajou looks like a little monkey but is actually related to the raccoon. This little mammal loves to slurp honey from beehives with its long, skinny tongue, earning it the nickname "honey bear." How sweet!

12 RED-EYED TREE FROG

When a hungry snake approaches a sleeping frog, one flash of its bright red eyes can startle the predator. Then, the frog can safely hop away.

13 DWARF FLYING SQUIRREL

With an elastic membrane between its forelegs and hind legs stretched out like a cape, this tiny flying squirrel flies from tree to tree to seek out seeds, fruits, and leaves.

14 AMERICAN PIKA

The American pika may look like a big mouse, but it's more closely related to the rabbit. As a baby, these animals are about as big as a walnut, and adults grow to be about as big as a baseball.

15 MOUNTAIN GORILLA

Young mountain gorillas spend their days having fun: climbing trees, chasing each other, and swinging from branches. This gentle species lives within family units and eats a mostly vegetarian diet.

16

PUDSEY

Give this pooch a bone! After winning *Britain's Got Talent* along with his human, Ashleigh, the dancing dog has starred in his own movie and even wrote an "autobi-*dog*-raphy" about his rise to fame.

17

LUNA THE SEA OTTER

Despite being abandoned on a California, U.S.A., beach at just one week old and weighing only two pounds (1 kg), Luna has made a remarkable recovery. Now living in an aquarium in Chicago, Illinois, U.S.A., the lively otter loves to play with everything from plastic toys to ice cubes.

ANIMAL RASCALS

(5) mischief-makers you'll never forget

Do you know people who are clever or sneaky, who enjoy pulling crazy pranks or fooling you? Sometimes animals exhibit this same type of behavior. See for yourself with these five stories about animal tricksters.

1

UP AND OVER

One day, Mavis Knight, of Toronto, Canada, spots a raccoon on her garage roof. From there the raccoon climbs a nearby tree until he reaches the utility lines. Then he stands up on the bottom of the wire, holds the top one, and sidesteps across—all the way to a neighbor's backyard. A week later, he does it again.

Why? A tall, wooden fence separates the properties. Instead of taking time to run around the barrier, this furry daredevil has found a quicker "highway" over the top. "He's very clever," Knight says. "I'm no longer angry at him. I just enjoy him." It's like having front-row seats at the circus.

A RACCOON USES A HIGH WIRE TO GET FROM YARD TO YARD.

2

PULLING TEETH

Bill Exner of Waterville, Maine, U.S.A., is eating a peanut butter sandwich in bed when he gets sleepy. So he takes out his false teeth, sets them on the nightstand, and falls asleep.

The next morning, his teeth are gone! He searches under the bed and behind the dressers. No pearly whites. Then, Exner remembers seeing a mouse near his bed the night before. He pries off the baseboard, shines a flashlight into the space behind the wall, and ... aha! Exner spots his dentures—safe and licked clean. He livetraps two sneaky little mice, then releases them on a college campus. Luckily, it's not a law school.

GONE FISHIN'

Bailey the Labrador retriever has eaten something he shouldn't. "His owners see it poking out behind his rib cage, but they don't know what it is," says Gary Sloniker, a veterinarian in Spooner, Wisconsin, U.S.A. The vet takes the dog in for an x-ray. What do they see? A 24-inch (61-cm) ice-fishing pole!

Sloniker thinks Bailey was chewing the handle when he stretched his neck, making the pole slide right into the puppy's mouth. His swallowing reflex kicked in, and down it went.

The vet reaches down Bailey's throat with long-handled tweezers and "fishes" out the hookless pole.

THIS X-RAY OF BAILEY'S INNARDS SHOWS THE ICE-FISHING POLE HE SWALLOWED.

THE ROD THAT BAILEY SWALLOWED WAS SIMILAR TO THIS ONE BUT DIDN'T HAVE THE REEL ATTACHED.

SWEET THIEF

Huh? Jo Adams opens her candy store in Estes Park, Colorado, U.S.A., to find dirt on the checkout counter and a candy tin on the floor. Curious, she plays the video from her surveillance cameras.

A small black bear can be seen sliding his claws under the locked front door and jiggling it open. The store is packed with yummy treats, but the bear chooses to chow down on only peanut butter cups, English toffee, fudge balls, and rice cereal treats. Then he tops it all off with four big cookies called—drumroll, please—cookie bears.

NIGHT MUSIC

It's a humid July evening in Katonah, New York, U.S.A. At the Caramoor Music Festival, an opera is being performed on an outdoor stage. The audience falls silent as one of the female stars begins to sing. *Tra-la-la ... CROAK! Tra ... CROAK! La ... CROAK!*

Operagoers look at each other. They shift in their seats. "The croaking sounds very loud and very close," says Paul Rosenblum, managing director of the festival. By Act 2, Michael Barrett, head of Caramoor at the time, can't stand it anymore. Wearing dress clothes, he leaves his seat and goes backstage. He climbs a ladder onto the roof of the nearest building. And there's the culprit: a lone frog no bigger than a golf ball. Barrett catches the little loudmouth and releases him in the woods. The opera continues. And the famous soloist no longer sounds like she has a frog in her throat.

EXTRAORDINARY Animals

SEA OTTER SHOOTS HOOPS

LEBRON JAMES "OTTER" WATCH OUT.

Portland, Oregon, U.S.A.
Someone alert the NBA: Eddie the sea otter is ready to go pro. His keepers at the Oregon Zoo taught the 18-year-old marine mammal to play basketball as a way to keep his arthritis from getting worse. Since he learned to shoot hoops, Eddie tosses anything he can get his paws on—especially his doggie chew toys—into the basket.

"In the wild, sea otters like Eddie would do a similar behavior we call the spy hop," says Jenny DeGroot, Eddie's keeper and trainer. "They come straight up out of the water, above the waves, to get a look around."

But at the zoo, Eddie's on the lookout for something else. If he scores a basket he gets a tasty treat, such as shrimp or clams. Swish!

Vertebrates
Animals WITH Backbones

Fish are cold-blooded and live in water. They breathe with gills, lay eggs, and usually have scales.

Amphibians are cold-blooded. Their young live in water and breathe with gills. Adults live on land and breathe with lungs.

Reptiles are cold-blooded and breathe with lungs. They live both on land and in water.

Birds are warm-blooded and have feathers and wings. They lay eggs, breathe with lungs, and usually are able to fly. Some birds live on land, some in water, and some on both.

Mammals are warm-blooded and feed on their mothers' milk. They also have skin that is usually covered with hair. Mammals live both on land and in water.

Bird: Bald eagle

Fish: Clown anemonefish

Invertebrates
Animals WITHOUT Backbones

Sponges are a very basic form of animal life. They live in water and do not move on their own.

Echinoderms have external skeletons and live in seawater.

Mollusks have soft bodies and can live either in or out of shells, on land or in water.

Arthropods are the largest group of animals. They have external skeletons, called exoskeletons, and segmented bodies with appendages. Arthropods live in water and on land.

Worms are soft-bodied animals with no true legs. Worms live in soil.

Cnidaria live in water and have mouths surrounded by tentacles.

Worm: Earthworms

Cnidaria: West Coast sea nettle

Cold-blooded
versus
Warm-blooded

Cold-blooded animals, also called ectotherms, get their heat from outside their bodies.

Warm-blooded animals, also called endotherms, keep their body temperature level regardless of the temperature of their environments.

RHINO

NATIONAL GEOGRAPHIC KiDS
MISSION ANIMAL RESCUE
Save ANIMALS >>
Save the WORLD

A threatened calf is flying high after he gets airlifted to a new, safe home.

A 15-month-old white rhinoceros gobbles grass next to his mother on a plain in South Africa. Everything appears calm, but the rhinos aren't safe. Poachers, which kill the rhinos for their horns, tend to lurk here. Last year more than 1,000 rhinos were killed in South Africa alone.

A HEAVY LIFT

Suddenly, a helicopter approaches. The pilot and passenger, a veterinarian, work for Rhinos Without Borders. This program plans to airlift a hundred rhinos from their current habitat to a protected reserve in the neighboring country of Botswana. They'll first be driven to a nearby refuge, where staff can make sure they're healthy enough for the trip.

The chopper nears, and the vet leans out and shoots a tranquilizer dart at each rhino. Both drop to the ground, completely sedated. Staff from Rhinos Without Borders rush over to give the rhinos a quick checkup. They then wake the drowsy animals to lead them into big crates. A crane on one truck must lift the heavy crates onto the other vehicle. Then the trucks and chopper take off.

RHINO REST STOP

Fifteen minutes later, the rhinos arrive at the two-acre (0.8-ha) refuge where they'll spend their "layover" in enclosures called bomas (BOH-mas) before going to Botswana. Staff monitor each rhino—if one gets sick, it can't travel.

For the next few weeks the rhinos—now named Kass and Draegon—rest and eat grass mixed with a plant called alfalfa. "We limit their contact with humans," says National Geographic Explorer-in-Residence Dereck Joubert, who founded an organization called Great Plains Conservation with his wife, National Geographic Explorer-in-Residence Beverly Joubert. Great Plains Conservation partnered with a group called andBeyond to launch Rhinos Without Borders and its rescue mission

WELCOME HOME

After two months, the rhinos are ready to go to Botswana. They're loaded onto a plane in crates, and arrive in their new home—a guarded reserve on a stretch of grassland—just two hours later.

Once staff open the crates, Draegon and his mother walk off into the wild. "They're much safer here," Beverly says. "We were so happy to give them a lift."

INTO THE CRATE

CHECKUP TIME

The term rhinoceros combines two Greek words meaning "nose" and "horn."

Adult white rhinos can weigh 5,000 pounds (2,268 kg).

SAVE ANIMALS, SAVE THE WORLD!

National Geographic Kids has an initiative called **Mission Animal Rescue** to show kids how to save endangered animals. You can help, too! Try out these cool rescue activities.

Write a script for a podcast on rhinos. Include fun facts about the animals and how people can help protect them. Record the podcast and play it for others.

Do the **Mission Animal Rescue challenge!** In November, go to our site **natgeo.com/kids/mission-animal-rescue** and take the "Which Wild Cat Are You?" personality quiz in support of Big Cat Week.

Create a rhino family photo album with pictures of the world's five rhino species. Add facts about each species to the album.

Check out the Nat Geo Kids book series **Mission Animal Rescue.** For more details or to donate to the cause, grab a parent and go online. **natgeo.com/kids/mission-animal-rescue**

MISSION: LION RESCUE

ALL ABOUT LIONS AND HOW TO SAVE THEM

Wild Hamsters

FARMERS TRY TO MAKE PEACE WITH THESE PESKY CRITTERS.

In a sun-dappled wheat field in France, a prowling barn cat meets a black-bellied hamster. Too far from her burrow to run for shelter, the wild hamster rises on her hind legs to face her enemy. She puffs out her cheeks, flashes her black underbelly, growls, and bares her teeth. The cat backs away. That black-bellied hamster is one tough rodent.

"They're afraid of nothing," says Alexandre Lehmann, a biologist who has worked with these wild hamsters for the past 12 years. "They fight against cars and dogs and even farmers. They try to fight against tractors. The Germans call them small bears."

Good thing the black-bellied hamster won't go down without a fight. Because in France, where only 500 to 1,000 remain in the wild, these cranky critters are in a fight for their lives.

During hibernation a hamster's heart beats only about six times a minute.

There are around 25 different species of wild hamsters.

TWO-DAY-OLD HAMSTERS

34

FOXES ON ICE

Clever arctic foxes survive snow, ice, and freezing cold temperatures.

N ot far from the North Pole, an arctic fox trots across the endless sea ice on a winter walkabout. It's been days since her last meal, and the whipping wind is relentless. She digs a hollow in the snow, curls up her cat-size body, and wraps her tail across her body and face to stay warm. Her fur acts like a warm sleeping bag, keeping her snug as temperatures dip below zero degrees. But warm fur alone might not keep this fox alive during the polar winter. Other freeze-defying strategies make this animal a champion of the cold.

FINDING FOOD

Arctic foxes prefer to eat small rodents called lemmings, but when times are tough, they'll take what they can get. This may be scraps of a seal that a polar bear has killed, or crabs and algae stuck to the bottom of ice. Sometimes, they'll stash dead lemmings near their dens for leaner times.

LEMMING

KEEPING WARM

In the toughest temps, this female fox digs a snow den and hunkers down for up to two weeks. She can slow her heart rate and metabolism to avoid burning more energy—similar to hibernation but not as long lasting. The fox's short legs provide heat exchange between warm blood flowing down from the body and cold blood flowing up from the legs.

When the fox emerges, she listens for scurrying sounds under the snow. Quietly, she takes a few steps, and then dives into the snow. Her head emerges with a brown fur ball in her mouth. With the energy tank refilled, this arctic fox has a better chance of making it through the long, dark winter.

Bet you didn't know

8 fab facts about bats

1 Ghost bats may be named for their translucent **wings** and ghostlike color.

2 The **pallid bat** is immune to **scorpion venom.**

3 **Bat** hibernation caves are called **hibernacula.**

4 Some **bats** can **live** for **30 years.**

5 Certain bats can **eat** more than **500 mosquitoes** in an hour.

6 The Malaysian flying fox's **wingspan** stretches up to **6 feet.** (1.8m)

7 Chiropto-phobia is the **fear** of **bats.**

8 The **spotted bat's** ears are about one-**third** the length of its body.

WOLVERINE!

How to track a wild, mysterious super-predator

Wolverines are small but ferocious bearlike animals. They're so mysterious that scientists don't even know how many there are in the wild. But researchers like Gregg Treinish are working to help this wild species continue to survive.

"It's February and I'm on the top of a mountain in Montana, U.S.A., all alone. The snow-caked forest is silent. All of a sudden I spot a wolverine track. I start following his trail.

"Tracking a wolverine is like following a ghost through the forest. They're so fast—covering 20 miles (32 km) in a day—and stealthy that I've never seen one in the wild. But if I pay close attention to the trail this one left, I can learn a lot about him.

"The tracks are grouped side by side instead of one after the other, showing that the wolverine was bounding fast, hunting something. I see another set of wolverine tracks. Then two more, crossing each other. Something was going on here. Ahead, I spot a four-foot (1.2-m) hole in the snow. Dirt and blood are scattered around the edge. I peer in to see an elk leg—a tasty meal for the wolverine.

"I search the hole and find two wolverine hairs, which I place in a bag. Later, scientists will extract DNA from the hairs and that will help them discover how many wolverines live in this area, what they're eating, and how far they're traveling.

"As climate change warms the planet, wolverines' snowy habitat is disappearing. The clues I find will help scientists track the population to learn whether we need to take action to prevent these phantoms of the forest from disappearing forever."

Wolverines are highly intelligent. People have reported seeing them climb trees, wait, and then pounce on deer that walk by.

A WOLVERINE CHOWS DOWN ON A LARGE ANIMAL'S LEG BONE.

41

FREAKY frogs!

Over 6,000 species of frogs hop, burrow, climb, swim, and even soar in exotic ecosystems around the world—and your own neighborhood. Their sometimes startling adaptations make them remarkable survivalists. Here are some frogs whose freakish good looks and bizarre lifestyles will make you become a frog fan.

WARNING LABEL

From the top, the Oriental fire-bellied toad from Korea, China, and southeastern Russia appears to be a mild-mannered frog. If threatened, though, it flashes its brightly colored belly to warn predators, "Look but don't touch." Not only is it toxic, it's also covered with sharp warts.

An amphibian is a **frog, toad,** newt, **salamander,** or caecilian.

CLEARLY SEE-THROUGH

From Central and South America, glass frogs are translucent (kind of see-through, like fogged glass). This type of camouflage makes them appear nearly invisible or like a bump on a leaf. Some even have green bones to blend in and trick predators. If you flip over a glass frog, you can see its heart beating through its skin.

FROG-ZILLA!

At 7 pounds (3.2 kg) and with a sitting length of 12.5 inches (31.8 cm), the Goliath frog from Cameroon and Equatorial Guinea is bigger than a Chihuahua. The world's largest frog, it can leap ten times its body length, or about 10 feet (3 m) each hop. Its body and legs can stretch 29.5 inches (7.5 cm) long, a little longer than a tennis racket.

AMAZING ANIMALS

Armadillos are mostly nocturnal. They stay inside their burrows when it's hot and come out at dawn or dusk or at night to look for food.

They turn into balls.

Armadillos usually aren't fighters. When threatened, the three-banded armadillo protects itself by rolling into a ball. The result looks so much like a soccer ball that a three-banded armadillo named Fuleco was the mascot of the 2014 World Cup in Brazil.

They're likely to get into traffic jams.

If you frighten an armadillo, it might run away to hide in the nearest burrow. But sometimes when one armadillo is trying to get into the burrow, another armadillo (or two!) is trying to get out. They get stuck!

Armadillos have been around for at least 65 million years.

They leap straight up when startled.

If something startles a nine-banded armadillo by touching it on the back, it responds by jumping straight up into the air, sometimes as high as four feet (1.2 m). It's a reflex that probably helps them get away from predators. (Or maybe it just makes the predators laugh so hard they forget to chase the armadillo.)

They stick out their tongues to eat.

Armadillos use their long, sticky tongues to feel around in ant nests, slurping up lots of ants at a time. A nine-banded armadillo can eat thousands of ants at one meal. Ants may not be *your* favorite food, but don't make fun of an armadillo's snack— it might stick out that extra-long tongue at you!

TONGUE

A nine-banded armadillo uses its huge front claws to dig its burrow. It might have several burrows but uses only one for its babies. That burrow is up to 25 feet (7.6 m) long and can have several rooms and connecting tunnels.

ROOM

TUNNEL

BIG CATS

A young male jaguar

Learn more about animals in peril and ways you can help with National Geographic Kids Mission: Animal Rescue series. Visit kids.nationalgeographic.com/mission-animal-rescue.

Not all wild cats are big cats, so what are big cats? To wildlife experts, they are the four living members of the genus *Panthera*: tigers, lions, leopards, and jaguars. They can all unleash a mighty roar and, as carnivores, they survive solely on the flesh of other animals. Thanks to powerful jaws; long, sharp claws; and daggerlike teeth, big cats are excellent hunters.

WHO'S WHO?

BIG CATS MAY HAVE a lot of features in common, but if you know what to look for, you'll be able to tell who's who in no time.

FUR

Most tigers are orange-colored with vertical black stripes on their bodies. This coloring helps the cats blend in with tall grasses as they sneak up on prey. These markings are like fingerprints: No two stripe patterns are alike.

TIGERS

JAGUARS

A jaguar's coat pattern looks similar to that of a leopard, as both have dark spots called rosettes. The difference? The rosettes on a jaguar's torso have irregularly shaped borders and at least one black dot in the center.

LEOPARDS

A leopard's yellowy coat has dark spots called rosettes on its back and sides. In leopards, the rosettes' edges are smooth and circular. This color combo helps leopards blend into their surroundings.

LIONS

Lions have a light brown, or tawny, coat and a tuft of black hair at the end of their tails. When they reach their prime, most male lions have shaggy manes that help them look larger and more intimidating.

JAGUAR
100 to 250 pounds
(45 TO 113 KG)

5 to 6 feet long
(1.5 TO 1.8 M)

LEOPARD
66 to 176 pounds
(30 TO 80 KG)

4.25 to 6.25 feet long
(1.3 TO 1.9 M)

BENGAL TIGER
240 to 500 pounds
(109 TO 227 KG)

5 to 6 feet long
(1.5 TO 1.8 M)

AFRICAN LION
265 to 420 pounds
(120 TO 191 KG)

4.5 to 6.5 feet long
(1.4 TO 2 M)

47

LION

Caged and neglected, an orphaned cub gets a second chance.

The female lion cub cowers in the corner of a cramped cage in a village in Ethiopia, Africa. People are paying money to see her up close, and she's hissing and snarling out of fear. While visiting the village, American humanitarian aid worker Jane Strachan hears rumors about the cub. When she catches sight of the terrified animal huddled on the dirt floor, Strachan becomes very worried. There's a chain circling the cub's neck, held by a padlock, and no one can find the key. One day the leash will interfere with her breathing. "If she stays here, she'll die," Strachan says.

SAVING THE LION

Rushing back to Ethiopia's capital, Addis Ababa, Strachan contacts the Born Free wildlife rescue team and tells them about the captive lioness. Soon after, a rescue worker and a federal wildlife officer confront the feline's keepers, informing them that it's illegal to house a lion. The keepers hand over the cub, and the worker places her in a pet carrier, then drives her to his rescue center.

Caretakers name the cub Safia and perform a checkup. They're concerned that the cub hasn't received enough calcium. "It's likely that Safia's mom was killed by hunters before the cub was done nursing, so she didn't get all the nutrients she needed," says Stephen Brend, who runs the center. Otherwise the 60-pound (27-kg) seven-month-old seems healthy.

CAGED CUB

LET FREEDOM ROAR

Since Safia never learned survival skills from her mom, she can't be released back into the wild. But her new home at the center will be a grassy area with bushes and trees, similar to a lion's natural habitat. When Safia is placed in her enclosure, she cautiously explores, diving for cover at every little noise. Soon, she gets playful, chasing birds and batting a plastic ball. Gobbling up two meat meals a day with calcium supplements helps Safia gain strength.

After nearly a year and a half, the now 275-pound (125-kg) Safia is released into another, permanent home. Safia meets Dolo, her big cat "roommate." Soon the two are close friends and spend their days playing and lounging together. And when Dolo lets out a mighty roar, Safia joins in. "Safia's finally happy in the way she deserves," Strachan says.

> The largest population of wild lions is in Tanzania, Africa.

PLAY BALL!

Lions spend about 20 hours a day resting.

THE LION QUEEN

Male lions live 10 to 12 years. Females can live up to 16 years.

NATIONAL GEOGRAPHIC KIDS
MISSION: LION RESCUE

STORIES of WILD LIONS

FACT IDEAS and PHOTOS

RESCUE ACTIVITIES and CHALLENGES

ALL ABOUT LIONS AND HOW TO SAVE THEM
by ASHLEE BROWN BLEWETT

SAVE ANIMALS, SAVE THE WORLD!

National Geographic Kids has a new initiative called **Mission: Animal Rescue** to show kids how to save lions and other threatened animals. Try out these activities to help the majestic lion.

Create a photo album of pet cats and lions from a local zoo. Share the album with friends to teach them about lions.

Find celebs with pet cats. Write a letter asking them to join the effort to help save their pets' big-cat relatives.

Get more lion rescue activities in the National Geographic Kids book **Mission: Lion Rescue.** To make a contribution in support of the mission initiative, grab a parent and go online. kids.nationalgeographic.com/mission-animal-rescue/

CHEETAHS: Built for SPEED

This wild cat's body makes it an incredible predator.

Breathing deeply, the cheetah prepares her body for the chase. Head low, eyes focused on an impala, she slowly inches forward. In three seconds this streamlined, superfast cat is sprinting at 60 miles an hour (96 km/h), eyes locked, laserlike, on the fleeing impala.

Long, muscular tail for balance in tight turns

The legendary Jamaican runner Usain Bolt is the world's fastest human. Bolt ran 200 meters in 19.19 seconds, about 23 miles an hour (37 km/h), but that's slow compared with the cheetah. Cheetahs can run about three times faster than Bolt. At top speed a sprinting cheetah can reach 70 miles an hour (113 km/h). Next time you're in a car on the highway, imagine a cheetah racing alongside you. That will give you an idea of how fast this speedy cat can run.

Several adaptations help cheetahs run so fast. A cheetah has longer legs than other cats. It also has a

Small, short face with enlarged nostrils to take in lots of air

long, extremely flexible spine. These features work together so a running cheetah can cover up to 23 feet (7 m) in one stride—about the length of five ten-year-olds lying head to feet in a row.

Most other cats can retract their claws when they're not using them. Cheetahs' claws stick out all the time, like dogs' claws. Cheetahs use these strong, blunt claws like an athlete uses cleats on track shoes—to help push off and quickly build up speed. The large center pad on the cheetah's foot is covered with long ridges that act like the treads on a car tire. A sprinting cheetah needs to be able to stop fast, too. It is able to spread its toes wide, and its toe pads are hard and pointed. This helps a cheetah turn

Strong, blunt claws and ridged footpads to grip the ground

quickly and brake suddenly. It can stop in a single stride from a speed of more than 20 miles an hour (32 km/h).

All of these body adaptations add up to extraordinary hunting abilities. A cheetah stalks up close to a herd of impalas, then streaks forward with lightning speed. As the herd bolts, the cat singles out one individual and follows its twists and turns precisely. As it closes in on its prey the cheetah strikes out with a forepaw, knocks the animal off its feet, and clamps its jaws over the prey's throat.

Snow Leopard SECRETS

High-tech tools help scientists understand how to save these big cats.

On a cool summer night, a snow leopard curiously sniffs an overhanging boulder for a strong scent sprayed by other cats. He rubs his cheeks on the boulder, scrapes the ground with his hind paws, and then urinates.

This act—called scraping—is how snow leopards communicate with one another. A scrape tells other snow leopards what they're doing and may reveal whether a snow leopard is male or female, has cubs, or is looking for a mate.

Recently, researchers studying the 4,000 to 6,500 snow leopards in the wild have set up motion-activated cameras at scraping sites in an effort to gather more information on these elusive cats and expose new details about how many snow leopards there are, how long they live, and how we can protect them.

Even though snow leopards live in some of the most rugged mountain terrain on Earth, people pose the biggest threat to their survival. Poachers can sell a snow leopard's hide and bones for thousands of dollars. Herders often kill any snow leopard that attacks their livestock. Hunters target ibex, wild sheep, and other animals for food and trophies—removing important snow leopard prey.

Like a snow leopard reality show, the cameras expose everything that happens. The images also help researchers count the number of snow leopards in an area and reveal whether prey animals, livestock, or poachers are nearby.

Other researchers will gently trap the wild cats and put satellite radio collars on them to track where the cats roam and to learn new things about how and where they live. Technology like this is essential to help researchers protect snow leopards in the wild and preserve their habitat.

MARKING TERRITORY

Despite their name, snow leopards are not snow-colored. Their spotted gray or beige fur actually stands out against a snowy background—but blends in with rocks.

TWO CUBS

CHASING DOWN PREY

51

SEA TURTLE

A lost and freezing loggerhead gets help from warmhearted volunteers.

The freezing sea turtle can barely manage another stroke as she struggles to keep herself warm in the frigid waters of Cape Cod Bay off Massachusetts, U.S.A. The reptile is suffering from the turtle version of human hypothermia—when body temperature falls below normal levels. Her strength is fading fast.

She bobs lifelessly on the surface of the water before a gust of wind propels her toward land. Washed up on the shore of Crosby Landing Beach, she lies motionless in the sand, bitterly cold. If she doesn't get help soon, she won't have a chance.

LIFEGUARDS ARRIVE

Taking a morning stroll along the beach, Brian Long spots the large turtle. He can't tell if she's alive, so he immediately phones the Massachusetts Audubon Society, a conservation organization. The call reaches director Bob Prescott, who rushes to the beach in a pickup truck and identifies the two-and-a-half-foot (0.76-m)-long creature as a loggerhead sea turtle. An endangered species, they spend their summers in the north and their winters in warmer southern waters, but this turtle likely got lost while navigating down the coast and missed the chance to migrate before cold weather set in. The animal's eyes are closed, and she's not visibly breathing. But when

Some Pacific loggerheads migrate over 7,500 miles (12,000 km) between nesting beaches.

A cooler loggerhead nest will produce more male hatchlings, while a warmer one will produce more females.

THE WEAK TURTLE ARRIVES AT THE REHAB CENTER.

Prescott gently touches her neck, the big-beaked reptile slowly raises her head. She's hanging on but urgently needs medical care. The two men hoist the huge animal onto the bed of the truck, and she's taken to New England Aquarium in Boston, Massachusetts. Here, she can begin her recovery.

SHELL-SHOCKED

At the aquarium's marine animal rehabilitation center, staff name the turtle Biscuits and give her an exam. She weighs in at 165 pounds (75 kg)—slightly underweight for a loggerhead of Biscuits's age. She has developed open wounds, she's dehydrated, and she has pneumonia. She is also cold-stunned, a condition that affects reptiles if their temperatures drop too low. As their bodies cool, the animals' blood circulation slows, causing the animals to enter a coma-like state, practically unable to move.

Now her caretakers' goal is to raise her body temperature from an extremely low 48°F (9°C) to between 70°F and 80°F (21°C and 25°C). But it won't be easy—warming her too quickly could be deadly. She's moved into a temperature-controlled pool set to 55°F (13°C).

These turtles may live for 50 years or more in the wild.

GEORGIA SEA TURTLE CENTER STAFF UNLOAD BISCUITS FROM THE PLANE.

TURTLE TAKEOFF

Soon, Biscuits is ready for to be moved to the Georgia Sea Turtle Center on Jekyll Island, which is located closer to her release site. Here the staff will continue to prepare her for reentry into the wild. Along with three other recovering turtles, she's flown to Georgia, U.S.A., on a private jet. Once there, Biscuits is placed in a tank where she can continue practicing her swimming strokes. Caretakers also put live blue crabs and horseshoe crabs in her tank so she can get used to catching prey again. These critters are some of a loggerhead's favorite foods in the wild, and Biscuits quickly remembers how to snatch up the tasty treats in her beak.

CARETAKERS LIFT BISCUITS INTO HER POOL AT THE AQUARIUM'S REHAB CENTER.

BISCUITS RETURNS TO THE SEA.

Each day the rehabbers raise the thermostat a little higher. As the temperature rises, Biscuits begins to move normally again.

To help her regain energy, the staff offer healthy meals of fish and squid, and they rehydrate her with daily injections of nutrient-filled fluids. Biscuits also receives antibiotics for her pneumonia and soothing ointment for her skin

BACK TO THE SEA

A month later Biscuits is ready to return to the ocean. She's heavier, now weighing 180 pounds (82 kg), and has proven she can catch live prey. She's driven by her rehabilitation team to a release site in Florida, U.S.A. When the team lowers her onto the sand at the water's edge, she immediately crawls into the crashing waves and swims off, healthy and happy at last.

Bottlenose dolphins live all over the world—near shore, far out to sea, and in warm water in both hemispheres.

Talking
Dolphin

Surprising new evidence suggests that each bottlenose dolphin creates its own name.

With a flick of its tail, a young bottlenose dolphin races through the ocean. The powerful dolphin easily cuts through water. At the surface, where it's sunny and clear, visibility is great—it's easy to see for miles. But deeper underwater, where the dolphin swims, visibility is down to a few feet. Yet the dolphin swiftly and easily zooms around boulders, dodges puffer fish, and avoids an enormous sea turtle without hesitation.

When it discovers a huge school of fish, the hungry dolphin whistles excitedly. In the distance a dolphin trills a reply. The two whistle back and forth, as the second dolphin rushes to locate its friend. Soon the two share a secret communication as they twist and turn in unison, eating, leaping, and gliding through the school with the perfect precision of ballet dancers.

Dolphins live in a dark, murky, underwater world. It's often impossible to see each other or anything else around them, so sound plays an essential role in their survival. To communicate with each other,

Bottlenose dolphins eat fish, squid, and shrimp.

A bottlenose dolphin is 8 to 12 feet (2.4 to 3.7 m) long.

dolphins produce a variety of whistles, squeaks, trills, and clicks.

Only other dolphins understand what the squeaks and squawks mean. Biologists haven't cracked their secret communication, except for one kind of whistle. It might last less than a second, but this whistle is a big deal. Why? Because these whistles are actually names of dolphins—and every bottlenose dolphin has one.

A mother dolphin whistles repeatedly to her newborn for several days after it's born. Biologists believe that this enables the calf to learn to recognize her through sound.

DOLPHIN RINGTONE

Think of a signature whistle as a special ringtone. When other dolphins hear it, they know which dolphin is calling or chattering. It's sort of a "Yo, it's Bob. I'm over here" kind of message. Other group members may reply with their own signature whistles, like a dolphin's version of Marco Polo.

Dolphins often hunt and explore solo, but they need to stay connected to the group. Their signature whistles allow them to check in with other dolphins who may be nearly five football fields away.

BABY NAMES

Many animal species have distinctive or shared calls. But a specific name for an individual is rare. Only humans, some parrot species, and a few other kinds of dolphins are known to have names for individuals.

Scientists believe that the calf itself comes up with the signature whistle. Like human babies, a calf plays with sounds throughout its first year, and dolphins have their own version of baby babble. So, while testing its sound skills, a baby dolphin is actually figuring out its signature whistle—and it may be nothing like its mother's or a group member's whistles. By the time the calf is a year old, its signature whistle is set.

Deciphering dolphin names is just the beginning of figuring out what dolphins communicate about with all their trills and squeaks. Do they chat about sharks? Discuss the tides? Maybe they even have a name for people. Someday scientists hope to decipher the rest of the mysteries of dolphin communication.

Dolphin Dictionary

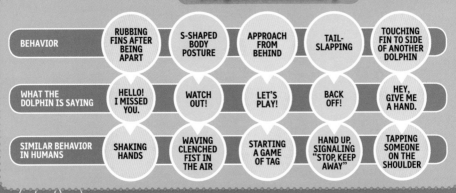

BEHAVIOR	RUBBING FINS AFTER BEING APART	S-SHAPED BODY POSTURE	APPROACH FROM BEHIND	TAIL-SLAPPING	TOUCHING FIN TO SIDE OF ANOTHER DOLPHIN
WHAT THE DOLPHIN IS SAYING	HELLO! I MISSED YOU.	WATCH OUT!	LET'S PLAY!	BACK OFF!	HEY, GIVE ME A HAND.
SIMILAR BEHAVIOR IN HUMANS	SHAKING HANDS	WAVING CLENCHED FIST IN THE AIR	STARTING A GAME OF TAG	HAND UP, SIGNALING "STOP, KEEP AWAY"	TAPPING SOMEONE ON THE SHOULDER

Parenting, PUFFIN Style

Tips for bringing up these little clowns of the sea

There comes a time, if you're a puffin, that **your beak changes** from dull gray to outrageous orange. **Your feet, too.** That means one thing—it's time to become a puffin parent. Here are **six pointers** for new puffin moms and dads.

1 Touch Down Carefully

When you're ready to become a parent, return to the islands of the North Atlantic where you hatched years before. Remember, landing on rocks isn't like your usual soft watery splashdown. So don't fly in at your full speed of 55 miles an hour. (88 km/h).

2 Show Your Affection

Sometime, maybe in the last year, you met that special someone. Each April you'll reunite. After racing toward each other, show your devotion by rubbing and tapping beaks. Other puffins will gather to enjoy this public display of affection.

③ Develop a Routine

Fly, dive, fly back, drop off fish. Repeat. Each day, you and your mate will make several trips to sea, easily diving 276 times. The usual catch is about ten fish per trip. By the time the chick is ready to leave the nest, each of you will have made 12,420 dives.

④ Land and Run

When returning from sea with a beak full of fish, don't forget to land close to the burrow, then race inside. Herring gulls would rather steal a quick meal from you than hunt for their own food.

"FLYING" THROUGH WATER

⑤ Prepare for Lots of Fishing

Congratulations! It's a *puffling!* This little fluffy ball of feathers needs you. It can't fly, swim, or hunt. To keep up with its ravenous appetite, it will take both you and your mate to bring it enough baby food: fish.

⑥ Let Your Puffling Go

You did it—you raised a puffling. Now it must survive on its own, so you have to let it leave the nest. Plus it's time for you to return to life at sea. See you next year!

A MESSAGE TO PUFFLINGS:

You're 45 days old; it's time to leave Mom and Dad. You've got sturdy, smooth feathers now—perfect for flying or diving into the cold sea. To avoid predators hanging around the burrow, be sure to fly or swim away in the dark. In four to six years, you'll return and become a puffin parent, too.

57

Name That
TIDE POOL ANIMAL

When the tide goes out in rocky, coastal areas, some water gets left behind in pools and crevices. These spots are called tide pools and many different creatures like to hang out in them. See if you can name these tide pool animals.

A

This creature is always on the lookout for a new home. Snail shells are usually its preference, but with five pairs of legs, you can't call it a slowpoke!

A tide pool is one tough neighborhood! When the tide is in, waves come crashing; when the tide is out, animals are exposed to sun, cold weather, and even fresh water from rain. When you look closely at tide pool creatures you'll find they all have adaptations to survive these harsh conditions.

C

The webbing between this animal's short, triangular arms is a clue to its name. Sensors on the end of each of its arms can sense light and detect prey.

B

These drifters don't have much say about where they end up, but often they show up in tide pools. They may be soft and squishy, but their tentacles are stunning.

D

Nemo and his father lived inside one of these. When their tentacles are open they are ready for food; when they're folded in, they're likely munching.

E

After grazing on algae, this tide pool creature finds the perfect parking spot on a rock and hunkers down, sealing water underneath itself to keep its body moist during low tide.

F

Call it a tide pool salad. This leafy green creature can get dry and stiff at low tide, but it bounces right back once the water comes in.

A. Hermit crab; B. Jellyfish; C. Bat star; D. Sea anemone; E. Limpet; F. Sea lettuce

59

Awesome
INSECT AWARDS

We're buggin' out! Our earth is crawling with over 800,000 species of insects. And whether they're teeny-tiny or superstrong, some of those six-legged species certainly stand out. Here are seven of the biggest, baddest, ickiest bugs out there!

Heavy Lifter

Sharp Shooter

The *rhinoceros beetle*, which gets its name from the hornlike structure on the male's head, is capable of carrying up to 850 times its own body weight.

If you spot a *bombardier beetle*, look out! When threatened, the bug shoots stinky, boiling-hot liquid out of its rear end at a distance up to eight inches (20 cm).

Is it a bird? A bat? No, it's the *Atlas moth*, who has a wingspan wider than a dinner plate—the largest moth wings on the planet.

Biggest Wings

They don't call it a *fly* for nothing! By beating its wings at over 200 times a second, a fly can pick up speeds faster than you can walk.

Fast Flier

Sharpest Defense

Coolest Camo

It's common to mistake the *walking leaf* for an actual leaf, thanks to its large, feathery wings. This clever camouflage provides protection from potential predators.

When clustered with others on a branch, a tiny *thorn bug* becomes part of a prickly pack no bird wants a bite of!

Colossal Crawler

The *Goliath beetle* weighs about as much as a quarter-pounder hamburger, making it one of the heaviest bugs on earth.

Monarchs Hit the Road!

Why did the monarch cross the road? To boost its population! At least that's what the U.S. Fish and Wildlife Service is hoping to do by creating a "Butterfly Highway" along U.S. Interstate 35, which runs between Texas and Minnesota.

Due to loss of habitat and food from herbicides that kill milkweed, the monarchs' numbers in North America have dramatically dwindled from 1 billion to about 100 million. But experts believe that they can bolster the butterfly's

numbers to 225 million by 2020 by helping them out along their epic 2,000-mile (3,219-km) migration each September and October from Canada and the northern United States to Mexico. Because I-35 follows the same route as the migration, researchers hope that lining the road with milkweed

To stay warm, thousands of monarchs gather together to "roost" on trees.

Monarchs can't fly if their body temperature is less than 86°F (30°C).

will provide a much-needed food source for the winged insects.

Plans for the Butterfly Highway are underway, and experts hope that the effort will extend beyond the interstate. People living within 100 miles (161 km) of I-35 are encouraged to plant milkweed and flowering plants in their yards so the butterflies can refuel during their migration. Simple steps like these will ensure that the majestic monarchs will be protected wherever they roam.

One monarch traveled 265 miles (427 km) in one day during migration.

MILKWEED'S MAGIC

Why is milkweed so important for monarchs? Not only does the plant keep them fueled for their epic migration, but it also serves as a host for the butterfly's eggs. Once they hatch, the caterpillars chomp on milkweed leaves, and toxins in the plant make the species foul-tasting and poisonous to predators. Simply put, without milkweed, there would be no monarchs.

Prehistoric TIME LINE

HUMANS HAVE WALKED on Earth for some 200,000 years, a mere blip in Earth's 4.5-billion-year history. A lot has happened during that time. Earth formed, and oxygen levels rose in the millions of years of the Precambrian time. The productive Paleozoic era gave rise to hard-shelled organisms, vertebrates, amphibians, and reptiles.

Dinosaurs ruled the Earth in the mighty Mesozoic. And 64 million years after dinosaurs became extinct, modern humans emerged in the Cenozoic era. From the first tiny mollusks to the dinosaur giants of the Jurassic and beyond, Earth has seen a lot of transformation.

THE PRECAMBRIAN TIME

4.5 billion to 542 million years ago

- The Earth (and other planets) formed from gas and dust left over from a giant cloud that collapsed to form the sun. The giant cloud's collapse was triggered when nearby stars exploded.
- Low levels of oxygen made Earth a suffocating place.
- Early life-forms appeared.

THE PALEOZOIC ERA

542 million to 251 million years ago

- The first insects and other animals appeared on land.
- 450 million years ago (m.y.a.), the ancestors of sharks began to swim in the oceans.
- 430 m.y.a., plants began to take root on land.
- More than 360 m.y.a., amphibians emerged from the water.
- Slowly the major landmasses began to come together, creating Pangaea, a single supercontinent.
- By 300 m.y.a., reptiles had begun to dominate the land.

What Killed the Dinosaurs?

It's a mystery that's boggled the minds of scientists for centuries: What happened to the dinosaurs? While various theories have bounced around, a new study confirms that the most likely culprit is an asteroid or comet that created a giant crater. Researchers say that the impact set off a series of natural disasters like tsunamis, earthquakes, and temperature swings that plagued the dinosaurs' ecosystem and disrupted their food chain. This, paired with intense volcano eruptions that caused drastic climate changes, is thought to be why half of the world's species—including the dinosaurs—died in a mass extinction.

DINO TIMES

THE MESOZOIC ERA

251 million to 65 million years ago

The Mesozoic era, or the age of the reptiles, consisted of three consecutive time periods (shown below). This is when the first dinosaurs began to appear. They would reign supreme for more than 150 million years.

TRIASSIC PERIOD

251 million to 199 million years ago

- Appearance of the first mammals. They were rodent-size.
- The first dinosaur appeared.
- Ferns were the dominant plants on land.
- The giant supercontinent of Pangaea began breaking up toward the end of the Triassic.

JURASSIC PERIOD

199 million to 145 million years ago

- Giant dinosaurs dominated the land.
- Pangaea continued its breakup, and oceans formed in the spaces between the drifting landmasses, allowing sea life, including sharks and marine crocodiles, to thrive.
- Conifer trees spread across the land.

CRETACEOUS PERIOD

145 million to 65 million years ago

- The modern continents developed.
- The largest dinosaurs developed.
- Flowering plants spread across the landscape.
- Mammals flourished, and giant pterosaurs ruled the skies over the small birds.
- Temperatures grew more extreme. Dinosaurs lived in deserts, swamps, and forests from the Antarctic to the Arctic.

THE CENOZOIC ERA—TERTIARY PERIOD

65 million to 2.6 million years ago

- Following the dinosaur extinction, mammals rose as the dominant species.
- Birds continued to flourish.
- Volcanic activity was widespread.
- Temperatures began to cool, eventually ending in an ice age.
- The period ended with land bridges forming, which allowed plants and animals to spread to new areas.

DINO Classification

Classifying dinosaurs and all other living things can be a complicated matter, so scientists have devised a system to help with the process. Dinosaurs are put into groups based on a very large range of characteristics.

Scientists put dinosaurs into two major groups: the bird-hipped ornithischians and the reptile-hipped saurischians.

Who Ate What?

Herbivores

- Primarily plant-eaters
- Weighed up to 100 tons (91 t)—the largest animals ever to walk on Earth
- Up to 1,000 blunt or flat teeth to grind vegetation
- Many had cheek pouches to store food.
- Examples: *Styracosaurus, Mamenchisaurus*

Carnivores

- Meat-eaters
- Long, strong legs to run faster than plant-eaters; ran up to 30 miles an hour (48 km/h)
- Most had good eyesight, strong jaws, and sharp teeth.
- Scavengers and hunters; often hunted in packs
- Grew to 45 feet (14 m) long
- Examples: *Velociraptor, Gigantoraptor, Tyrannosaurus rex*

Ornithischian

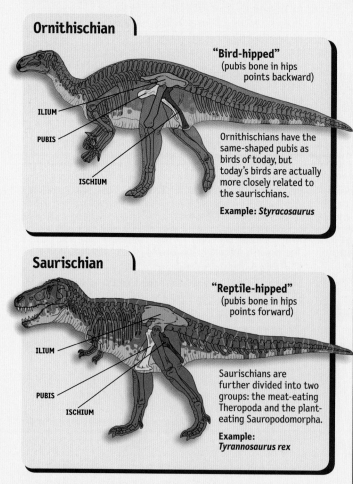

ILIUM

PUBIS

ISCHIUM

"Bird-hipped"
(pubis bone in hips points backward)

Ornithischians have the same-shaped pubis as birds of today, but today's birds are actually more closely related to the saurischians.

Example: *Styracosaurus*

Saurischian

ILIUM

PUBIS

ISCHIUM

"Reptile-hipped"
(pubis bone in hips points forward)

Saurischians are further divided into two groups: the meat-eating Theropoda and the plant-eating Sauropodomorpha.

Example: *Tyrannosaurus rex*

Within these two main divisions, dinosaurs are then separated into orders and then families, such as Stegosauria. Like other members of the Stegosauria, *Stegosaurus* had spines and plates along the back, neck, and tail.

4 NEWLY DISCOVERED DINOS

Humans have been searching for—and discovering—dinosaur remains for hundreds of years. In that time, at least 1,000 species of dinos have been found all over the world, and thousands more may still be out there waiting to be unearthed. Recent discoveries include the *Dreadnoughtus schrani*. Found in Argentina, it is one of the world's largest dinosaurs. For more exciting dino discoveries, read on.

3 *Regaliceratops peterhewsi*
(Ornithischian)

Royal horned face, geologist Peter Hews

Length: 16 feet (5 m)

Time Range: Late Cretaceous

Where: Alberta, Canada

1 *Chilesaurus diegosuarezi*
(Ornithischian)

Chile dinosaur and Diego Suárez, the 7-year-old who helped discover it

Length: 9.8 feet (3 m)

Time Range: Late Jurassic

Where: Chile

2 *Qijianglong guokr*
(Saurischian)

Dragon of Qijiang

Length: 50 feet (15 m)

Time Range: Late Jurassic

Where: China

4 *Yi qi*
(Saurischian)

Strange wing

Length: 2.1 feet (63 cm)

Time Range: Late Jurassic

Where: China

DINOSAUR FAMILY TREE

Experts believe the first dinosaurs to roam the planet some 230 million years ago were dog-size carnivores with reptilian traits. Eventually, those early dinosaurs changed enough to be divided into two groups based on the design of their hip bones: Ornithischia (bird-hipped) and Saurischia (reptile-hipped). Over time, these groups continued to branch out, and, as Earth's environment shifted, the size and shape of dinosaurs did, too.

SMALL & LARGE CERATOPSIANS
PLANT
Covered in bony plates with a birdlike beak.

ANKYLOSAURS
PLANT
As big as a tank, slow-moving with short front legs.

STEGOSAURS
PLANT
Armored herbivore with bony plates along its spine and a powerful spiked tail.

PACHYCEPHALOSAURS
PLANT
Dome-headed, thick-skulled plant-eaters that lived in packs.

ORNITHISCHIA (Bird-Hipped Dinosaurs)

EARLY DINOSAURS
MEAT
Dog-sized, two-legged meat-eaters.

DINOSAURIA

SAUROPODS
PLANT
Large four-legged plant-eaters with small head, and a long neck and tail.

PROSAUROPODS
PLANT
The biggest plant-eaters of their time; walked on two legs.

CERATOSAURIANS
MEAT
These "horned lizards" had sharp teeth and claws.

SAURISCHIA (Reptile-Hipped Dinosaurs)

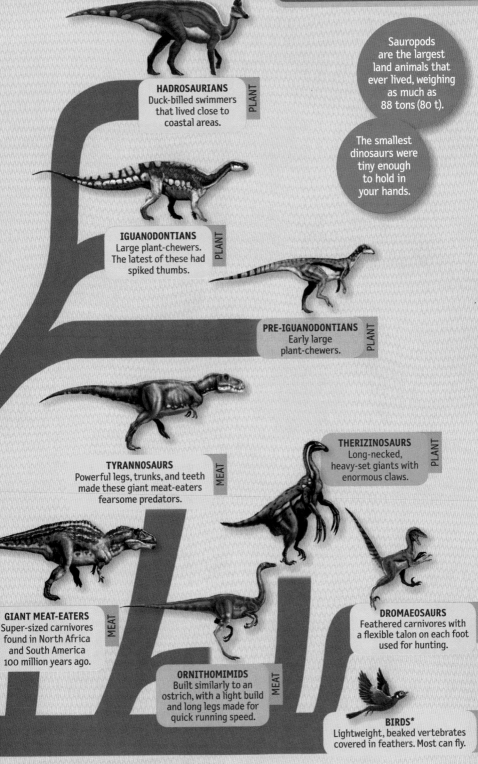

HADROSAURIANS
Duck-billed swimmers that lived close to coastal areas.

PLANT

Sauropods are the largest land animals that ever lived, weighing as much as 88 tons (80 t).

The smallest dinosaurs were tiny enough to hold in your hands.

IGUANODONTIANS
Large plant-chewers. The latest of these had spiked thumbs.

PLANT

PRE-IGUANODONTIANS
Early large plant-chewers.

PLANT

TYRANNOSAURS
Powerful legs, trunks, and teeth made these giant meat-eaters fearsome predators.

MEAT

THERIZINOSAURS
Long-necked, heavy-set giants with enormous claws.

PLANT

GIANT MEAT-EATERS
Super-sized carnivores found in North Africa and South America 100 million years ago.

MEAT

DROMAEOSAURS
Feathered carnivores with a flexible talon on each foot used for hunting.

MEAT

ORNITHOMIMIDS
Built similarly to an ostrich, with a light build and long legs made for quick running speed.

MEAT

BIRDS*
Lightweight, beaked vertebrates covered in feathers. Most can fly.

MEAT

*Despite a backward pointing "bird-hipped" pubis bone, birds are actually more closely related to "reptile-hipped" dinosaurs.

69

1

A fossil IS THE REMAINS OF AN ANCIENT ANIMAL OR PLANT THAT HAS BEEN PRESERVED.

2 FOSSILS SHOW THAT EEL-LIKE HAGFISH HAVE BEEN LIVING ON EARTH FOR 330 MILLION YEARS.

4 HORSESHOE CRABS, which are living fossils, are not crabs at all. They're actually in the spider family.

3 A LIVING FOSSIL is an animal or plant that hasn't changed much from its prehistoric ancestors.

5 Amber, FOSSILIZED TREE RESIN FROM AS LONG AS 70 MILLION YEARS AGO, SOMETIMES CONTAINS INSECTS THAT WERE TRAPPED IN THE STICKY STUFF.

17 AGE-OLD FACTS ABOUT

6 The skull of a 246-million-year-old marine animal called a placodont was discovered in the Netherlands in 2013.

7 Australia's famous koalas are living fossils that have been around for at least 20 million years.

8 AARDVARKS have an ancient arrangement of chromosomes—the material in cells that determines what an animal looks like—that make this ONE-OF-A-KIND animal a living fossil.

9 Horsetails, a kind of living fossil plant, have been on Earth since the Mesozoic era, more than 100 million years ago.

10 A population of living fossils, eight-inch (20-cm)-long fluorescent pink slugs, has been isolated for millions of years atop Mount Kaputor in Australia.

11 THE PURPLE FROG, A LIVING FOSSIL FOUND IN INDIA, HAS BEEN DESCRIBED AS LOOKING LIKE A "BLOATED DOUGH-NUT." IT EVOLVED FROM A CREATURE THAT LIVED ABOUT 130 MILLION YEARS AGO.

12 A fossil of an elephant bird egg sold at auction for over $100,000. It's so large, 120 chicken eggs could fit inside it.

13 Most of America's 50 states have an official state fossil. Alaska, Nebraska, and Washington gave this honor to the MAMMOTH.

14 The first discovery of fossilized tree stumps in the United States was made in 1850 by an amateur naturalist in the town of Gilboa, New York.

FOSSILS

15 BODY FOSSILS contain the remains of creatures that were once alive. Trace fossils are signs of prehistoric creatures, like footprints.

16 ONE OF THE MOST BEAUTIFUL SEASHELLS IS HOME TO A KIND OF CEPHALOPOD CALLED A NAUTILUS. THIS LIVING FOSSIL HAS BEEN AROUND FOR AT LEAST 500 million years.

17 THE BIGGEST FOSSIL OF A SPIDER— MEASURING ONE INCH (2.5 CM) IN LENGTH—WAS FOUND IN CHINA AND IS 165 MILLION YEARS OLD.

HoW TO SPEAk CaT

COME ON, LET'S PLAY!

CHECK OUT THE BOOK!

HoW TO SPEAk CaT
A GUIDE TO DECODING CAT LANGUAGE

Cats are on a roll. All around the globe, kitties now rank as the most popular pet. And no wonder: Everyone feels good when a friendly cat purrs, rubs against their legs, or snuggles in their lap.

But let's get one thing straight. Cats are not dogs! They look, act, and (we're pretty sure) think differently. Dogs depend on us to take care of them; cats maintain a lot of their wildness.

Because they're so independent, cats hide their feelings. Unless you know exactly what to look for, a happy cat and a miserable one can look very much the same. But cats do communicate. Check out how to read your cat's moods by recognizing five ways it "talks" to you.

AAH. THIS IS THE LIFE.

THE PLAYFUL KITTEN

Kittens are always in the mood for fun. They spend almost every waking minute playing. They love to run and chase, pounce and wrestle, attack and retreat. At about seven weeks old, kittens learn the signs for inviting each other to play. Watch for a kitten with a relaxed, content look. That's its play face. Rolling onto its back or standing up on its hind legs are also signs that a cat's ready for fun. Holding its tail like a question mark and hopping sideways might be other ways of telling a playmate to let the games begin!

HAPPY CAT

You can tell a happy cat by its relaxed body, half-perked ears, and droopy whiskers. He'll greet you with a chipper "Hi, there" meow and a straight-up tail. Then he'll jump on your lap, purr loudly, and move his body under your hand. Keep your cat happy by petting him—just where he likes it.

Some of the best cat toys are free: a crumpled-up newspaper or a paper bag.

All cats, no matter the breed, are born with blue eyes. Their true color appears at about 12 weeks.

72

CAT ON THE HUNT

Shh! This cat is after something. You can tell by his intense stare, twitching tail, and forward-pointing ears and whiskers. All his senses are alert as he crouches low to the ground and pads silently toward his prey. Hunting is difficult, dangerous work. Humans have long admired cats for their courage and predatory skills. Without cats, early Egyptians would have lost much of their food supply to rats. So would sailors, who took the little rodent killers with them to sea, spreading the animals around the world. Your cat can hunt pesky houseflies or other insects that sneak into your home—keeping both you and your cat happy.

Cats hunt what they can get: rats in New York City, lizards in Georgia, U.S.A., and baby turtles on Africa's Seychelles islands.

HEH, HEH. HE CAN'T HEAR ME COMING.

THE FRUSTRATED FELINE

A frustrated cat will have wide eyes and forward, pricked ears. It'll bat its paws, its teeth might chatter, and it may slowly thrash its tail. Like humans, cats get frustrated when they don't get what they expect. For instance, an indoor cat stares out the window at a bird, but she can't reach the prey outside. The longer the cat sits and watches, the greater her frustration, until she's ready to attack someone.

A cat can get frustrated often. But if you know the signs, you can turn your irritated cat into a contented kitty. When she's annoyed that she can't get to a bird, distract your feline by playing with a fishing-pole toy. Let your kitty catch the "mouse" at the end, and that bird will soon be forgotten.

The word for "cat" is *mio* in Chinese, *gatto* in Italian, *poes* in Dutch, and *kedi* in Turkish.

I'D RATHER BE HUNTING.

NauGHty PETS

CAUGHT ON CAMERA

ONCE I SCALE THIS TREE, WALKING ON THE CEILING SHOULD BE EASY.

IF YOU DON'T LIKE DOGGY DROOL, YOU MIGHT WANT TO SLEEP ON THE COUCH.

NAME Smoochiepoo

FAVORITE ACTIVITY
Washing the sheets with his slobber

FAVORITE TOY
Chewy pillows

PET PEEVE
Alarm clocks

NAME Master Meow

FAVORITE ACTIVITY
Competing in the Extreme Cat Olympics

FAVORITE TOY
Half-pipe litter box

PET PEEVE Gravity

THE PILLOW STARTED IT.

NAME Weasley

FAVORITE ACTIVITY
Pillow fights with imaginary pooch pals

FAVORITE TOY
A blanket—it's for playing tug-of-war, right?

PET PEEVE
Time-outs in his crate

REAL ANIMAL HEROES!

THESE ANIMALS SHOW AMAZING BRAVERY.

DOG SAVES KID FROM TRUCK

Geo the German shepherd mix follows ten-year-old Charlie Riley everywhere. Naturally the pup goes along on family walks.

One day Charlie, his mom, and two younger brothers are standing at a street corner. Geo is sitting at Charlie's side. Suddenly ...

"We hear a roar," Charlie's mother says. An out-of-control pickup jumps the curb. It's heading straight for Charlie!

But Geo makes a flying leap. "He hits me so hard I fall over," Charlie says. The speeding truck slams into Geo instead. They rush an injured Geo to the animal hospital for emergency surgery.

"My dog could have died," Charlie says. *And my son could have too,* thinks his mother. But he didn't—thanks to Geo.

CAT DETECTS LOW BLOOD SUGAR

Patricia Peter is asleep when her cat, Monty, bites her hand. "It's the hand I poke to test my blood sugar level," she says. Peter has diabetes, a serious disease that requires frequent blood testing. Peter pushes the cat away, but Monty bites harder. Peter gets up and Monty leads her to the kitchen, then jumps on the counter beside Peter's testing kit.

Peter tests, and her sugar level is dangerously low. She pops some sugar pills, and her level returns to normal. According to Peter's doctor, Monty knew something was wrong by smelling her breath and tasting her skin. "He's my guardian angel," Peter says.

PUP DETECTS SEIZURES

Zoe the pit bull mix is Gretchen Jett's best gift ever. Born deaf, the 11-year-old girl from Nevada, U.S.A., also has epilepsy, a brain disease that causes seizures. Because of this, she usually has to play indoors. So her dad gets a dog to keep his daughter company.

Just two nights later, Zoe bursts into Gretchen's parents' room. "I get up, thinking she needs to go outside," Gretchen's dad says. "Instead, Zoe runs in a circle and bolts straight into Gretchen's room. She's suffering a bad seizure." Circling and running becomes Zoe's signal. "When she does that we know something is wrong with Gretchen," her dad says. Zoe knows that Gretchen needs her.

Lifestyles of the RICH and FURRY

OUTRAGEOUS WAYS TO PAMPER YOUR PET

From canine country clubs to tabby tiaras, pets today are living in the lap of luxury. In 2014, pet owners spent about $58 billion—almost twice what they spent in 2002—on supplies and services to pamper their pets. "Pets improve our lives," says Bob Vetere of the American Pet Products Association. "So we want to improve theirs." *NG Kids* tracks just how far some owners go to give their pets the royal treatment.

WHAT TO WEAR

When Selena Gomez and Amanda Seyfried need fashion for their dogs, they don't have to look far. That's because many stores now cater exclusively to the pampered pet. At Fifi & Romeo (left) in Los Angeles, California, dogs in handmade cashmere sweaters and colorful raincoats are considered fashionable, not funny-looking, and are sure to please the most finicky pooch.

Will your pet be less happy if you don't shower it with expensive stuff?

Absolutely not! "As long as your pet has food, comfort, and friendship, that's what's most important," says pet psychologist John C. Wright.

IN THE HOUSE

Skeeter the cairn terrier hangs out in a two-story doghouse with floor-to-ceiling windows, and heated floors. It's just one of many custom-made cribs owners are building for their pets. "One owner asked for a cat house with a separate dining room, litter box room, and bedroom," says Michelle Pollak of La Petite Maison, which builds luxury pet homes (above). "Some pet owners spare nothing to make sure their pets are comfortable and happy."

KENNEL—OR VACATION?

Sampson the Yorkshire terrier loves a good massage. His sister, Delilah, likes to get her toenails painted. They can do it all at the Olde Towne Pet Resort in Virginia, U.S.A. (below), one of many "pet spas" around the country that act more like luxury hotels than kennels.

CHOW TIME

Plain old dog chow just won't do for canines like Clementine the beagle. Gourmet pet food has become all the rage. Places like Three Dog Bakery offer biscuits made of carob chips, apples, oatmeal, and peanut butter, and cats munch on Alaskan salmon bites.

Pampering your pet could cost you an arm and a paw!

LUXURY SUITE AT PET SPA	$110 A NIGHT
PROFESSIONAL MASSAGE	$35
CUSTOM-BUILT DOGHOUSE	$10,000
HAND-KNITTED SWEATER	$280
GOURMET DOG TREATS	$6.99

PET TECH

Think you're tech-savvy? With all the gadgets owners are buying for their pets, some animals may have you beat. Some owners set up webcams so their pets can watch them at work. And Petzila, a company dedicated to connecting pets with their owners, offers a device that allows away-from-home owners to see, talk to, and surprise a pet with a treat—all through Wi-Fi and the click of an app.

QUIZ WHIZ

How much do you know about all things animals? Quiz yourself!

ANSWERS BELOW

1 **True or false?** Male seahorses carry eggs in a kangaroo-like pouch.

2 **Which of the following is not an invertebrate?**
a. sponge
b. worm
c. echinoderm
d. Minion

3 **Bat hibernation caves are called _____.**
a. dens
b. grottoes
c. labyrinths
d. hibernacula

4 **What name do Kermode bears also go by?**
a. Kermit the Frog bears
b. brown bears
c. spirit bears
d. white bears

5 **Koalas eat one to two pounds (450 to 900 g) of _____ in a day.**
a. eucalyptus leaves
b. bamboo
c. grass
d. potato chips

Not **STUMPED** yet? Check out the *NATIONAL GEOGRAPHIC KIDS QUIZ WHIZ* collection for more crazy **ANIMAL** questions!

ANSWERS: 1. True ; 2. d ; 3. d ; 4. c ; 5. a

HOMEWORK HELP

Wildly Good Animal Reports

beluga whale

Your teacher wants a written report on the beluga whale. Not to worry. Use these organizational tools so you can stay afloat while writing a report.

STEPS TO SUCCESS: Your report will follow the format of a descriptive or expository essay (see p. 141 for "How to Write a Perfect Essay") and should consist of a main idea, followed by supporting details and a conclusion. Use this basic structure for each paragraph as well as the whole report, and you'll be on the right track.

1. Introduction
State your **main idea.**
The beluga whale is a common and important species of whale.

2. Body
Provide **supporting points** for your main idea.
The beluga whale is one of the smallest whale species.
It is also known as the "white whale" because of its distinctive coloring.
These whales are common in the Arctic Ocean's coastal waters.

Then **expand** on those points with further description, explanation, or discussion.
The beluga whale is one of the smallest whale species.
Belugas range in size from 13 to 20 feet (4 to 6.1 m) in length.
It is also known as the "white whale" because of its distinctive coloring.
Belugas are born gray or brown. They fade to white at around five years old.
These whales are common in the Arctic Ocean's coastal waters.
Some Arctic belugas migrate south in large herds when sea ice freezes over.

3. Conclusion
Wrap it up with a **summary** of your whole paper.
Because of its unique coloring and unusual features, belugas are among the most familiar and easily distinguishable of all the whales.

KEY INFORMATION

Here are some things you should consider including in your report:

> What does your animal look like?
> To what other species is it related?
> How does it move?
> Where does it live?
> What does it eat?
> What are its predators?
> How long does it live?
> Is it endangered?
> Why do you find it interesting?

SEPARATE FACT FROM FICTION: Your animal may have been featured in a movie or in myths and legends. Compare and contrast how the animal has been portrayed with how it behaves in reality. For example, penguins can't dance the way they do in *Happy Feet*.

PROOFREAD AND REVISE: As with any great essay, when you're finished, check for misspellings, grammatical mistakes, and punctuation errors. It often helps to have someone else proofread your work, too, as he or she may catch things you have missed. Also, look for ways to make your sentences and paragraphs even better. Add more descriptive language, choosing just the right verbs, adverbs, and adjectives to make your writing come alive.

BE CREATIVE: Use visual aids to make your report come to life. Include an animal photo file with interesting images found in magazines or printed from websites. Or draw your own! You can also build a miniature animal habitat diorama. Use creativity to help communicate your passion for the subject.

THE FINAL RESULT: Put it all together in one final, polished draft. Make it neat and clean, and remember to cite your references.

Plastic bottles can be creatively reused as hanging cactus planters.

WHERE HAVE THE ANIMALS GONE?

All around the world, animals face threats to their habitat, many of which are caused by humans. Read on about two animals and their fight for survival.

Habitat

The name "jaguar" comes from the Native American word *yaguar*, which means "he who kills with one leap."

Jaguars are good swimmers.

Jaguars have specialized eyes that are nearly twice as powerful at night as during the day to stalk and ambush prey in the dark.

Jaguars live to be 12 to 15 years old in the wild.

JAGUAR CUB

SAVING THE JAGUARS

Deep in the rain forest of Paraguay, jaguars stealthily sneak through the lush green plants and trees, stalking prey like peccaries and tapir, or take a cooling dip in the river. Here, the government and other organizations are striving to protect the forests in which the jaguars live. Other parts of the jaguar's range have not fared as well. Deforestation—humans chopping down trees to build farms, ranches, roads, and subdivisions—is destroying the jaguars' habitat and blocking their migration routes. This is leaving the cats stranded and vulnerable in the wild throughout their range—which extends through parts of North, South, and Central America—where they're exposed to humans who hunt them to protect their livestock. Facing this and other threats, jaguars have been all but eliminated in the United States, and experts estimate fewer than 15,000 remain in the wild.

In Paraguay, people are working to protect the forests of San Rafael National Park, a sanctuary for the hundreds of species of animals that live there, including jaguars. Further north, in Sonora, Mexico, six former cattle ranches have been combined to create 90 square miles (235 sq km) of rugged wilderness, known as the Northern Jaguar Reserve. Still, many jaguars live outside the protected boundaries, exposing them to human threats. Fortunately, conservation groups like the Northern Jaguar Project and Naturalia are stepping in to educate locals on the importance of saving the species and to stop illegal killing. And as their efforts intensify, the focus remains on securing a brighter future for the spotted cats.

Destruction

MANATEE RESCUE!

DRINK UP!

Swimming along a river in western Florida, U.S.A., a female manatee floats just beneath the water's surface. Dark in color and moving slowly, the manatee is hard to spot. Above the surface, a boat is heading straight toward her. The people on the boat don't see the manatee just below the surface. Suddenly, the boat collides with the manatee.

Luckily, this manatee, named Della, is rescued and treated at a rehabilitation center. Caretakers determine that she's just weeks away from having a baby. Soon, Della gives birth to a calf, named Pal. She also becomes an adoptive mom to Kee, a rescued orphaned calf. Della regains strength as she spends her days with the two calves, gliding around the water with them, and even napping with them at the bottom of their pool.

Five months later, it's time to release the trio back into the wild. Once submerged in their new stream, the manatee family happily paddles away.

Della, Pal, and Kee are lucky. They were rescued, treated, and given a new home. But that's not always the case. People are living in manatees' habitats. They are driving boats, fishing, and swimming in the water. That puts manatees at risk. Learning to share space with animals is important. Driving boats slowly and carefully in manatee habitats can help save these gentle giants.

When resting, manatees can stay submerged for up to 20 minutes.

Average adult manatees are about 10 feet (3 m) long and weigh 1,000 pounds (454 kg).

Manatees breathe only through their nostrils.

1 YOU CAN BUY JEANS MADE FROM PLASTICS FOUND FLOATING IN THE SEA.

2 Dogs have been trained to sniff out pollutants in waterways so the waste can be removed.

3 Scientists are trying to **convert sugar** into **clean fuel.**

4 Turning off the tap while brushing your teeth can conserve up to eight gallons (30 L) of water a day.

17 COOL THINGS ABOUT

5 The "Great Green Wall," a 4,400-mile (7,080-km)-long line of trees and vegetation, is being planted along the edge of Africa's Sahara.

6 A COMPANY IN DENMARK MAKES PLASTIC DINNER PLATES FROM RECYCLED PIG URINE.

7 The FIRST recorded PAPER RECYCLING happened in JAPAN in 1031.

8 In its lifetime, one reusable bag can prevent the use of 600 plastic bags.

9 THE *FASTEST* ELECTRIC CAR CAN TRAVEL OVER 300 MILES AN HOUR (483 KM/H).

10 Shower water at a Chumbe Island eco-resort in Zanzibar, Africa, comes from filtered rainwater.

11 An airport in England collects chewed gum that's RECYCLED INTO TOYS AND TIRES.

12 CITIES MAY ONE DAY BUILD FARMSCRAPERS—HIGH-RISES IN WHICH FARMERS GROW CROPS—TO CONSERVE LAND.

GOING GREEN

13 RECYCLING ONE CAN OF SODA WILL SAVE ENOUGH ENERGY TO POWER A TV FOR THREE HOURS.

14 **Environmentalists** sometimes use mushrooms to soak up oil spills and toxic waste.

15 IN 2014 THE UNITED STATES CREATED A PACIFIC OCEAN MARINE RESERVE NEARLY TWICE THE SIZE OF TEXAS.

16 The **TOKELAU ISLANDS** in the Pacific Ocean **RUN ON SOLAR POWER AND** COCONUT OIL.

17 A VERMONT, U.S.A., TOWN USES GRAZING SHEEP TO REDUCE THE NEED FOR GAS-GUZZLING LAWN MOWERS.

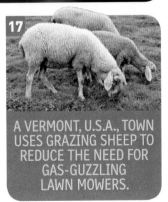

THE ARCTIC'S
DISAPPEARING ICE

In the past few decades, sea ice cover in the Arctic has shrunk because of global climate change. Arctic sea ice freezes up and expands in the winter and melts and shrinks in the summer. It typically reaches its smallest size every September. Scientists call this the "Arctic sea ice minimum." This minimum has shrunk from 3.02 million square miles (7.83 million sq km) in 1980 to about 1.4 million square miles (3.62 million sq km) in 2012. The change is so significant that cartographers at the National Geographic Atlas of the World redrew the map of the Arctic to reflect the smaller sea ice coverage. So what's behind this ice loss in the Arctic? Scientists point to a phenomenon known as the "positive feedback loop."

Sea ice's bright surface reflects sunlight back into space. This means icy areas absorb less solar energy and remain cool. But when air and ocean temperatures rise over time and more sea ice melts, fewer bright surfaces reflect sunlight back into space. The ice and exposed seawater absorb more solar energy, and this causes a feedback loop of more melting and more warming.

If the ice loss continues at the current rate, scientists are concerned the Arctic will become ice free during the summer at some point within this century. As the ice melts, it's essential that we find ways to protect the indigenous people and animals—such as polar bears and seals—that rely on the Arctic's ice for food and survival.

ARCTIC SEA ICE MINIMUM IN 1980

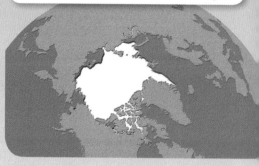

ARCTIC SEA ICE MINIMUM IN 2012

COMPARISON OF ARCTIC SEA ICE MINIMUMS

Arctic sea ice minimum in 1980

Arctic sea ice minimum in 2012

Pollution
Cleaning Up Our Act

So what's the big deal about a little dirt on the planet? Pollution can affect animals, plants, and people. In fact, some studies show that more people die every year from diseases linked to air pollution than from car accidents. And right now nearly one billion of the world's people don't have access to clean drinking water.

A LITTLE POLLUTION = BIG PROBLEMS
You can probably clean your room in a couple of hours. (At least we hope you can!) But you can't shove air and water pollution under your bed or cram them into the closet. Once released into the environment, pollution—whether it's oil leaking from a boat or chemicals spewing from a factory's smokestack—can have a lasting environmental impact.

KEEP IT CLEAN
It's easy to blame things like big factories for pollution problems. But some of the mess comes from everyday activities. Exhaust fumes from cars and garbage in landfills can seriously trash the Earth's health. We all need to pitch in and do some house-cleaning. It may mean bicycling more and riding in cars less. Or not dumping water-polluting oil or household cleaners down the drain. Look at it this way: Just as with your room, it's always better not to let Earth get messed up in the first place.

What a Prince!

The heir to the British throne is doing his part to save Earth's oceans. Working to combat both overfishing and the amount of plastic that lands in the ocean every year—8.8 million tons (8 million t) by some estimates—Prince Charles is leading a charitable drive to protect the seas with a focus on sustainable fishing. We'd say that's a quite a royal effort.

FOOD FOR THOUGHT

It may seem as if the world's oceans are so vast that nothing could hurt them. Unfortunately, that's not true. The oceans suffer from people dumping stuff in them that they don't want (pollution) and taking too much from them that they do want (overfishing). You can help turn this problem around.

BE AN OCEAN HERO!

You can be part of the solution if you carefully choose what fish to eat. Some are okay to eat; others you should avoid because they're overfished or caught in ways that harm the ocean. Check out the list below to help guide your seafood choices. To get the most up-to-date info, check out our Seafood Decision Guide at www.natgeoseafood.com. Ask your parents to consult it when they buy fish at the market or order it at a restaurant. Ask the grocer or chef where and how the fish was caught. Saving marine life is hard, but if everyone helps, it will make a difference.

BEST CHOICES

abalone (farmed)
catfish (U.S.)
clams (farmed)
clams, softshell
crab, Dungeness
crab, stone
crawfish (U.S.)
halibut, Pacific
lobster, spiny
   (Australia, Baja, U.S.)

mackerel, Atlantic
mahimahi (U.S. troll)
mullet (U.S.)
mussels (farmed)
oysters (farmed)
pollock, Alaska
sablefish/black cod
   (Alaska, Canada)
salmon (Alaska wild)
salmon, canned pink/sockeye

sardines (U.S.)
scallops, bay (farmed)
shrimp, pink (Oregon)
shrimp (U.S. farmed)
squid, longfin (U.S.)
striped bass (farmed)
tilapia (U.S.)
trout, rainbow (farmed)
tuna, albacore (Canada, U.S.)
tuna, yellowfin (U.S. troll)

WORST CHOICES

cod, Atlantic
crab, king (imported)
crawfish (China)
flounder/sole (Atlantic)
grouper
haddock (trawl)

halibut, Atlantic
mahimahi (imported longline)
orange roughy
salmon (farmed or Atlantic)
shark
shrimp/prawns (imported)

swordfish (imported)
tilapia (Asia)
tuna, bigeye (longline)
tuna, bluefin
tuna, yellowfin
   (imported longline)

In the first ever Almanac Newsmaker Challenge, we asked kids to Step Up to the Plate to Fight Food Waste. National Geographic Explorer Tristram Stuart inspired kids with the facts—***Enough food is wasted to feed all the 1 billion malnourished people on the planet three times over!***—and offered ideas on how we can all make a difference. Hundreds of kids from around the world went to our website and took the pledge to waste less food and inspire others to do the same. Here's who stepped up.

FIGHTING FOOD WASTE

About one-third of the world's food is wasted. And National Geographic Emerging Explorer Tristram Stuart wants to do something about that. To feed some of the one billion hungry people in the world, Stuart has started a global movement against food waste. This includes the campaign Feeding the 5,000, which offers free feasts featuring foods salvaged from farm waste piles, like surplus veggies, imperfect apples, and dinged-up tomatoes. With these types of events, Stuart hopes that everyone around the world will become just as fed up as he is about food waste and do something about it.

COUNTRIES REPRESENTED

15 countries were represented. Top countries: U.S., Canada, India, Japan, Philippines, and Vietnam. Top U.S. states: California and Florida.

Ireland · Canada · United States · California · Mexico · Florida · Trinidad & Tobago · Italy · Libya · Uganda · Egypt · India · Singapore · Philippines · Vietnam · Hong Kong · Japan

TRISTRAM STUART

BOYS VS GIRLS

30% more girls than boys participated.

AGES

11

Newsmakers were as young as 4 and as old as 68. The average age was 11.

FAMILIES

Average number of people in household: 4.3
Two families had 13 people!

FAVORITE VEGETABLE*

Broccoli 20% · Carrots 15% · Potatoes 9%
Corn 7% · Cucumber 6% · Spinach 6%
Beans 5% · Peas 3% · Other 30%

*This survey question was open-ended, so we got lots of responses!

6 TIPS to Save the Earth

The Earth needs your help! Here are six ways to protect our planet.

1 Take a Walk — Usually get a ride to your friend's house down the street? Ask your parents if you can walk or ride your bike there instead. Skipping the car ride not only saves gas, but it also cuts back on air pollution. Just make sure to always have an adult with you on longer walks or rides, and stick to the sidewalks—especially on busy roads.

2 Fill It Up — Of the billions of bottles of water consumed in the United States every year, only about 30 percent of those are actually recycled. The rest clog up landfills or wind up in the ocean, where they may harm sea animals. An easy fix? Drink from a reusable water bottle. Experts say tap water is totally safe to drink, and you'll do your part to reduce the waste.

3 Bag It — Like water bottles, plastic grocery bags are likely to become hazards to the environment, as they take many years to degrade. Next time you go the grocery store with Mom or Dad, remind them to bring along reusable shopping totes.

4 Eat Up — Mom's right: You really should eat everything on your plate! Around the world, 1.4 billion tons (1.3 billion t) of food is lost or wasted every year. And all of that rotting food is filling up landfills and releasing harmful greenhouse gases into the environment. Coming up with creative ways to use up food that would otherwise be tossed—like making muffins out of ripe bananas—can make a big impact on the future of our planet.

5 Go Portable — Laptop computers use 50 to 90 percent less energy than desktop computers.

6 Pick It Up — Every year, people around the world generate 2.6 trillion pounds (1.2 trillion kg) of garbage—equal to the weight of more than 6 million blue whales. And some of that will wind up in your local creeks and playgrounds. So grab some gloves and a trash bag and pick up trash. You'll get some fresh air and exercise—and help the environment, too.

DID YOU KNOW?
If food waste were a country, it would be the third largest emitter of greenhouse gases behind China and the United States.

TRY MAKING YOUR OWN SOAP

Don't trash your leftover bits of soap! Combine soap slivers to keep pieces of soap from going into the garbage—and adding to landfill. Squish the slivers into cool shapes when they're wet.

Try This!

By the Numbers
TRASH BREAKDOWN

After you toss out a banana peel, a soda can, or a smelly sock, it's out of sight, but it's still around—sometimes for weeks, and other times for hundreds of years! Here's a timeline of how long it takes everyday trash to decompose—or completely break down—in a landfill.

BANANA PEEL
2–5 WEEKS

APPLE CORE
2 MONTHS

WOOL SOCKS
1–5 YEARS

PLASTIC BAG
10–20 YEARS

LEATHER
50 YEARS

RUBBER BOOT SOLE
50–80 YEARS

ALUMINUM CAN
80–200 YEARS

PLASTIC FISHING LINE
600 YEARS

GLASS BOTTLE
1 MILLION YEARS OR MORE

GREEN Extremes

THESE OVER-THE-TOP IDEAS TAKE ECO-FRIENDLY TO A WHOLE NEW LEVEL. FIND OUT HOW FAR SOME PEOPLE WILL GO TO REUSE AND RECYCLE.

Recycled Art

This may look like a regular portrait, but look closely and you'll see it's actually made of discarded pieces of junk. Artist Zac Freeman collects objects like buttons, bike chains, and safety pins, and then glues them to a wooden canvas to create giant works of eco-friendly art.

Green Mile

A company in the Netherlands has plans to turn trash fished from the ocean into roads. Made from recycled plastic, the roads will provide an eco-friendly alternative to asphalt, which generates 1.6 million tons (1.5 million t) of CO_2 per year. Even cooler? The roads come in connectable pieces like Legos, so installing and fixing them will be a snap.

With the Ecocapsule, you can live anywhere in the world and leave no carbon footprints behind. This egg-shaped home—complete with a fold-up bed, mini kitchen, dining area, a toilet, and shower—generates its own clean energy, thanks to solar cells on the roof and a retractable wind turbine. As for running water? That comes from rain, captured and filtered from the capsule's curved roof.

Cool Capsule

No-Waste Home

This house is made completely out of recycled products and trash, including 4,000 VHS tapes, 500 bike tires, and 20,000 toothbrushes.

WASTE

93

QUIZ WHIZ

What's your eco-friendly IQ? Find out with this quiz!
ANSWERS BELOW

1 It can take up to _____ years for an aluminum can to decompose in a landfill.
a. 2
b. 20
c. 200
d. 2,000

2 True or false?
Jaguars are poor swimmers.

3 An airport in England makes recycled toys and tires out of which found items?
a. safety pins
b. coins
c. batteries
d. used chewing gum

4 About how many people around the world are lacking access to clean drinking water?
a. one billion
b. one million
c. one thousand
d. one hundred

5 Which famous royal figure is taking a stand to protect Earth's oceans?
a. Queen Elizabeth
b. King Kong
c. Prince Charles
d. Catherine Middleton

Not **STUMPED** yet? Check out the *NATIONAL GEOGRAPHIC KIDS QUIZ WHIZ* collection for more crazy **ENVIRONMENT** questions!

ANSWERS:
1. c; 2. False; 3. d; 4. a; 5. c

Write a Letter That Gets Results

Knowing how to write a good letter is a useful skill. It will come in handy anytime you want to persuade someone to understand your point of view. Whether you're emailing your congressperson or writing a letter for a school project or to your grandma, a great letter will help you get your message across. Most important, a well-written letter leaves a good impression.

Check out the example below for the elements of a good letter.

Your address

Date

Salutation
Always use "Dear" followed by the person's name; use Mr., Mrs., Ms., or Dr. as appropriate.

Introductory paragraph
Give the reason you're writing the letter.

Body
The longest part of the letter, which provides evidence that supports your position. Be persuasive!

Closing paragraph
Sum up your argument.

Complimentary closing
Sign off with "Sincerely" or "Thank you."

Your signature

Abby Jones
1204 Green Street
Los Angeles, CA 90045

March 31, 2017

Dear Mr. School Superintendent,

I am writing to you about how much excess energy our school uses and to offer a solution.

Every day, we leave the computers on in the classroom, the TVs are plugged in all the time, and the lights are on all day. All of this adds up to a lot of wasted energy, which is not only harmful for the Earth, as it increases the amount of harmful greenhouse gas emissions into the environment, but is also costly to the school. In fact, I read that schools spend more on energy bills than on computers and textbooks combined!

I am suggesting that we start an Energy Patrol to monitor the use of lighting, air-conditioning, heating, and other energy systems within our school. My idea is to have a group of students dedicated to figuring out ways we can cut back on our energy use in the school. We can do room checks, provide reminders to students and teachers to turn off lights and computers, replace old lightbulbs with energy-efficient products, and even reward the classrooms that do the most to save energy.

Above all, I think our school could help the environment tremendously by cutting back on how much energy we use. Let's see an Energy Patrol at our school soon. Thank you.

Sincerely,

Abby Jones

Abby Jones

COMPLIMENTARY CLOSINGS

Sincerely, Sincerely yours, Thank you, Regards, Best wishes, Respectfully,

Stilt fishermen wait for their catch among the reefs of the Sri Lankan coast. They fish from narrow bamboo benches built between two stilts.

Culture
Connection

CELEBRATIONS

1 CHINESE NEW YEAR
January 28
Also called Lunar New Year, this holiday marks the new year according to the lunar calendar. Families celebrate with parades, feasts, and fireworks. Young people may receive gifts of money in red envelopes.

2 HOLI
March 13
This festival in India celebrates spring and marks the triumph of good over evil. People cover one another with powdered paint, called *gulal,* and douse one another with buckets of colored water.

3 NAURYZ
March 21
This ancient holiday is a major moment on the Kazakhstan calendar. To usher in the start of spring, the people of this Asian country set up tentlike shelters called yurts, play games, go to rock concerts, and feast on rich foods.

4 QINGMING FESTIVAL
April 5
Also known as "Grave Sweeping Day," this Chinese celebration calls on people to return to the graves of their deceased loved ones. There, they tidy up the grave, as well as light firecrackers, burn fake money, and leave food as an offer to the spirits.

5 EASTER
April 16
A Christian holiday that honors the resurrection of Jesus Christ, Easter is celebrated by giving baskets filled with gifts, decorated eggs, or candy to children.

6 KONINGSDAG
April 27

Orange you glad it's King's Day? People across the Netherlands celebrate the monarchy with street parties and by wearing all things orange.

7 VESAK DAY
May 10
Buddhists around the world observe Buddha's Birthday with special rituals including chanting and prayer, candlelight processions, and meditation.

8 RAMADAN AND EID AL-FITR
May 27*–June 26**
A Muslim holiday, Ramadan is a month long, ending in the Eid Al-Fitr celebration. Observers fast during this month— eating only after sunset. People pray for forgiveness and hope to purify themselves through observance.

9 TANABATA
July 7
To commemorate this Star Festival, people in Japan first write wishes on colorful strips of paper. Then, they hang the paper on bamboo branches in their yards and around their homes in the hopes that their wishes will come true.

10 BASTILLE DAY
July 14
The French call this day *La Fête Nationale,* as it is the celebration of the start of the French Revolution in 1789. In Paris, fireworks light up the night skies while dance parties spill into the streets.

*Begins at sundown.
**Dates may vary slightly by location.

Around the World

11 NAG PANCHAMI
July 27
In Nepal and India, Hindus worship snakes—and keep evil spirits out of their homes—by sticking images of serpents on their doors and making offerings to the revered reptiles.

12 VERSLUNARMANNAHELGI
August 4–5
During Verslunarmannahelgi—also known as Iceland's Labor Day—people head to the great outdoors for camping trips, cookouts, and massive music festivals.

13 ROSH HASHANAH
September 20*–22
A Jewish holiday marking the beginning of a new year on the Hebrew calendar. Celebrations include prayer, ritual foods, and a day of rest.

14 HANUKKAH
December 12*–20
This Jewish holiday is eight days long. It commemorates the rededication of the Temple in Jerusalem. Hanukkah celebrations include the lighting of menorah candles for eight days and the exchange of gifts.

15 CHRISTMAS DAY
December 25
A Christian holiday marking the birth of Jesus Christ, Christmas is usually celebrated by decorating trees, exchanging presents, and having festive gatherings.

2017 CALENDAR

JANUARY
S	M	T	W	T	F	S
1	2	3	4	5	6	7
8	9	10	11	12	13	14
15	16	17	18	19	20	21
22	23	24	25	26	27	28
29	30	31				

FEBRUARY
S	M	T	W	T	F	S
			1	2	3	4
5	6	7	8	9	10	11
12	13	14	15	16	17	18
19	20	21	22	23	24	25
26	27	28	29			

MARCH
S	M	T	W	T	F	S
			1	2	3	4
5	6	7	8	9	10	11
12	13	14	15	16	17	18
19	20	21	22	23	24	25
26	27	28	29	30	31	

APRIL
S	M	T	W	T	F	S
						1
2	3	4	5	6	7	8
9	10	11	12	13	14	15
16	17	18	19	20	21	22
23	24	25	26	27	28	29
30						

MAY
S	M	T	W	T	F	S
	1	2	3	4	5	6
7	8	9	10	11	12	13
14	15	16	17	18	19	20
21	22	23	24	25	26	27
28	29	30	31			

JUNE
S	M	T	W	T	F	S
				1	2	3
4	5	6	7	8	9	10
11	12	13	14	15	16	17
18	19	20	21	22	23	24
25	26	27	28	29	30	

JULY
S	M	T	W	T	F	S
						1
2	3	4	5	6	7	8
9	10	11	12	13	14	15
16	17	18	19	20	21	22
23	24	25	26	27	28	29
30	31					

AUGUST
S	M	T	W	T	F	S
		1	2	3	4	5
6	7	8	9	10	11	12
13	14	15	16	17	18	19
20	21	22	23	24	25	26
27	28	29	30	31		

SEPTEMBER
S	M	T	W	T	F	S
					1	2
3	4	5	6	7	8	9
10	11	12	13	14	15	16
17	18	19	20	21	22	23
24	25	26	27	28	29	30

OCTOBER
S	M	T	W	T	F	S
1	2	3	4	5	6	7
8	9	10	11	12	13	14
15	16	17	18	19	20	21
22	23	24	25	26	27	28
29	30	31				

NOVEMBER
S	M	T	W	T	F	S
			1	2	3	4
5	6	7	8	9	10	11
12	13	14	15	16	17	18
19	20	21	22	23	24	25
26	27	28	29	30		

DECEMBER
S	M	T	W	T	F	S
					1	2
3	4	5	6	7	8	9
10	11	12	13	14	15	16
17	18	19	20	21	22	23
24	25	26	27	28	29	30
31						

HOWL-OWEEN
PET PARTY

BARK! I MEAN, BOO!

You expect to see ghosts, vampires, and pirates on Halloween. What you *don't* expect is for those creatures to have four legs. Millions of pets will be dressed up for the holiday—here are some of the funniest getups.

LANEY THE POMERANIAN ISN'T FOOLING ANYONE IN HER GHOST GETUP.

I THINK I COULD USE MORE HAIR SPRAY.

These pets like wearing costumes but yours may not. Never force your pet to do something it doesn't want to do.

FORGET BATMAN, I'M BATDOG!

MASON THE CHIHUAHUA MAKES GOING BATTY LOOK SUPERCUTE.

TOBY THE ENGLISH BULLDOG IS HAVING A SERIOUSLY AWESOME HAIR DAY.

THERE'S NO PLACE LIKE THE DOGGIE PARK!

I NOW PRONOUNCE ME THE CUTEST PUP EVER.

DRESSED AS DOROTHY FROM *THE WIZARD OF OZ*, NELLIE THE MIXED BREED IS ON THE LOOKOUT FOR A YELLOW BRICK ROAD.

TINSLEY THE TERRIER TAKES THE CAKE IN HER WEDDING-THEMED COSTUME.

TREAT YOUR PET

Instead of candy, which will hurt your pet's tummy, give your furry friend its own Halloween snack. Check out pet stores for ideas, or grab a parent and try one of the recipes below from the American Society for the Prevention of Cruelty to Animals.

CREEPY CAT COOKIES

- ¼ cup (60 ml) of warm water
- 5 tablespoons (75 ml) of grated Parmesan cheese
- 3 tablespoons (45 ml) of margarine
- 1 tablespoon (15 ml) of cod liver oil
- 1 cup (240 ml) of white flour
- ¼ cup (80 ml) of soy flour

Preheat the oven to 300°F (150°C). Combine the water, cheese, margarine, and oil, then add the flour. Roll the dough ¼ inch (6 mm) thick and cut it with spooky-shaped cookie cutters. Bake the cookies on an ungreased cookie sheet for 20 to 25 minutes.

PUMPKIN POOCH BITES

- 2½ cups (600 ml) of whole wheat flour
- ½ cup (120 ml) of fresh or canned pumpkin
- ½ cup (120 ml) of peanut butter
- 2 teaspoons (10 ml) of cinnamon
- 1 teaspoon (5 ml) of baking powder
- ½ cup (120 ml) of water

Preheat the oven to 350°F (180°C). In a bowl, whisk together the flour, pumpkin, peanut butter, cinnamon, and baking powder. Add water as needed, but the dough should be stiff and dry. Roll the dough until it's ½ inch (1 ¼ cm) thick and cut it with cookie cutters. Bake the treats for about 40 minutes.

If you dress up your pet, check that the outfit is comfortable and allows the animal to breathe and walk safely.

...d not ...gular ...our ...et has ...s or

101

What's Your Chinese Horoscope?
Locate your birth year to find out.

In Chinese astrology the zodiac runs on a 12-year cycle, based on the lunar calendar. Each year corresponds to one of 12 animals, each representing one of 12 personality types. Read on to find out which animal year you were born in and what that might say about you.

RAT
1972, '84, '96, 2008
Say cheese! You're attractive, charming, and creative. When you get mad, you can have really sharp teeth!

RABBIT
1975, '87, '99, 2011
Your ambition and talent make you jump at opportunity. You also keep your ears open for gossip.

HORSE
1966, '78, '90, 2002, '14
Being happy is your "mane" goal. And while you're smart and hardworking, your teacher may ride you for talking too much.

ROOSTER
1969, '81, '93, 2005, '17

You crow about your adventures, but inside you're really shy. You're thoughtful, capable, brave, and talented.

OX
1973, '85, '97, 2009
You're smart, patient, and as strong as an ... well, you know what. Though you're a leader, you never brag.

DRAGON
1976, '88, 2000, '12
You're on fire! Health, energy, honesty, and bravery make you a living legend.

SHEEP
1967, '79, '91, 2003, '15
Gentle as a lamb, you're also artistic, compassionate, and wise. You're often shy.

DOG
1970, '82, '94, 2006, '18
Often the leader of the pack, you're loyal and honest. You can also keep a secret.

TIGER
1974, '86, '98, 2010
You may be a nice person, but no one should ever enter your room without asking—you might attack!

SNAKE
1977, '89, 2001, '13

You may not speak often, but you're very smart. You always seem to have a stash of cash.

MONKEY
1968, '80, '92, 2004, '16
No "monkey see, monkey do" for you. You're a clever problem-solver with an excellent memory.

PIG
1971, '83, '95, 2007

Even though you're courageous, honest, and kind, you never hog all the attention.

Make a 3-D Valentine!

Be sweet to your loved ones and the Earth this Valentine's Day by turning everyday items around your house into something heartfelt. Show how much you care about the environment by creating recycled cards for your family and friends.

YOU WILL NEED

- Old newspaper or leftover tissue paper
- Heart-shaped cookie cutter
- A clean plate
- Bowl of water
- Paintbrush
- Glue wash (equal parts glue and water)
- An old greeting card

WHAT TO DO

1 Tear newspaper or tissue paper into small pieces. Place the cookie cutter on the plate. Making sure each piece overlaps, position a few pieces of the paper inside the cookie cutter to create a thin layer. Dip your finger into the bowl of water and then press it gently on the paper layer, making the paper damp. Continue layering, dipping, and pressing until the cookie cutter is about half full. Let it dry for at least a day.

2 When the paper mold is completely dry, gently press down on the mold and carefully lift off the cookie cutter. Using a clean paintbrush, apply a light coat of glue wash to the mold. As it dries, move on to Step 3.

3 Cover an old greeting card with things from around the house—such as construction paper, magazines, newspapers, or doilies. Write a poem or message inside the card and then glue your 3-D heart to the front. Now you're ready to give this Earth-friendly valentine to someone you love!

Archaeologist
Fred Hiebert
digs the past

Imagine traveling to a far-flung destination and searching for artifacts in some of the planet's most remote places: deep, dark caves, desert oases, and even the bottom of the ocean.

That's just what Fred Hiebert does as a National Geographic explorer and archaeologist. His mission? Exploring the world in the hopes of unearthing artifacts so he can piece together critical information about the past.

Hiebert's work has spanned from Asia—where he led excavations along the Silk Road—to South America as he searched for signs of submerged settlements in Lake Titicaca, the continent's highest lake. His excavations have been applauded for unlocking mysteries surrounding ancient cultures, giving us a deeper understanding of what life was like thousands of years ago.

TIMELESS TREASURES

In many ways, archaeologists—and anthropologists, who study human civilization and cultures—are like treasure hunters. But the bounty isn't always shiny pieces of gold or glittering jewels. Many times, the most impressive artifacts are extremely simple, like a

piece of pottery. Hiebert's current excavations are at an ancient palace submerged along the edge of a lake in Kyrgyzstan, west of China.

"Along the ancient Silk Road in Central Asia is a valley where caravans and armies had to go around a lake. At one place along the lakeshore, the locals told us stories of a fantastic building underwater. Too good to be true?" Hiebert says.

NATIONAL GEOGRAPHIC KiDS

ALMANAC NEWSMAKER CHALLENGE

A Present for the Future

Calling all future explorers! Help us preserve our past by participating in the 2017 Almanac Newsmaker Challenge, led by Fred Hiebert. What you'll do: Create a virtual time capsule with up to ten key items that tell us about you, your family, friends, or community. Photograph it, then submit your shot by March 1, 2017, to ngkidsmyshot.com with the hashtag #timecapsule. Highlights will be featured in the 2018 National Geographic Kids' Almanac.

Time Capsule
Buried November 2000
Open on Veterans Day
November 11, 2050
Sponsored by Veterans of the Tri-State
And
The Greater Huntington Park and Recreation District

What items (or "artifacts") represent the things that are important to you today and would tell kids in 2050 about what life was like in 2017?

"Our underwater archaeological expedition is finding actual remains of a huge building which is 600 years old. It was built along the shore when the lake level was lower. This expedition is proving that sometimes legends are true!"

Unexpected discoveries like these can offer archaeologists and anthropologists the key to understanding ancient cultures. And it's the work of experts like Hiebert that brings to light new stories and details that might otherwise remain buried in the past.

World's Wackiest
HOUSES

Check out these not-so-humble abodes from around the globe.

Your house is a place to kick back and get cozy. But what if it also had 27 floors, a replica of King Tut's burial chamber, or an indoor garden? Make yourself at home in some of the coolest dwellings from around the world.

Nearly 30,000 registered archaeological sites are spread across Mexico.

SEA CREATURE SHACK

Naucalpan, Mexico
Here's what it'd be like to dwell in a shell. Architect Javier Senosiain designed this home to look like a real shelled sea creature called the nautilus. The house has curved rooms and looping hallways, plus a large front window with multicolored glass. There's even an indoor garden. The center of the house holds a circular TV room lined with soft couches. If you lived here, you'd never want to come out of your shell.

HOBBIT HOME

Pembrokeshire, Wales

Not all hobbit houses are located in mythical Middle Earth. Simon Dale constructed a family home that looks as if it came straight from *The Lord of the Rings* movies. The grass-covered dwelling was made from scrap wood, twisty tree limbs, and plaster. Inside, floor-to-ceiling tree trunks hold up the roof. Dale built the home in four months with mainly a hammer, chain saw, and chisel—no wizards necessary.

Wales is said to have more castles per square mile than any other European country.

TOWER POWER

Mumbai, India

For a billionaire looking for new digs, the sky's the limit. One wealthy businessman even had a 27-story skyscraper built as a private home for his family of five. The tower—which supposedly cost one billion dollars—boasts a spa, ballroom, movie theater, and yoga studio. Literally living the high life comes at a price, though. The building's first electric bill reportedly totaled $115,000!

Some 447 languages are spoken in India.

Brazil's soccer team has won five World Cups—that's more than any other nation.

ROUND RESIDENCE

São Paulo, Brazil

Sculpted from cement and iron by Eduardo Longo, the 32-foot (9.8-m)-tall house known as the Sphere has three stories and a sleek interior. Instead of a staircase, levels are linked by a winding ramp. For outdoor fun, you can grab onto a rope swing attached to the exterior and go flying around the orb. Longo hopes to create neighborhoods of stacked Sphere houses as a way to save space in his jam-packed city.

1 You can find "Sunday Best Roast Chicken" and "Chilli & Chocolate" **POTATO CHIPS** in Great Britain.

2 IF YOU THINK YOU'VE TRIED EVERY KIND OF POPSICLE, THINK AGAIN: YOU CAN BUY A **pickle-flavored** ONE IN THE UNITED STATES!

3 **BEEF TONGUE** is a popular flavor of ice cream in Tokyo, Japan.

4 THE "FAT ELVIS ON-A-STICK" IS A DEEP-FRIED, BANANA-BATTERED PEANUT BUTTER CUP WITH BACON.

17 ZANY FACTS ABOUT

5 You can order **FRIED WILD EEL SPINE** at a restaurant in New York City, U.S.A.

6 Silkworm larvae are steamed or boiled and sold at street markets in South Korea. In China and Vietnam, they're fried.

7 **BIRD'S NEST SOUP,** a Chinese delicacy, is made with a swiftlet's nest floating in broth. Swiftlets make their nests entirely out of sticky saliva.

8 During Roman times, people ate dormice—as appetizers and for dessert!

9

Oreo cookies
TASTE—AND LOOK—DIFFERENT AROUND THE GLOBE. IN INDONESIA, SOME ARE FLAVORED LIKE BLUEBERRY ICE CREAM.

IN ARGENTINA, OREOS "x3" HAVE 3 COOKIES AND 2 LAYERS OF FILLING.

10

Fried Kool-Aid balls— MADE WITH A DEEP-FRIED COMBO OF FLOUR, WATER, AND KOOL-AID MIX—ARE SOLD AT SOME U.S. COUNTY FAIRS.

11

TUNA EYEBALLS are served up with garlic and soy sauce in Japan.

12

Fairgoers in Arizona, U.S.A., can buy caramel apples dipped in **MEALWORMS!**

FAR-OUT FOOD

13

At a restaurant in Taiwan, food is SERVED IN MINI-TOILETS.

14

You can buy jam infused with sand from near the Great Pyramid at Giza, Egypt.

15

Bananas, curry, and mashed potatoes are **TOPPINGS** served on pizza in Sweden.

16

WASABI-INFUSED KIT KAT CANDY BARS ARE SOLD IN JAPAN.

17

ROCKET FIZZ SODA POP OFFERS UP SODA FLAVORS RANGING FROM PEANUT BUTTER AND JELLY TO BACON!

109

CHEW ON THIS

SUSHI!

"Sushi" means "raw fish," right? Wrong! It's believed to come from the Japanese word *su*, meaning "vinegar," and *meshi*, the Japanese word for "rice." So sushi is really "vinegar rice," or sticky rice. Some sushi has raw fish in it, but plenty has no seafood at all. You can roll in whatever ingredients you want—chicken, vegetables, even candy!

GINGER has been used to treat things such as bellyaches and burns.

WASABI, the spicy green herb eaten with sushi, is sometimes faked using horseradish and food coloring.

Ancient Japanese warriors called samurai were paid with **RICE.**

SEAWEED has been used to polish shoes.

CUCUMBERS are 96 percent water.

CHECK OUT THE BOOK!

NATIONAL GEOGRAPHIC KIDS

COOK BOOK

COOL THINGS ABOUT JAPAN

The first known people to live in Japan arrived about 35,000 years ago.	The capital city of Tokyo was once a small fishing village named Edo.	It's considered polite to slurp your noodles in Japan.	In 2012 more than 50,000 people in Japan were at least 100 years old.	More pets live in Japan than children.

CREPES!

It might sound fancy, but the crepe is basically a paper-thin take on the pancake. The French dish was once served in place of bread, but today it's topped or stuffed with a variety of sweet or savory ingredients. Bon appétit!

In 1493, Christopher Columbus took chickens on his second voyage to the New World so his sailors would have **EGGS** to eat during their travels.

The old London Stock Exchange was nicknamed **"GORGONZOLA** Hall" because its marble walls resembled the Italian cheese.

In the 18th century, **ASPARAGUS** was called "sparrow-grass."

Europeans once believed that dried bunches of **CHIVES** hanging in a home would drive away evil influences.

The world record for the most slices of **HAM** cut in one hour is 2,160.

MAKE YOUR OWN CREPES

Get a parent's help to whip up some delicious crepes.

1 Mix 1½ cups (240 ml) of flour, 1 tablespoon (15 ml) of sugar, 1 teaspoon (5 ml) of baking powder, ½ teaspoon (2.5 ml) each of salt and vanilla, and 2 cups (480 ml) of milk into a large mixing bowl.

2 In a smaller bowl, beat 2 eggs, breaking up the yolks. Pour them into the large bowl, and whisk with the other ingredients until the batter is smooth.

3 Add 1 teaspoon (5 ml) of margarine to a medium-size frying pan and heat until bubbly. Add ½ cup (120 ml) of the crepe batter, covering the bottom of the pan.

4 Cook for 30 seconds until lightly browned. Use a spatula to flip and cook the other side. Repeat until you run out of batter.

5 Roll the crepes with ham, egg, cheese, or any other filling you'd like. Sprinkle a handful of chopped chives on top.

MONEY Around the World!

Jordan's **HALF-DINAR COIN** has seven sides.

TO SPEND $1 BILLION A DOLLAR AT A TIME, YOU'D HAVE TO PAY A BUCK A SECOND FOR NEARLY 32 YEARS.

IN THAILAND, OVAL BARS OF SILVER ONCE USED AS MONEY WERE CALLED **"TIGER TONGUES."**

IN ARGENTINA, **"MANGO"** IS SLANG FOR **"PESO."**

BANCO CENTRAL DE CHILE
FA6876603
20 MIL PESOS
2006
20000
VEINTE MIL PESOS

A **20,000**-PESO **BANKNOTE FROM** CHILE **CONTAINS INK THAT CHANGES COLOR WHEN TILTED.**

The **INCA** called gold **"THE SWEAT OF THE SUN"** and silver **"THE TEARS OF THE MOON."**

112

DENMARK'S 50-ORE COIN has a **HEART** on it.

I KNEW I SHOULD'VE TRIED A FAKE ATM INSTEAD.

IN 2002, A MAN OPENED A FAKE BANK AND TOOK IN **$650,000** BEFORE HE WAS CAUGHT.

POTATOES were once used as **CURRENCY** on the **SOUTH ATLANTIC ISLAND** of **TRISTAN DA CUNHA.**

A 1913 U.S. LIBERTY HEAD NICKEL—ONE OF ONLY FIVE IN EXISTENCE— **SOLD AT** AUCTION FOR MORE THAN **$3.1 MILLION.**

THE PHRASE **"BRING HOME THE BACON"** STARTED AFTER A 12TH-CENTURY PRIEST REWARDED A MARRIED COUPLE WITH A SIDE OF BACON.

BRICKS OF COMPRESSED TEA LEAVES WERE ONCE USED AS CURRENCY IN SIBERIA, MONGOLIA, AND CHINA.

MONEY TIP!

ANYTIME YOU BUY SOMETHING **ON SALE,** PUT WHAT YOU SAVED IN YOUR PIGGY BANK.

12 Ways to Say Friend

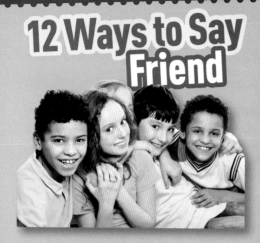

1. AFRIKAANS: **vriend** (male) / **vriendin** (female)
2. CANTONESE: **pung yau**
3. GERMAN: **Freund** (male) / **Freundin** (female)
4. HAWAIIAN: **hoaloha**
5. HINDI: **dost**
6. ICELANDIC: **vinur** (male) / **vinkona** (female)
7. MALAY: **kawan**
8. SPANISH: **amigo** (male) / **amiga** (female)
9. SWAHILI: **rafiki**
10. TAGALOG (Filipino): **kaibigan**
11. AKUAPIM TWI (Ghana): **adamfo**
12. WELSH: **ffrind**

LANGUAGES IN PERIL

TODAY, there are more than 7,000 languages spoken on Earth. But by 2100, more than half of those may disappear. In fact, experts say one language dies every two weeks, due to the increasing dominance of larger languages, such as English, Spanish, and Mandarin. So what can be done to keep dialects from disappearing? Efforts like National Geographic's Enduring Voices Project are now tracking down and documenting the world's most threatened indigenous languages, such as Tofa, spoken only by people in Siberia, and Magati Ke, from Aboriginal Australia. The hope is to preserve these languages— and the cultures they belong to.

10 LEADING LANGUAGES

Approximate population of first-language speakers (in millions)

1. Chinese*	1,197
2. Spanish	414
3. English	335
4. Hindi	260
5. Arabic	237
6. Portuguese	203
7. Bengali	193
8. Russian	167
9. Japanese	122
10. Javanese	83

Some languages have only a few hundred speakers, while Chinese has nearly one billion two hundred million native speakers worldwide. That's about triple the next largest group of language speakers. Colonial expansion, trade, and migration account for the spread of the other most widely spoken languages. With growing use of the Internet, English is becoming the language of the technology age.

*Includes all forms of the language.

Bet you **didn't know**

6 epic facts
about mythology

1 One **cyclops** from Greek mythology **liked to snack** on humans.

2 To live **forever,** gods in ancient Chinese myths **ate** peaches from a **magic tree.**

3 An Irish folklore **hero** carried a **spear** made of **sea monster bones.**

4 The spirits of **old umbrellas** appear in some **Japanese myths.**

5 Certain African tales feature a **snake** that **belches out rainbows.**

6 According to **Viking** lore, the god Odin rode an **eight-legged horse.**

115

MONSTER MYTHS

5 TERRIFYING TALES DEBUNKED

BUSTED!

Are monsters more than just the stuff of freaky films? Some people think so. They believe that big, bad beasts—hairy giants, pterodactyl-like brutes, and more—lurk just out of sight in areas around the world. Luckily scientists have explanations that bust these tales. Check out five monster myths that have been defanged.

The Nepali name for Mount Everest in the Himalaya means "Forehead of the Sky."

MYTH 1

THE LOVELAND FROG, A BIG AMPHIBIOUS CREATURE, PROWLS AN OHIO, U.S.A., TOWN.

HOW IT MAY HAVE STARTED

This slimy, froglike beast is said to stand four feet (1.2 m) tall and walk on two legs. In 1972 a police officer claimed he caught sight of it on a roadside while driving through Loveland, Ohio, U.S.A. at night. When another officer also reported seeing the freaky frog, the rumor took off.

WHY IT'S NOT TRUE

An investigation by local police found no evidence of the creature. Later, one of the police officers stated that he didn't actually believe that he had seen a monster, and that people had exaggerated his story. It's probable that the Loveland Frog was actually an escaped pet monitor lizard—some types can stretch ten feet (3 m).

SHAGGY-HAIRED BEASTS CALLED YETIS ROAM ASIA'S PEAKS.

HOW IT MAY HAVE STARTED

Yetis are allegedly hairy ogres that look like a human-bear hybrid with jagged fangs. The legend of the yeti probably originated in Tibet, a territory nestled near Asia's Himalaya mountain range. Sherpas, a once-nomadic people from the area, may have spread the myth during their travels in the 16th century. People still claim to see yetis today.

WHY IT'S NOT TRUE

In 2014 scientists did DNA tests on strands of hair found where yetis were supposedly spotted. Results showed that the hairs came not from an unknown beast, but from a rare sub-species of brown bear that lives in the area. It's likely that those who claimed to have seen a yeti really just saw this bear.

MYTH 2

MYTH 3

THE DOBHAR-CHÚ—PART DOG, PART OTTER, ALL MONSTER—LURKS IN IRELAND.

HOW IT MAY HAVE STARTED
An otter-dog mix, the Dobhar-Chú (Gaelic for "water hound") supposedly inhabits Ireland's lakes. It's known for unleashing eerie whistles and having an appetite for humans. No one knows where the legend of this beast came from, but it dates back to at least the 1700s, when a carved image of the creature appeared on the tombstone of one of its alleged victims.

WHY IT'S NOT TRUE
It's more likely that Dobhar-Chú is a Eurasian otter. The animal is found in Ireland's rivers and lakes and often whistles to communicate.

Lough Corrib, a huge lake in western Ireland, contains more than 360 islands.

The wetlands of Lake Bangweulu in Zambia are home to roughly 390 species of birds.

MYTH 4

THE KONGAMATO, A FLYING REPTILIAN MONSTER, ATTACKS BOATERS IN AFRICA.

HOW IT MAY HAVE STARTED
Reportedly seen soaring over southern and central African swamps, the Kongamato is said to have leathery wings, sharp teeth, and a bad habit of swooping down to smash boats that paddle into its territory. Some say the creature is a pterodactyl—a prehistoric flying reptile. Although the myth has circulated for about a century, its origins are unknown.

WHY IT'S NOT TRUE
Scientists know the Kongamato couldn't be a long-extinct pterodactyl. It's more likely a swamp-dwelling hammerhead bat, the largest bat in Africa. It could also be a big type of stingray that tips boats as it leaps from the water.

MYTH 5

IN THE AMERICAS, THE BEASTLY CHUPACABRA DRINKS THE BLOOD OF FARM ANIMALS.

HOW IT MAY HAVE STARTED
When several goats and chickens in areas of Puerto Rico turned up dead with their blood seemingly drained in the 1990s, rumors spread that the culprit was a vampire-like monster with fangs, a forked tongue, and quills running down its back. A rash of similar deaths that occurred a few years later in Texas were also blamed on the Chupacabra (which roughly translates to "goat sucker" in Spanish).

WHY IT'S NOT TRUE
Investigators looking into the deaths of chickens in Texas found no real evidence that the animals' blood had been drained, making the possibility of a vampire-like slayer way less likely. And sightings of the Chupacabra have usually turned out to be sickly coyotes or dogs suffering from mange, a skin condition that gives them a sinister appearance.

117

World Religions

Around the world, religion takes many forms. Some belief systems, such as Christianity, Islam, and Judaism, are monotheistic, meaning that followers believe in just one supreme being. Others, like Hinduism, Shintoism, and most native belief systems, are polytheistic, meaning that many of their followers believe in multiple gods.

All of the major religions have their origins in Asia, but they have spread around the world. Christianity, with the largest number of followers, has three divisions—Roman Catholic, Eastern Orthodox, and Protestant. Islam, with about one-fifth of all believers, has two main divisions—Sunni and Shiite. Hinduism and Buddhism account for almost another one-fifth of believers. Judaism, dating back some 4,000 years, has more than 13 million followers, less than one percent of all believers.

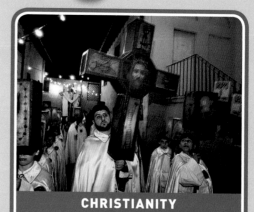

CHRISTIANITY

Based on the teachings of Jesus Christ, a Jew born some 2,000 years ago in the area of modern-day Israel, Christianity has spread worldwide and actively seeks converts. Followers in Switzerland (above) participate in an Easter season procession with lanterns and crosses.

BUDDHISM

Founded about 2,400 years ago in northern India by the Hindu prince Gautama Buddha, Buddhism spread throughout East and Southeast Asia. Buddhist temples have statues, such as the Mihintale Buddha (above) in Sri Lanka.

HINDUISM

Dating back more than 4,000 years, Hinduism is practiced mainly in India. Hindus follow sacred texts known as the Vedas and believe in reincarnation. During the festival of Navratri, which honors the goddess Durga, the Garba dance is performed (above).

CLOSE-UP

Technology Meets Tradition

It has been 1,200 years since the bishop of Rome became known as the pope. Pope Francis became the head of the Roman Catholic Church in 2013 and has embraced technology as a way to reach Catholics around the globe. He's the first pope to pose for a selfie and has more than 22 million Twitter followers.

ISLAM

Muslims believe that the Koran, Islam's sacred book, records the words of Allah (God) as revealed to the Prophet Muhammad beginning around A.D. 610. Believers (above) circle the Kaaba in the Haram Mosque in Mecca, Saudi Arabia, the spiritual center of the faith.

JUDAISM

The traditions, laws, and beliefs of Judaism date back to Abraham (the Patriarch) and the Torah (the first five books of the Old Testament). Followers pray before the Western Wall (above), which stands below Islam's Dome of the Rock in Jerusalem.

119

QUIZ WHIZ

Take this quiz to find out how much you know about the world around you!

ANSWERS BELOW

1 **True or false?** Beef tongue ice cream is a popular flavor in Tokyo, Japan.

2 Wales is said to have more _____ per square mile than any other European country?
a. sheep
b. people
c. castles
d. whales

3 Why was the old London Stock Exchange nicknamed "Gorgonzola Hall?"
a. It smelled like stinky Italian cheese.
b. A cheese monger sold gorgonzola from the lobby of the building.
c. Its marble resembled the cheese.
d. It was owned by Mr. Alfred Gorgonzola.

4 Bricks of _____ were once used as currency in Siberia.
a. tea leaves
b. concrete
c. clay
d. gold

5 In Greek mythology, what was one cyclops's favorite snack?
a. peaches
b. humans
c. snakes
d. bubble gum

Not **STUMPED** yet? Check out the *NATIONAL GEOGRAPHIC KIDS QUIZ WHIZ* collection for more crazy **CULTURE** questions!

ANSWERS:
1. True; 2. c; 3. c; 4. a; 5. b

HOMEWORK HELP

Explore a New Culture

You're a student, but you're also a citizen of the world. Writing a report on a foreign nation or your own country is a great way to better understand and appreciate how different people live. Pick the country of your ancestors, one that's been in the news, or one that you'd like to visit someday.

Passport to Success
A country report follows the format of an expository essay because you're "exposing" information about the country you choose.

Simple Steps

1. **RESEARCH** Gathering information is the most important step in writing a good country report. Look to Internet sources, encyclopedias, books, magazine and newspaper articles, and other sources to find important and interesting details about your subject.

2. **ORGANIZE YOUR NOTES** Put the information you gathered into a rough outline. For example, sort everything you found about the country's system of government, climate, etc.

3. **WRITE IT UP** Follow the basic structure of good writing: introduction, body, and conclusion. Remember that each paragraph should have a topic sentence that is then supported by facts and details. Incorporate the information from your notes, but make sure it's in your own words. And make your writing flow with good transitions and descriptive language.

4. **ADD VISUALS** Include maps, diagrams, photos, and other visual aids.

5. **PROOFREAD AND REVISE** Correct any mistakes, and polish your language. Do your best!

6. **CITE YOUR SOURCES** Be sure to keep a record of your sources.

A mountaineer stands at the summit of Barrhorn in the Swiss Alps. At 11,844 feet (3,610 m), Barrhorn is one of the highest hiking mountains in Europe.

DARE to EXPLORE

KENNETH SIMS
Geologist / geochemist

Do you have what it takes to be a great explorer? Read these stories of four adventurers, and see how you can get started on the exploration path.

WANT TO BE A GEOLOGIST?
STUDY: Geology, math, and physics
WATCH: PBS's *The Volcano Watchers*
READ: *Endurance: Shackleton's Incredible Voyage* by Alfred Lansing

"**Don't ever let** fear of failure **get in the way of** your goals. **There are no defeats,** only setbacks."

A SWELTERING LAVA LAKE

SIMS REACHES A CRATER'S RIM.

"**M**y job is to investigate something called radioactive isotopes. These are unstable atoms that are found in volcanic rock and lava. Researching them can give us clues about how volcanoes work and help us predict future eruptions.

"Collecting samples to study can be dangerous but exciting. I've climbed down ropes into the mouths of volcanoes, dived to volcanic vents on the ocean floor, and traveled to a frozen peak in Antarctica where molten lava bubbles within. To stare into an active volcano is like standing at the top of a football stadium filled with seething lava.

"Some of my experiences have been scary. But I try to stay unafraid. You do the best you can to keep safe while getting the job done. It's important to live life to its fullest."

EARTH HAS ABOUT 1,500 ACTIVE VOLCANOES.

LALY LICHTENFELD
Conservationist

WANT TO BE A CONSERVATIONIST?

STUDY: Biology, ecology, and history

WATCH: *Game of Lions,*
a National Geographic film

READ: *Facing the Lion* by
Joseph Lemasolai Lekuton

"Stay curious and always try to **learn new things.** Being open to **new experiences** will lead to **amazing opportunities.**"

"**S**itting in my tent during an expedition into the wilderness of Tanzania, I was startled by a big, beautiful lioness ambling through our campsite. Lions usually try to avoid close encounters with humans. But this one padded right up to me. I sat very still, but my heart was pounding. Would she pounce or swipe at me? The animal just stood motionless for some time, looking into my eyes. Then she turned around and trotted off. It was a very special moment.

"My job is to protect big cats such as lions in Tanzania. Humans pose a big threat to these animals. That's because the big cats sometimes hunt cows and other livestock owned by people. When the humans try to stop them, the felines can get hurt—or worse. My team and I work to resolve conflicts between people and cats peacefully. For instance, we teach farmers how to build special fences called bomas around their livestock that keep lions out.

"Big cats around the world face threats. But there's so much we can do to help."

BUILDING A BOMA

LIONS ARE THE ONLY CATS THAT LIVE IN GROUPS.

CORY RICHARDS
Adventure photographer

WANT TO BE A PHOTOGRAPHER?

STUDY: Photography, anthropology, and geology

WATCH: The documentary *Cave People of the Himalaya*

READ: *Banner in the Sky* by James Ramsey Ullman

"Don't let **obstacles** discourage you from reaching your **goals**. Anything is **possible** if you put your **heart** into it."

RICHARDS SCALES A PEAK IN THE ROCKY MOUNTAINS IN CANADA ON A PHOTO EXPEDITION.

RICHARDS' STUNNING PHOTOGRAPHY

CANADA

EUROPE'S CRIMEAN PENINSULA

"**O**ne time I was rappelling, or descending by rope, down a seaside cliff in Spain to photograph some climbers. Suddenly the rock that my rope was anchored to at the top of the cliff broke away. My stomach lurched as I went into a free fall, plummeting 50 feet (15 m) into the ocean. Once I hit the water, the heavy camera equipment strapped to my body dragged me under the waves. With my heart hammering, I freed myself from the gear and swam to the surface. My cameras were ruined, but I was alive.

"Working as a photographer can be a nonstop adventure. My career has taken me to every terrain imaginable, from icy peaks in Asia to the vast plains of Africa to coral reefs in the South Pacific Ocean. I've snapped pictures of people scaling mountains, diving, and skiing across Antarctica. I love using photography to show the incredible things humans are capable of doing.

"Getting the right shot involves creativity and sometimes danger. Stay open to new experiences, and you'll never be disappointed."

IN EXTREME COLD, CAMERAS CAN PACK UP WITH ICE.

MEAVE AND LOUISE LEAKEY

WANT TO BE A PALEONTOLOGIST?
STUDY: Geology, biology, and chemistry
WATCH: National Geographic's *Mysteries of Mankind*
READ: *The Skull in the Rock* by Lee R. Berger and Marc Aronson; *The Tree of Life: Charles Darwin* by Peter Sís

LOUISE MEAVE

"Important lessons about **our existence** today can only **be learned** by studying the past."

LOUISE LEAKEY WORKING IN THE FIELD

"Searching for clues to our human ancestry is a lot like putting together complex, 3-D puzzles in which all the pieces are buried deep in the ground.

"One particular morning my mother and I had been out collecting fossils. Our bags were heavy, our water had run out, it was hot, and we still had a 20-minute walk to the car. But we stopped to look at the two final points on our list. We found the fossil of a piece of a skull barely visible on the surface and we dug out the large block of sandstone containing what we hoped was the entire fossil to carry back to camp. After several months of cleaning the fossil under a microscope, we realized what we'd discovered: the preserved, small skull of *Homo erectus*, one of the closest relatives to today's human beings.

"Paleontology requires patience and concentration, a love of the outdoors, and a deep curiosity about our past and what life was like before humans. In the field, you need to be comfortable with a rugged existence, away from all the comforts of home—and most important: You have to be a team player."

A 4.1-MILLION-YEAR-OLD JAW

A MORE THAN 3-MILLION-YEAR-OLD SKULL

SOME FOSSILS ARE 3.5 BILLION YEARS OLD.

National Geographic Emerging Explorer **Jessica Cramp** spends most of her time on the water in exotic locations tracking sharks. Here's a glimpse at all of the must-haves found inside her backpack.

1 LONG SARONG.
"I use it as a towel, drape it over my head and shoulders to act as a sunshade, and dip it in water to cool down. And it serves as a wrap when I get cold."

2 KEVLAR GLOVES.
"To avoid cuts from fishing line and hooks."

3 ZIPLOC BAGS.
"FLEXIBLE AND WATERPROOF, THEY'RE GOOD FOR KEEPING THINGS DRY ON BOATS, ESPECIALLY IF WE GET CAUGHT IN A RAINSTORM."

17 THINGS IN AN EXPLORER'S

4 TWO WATER BOTTLES.
"You have to stay hydrated out there."

5 BATHYMETRIC MAPS OF ISLANDS.
"TO NAVIGATE, TO MAKE CLEAR MARKS ON WHERE WE HAVE SURVEYED AND CAUGHT SHARKS, AND TO LOOK AT THE BOTTOM/REEF CONTOURS FOR AREAS THAT WOULD BE GOOD SHARK HABITAT."

6 MASK AND SNORKEL.
"I'm always prepared to get in!"

7 WATERPROOF NOTEBOOK AND PERMANENT MARKERS.
"FOR CAPTURING DATA. I ALWAYS BRING EXTRAS— SALT WATER IS NOT NICE TO MARKERS."

8 WATERPROOF BLUETOOTH SPEAKER.
"Long hours on boats are made easier with music or podcasts."

9

GOPRO AND EXTENDABLE POLE.

"THE CAMERA IS WATERPROOF, AND THE POLE ALLOWS ME TO EXTEND INTO THE WATER TO CAPTURE SHARK ACTIVITY."

10

BABY WIPES.

"TO GET THE FISH SMELL OFF OF MY HANDS AFTER I'VE BEEN CHOPPING BAIT FOR HOURS. AND TO WIPE DRIED SALT OFF OF MY SKIN SO I CAN REAPPLY A FRESH COAT OF SUNSCREEN."

11

RAINCOAT AND EXTRA LAYERS.

"Getting soaking wet and then traveling long distances on boats gets you cold, quickly."

12

ANTIBIOTIC OINTMENT.

"If I do get cuts, I always have this on me to keep them from getting infected."

13

HEADLAMP.

"YOU NEVER KNOW WHEN YOU WILL BE STUCK PAST SUNSET."

BACKPACK

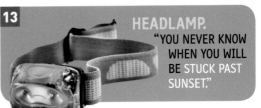

14

SUNSCREEN, HAT, AND SUNGLASSES.

"THE SUN IS SO STRONG ON THE WATER AND I DON'T WANT TO GET SKIN CANCER. I PROTECT MY SKIN, FACE, AND EYES AT ALL TIMES."

15

PHONE IN A WATERPROOF CASE.

"For photos and emergencies; also, it has a calculator and good quick note taking/ voice memo function."

16

PEPPERMINT AND COCONUT OIL.

"On hot days, I mix a few drops together and rub it on my chest and back to cool me down. Also, it acts as a natural mosquito repellent."

17

BANANAGRAMS. "WHEN I'M ON AN EXPEDITION, I LOVE TO HAVE A GAME AND THIS ONE IS COMPACT AND CAN BE USED TO LEARN NEW LANGUAGES, TOO."

RHIAN WALLER: KEEPING YOUR COOL!

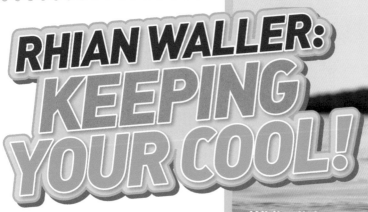

While diving to study cold-water corals off the coast of Chile, Rhian Waller is pushed to her limits. Check out this excerpt from National Geographic Kids Chapters Diving With Sharks!

Rhian's alarm went off again. Now they only had ten minutes of air left. Time was nearly up. She and her buddy would need to keep swimming toward the surface if they were going to make it back safely.

As they swam upward, they scanned their flashlights back and forth below them and to the side, trying to catch sight of their missing partner. But their beams of light were no match for the dark water.

Only five minutes remained on their timer. Rhian couldn't leave her missing buddy behind. But if she stayed much longer, both she and her remaining buddy would die.

Rhian gripped her buddy's hand tighter. They hadn't lost each other. But they hadn't found their teammate, either. They were getting close to the surface now. The timer was counting down. Suddenly, Rhian and her buddy broke through the top of the water.

The rain was still driving down. The winds were still kicking up waves. She frantically looked around. Then, she saw him. The missing diver was clinging to the wall just above the water's surface.

Rhian felt flooded with a sense of relief. She and the other diver swam to the wall. They joined their missing teammate. Before long, their boat captain had pulled the boat alongside them.

Rhian and her teammates dragged themselves onto the boat. They lay shivering and exhausted but ready for the long, choppy ride back. As they sped along, the missing teammate told Rhian his story.

When he reached the surface of the water, he didn't think he could

Did You Know?

After a cold dive, it's important to replenish the nutrients in your body with a high-calorie meal. Rhian's favorite is a bacon sandwich and cookies!

risk swimming to the boat alone in the choppy waters. So he found something to hold on to. He had been searching for them, too. He had been just as worried and panicked as they were!

Rhian thought about the dive. It had certainly been dangerous. But during the worst moments, she and her teammates had remembered their training. They had looked out for one another and kept each other safe.

CHECK OUT THE BOOK!

NATIONAL GEOGRAPHIC KIDS **CHAPTERS**

DIVING WITH SHARKS!

And More True Stories of Extreme Adventures!

CAVE of SECRETS

Explorers discover towering **cliffs and poisonous ooze** in the world's largest cave

Hidden deep in the dense mountain jungle of Vietnam, a massive underworld waits to be explored. A team of scientists and cave experts boldly enters to explore the largest cave ever found, where they'll face dangerous drop-offs and freaky fungus.

No other cave comes close to Hang Son Doong in total size. Using precise laser measuring devices, the team determines that the 5.5-mile (8.9-km)-long cavern soars more than 600 feet (180 m) high and spreads almost 500 feet (150 m) wide in sections. An entire New York City block, complete with 40-story skyscrapers, could fit inside one of Hang Son Doong's vast chambers.

Near the entrance, the team members fight to keep their balance as they wade through a swift underground river. Then they make their way through a field of boulders—some the size of houses—and scramble around stalagmites and slippery rock formations. A wrong step can lead to a fall of over a hundred feet (30 m).

Deeper in the cavern the team slogs through a muddy trench a mile (1.6 km) long. A poisonous fungus lives in the mud that can cause the skin to fall off their feet. The team pushes on.

The other, larger sinkhole eventually brought some of the jungle down with it. A fantastic forest of 100-foot (30-m) trees rises from the rubble pile toward the bright sun. Monkeys, snakes, and birds inhabit the cave jungle.

JOURNEY'S END

The final hurdle is probably the toughest: climbing a slimy 200-foot (61-m) cliff made of solidified, waterborne minerals. Climbers drill in security anchors as they scale the cliff, which resembles a frozen, brown waterfall. After a two-day climb, they literally see light at the end of a tunnel as they reach the cave's exit. Satisfied with the expedition to explore, map, and photograph the world's largest cave, the team climbs out into the sunlight.

HIDDEN JUNGLE

The cavern's roof fell in at two places, creating spectacular natural skylights. The first, which features a mossy green rock mound at the bottom, is jokingly named "Watch Out for Dinosaurs." In the otherworldly setting, prehistoric reptiles seem likely to appear at any moment.

Getting the Shot

The cave passage becomes pitch black in areas—a big problem for a photographer who needs lots of light. Even the most powerful electric flashes can't do the job. "It was a nightmare for me to think about," photographer Carsten Peter says. His solution? Single-use flashbulbs (the kind you might see photographers popping in old movies) from the one company that still makes them.

All About Vietnam

Vietnam is located in Southeast Asia, bordered by China, Laos, and Cambodia.	About 40 percent of people in Vietnam have the last name Nguyen (NWEN).	The Tonkin snub-nosed monkey, one of the more endangered primates in the world, lives only in Vietnam.

Bet you didn't know

8 deep facts about caves

1 Certain ice caves in Iceland are filled with hot springs.

2 1,000-year-old popcorn was found in a Utah cave.

3 Cave bears, which are now extinct, weighed around 1,500 (680 kg) pounds.

4 A cave in American Fork Canyon was used as a dance hall during World War II.

5 Caves can be formed by earthquakes.

6 Many cave-dwelling fish don't have eyes.

7 Ancient cave paintings in Australia show an almost 8-foot-tall (2.4-m) bird.

8 Some doctors in the 1800s thought cave air could cure illness.

AN ICE CAVE INSIDE ICELAND'S LANGJÖKULL GLACIER

FROZEN IN TIME

ERNEST SHACKLETON'S PRESERVED HUT IN CAPE ROYDS, ANTARCTICA

ANTARCTIC EXPLORERS ERNEST SHACKLETON, ROBERT FALCON SCOTT, AND EDWARD WILSON, CIRCA 1903

When British adventurers Ernest Shackleton and Robert Falcon Scott explored Antarctica in the early 1900s, they set up camp in wooden huts, which they left behind in the icy environs once the expeditions were over.

One would think that over time, the huts would completely deteriorate in the harsh conditions of the coldest continent. But the structures remained upright, albeit damaged by water, wind, and snow over the years. Now, a team of conservationists have completely restored them, offering a time capsule into the explorers' lives a century ago.

So what's inside the huts? Thousands of artifacts, like clothes, scientific equipment, photographs, and even frozen butter. Here's a closer look at some of the items originally used—and how they compare to the gear used by today's Antarctic explorers.

THE FOOD
THEN: Scott's crew mostly munched on pemmican, a mixture of dried beef and fat plus water, and plenty of biscuits.

NOW: Explorers eat a customized diet fine-tuned to give them enough calories to withstand the cold conditions and physical demands. On the menu? Porridge and cream for breakfast, energy bars, electrolyte drinks, and chicken curry for dinner.

THE SLEDS
THEN: Shackleton and Scott's teams hauled heavy loads in wooden sleds dragged by ponies and dogs.
NOW: Modern lightweight sleds are made of carbon fiber and are capable of carrying more equipment while still being sleek enough to smoothly travel over the ice.

THE CLOTHES
THEN: Early explorers wore wool, cotton, and animal fur. Gloves, boots, and sleeping bags were lined with reindeer fur.
NOW: High-tech mountaineering clothing is made from breathable fabrics that have been specially designed for the Antarctic's cold and dry environment.

Scientist at Base Orcadas in Antarctica

THE COMMUNICATION
THEN: Completely isolated in the Antarctic, explorers had no means of communicating with the outside world and could only write the details of their journey in notebooks.
NOW: Ultralight laptops connected to a mobile satellite hub help explorers stay connected, post pictures, and even watch movies.

Meerkat Close Encounter

Wildlife photographer Will Burrard-Lucas gives new meaning to the term "up close and personal" while photographing meerkats in the wild.

Makgadikgadi Pans, Botswana

When a family of meerkats discovered a wildlife photographer on his stomach angling for a picture outside their burrow, they didn't hide. Instead they used him as a lookout rock!

Baby meerkat pups venturing aboveground for the first time took turns playing with photographer Will Burrard-Lucas's camera. One bold adult hoisted himself onto Burrard-Lucas's head and scaled to the top of the camera lens he was holding. "They were trying to get as high as they could to have a good look around," Burrard-Lucas says.

"For meerkats, the higher you get, the safer you are, because you can hopefully spot a predator before it spots you," says Kenton Kerns, a biologist at the Smithsonian's National Zoo in Washington, D.C. "If they can find a stable spot that's higher than their normal places, they'll do anything to get there— including climbing a human."

Before packing up for the day, Burrard-Lucas waited patiently while one curious meerkat peered through the lens of his camera on the ground. Another meerkat walked right in front of it. How's that for a close-up?

136

HOW TO
SURVIVE A
KILLER BEE ATTACK!

1 Buzz Off
Killer bees—or Africanized honey-bees—only attack when their hive is being threatened. If you see several bees buzzing near you, a hive is probably close by. Heed their "back off" attitude and slowly walk away.

2 Don't Join the Swat Team
Your first instinct might be to start swatting and slapping the bees. But that just makes the buzzers angry. Loud noises have the same effect, so don't start screaming, either. Just get away.

3 Don't Play Hide-and-Seek
Hives are often near water, but don't even think about outlasting the bees underwater. They'll hover and attack when you come up for air, even if you try to swim for it.

4 Make Like Speedy Gonzalez
Killer bees will chase you, but they'll give up when you're far enough away from the hive (usually about 200 yards [183 m]). Take off running and don't stop until the buzzing does.

5 Create a Cover-Up
Killer bees often go for the face and throat, which are the most dangerous places to be stung. While you're on the run, protect your face and neck with your hands, or pull your shirt over your head.

HOW TO SURVIVE A
BEE STING!

1. De-Sting Yourself
First, get inside or to a cool place. Then, remove the stinger by scraping a fingernail over the area, like you would to get a splinter out. Do not squeeze the stinger or use tweezers unless you absolutely can't get it out any other way because squeezing it may release more venom.

2. Put It on Ice
Wash the area with soap and water and apply a cool compress to reduce swelling. Continue icing the spot for 20 minutes every hour. Place a washcloth or towel between the ice and your skin.

3. Treat It Right
With a parent's permission, take an antihistamine and gently rub a hydrocortisone cream on the sting site.

4. Hands Off
Make sure you don't scratch the sting. You'll just increase the pain and swelling.

5. Recognize Danger
If you experience severe burning and itching, swelling of the throat and/or mouth, difficulty breathing, weakness, or nausea, or if you already know you are allergic to bees, get to an emergency room immediately.

137

GETTING the SHOT

Capturing good photographs of wild animals can be tough. To get amazing pictures of them, nature photographers often tap into their wild side, thinking and even acting like the creatures they're snapping. Whether tracking deadly snakes or swimming with penguins, the artists must be daring—but they also need to know when to keep their distance. Three amazing photographers tell NG KIDS the behind-the-scenes stories of how they got these incredible shots.

MY SHOT

EARN BADGES FOR YOUR CRITTER PICS.

ngkidsmyshot.com

FANG FOCUS

PHOTOGRAPHER: Mattias Klum
ANIMAL: Jameson's mamba
SHOOT SITE: Cameroon, Africa

"The Jameson's mamba is beautiful but dangerous. It produces highly toxic venom. My team searched for weeks for the reptile, asking locals about the best spots to see one. At last we came across a Jameson's mamba peeking out from tree leaves. Carefully, I inched closer. It's important to make this kind of snake think that you don't see it. Otherwise it might feel threatened and strike you. At about four and a half feet (1.4 m) away, I took the picture. Then I backed up and the snake slid off."

SECRETS FROM AMAZING WILDLIFE PHOTOGRAPHERS

Usually solitary creatures, oceanic whitetip sharks have been observed swimming with pods of pilot whales.

SHARK **TALE**

PHOTOGRAPHER: Brian Skerry
ANIMAL: Oceanic whitetip shark
SHOOT SITE: The Bahamas

"I wanted to photograph an endangered oceanic whitetip shark. So I set sail with a group of scientists to an area where some had been sighted. Days later, the dorsal fin of a whitetip rose from the water near our boat. One scientist was lowered in a metal cage into the water to observe the fish. Then I dived in. Because I wasn't behind the protective bars, I had to be very careful. These nine-foot (2.7-m) sharks can be aggressive, but this one was just curious. She swam around us for two hours and allowed me to take pictures of her. She was the perfect model."

LEAPS and **BOUNDS**

PHOTOGRAPHER: Nick Nichols
ANIMAL: Bengal tiger
SHOOT SITE: Bandhavgarh
National Park, India

Fewer than 2,500 Bengal tigers are left in the wild.

"While following a tiger along a cliff, I saw him leap from the edge to his secret watering hole and take a drink. I wanted a close-up of the cat, but it wouldn't have been safe to approach him. Figuring he'd return to the spot, I set up a camera on the cliff that shoots off an infrared beam. Walking into the beam triggers the camera to click. The device was there for three months, but this was the only shot I got of the cat. Being near tigers makes the hair stand up on my arm. It was a gift to encounter such a magnificent creature."

QUIZ WHIZ

Explore just how much you know about adventure with this quiz!
ANSWERS BELOW

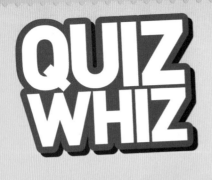

1 What did the earliest Antarctic explorers eat during their expeditions?
a. porridge
b. pemmican
c. blubber
d. energy bars

2 **True or false?** The world's largest cave is hidden deep in a mountain jungle in Cambodia.

3 1,000-year-old _____ was found in a Utah cave.
a. animal dung
b. sausage
c. popcorn
d. butter

4 Which of the following is a useful item for an ocean explorer?
a. Ziploc bags
b. baby wipes
c. peppermint oil
d. all of the above

5 How could you help your body recover after a cold dive?
a. elevate your feet
b. replenish nutrients with a bacon sandwich
c. sunbathe
d. Read the *National Geographic Kids Almanac 2017*

Not **STUMPED** yet? Check out the *NATIONAL GEOGRAPHIC KIDS QUIZ WHIZ* collection for more crazy **ADVENTURE** questions!

ANSWERS: 1. b; 2. False. The largest cave is Hang Son Doong in Vietnam; 3. c; 4. d; 5. b

HOMEWORK HELP

How to Write a Perfect Essay

Need to write an essay? Does the assignment feel as big as climbing Mount Everest? Fear not. You're up to the challenge! The following step-by-step tips will help you with this monumental task.

1 **BRAINSTORM.** Sometimes the subject matter of your essay is assigned to you, sometimes it's not. Either way, you have to decide what you want to say. Start by brainstorming some ideas, writing down any thoughts you have about the subject. Then read over everything you've come up with and consider which idea you think is the strongest. Ask yourself what you want to write about the most. Keep in mind the goal of your essay. Can you achieve the goal of the assignment with this topic? If so, you're good to go.

2 **WRITE A TOPIC SENTENCE.** This is the main idea of your essay, a statement of your thoughts on the subject. Again, consider the goal of your essay. Think of the topic sentence as an introduction that tells your reader what the rest of your essay will be about.

3 **OUTLINE YOUR IDEAS.** Once you have a good topic sentence, you then need to support that main idea with more detailed information, facts, thoughts, and examples. These supporting points answer one question about your topic sentence—"Why?" This is where research and perhaps more brainstorming come in. Then organize these points in the way you think makes the most sense, probably in order of importance. Now you have an outline for your essay.

4 **ON YOUR MARK, GET SET, WRITE!** Follow your outline, using each of your supporting points as the topic sentence of its own paragraph. Use descriptive words to get your ideas across to the reader. Go into detail, using specific information to tell your story or make your point. Stay on track, making sure that everything you include is somehow related to the main idea of your essay. Use transitions to make your writing flow.

5 **WRAP IT UP.** Finish your essay with a conclusion that summarizes your entire essay and restates your main idea.

6 **PROOFREAD AND REVISE.** Check for errors in spelling, capitalization, punctuation, and grammar. Look for ways to make your writing clear, understandable, and interesting. Use descriptive verbs, adjectives, or adverbs when possible. It also helps to have someone else read your work to point out things you might have missed. Then make the necessary corrections and changes in a second draft. Repeat this revision process once more to make your final draft as good as you can.

FUN and GAMES

KNOCK, KNOCK.

Who's there?
Ben.
Ben who?
Ben ringing your doorbell for ten minutes!

EXPLORE!

NATIONAL GEOGRAPHIC KIDS' virtual world online: **AnimalJam.com**

Enter the special code **NGKAJ17** for a bonus!

Find the HIDDEN ANIMALS

Animals often blend into their environments for protection. Find the animals listed below in the photographs. Write the letter of the correct photo next to each animal's name.

ANSWERS ON PAGE 338

1. sawblade shrimp
2. sand cat
3. black bear
4. flounder
5. white-tailed deer
6. white-tailed ptarmigan*

*Hint: A white-tailed ptarmigan is a type of bird that lives in mountain areas.

What in the World?

BIRD'S-EYE VIEW

These photos show views of how things look from up in the sky. Unscramble the letters to identify what's in each picture.

Bonus: Use the highlighted letters to solve the puzzle below. ANSWERS ON PAGE 338

NSDLIA
_____

ETSOFR
_____

THENEPAL DHRE
_____

OGNALMSFI
_____

LMSAEC
_____

ALOCR EFER
_____

WRFEOL LSEFDI
_____

GRIESEBC
_____

THO-IRA OLNBLOA
_____

HINT: What does the ground say to an earthquake?

ANSWER: Y _ _ U _ _ _ _ _ K _ _ _ U _ _!

A-MAZE-ing Mind

START

EMOTION

TOUCH

TEMPERATURE

SMELL

HI! HOLA! BONJOUR!
LANGUAGE

SIGHT

HEARING

COORDINATION

BREATHING

END

Feeling brainy? Find the path through this maze that leads you from the top of the brain to the bottom without running into any obstacles. (Bonus! The illustrations show which functions each part of your brain is responsible for.) Ready, set, think!

ANSWER ON PAGE 338

Funny FILL-IN

Here, Kitty!

Ask a friend to give you words to fill in the blanks in this story without showing it to him or her. Then read it out loud for a laugh.

We've been trekking through this forest so long, we need a break. So we sit _____
adverb ending in –ly

on a(n) _____ . I suddenly get the feeling I'm being watched and turn around.
something soft

There's a(n) _____ huge wild cat with _____ spots creeping up on us!
adjective _color_

"Don't worry, I've got this," _____ says _____ . _____
friend's name _adverb ending in –ly_ _same friend's name_

unzips a suitcase and pulls out a tin of _____ . He's/she's kind of
type of food, plural

_____ , but sometimes that's good. "Got anything else in there? Some
adjective

_____ or _____ ?" I ask. My friend just _____ and
noun, plural _noun, plural_ _verb ending in –s_

tosses the tin to the wild cat, which is looking very hungry. It starts _____
verb ending in –ing

and chomping _____ on the tin. Then it starts _____ and
adverb ending in –ly _verb ending in –ing_

_____ like a little kitten! We slowly back away. Nice kitty!
verb ending in –ing

Noun Town

This city is full of nouns, or people, places, and things. But twelve compound nouns—nouns made up of two or more words, or two words combined to make one word—have been drawn exactly as they're named. Can you guess the compound nouns illustrated in each of the numbered scenes? Here's a hint: The answer to number 1 is "sleeping bag."

ANSWERS ON PAGE 338

Attention on Set

At least ten objects at the rehearsal for *Giant Squid Versus Aliens* have the word "ten" in their names—for example, the squid's *ten*tacles. Can you spot the rest?

ANSWERS ON PAGE 338

WELCOME TO MEMPHIS

DIRECTOR

PROPS PROPS

MELLOW YELLOW

These photos show close-up views of yellow things. Unscramble the letters to identify what's in each picture.
Bonus: Use the highlighted letters to solve the puzzle below. ANSWERS ON PAGE 338

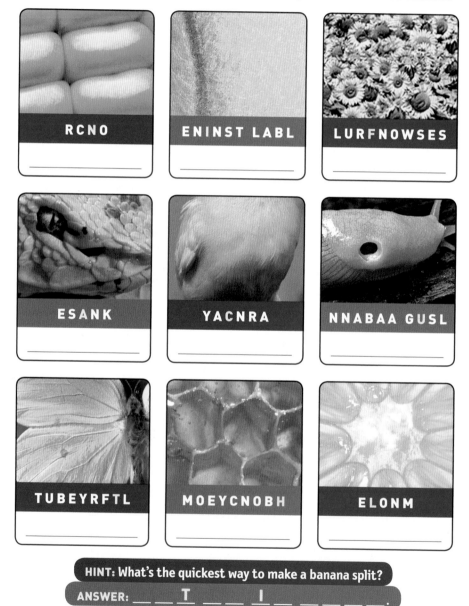

RCNO

ENINST LABL

LURFNOWSES

ESANK

YACNRA

NNABAA GUSL

TUBEYRFTL

MOEYCNOBH

ELONM

HINT: What's the quickest way to make a banana split?

ANSWER: __ __ __ T __ __ __ I __ __ __ __ __ __.

150

Just Joking

Red Panda

KNOCK,
KNOCK.

Who's there?
Hugo
Hugo who?
Hugo-ing to let
me in or not?

Two thieves robbing an apartment hear the owner coming home.

"Quick, jump out the window," says the first robber.

"Are you crazy? We're on the 13th floor!" says the second robber.

The first one replies, "This is no time to be superstitious!"

TONGUE TWISTER!

Say this fast three times:

Chimp chomps chips.

Q Why wouldn't they let the butterfly into the dance?

A Because it was a moth ball.

WANT MORE?

Check out the NG Kids book *Just Joking Cats* and the Just Joking app.

Q

What kind of insect eats brains?

A zom-bee.

A

Riddle Me This

Answer these riddles! Read the questions at right, then find their corresponding punch lines illustrated and marked with yellow dots throughout this museum scene. The first one has been done for you.
ANSWERS ON PAGE 338

1. What kind of shoes do spies wear? *Sneak*-ers
2. What's black and white and pink all over? An embarrassed _ _ _ _ _
3. What has bark but no bite? A _ _ _ _
4. What comes down but never goes up? _ _ _ _
5. What's tall when it's young and short when it's old? A _ _ _ _ _
6. The more you take of these, the more you leave behind. _ _ _ _ _ _ _ _ _
7. What has a face and two hands but no arms or legs? A _ _ _ _ _
8. What can honk without a horn? A _ _ _ _ _ _
9. What has a neck but no head? A _ _ _ _ _
10. What invention lets you look right through a wall? A _ _ _ _ _ _

"I DON'T KNOW. I THINK THE BOW TIE MIGHT BE A BIT TOO MUCH!"

I NEED A GIFT FOR A FRIEND. WHAT DO YOU SUGGEST?

flowers

OH!

"DIDN'T I TELL YOU TO CLEAN OFF YOUR BELLY BEFORE DINNER?"

"HEY, EVERYBODY! IF YOU TURN YOUR HEAD THIS WAY, EVERYTHING LOOKS UPSIDE DOWN!"

FUNNY FILL-IN
Wild Ride

Ask a friend to give you words to fill in the blanks in this story without showing it to him or her. Then read it out loud for a laugh.

NEW RIDE

My friends and I were waiting to ride the _____ (noun, plural) at the amusement park. But when

we got to the front of the line, a park employee asked us if we would like to test a(n)

_____ (adjective) new ride instead. As we climbed into a(n) _____ (noun) -shaped car, another park

employee said, "Welcome to the _____ (noun), the world's _____ (adjective ending in –est) roller coaster!"

Our car suddenly _____ (past-tense verb). Then the car shot up _____ (large number) feet—we were so

high, I thought I could touch the _____ (something in the sky, plural). The people below looked like

_____ (animal, plural). Next we did a barrel roll over the _____ (verb ending in -ing) teacups and flew over

the _____ (mythical creature) waterslide. Finally our car _____ (past-tense verb) backward as fast as

a(n) _____ (noun) before coming to a stop where we started. What a hair-raising experience!

My _____ (body part) felt a little _____ (adjective), but I still went on the ride again—twice.

THE SWOOPING SPACESHIP

CHECK OUT THE BOOK!

Book Boggle

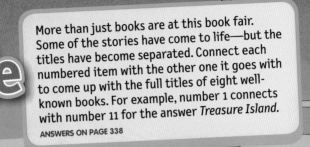

More than just books are at this book fair. Some of the stories have come to life—but the titles have become separated. Connect each numbered item with the other one it goes with to come up with the full titles of eight well-known books. For example, number 1 connects with number 11 for the answer *Treasure Island*.

ANSWERS ON PAGE 338

155

Just Joking

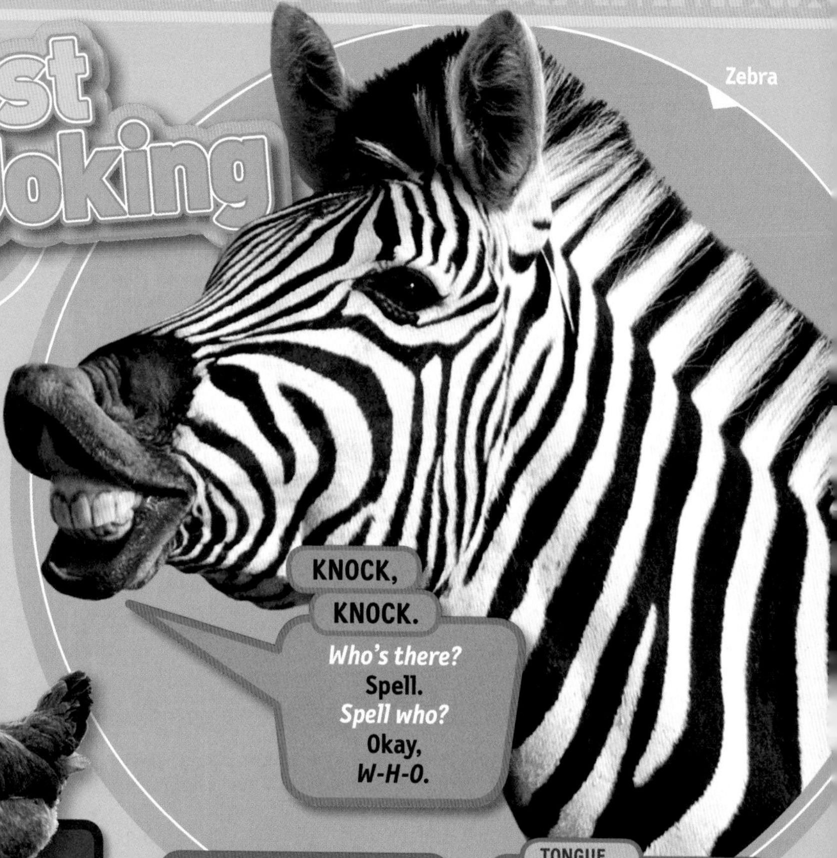

Zebra

KNOCK, KNOCK.

Who's there?
Spell.
Spell who?
Okay,
W-H-O.

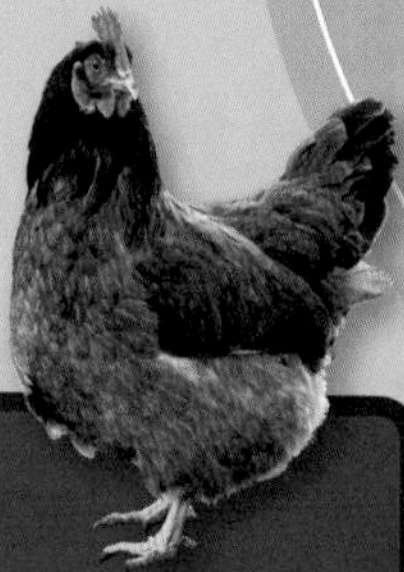

What do you get if you cross a **chicken** with a **skunk?**

Q

A A fowl smell.

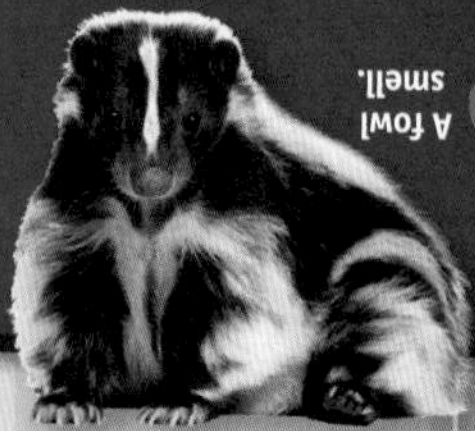

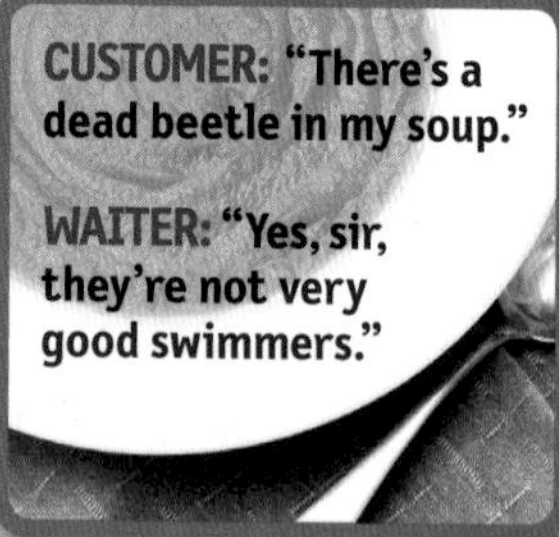

CUSTOMER: "There's a dead beetle in my soup."

WAITER: "Yes, sir, they're not very good swimmers."

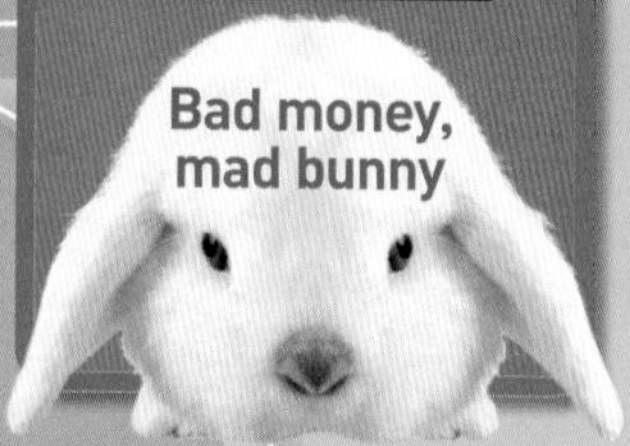

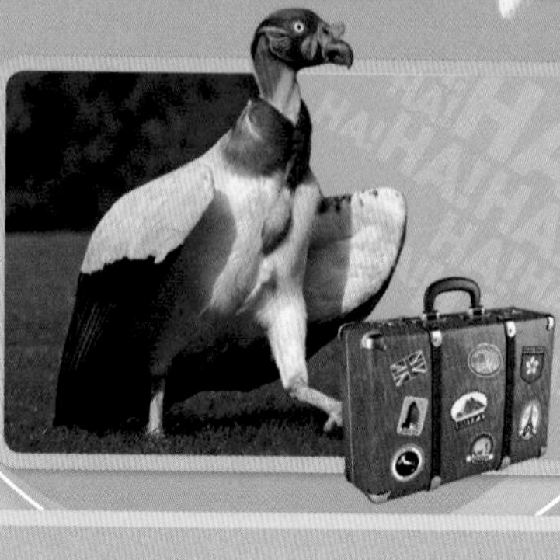

What does a **vulture pack** for a **vacation?**

Q

A Carrion luggage.

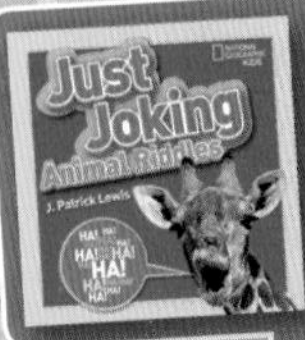

156

Dog Daze

The eight snapshots above were taken at this dog park. Find the scene that appears in each picture. Hint: Some of the snapshots are upside down or sideways. ANSWERS ON PAGE 338

Just Joking

Snake

KNOCK, KNOCK.

Who's there?
Metaphors.
Metaphors who?
Mataphors be with you.

Q What did one **math book** say to the other math book?

A I've got a lot of problems.

CATHIE: Did your party guests enjoy the piñata?
DOUG: It was a huge hit!

Q What **chews on trees and sings?**

A Justin beaver.

You've **got** to be joking...

Q How do **turtles talk to** each other?

A On their shell phones.

CHECK OUT THE BOOK!

Just Joking

NATIONAL GEOGRAPHIC KIDS

300 hilarious jokes about everything, including tongue twisters, riddles, and more!

Funny FiLL-IN
Birds to the Rescue!

Ask a friend to give you words to fill in the blanks in this story without showing it to him or her. Then read it out loud for a laugh.

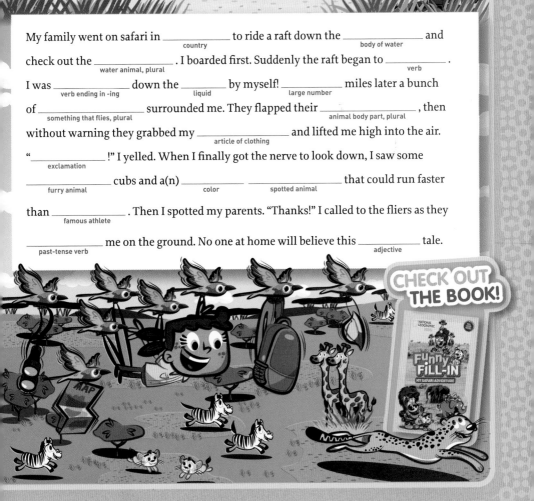

My family went on safari in _____ to ride a raft down the _____ and
                                       country   body of water

check out the _____ . I boarded first. Suddenly the raft began to _____ .
                      water animal, plural   verb

I was _____ down the _____ by myself! _____ miles later a bunch
        verb ending in -ing   liquid   large number

of _____ surrounded me. They flapped their _____ , then
    something that flies, plural   animal body part, plural

without warning they grabbed my _____ and lifted me high into the air.
                                article of clothing

"_____ !" I yelled. When I finally got the nerve to look down, I saw some
   exclamation

_____ cubs and a(n) _____ _____ that could run faster
 furry animal   color   spotted animal

than _____ . Then I spotted my parents. "Thanks!" I called to the fliers as they
    famous athlete

_____ me on the ground. No one at home will believe this _____ tale.
 past-tense verb   adjective

CHECK OUT THE BOOK!

159

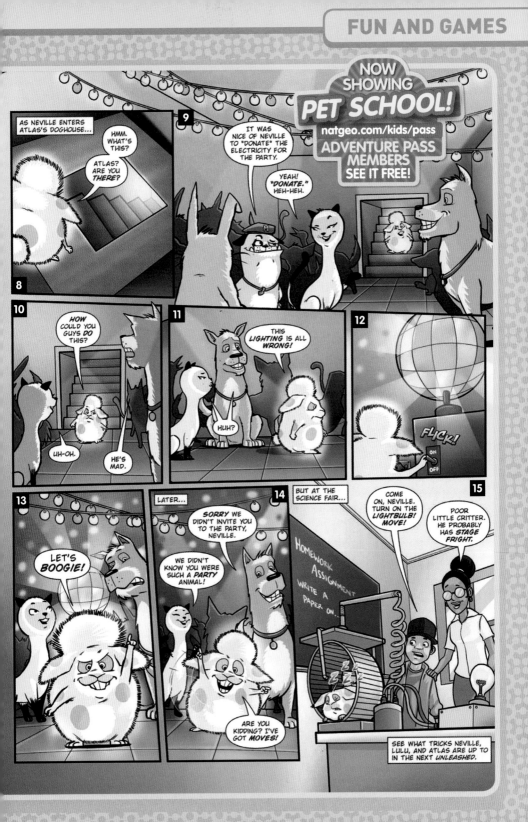

Cosmonauts undergo weightlessness training in a pool in Moscow, Russia.

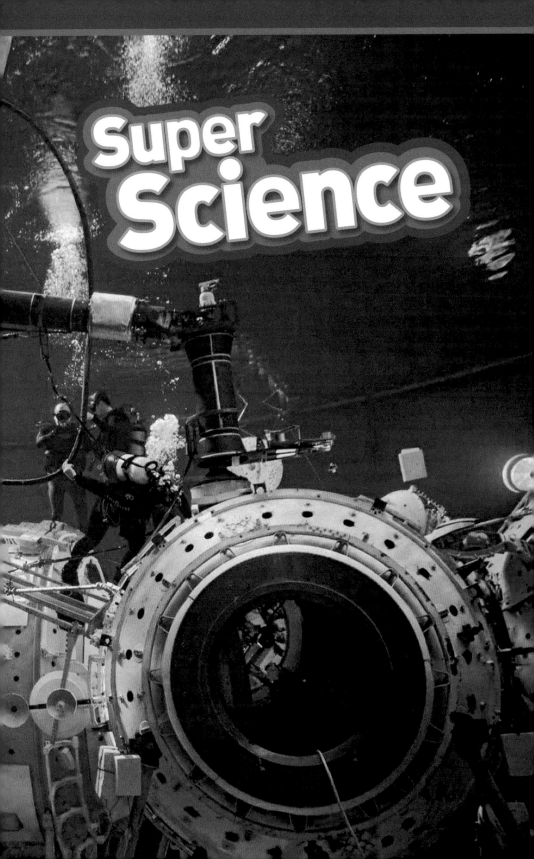

Super
Science

1

One of U.S. president Lyndon Johnson's favorite gadgets was his **AMPHIBIOUS CAR.** He surprised unsuspecting riders by yelling that the brakes didn't work as he drove straight into a lake.

2

THE RED SCHUMACHER MI3 IS THE FASTEST REMOTE-CONTROL CAR IN THE WORLD, ZOOMING AT A SPEED OF 161.76 MILES AN HOUR (260.32 KM/H).

3
LEARN TO PLAY GUITAR ON YOUR T-SHIRT.
The electronic guitar T-shirt lets you play all major chords while the sound comes from a mini-amplifier attached to your belt.

4

Smartwatches let users read their email, check social media, monitor their health, and even pay for a cup of coffee.

17 FACTS ABOUT EXTREME

5

GOOGLE CARDBOARD
Pop your phone into a GOOGLE CARDBOARD headpiece, strap it on your face, and go anywhere in the world without taking a step, thanks to special virtual reality apps.

6

Shaped like a shark, dolphin, or orca whale, the Seabreacher watercraft jumps, dives, rolls, and speeds across the water at up to 55 miles an hour (89 km/h).

7
A company has developed **unmanned robotic helicopters** that can deliver food, medicine, mail, and more where roads don't go.

8

Ever played ANGRY BIRDS on water? The Displair is a touch screen made of mist that needs up to a half gallon (2 L) of water every hour to keep it going.

9

YOU CAN RIDE AROUND IN YOUR VERY OWN MONDO SPIDER, AN **8-legged,** (726-kg) **1,600-pound** ROBOT ARACHNID THAT MOVES AT 5 MILES AN HOUR (8 KM/H).

10

JetLev is a water-propelled jetpack that pumps 1,000 gallons (3,785 L) of water a minute through a backpack, launching the wearer 30 feet (9 m) into the air.

11 A company makes a **HARRY POTTER– LIKE WAND** that can learn up to 13 commands that will turn up the volume, change the channel, and do more on your TV.

12 A DISAPPEARING TELEVISION COULD SOON BE A REALITY. ONE CONCEPT IN DEVELOPMENT IS A SEE-THROUGH TV, WHICH USES TRANSPARENT LCD TECHNOLOGY TO LOOK LIKE GLASS WHEN TURNED OFF.

GADGETS

13 SMART LOCKS ARE CONTROLLED BY YOUR SMARTPHONE, NOT KEYS. SOME LOCKS CAN TELL WHO'S ENTERING YOUR HOUSE AND EVEN TAKE A PICTURE.

14 The HAPIfork aims to manage weight loss by measuring how often you raise your fork to your mouth and vibrating when you eat too quickly.

15 There's a basketball that records every dribble and shot you make, then transmits the data to your mobile device to help you achieve the perfect game.

16 A car company created **a self-driving model car called Shelley** that allows the company to test performance at speeds up to 155 miles an hour (249 km/h).

17 The BeBionic3—the world's MOST ADVANCED PROSTHETIC HAND—mimics real hand and wrist movements and is controlled by the wearer's actual muscles.

COOL inventions

CAR FOLDS UP

Pulling up to your favorite restaurant for dinner, you see that cars parked along the curb haven't left enough space for a regular auto to fit into. Luckily you have a CityCar. This prototype fold-up vehicle may help drivers get into tight spots and replace bigger cars that crowd cities. The electric two-seater features an oval pod for a driver and passenger. With the press of a button, the front and rear wheels slide toward each other, and the pod is pushed up vertically. Folded, the Transformer-like car is five feet (1.5 m) long. (Most other autos take up 16 feet [5 m].) With its tiny, flexible frame, the CityCar saves space, fuel—and your dinner plans.

PARKED

A PEN "DREW" THIS!   AND THIS!

3-D PEN

Doodles with a regular pen are, well, flat. But not when you use the 3Doodler. This cool electronic pen produces plastic to draw three-dimensional objects. As you sketch in the air, a string of heated plastic flows like ink. Use the flexible material to create shapes such as pyramids or boxes. You can also twirl the pen to make a coil. The plastic quickly hardens into whatever objects you've drawn. Artists have even made replicas of the Eiffel Tower (left) and model dinosaurs with the pen. Just pick a good spot to display your doodle masterpieces, because these drawings definitely won't fit on the pages of your notebook.

166

ACCIDENTS Happen

Hey, they happen. Sometimes accidents are totally embarrassing. But other times they lead to something awesome. Check out these fortunate mistakes.

BUT SOMETIMES THEY RESULT IN AMAZING DISCOVERIES.

THE INVENTION: ARTIFICIAL SWEETENER

THE MOMENT OF "OOPS": Dirty hands

THE DETAILS: In the late 1870s, Constantin Fahlberg was working in his lab when he tipped over a beaker of chemicals, spilling them all over his hands. Without pausing to wash, Fahlberg went on with his work. When he went home to eat, the chemical residue was still on his fingers. After biting into a piece of bread, he noticed that it tasted strangely sweet. It wasn't the bread—it was something on his hands.

Fahlberg rushed back to work and found that the substance in the beaker that had spilled was sweet—much sweeter than sugar. He named his discovery saccharin—the first artificial sweetener.

THE INVENTION: MICROWAVE OVEN

THE MOMENT OF "OOPS": Accidentally melting a chocolate bar in a pocket

THE DETAILS: In the 1940s, Percy Spencer was experimenting with radar—radio waves used to detect objects. When he stepped in front of a magnetron—a device that makes waves called microwaves—the chocolate bar in his pocket melted! Spencer then aimed a beam of microwaves at some kernels of popping corn. They burst. Then he zapped a raw egg, which exploded. This proved that microwaves could heat food superfast, leading to the first microwave oven.

167

WHAT IS LIFE?

This seems like such an easy question to answer. Everybody knows that singing birds are alive and rocks are not. But when we start studying bacteria and other microscopic creatures, things get more complicated.

SO WHAT EXACTLY IS LIFE?

Most scientists agree that something is alive if it can do the following: reproduce; grow in size to become more complex in structure; take in nutrients to survive; give off waste products; and respond to external stimuli, such as increased sunlight or changes in temperature.

KINDS OF LIFE

Biologists classify living organisms by how they get their energy. Organisms such as algae, green plants, and some bacteria use sunlight as an energy source. Animals (like humans), fungi, and some Archaea use chemicals to provide energy. When we eat food, chemical reactions within our digestive system turn our food into fuel.

Living things inhabit land, sea, and air. In fact, life also thrives deep beneath the oceans, embedded in rocks miles below the Earth's crust, in ice, and in other extreme environments. The life-forms that thrive in these challenging environments are called extremophiles. Some of these draw directly upon the chemicals surrounding them for energy. Since these are very different forms of life than what we're used to, we may not think of them as alive, but they are.

HOW IT ALL WORKS

To try and understand how a living organism works, it helps to look at one example of its simplest form—the single-celled bacterium called *Streptococcus*. There are many kinds of these tiny organisms, and some are responsible for human illnesses. What makes us sick or uncomfortable are the toxins the bacteria give off in our bodies.

A single *Streptococcus* bacterium is so small that at least 500 of them could fit on the dot above this letter *i*. These bacteria are some of the simplest forms of life we know. They have no moving parts, no lungs, no brain, no heart, no liver, and no leaves or fruit. Yet this life-form reproduces. It grows in size by producing long chain structures, takes in nutrients, and gives off waste products. This tiny life-form is alive, just as you are alive.

What makes something alive is a question scientists grapple with when they study viruses, such as the ones that cause the common cold and smallpox. They can grow and reproduce within host cells, such as those that make up your body. Because viruses lack cells and cannot metabolize nutrients for energy or reproduce without a host, scientists ask if they are indeed alive. And don't go looking for them without a strong microscope— viruses are a hundred times smaller than bacteria.

Scientists think life began on Earth some 3.9 to 4.1 billion years ago, but no fossils exist from that time. The earliest fossils ever found are from the primitive life that existed 3.6 billion years ago. Other life-forms, some of which are shown below, soon followed. Scientists continue to study how life evolved on Earth and whether it is possible that life exists on other planets.

MICROSCOPIC ORGANISMS*

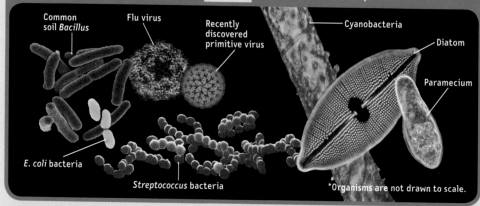

Common soil *Bacillus*
Flu virus
Recently discovered primitive virus
Cyanobacteria
Diatom
Paramecium
E. coli bacteria
Streptococcus bacteria
*Organisms are not drawn to scale.

168

The Three Domains of Life

Biologists divide all living organisms into three domains: Bacteria, Archaea, and Eukarya. Archaean and Bacterial cells do not have nuclei; they are so different from each other that they belong to different domains. Since human cells have a nucleus, humans belong to the Eukarya domain.

1

BACTERIA

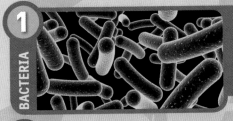

Domain Bacteria: These single-celled microorganisms are found almost everywhere in the world. Bacteria are small and do not have nuclei. They can be shaped like rods, spirals, or spheres. Some of them are helpful to humans, and some are harmful.

2

ARCHAEA

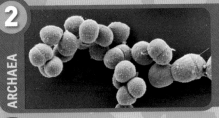

Domain Archaea: These single-celled micro-organisms are often found in extremely hostile environments. Like Bacteria, Archaea do not have nuclei, but they have some genes in common with Eukarya. For this reason, scientists think the Archaea living today most closely resemble the earliest forms of life on Earth.

3

EUKARYA

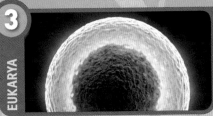

Domain Eukarya: This diverse group of life-forms is more complicated than Bacteria and Archaea, as Eukarya have one or more cells with nuclei. These are the tiny cells that make up your whole body. Eukarya are divided into four groups: fungi, protists, plants, and animals.

What is a domain? Scientifically speaking, a domain is a major taxonomic division into which natural objects are classified (see p. 30 for "What Is Taxonomy?").

FYI

FUNGI

Kingdom Fungi (about 100,000 species): Mainly multicellular organisms, fungi cannot make their own food. Mushrooms and yeast are fungi.

PROTISTS

Protists (about 250,000 species): Once considered a kingdom, this group is a "grab bag" that includes unicellular and multicellular organisms of great variety.

PLANTS

Kingdom Plantae (about 300,000 species): Plants are multicellular, and many can make their own food using photosynthesis (see p. 210 for "Photosynthesis").

ANIMALS

Kingdom Animalia (about 1,000,000 species): Most animals, which are multicellular, have their own organ systems. Animals do not make their own food.

YOU AND YOUR CELLS

Your body is made up of microscopically tiny structures called cells— many trillions of them!

Every living thing—from the tiniest bug to the biggest tree—is made up of cells, too. Cells are the smallest building blocks of life. Some living things, such as an amoeba, are made up of just one cell. Other living things contain many more. Estimates for an adult human, for example, range from 10 trillion to 100 trillion cells!

An animal cell is a bit like the world's tiniest water balloon. It's a jellylike blob surrounded by an oily "skin" called a cell membrane. The membrane works to let some chemicals into the cell and keep others out. The "jelly" on the inside is called cytoplasm. It's speckled with tiny cell parts, called organelles. Some organelles make energy. Others take apart and put together various chemicals, which become ingredients for different body functions such as growth and movement.

CHECK OUT THE BOOK!

ULTIMATE BODY-PEDIA

SEEING CELLS

The first microscope that clearly showed anything smaller than a flea was invented in the late 1500s. Later, people tinkered with microscopes and lenses to make them even more powerful. One of these people was the English scientist Robert Hooke.

Hooke designed a microscope of his own and drew detailed pictures of what he saw. In 1665, he published his illustrations in a book called *Micrographia*, which means "little pictures." One picture shows boxy spaces in a slice of cork from a tree. Hooke called the spaces "cells" because they looked like little rooms. It would be another 200 years before scientists realized that cells make up all living things.

YOU HAVE A LOT OF NERVE!

Different parts of your brain control different activities, but how does your brain tell all the parts of your body what to do?

And, in return, how do your eyes, ears, and nose tell your brain what they see, hear, and smell? The answer is your nerves!

Nerves—thin, threadlike structures—carry messages between your brain and the rest of your body, in both directions. Nerves run down your spine and branch out all the way to your fingers and toes. This system of nerves controls your body, tells your muscles to move, and lets you experience the wonderful world around you. Nerves are part of your nervous system, which also includes your brain and spinal cord.

Your nerves are made of cells called neurons. Neurons send and receive messages between your brain and the other parts of your body by sending out alternating electrical and chemical signals.

Messages flash from neuron to neuron along your nerves and inside your brain. Signals from your eyes might tell the brain, "There's my school bus." The brain then sends signals that zoom from cell to cell making sense of the message. Then the brain sends signals back down to the nerves connected to your leg muscles to say, "Run to the bus stop!"

TOUR A NEURON

Neurons have four parts:

CELL BODY Contains the nucleus, which controls the activity of the cell and contains its DNA, or deoxyribonucleic acid

AXON Fiber that transmits impulses from the cell body to another nerve cell

DENDRITE Branchlike fiber extending from the cell body that receives signals from other neurons

MYELIN A fatty covering around the axons that insulate the axon, giving the white matter its characteristic color

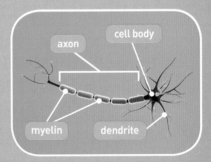

171

Your Amazing
brain

Inside your body's supercomputer

Y ou carry around
a three-pound
(1.4-kg) mass of
wrinkly material
in your head that controls
every single thing you will
ever do. From enabling you
to think, learn, create, and
feel emotions to controlling
every blink, breath, and
heartbeat—this fantastic
control center is your brain.
It is a structure so amazing
that a famous scientist
once called it the "most
complex thing we have yet
discovered in our universe."

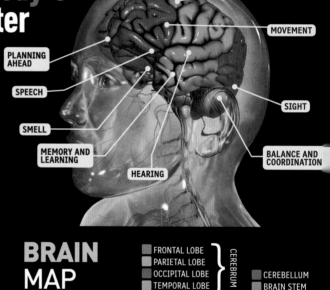

TOUCH

MOVEMENT

PLANNING AHEAD

SPEECH

SIGHT

SMELL

MEMORY AND LEARNING

BALANCE AND COORDINATION

HEARING

BRAIN MAP

FRONTAL LOBE
PARIETAL LOBE   CEREBRUM
OCCIPITAL LOBE
TEMPORAL LOBE

CEREBELLUM
BRAIN STEM

THE BIG QUESTION

WHAT TAKES UP TWO-THIRDS OF YOUR BRAIN'S WEIGHT AND ALLOWS YOU TO SWIM, EAT, AND SPEAK?

Answer: The huge hunk of your brain called the cerebrum. It's definitely the
biggest part of the brain. The four lobes of the cerebrum house the centers
for memory, the senses, movement, and emotion, among other things.

The cerebrum is made up of two hemispheres—the right and the left.
Each side controls the muscles of the opposite side of the body.

CHECK YOUR
MEMORY

How much can your
brain remember?
Put it to the test.

CHALLENGE

Take 30 seconds.
Memorize as many of
these pictures as
you can. Cover the
pictures. Now get
a pencil and a piece
of paper. Write
down the pictures you
remember. How many
did you get right?

WHAT EXACTLY IS HAPPENING?

Looking at pictures actually helps your brain to remember better. Short-term memory, also called working memory, relies heavily on the visual cortex. Words that are read are processed very quickly by our brains. They don't stick around for very long. But recording a picture in your brain takes longer. The more time spent looking at the picture, the better the memory. Saying a word out loud does the same thing. It takes longer to speak a word than it does to read it. That's why you remember it better when you say it aloud. The lesson? When you are doing last-minute cramming for a test, look at pictures and

CHECK OUT
THE BOOK!

YOUR
SHORT-TERM
MEMORY
CAN HOLD ONLY ABOUT

Your Amazing Ears

OUTER EAR

INNER EAR

COCHLEA

MIDDLE EAR

EAR DRUM

Listen up! Your ears are so much more than just two funny-looking things stuck to the side of your head. Here's an earful on all that's cool about these awesome organs.

Your entire inner ear can fit inside the tip of your pinkie.

Some people can hear their own eyeballs move.

TRIPLE PLAY. The ears are made up of three sections: the outer ear, the middle ear, and the inner ear. Each part plays separate and equally important roles to keep your hearing sharp. Here's how sound travels through your ears.

OUTER EAR: The part you can see and feel, the outer ear consists of the pinna and the ear canal. Sound waves enter here and travel down the ear canal to the ear drum.

MIDDLE EAR: Sound waves create vibrations that strike the ear drum, causing the three tiny bones located here to move. The movement amplifies the sound and delivers it to the inner ear.

INNER EAR: Sound vibrations enter the cochlea, the small, snail-shaped, liquid-filled tube that's lined with tiny hairs. The vibrations make the tiny hairs wave back and forth and tickle the nerve cells. This causes the nerve cells to send messages to your brain that are interpreted as sound.

feeling you get when you've spun around in circles one too many times? That happens because the fluid in the semicircular canals continues to swish around even after you stop, confusing your brain into thinking that you're still spinning.

DRUM ROLL. Despite its name, the ear drum has nothing to do with percussion. Rather, this tiny piece of skin located between the outer and middle ear is called a "drum" because it's such a tightly stretched membrane. Bad ear infections or trauma can cause it to tear, or perforate, but the ear drum usually heals itself within a few months.

⑦ popping facts to sound off about

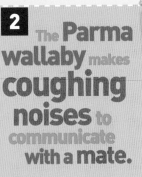

1 Some **radio signals coming** from **Jupiter** make a sound like **popping popcorn.**

2 The **Parma wallaby** makes **coughing noises** to communicate with a **mate.**

3 The **longest recorded echo lasted for** nearly **2 minutes.**

4 An **orchestra** in the Washington, D.C., area **performs** only music from **video games.**

5 Certain **sand dunes** occasionally **hum.**

6 Hot **water and cold** water make **different** sounds when **poured.**

7 The **western diamondback rattlesnake** can **vibrate** its **rattle** about **60** times a second.

175

That's GROSS!

WHO NEEDS SLOBBERING ZOMBIES AND SLIMY MONSTERS THIS HALLOWEEN? THE BACTERIA LIVING INSIDE YOUR BODY ARE ICKY ENOUGH.

Don't panic, but you're outnumbered by alien life-forms. They look like hairy hot dogs, spiky blobs, and oozing spirals, and they're crawling across—and deep inside—your body right this very minute. They're bacteria!

Your body is built of trillions of itty-bitty living blobs, called cells, that work together to do amazing things, such as hold in your organs or help beat your brother at *Clash of Clans.* But for every cell you call your own, about ten foreign bacteria are clustering around or near it. You can't see these hitchhikers, but you sure can smell a lot of them. Like any living thing, bacteria eat, reproduce, die, and create waste. A lot of this waste is the source of your body odor, bad breath, and torturous toots. In other words, some bacteria can make your life stink!

If the thought of being a human-shaped planet for microscopic inhabitants makes you queasy, relax. Most of your body's microbes have been harmlessly hanging out in your body for years and are essential for good health. And just like a fingerprint, your bacteria make you who you are, because no two people host the same mix of microorganisms. But that doesn't make things any less disgusting!

Little Monsters

Meet **four** famous bacteria that **call your body "home sweet home..."**

1 ACTINOMYCES VISCOSUS
When your dentist breaks out the power tools to jackhammer the brownish coat of slime known as plaque from your teeth, she's really attacking these mouth-dwelling bacteria.

4 BREVIBACTERIUM LINENS

This foul-smelling microbe thrives in the sweat simmering in your sneakers, unleashing an awful stink when you kick off your shoes. It's also used to ferment stinky Limburger cheese.

2 METHANOGENS

About half of all people have these supersimple microbes living in their guts. Methanogens produce methane, a greenhouse gas that animals—including humans—pass into the atmosphere when they, um, toot.

3 ESCHERICHIA COLI

This rod-shaped microbe lives deep in your guts, the body's busiest bacterial neighborhood. Helpful *E. coli* strains produce an important vitamin. Harmful ones make you vomit for days.

More Grossness

Your body's bacterial zoo begins when you're born, as you ingest bacteria from your mom's skin and milk. You also consume lots of harmless and helpful bacteria through food and water every day.

Some bacteria are used by scientists to help produce new vaccines and other medicine.

Your body's bacteria eat everything from salt inside your intestines to chemicals in your sweat.

Belly-button lint—a mix of clothing fibers and dead skin cells—is a hot spot for bacteria. Scientists recently found more than 1,400 species of microbes living in people's navels.

177

THE UNIVERSE BEGAN WITH A BIG BANG

Clear your mind for a minute and try to imagine this: All the things you see in the universe today—all the stars, galaxies, and planets—are not yet out there. Everything that now exists is concentrated in a single, incredibly hot, dense state that scientists call a singularity. Then, suddenly, the basic elements that make up the universe flash into existence. Scientists say that actually happened about 13.8 billion years ago, in the moment we call the big bang.

For centuries scientists, religious scholars, poets, and philosophers have wondered how the universe came to be. Was it always there? Will it always be the same, or will it change? If it had a beginning, will it someday end, or will it go on forever?

These are huge questions. But today, because of recent observations of space and what it's made of, we think we may have some of the answers. Everything we can see or detect around us in the universe began with the big bang. We know the big bang created not only matter but also space itself. And scientists think that in the very distant future, stars will run out of fuel and burn out. Once again the universe will become dark.

POWERFUL PARTICLE

It's just one tiny particle, but without it the world as we know it would not exist. That's what scientists are saying after the recent discovery of the Higgs boson particle, a subatomic speck related to the Higgs field, which is thought to give mass to everything around us. Without the Higgs boson, all the atoms created in the big bang would have zipped around the cosmos too quickly to collect into stars and planets. So you can think of it as a building block of the universe—and of us!

EARLY LIFE ON EARTH

About 3.5 billion years ago Earth was covered by one gigantic reddish ocean. The color came from hydrocarbons.

The first life-forms on Earth were Archaea that could live without oxygen. They released large amounts of methane gas into an atmosphere that would have been poisonous to us.

About 3 billion years ago erupting volcanoes linked together to form larger landmasses. And a new form of life appeared— cyanobacteria, the first living things that used energy from the sun.

Some 2 billion years ago the cyanobacteria algae filled the air with oxygen, killing off the methane-producing Archaea. Colored pools of greenish brown plant life floated on the oceans. The oxygen revolution that would someday make human life possible was now under way.

About 530 million years ago the Cambrian explosion occurred. It's called an explosion because it's the time when most major animal groups first appeared in our fossil records. Back then, Earth was made up of swamps, seas, a few active volcanoes, and oceans teeming with strange life.

More than 450 million years ago life began moving from the oceans onto dry land. About 200 million years later dinosaurs began to appear. They would dominate life on Earth for more than 150 million years.

PLANETS

MERCURY

VENUS

EARTH

MARS

CERES

JUPITER

SUN

MERCURY

Average distance from the sun:
35,980,000 miles (57,900,000 km)
Position from the sun in orbit: first
Equatorial diameter: 3,030 miles (4,878 km)
Length of day: 59 Earth days
Length of year: 88 Earth days
Surface temperatures: -300°F (-184°C)
to 800°F (427°C)
Known moons: 0
Fun fact: Mercury has shrunk by about
9 miles (14 km) in diameter since it
was first formed billions of years ago.

VENUS

Average distance from the sun:
67,230,000 miles (108,200,000 km)
Position from the sun in orbit: second
Equatorial diameter: 7,520 miles (12,100 km)
Length of day: 243 Earth days
Length of year: 224.7 Earth days
Average surface temperature: 864°F (462°C)
Known moons: 0
Fun fact: There's a mountain on Venus that's
1.25 times taller than Mount Everest.

EARTH

Average distance from the sun:
93,000,000 miles (149,600,000 km)
Position from the sun in orbit: third
Equatorial diameter: 7,900 miles (12,750 km)
Length of day: 24 hours
Length of year: 365 days
Surface temperatures: -126°F (-88°C)
to 136°F (58°C)
Known moons: 1
Fun fact: 40,000 tons (36,300 t) of cosmic
dust falls on Earth every year.

MARS

Average distance from the sun:
141,633,000 miles (227,936,000 km)
Position from the sun in orbit: fourth
Equatorial diameter: 4,221 miles (6,794 km)
Length of day: 25 Earth hours
Length of year: 1.9 Earth years
Surface temperatures: -270°F (-168°C)
to 80°F (27°C)
Known moons: 2
Fun fact: In 2015, scientists confirmed
evidence of liquid water on Mars.

This artwork shows the
13 planets and dwarf planets.
The relative sizes and positions
of the planets are shown but
not the relative distances
between them.

SATURN

URANUS

NEPTUNE

PLUTO

HAUMEA

MAKEMAKE

ERIS

JUPITER
Average distance from the sun:
  483,682,000 miles (778,412,000 km)
Position from the sun in orbit: sixth
Equatorial diameter: 88,840 miles (142,980 km)
Length of day: 9.9 Earth hours
Length of year: 11.9 Earth years
Average surface temperature: -235°F (-148°C)
Known moons: 67*
Fun fact: Droplets of neon dissolved in helium
  fall like rain on the planet Jupiter.

SATURN
Average distance from the sun:
  890,800,000 miles (1,433,500,000 km)
Position from the sun in orbit: seventh
Equatorial diameter: 74,900 miles (120,540 km)
Length of day: 10.7 Earth hours
Length of year: 29.5 Earth years
Average surface temperature: -218°F (-139°C)
Known moons: 62*
Fun fact: Saturn's outermost ring is roughly
  7,000 times larger than the planet itself.

*Includes provisional moons, which await confirmation
and naming from the International Astronomical Union.

URANUS
Average distance from the sun:
  1,784,000,000 miles (2,870,970,000 km)
Position from the sun in orbit: eighth
Equatorial diameter: 31,760 miles (51,120 km)
Length of day: 17.2 Earth hours
Length of year: 84 Earth years
Average surface temperature: -323°F (-197°C)
Known moons: 27
Fun fact: Some methane storms on Uranus
  are so big and bright, you can see them
  from telescopes on Earth.

NEPTUNE
Average distance from the sun:
  2,795,000,000 miles (4,498,250,000 km)
Position from the sun in orbit: ninth
Equatorial diameter: 30,775 miles (49,528 km)
Length of day: 16 Earth hours
Length of year: 164.8 Earth years
Average surface temperature: -353°F (-214°C)
Known moons: 14*
Fun fact: Neptune experiences the strongest
  sustained winds of any planet in the solar
  system.

For information about dwarf planets—Ceres,
Pluto, Haumea, Makemake, and Eris—see p. 183. **181**

NUMBERS

SOLAR SYSTEM

Check out **how long** it would take **for the planets** in our solar system **to race around the sun** if they were runners **on a track.**

Psst! Did you notice that the planets seem too close to the sun—and to each other? You're right! To help show how long it takes each planet to fully orbit the sun, we fudged a little and illustrated the planets as if they were running a race—instead of showing their correct distances. To find out their *real* distances from the sun and each other, go online to check out a video and get even more scoop on our solar system.

natgeo.com/kids/solar-system

A season on Uranus lasts roughly 21 years.

NEPTUNE 164.8 YEARS

URANUS 84 YEARS

Earth orbits the sun almost 165 times before Neptune orbits it once.

JUPITER 11.9 YEARS

SATURN 29.5 YEARS

MARS 1.9 YEARS

EARTH 1 YEAR

VENUS 224.7 DAYS

MERCURY 88 DAYS

Temperatures on Mercury can range from about minus 280°F (-173°C) at night to 800°F (427°C) during the day.

DWARF PLANETS

Haumea

Eris

Pluto

Thanks to advanced technology, astronomers have been spotting many never-before-seen celestial bodies with their telescopes. One new discovery? A population of icy objects orbiting the sun beyond Pluto. The largest, like Pluto itself, are classified as dwarf planets. Smaller than the moon but still massive enough to pull themselves into a ball, dwarf planets nevertheless lack the gravitational "oomph" to clear their neighborhood of other sizable objects. So, while larger, more massive planets pretty much have their orbits to themselves, dwarf planets orbit the sun in swarms that include other dwarf planets as well as smaller chunks of rock or ice.

So far, astronomers have identified five dwarf planets: Ceres (which circles the sun in the asteroid belt between Mars and Jupiter), Pluto, Haumea, Makemake, and Eris. Astronomers are studying hundreds of newly found objects in the frigid outer solar system, trying to figure out just how big they are. As time and technology advance, the family of known dwarf planets will surely continue to grow.

CERES
Position from the sun in orbit: fifth
Length of day: 9.1 Earth hours
Length of year: 4.6 Earth years
Known moons: 0

PLUTO
Position from the sun in orbit: tenth
Length of day: 6.4 Earth days
Length of year: 248 Earth years
Known moons: 5

HAUMEA
Position from the sun in orbit: eleventh
Length of day: 3.9 Earth hours
Length of year: 282 Earth years
Known moons: 2

MAKEMAKE
Position from the sun in orbit: twelfth
Length of day: 22.5 Earth hours
Length of year: 305 Earth years
Known moons: 0

ERIS
Position from the sun in orbit: thirteenth
Length of day: 25.9 Earth hours
Length of year: 561 Earth years
Known moons: 1

ALIEN SEA

Orange haze blurs the view outside your spaceship's window. You're descending to Titan, the largest of Saturn's 62 moons and 1.5 times bigger than Earth's moon. The smog beneath you thins, and you gasp in amazement: On the alien surface below, rivers flow through canyons. Waves crash in oceans. But Titan is no place like home.

Your special spacecraft splashes down in Kraken Mare, Titan's largest sea. The pumpkin-orange coastline is lined by craggy cliffs. Rocks dot the shore. But because it's a frigid minus 290°F (179°C) here, the rocks are made of solid ice.

Rain begins to fall. It isn't water—it's methane and ethane. On Earth these are polluting gases. On Titan they form clouds and fall as rain that fills the rivers and oceans. You scoop up a sample of ocean liquid for a closer look: Scientists think there's a chance that Titan's seas might be home to alien life.

It'd be very strange if something did live here. On Earth everything living is partly made of water. Since there's no liquid water on Titan's surface, creatures here would be formed of methane or ethane. And because it's so cold, they'd move in slow motion.

Before you can get a good look at your sample, you hear a rumble. It's an ice volcano, thousands of feet tall. It shoots out a slurry of ice and ammonia (a chemical used as a cleaning product on Earth). You'd better get away before the icy blasts sink your boat!

Destination
Titan

Location
Orbiting the planet Saturn

Distance
886 million miles
(1.43 billion km)
from Earth

Time to reach
3 years

Weather
minus 290°F (-179°C),
with scattered methane
rainstorms

THE MOON
TITAN

At minus 290°F (-179°C), Titan seems way too cold for alien life. But it might not be. Even on Earth, creatures called **cryophiles** thrive in below-freezing temperatures. *Brr!*

SEE PHOTOS TAKEN BY
Hubble!
natgeo.com
/kids/hubble

Sky Calendar
2017

Jupiter

Leonid meteor shower

Partial solar eclipse

January 3–4 Quadrantids Meteor Shower Peak. Featuring up to 40 meteors and hour, this shower is best viewed when the moon sets after midnight.

April 1 Mercury at Greatest Eastern Elongation. Visible low in the western sky just after sunset, Mercury will be at its highest point on the horizon.

April 7 Jupiter at Opposition. The giant planet is at its closest approach to Earth.

May 6–7 Eta Aquarids Meteor Shower Peak. View about 30 to 60 meteors an hour.

June 15 Saturn at Opposition. The best time to view the ringed planet. It makes its closest approach to Earth.

August 12–13 Perseid Meteor Shower Peak. One of the best! Up to 60 meteors an hour. Best viewing is in the direction of the constellation Perseus.

August 21 Total Solar Eclipse. Beginning at the Pacific Ocean then moving through the central United States, the eclipse can be viewed in parts of Oregon, Idaho, Wyoming, Nebraska, Missouri, Kentucky, Tennessee, North Carolina, and South Carolina. A partial eclipse may be visible in most of North America and some of northern South America.

October 21–22 Orionid Meteor Shower Peak. View up to 20 meteors an hour. Look toward the constellation Orion for the best show.

November 13 Conjunction of Venus and Jupiter. These two bright planets will appear very close together in the eastern sky just before sunrise.

November 17–18 Leonid Meteor Shower Peak. View up to 15 meteors an hour.

December 3 Supermoon, Full Moon. The moon will be full and at its closest approach to Earth, likely appearing bigger and brighter than usual.

December 13–14 Geminid Meteor Shower Peak. A spectacular show! Up to 120 multicolored meteors an hour.

Various dates throughout 2017
View the International Space Station. Visit spotthestation.nasa.gov to find out when the ISS will be flying over your neighborhood.

Dates may vary slightly depending on your location. Check with a local planetarium for the best viewing time in your area.

CONSTELLATIONS

Nothing to do on a clear night? Look up! There's so much to see in that starry sky. The constellations you can see among the stars vary with the season. As the following maps show, some are more visible in the winter and spring, while others can be spotted in the summer and fall.

NORTH

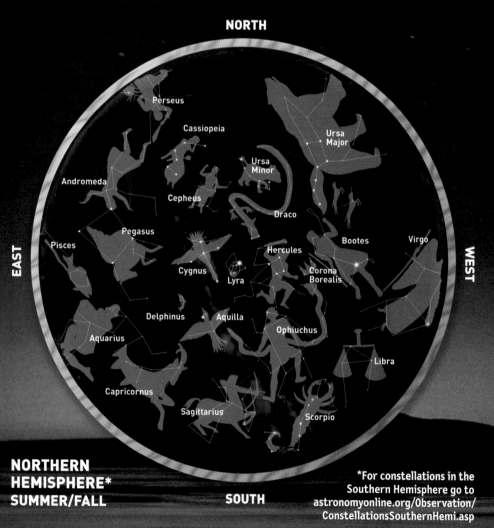

Perseus
Cassiopeia
Ursa Major
Ursa Minor
Andromeda
Cepheus
Draco
Pegasus
Bootes
Virgo
Pisces
Hercules
Cygnus
Corona Borealis
Lyra
Delphinus
Aquilla
Ophiuchus
Aquarius
Libra
Capricornus
Sagittarius
Scorpio

EAST

WEST

SOUTH

NORTHERN HEMISPHERE* SUMMER/FALL

*For constellations in the Southern Hemisphere go to astronomyonline.org/Observation/ConstellationsSouthernHemi.asp

186

Planet or Star?

On a clear night, you'll see a sky filled with glittering lights. But not every bright spot is a star—you may be peeking at a planet instead. How do you tell a star from a planet? While stars twinkle, planets shine more steadily and tend to be the brightest objects in the sky, other than the moon. Planets also move slowly across the sky from night to night. If you think you've spotted one, keep checking on it as the week goes by. If it has moved closer or farther from the moon, then it's probably a planet.

WANT TO SPOT A SATELLITE? Look for an **OBJECT** that travels quickly and steadily among **THE STARS.**

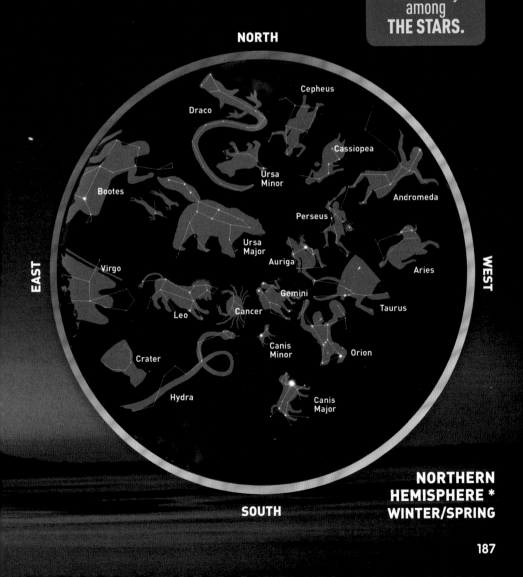

NORTH

Cepheus

Draco

Cassiopea

Ursa Minor

Bootes

Andromeda

Perseus

Virgo

Ursa Major

Auriga

Aries

EAST

WEST

Gemini

Leo

Cancer

Taurus

Crater

Canis Minor

Orion

Hydra

Canis Major

SOUTH

NORTHERN HEMISPHERE * WINTER/SPRING

Continents on the Move

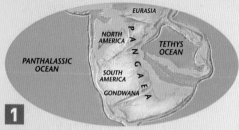

1 PANGAEA About 240 million years ago, Earth's landmasses were joined together in one super-continent that extended from Pole to Pole.

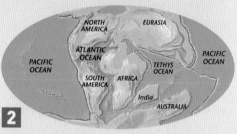

2 BREAKUP By 94 million years ago, Pangaea had broken apart into landmasses that would become today's continents. Dinosaurs roamed Earth during a period of warmer climates.

3 EXTINCTION About 65 million years ago, an asteroid smashed into Earth, creating the Gulf of Mexico. Scientists think this impact resulted in the extinction of half the world's species, including the dinosaurs. This was one of several mass extinctions.

4 ICE AGE By 18,000 years ago, the continents had drifted close to their present positions, but most far northern and far southern lands were buried beneath huge glaciers.

A LOOK INSIDE

The distance from Earth's surface to its center is 3,963 miles (6,378 km) at the Equator. There are four layers: a thin, rigid crust; the rocky mantle; the outer core, which is a layer of molten iron; and finally the inner core, which is believed to be solid iron.

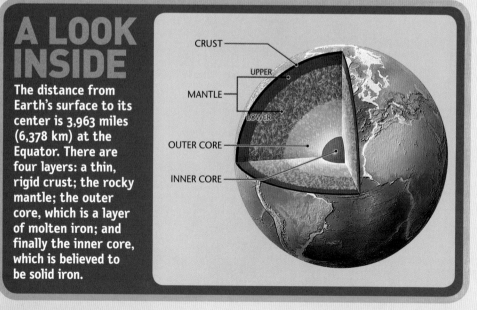

CRUST
UPPER
MANTLE
LOWER
OUTER CORE
INNER CORE

ROCK STARS

The world is full of rocks—some big, some small, some formed deep beneath the Earth, and some formed at the surface. While they may look similar, not all rocks are created equal. Look closely, and you'll see differences between every boulder, stone, and pebble. Here's more about the three top varieties of rocks.

Igneous

Named for the Greek word meaning "from fire," igneous rocks form when hot, molten liquid called magma cools. Pools of magma form deep underground and slowly work their way to the Earth's surface. If they make it all the way, the liquid rock erupts and is called lava. As the layers of lava build up they form a mountain called a volcano. Typical igneous rocks include obsidian, basalt, and pumice, which is so chock-full of gas bubbles that it actually floats in water.

OBSIDIAN   **PUMICE**

Metamorphic

Metamorphic rocks are the masters of change! These rocks were once igneous or sedimentary, but thanks to intense heat and pressure deep within the Earth, they have undergone a total transformation from their original form. These rocks never truly melt; instead, the heat twists and bends them until their shapes substantially change. Metamorphic rocks include slate as well as marble, which is used for buildings, monuments, and sculptures.

MARBLE   **SLATE**

Sedimentary

When wind, water, and ice constantly wear away and weather rocks, smaller pieces called sediment are left behind. These are sedimentary rocks, also known as gravel, sand, silt, and clay. As water flows downhill it carries the sedimentary grains into lakes and oceans, where they get deposited. As the loose sediment piles up, the grains eventually get compacted or cemented back together again. The result is new sedimentary rock. Sandstone, gypsum, limestone, and shale are sedimentary rocks that have formed this way.

SANDSTONE   **GYPSUM**

Name That ROCK

Whether you're kicking one down the road or climbing on top of one at the park, rocks are all around you. But what kind of rocks are they? Can you identify the variety of rocks on this page?

Answers are at the bottom of page 191.

A
This is the stuff of hopscotch and tic-tac-toe. It was formed with the skeletons of microorganisms.

B
This volcanic rock forms after lava has cooled quickly, and it is the only rock that floats!

GET OUTSIDE GUIDE

CHECK OUT THE BOOK!

C This rock formed in a similar way to granite, but you can see large crystals in it.

D This rock is so soft it can break up in water.

fun fact

Diamonds are the hardest rocks on Earth. They come in a variety of colors, including yellow, red, and even green.

E Some of the oldest fossils found on Earth are preserved in this soft sedimentary rock.

F The most common volcanic rock on Earth, it formed by cooling quickly, but it has fine grains on the surface.

G A seated Abraham Lincoln and Michelangelo's "David" were both carved out of this white, metamorphic rock.

A. Chalk; B. Pumice; C. Gabbro; D. Mudstone; E. Shale; F. Basalt; G. Marble

Volcano!

Fiery hot lava flows down a Hawaiian mountainside like dark, thick syrup. **When it reaches the sea, it hisses and explodes** in scalding jets of steam.

Lava flowing from a volcano can be hotter than **2100°F** (1149°C).

Farther up the slope, volcanologist Ken Hon picks his way slowly across the rough surface. The hot lava is slippery to walk on. "It's like walking on ice," Hon says. "But the bottom part of your boots starts to melt a little. If you fall, you'll get burned."

Hon plants his feet carefully and slowly. He is collecting data on the lava flowing out of Kilauea (kee-luh-WAY-uh, shown here), a volcano that has been erupting since 1983. Knowing the lava's movements can save lives on the slopes below. But Hon must be careful. New waves of lava are flowing down toward him. Every few minutes he looks up to see where the streams are and makes sure the moving lava hasn't cut off his escape route.

"It's searing hot out there—like the heat from an oven," Hon says. "Up close, you have to wear firefighters' gear so the clothes you're wearing don't catch on fire or melt."

SLOW FLOW

Earth's interior is so hot that rock softens and flows. Volcanoes form at certain places where liquid rock, or magma, pushes through cracks to the Earth's surface. The cracks eject lava, which is what magma is called when it reaches the surface. Ash that forms volcanic mountains also explodes from the crater. Some volcanoes, such as Kilauea, typically erupt gently. But they can pour out rivers of lava that engulf everything in their path.

LAVA ON ROAD

"Back in 1990, lava entered the town of Kalapana," Hon says. "We had to evacuate people from about 150 homes. The lava inched forward and consumed all of the houses." Everyone escaped. But today Kalapana is buried under 30 feet (9.1 m) of lava.

In 2014, about 20 families in Pahoa, Hawaii, were evacuated as Kīlauea's lava once again threatened homes.

Volcanoes aren't scary to Hon. They're fascinating and exciting. Still, Hon knows how to keep safe—and knows when the lava is too close. But the danger is worth it, because the more Hon and other scientists can learn about volcanoes, the safer they can keep the people who live around these powerful forces of nature.

Hawaii's Mauna Loa is the world's largest active volcano.

More than **1,500** volcanoes on Earth are active.

DOOMED HOUSE

LAVA LAMPS

FOUR WAYS VOLCANOES ERUPT

1. FIERY FLOW
Lava sprays through cracks in the Earth and flows down the slopes.

2. SHORT BURST
The pressure in the gas inside stickier magma increases, causing small but frequent bursts of lava.

3. ROCKY RUSH
Stickier magma forms a dome in the volcano's opening. The dome collapses and then explodes, sending ash and rock down the volcano's sides.

4. HUGE *KABOOM!*
The stickiest magma traps large amounts of gas and produces great pressure in the magma chamber. The gas blows the magma into pieces, shooting ash and rock miles into the air.

Get Out of the Way!

As magma moves upward inside a volcano, the volcano becomes more likely to erupt. Here are signs that it might be happening.

- Many small or moderate earthquakes
- Bulges and other deformations in the volcano's surface
- Major changes in the release of gases from cracks and other openings

193

HOT SPOT

FOUNTAINS OF SUPERHEATED WATER CREATE A WEIRD LANDMARK.

A bizarre blob of steaming fountains bursts with water and color from the barren landscape. It may look like a scene from another planet, but the surreal Fly Geyser unexpectedly gushes up from the Nevada, U.S.A., desert. The mounds stand 12 feet (3.7 m) tall, spouting scalding water 5 feet (1.5 m) higher. At first glance, Fly Geyser seems to be a natural wonder, but it's not quite natural. It's technically not a geyser either. It's an accident.

BIRTH OF FLY GEYSER Although Fly Geyser is powered by nature, it got a kick start from humans. The fountains spew water that continuously flows from a single underground hole, which was drilled by workers about 50 years ago. They had hoped to strike water that was so hot it could power an electrical plant with geothermal energy. The boiling water spurting from the Fly Geyser originates deep below the surface, where it is heated by shallow magma—hot, liquid rock. This wet zone is covered by a hard layer of rock, which traps the hot water. Because it can't escape as steam, the pressurized water's temperature rises far above the normal boiling point. The artificial, drilled hole gives the water a way out, like the opening of a soda bottle.

IT'S ALIVE! Even though the water spewing from Fly Geyser tops 200°F (93°C), the temperature turned out to be too low for a geothermal plant. The hole was plugged, but the hot water eventually forced its way up. Minerals that dissolved in the exiting water gradually built the mounds and surrounding terraces.

Fly Geyser's mounds and terraces aren't only alive with color—they're literally alive. The brilliant reds, yellows, and greens are caused by organisms called thermophiles, or "heat lovers." They are the only life-forms that can survive in such high, deadly temperatures. Different colors of thermophiles live in water at different temperatures, creating Fly Geyser's changing colors.

THEY'RE GONNA BLOW!

Natural geysers are more complicated than Fly Geyser. The world's most famous geyser, Wyoming's Old Faithful in Yellowstone National Park, doesn't spray continuously like Fly Geyser. Instead, it erupts about 16 times a day, shooting a steamy torrent of water more than 130 feet (40 m) into the air. What makes Old Faithful and other natural geysers different from Fly Geyser is their complex plumbing systems. The hot water's path to the surface becomes constricted, and the pressure builds. The heated water begins to bubble, and then explodes up and out. "It's like a volcano," explains U.S. Geological Survey researcher Shaul Hurwitz. "Once it starts erupting, all the stored water is released rapidly."

HOT PURSUIT Fly Geyser wasn't hot enough to support a geothermal plant, but it was a necessary step in a hit-or-miss process. Other heat-seeking holes in the area tapped into hotter water and were put to use. That water makes steam that cranks big machines to create electricity. Most power plants use steam, but geothermal ones don't burn coal or gas to make it, so they're much cleaner.

QUIZ WHIZ

Discover your science smarts by taking this quiz!
ANSWERS BELOW

1 **True or false?** Your short-term memory can hold about twelve things at a time.

2 _____ is/are the hardest type of rock on earth.
a. Diamonds
b. Pumice
c. Marble
d. Sandstone

3 Ceres is a _____.
a. mineral
b. volcano
c. dwarf planet
d. smart phone feature

4 Adult humans have up to _____ cells in their body.
a. 100
b. 1,000
c. 1 million
d. 100 trillion

5 What falls like rain on Jupiter?
a. hydrogen combined with oxygen
b. neon dissolved in helium
c. methane
d. cats and dogs

Not **STUMPED** yet? Check out the *NATIONAL GEOGRAPHIC KIDS QUIZ WHIZ* collection for more crazy **SCIENCE** questions!

ANSWERS:
1. False. Your short-term memory can only hold about seven things at a time. 2. a; 3. c; 4. d; 5. b

Research Like a Pro

There is so much information on the Internet. How do you find what you need and make sure it's accurate?

Be Specific
To come up with the most effective key-words—words that describe what you want to know more about—write down what you're looking for in the form of a ques-tion, and then circle the most important words in that sentence. Those are the key-words to use in your search. And for best results, use words that are specific rather than general.

Research
Research on the Internet involves "looking up" information using a search engine (see list below). Type one or two keywords, and the search engine will provide a list of websites that contain information related to your topic.

Use Trustworthy Sources
When conducting Internet research, be sure the website you use is reliable and the information it provides can be trusted. Sites produced by well-known, established organizations, companies, publications, educational institutions, or the government are your best bets.

Don't Copy
Avoid Internet plagiarism. Take careful notes and cite the websites you use to conduct research.

HELPFUL AND SAFE SEARCH ENGINES FOR KIDS

Google Safe Search
squirrelnet.com/search/Google_SafeSearch.asp

GoGooligans
gogooligans.com

AOL Kids
kids.aol.com

Flowering namaqua daisies create a spectacular display at the Goegap Nature Reserve in Namaqualand, South Africa.

Wonders of Nature

1

A HEAT WAVE CAN MAKE TRAIN TRACKS BEND.

2

A hurricane in Florida caused 900 captive pythons to escape.

3

SOME TORNADOES CAN BE FASTER THAN FORMULA ONE RACE CARS.

17

4

You can tell the TEMPERATURE by COUNTING a cricket's CHIRPS.

FREAKY FACTS ABOUT

5

A 2003 heat wave turned grapes to raisins before they were picked from the vine.

6

SANDSTORMS CAN SWALLOW UP ENTIRE CITIES.

7

A MUDSLIDE CAN CARRY ROCKS, TREES, VEHICLES, AND ENTIRE BUILDINGS.

8

A spiderweb INSIDE your HOUSE may be a SIGN that COLDER WEATHER is coming.

9 CATS AND DOGS HAVE BEEN KNOWN TO SENSE WHEN A TORNADO IS APPROACHING.

11 In 525 B.C., a SANDSTORM BURIED hundreds of SOLDIERS in an EGYPTIAN DESERT.

12 Lava from volcanoes can start wildfires.

13 About **2,000** thunderstorms rain down on Earth every minute.

10 In ANTARCTICA, SNOW can fall so hard YOU CAN'T SEE your hand IN FRONT OF YOUR FACE.

WEATHER

14 Worms CRAWL UP from UNDERGROUND when a FLOOD IS COMING.

15 Some frogs get noisier just before it rains.

16 RAINDROPS can be the SIZE OF A HOUSEFLY and fall at roughly 20 miles an hour (32 km/h).

17 WILDFIRES SOMETIMES CREATE FLAME-THROWING TORNADOES CALLED FIRE WHIRLS.

Weather and Climate

Weather is the condition of the atmosphere—temperature, wind, humidity, and precipitation—at a given place at a given time. Climate, however, is the average weather for a particular place over a long period of time. Different places on Earth have different climates, but climate is not a random occurrence. It is a pattern that is controlled by factors such as latitude, elevation, prevailing winds, the temperature of ocean currents, and location on land relative to water. Climate is generally constant, but evidence indicates that human activity is causing a change in the patterns of climate.

WEATHER EXTREMES

BIGGEST SNOWFLAKE: The biggest snowflake ever recorded was 15 inches (38.1 cm) wide.

LIGHTNING HOT: Temperatures in the air around a lightning bolt can hit 50,000°F (27,760°C)

RAINIEST DAY: 72 inches (183 cm) of rain was recorded in a 24-hour period in 1966 on Reunion Island, a French island in the Indian Ocean, during Tropical Cyclone Denise.

GLOBAL CLIMATE ZONES

Climatologists, people who study climate, have created different systems for classifying climates. One often-used system is called the Köppen system, which classifies climate zones according to precipitation, temperature, and vegetation. It has five major categories—Tropical, Dry, Temperate, Cold, and Polar—with a sixth category for locations where high elevations override other factors.

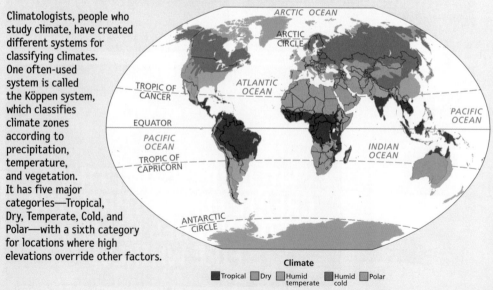

ARCTIC OCEAN
ARCTIC CIRCLE
ATLANTIC OCEAN
TROPIC OF CANCER
PACIFIC OCEAN
EQUATOR
PACIFIC OCEAN
TROPIC OF CAPRICORN
INDIAN OCEAN
PACIFIC OCEAN
ANTARCTIC CIRCLE

Climate
■ Tropical □ Dry □ Humid temperate ■ Humid cold □ Polar

WATER CYCLE

Precipitation falls

Water storage in ice and snow

Water vapor condenses in clouds

Water filters into the ground

Meltwater and surface runoff

Fresh water storage

Evaporation

Ground water discharge

Water storage in ocean

The amount of water on Earth is more or less constant—

only the form changes. As the sun warms Earth's surface, liquid water is changed to water vapor in a process called **evaporation.** Water on the surface of plants' leaves turn into water vapor in a process called **transpiration.** As water vapor rises into the air, it cools and changes form again. This time it becomes clouds in a process called **condensation.** Water droplets fall from the clouds as **precipitation,** which then travels as groundwater or runoff back to the lakes, rivers, and oceans, where the cycle (shown above) starts all over again.

To a meteorologist— a person who studies the weather— a "light rain" is less than 1/48 of an inch (0.5 mm). A "heavy rain" is more than 1/6 of an inch (4 mm).

Weather Sayings

These words of weather wisdom have been passed down for generations. But they're not always accurate—be sure to check the forecast!

- Red sky in the morning, sailors take warning. Red sky at night, sailors' delight.

- Clear nights mean cold days.

- If a circle forms 'round the moon, then it will rain very soon.

- Rain before seven stops by eleven.

- In a green sky, the cows will fly.

Types of Clouds

If you want a clue about the weather, look up at the clouds. They'll tell a lot about the condition of the air and what weather might be on the way. Clouds are made of both air and water. On fair days, warm air currents rise up and push against the water in clouds, keeping it from falling. But as the raindrops in a cloud get bigger, it's time to set them free. The bigger raindrops become too heavy for the air currents to hold up, and they fall to the ground.

How Much Does a Cloud Weigh?

A light, fluffy, cumulus cloud typically weighs about 216,000 pounds (97,975 kg). That's about the weight of 18 elephants. A rain-soaked cumulonimbus cloud typically weighs 105.8 million pounds (48,000,000 kg), or about 9,000 elephants.

1 STRATUS These clouds make the sky look like a bowl of thick gray porridge. They hang low in the sky, blanketing the day in dreary darkness. Stratus clouds form when cold, moist air close to the ground moves over a region.

2 CIRRUS These wispy tufts of clouds are thin and hang high up in the atmosphere where the air is extremely cold. Cirrus clouds are made of tiny ice crystals.

3 CUMULONIMBUS These are the monster clouds. Rising air currents force fluffy cumulus clouds to swell and shoot upward, as much as 70,000 feet (21,000 m). When these clouds bump against the top of the troposphere, or the tropopause, they flatten out on top like tabletops.

4 CUMULUS These white, fluffy clouds make people sing, "Oh, what a beautiful morning!" They form low in the atmosphere and look like marshmallows. They often mix with large patches of blue sky. Formed when hot air rises, cumulus clouds usually disappear when the air cools at night.

Make a Barometer

ARE YOU FASCINATED BY WEATHER? Then you should make your own barometer to track the weather where you live!

SUPPLY LIST

- Ruler
- Tall glass
- Drinking straw
- Bubble gum
- Tape
- Water and blue food coloring

STEPS

1. Tape a clear drinking straw to a ruler. The bottom of the straw should line up with the ½-inch (12–13 mm) mark on the ruler.

2. Stand the ruler up in a tall glass and tape it to the inside of the glass so it stays straight. Fill the glass ¾ full with water.

3. Here's the fun part: Chew on a piece of gum for a while, then stick it to the top of the straw.

4. Pour out ¼ of the water so that the water in the straw is higher than the water in the cup.

5. Keep an eye on your barometer. When atmospheric pressure increases, the water level in your straw will rise (which usually means fair weather). When atmospheric pressure decreases, the water level will fall (and can mean clouds or rain are on the way). Record your findings in your meteorologist notebook!

> Barometers were invented in Italy in the early 1600s by Evangelista Torricelli.

Time: about 10 minutes

KEEP A WEATHER JOURNAL

Recording the daily temperature, rainfall, and barometric changes will help you track patterns in the weather. Try to take a measurement every day and record it in a journal. Set up a chart for each component of your weather station. After a few weeks, you might start to see some patterns, and soon you'll be making predictions—like a regular meteorologist!

TOP OF STRAW

Natural Disasters

Every world region has its share of natural disasters—the mix just varies from place to place. And the names of similar storms may vary as well. Take, for example, cyclones, typhoons, and hurricanes. The only difference among these disasters is where in the world they strike. In the Atlantic and the Northeast Pacific, they're hurricanes; in the Northwest Pacific near Asia they're typhoons; and in the South Pacific and Indian Oceans, they're cyclones.

Despite their distinct titles, these natural disasters are each classified by violent winds, massive waves, torrential rain, and floods. The only obvious variation among these storms? They spin in the opposite direction if they're south of the Equator.

TYPHOON!

HURRICANES IN 2017

HELLO, MY NAME IS . . .

Hurricane names come from six official international lists. The names alternate between male and female.

When a storm becomes a hurricane, a name from the list is used, in alphabetical order. Each list is reused every six years. A name "retires" if that hurricane caused a lot of damage or many deaths.

Arlene
Bret
Cindy
Don
Emily
Franklin
Gert
Harvey
Irma
Jose
Katia
Lee
Maria
Nate
Ophelia
Philippe
Rina
Sean
Tammy
Vince
Whitney

A monster storm with gusts of 235 miles an hour (380 km/h) barrels down onto a cluster of islands in the heart of the Philippines in November 2013. Howling winds whip debris into the street as palm trees bend nearly in half, and seawater rises as high as a two-story building. This is Super Typhoon Haiyan, and it's about as dangerous as they come.

When does a typhoon become a super-typhoon? According to the U.S. National Oceanic and Atmospheric Administration (NOAA), winds must sustain speeds of over 150 miles an hour (240 km/h) for at least a minute. And not only is Haiyan powerful, it's also gigantic: The storm's clouds cover at least two-thirds of the Philippines, which is roughly the size of Arizona, U.S.A.

The word "typhoon" comes from the Greek *typhon*, meaning "whirlwind." These superstrong storms form when tropical winds suck up moisture as they pass over warm water. Increasing in speed and strength as they near the coast, typhoons can topple homes and cause massive flooding once they hit land.

The Philippines endures an average of eight or nine tropical storms every year. But none have been as disastrous as Haiyan. Resulting in over 6,300 casualties, affecting 16 million people, and racking up millions of dollars in damage, the storm was one of the strongest typhoons to ever hit land anywhere in the world.

Scale of Hurricane Intensity

CATEGORY	ONE	TWO	THREE	FOUR	FIVE
DAMAGE	Minimal	Moderate	Extensive	Extreme	Catastrophic
WINDS	74–95 mph (119–153 kph)	96–110 mph (154–177 kph)	111–129 mph (178–208 kph)	130–156 mph (209–251 kph)	157 mph or higher (252+ kph)
	(DAMAGE refers to wind and water damage combined.)				

EARTHQUAKE!

It was a force strong enough to move Mount Everest. When a 7.8-magnitude earthquake rocked Nepal in April 2015 the world's tallest mountain actually shifted more than an inch (3 cm) southwest.

The damage below the mountain was much more significant, however. The earthquake was the worst to hit the Himalayan nation in nearly a century.

More than 8,500 died and scores more were injured in the aftermath of the earthquake and its aftershocks. Villages were reduced to rubble, and more than half a million homes around the country were seriously damaged. The earthquake and its aftershocks also triggered landslides and a deadly avalanche on Mount Everest, causing even more damage and taking the lives of dozens of villagers and trekkers aiming to reach the peak.

No doubt, Nepal was devastated by the earthquake. But the resilient nation reopened schools within five weeks, and humanitarian efforts are helping to rebuild homes and businesses—and resume life as normal in Nepal.

BLIZZARD!

Buffalo, New York, U.S.A., is no stranger to snow. In fact, the town typically receives an average of about seven feet (2.1 m) per year. But no one was quite prepared for the massive snowstorm that hit the region in November 2014, burying parts of Buffalo in more than five feet (1.5 m) of heavy snow. With freezing winds whipping off of nearby Lake Erie, bands of heavy snow fell at a rate of up to five inches (12.7 cm) per hour at times. The snow trapped people in their homes, stranding cars on the highway, closing schools for a week, and stalling almost all activity in the town and surrounding areas. All told, 13 people died during the blizzard.

And once the snow stopped? Massive loads of snow—estimated to match the weight of two cars—caused rooftops to buckle, forcing people to evacuate from apartment buildings and homes. It took thousands of truckloads to remove the snow from city streets before unseasonably warm temperatures that hit the region just one week later melted the rest away.

What is a tornado?

TORNADOES, ALSO KNOWN AS TWISTERS, are funnels of rapidly rotating air that are created during a thunderstorm. With wind speeds of up to 300 miles an hour (483 km/h), tornadoes have the power to pick up and destroy everything in their path.

Supercell

A massive rotating thunderstorm that generates the most destructive of all tornadoes. A series of supercells in the southern United States caused an outbreak of 92 tornadoes in ten states over a 15-hour period in 2008.

Weather Alert

TORNADOES HAVE OCCURRED IN ALL 50 U.S. STATES AND ON EVERY CONTINENT EXCEPT ANTARCTICA.

Funnel cloud

This rotating funnel of air formed in a cumulus or cumulonimbus cloud becomes a tornado if it touches the ground.

Fire whirls

These tornadoes made of wind and fire occur during a wildfire. Their flaming towers can be five to ten stories tall and can last for more than an hour. They are also called fire devils.

Waterspout

This funnel-shaped column forms over water and is usually weaker than a land tornado.

THE ENHANCED FUJITA SCALE

The Enhanced Fujita (EF) Scale, named after tornado expert T. Theodore Fujita, classifies tornadoes based on wind speed and the intensity of damage that they cause.

EF0
65–85 mph winds
(105–137 kph)
Slight damage

EF1
86–110 mph winds
(138–177 kph)
Moderate damage

EF2
111–135 mph winds
(178–217 kph)
Substantial damage

EF3
136–165 mph winds
(218–266 kph)
Severe damage

EF4
166–200 mph winds
(267–322 kph)
Massive damage

EF5
More than
200 mph winds
(322+ kph)
Catastrophic damage

HOW DOES YOUR GARDEN GROW?

Three characteristics make plants distinct:

1. Most have chlorophyll (a green pigment that makes photosynthesis work and turns sunlight into energy), while some are parasitic.

2. They cannot change their location on their own.

3. Their cell walls are made from a stiff material called cellulose.

The plant kingdom is more than 300,000 species strong, growing all over the world: on top of mountains, in the sea, in frigid temperatures—everywhere. Without plants, life on Earth would not be able to survive. Plants provide food and oxygen for animals and humans.

Photosynthesis

Plants are lucky—they don't have to hunt or shop for food. Most use the sun to produce their own food. In a process called photosynthesis, the plant's chloroplast (the part of the plant where the chemical chlorophyll is located) captures the sun's energy and combines it with carbon dioxide from the air and nutrient-rich water from the ground to produce a sugar called glucose. Plants burn the glucose for energy to help them grow. As a waste product, plants emit oxygen, which humans and other animals need to breathe. When we breathe, we exhale carbon dioxide, which the plants then use for more photosynthesis—it's all a big, finely tuned system. So the next time you pass a lonely houseplant, give it thanks for helping you live.

Bet you didn't know

6 facts about plants that will grow on you

1 **Medicine** made with certain **passion-flowers** is used to **help** people **sleep.**

2 **Leaves** of a species of **mimosa** plant curl when **touched.**

3 **Attenborough's** pitcher plant secretes nectar to lure **bugs** and **rodents** into its **"mouth."**

4 **A common sunflower's** main head consists of up to **4,000** tiny **flowers.**

5 **The seed pods** of some **snap-dragon** plants can look like human skulls.

6 **One** kind of **eucalyptus tree** can have **rainbow-colored** bark.

211

CARNIVOROUS Plants

Most plants get their nutrients from soil. But many carnivorous plants grow in places where the soil is poor, so they eat insects instead. Here's more about these meat-eaters!

Sarracenia

Sarracenia is a genus of plants that trap bugs with their pitchers, or pitcher-shaped leaves, but that's not all. Some species contain a chemical-laced nectar that dazes their prey. After a few sips, a woozy insect becomes less steady on its feet, leaving it little chance to fend off an inevitable—and untimely—death.

The "dew" on this plant is inviting to insects. But those droplets—made of a thick, sticky substance attached to the tips of the plant's hairs—are deadly. After landing on the plant's narrow leaves to suck up moisture, the insect gets stuck in the hairs and eventually suffocates or dies from exhaustion. Digestive enzymes in the droplets break down the insect, completing the meal.

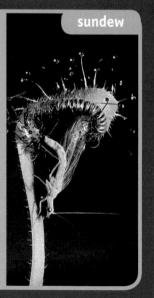

sundew

cobra lily

This plant picks up its ferocious name from its pitcher, which is formed from a modified leaf that looks like a cobra ready to strike. Instead of using fangs to attack its prey, the cobra lily draws insects into its sunny pitcher, thanks to transparent windows on top of its trap that work like a skylight. The insects are drawn to the light, but once they're trapped inside, it's, uh, lights out.

butterwort

The shiny leaves on this plant may look inviting to a thirsty insect, but watch out! Things are not what they seem. The butterwort's leaves are covered with short hairs that are topped with a gluey fluid that acts as a trap. The fluid also contains enzymes that slowly digest the victim.

monkey cup

These plants, native to Southeast Asia, typically trap insects. But they've also been known to eat much bigger species, including small mammals like mice, rats, and occasionally even birds that come to sip at its pitcher. At least the monkeys who are said to drink rainwater out of the plant's pitcher manage to stay out of harm's way!

pitcher plant

Bugs beware! There are many kinds of pitcher plants, but they're all dangerous places to dine. A bug is attracted to the plant's delicious nectar, but if a hungry insect crawls too close to the edge, it slips down the plant's slick insides and becomes trapped at the bottom of the pitcher.

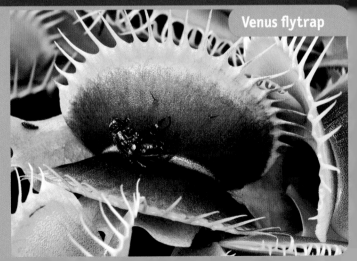

Venus flytrap

No wonder this plant shares a name with a planet—it's truly out of this world! Its leaves are like trapdoors, drawing small insects in with sweet-smelling nectar. If tiny hairs on the surface of the trap are brushed twice in quick succession, the leaves snap shut in the blink of an eye. This sophisticated system ensures that the plant won't waste energy on nonfood items.

Biomes

A BIOME, OFTEN CALLED A MAJOR LIFE ZONE, is one of the natural world's major communities where plants and animals adapt to their specific surroundings. Biomes are classified depending on the predominant vegetation, climate, and geography of a region. They can be divided into six major types: forest, freshwater, marine, desert, grassland, and tundra. Each biome consists of many ecosystems.

Biomes are extremely important. Balanced ecological relationships among biomes help to maintain the environment and life on Earth as we know it. For example, an increase in one species of plant, such as an invasive one, can cause a ripple effect throughout the whole biome.

FOREST

Forests occupy about one-third of Earth's land area. There are three major types of forests: tropical, temperate, and boreal (taiga). Forests are home to a diversity of plants, some of which may hold medicinal qualities for humans, as well as thousands of animal species, some still undiscovered. Forests can also absorb carbon dioxide, a greenhouse gas, and give off oxygen.

> The rabbit-size royal antelope lives in West Africa's dense forests.

FRESHWATER

Most water on Earth is salty, but freshwater ecosystems—including lakes, ponds, wetlands, rivers, and streams—usually contain water with less than one percent salt concentration. The countless animal and plant species that live in a freshwater biome vary from continent to continent, but they include algae, frogs, turtles, fish, and the larvae of many insects.

> The place where fresh and salt water meet is called an estuary.

MARINE

The marine biome covers almost three-fourths of Earth's surface, making it the largest habitat on our planet. Oceans make up the majority of the saltwater marine biome. Coral reefs are considered to be the most biodiverse of any of the biome habitats. The marine biome is home to more than one million plant and animal species.

Estimated to be up to 100,000 years old, sea grass growing in the Mediterranean Sea may be the oldest living thing on Earth.

DESERT

Covering about one-fifth of Earth's surface, deserts are places where precipitation is less than ten inches (25 cm) per year. Although most deserts are hot, there are other kinds as well. The four major kinds of deserts are hot, semiarid, coastal, and cold. Far from being barren wastelands, deserts are biologically rich habitats.

Some sand dunes in the Sahara are tall enough to bury a 50-story building.

GRASSLAND

Biomes called grasslands are characterized by having grasses instead of large shrubs or trees. Grasslands generally have precipitation for only about half to three-fourths of the year. If it were more, they would become forests. Grasslands can be divided into two types: tropical (savannas) and temperate. Some of the world's largest land animals, such as elephants, live there.

Grasslands in North America are called prairies; in South America, they're called pampas.

TUNDRA

The coldest of all biomes, a tundra is characterized by an extremely cold climate, simple vegetation, little precipitation, poor nutrients, and a short growing season. There are two types of tundra: arctic and alpine. A tundra is home to few kinds of vegetation. Surprisingly, though, there are quite a few animal species that can survive the tundra's extremes, such as wolves, caribou, and even mosquitoes.

Formed 10,000 years ago, the arctic tundra is the world's youngest biome.

THE OC

PACIFIC OCEAN

STATS

Surface area
65,436,200 sq mi (169,479,000 sq km)

Portion of Earth's water area
47 percent

Greatest depth
**Challenger Deep
(in the Mariana Trench)
-36,070 ft (-10,994 m)**

Surface temperatures
**Summer high: 90°F (32°C)
Winter low: 28°F (-2°C)**

Tides
**Highest: 30 ft (9 m) near Korean peninsula
Lowest: 1 ft (0.3 m) near Midway Islands**

Cool creatures: **giant Pacific octopus,
bottlenose whale, clownfish, great
white shark**

ATLANTIC OCEAN

STATS

Surface area
35,338,500 sq mi (91,526,300 sq km)

Portion of Earth's water area
25 percent

Greatest depth
**Puerto Rico Trench
-28,232 ft (-8,605 m)**

Surface temperatures
**Summer high: 90°F (32°C)
Winter low: 28°F (-2°C)**

Tides
**Highest: 52 ft (16 m)
Bay of Fundy, Canada
Lowest: 1.5 ft (0.5 m)
Gulf of Mexico and Mediterranean Sea**

Cool creatures: **blue whale, Atlantic spotted
dolphin, sea turtle**

GREAT WHITE SHARK

GREEN SEA TURTLE

EANS

INDIAN OCEAN

STATS

Surface area
28,839,800 sq mi (74,694,800 sq km)

Portion of Earth's water area
21 percent

Greatest depth
Java Trench
-23,376 ft (-7,125 m)

Surface temperatures
Summer high: 93°F (34°C)
Winter low: 28°F (-2°C)

Tides
Highest: 36 ft (11 m)
Lowest: 2 ft (0.6 m)
Both along Australia's west coast

Cool creatures: humpback whale, Portuguese man-of-war, dugong (sea cow)

DUGONG

ARCTIC OCEAN

STATS

Surface area
5,390,000 sq mi (13,960,100 sq km)

Portion of Earth's water area
4 percent

Greatest depth
Molloy Deep
-18,599 ft (-5,669 m)

Surface temperatures
Summer high: 41°F (5°C)
Winter low: 28°F (-2°C)

Tides
Less than 1 ft (0.3 m) variation throughout the ocean

Cool creatures: beluga whale, orca, harp seal, narwhal

ORCA

To see the major oceans and bays in relation to landmasses, look at the map on pages 258 and 259.

PRISTINE SEAS

Explorers work to protect the last truly wild places in the ocean.

Around the world, only one percent of the ocean is fully protected from fishing.

A YELLOW-EDGED LYRETAIL PROWLS CORAL NEAR PITCAIRN ISLAND.

DR. ENRIC SALA

KEEPING OUR OCEANS PRISTINE

Oceans cover more than 70 percent of Earth's surface. Even with all of that water, only a tiny percentage is not impacted by human activity—but conservationists are working to change that. The National Geographic Pristine Seas team, led by National Geographic Explorer-in-Residence Enric Sala, travels to some of the most remote parts of the oceans to explore life underwater and create protected areas. One such location? The Pitcairn Islands in the South Pacific, where the Pristine Seas squad created the world's largest marine reserve, setting aside a swath of sea bigger than the entire state of California, U.S.A., for special protection. That means that there is no fishing or seafloor mining allowed in the reserve, a move meant to keep the thousands of fish, plants, and coral living there healthy and thriving.

PITCAIRN ISLAND

More than 102 million tons (92.6 million t) of wild fish and shellfish are caught in the oceans every year.

A DIVER EXPLORES BOUNTY BAY NEAR PITCAIRN ISLAND.

GREY REEF SHARK

Ninety percent of the large predators in the ocean, like sharks and tuna, are gone.

SAVING THE SHARKS

The Pristine Seas expedition has also made its mark on the uninhabited Southern Line Islands, an archipelago deep in the South Pacific. Dozens of grey reef sharks swirl around these islands, feeding on the fish around the coral reefs. But they face constant danger. Sought out by humans for their fins—considered a delicacy in some parts of Asia—these sharks are vulnerable to overfishing, which is when people catch them at too fast a rate for the species to replace themselves. But by working with the local government, Sala and his crew have established a 12-nautical-mile fishing exclusion zone around each island. It's a step in the right direction for protecting the ecology of the island and, ultimately, boosting the shark's dwindling population.

QUIZ WHIZ

Quiz yourself to find out if you're a natural when it comes to nature knowledge!
ANSWERS BELOW

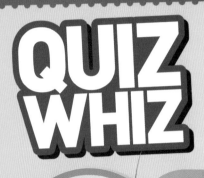

1 **True or false?** You can tell the temperature by counting a cricket's chirps.

2 A light, fluffy cumulus cloud can weigh as much as what?
- **a.** a feather
- **b.** 18 elephants
- **c.** 5 trucks
- **d.** 9,000 rhinos

3 Monkey cups, butterworts, and sundews are all types of what?
- **a.** flowers
- **b.** mushrooms
- **c.** carnivorous plants
- **d.** cookies

4 A tornado made of wind and fire is also known as a _____.

5 _____ percent of the large predators in the ocean are gone.
- **a.** 90
- **b.** 10
- **c.** 5
- **d.** 50

Not **STUMPED** yet? Check out the
NATIONAL GEOGRAPHIC KIDS QUIZ WHIZ collection
for more crazy **NATURE** questions!

ANSWERS:
1. True; 2. b; 3. c; 4. fire whirl; 5. a

SPEAK NATURALLY

Oral Reports Made Easy

Does the thought of public speaking start your stomach churning like a tornado? Would you rather get caught in an avalanche than give a speech?

Giving an oral report does not have to be a natural disaster. The basic format is very similar to that of a written essay. There are two main elements that make up a good oral report—the writing and the presentation. As you write your oral report, remember that your audience will be hearing the information as opposed to reading it. Follow the guidelines below, and there will be clear skies ahead.

> **TIP:**
> Make sure you practice your presentation a few times. Stand in front of a mirror or have a parent record you so you can see if you need to work on anything, such as eye contact.

Writing Your Material

Follow the steps in the "How to Write a Perfect Essay" section on p. 141, but prepare your report to be spoken rather than written. Try to keep your sentences short and simple. Long, complex sentences are harder to follow. Limit yourself to just a few key points. You don't want to overwhelm your audience with too much information. To be most effective, hit your key points in the introduction, elaborate on them in the body, and then repeat them once again in your conclusion.

An oral report has three basic parts:

- **Introduction**—This is your chance to engage your audience and really capture their interest in the subject you are presenting. Use a funny personal experience or a dramatic story, or start with an intriguing question.

- **Body**—This is the longest part of your report. Here you elaborate on the facts and ideas you want to convey. Give information that supports your main idea, and expand on it with specific examples or details. In other words, structure your oral report in the same way you would a written essay so that your thoughts are presented in a clear and organized manner.

- **Conclusion**—This is the time to summarize the information and emphasize your most important points to the audience one last time.

Preparing Your Delivery

1 Practice makes perfect.
Practice! Practice! Practice! Confidence, enthusiasm, and energy are key to delivering an effective oral report, and they can best be achieved through rehearsal. Ask family and friends to be your practice audience and give you feedback when you're done. Were they able to follow your ideas? Did you seem knowledgeable and confident? Did you speak too slowly or too fast, too softly or too loudly? The more times you practice giving your report, the more you'll master the material. Then you won't have to rely so heavily on your notes or papers, and you will be able to give your report in a relaxed and confident manner.

2 Present with everything you've got.
Be as creative as you can. Incorporate videos, sound clips, slide presentations, charts, diagrams, and photos. Visual aids help stimulate your audience's senses and keep them intrigued and engaged. They can also help to reinforce your key points. And remember that when you're giving an oral report, you're a performer. Take charge of the spotlight and be as animated and entertaining as you can. Have fun with it.

3 Keep your nerves under control.
Everyone gets a little nervous when speaking in front of a group. That's normal. But the more preparation you've done—meaning plenty of researching, organizing, and rehearsing—the more confident you'll be. Preparation is the key. And if you make a mistake or stumble over your words, just regroup and keep going. Nobody's perfect, and nobody expects you to be.

2017 marks the 20th anniversary of the Hong Kong handover. On July 1, 1997, the United Kingdom returned the city to China after more than 150 years of British control.

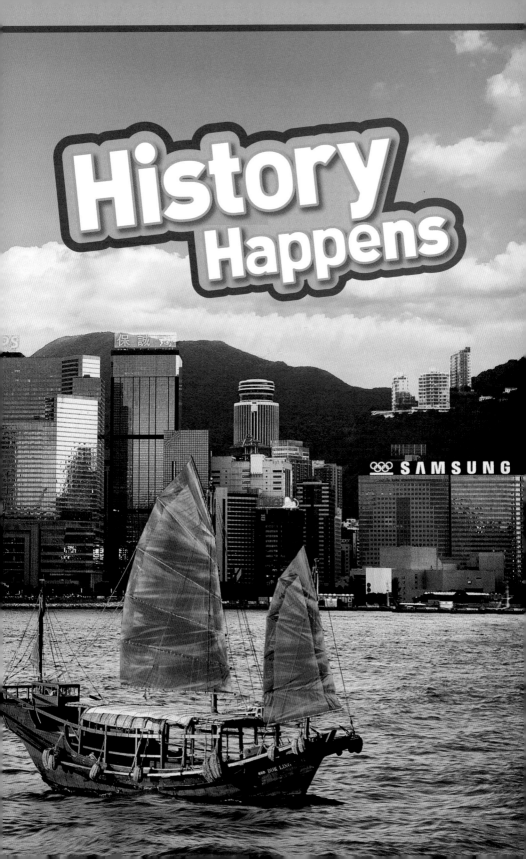

Jungle of Secrets

Scientists uncover a hidden city near a temple called ANGKOR WAT.

In the midst of Cambodia's steamy jungle looms a majestic medieval temple. Called Angkor Wat, the nearly 900-year-old structure was built in the capital of the Khmer Empire, a powerful civilization in Southeast Asia. But until recently, few were aware of something tucked in the forest beyond the temple—a hidden city.

MISSING METROPOLIS

The Khmer Empire thrived between the 9th and 15th centuries. Many people worshipped at the temple of Angkor Wat in the capital city of Angkor, which was about the size (area) of New York City. Scientists believe that in the 14th and 15th centuries, droughts and other extreme natural disasters caused many people to abandon the region and move south. Eventually, thick

In this nation, it's considered an insult to touch someone's head.

forests grew over much of the area.

Built in the 12th century to honor a god, Angkor Wat was in continual use even after the capital city was abandoned. When a French explorer came across the temple in the 1800s, he spread word of its beauty, drawing visitors and archaeologists to the area.

Scientists suspected that another, older city from the Khmer Empire called Mahendraparvata was hidden in the jungle around the temple. According to writings found in old texts, the city was built in A.D. 802 and served as the Khmer Empire's capital before it moved to Angkor.

AIRBORNE DETECTIVES

In 2012 a team of scientists wanted to investigate the region in search of the remains of Mahendraparvata. A thick tangle of trees

Angkor Wat appears on Cambodia's flag (left).

TREE ROOTS GROW OVER RUINS IN A JUNGLE NEAR ANGKOR WAT.

ASIA

PACIFIC OCEAN

CAMBODIA

INDIAN OCEAN

THAILAND

LAOS

Angkor Wat

Tonle Sap

CAMBODIA

Phnom Penh ★

VIETNAM

Gulf of Thailand

South China Sea

covering the land made exploring on foot difficult. So instead the team took to the skies.

Crisscrossing over forest canopies in a helicopter, archaeologist Damian Evans used an instrument called LIDAR to scan the ground. LIDAR works by rapidly firing off pulses of laser light. A sensor on the instrument measures how long it takes for each pulse to bounce back from the ground. If a set of laser beams has a shorter return time than the previous pulses sent, it could mean the beams have hit something elevated, such as a building. A longer return time could mean that the beams are bouncing off of a low valley or deep riverbed. Using GPS technology, cartographers then combined all of the measurements to create a map of the terrain.

As the scientists analyzed the map, they noticed an area with a network of roads and canals built into a mountain. It appeared to

match the description of Mahendraparvata found in the old texts. Evans and his team knew this had to be the hidden city.

IT'S A JUNGLE OUT THERE

The archaeologists started their expedition north of Angkor Wat under the heat of a sizzling sun. They cut away tree leaves blocking their path with machetes, waded knee-deep in bogs, and dodged dangerous land mines that had been left in the jungle after a war.

Finally they stumbled upon dozens of crumbled temples and evidence of roads and canals, all organized into city blocks. They had reached their destination, and it was indeed Mahendraparvata.

In the coming years, Evans and his team will continue to investigate the area. But the scientists will have their work cut out for them. After all, this jungle is very good at keeping secrets.

225

Knight Life

Protector of the Castle

It started with a childhood full of boring chores and ended at age 21 with a ceremonial smack to the head that knocked some men on their tails. The road to knighthood was long and rough, but the journey was often worth the trouble. Successful knights found fortune and glory.

In times of war and peace, knights led a dangerous life. These professional warriors were charged with protecting the lord's land from invaders, leading the castle's men-at-arms during sieges, and fighting on behalf of the church. Between battles, they competed in deadly games called tournaments to sharpen their skills.

In exchange for military service, knights were granted their own lands—along with peasants to farm it—and noble titles. The mightiest knights rose to rival lords in power and property. Sir Ulrich von Liechtenstein, one of the 13th century's most famous knights, owned three castles.

Not just anyone could become a knight. Armor, weapons, and warhorses cost more than a typical peasant might earn in a lifetime, so knights often hailed from noble families. They started their training early in life—at the age most kids today begin first grade.

Lord Lore

England's royal family still grants knighthood to actors, scientists, and other accomplished citizens.

How to Become a Knight

1. Serve as a Page

A boy destined for knighthood left home at age seven to become a servant in a great lord's castle. The page learned courtly manners, received a basic education, and played rough with other pages.

2. Squire for a Knight

Once he turned 14, a page became a squire for a knight. He learned about armor by cleaning his master's suit and helping him dress for battle. He practiced fighting with swords, shields, and other weaponry. Most important of all, he learned to attack from the saddle of a huge warhorse—the type of mounted combat knights were famous for.

3. Get Dubbed

By age 21, a squire was ready for his dubbing ceremony. He knelt before his lord or lady and received a hard slap to help him remember his oath. (This brutal blow later evolved into a friendlier sword tap on the shoulders.) The newly dubbed knight was given the title "sir" and could seek service at a lord's castle.

Knightly Numb

55 pounds (25 kg) of ar weighed down a kni the battlefield.

45 years was the life expectancy of the average knight.

45 days per year was th typical term of servi knight owed his lord.

Good knights acted chivalrously, which meant they protected the weak, treated women with respect, served the church, and were generous and humble.

Must-See SIGHTS

WHAT: HERCULANEUM
WHERE: Ercolano, Italy

WHY IT'S COOL: Buried by ash and lava from the eruption of Mount Vesuvius in A.D. 79, this port town is said to be better preserved than its neighbor Pompeii. Some ruins here stand up to two stories high.

WHAT: THE GREAT BUDDHA
WHERE: Kamakura, Japan

WHY IT'S COOL: More than 760 years old, this giant bronze statue has stayed standing through a lot—even surviving a giant tsunami. At 44 feet (13.35 m) tall, it's one of Japan's most famous icons.

USS ARIZONA BB 39

WHAT: U.S.S. *ARIZONA* MEMORIAL
WHERE: Honolulu, Hawaii, U.S.A.

WHY IT'S COOL: This site, which can be reached by ferry from the visitor's center, marks the memory of Japan's attack on the United States on December 7, 1941.

When you visit these historical landmarks around the world, you'll step into places almost untouched by time.

WHAT: PETRA
WHERE: Jordan

WHY IT'S COOL: You have to walk in the desert to reach this more than 2,000-year-old ancient city. But the trek is worth it as it reveals awe-inspiring buildings carved into cliffs.

WHAT: TEMPLO MAYOR
WHERE: Mexico City, Mexico

WHY IT'S COOL: With a pyramid as tall as a 15-story building as its centerpiece, this site was the heart of the Aztec community. The pyramid and temples have since been destroyed, but the artifacts and ruins that remain offer a glimpse of Aztec life over 600 years ago.

WHAT: ST. BASIL'S CATHEDRAL
WHERE: Moscow, Russia

WHY IT'S COOL: This colorful cathedral was commissioned by Ivan the Terrible in 1552 to celebrate a military victory. Today, it remains a stunning symbol of classic Russian architecture.

1

BLACKBEARD put **BURNING FUSES** on the ends of his beard to scare his enemies.

2

HARDTACK BISCUITS were a staple on pirate ships, but pirates had to be careful when taking a bite. The biscuits were often infested with **GRUBBY MAGGOTS.**

3

THE GOLDEN AGE OF PIRACY HAPPENED BETWEEN 1660 AND 1730. PIRATES WOULD ATTACK SHIPS CARRYING TREASURE FROM THE AMERICAS TO EUROPE.

4

To a pirate, a ship's medicine cabinet was just as valuable as money or jewels. Disease, injuries, food poisoning, and flea or rat bites were common.

ARRRGH!
17 FACTS ABOUT

5

Two women pirates—*ANNE BONNY AND MARY READ*—sailed with Captain John "Calico Jack" Rackham in the early 1700s. Dressed like men, they fought alongside the rest of the crew.

6

THE PRIVATEER **FRANCIS DRAKE** BROUGHT MUCH WEALTH TO ENGLAND'S QUEEN ELIZABETH I BY RAIDING SPANISH SHIPS. THE QUEEN KNIGHTED HIM IN 1581, CALLING HIM "MY PIRATE."

7

Some of the first flags on pirate ships were **RED,** not black.

8

The city of **Port Royal, Jamaica,** was a thriving town for pirates until 1692 when it was **destroyed** by a combination *EARTHQUAKE AND TSUNAMI.*

9 Cutlasses are the short, sharp swords pirates used to fight with.

10

The Welshman **BARTHOLOMEW ROBERTS** was captured by pirates who forced him to join them. As the pirate **BLACK BART**, he captured more than 400 ships.

11 Pirates who broke ship rules were **OFTEN LEFT ON DESERTED ISLANDS** with no food or water. Sometimes they were given a **PISTOL WITH 1 BULLET.**

12 In battles, pirates used *pistols* that fired *only 1 shot* before they had to be reloaded.

13 **PIRATES DRANK GROG,** a mixture of **rum, lime juice, and water.** Vitamin C from the lime helped prevent scurvy, a disease that can cause swelling, bleeding, and tooth loss.

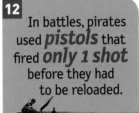

PIRATES

14 THERE IS NO DOCUMENTED RECORD OF PIRATES HAVING TO **"walk the plank"** TO THEIR DEATH.

15 The nickname "JOLLY ROGER" for pirate flags likely comes from the French words *jolie rouge,* which means "PRETTY RED."

16 The skull and crossbones on many pirate flags was a **SYMBOL OF DEATH.** Today, it is used to warn of poison or danger.

17

"Barbarossa," which means "red beard," was the name of two fearsome pirate brothers who operated along **North Africa's Barbary Coast** in the 16th century.

HORUSCE und HAREADEN BARBAROSSA

MYSTERY OF THE STONE GIANTS

WHO PLACED THE STATUES ON EASTER ISLAND? SCIENTISTS WEIGH IN.

MOAI HEAD

A strange army of jumbo-size stones carved to look like humans have "guarded" the coast of Easter Island in the Pacific Ocean for centuries. But not even the island's inhabitants are sure how they got there.

Scientists think islanders began creating the *moai*—which can weigh more than 90 tons (81,647 kg) and stand as tall as a three-story building—some 800 years ago to honor their ancestors. Inland, archaeologists unearthed ancient tools used to carve figures from volcanic rock. But that was about 11 miles (18 km) from where most of the statues now stand. And back then, the islanders didn't have wheels, cranes, or animals to move the rock giants.

Wondering if the islanders could have transported the statues upright with just rope and muscle power, one group of archaeologists attempted to move a ten-foot (3-m)-tall moai replica by wrapping three cords around the statue's forehead.

TINY TOURIST!

ROW OF MOAI

Easter Island's first inhabitants arrived between 800 and 1,200 years ago. They canoed from other Pacific islands for more than 1,000 miles (1,600 km).

With a team of people pulling each rope they were able to "walk" the moai a short distance by rocking it side to side. Another team laid an actual moai onto a giant log and pulled the log forward. But these techniques might have worked only over short distances and on flat land, or would have damaged the moai. Some researchers suggest the statues were laid on wooden sleds, which were dragged across log tracks. But the truth may never be revealed. Today the only remaining witnesses to the event are the moai themselves. And their stone lips are sealed.

CAN AN ISLAND PARADISE DISAPPEAR IN A DAY? THAT'S WHAT ONE ANCIENT LEGEND SAYS ABOUT THE EMPIRE OF ATLANTIS. TODAY, SCIENTISTS CONTINUE TO TRY TO LOCATE THE LOST ISLAND.

MYSTERY OF
ATLANTIS

Plato, an ancient Greek philosopher, described Atlantis as a wealthy city with palaces, a silver-and-gold temple, abundant fruit trees, and elephants roaming the land. But the good times didn't last. Plato wrote that sudden earthquakes jolted Atlantis and whipped up waves that sank the island within a day.

Was Plato's story true? Recently, researchers in Spain used underground radar in search of buried buildings. Results showed something like a crumbled wall in the soil 40 feet (12.1 m) below, but because there was water beneath the site, a dig seemed improbable.

Other explorers think Atlantis is in the Mediterranean Sea, where images supposedly show remains of canals and walls. Others are skeptical about the story entirely. Such an advanced city, they say, couldn't have been built in the Stone Age, when Plato's story was set.

So, was Atlantis real, fake, or something in between? The search continues.

233

TREASURE!

Check out these stories of lost treasures found!

SUNKEN GOLD

In the summer of 2013, Rick Schmitt was scuba diving off the coast of eastern Florida when he discovered $300,000 worth of gold chains, coins, and jewelry on the ocean floor. The riches date back to the 1700s, when Spanish ships called galleons often ferried treasure from North and South America to Europe. In July 1715 a hurricane sank 11 galleons near Florida's coast, scattering valuables along the seafloor. Nearly 300 years later, Schmitt found only a portion of this loot. Many more riches still linger at the bottom of the ocean.

MAYA RICHES

During a 2012 expedition to the jungles of northern Guatemala, a team of archaeologists discovered a tomb filled with precious stones and ancient bones dating back to the seventh century. Maya hieroglyphics on a jar in the burial chamber revealed that the bones may have belonged to a warrior queen. The exact worth of the treasure hasn't been calculated—but most people agree that this find is priceless.

PALACE PRIZE

In 2011, workers renovating Hanuman Dhoka, a palace that once housed Nepal's royal family, came upon three safes and a tank filled with gold jewelry, bows with silver arrows, and gold masks. The loot was thought to be at least 500-year-old offerings made to Hindu gods and goddesses, and no one knows for sure why it was placed here. But with the treasure soon on exhibit, the renovated palace museum won't just be spruced up— it'll be blinged out!

THE SECRETS OF
STONEHENGE

Could a new discovery help solve this ancient puzzle?

Dazzling rays from the sun burst through a strange ring of stones set on a grassy field. This huge monument, called Stonehenge, has towered above England's Salisbury Plain for thousands of years—but it's still one of the world's biggest mysteries.

THE UNEXPLAINED

For centuries people have tried to unlock Stonehenge's secrets.

Some theories have suggested that migrants from continental Europe built the site as an astronomical observatory or as a temple to the sun and moon gods. No theories have been proven. But a new discovery may provide more information about the builders of Stonehenge and could help explain why the monument was constructed in this region.

HUNTING FOR CLUES

While digging around a spring about a mile and a half (2.4 km) from Stonehenge, archaeologist David Jacques and his team uncovered hundreds of bones belonging to aurochs—a species of cattle twice the size of a modern-day bull that thrived in ancient times. In fact the site held the largest collection of auroch bones ever found in Europe. That suggests that the spring was a pit stop along an auroch migration route where the animals drank water.

The team also unearthed 31,000 flints, a stone tool used for hunting. "We started to wonder if the area was also a hunting ground and feasting site for ancient people," Jacques says. "Just one auroch could've fed a hundred people, so the place would've been a big draw."

The animal bones and tools date back to 7500 B.C. The age of the artifacts caused Jacques to conclude that people moved to the region around 9,500 years ago to hunt auroch. And he thinks descendants of these settlers assembled the mysterious stone ring.

MONARCHS OF ENGLAND AND GREAT BRITAIN

The idea of a single, unifying leader over England first arose in the ninth century, when King Egbert of Wessex became what most people recognize as the country's first ruler. A long succession of leaders have followed, culminating in the reign of the House of Windsor, which has held the throne since 1917. Elizabeth II, queen for more than 60 years, became the longest reigning British monarch in September 2015. Hail to the Queen!

HOUSE OF WESSEX

Egbert (802–839)
Aethelwulf (839–855)
Aethelbald (855–860)
Aethelbert (860–866)
Aethelred (866–871)
Alfred the Great (871–899)
Edward the Elder (899–925)
Athelstan (925–940)
Edmund the Magnificent (940–946)
Eadred (946–955)
Eadwig (Edwy) All-Fair (955–959)
Edgar the Peaceable (959–975)
Edward the Martyr (975–978)
Aethelred the Unready (978–1013)

HOUSE OF DENMARK

Svein Forkbeard (1014)

HOUSE OF WESSEX Restored, First Time

Aethelred the Unready (1014–1016)
Edmund Ironside (1016)

HOUSE OF DENMARK Restored

Canute the Great (1016–1035)
Harold Harefoot (1035–1040)
Hardicanute (1040–1042)

HOUSE OF WESSEX Restored, Second Time

Edward the Confessor (1042–1066)
Harold II (1066)

Norman Line

William I the Conqueror (1066–1087)
William II Rufus (1087–1100)
Henry I Beauclerc (1100–1135)
Stephen (1135–1154)
Empress Matilda (1141)

PLANTAGENET

Angevin Line

Henry II Curtmantle (1154–1189)
Richard I the Lionheart (1189–1199)
John Lackland (1199–1216)
Henry III (1216–1272)
Edward I Longshanks (1272–1307)
Edward II (1307–1327)
Edward III (1327–1377)
Richard II (1377–1399)

Lancastrian Line

Henry IV Bolingbroke (1399–1413)
Henry V (1413–1422)
Henry VI (1422–1461, 1470–1471)

Yorkist Line

Edward IV (1461–1470, 1471–1483)
Edward V (1483)
Richard III Crookback (1483–1485)

HOUSE OF TUDOR

Henry VII Tudor (1485–1509)
Henry VIII (1509–1547)
Edward VI (1547–1553)
Lady Jane Grey (1553)
Mary I Tudor (1553–1558)
Elizabeth I (1558–1603)

HOUSE OF STUART

James I (1603–1625)
Charles I (1625–1649)

James IV of Scotland was also James I of England.

KING WILLIAM I THE CONQUEROR

KING JOHN LACKLAND

THE COMMONWEALTH
Oliver Cromwell (1649–1658)
Richard Cromwell (1658–1659)

HOUSE OF STUART Restored
Charles II (1660–1685)
James II (1685–1688)

HOUSE OF ORANGE AND STUART
William III, Mary II (1689–1702)

HOUSE OF STUART
Anne (1702–1714)

HOUSE OF BRUNSWICK
Hanover Line
George I (1714–1727)
George II (1727–1760)
George III (1760–1820)
George IV (1820–1830)
William IV (1830–1837)
Victoria (1837–1901)

HOUSE OF SAXE-COBURG-GOTHA
Edward VII (1901–1910)

HOUSE OF WINDSOR
George V (1910–1936)
Edward VIII (1936)
George VI (1936–1952)
Elizabeth II (1952–present)

The birth of Princess Charlotte in 2015 marks the first time a British princess has been named Charlotte in about 200 years.

Queen Elizabeth II can travel the world without a passport.

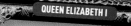

QUEEN ELIZABETH I

QUEEN VICTORIA

KING HENRY VIII

QUEEN ELIZABETH II

237

LEADERS OF THE WORLD

Each of the 195 independent countries in the world has its own leader or leaders. Whatever the leader is called, he or she is called upon to take charge of the direction of the country's growth—politically, economically, and socially.

Some countries have more than one person who has an executive role in the government. That second person is often a prime minister or a chancellor. This varies depending on the type of government in the country.

Over the next several pages, the countries and their leaders are listed in alphabetical order according to the most commonly used version of each country's name. Disputed areas such as Northern Cyprus and Taiwan, and dependencies such as Bermuda, Greenland, and Puerto Rico, which belong to independent nations, are not included in this listing. The date given for leaders

taking office is the date of their first term.

Note the color key at the bottom of the pages, which assigns a color to each country based on the continent on which it is located.

NOTE: These facts are current as of press time.

Color Key by Continent

Afghanistan

President
Ashraf Ghani Ahmadzai
Took office: September 29, 2014

Albania

President
Bujar Nishani
Took office: July 24, 2012

Prime Minister
Edi Rama
Took office: September 10, 2013

Algeria

President
Abdelaziz Bouteflika
Took office: April 28, 1999

Prime Minister
Abdelmalek Sellal
Took office: April 28, 2014

To learn more about world leaders, go online:
cia.gov/library/
publications/
world-leaders-1

Andorra

Co-Prince
François Hollande
Took office: May 15, 2012

Co-Prince
Archbishop Joan-Enric Vives i Sicília
Took office: May 12, 2003

Executive Council President
Antoni Marti Petit
Took office: May 12, 2011

Angola

President
José Eduardo Dos Santos
Took office: September 21, 1979

Antigua and Barbuda

Governor General
Rodney Williams
Took office: August 14, 2014

Prime Minister
Gaston Browne
Took office: June 13, 2014

Argentina

President
Mauricio Macri
Took office: December 10, 2015

Armenia

President Serzh Sargsian
Took office: April 9, 2008

Prime Minister
Hovik Abrahamyan
Took office: April 13, 2014

Australia

Governor General
Sir Peter Cosgrove
Took office: March 28, 2014

Prime Minister
Malcolm Turnbull
Took office: September 15, 2015

As a barrister, **MALCOLM TURNBULL** once defended a **FORMER SPY.**

COLOR KEY ● Africa ● Australia, New Zealand, and Oceania

Austria

President Heinz Fischer
Took office: July 8, 2004

Chancellor Werner Faymann
Took office: December 2, 2008

Azerbaijan

President Ilham Aliyev
Took office: October 31, 2003

Prime Minister Artur Rasizade
Took office: November 4, 2003

Bahamas

Governor General Dame Marguerite Pindling
Took office: July 8, 2014

Prime Minister Perry Christie
Took office: May 8, 2012

Bahrain

King Hamad bin Isa al-Khalifa
Began reign: March 6, 1999

Prime Minister Khalifa bin Salman al-Khalifa
Took office: 1971

Bangladesh

President Abdul Hamid
Took office: April 24, 2013

Prime Minister Sheikh Hasina
Took office: January 6, 2009

Barbados

Governor General Elliot Belgrave
Took office: June 1, 2012

Prime Minister Freundel Stuart
Took office: October 23, 2010

Belarus

President Aleksandr Lukashenko
Took office: July 20, 1994

Prime Minister Andrey Kabyakow
Took office: December 27, 2014

Belgium

King Philippe
Began reign: July 21, 2013

Prime Minister Charles Michel
Took office: October 11, 2014

ELECTED AT AGE 38, **CHARLES MICHEL** is Belgium's **YOUNGEST PM** since 1841.

Belize

Governor General Sir Colville Young, Sr.
Took office: November 17, 1993

Prime Minister Dean Oliver Barrow
Took office: February 8, 2008

Benin

President Thomas Yayi Boni
Took office: April 6, 2006

Bhutan

King Jigme Khesar Namgyel Wangchuck
Began reign: December 14, 2006

Prime Minister Tshering Tobgay
Took office: July 2013

Bolivia

President Juan Evo Morales Ayma
Took office: January 22, 2006

Bosnia and Herzegovina

Presidency members:
Dragan Covic
Mladen Ivanic
Took office: November 17, 2014

Bakir Izetbegović
Took office: November 10, 2010

Chairman of the Council of Ministers Denis Zvizdic
Took office: February 11, 2015

Botswana

President Seretse Khama Ian Khama
Took office: April 1, 2008

Brazil

President Dilma Rousseff
Took office: January 1, 2011

DILMA ROUSSEFF once aspired to be a **BALLERINA.**

Brunei

Sultan Hassanal Bolkiah
Began reign: October 5, 1967

Bulgaria

President Rosen Plevneliev
Took office: January 22, 2012

Prime Minister Boiko Borisov
Took office: November 6, 2014

Burkina Faso

Interim Civilian President Michel Kafando
Took office: November 18, 2014

Prime Minister Yacouba Isaac Zida
Took office: November 19, 2014

Burundi

President Pierre Nkurunziza
Took office: August 26, 2005

Cabo Verde

President
Jorge Carlos Fonseca
Took office: September 9, 2011

Prime Minister
José Maria Pereira Neves
Took office: February 1, 2001

Cambodia

King Norodom Sihamoni
Began reign: October 29, 2004

Prime Minister Hun Sen
Took office: January 14, 1985

HUN SEN, in office since 1985, is one of the longest serving prime ministers in the world.

Cameroon

President Paul Biya
Took office: November 6, 1982

Prime Minister Philémon Yang
Took office: June 30, 2009

Canada

Governor General
David Johnston
Took office: October 1, 2010

Prime Minister
Justin Trudeau
Took office: November 4, 2015

JUSTIN TRUDEAU once worked as a SNOWBOARDING INSTRUCTOR.

Central African Republic

Interim President
Catherine Samba-Panza
Took office: January 23, 2014

Interim Prime Minister
Mahamat Kamoun
Took office: August 10, 2014

Chad

President
Lt. Gen. Idriss Déby Itno
Took office: December 4, 1990

Prime Minister
Kalzeube Pahimi Deubet
Took office: November 21, 2013

Chile

President
Michelle Bachelet Jeria
Took office: March 11, 2014

Ni Hao from China

Shanghai

COLOR KEY ● Africa ● Australia, New Zealand, and Oceania

China

President Xi Jinping
Took office: March 14, 2013

Premier Li Keqiang
Took office: March 16, 2013

Xi Jinping spent seven years living in a cave house.

Colombia

President Juan Manuel Santos Calderón
Took office: August 7, 2010

Comoros

President Ikililou Dhoinine
Took office: May 26, 2011

Congo

President Denis Sassou-Nguesso
Took office: October 25, 1997

Costa Rica

President Luis Guillermo Solis Rivera
Took office: May 8, 2014

Côte d'Ivoire (Ivory Coast)

President Alassane Ouattara
Took office: December 4, 2010

Prime Minister Daniel Kablan Duncan
Took office: November 21, 2012

Croatia

President Kolinda Grabar-Kitarovic
Took office: February 19, 2015

Prime Minister Zoran Milanović
Took office: December 23, 2011

Cuba

President Raúl Castro Ruz
Took office: February 24, 2008

Cyprus

President Nicos Anastasiades
Took office: February 28, 2013

NICOS ANASTASIADES has a TWIN BROTHER.

Czech Republic (Czechia)

President Milos Zeman
Took office: March 8, 2013

Prime Minister Bohuslav Sobotka
Took office: January 17, 2014

Democratic Republic of the Congo

President Joseph Kabila
Took office: January 17, 2001

Prime Minister Augustin Matata Ponyo Mapon
Took office: April 18, 2012

Denmark

Queen Margrethe II
Began reign: January 14, 1972

Prime Minister Helle Thorning-Schmidt
Took office: October 3, 2011

HELLE THORNING-SCHMIDT has been called "Gucci Helle" because of her taste for designer clothes.

Djibouti

President Ismail Omar Guelleh
Took office: May 8, 1999

Prime Minister Abdoulkader Kamil Mohamed
Took office: April 1, 2013

Dominica

President Charles Savarin
Took office: October 2, 2013

Prime Minister Roosevelt Skerrit
Took office: January 8, 2004

Dominican Republic

President Danilo Medina Sánchez
Took office: August 16, 2012

Ecuador

President Rafael Correa Delgado
Took office: January 15, 2007

Egypt

President Abdelfattah Said Elsisi
Took office: June 8, 2014

Prime Minister Sherif Ismail
Took office: September 12, 2015

PRESIDENT ABDELFATTAH SAID ELSISI had a type of orchid named after him.

El Salvador

President
Salvador Sanchez Ceren
Took office: June 1, 2014

Equatorial Guinea

President Teodoro Obiang Nguema Mbasogo
Took office: August 3, 1979

Prime Minister Vicente Ehate Tomi
Took office: May 22, 2012

TEODORO OBIANG NGUEMA MBASOGO is Africa's longest serving head of state.

Eritrea

President Isaias Afworki
Took office: June 8, 1993

Estonia

President Toomas Hendrik Ilves
Took office: October 9, 2006

Prime Minister Taavi Roivas
Took office: March 26, 2014

Ethiopia

President Mulatu Teshome Wirtu
Took office: October 7, 2013

Prime Minister Hailemariam Desalegn
Took office: September 21, 2012

Fiji

President Jioji Konrote
Took office: November 12, 2015

Prime Minister Voreqe "Frank" Bainimarama
Took office: September 22, 2014

Finland

President Sauli Niinisto
Took office: March 1, 2012

Prime Minister Juha Sipila
Took office: May 29, 2015

France

President François Hollande
Took office: May 15, 2012

Prime Minister Manuel Valls
Took office: April 1, 2014

François Hollande traveled to the United States to study American FAST-FOOD RESTAURANTS.

Gabon

President Ali Ben Bongo Ondimba
Took office: October 16, 2009

Prime Minister Daniel Ona Ondo
Took office: January 27, 2014

Gambia

President Yahya Jammeh
Took office: October 18, 1996

Georgia

President Giorgi Margvelashvili
Took office: November 17, 2013

Prime Minister Irakli Garibashvili
Took office: November 20, 2013

Germany

President Joachim Gauck
Took office: March 23, 2012

Chancellor Angela Merkel
Took office: November 22, 2005

Ghana

President John Dramani Mahama
Took office: July 24, 2012

Greece

President Karolos Papoulias
Took office: March 12, 2005

Prime Minister Alexis Tsipras
Took office: September 21, 2015

Grenada

Governor General Cecile La Grenade
Took office: May 7, 2013

Prime Minister Keith Mitchell
Took office: February 20, 2013

Guatemala

President Alejandro Maldonado Aguirre
Took office: September 3, 2015

Guinea

President Alpha Condé
Took office: December 21, 2010

Prime Minister Mohamed Said Fofana
Took office: December 24, 2010

Guinea-Bissau

President Josse Mario Vaz
Took office: June 17, 2014

Prime Minister Carlos Correia
Took office: September 17, 2015

Guyana

President Donald Ramotar
Took office: December 3, 2011

Prime Minister Samuel Hinds
Took office: October 9, 1992

Haiti

President Michel Martelly
Took office: May 14, 2011

**Prime Minister
Evans Paul**
Took office: January 16, 2015

> **EVANS PAUL**
> **is a former**
> **theater director**
> **and radio host.**

Honduras

**President
Juan Orlando Hernandez
Alvarado**
Took office: January 27, 2014

Hungary

President Janos Ader
Took office: May 10, 2012

**Prime Minister
Viktor Orban**
Took office: May 29, 2010

Iceland

**President
Ólafur Ragnar Grímsson**
Took office: August 1, 1996

**Prime Minister
Sigmundur Davíd
Gunnlaugsson**
Took office: May 23, 2013

India

**President
Pranab Mukherjee**
Took office: July 22, 2012

**Prime Minister
Narendra Modi**
Took office: May 26, 2014

> **NARENDRA
> MODI
> is known to
> POST SELFIES
> on his
> TWITTER
> ACCOUNT.**

Indonesia

**President
Joko "Jokowi" Widodo**
Took office: October 20, 2014

Iran

**Supreme Leader Ayatollah
Ali Hoseini-Khamenei**
Took office: June 4, 1989

**President
Hasan Fereidun Ruhani**
Took office: August 3, 2013

Iraq

President Fuad Masum
Took office: July 24, 2014

**Prime Minister
Haider al-Abadi**
Took office: September 8, 2014

Ireland

President Michael D. Higgins
Took office: October 29, 2011

Prime Minister Enda Kenny
Took office: March 9, 2011

Greetings from
Guatemala

Chichicastenango

● Asia ● Europe ● North America ● South America

Israel

President
Reuben Rivlin
Took office: July 27, 2014

Prime Minister
Binyamin Netanyahu
Took office: March 31, 2009

Italy

President
Sergio Mattarella
Took office: February 3, 2015

Prime Minister
Matteo Renzi
Took office: February 22, 2014

MATTEO RENZI once won the Italian version of WHEEL OF FORTUNE.

Jamaica

Governor General
Dr. Patrick L. Allen
Took office: February 26, 2009

Prime Minister
Portia Simpson-Miller
Took office: January 5, 2012

Japan

Emperor Akihito
Began reign: January 7, 1989

Prime Minister
Shinzo Abe
Took office: December 26, 2012

AKIHITO has published ACADEMIC PAPERS ABOUT FISH.

Jordan

King Abdullah II
Began reign: February 7, 1999

Prime Minister
Abdullah Nsour
Took office: October 11, 2012

Kazakhstan

President
Nursultan A. Nazarbayev
Took office: December 1, 1991

Prime Minister
Karim Masimov
Took office: April 2, 2014

Kenya

President
Uhuru Kenyatta
Took office: April 9, 2013

WELCOME TO
ITALY

Ponte Vecchio in Florence

COLOR KEY ● Africa ● Australia, New Zealand, and Oceania

Kiribati

President
Anote Tong
Took office: July 10, 2003

Kosovo

President
Atifete Jahjaga
Took office: April 7, 2011

Prime Minister
Isa Mustafa
Took office: December 9, 2014

Kuwait

Emir Sabah al-Ahmad al-Jabir al-Sabah
Began reign: January 29, 2006

Prime Minister
Jabir al-Mubarak al-Hamad al-Sabah
Took office: November 30, 2011

Kyrgyzstan

President
Almazbek Atambayev
Took office: December 1, 2011

Prime Minister
Temir Sariev
Took office: May 1, 2015

Laos

President
Choummali Saignason
Took office: June 8, 2006

Prime Minister
Thongsing Thammavong
Took office: December 24, 2010

Latvia

President
Raimonds Vejonis
Took office: July 8, 2015

Prime Minister
Laimdota Straujuma
Took office: January 22, 2014

Lebanon

President: The prime minister and his cabinet are temporarily taking over the duties of the president.

Prime Minister
Tammam Salam
Took office: April 6, 2013

Lesotho

King Letsie III
Began reign: February 7, 1996

Prime Minister
Pakalitha Mosisili
Took office: March 18, 2015

Liberia

President
Ellen Johnson Sirleaf
Took office: January 16, 2006

ELLEN JOHNSON SIRLEAF once worked in a DRUGSTORE to help pay the bills.

Libya

Speaker of the House of Representatives
Aqilah Salah Issa
Took office: August 5, 2014

Prime Minister
Abdullah al-Thani
Took office: March 11, 2014

Liechtenstein

Prince Hans Adam II
Began reign: November 13, 1989

Prime Minister
Adrian Hasler
Took office: March 27, 2013

Lithuania

President
Dalia Grybauskaite
Took office: July 12, 2009

Prime Minister
Algirdas Butkevičius
Took office: November 22, 2012

Luxembourg

Grand Duke Henri
Began reign: October 7, 2000

Prime Minister
Xavier Bettel
Took office: December 4, 2013

Macedonia

President
Gjorge Ivanov
Took office: May 12, 2009

Prime Minister
Nikola Gruevski
Took office: August 26, 2006

Madagascar

President
Hery Martial Rajaonarimampianina Rakotoarimana
Took office: January 25, 2014

Prime Minister
Jean Ravelonarivo
Took office: January 17, 2015

Malawi

President
Arthur Peter Mutharika
Took office: May 31, 2014

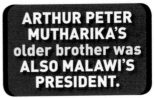

ARTHUR PETER MUTHARIKA'S older brother was ALSO MALAWI'S PRESIDENT.

Malaysia

King Tuanku Abdul Halim Mu'adzam Shah
Began reign: December 13, 2011

**Prime Minister
Mohamed Najib bin
Abdul Razak**
Took office: April 3, 2009

Maldives

**President
Abdulla Yameen
Abdul Gayoom**
Took office: November 17, 2013

Mali

**President
Ibrahim Boubacar Keita**
Took office: September 4, 2013

**Prime Minister
Modibo Keita**
Took office: January 8, 2015

Malta

**President
Marie-Louise Coleiro Preca**
Took office: April 4, 2014

**Prime Minister
Joseph Muscat**
Took office: March 11, 2013

Marshall Islands

**President
Christopher J. Loeak**
Took office: January 17, 2012

Mauritania

**President
Mohamed Ould Abdel Aziz**
Took office: August 5, 2009

**Prime Minister
Yahya Ould Hademine**
Took office: August 21, 2014

Mauritius

**President
Ameenah Gurib-Fakim**
Took office: June 5, 2015

**Prime Minister
Sir Aneerood Jugnauth**
Took office: December 17, 2014

Mexico

**President
Enrique Peña Nieto**
Took office: December 1, 2012

ENRIQUE PEÑA NIETO has more than **FOUR MILLION FOLLOWERS** on **TWITTER.**

Micronesia

**President
Peter M. Christian**
Took office: May 12, 2015

Moldova

**President
Nicolae Timofti**
Took office: March 23, 2012

**Interim Prime Minister
Gheorghe Brega**
Took office: October 30, 2015

Monaco

Prince Albert II
Began reign: April 6, 2005

**Minister of State
Michel Roger**
Took office: March 29, 2010

Mongolia

**President
Tsakhia Elbegdorj**
Took office: June 18, 2009

**Prime Minister
Chimed Saikhanbileg**
Took office: November 21, 2014

TSAKHIA ELBEGDORJ and his wife **ARE FOSTER PARENTS** to 20 orphans.

Montenegro

President Filip Vujanović
Took office: April 6, 2008

**Prime Minister
Milo Djukanovic**
Took office: December 4, 2012

Morocco

King Mohammed VI
Began reign: July 30, 1999

**Prime Minister
Abdelilah Benkirane**
Took office: November 29, 2011

Mozambique

**President Filipe
Jacinto Nyusi**
Took office: January 15, 2015

**Prime Minister
Carlos Agostinho Do Rosario**
Took office: October 8, 2012

Myanmar (Burma)

President Thein Sein
Took office: February 4, 2011

Namibia

President Hage Geingob
Took office: March 21, 2005

COLOR KEY ● Africa ● Australia, New Zealand, and Oceania

Nauru

President Baron Waqa
Took office: June 11, 2013

Nepal

**President
Bidhya Devi Bhandari**
Took office: October 29, 2015

**Prime Minister
Khadga Prasad Oli**
Took office: October 12, 2015

Netherlands

King Willem-Alexander
Began reign: April 30, 2013

Prime Minister Mark Rutte
Took office: October 14, 2010

KING WILLEM-ALEXANDER once ran the **New York City Marathon.**

New Zealand

**Governor General
Sir Jerry Mateparae**
Took office: August 31, 2011

**Prime Minister
John Phillip Key**
Took office: November 19, 2008

Nicaragua

**President
Daniel Ortega Saavedra**
Took office: January 10, 2007

Niger

**President
Issoufou Mahamadou**
Took office: April 7, 2011

**Prime Minister
Brigi Rafini**
Took office: April 7, 2011

Nigeria

**President Maj. Gen. (ret.)
Muhammadu Buhari**
Took office: May 29, 2015

North Korea

**Supreme Leader
Kim Jong-un**
Took office: December 17, 2011

**Premier
Pak Pong Ju**
Took office: April 2, 2013

Norway

King Harald V
Began reign: January 17, 1991

**Prime Minister
Erna Solberg**
Took office: October 16, 2013

Oman

**Sultan
Qaboos bin Said al-Said**
Began reign: July 23, 1970

Pakistan

**President
Mamnoon Hussain**
Took office: September 9, 2013

**Prime Minister
Mohammad Nawaz Sharif**
Took office: June 5, 2013

Palau

**President
Tommy Remengesau**
Took office: January 17, 2013

TOMMY REMENGESAU is the first **PALAUAN** to be elected president **THREE TIMES.**

Panama

**President
Juan Carlos Varela**
Took office: July 1, 2014

Papua New Guinea

**Governor General
Michael Ogio**
Took office: February 25, 2011

**Prime Minister
Peter O'Neill**
Took office: August 2, 2011

Paraguay

**President
Horacio Cartes**
Took office: August 15, 2013

HORACIO CARTES started his own business **AT AGE 19.**

Peru

**President
Ollanta Humala Tasso**
Took office: July 28, 2011

Philippines

**President
Benigno Aquino**
Took office: June 30, 2010

Poland

**President
Andrzej Duda**
Took office: August 6, 2015

**Prime Minister
Beata Szydlo**
Took office: November 16, 2015

● Asia ● Europe ● North America ● South America

Portugal

President
Aníbal Cavaco Silva
Took office: March 9, 2006

Prime Minister
António Costa
Took office: November 26, 2015

Qatar

Amir Tamim bin Hamad Al Thani
Began reign: June 25, 2013

Prime Minister Abdallah bin Nasir bin Khalifa Al Thani
Took office: June 26, 2013

Romania

President Klaus Iohannis
Took office: December 21, 2014

Prime Minister
vacant

Russia

President Vladimir Vladimirovich Putin
Took office: May 7, 2012

Premier Dmitriy Anatolyevich Medvedev
Took office: May 8, 2012

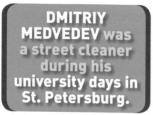

DMITRIY MEDVEDEV was a street cleaner during his university days in St. Petersburg.

Rwanda

President Paul Kagame
Took office: April 22, 2000

Prime Minister
Anastase Murekezi
Took office: July 24, 2014

Samoa

Head of State
Tui Atua Tupua Tamasese
Took office: June 20, 2007

Prime Minister Tuila'epa Lupesoliai Sailele Malielegaoi
Took office: 1998

San Marino

Co-chiefs of State: Captain Regent Lorella Stefanelli

Captain Regent Nicola Renzi
Took office: October 1, 2015

Secretary of State for Foreign and Political Affairs Pasquale Valentini
Took office: December 5, 2012

Sao Tome and Principe

President
Manuel Pinto da Costa
Took office: September 3, 2011

Prime Minister
Patrice Emery Trovoada
Took office: November 25, 2014

Saudi Arabia

King and Prime Minister Salman bin Abd al-Aziz Al Saud
Began reign: January 23, 2015

Senegal

President Macky Sall
Took office: April 2, 2012

Prime Minister Mohammed Abdallah Boun Dionne
Took office: July 6, 2014

MOHAMMED DIONNE trained as a **COMPUTER ENGINEER** before entering politics.

Serbia

President
Tomislav Nikolic
Took office: May 31, 2012

Prime Minister
Aleksandar Vucic
Took office: April 22, 2014

Seychelles

President
James Alix Michel
Took office: April 14, 2004

Sierra Leone

President
Ernest Bai Koroma
Took office: September 17, 2007

Singapore

President Tony Tan Keng Yam
Took office: September 1, 2011

Prime Minister
Lee Hsien Loong
Took office: August 12, 2004

Slovakia

President Andrej Kiska
Took office: June 15, 2014

Prime Minister Robert Fico
Took office: April 4, 2012

Slovenia

President Borut Pahor
Took office: December 22, 2012

Prime Minister Miro Cerar
Took office: September 18, 2014

Solomon Islands

Governor General
Frank Kabui
Took office: July 7, 2009

Prime Minister
Manasseh Sogavare
Took office: December 9, 2014

COLOR KEY ● Africa ● Australia, New Zealand, and Oceania

Somalia

President
Hassan Sheikh Mahamud
Took office: September 10, 2012

Prime Minister
Omar Abdirashid Ali Sharmarke
Took office: December 24, 2014

South Africa

President
Jacob Zuma
Took office: May 9, 2009

JACOB ZUMA taught himself how to READ and WRITE.

South Korea

President
Park Geun-hye
Took office: February 25, 2013

Prime Minister
Hwang Kyo-ahn
Took office: June 18, 2015

South Sudan

President
Salva Kiir Mayardit
Took office: July 9, 2011

Spain

King Felipe VI
Began reign: June 19, 2014

President of the Government
Mariano Rajoy
Took office: December 20, 2011

Sri Lanka

President
Maithripala Sirisena
Took office: January 9, 2015

St. Kitts and Nevis

Governor General
Samuel W. T. Seaton
Took office: January 2, 2013

Prime Minister
Timothy Harris
Took office: February 18, 2015

St. Lucia

Governor General
Dame Pearlette Louisy
Took office: September 17, 1997

Prime Minister
Kenny Anthony
Took office: November 30, 2011

Postcard from SAMOA!

Pago Pago Harbor

● Asia ● Europe ● North America ● South America

St. Vincent and the Grenadines

Governor General
Sir Frederick Nathaniel Ballantyne
Took office: September 2, 2002

Prime Minister
Ralph Gonsalves
Took office: March 29, 2001

Ralph Gonsalves played in his UNIVERSITY'S STEEL BAND.

Sudan

President
Umar Hassan Ahmad al-Bashir
Took office: October 16, 1993

Suriname

President
Desiré Delano Bouterse
Took office: August 12, 2010

Swaziland

King Mswati III
Began reign: April 25, 1986

Prime Minister
Barnabas Sibusiso Dlamini
Took office: October 16, 2008

KING MSWATI III is the second of 67 sons of KING SOBHUZA II.

Sweden

King Carl XVI Gustaf
Began reign: September 19, 1973

Prime Minister
Stefan Löfven
Took office: October 3, 2014

Switzerland

President of the Swiss Confederation
Simonetta Sommaruga
Took office: January 1, 2015

Federal Council members:
Doris Leuthard, Didier Burkhalter, Johann Schneider-Ammann, Simonetta Sommaruga, Alain Berset, Eveline Widmer-Schlumpf, Ueli Maurer
Took office: dates vary

SIMONETTA SOMMARUGA is a former CONCERT PIANIST.

Syria

President
Bashar al-Asad
Took office: July 17, 2000

Prime Minister
Wael al-Halqi
Took office: August 9, 2012

Tajikistan

President
Emomali Rahmon
Took office: November 19, 1992

Prime Minister
Qohir Rasulzoda
Took office: November 23, 2013

EMOMALI RAHMON has nine children— SEVEN daughters and TWO sons.

Tanzania

President
John Pombe Magufuli
Took office: November 5, 2015

Thailand

King Phumiphon Adunyadet
Began reign: June 9, 1946

Prime Minister
Prayut Chan-ocha
Took office: August 25, 2014

Timor-Leste (East Timor)

President
Taur Matan Ruak (Jose Maria de Vasconcelos)
Took office: May 20, 2012

Prime Minister
Kay Rala Xanana Gusmão
Took office: August 8, 2007

Togo

President
Faure Gnassingbé
Took office: May 4, 2005

Prime Minister
Komi Klassou
Took office: June 5, 2015

Tonga

King George Tupou VI
Began reign: March 18, 2012

Prime Minister
Lord Tu'ivakano
Took office: December 22, 2010

Trinidad and Tobago

President
Anthony Carmona
Took office: March 18, 2013

Prime Minister
Keith Rowley
Took office: September 9, 2015

COLOR KEY ● Africa ● Australia, New Zealand, and Oceania

Tunisia

**President
Beji Caid Essebs**
Took office: December 31, 2014

**Prime Minister
Habib Essid**
Took office: February 6, 2015

Turkey

**President
Recep Tayyip Erdogan**
Took office: August 10, 2014

**Prime Minister
Ahmet Davutoglu**
Took office: August 28, 2014

RECEP TAYYIP ERDOGAN once played **SEMI-PRO SOCCER.**

Turkmenistan

President Gurbanguly Berdimuhamedow
Took office: February 14, 2007

Tuvalu

**Governor General
Iakoba Taeia Italeli**
Took office: April 16, 2010

**Prime Minister
Enele Sopoaga**
Took office: August 5, 2013

Uganda

**President
Yoweri Kaguta Museveni**
Took office: January 26, 1986

**Prime Minister
Amama Mbabazi**
Took office: May 24, 2011

Ukraine

**President
Petro Poroshenko**
Took office: June 7, 2014

**Prime Minister
Arseniy Yatsenyuk**
Took office: February 27, 2014

United Arab Emirates

President Khalifa bin Zayid al-Nuhayyan
Took office: November 3, 2004

**Prime Minister
Muhammad bin Rashid al-Maktum**
Took office: January 5, 2006

United Kingdom

Queen Elizabeth II
Began reign: February 6, 1952

**Prime Minister
David Cameron**
Took office: May 11, 2010

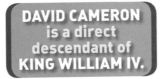

DAVID CAMERON is a direct descendant of **KING WILLIAM IV.**

United States

President Barack H. Obama
Took office: January 20, 2009

Uruguay

President Tabare Vazquez
Took office: March 1, 2015

Uzbekistan

President Islom Karimov
Took office: March 24, 1990

**Prime Minister
Shavkat Mirziyoyev**
Took office: December 11, 2003

Vanuatu

**President
Baldwin Lonsdale**
Took office: September 22, 2014

**Prime Minister
Sato Kilman**
Took office: June 11, 2015

Vatican City

**Supreme Pontiff
Pope Francis**
Took office: March 13, 2013

**Secretary of State
Archbishop Pietro Parolin**
Took office: October 15, 2013

Venezuela

**President
Nicolas Maduro Moros**
Took office: April 19, 2013

Vietnam

**President
Trong Tan Sang**
Took office: June 25, 2011

**Prime Minister
Nguyen Tan Dung**
Took office: June 27, 2006

Yemen

President Abd Rabuh Mansur Hadi
Took office: February 21, 2012

**Prime Minister
Khalid Mahfuz Bahah**
Took office: October 2014

Zambia

**President
Edgar Lungu**
Took office: January 25, 2015

Zimbabwe

**Executive President
Robert Gabriel Mugabe**
Took office: December 31, 1987

QUIZ WHIZ

Go back in time to seek the answers to this history quiz!
ANSWERS BELOW

① What was the life expectancy of the average medieval knight?

a. 45 years
b. 100 years
c. 30 years
d. 78 years

② True or false? In Cambodia, it's considered an insult to touch someone's head.

③ Japan's 760-year-old Great Buddha statue once withstood which kind of natural disaster?

a. an earthquake
b. a blizzard
c. a tsunami
d. a tornado

④ Fill in the blank. Some of the first flags on pirate ships were _____, not black.

⑤ What's the name of the jumbo-size stone statues lining the coast of Easter Island?

a. Stone Guardians
b. Moai
c. Rock Stars
d. Easter Bunnies

Not **STUMPED** yet? Check out the *NATIONAL GEOGRAPHIC KIDS QUIZ WHIZ* collection for more crazy **HISTORY** questions!

ANSWERS:
1. a; 2. True; 3. c; 4. red; 5. b

Brilliant Biographies

A biography is the story of a person's life.
It can be a brief summary or a long book.
Biographers—those who write biographies—
use many different sources to learn about their
subjects. You can write your own biography of
a famous person whom you find inspiring.

How to Get Started

Choose a subject you find interesting. If you
think Cleopatra is cool, you have a good chance
of getting your reader interested, too. If you're
bored by ancient Egypt, your reader will be
snoring after your first paragraph.

Your subject can be almost anyone: an author,
an inventor, a celebrity, a politician, or a member of your family. To find someone to write
about, ask yourself these simple questions:

1. Whom do I want to know more about?
2. What did this person do that was special?
3. How did this person change the world?

Do Your Research

• Find out as much about your subject as
possible. Read books, news articles, and
encyclopedia entries. Watch video clips and
movies, and search the Internet. Conduct
interviews, if possible.

• Take notes, writing down important facts
and interesting stories about your subject.

Write the Biography

• Come up with a title. Include the
person's name.

• Write an introduction. Consider asking a
probing question about your subject.

• Include information about the person's childhood. When was this person born? Where did
he or she grow up? Whom did he or she admire?

• Highlight the person's talents, accomplishments, and personal attributes.

• Describe the specific events that helped to
shape this person's life. Did this person ever
have a problem and overcome it?

• Write a conclusion. Include your thoughts about
why it is important to learn about this person.

• Once you have finished your first draft,
revise and then proofread your work.

Author
Rick Riordan

Here's a SAMPLE BIOGRAPHY of
Rick Riordan, best-selling author
of series such as Percy Jackson and
the Olympians and Magnus Chase
and the Gods of Asgard.
Of course, there is so much more
for you to discover, and write
about on your own!

Rick Riordan—Author

Rick Riordan was born on June 5, 1964,
in San Antonio, Texas, U.S.A. Born into a
creative family—his mom was a musician
and artist and his dad was a ceramicist—
Riordan began writing in middle school,
and he published his first short stories
while attending college.

After graduating from University of
Texas at Austin, Riordan went on to teach
English to middle schoolers, spending his
summers as a music director at a summer
camp. Writing adult mysteries on the side,
Riordan soon discovered his knack for
writing for younger readers and published
The Lightning Thief, the first book in the
Percy Jackson series, in 2005. *The Sea
of Monsters* soon followed. Before long,
Riordan quit his teaching job to become
a full-time writer.

Today Riordan has penned dozens of
books, firmly establishing himself as one
of the most accomplished and well-known
authors of our time. When he's not writing,
Riordan likes to read, swim, play guitar,
and travel with his wife, Becky, and their
sons Haley and Patrick.

Sunrise illuminates terraced rice fields in Longsheng, Guangxi Province, China.

THE POLITICAL WORLD

Earth's land area is made up of seven continents, but people have divided much of the land into smaller political units called countries. Australia is a continent made up of a single country, and Antarctica is used for scientific research. But the other five continents include almost 200 independent countries. The political map shown here depicts boundaries—imaginary lines created by treaties—that separate countries. Some boundaries, such as the one between the United States and Canada, are very stable and have been recognized for many years.

See Europe map for more detail.

Winkel Tripel Projection

miles 2000
kilometers 3000

Map labels:

ARCTIC
Queen Elizabeth Is.
Chukchi Sea
Beaufort Sea
Greenland (Denmark)
Greenland Sea
RUSSIA
Baffin Bay
Alaska (U.S.)
Bering Sea
Gulf of Alaska
Great Bear Lake
Great Slave Lake
Labrador Sea
CANADA
Hudson Bay
ARCTIC CIRCLE
ICELAND
UNITED KINGDOM
IRELAND (ÉIRE)
FRANCE
PORT. SPAIN
Lake Winnipeg
Great Salt Lake
UNITED STATES
MOROCCO
TROPIC OF CANCER
Hawai'i (U.S.)
Gulf of Mexico
MEXICO
BAHAMAS
CUBA
DOMINCAN REP.
Puerto Rico (U.S.)
Western Sahara (Morocco)
BELIZE
JAMAICA
HAITI
ST. KITTS & NEVIS
ANTIGUA & BARBUDA
Guadeloupe (France)
DOMINICA
Martinique (France)
ST. LUCIA
BARBADOS
ST. VINCENT & THE GRENADINES
TRINIDAD AND TOBAGO
CABO VERDE
MAURITANIA
MALI
GUATEMALA
HONDURAS
EL SALVADOR
NICARAGUA
Caribbean Sea
GRENADA
SENEGAL
GAMBIA
GUINEA-BISSAU
BURKINA FASO
COSTA RICA
PANAMA
VENEZUELA
GUYANA
GUINEA
SIERRA LEONE
LIBERIA
COLOMBIA
French Guiana (France)
SURINAME
PACIFIC
KIRIBATI
OCEAN
Galápagos Islands (Ecuador)
ECUADOR
EQUATOR
CÔTE D'IVOIRE (IVORY COAST)
EQ. GUINEA
SAO TOME AND PRINCIPE
Marquesas Islands (France)
PERU
BRAZIL
ATLANTIC
SAMOA
American Samoa (U.S.)
French Polynesia (France)
BOLIVIA
OCEAN
TONGA
PARAGUAY
TROPIC OF CAPRICORN
URUGUAY
CHILE
ARGENTINA
30°
Chatham Is. (N.Z.)
Falkland Islands (U.K.)
Tierra del Fuego
Strait of Magellan
Drake Passage
ANTARCTIC
Weddell Sea
Ross Sea
ANT
Meridian of Greenwich (London)

Coordinates: 60°, 30°, 0° EQUATOR, 150°, 120°, 90°, 30°, 0°

Other boundaries, such as the one between Sudan and South Sudan in northeast Africa, are relatively new and still disputed. Countries come in all shapes and sizes. Russia and Canada are giants; others, such as El Salvador and Qatar, are small. Some countries are long and skinny—look at Chile in South America! Still other countries—such as Indonesia and Japan in Asia—are made up of groups of islands. The political map is a clue to the diversity that makes Earth so fascinating.

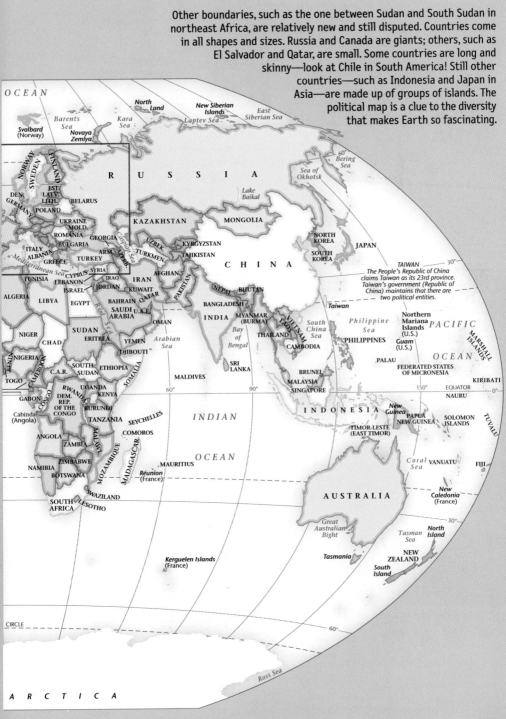

TAIWAN
The People's Republic of China claims Taiwan as its 23rd province. Taiwan's government (Republic of China) maintains that there are two political entities.

THE PHYSICAL WORLD

Earth is dominated by large landmasses called continents—seven in all—and by an interconnected global ocean that is divided into four parts by the continents. More than 70 percent of Earth's surface is covered by oceans, and the rest is made up of land areas.

Different landforms give variety to the surface of the continents. The Rocky Mountains divide North America, the Andes mark the western edge of South America, and the Himalaya tower above South Asia. The Plateau of Tibet forms the rugged core of Asia, while

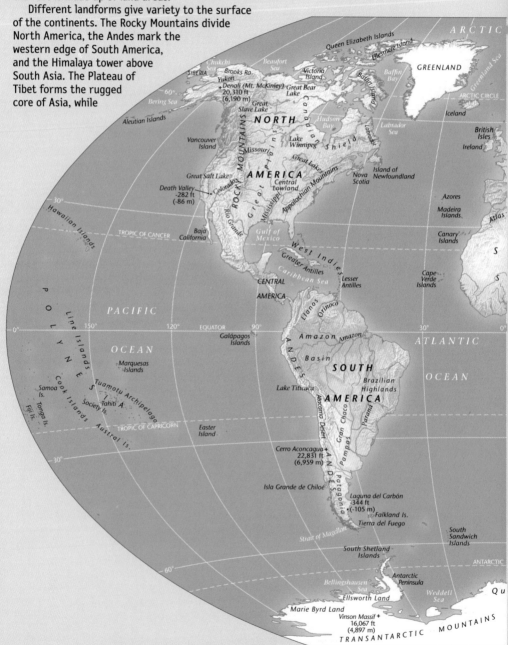

the Northern European Plain extends from the North Sea to the Ural Mountains. Much of Africa is a plateau, and dry plains cover large areas of Australia. Mountains rise more than 16,000 feet (4,877 m) above Antarctica's massive ice sheets. Mountains and trenches make the ocean floors as varied as any continent. A mountain chain called the Mid-Atlantic Ridge runs the length of the Atlantic Ocean. In the western Pacific, trenches drop deep into the ocean floor.

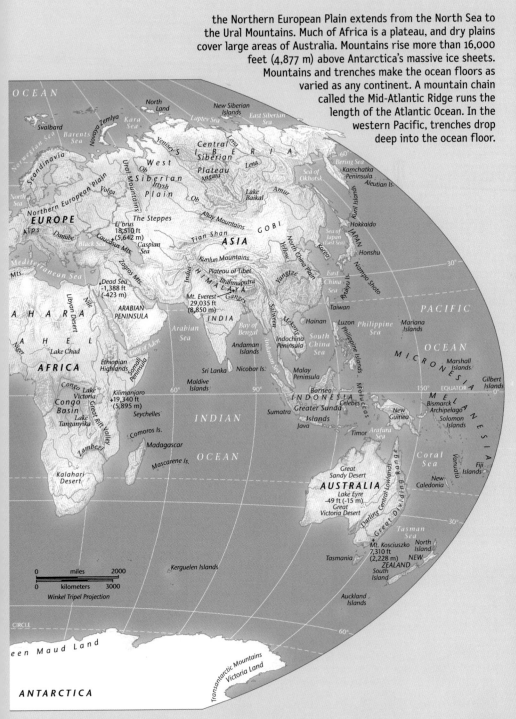

OCEAN

North Land

New Siberian Islands

Svalbard

Barents Sea

Kara Sea

Novaya Zemlya

Laptev Sea

East Siberian Sea

Norwegian Sea

Scandinavia

Yenisey

Ob

Irtysh

Central SIBERIA

West Siberian Plateau

Lena

Lena

Bering Sea

Kamchatka Peninsula

Aleutian Is.

Ural Mountains

Plain

Angara

Sea of Okhotsk

Kuril Islands

North Sea

Northern European Plain

Volga

EUROPE

Alps

Danube

Black Sea

Caucasus Mts.

El'brus 18,510 ft (5,642 m)

The Steppes

Caspian Sea

Ob

Altay Mountains

Tian Shan

ASIA

GOBI

North China Plain

Yellow

Sea of Japan (East Sea)

Hokkaido

Honshu

JAPAN

Korea

Nampo Shoto

Mediterranean Sea

Mts.

Zagros Mts.

Kunlun Mountains

Plateau of Tibet

Dead Sea -1,388 ft (-423 m)

India

Brahmaputra

HIMALAYA

Mt. Everest 29,035 ft (8,850 m)

Ganges

Salween

Yangtze

Mekong

East China Sea

Taiwan

PACIFIC

SAHARA

Libyan Desert

Nile

ARABIAN PENINSULA

INDIA

Arabian Sea

Bay of Bengal

Andaman Islands

Hainan

Luzon

Philippine Sea

Mariana Islands

OCEAN

SAHEL

Niger

Lake Chad

AFRICA

Ethiopian Highlands

Gulf of Aden

Somali Peninsula

Sri Lanka

Nicobar Is.

Indochina Peninsula

South China Sea

Philippine Islands

MICRONESIA

Marshall Islands

Congo

Lake Victoria

Congo Basin

Great Rift Valley

Kilimanjaro 19,340 ft (5,895 m)

Maldive Islands

Malay Peninsula

Borneo

INDONESIA

Greater Sunda Islands

Celebes

Moluccas

EQUATOR

Gilbert Islands

MELANESIA

Bismarck Archipelago

Solomon Islands

Lake Tanganyika

Seychelles

Sumatra

Java

New Guinea

Zambezi

Comoros Is.

INDIAN

Madagascar

Mascarene Is.

OCEAN

Timor

Arafura Sea

Coral Sea

Vanuatu

New Caledonia

Fiji Islands

Kalahari Desert

Great Sandy Desert

AUSTRALIA

Lake Eyre -49 ft (-15 m)

Great Victoria Desert

Darling

Central Lowlands

Great Dividing Range

Tasman Sea

New Zealand

Kerguelen Islands

Mt. Kosciuszko 7,310 ft (2,228 m)

North Island

NEW ZEALAND

South Island

Tasmania

Auckland Islands

0 miles 2000
0 kilometers 3000

Winkel Tripel Projection

CIRCLE

een Maud Land

Transantarctic Mountains

Victoria Land

ANTARCTICA

KINDS OF MAPS

Maps are special tools that geographers use to tell a story about Earth. Maps can be used to show just about anything related to places. Some maps show physical features, such as mountains or vegetation. Maps can also show climates or natural hazards and other things we cannot easily see. Other maps illustrate different features on Earth—political boundaries, urban centers, and economic systems.

AN IMPERFECT TOOL

Maps are not perfect. A globe is a scale model of Earth with accurate relative sizes and locations. Because maps are flat, they involve distortions of size, shape, and direction. Also, cartographers—people who create maps—make choices about what information to include. Because of this, it is important to study many different types of maps to learn the complete story of Earth. Three commonly found kinds of maps are shown on this page.

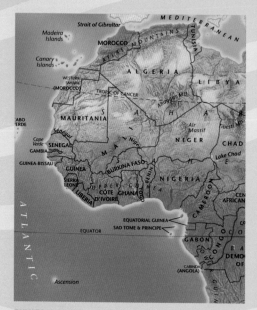

PHYSICAL MAPS. Earth's natural features—landforms, water bodies, and vegetation—are shown on physical maps. The map above uses color and shading to illustrate mountains, lakes, rivers, and deserts of western Africa. Country names and borders are added for reference, but they are not natural features.

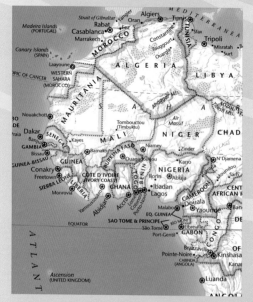

POLITICAL MAPS. These maps represent characteristics of the landscape created by humans, such as boundaries, cities, and place-names. Natural features are added only for reference. On the map above, capital cities are represented with a star inside a circle, while other cities are shown with black dots.

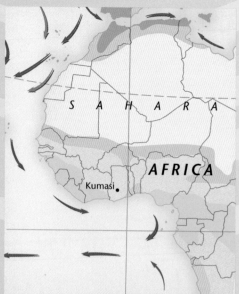

THEMATIC MAPS. Patterns related to a particular topic or theme, such as population distribution, appear on these maps. The map above displays the region's climate zones, which range from tropical wet (bright green) to tropical wet and dry (light green) to semiarid (dark yellow) to arid or desert (light yellow).

MAKING MAPS

Long ago, cartographers worked with pen and ink, carefully handcrafting maps based on explorers' observations and diaries. Today, mapmaking is a high-tech business. Cartographers use Earth data stored in "layers" in a Geographic Information System (GIS) and special computer programs to create maps that can be easily updated as new information becomes available. The cartographers at right are changing country labels on a map of the Balkans.

Satellites in orbit around Earth act as eyes in the sky, recording data about the planet's land and ocean areas. The data is converted to numbers that are transmitted back to computers that are specially programmed to interpret the data. They record it in a form that cartographers can use to create maps.

MAP PROJECTIONS

To create a map, cartographers transfer an image of the round Earth to a flat surface, a process called projection. All projections involve distortion. For example, an interrupted projection (bottom map) shows accurate shapes and relative sizes of land areas, but oceans have gaps. Other types of projections are cylindrical, conic, or azimuthal—each with certain advantages, but all with some distortion.

261

GEOGRAPHIC FEATURES

From roaring rivers to parched deserts, from underwater canyons to jagged mountains, Earth is covered with beautiful and diverse environments. Here are examples of the most common types of geographic features found around the world.

DESERT

Deserts are land features created by climate, specifically by a lack of water. Here, a camel caravan crosses the Sahara in North Africa.

VALLEY

Valleys, cut by running water or moving ice, may be broad and flat or narrow and steep, such as the Indus River Valley in Ladakh, India (above).

RIVER

As a river moves through flatlands, it twists and turns. Above, the Rio Los Amigos winds through a rain forest in Peru.

MOUNTAIN

Mountains are Earth's tallest landforms, and Mount Everest (above) rises highest of all, at 29,035 feet (8,850 m) above sea level.

GLACIER

Glaciers—"rivers" of ice—such as Alaska's Hubbard Glacier (above) move slowly from mountains to the sea. Global warming is shrinking them.

CANYON

Steep-sided valleys called canyons are created mainly by running water. Buckskin Gulch in Utah (above) is the deepest "slot" canyon in the American Southwest.

WATERFALL

Waterfalls form when a river reaches an abrupt change in elevation. Above, Kaieteur Falls, in Guyana, has a sheer drop of 741 feet (226 m).

Bet you didn't know

7 extreme facts about Earth

1 You can find **pink lakes** in western Australia.

2 There is **3 times more air** at sea level than at the **top of Mt. Everest.**

3 About 12,000 years ago, the **Sahara** had a **wetter climate** and was covered with forests.

4 **Finland** has more than **185,000 lakes.**

5 **Indonesia** is home to more than **78 active volcanoes.**

6 **Canada's Mt. Thor** has a **4,100-ft. (1,250-m) vertical drop** that is considered the world's **tallest and steepest cliff.**

7 **Parts of Chile's Atacama Desert** have gone hundreds of years without rain.

263

SPOTLIGHT ON
AFRICA

> Elephants can sleep both standing up and lying down.

> Zanzibar, an island off Africa's east coast, is made up entirely of coral.

African elephants in Zambia

The massive continent of Africa, where humankind began millions of years ago, is second to only Asia in size. Stretching nearly as far from west to east as it does from north to south, Africa is home to both the longest river in the world (the Nile) and the largest hot desert on Earth (Sahara).

Namibian woman in traditional dress

Speedy Species

Some of the world's fastest animals live in Africa, such as cheetahs, pronghorn antelopes, wildebeests, and lions. Each of these species can reach speeds topping 50 miles an hour (80 km/h).

Cheetah

Fast Growth

Thanks to better quality health care and more access to medicine, Africa's population is expected to more than double to at least 2.4 billion people by 2050.

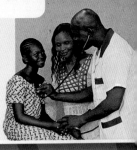

Star Struck

The force is strong in Tunisia, where the parts of the original Star Wars movies were filmed. The sandy scenes were created in various desert locations in the North African nation.

Sea Life

Africa may have one of the shortest coastlines of all the continents, but its coastal waters are packed with wildlife that includes sea turtles, dolphins, humpback whales, and whale sharks.

Whale shark

Protecting the Environment

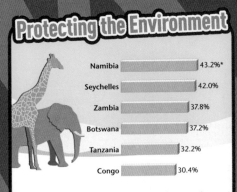

Country	Percent
Namibia	43.2%*
Seychelles	42.0%
Zambia	37.8%
Botswana	37.2%
Tanzania	32.2%
Congo	30.4%

*Figures represent percent of total land area set aside as protected area

The Great Sphinx at Giza in Egypt

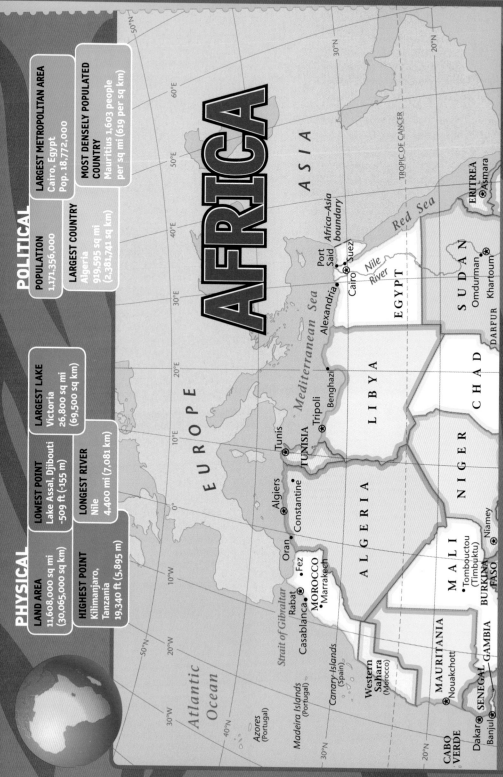

AFRICA

PHYSICAL

LAND AREA
11,608,000 sq mi
(30,065,000 sq km)

HIGHEST POINT
Kilimanjaro,
Tanzania
19,340 ft (5,895 m)

LOWEST POINT
Lake Assal, Djibouti
-509 ft (-155 m)

LONGEST RIVER
Nile
4,400 mi (7,081 km)

LARGEST LAKE
Victoria
26,800 sq mi
(69,500 sq km)

POLITICAL

POPULATION
1,171,356,000

LARGEST COUNTRY
Algeria
919,595 sq mi
(2,381,741 sq km)

LARGEST METROPOLITAN AREA
Cairo, Egypt
Pop. 18,772,000

MOST DENSELY POPULATED COUNTRY
Mauritius 1,603 people
per sq mi (619 per sq km)

Atlantic Ocean

Azores (Portugal)

Madeira Islands (Portugal)

Canary Islands (Spain)

Strait of Gibraltar

EUROPE

ASIA

Mediterranean Sea

Red Sea

TROPIC OF CANCER

Oran
Rabat
Casablanca
Fez
MOROCCO
Marrakech

Western Sahara (Morocco)

MAURITANIA
Nouakchott

CABO VERDE
Dakar
Banjul
SENEGAL
GAMBIA

Algiers
Constantine

Tunis
TUNISIA
Tripoli

Benghazi

A L G E R I A

L I B Y A

EGYPT

Alexandria
Cairo
Port Said
Suez
Africa-Asia boundary
Nile River

SUDAN
Omdurman
Khartoum
DARFUR

ERITREA
Asmara

M A L I
Tombouctou (Timbuktu)
Niamey
BURKINA FASO

N I G E R

C H A D

Gulf of Aden

SOMALIA

⊛ Mogadishu

Lake Assal
(–155 m) –509 ft.▼
DJIBOUTI Djibouti ⊛

Victoria ⊛

SEYCHELLES

MAURITIUS
Port Louis ⊛
Réunion
(France)

MADAGASCAR

Antananarivo ⊛

COMOROS
Moroni ⊛

Indian
Ocean

ETHIOPIA

Addis
Ababa ⊛

Mombasa ⊛

Dar es Salaam ⊛

Mozambique Channel

KENYA

Nairobi ⊛

Kilimanjaro
19,340 ft.▲
(5,895 m)

TANZANIA

Dodoma ⊛

MALAWI
Lilongwe ⊛

MOZAMBIQUE

SOUTH
SUDAN

Juba ⊛

UGANDA

Kampala ⊛

Lake
Victoria

RWANDA
Kigali ⊛
BURUNDI
Bujumbura ⊛

Kisangani •

DEMOCRATIC
REPUBLIC
OF THE CONGO

Mbuji-Mayi •

Kananga •

Kinshasa ⊛

Luanda ⊛

Lubumbashi •

Kolwezi •

Kitwe •

Lusaka ⊛

ZAMBIA

Harare ⊛

ZIMBABWE

SWAZILAND

Maputo ⊛

Lobamba ⊛
Mbabane ⊛

Pretoria
(Tshwane) ⊛

LESOTHO

Maseru ⊛

Durban •

CENTRAL
AFRICAN REPUBLIC

N'Djamena ⊛

Bangui ⊛

CONGO

Brazzaville ⊛

Pointe-Noire •

Cabinda
(Angola)

CAMEROON

Yaoundé ⊛

Douala •

Libreville ⊛

GABON

ANGOLA

NAMIBIA

Windhoek ⊛

BOTSWANA

Gaborone ⊛

Johannesburg •

Bloemfontein ⊛

SOUTH
AFRICA

Port
Elizabeth •

Cape Town ⊛

NIGERIA

Kano •

Abuja ⊛

Ogbomosho •

Lagos •

Porto-
Novo ⊛

Cotonou •

Malabo ⊛

EQUATORIAL GUINEA

SAO TOME & PRINCIPE

São Tomé ⊛

BENIN

TOGO

Lomé ⊛

GHANA

Accra ⊛

CÔTE D'IVOIRE
(IVORY COAST)

Yamoussoukro ⊛

Abidjan •

Ouagadougou ⊛

Bamako ⊛

GUINEA-
BISSAU

Bissau ⊛

GUINEA

Conakry ⊛

SIERRA
LEONE

Freetown ⊛

LIBERIA

Monrovia ⊛

Atlantic
Ocean

St. Helena
(U.K.)

Ascension
(U.K.)

EQUATOR

TROPIC OF CAPRICORN

Map Key

⊛ National capital
• Other city
▲ Highest point
▼ Lowest point

800 Miles

800 Kilometers

Azimuthal Equal-Area Projection

SPOTLIGHT ON
ANTARCTICA

Emperor penguin
with chick

Apart from humans, emperor penguins are the only warm-blooded animal to stay on Antarctica for the winter.

Millions of years ago, forests grew on Antarctica.

268

This frozen continent may be a cool place to visit, but unless you're a penguin, you probably wouldn't want to hang out in Antarctica for long. The fact that it's the coldest, windiest, and driest continent helps explain why humans never colonized this ice-covered land surrounding the South Pole.

Russian Orthodox church, South Shetland Islands

Slippery Landing

Flying into Antarctica is tricky, as many airport runways are made of blue ice. These runways need to be specially prepared to keep the planes from skidding.

Supersize Seals

Southern elephant seals spend most of their time in the frigid Antarctic waters. Adult males can grow to be 20 feet (6 m) long and weigh as much as a hippo.

Going the Distance

Each year, a few hundred runners from around the world compete in the Antarctica Marathon and Half-Marathon, a hilly and twisty race along the continent's icy peninsula.

Not All Ice

The Antarctic Peninsula is called the "Banana Belt" since it has a milder climate and gets just 14 to 20 inches (35 to 50 cm) of annual precipitation, about the same as Denver, Colorado, U.S.A.

Earth's Largest Deserts

Largest hot desert:
Sahara, Africa
3,475,000 square miles
(9,000,000 sq km)

Largest cold desert:
Antarctica
5,100,000 square miles
(13,209,000 sq km)

Not to scale

Weddell seal

269

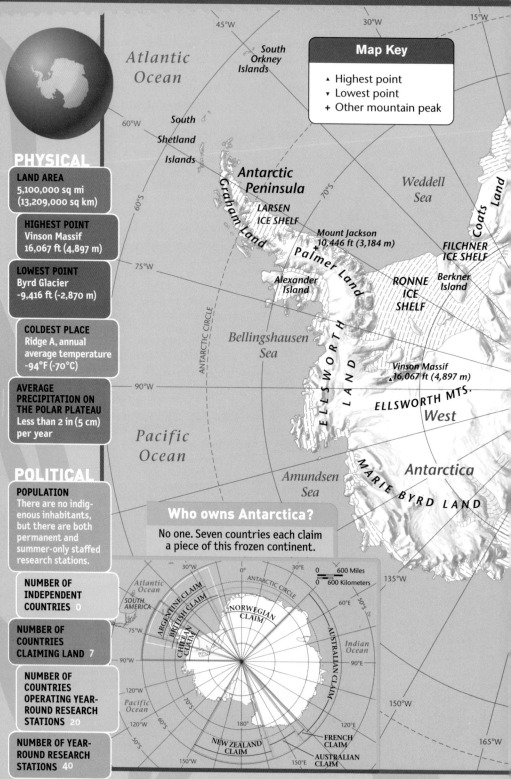

Atlantic
Ocean

South
Orkney
Islands

Map Key

▲ Highest point
▼ Lowest point
+ Other mountain peak

60°W

South
Shetland
Islands

**Antarctic
Peninsula**

Graham Land

LARSEN
ICE SHELF

Mount Jackson
10,446 ft (3,184 m)

Palmer Land

Weddell
Sea

Coats Land

FILCHNER
ICE SHELF

PHYSICAL

LAND AREA
5,100,000 sq mi
(13,209,000 sq km)

HIGHEST POINT
Vinson Massif
16,067 ft (4,897 m)

LOWEST POINT
Byrd Glacier
-9,416 ft (-2,870 m)

COLDEST PLACE
Ridge A, annual
average temperature
-94°F (-70°C)

**AVERAGE
PRECIPITATION ON
THE POLAR PLATEAU**
Less than 2 in (5 cm)
per year

75°W

Alexander
Island

ANTARCTIC CIRCLE

*Bellingshausen
Sea*

RONNE
ICE
SHELF

Berkner
Island

90°W

*Pacific
Ocean*

E L L S W O R T H   L A N D

Vinson Massif
▲16,067 ft (4,897 m)

ELLSWORTH MTS.
West

Antarctica

POLITICAL

POPULATION
There are no indig-
enous inhabitants,
but there are both
permanent and
summer-only staffed
research stations.

*Amundsen
Sea*

M A R I E   B Y R D   L A N D

**NUMBER OF
INDEPENDENT
COUNTRIES** 0

**NUMBER OF
COUNTRIES
CLAIMING LAND** 7

Who owns Antarctica?

No one. Seven countries each claim
a piece of this frozen continent.

30°W   0°   30°E
ANTARCTIC CIRCLE

*Atlantic
Ocean*

SOUTH
AMERICA

ARGENTINE CLAIM
BRITISH CLAIM
CHILEAN CLAIM

NORWEGIAN
CLAIM

60°E

AUSTRALIAN CLAIM

*Indian
Ocean*

0   600 Miles
0   600 Kilometers

135°W

90°E

**NUMBER OF
COUNTRIES
OPERATING YEAR-
ROUND RESEARCH
STATIONS** 20

90°W

120°W

*Pacific
Ocean*

120°W

180°

NEW ZEALAND
CLAIM

120°E

FRENCH
CLAIM

150°E

AUSTRALIAN
CLAIM

150°W

165°W

**NUMBER OF YEAR-
ROUND RESEARCH
STATIONS** 40

ANTARCTICA

FIMBUL
ICE SHELF

RIISER-LARSEN
ICE SHELF

QUEEN MAUD LAND

ENDERBY
LAND

*Indian
Ocean*

Valkyrie
Dome

MacKenzie Bay

AMERY ICE SHELF

Lambert
Glacier

AMERICAN

HIGHLAND

WEST
ICE SHELF

Ridge A

POLAR PLATEAU

*East

Antarctica*

South Pole

SHACKLETON
ICE SHELF

TRANSANTARCTIC MOUNTAINS

ROSS
ICE
SHELF

Roosevelt
Island

Taylor
Glacier

Byrd Glacier
-9,416 ft (-2,870 m)

Ross Island

Mount Erebus
12,448 ft
(3,794 m)

VICTORIA LAND

WILKES LAND

*Ross
Sea*

Talos
Dome

*South
Magnetic
Pole (2015)*

*Indian
Ocean*

0 _____ 600 Miles
0 _____ 600 Kilometers

Azimuthal Equidistant Projection

0°   15°E   30°E   45°E   60°E   75°E   90°E   105°E   120°E   135°E   150°E   180°

80°S   70°S   60°S

SPOTLIGHT ON
ASIA

The Chinese name for red panda is *hun-ho*, which means "fire fox."

Mountains cover 75 percent of Kyrgyzstan.

Red panda

Made up of 46 countries, Asia is the world's largest continent. Just how big is it? From western Turkey to the eastern tip of Russia, Asia spans nearly half the globe! Home to four billion citizens—that's three out of five people on the planet—Asia's population is bigger than that of all the other continents combined.

Safdarjung's Tomb, Delhi, India

Bear It

The dog-size sun bear is native to the dense forests of Southeast Asia. Its short fur keeps it cool in the tropical heat. Contrary to their name, they are mostly active at night.

Stellar Schools

A recent study shows that Asian schools are the top of the class in math and science. Singapore schools rank the highest in the world, followed by Hong Kong, South Korea, and Japan.

Young Mountains

Stretching across South Asia, the Himalaya include Mount Everest, the world's tallest peak. Formed about 50 million years ago, it's one of the youngest mountain ranges on Earth.

Flower Power

Thailand is one of the world's top orchid exporters. You can find more than 1,000 species of the flower growing wild in Thai forests.

World's Tallest Buildings

Asia is home to four of the five tallest buildings in the world.

Burj Khalifa	Shanghai Tower	Makkah Clock Royal Tower	One World Trade Center	CTF Finance Center
Dubai, U.A.E.	Shanghai, China	Mecca, Saudi Arabia	New York, U.S.A.	Guangzhou, China
2,717 feet (828 m)	2,073 feet (632 m)	1,972 feet (601 m)	1,776 feet (541 m)	1,739 feet (530 m)

Kuala Lumpur, Malaysia

273

ASIA

PHYSICAL

LAND AREA
17,208,000 sq mi
(44,570,000 sq km)

HIGHEST POINT
Mount Everest,
China–Nepal
29,035 ft (8,850 m)

LOWEST POINT
Dead Sea,
Israel–Jordan
-1,388 ft (-423 m)

LONGEST RIVER
Yangtze, China
3,880 mi (6,244 km)

**LARGEST LAKE
ENTIRELY IN ASIA**
Lake Baikal, Russia
12,200 sq mi
(31,500 sq km)

POLITICAL

POPULATION
4,396,678,000

**LARGEST
METROPOLITAN AREA**
Tokyo, Japan
Pop. 38,001,000

**LARGEST COUNTRY
ENTIRELY IN ASIA**
China
3,705,405 sq mi
(9,596,960 sq km)

**MOST DENSELY
POPULATED COUNTRY**
Singapore
21,729 people
per sq mi
(8,395 per sq km)

EUROPE

Mediterranean Sea

Dardanelles

Bosporus

İzmir

TURKEY

Ankara

ARMENIA

GEORGIA

Tbilisi

Yerevan

Baku

AZERBAIJAN

LEBANON

Beirut

Jerusalem

SYRIA

Damascus

ISRAEL

Amman

Dead Sea
-1,388 ft
(-423 m)

JORDAN

Baghdad

IRAQ

Basra

Medina

KUWAIT

Kuwait
City

Manama

Doha

IRAN

Tehran

Mashhad

Jeddah

SAUDI ARABIA

Mecca

Riyadh

BAHRAIN

QATAR

Dubai

Abu Dhabi

Sanaa

YEMEN

OMAN

Muscat

UNITED ARAB
EMIRATES

Aden

AFRICA

Arabian
Sea

EQUATOR

Europe
Asia

R U

Yekaterinburg

Nizhniy Tagil

Tyumen'

Magnitogorsk

Chelyabinsk

Omsk

Astana

TURKMENISTAN

Qaraghandy

KAZAKHSTAN

UZBEKISTAN

Ashgabat

Tashkent

Bishkek

Almaty

Samarqand

Dushanbe

KYRGYZSTAN

TAJIKISTAN

AFGHANISTAN

Kabul

Islamabad

Hotan

Rawalpindi

Faisalabad

Lahore

PAKISTAN

Delhi

New Delhi

Jaipur

NEPAL

Karachi

Kanpur

Indore

Bhopal

Surat

Mumbai
(Bombay)

Pune

I N D I A

Hyderabad

Bengaluru
(Bangalore)

Chennai
(Madras)

SRI
LANKA

Colombo

Sri Jayewardenepura Kotte

Male

MALDIVES

Indian Ocean

0   800 Miles

0   800 Kilometers

Two-point Equidistant Projection

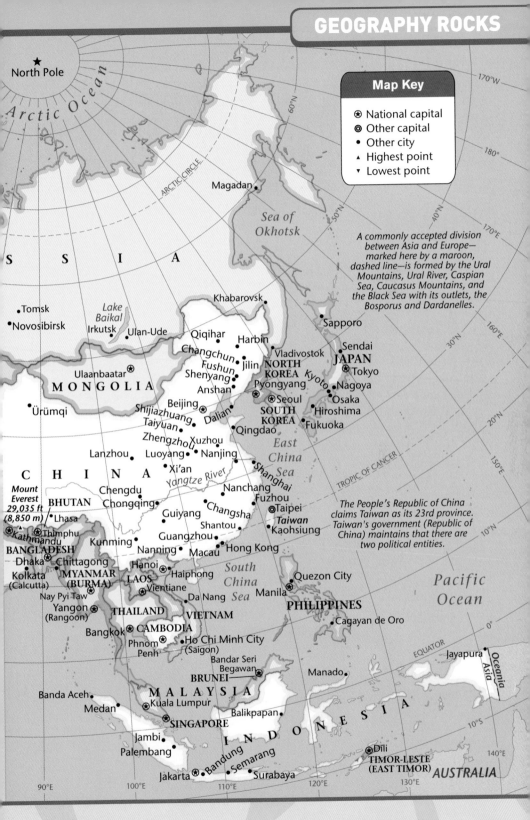

Map Key

⊛ National capital
◎ Other capital
• Other city
▲ Highest point
▼ Lowest point

North Pole

Arctic Ocean

ARCTIC CIRCLE

Magadan

Sea of Okhotsk

A commonly accepted division between Asia and Europe—marked here by a maroon, dashed line—is formed by the Ural Mountains, Ural River, Caspian Sea, Caucasus Mountains, and the Black Sea with its outlets, the Bosporus and Dardanelles.

RUSSIA

Tomsk
Novosibirsk
Irkutsk
Ulan-Ude
Lake Baikal
Khabarovsk
Sapporo
Vladivostok
Sendai
JAPAN
Qiqihar
Harbin
Changchun
Jilin
Fushun
Shenyang
Anshan
NORTH KOREA
Pyongyang
Kyoto
Tokyo
Nagoya
Osaka
Hiroshima
Fukuoka
Seoul
SOUTH KOREA
Ulaanbaatar
MONGOLIA
Ürümqi
Beijing
Shijiazhuang
Dalian
Taiyuan
Qingdao
Zhengzhou
Xuzhou
Lanzhou
Luoyang
Nanjing
East China Sea
Xi'an
Shanghai
Yangtze River
TROPIC OF CANCER
CHINA
Chengdu
Chongqing
Nanchang
Fuzhou
Taipei
Taiwan
Kaohsiung
Guiyang
Changsha
Shantou
Mount Everest 29,035 ft (8,850 m)
BHUTAN
Lhasa
Thimphu
Kathmandu
BANGLADESH
Dhaka
Chittagong
Kolkata (Calcutta)
MYANMAR (BURMA)
Nay Pyi Taw
Yangon (Rangoon)
Kunming
Nanning
Guangzhou
Macau
Hong Kong
Hanoi
Haiphong
LAOS
Vientiane
Da Nang
South China Sea
Manila
Quezon City
PHILIPPINES
Cagayan de Oro
THAILAND
Bangkok
CAMBODIA
Phnom Penh
Ho Chi Minh City (Saigon)
VIETNAM
Bandar Seri Begawan
BRUNEI
Manado
Pacific Ocean
EQUATOR
Jayapura
Oceania
Asia
Banda Aceh
Medan
MALAYSIA
Kuala Lumpur
Balikpapan
SINGAPORE
Jambi
Palembang
INDONESIA
Jakarta
Bandung
Semarang
Surabaya
Dili
TIMOR-LESTE (EAST TIMOR)
AUSTRALIA

The People's Republic of China claims Taiwan as its 23rd province. Taiwan's government (Republic of China) maintains that there are two political entities.

90°E 100°E 110°E 120°E 130°E 140°E 150°E 160°E 170°E 180° 170°W

0° 10°N 20°N 30°N 40°N 50°N 60°N

SPOTLIGHT ON
AUSTRALIA,
NEW ZEALAND, AND OCEANIA

In Australia, "Bluey" is a nickname for redheads.

The Twelve Apostles limestone rock stacks were once called the Sow and Piglets.

Twelve Apostles rock stacks, Victoria, Australia

G'day, mate! This vast region, covering almost 3.3 million square miles (8.5 million sq km), includes Australia—the world's smallest and flattest continent—and New Zealand, as well as a fleet of mostly tiny islands scattered across the Pacific Ocean. Also known as "down under," all of the countries in this region are in the Southern Hemisphere, and below the Equator.

Maori children of New Zealand in ceremonial costume

Snowy Spot

It does snow down under! From June through September, the Australian Alps, stretching through New South Wales and into Victoria, gets about 6.5 feet (2 m) of snow.

Horse Country

Mobs of wild horses, known as brumbies, roam throughout Australia. It's believed they escaped into the bush when European settlers arrived in the country 150 years ago.

Plenty of Wool

With more sheep than people, Australia and New Zealand are among the world's top producers of wool. Sheep shearing and wool handling competitions are held in both countries.

Protected Waters

The South Pacific island nation of Palau is making big waves as the future home of what may be the world's largest marine sanctuary. Plans include a block on fishing and drilling.

Australia
Sizing Up the Great Barrier Reef

Just how big is the Great Barrier Reef Marine Park? It's approximately as large as:

Great Barrier Reef Marine Park

Germany

Australia

Vietnam

or the Republic of Congo

*Based on an area of 133,000 square miles (344,400 sq km)

Sydney Harbour Bridge in Sydney, Australia

Map Key

- ⊛ National capital
- • Other city
- ▲ Highest point
- ▼ Lowest point

PHYSICAL

LAND AREA
3,278,000 sq mi
(8,490,000 sq km)

HIGHEST POINT
Mount Wilhelm,
Papua New Guinea
14,793 ft (4,509 m)

LOWEST POINT
Lake Eyre, Australia
-49 ft (-15 m)

LONGEST RIVER
Murray-Darling,
Australia 2,282 mi
(3,672 km)

LARGEST LAKE
Lake Eyre, Australia
3,741 sq mi
(9,690 sq km)

POLITICAL

POPULATION
39,506,000

**LARGEST
METROPOLITAN AREA**
Sydney, Australia
Pop. 4,505,000

LARGEST COUNTRY
Australia
2,988,901 sq mi
(7,741,220 sq km)

**MOST DENSELY
POPULATED COUNTRY**
Nauru
1,375 people per sq
mi (524 per sq km)

A S I A

M i c r o n e s i a

Northern Mariana
Islands
(U.S.)
• Capital Hill
Guam
(U.S.)

PALAU ⊛
Melekeok

Yap
Islands

Truk Islands

Caroline Islands

⊛ Palikir

FEDERATED STATES
OF MICRONESIA

M e l a n

Oceania–Asia
boundary

PAPUA NEW GUINEA
▲ Mount Wilhelm
14,793 ft
(4,509 m)

Honiara
⊛
Solomon Islands

Port Moresby ⊛

Coral Sea
Islands
Territory
(Australia)

C o r a l   S e a

AUSTRALIA

• Brisbane

-49 ft
(-15 m)

▼ Lake
Eyre

Darling
River

Lord Howe
Island
(Australia)

• Perth

Sydney •

Adelaide •

Murray
River

Canberra, ⊛
A.C.T.

Tasman
Sea

Melbourne •

Indian
Ocean

Tasmania

Hobart •

0   800 Miles
0   800 Kilometers

Mercator Projection

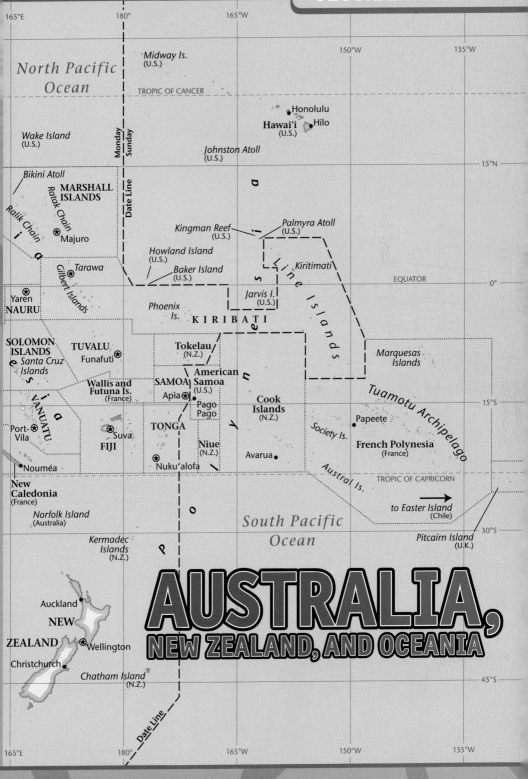

165°E   180°   165°W   150°W   135°W

North Pacific Ocean

Midway Is.
(U.S.)

TROPIC OF CANCER

Honolulu
Hawai'i Hilo
(U.S.)

Wake Island
(U.S.)

Johnston Atoll
(U.S.)

15°N

Monday Sunday

Bikini Atoll

MARSHALL ISLANDS

Ratak Chain

Ralik Chain

Date Line

Kingman Reef
(U.S.)

Palmyra Atoll
(U.S.)

Majuro

Howland Island
(U.S.)

Kiritimati

Tarawa

Baker Island
(U.S.)

EQUATOR

0°

Gilbert Islands

Yaren
NAURU

Phoenix
Is.

Jarvis I.
(U.S.)

Line Islands

K I R I B A T I

SOLOMON ISLANDS

TUVALU
Funafuti

Tokelau
(N.Z.)

Marquesas
Islands

Santa Cruz
Islands

SAMOA

American Samoa
(U.S.)

Wallis and
Futuna Is.
(France)

Apia

Pago
Pago

VANUATU

Port-
Vila

Suva

TONGA

**Cook
Islands**
(N.Z.)

Papeete

Tuamotu Archipelago

15°S

Society Is.

FIJI

Niue
(N.Z.)

French Polynesia
(France)

Nouméa

Nuku'alofa

Avarua

Austral Is.

TROPIC OF CAPRICORN

**New
Caledonia**
(France)

Norfolk Island
(Australia)

*South Pacific
Ocean*

to Easter Island
(Chile)

Kermadec
Islands
(N.Z.)

Pitcairn Island
(U.K.)

30°S

Auckland

**NEW
ZEALAND**
Wellington

AUSTRALIA,
NEW ZEALAND, AND OCEANIA

Christchurch

Chatham Island
(N.Z.)

45°S

Date Line

165°E   180°   165°W   150°W   135°W

279

SPOTLIGHT ON
EUROPE

Amsterdam, Netherlands, is home to 165 canals.

The first circus was held in Rome, Italy.

Amsterdam, Netherlands

A cluster of islands and peninsulas jutting west from Asia, Europe is bordered by the Atlantic and Arctic Oceans and more than a dozen seas. Here you'll find a variety of scenery, from mountains to countryside to coastlines. Europe is also known for its rich culture and fascinating history, which make it one of the most visited continents on Earth.

Hedgehog

Blue Bloods

There are 12 surviving monarchies in western Europe. Denmark's royal family takes the crown for Europe's longest-running monarchy, having lasted more than 1,000 years.

Fiery Mountain

Italy's Mount Etna, one of the most active volcanoes on Earth, erupts almost every year. Towering 10,900 feet (3,322 m) above Sicily, it can be seen from much of the island.

Magic Kingdom

Disney World's famous Cinderella castle was modeled after the Neuschwanstein Castle, a 19th-century fortress built for King Ludwig II in southwest Bavaria in Germany.

Just Visiting

More than 580 million people visit Europe each year, making it the most popular continent to travel to. The top destinations within Europe? France, Spain, and Italy.

Europe's 6 Most-Visited Cities*

1. **London, England**
   18.82 million visitors

2. **Paris, France**
   16.06 million visitors

3. **Istanbul, Turkey**
   12.56 million visitors

4. **Barcelona, Spain**
   7.63 million visitors

5. **Amsterdam, Netherlands**
   7.44 million visitors

6. **Rome, Italy**
   7.41 million visitors

*International visitors in 2015

Traditional dance performed in Greece

Map Key

- ⊛ National capital
- • Other city
- ▫ Small country
- ▲ Highest point
- ▼ Lowest point

PHYSICAL

LAND AREA
3,841,000 sq mi
(9,947,000 sq km)

HIGHEST POINT
El'brus, Russia
18,510 ft (5,642 m)

LOWEST POINT
Caspian Sea
-92 ft (-28 m)

LONGEST RIVER
Volga, Russia
2,290 mi
(3,685 km)

**LARGEST LAKE
ENTIRELY IN EUROPE**
Ladoga, Russia
6,900 sq mi
(17,872 sq km)

POLITICAL

POPULATION
741,652,000

**LARGEST
METROPOLITAN AREA**
Moscow, Russia
Pop. 12,166,000

**LARGEST COUNTRY
ENTIRELY IN EUROPE**
Ukraine
233,030 sq mi
(603,550 sq km)

**MOST DENSELY
POPULATED COUNTRY**
Monaco
47,500 people per sq
mi (19,000 per sq km)

Jan Mayen
(Norway)

Reykjavík
ICELAND

*Norwegian
Sea*

ARCTIC CIRCLE

Faroe Islands
(Denmark)

Shetland
Islands

Orkney Islands

*North
Sea*

Oslo

Göteborg

SCOTLAND
Glasgow
•Edinburgh

N. IRELAND
•Belfast

DENMARK
Copenhagen

**IRELAND
(ÉIRE)**
Dublin

UNITED KINGDOM

Kiel

Liverpool •Manchester
WALES •Birmingham
Cardiff• •ENGLAND

Hamburg
The •NETH.
Hague•Amsterdam•

Berlin

London⊛

*Atlantic
Ocean*

Brussels⊛
BELGIUM

GERMANY

⊛Paris

LUX.

Frankfurt
Prague

•Nantes

*Bay of
Biscay*

FRANCE Zürich
Bern•

Munich
LIECH.

SWITZ.

AUSTRIA

•Bordeaux Lyon•

Milan
•Turin

Ljubljana
SLOV.
Venice•

Oporto

Bilbao

•Toulouse

MONACO

Genoa
SAN
MARINO

•Valladolid

ANDORRA

Nice

40°N

Lisbon

PORTUGAL

Madrid⊛

•Zaragoza

Marseille

ITALY

VATICAN
CITY

S P A I N

Barcelona

Corsica
(France)

Rome

Valencia

•Seville Murcia•

•Málaga

*Sardinia
(Italy)*

Naples•

•Gibraltar (U.K.)

*Balearic Is.
(Spain)*

M e d i t e r r a

Messina
Palermo•

•Catania
Sicily

| 0 | | | 400 Miles |
| 0 | | 400 Kilometers | |

Azimuthal Equidistant Projection

A F R I C A

Valletta⊛
MALTA

EUROPE

A commonly accepted division
between Asia and Europe—
marked here by a maroon,
dashed line—is formed by the
Ural Mountains, Ural River, Caspian
Sea, Caucasus Mountains, and
the Black Sea with its outlets, the
Bosporus and Dardanelles.

SPOTLIGHT ON
NORTH AMERICA

Chichén Itzá, a Maya temple on Mexico's Yucatan Peninsula, has 365 steps —one for each day of the calendar year.

Honduras is the only Central American country that doesn't have a volcano.

Castillo Kukulkan Temple of Chichén Itzá, Mexico

From the Great Plains of the United States and Canada to the rain forests of Panama, North America stretches 5,500 miles (8,850 km) from north to south. The third largest continent, North America can be divided into five regions: the mountainous west (including parts of Mexico and Central America's western coast), the Great Plains, the Canadian Shield, the varied eastern region (including Central America's lowlands and coastal plains), and the Caribbean.

Rodeo cowboy

Early Life

The 20,000-year-old stone tools and animal bones discovered in the Bluefish caves in Yukon Territory, Canada, may be the continent's first evidence of human activity.

Horse jawbone

Taking Flight

Millions of monarchs migrate up to 3,000 miles (4,828 km) to Mexico every year from the United States and Canada. They're the only butterflies to make such a massive journey.

Back to Its Roots

Same mountain, new official name: Formerly called Mount McKinley, Denali now officially goes by the Native Alaskan name it was given thousands of years ago.

Tale of the Shrew

Found throughout most of Canada and the U.S., the northern short-tailed shrew is North America's only native venomous mammal. The mouse-size animal uses its venom to paralyze prey.

North America's 5 Most Visited National Parks*

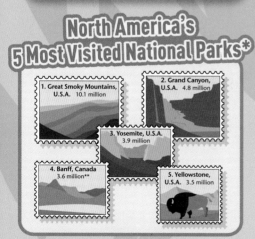

1. Great Smoky Mountains, U.S.A.   10.1 million
2. Grand Canyon, U.S.A.   4.8 million
3. Yosemite, U.S.A.   3.9 million
4. Banff, Canada   3.6 million**
5. Yellowstone, U.S.A.   3.5 million

Snowy owl

*2014 (National Park Service); **2014-2015 Parks Canada

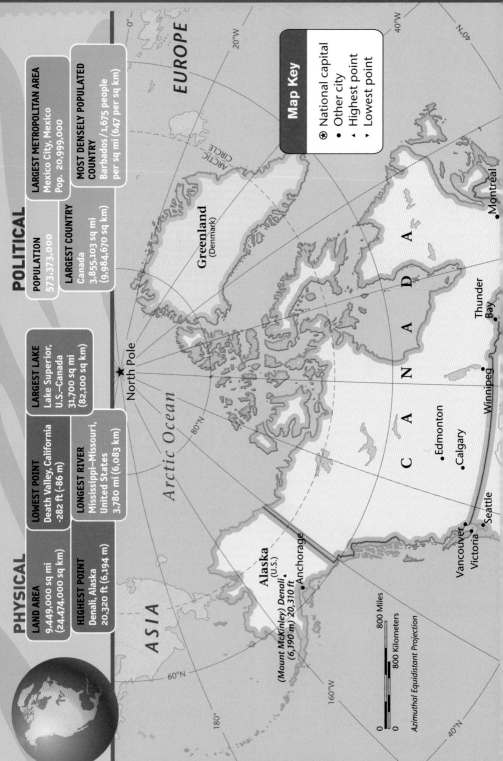

PHYSICAL

LAND AREA
9,449,000 sq mi
(24,474,000 sq km)

HIGHEST POINT
Denali, Alaska
20,320 ft (6,194 m)

LOWEST POINT
Death Valley, California
−282 ft (−86 m)

LONGEST RIVER
Mississippi–Missouri,
United States
3,780 mi (6,083 km)

LARGEST LAKE
Lake Superior,
U.S.–Canada
31,700 sq mi
(82,100 sq km)

POLITICAL

POPULATION
573,373,000

LARGEST COUNTRY
Canada
3,855,103 sq mi
(9,984,670 sq km)

LARGEST METROPOLITAN AREA
Mexico City, Mexico
Pop. 20,999,000

**MOST DENSELY POPULATED
COUNTRY**
Barbados / 1,675 people
per sq mi (647 per sq km)

Map Key

⊛ National capital
• Other city
▲ Highest point
▼ Lowest point

EUROPE

ASIA

Arctic Ocean

North Pole

Greenland
(Denmark)

CANADA

Alaska
(U.S.)

(Mount McKinley) Denali ▲
(6,190 m) 20,310 ft
•Anchorage

•Edmonton
•Calgary

Seattle
Vancouver
Victoria

Winnipeg

Thunder
Bay

•Montréal

ARCTIC
CIRCLE

800 Miles
800 Kilometers

Azimuthal Equidistant Projection

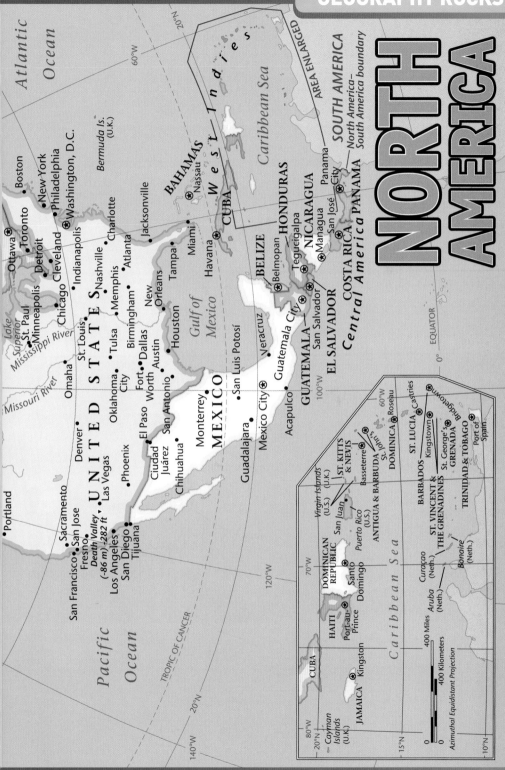

NORTH AMERICA

AREA ENLARGED

SOUTH AMERICA

North America–
South America boundary

Atlantic Ocean

Pacific Ocean

Caribbean Sea

Gulf of Mexico

Lake Superior

Mississippi River

Missouri River

West Indies

UNITED STATES

MEXICO

BAHAMAS

CUBA

BELIZE

GUATEMALA

EL SALVADOR

HONDURAS

NICARAGUA

COSTA RICA

PANAMA

Central America

Portland
Sacramento
San Jose
San Francisco
Fresno
Las Vegas
Death Valley
(−86 m) −282 ft
Los Angeles
San Diego
Tijuana
Phoenix
Denver
El Paso
Ciudad Juárez
Chihuahua
Oklahoma City
Tulsa
Fort Worth
Dallas
Austin
San Antonio
Omaha
St. Louis
Memphis
Birmingham
New Orleans
Houston
Nashville
Indianapolis
Chicago
St. Paul
Minneapolis
Detroit
Cleveland
Atlanta
Charlotte
Jacksonville
Tampa
Miami
Ottawa
Toronto
Boston
New York
Philadelphia
Washington, D.C.
Bermuda Is. (U.K.)

Monterrey
Guadalajara
San Luis Potosí
Mexico City
Acapulco
Veracruz
Guatemala City
San Salvador
Belmopan
Tegucigalpa
Managua
San José
San José
Panama City

Nassau
Havana

20°N
20°N
15°N
10°N
60°W
80°W
100°W
120°W
140°W
0°
20°W
60°W
70°W
EQUATOR
TROPIC OF CANCER

Caribbean Sea

Virgin Islands (U.S.) (U.K.)
ST. KITTS & NEVIS
Basseterre
ANTIGUA & BARBUDA
St. John's
DOMINICA
Roseau
ST. LUCIA
Castries
BARBADOS
Bridgetown
ST. VINCENT & THE GRENADINES
Kingstown
St. George's
GRENADA
TRINIDAD & TOBAGO
Port of Spain
San Juan
Puerto Rico (U.S.)
DOMINICAN REPUBLIC
Santo Domingo
HAITI
Port-au-Prince
CUBA
JAMAICA
Kingston
Cayman Islands (U.K.)
Curaçao (Neth.)
Aruba (Neth.)
Bonaire (Neth.)

0   400 Miles
0   400 Kilometers
Azimuthal Equidistant Projection

287

SPOTLIGHT ON
SOUTH AMERICA

In addition to llamas and alpacas, you might find ocelots, condors, and spectacled bears at Machu Picchu.

More than 700,000 different kinds of insects live in Brazil.

Llamas and alpacas, Machu Picchu, Peru

288

South America is bordered by three major bodies of water—the Caribbean Sea, Atlantic Ocean, and Pacific Ocean. The world's fourth largest continent extends over a range of climates from tropical in the north to subarctic in the south. South America produces a rich diversity of natural resources, including nuts, fruits, sugar, grains, coffee, and chocolate.

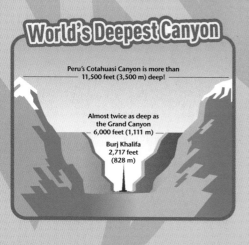

A boy celebrates Carnival in Rio de Janeiro, Brazil.

High Sands

Peru's Cerro Blanco is home to the world's highest sand dune. At 3,858 feet (1,176 m), it's more than 1,000 feet (305 m) taller than Dubai's Burj Khalifa—the world's tallest building.

Clean Air

The southern tip of South America has some of the world's freshest air. Ushuaia, Argentina, has no pollutants in the air much of the year. A remote location and frequent rain play a part.

Big Bird

The Andean condor, which lives exclusively in the mountains and valleys of the Andes, is the largest raptor in the world and the largest flying bird in South America.

Living in Isolation

Brazil's Amazon rain forest is home to more isolated tribes than anywhere on the planet. There are thought to be at least 77 groups with little to no contact with the outside world.

World's Deepest Canyon

Peru's Cotahuasi Canyon is more than 11,500 feet (3,500 m) deep!

Almost twice as deep as the Grand Canyon 6,000 feet (1,111 m)

Burj Khalifa 2,717 feet (828 m)

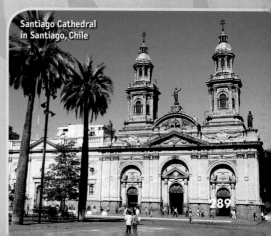

Santiago Cathedral in Santiago, Chile

PHYSICAL

LAND AREA
6,880,000 sq mi
(17,819,000 sq km)

HIGHEST POINT
Cerro Aconcagua,
Argentina
22,831 ft (6,959 m)

LOWEST POINT
Laguna del Carbón,
Argentina
-344 ft (-105 m)

LONGEST RIVER
Amazon
4,150 mi (6,679 km)

LARGEST LAKE
Lake Maracaibo,
Venezuela
5,127 sq mi
(13,280 sq km)

POLITICAL

POPULATION
413,870,000

LARGEST COUNTRY
Brazil
3,287,612 sq mi
(8,514,877 sq km)

LARGEST METROPOLITAN AREA
São Paulo, Brazil
Pop. 21,066,000

MOST DENSELY POPULATED COUNTRY
Ecuador / 149 people per
sq mi (57 per sq km)

Map Key

- ⊛ National capital
- • Other city
- ▲ Highest point
- ▼ Lowest point

Central
America

Caribbean
Sea

Barranquilla

Maracaibo
Lake
Maracaibo

South America–
North America
boundary

Medellín

Bogotá

Cali

COLOMBIA

ECUADOR

Quito

Guayaquil

Caracas

Valencia

Barquisimeto

VENEZUELA

Georgetown

GUYANA

Paramaribo

SURINAME

Cayenne

French Guiana
(France)

Manaus

Amazon River

Belém

B R A Z I L

Fortaleza

Natal

Recife

Salvador
(Bahia)

Brasília

Trujillo

Lima

Cusco

P E R U

BOLIVIA

EQUATOR

EQUATOR

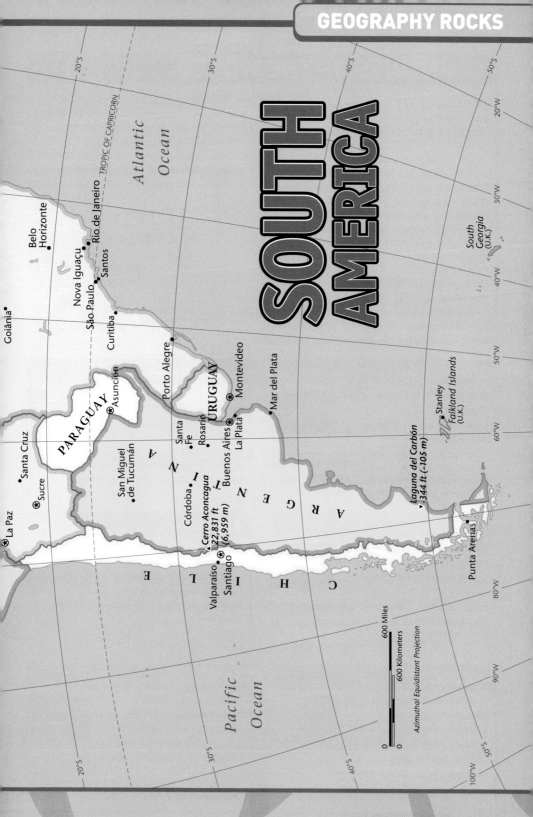

SOUTH AMERICA

Atlantic Ocean

Pacific Ocean

TROPIC OF CAPRICORN

20°S
30°S
40°S
50°S

La Paz
Santa Cruz
Sucre
Goiânia
Belo Horizonte
Nova Iguaçu
Rio de Janeiro
São Paulo
Santos
Curitiba
Porto Alegre

PARAGUAY
Asunción

San Miguel de Tucumán
Córdoba
Santa Fe
Rosario
URUGUAY
Montevideo
Mar del Plata

A R G E N T I N A

C H I L E

Cerro Aconcagua
22,831 ft (6,959 m)
Valparaíso
Santiago
Buenos Aires
La Plata

Laguna del Carbón
-344 ft (-105 m)

Punta Arenas

Stanley
Falkland Islands (U.K.)

South Georgia (U.K.)

600 Miles
600 Kilometers
Azimuthal Equidistant Projection

0

20°W
30°W
40°W
50°W
60°W
70°W
80°W
90°W
100°W

30°S
40°S
50°S

COUNTRIES OF THE WORLD

The following pages present a general overview of all 195 independent countries recognized by the National Geographic Society, including the newest nation, South Sudan, which gained independence in 2011.

The flags of each independent country symbolize diverse cultures and histories. The statistical data cover highlights of geography and demography and provide a brief overview of each country. They present general characteristics and are not intended to be comprehensive. For example, not every language spoken in a specific country can be listed. Thus, languages shown are the most representative of that area. This is also true of the religions mentioned.

A country is defined as a political body with its own independent government, geographical space, and, in most cases, laws, military, and taxes.

Disputed areas such as Northern Cyprus and Taiwan, and dependencies of independent nations, such as Bermuda and Puerto Rico, are not included in this listing.

Note the color key at the bottom of the pages and the locator map below, which assign a color to each country based on the continent on which it is located. All information is accurate as of press time.

Color Key by Continent

Afghanistan

Area: 251,773 sq mi (652,090 sq km)
Population: 32,247,000
Capital: Kabul, pop. 4,436,000
Currency: afghani
Religions: Sunni Muslim, Shiite Muslim
Languages: Afghan Persian (Dari), Pashto, Turkic languages (primarily Uzbek and Turkmen), Baluchi, 30 minor languages (including Pashai)

Albania

Area: 11,100 sq mi (28,748 sq km)
Population: 2,892,000
Capital: Tirana, pop. 445,000
Currency: lek
Religions: Muslim, Albanian Orthodox, Roman Catholic
Languages: Albanian, Greek, Vlach, Romani, Slavic dialects

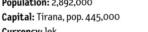

Algeria

Area: 919,595 sq mi (2,381,741 sq km)
Population: 39,948,000
Capital: Algiers, pop. 2,559,000
Currency: Algerian dinar
Religion: Sunni Muslim
Languages: Arabic, French, Berber dialects

Andorra

Area: 181 sq mi (469 sq km)
Population: 78,000
Capital: Andorra la Vella, pop. 23,000
Currency: euro
Religion: Roman Catholic
Languages: Catalan, French, Castilian, Portuguese

Angola

Area: 481,354 sq mi (1,246,700 sq km)
Population: 25,000,000
Capital: Luanda, pop. 5,288,000
Currency: kwanza
Religions: indigenous beliefs, Roman Catholic, Protestant
Languages: Portuguese, Bantu, and other African languages

Antigua and Barbuda

Area: 171 sq mi (442 sq km)
Population: 90,000
Capital: St. John's, pop. 22,000
Currency: East Caribbean dollar
Religions: Anglican, Seventh-day Adventist, Pentecostal, Moravian, Roman Catholic, Methodist, Baptist, Church of God, other Christian
Languages: English, local dialects

COLOR KEY ● Africa ● Australia, New Zealand, and Oceania

Argentina

Area: 1,073,518 sq mi
(2,780,400 sq km)
Population: 42,426,000
Capital: Buenos Aires,
pop. 15,024,000
Currency: Argentine peso
Religion: Roman Catholic
Languages: Spanish, English, Italian, German, French

Armenia

Area: 11,484 sq mi
(29,743 sq km)
Population: 3,017,000
Capital: Yerevan,
pop. 1,049,000
Currency: dram
Religions: Armenian Apostolic, other Christian
Language: Armenian

Australia

Area: 2,988,901 sq mi
(7,741,220 sq km)
Population: 23,888,000
Capital: Canberra, A.C.T.,
pop. 415,000
Currency: Australian dollar
Religions: Roman Catholic, Anglican
Language: English

5 cool things about AUSTRALIA

1. Australia's outback is home to the world's largest population of wild camels.

2. The dangerous bulldog ant—whose bite can be fatal to humans—is found exclusively in Australia.

3. Kangaroos as tall as a professional basketball player once roamed around Australia.

4. You can ride a single train from one coast of Australia to another—a total of 2,704 miles (4,352 km).

5. The term "selfie" is said to have originated in Australia.

Austria

Area: 32,378 sq mi (83,858 sq km)
Population: 8,616,000
Capital: Vienna, pop. 1,743,000
Currency: euro
Religions: Roman Catholic, Protestant, Muslim
Language: German

Azerbaijan

Area: 33,436 sq mi
(86,600 sq km)
Population: 9,651,000
Capital: Baku, pop. 2,317,000
Currency: Azerbaijani manat
Religion: Muslim
Language: Azerbaijani (Azeri)

Bahamas

Area: 5,382 sq mi
(13,939 sq km)
Population: 377,000
Capital: Nassau, pop. 267,000
Currency: Bahamian dollar
Religions: Baptist, Anglican, Roman Catholic, Pentecostal, Church of God
Languages: English, Creole

Bahrain

Area: 277 sq mi (717 sq km)
Population: 1,412,000
Capital: Manama, pop. 398,000
Currency: Bahraini dinar
Religions: Shiite Muslim, Sunni Muslim, Christian
Languages: Arabic, English, Farsi, Urdu

Bangladesh

Area: 55,598 sq mi
(143,998 sq km)
Population: 160,411,000
Capital: Dhaka, pop. 16,982,000
Currency: taka
Religions: Muslim, Hindu
Languages: Bangla (Bengali), English

Barbados

Area: 166 sq mi (430 sq km)
Population: 278,000
Capital: Bridgetown, pop. 90,000
Currency: Barbadian dollar
Religions: Anglican, Pentecostal, Methodist, other Protestant, Roman Catholic
Language: English

Belarus

Area: 80,153 sq mi (207,595 sq km)
Population: 9,524,000
Capital: Minsk, pop. 1,905,000
Currency: Belarusian ruble
Religions: Eastern Orthodox, other (includes Roman Catholic, Protestant, Jewish, Muslim)
Languages: Belarusian, Russian

Belgium

Area: 11,787 sq mi (30,528 sq km)
Population: 11,211,000
Capital: Brussels, pop. 2,029,000
Currency: euro
Religions: Roman Catholic, other (includes Protestant)
Languages: Dutch, French

Belize

Area: 8,867 sq mi (22,965 sq km)
Population: 368,000
Capital: Belmopan, pop. 17,000
Currency: Belizean dollar
Religions: Roman Catholic, Protestant (includes Pentecostal, Seventh-day Adventist, Mennonite, Methodist)
Languages: Spanish, Creole, Mayan dialects, English, Garifuna (Carib), German

Benin

Area: 43,484 sq mi (112,622 sq km)
Population: 10,583,000
Capitals: Porto-Novo, pop. 268,000; Cotonou, pop. 680,000
Currency: Communauté Financière Africaine franc
Religions: Christian, Muslim, Vodoun
Languages: French, Fon, Yoruba, tribal languages

Bhutan

Area: 17,954 sq mi (46,500 sq km)
Population: 757,000
Capital: Thimphu, pop. 152,000
Currencies: ngultrum; Indian rupee
Religions: Lamaistic Buddhist, Indian- and Nepalese-influenced Hindu
Languages: Dzongkha, Tibetan dialects, Nepalese dialects

Bolivia

Area: 424,164 sq mi (1,098,581 sq km)
Population: 10,476,000
Capitals: La Paz, pop. 1,800,000; Sucre, pop. 358,000
Currency: boliviano
Religions: Roman Catholic, Protestant (includes Evangelical Methodist)
Languages: Spanish, Quechua, Aymara

There are **NO MOTOR VEHICLES** on Bolivia's Isla del Sol—**VISITORS MUST HIKE OR TRAVEL BY BOAT.**

Bosnia and Herzegovina

Area: 19,741 sq mi (51,129 sq km)
Population: 3,650,000
Capital: Sarajevo, pop. 322,000
Currency: konvertibilna marka (convertible mark)
Religions: Muslim, Orthodox, Roman Catholic
Languages: Bosnian, Croatian, Serbian

Botswana

Area: 224,607 sq mi (581,730 sq km)
Population: 2,140,000
Capital: Gaborone, pop. 247,000
Currency: pula
Religions: Christian, Badimo
Languages: Setswana, Kalanga

Brazil

Area: 3,287,612 sq mi
(8,514,877 sq km)
Population: 204,519,000
Capital: Brasília, pop. 4,074,000
Currency: real
Religions: Roman Catholic, Protestant
Language: Portuguese

Bulgaria

Area: 42,855 sq mi
(110,994 sq km)
Population: 7,181,000
Capital: Sofia, pop. 1,222,000
Currency: lev
Religions: Bulgarian Orthodox, Muslim
Languages: Bulgarian, Turkish, Roma

Brunei

Area: 2,226 sq mi (5,765 sq km)
Population: 413,000
Capital: Bandar Seri Begawan,
pop. 14,000
Currency: Bruneian dollar
Religions: Muslim, Buddhist, Christian, other
(includes indigenous beliefs)
Languages: Malay, English, Chinese

Burkina Faso

Area: 105,869 sq mi
(274,200 sq km)
Population: 18,450,000
Capital: Ouagadougou,
pop. 2,565,000
Currency: Communauté Financière Africaine franc
Religions: Muslim, indigenous beliefs, Christian
Languages: French, native African languages

You Are There!

The Amazon, Brazil

Pink river dolphins

Cruising along the Amazon River on a boat, you look down to spot a large, shadowy figure lurking just beneath the water's surface. Is it a massive fish? A dolphin? A manatee? In the Amazon, it just may be any of those things. This iconic river is home to thousands of species, including threatened animals like the giant arapaima fish, the Amazonian manatee, and the pink river dolphin. A trip along any stretch of this 4,150-mile (6,679-km) waterway is an ideal way to spot such rare species in their natural habitat. Just make sure you stay safe inside the boat: There are plenty of alligators and piranhas in that water, too, so you're better off admiring everything from afar—and above.

● Asia ● Europe ● North America ● South America

Burundi

Area: 10,747 sq mi (27,834 sq km)
Population: 10,742,000
Capital: Bujumbura, pop. 707,000
Currency: Burundi franc
Religions: Roman Catholic, indigenous beliefs, Muslim, Protestant
Languages: Kirundi, French, Swahili

Cambodia

Area: 69,898 sq mi (181,035 sq km)
Population: 15,417,000
Capital: Phnom Penh, pop. 1,684,000
Currency: riel
Religion: Theravada Buddhist
Language: Khmer

Cabo Verde

Area: 1,558 sq mi (4,036 sq km)
Population: 514,000
Capital: Praia, pop. 145,000
Currency: Cape Verdean escudo
Religions: Roman Catholic (infused with indigenous beliefs), Protestant (mostly Church of the Nazarene)
Languages: Portuguese, Crioulo

Cameroon

Area: 183,569 sq mi (475,442 sq km)
Population: 23,739,000
Capital: Yaoundé, pop. 2,930,000
Currency: Communauté Financière Africaine franc
Religions: indigenous beliefs, Christian, Muslim
Languages: 24 major African language groups, English, French

You Are There!

Vancouver Island, British Columbia, Canada

Picture this: You're cruising along around Vancouver Island on a ferry boat when you head out to the deck just in time to see a giant, shiny, black and white object go flying in the air before plunging back into the water with a huge splash. An orca! Hundreds of these massive mammals—plus other whales including humpbacks, greys and minkes—can be found in the waters surrounding Vancouver Island. So it's no wonder this place is one of the world's top whale-watching spots. But there's more than just whales to see as you wonder around Vancouver Island: Sea lions swim alongside octopuses, and you may spot a bald eagle soaring up above or a grizzly bear snagging salmon along the shores. So keep your eyes peeled— and be sure to bring your binoculars!

COLOR KEY ● Africa ● Australia, New Zealand, and Oceania

Canada

Area: 3,855,101 sq mi
(9,984,670 sq km)
Population: 35,833,000
Capital: Ottawa, pop. 1,306,000
Currency: Canadian dollar
Religions: Roman Catholic, Protestant (includes United Church, Anglican), other Christian
Languages: English, French

Central African Republic

Area: 240,535 sq mi
(622,984 sq km)
Population: 5,552,000
Capital: Bangui, pop. 781,000
Currency: Communauté Financière Africaine franc
Religions: indigenous beliefs, Protestant, Roman Catholic, Muslim
Languages: French, Sangho, tribal languages

Chad

Area: 495,755 sq mi
(1,284,000 sq km)
Population: 13,707,000
Capital: N'Djamena, pop. 1,212,000
Currency: Communauté Financière Africaine franc
Religions: Muslim, Catholic, Protestant, animist
Languages: French, Arabic, Sara, more than 120 languages and dialects

Chile

Area: 291,930 sq mi
(756,096 sq km)
Population: 18,025,000
Capital: Santiago, pop. 6,472,000
Currency: Chilean peso
Religions: Roman Catholic, Evangelical
Language: Spanish

China

Area: 3,705,406 sq mi
(9,596,961 sq km)
Population: 1,371,920,000
Capital: Beijing, pop. 19,520,000
Currency: renminbi (yuan)
Religions: Taoist, Buddhist, Christian
Languages: Standard Chinese or Mandarin, Yue, Wu, Minbei, Minnan, Xiang, Gan, Hakka dialects

Colombia

Area: 440,831 sq mi
(1,141,748 sq km)
Population: 48,218,000
Capital: Bogotá, pop. 9,558,000
Currency: Colombian peso
Religion: Roman Catholic
Language: Spanish

Comoros

Area: 863 sq mi (2,235 sq km)
Population: 764,000
Capital: Moroni, pop. 56,000
Currency: Comoran franc
Religion: Sunni Muslim
Languages: Arabic, French, Shikomoro

Congo

Area: 132,047 sq mi (342,000 sq km)
Population: 4,755,000
Capital: Brazzaville, pop. 1,827,000
Currency: Communauté Financière Africaine franc
Religions: Christian, animist
Languages: French, Lingala, Monokutuba, local languages

Costa Rica

Area: 19,730 sq mi
(51,100 sq km)
Population: 4,832,000
Capital: San José, pop. 1,160,000
Currency: Costa Rican colón
Religions: Roman Catholic, Evangelical
Languages: Spanish, English

Côte d'Ivoire (Ivory Coast)

Area: 124,503 sq mi
(322,462 sq km)
Population: 23,281,000
Capitals: Abidjan, pop. 4,708,000; Yamoussoukro, pop. 259,000
Currency: Communauté Financière Africaine franc
Religions: Muslim, indigenous beliefs, Christian
Languages: French, Dioula, other native dialects

Croatia

Area: 21,831 sq mi
(56,542 sq km)
Population: 4,215,000
Capital: Zagreb, pop. 687,000
Currency: kuna
Religions: Roman Catholic, Orthodox
Language: Croatian

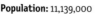

NECKTIES
ORIGINATED IN
CROATIA.

Cuba

Area: 42,803 sq mi
(110,860 sq km)
Population: 11,139,000
Capital: Havana, pop. 2,146,000
Currency: Cuban peso
Religions: Roman Catholic, Protestant, Jehovah's
Witnesses, Jewish, Santería
Language: Spanish

Cyprus

Area: 3,572 sq mi (9,251 sq km)
Population: 1,153,000
Capital: Nicosia, pop. 251,000
Currencies: euro; new Turkish
lira in Northern Cyprus
Religions: Greek Orthodox, Muslim, Maronite,
Armenian Apostolic
Languages: Greek, Turkish, English

Czech Republic (Czechia)

Area: 30,450 sq mi (78,866 sq km)
Population: 10,551,000
Capital: Prague, pop. 1,303,000
Currency: koruny
Religion: Roman Catholic
Language: Czech

Democratic Republic of the Congo

Area: 905,365 sq mi
(2,344,885 sq km)
Population: 73,340,000
Capital: Kinshasa, pop. 11,116,000
Currency: Congolese franc
Religions: Roman Catholic, Protestant, Kimbanguist,
Muslim, syncretic sects, indigenous beliefs
Languages: French, Lingala, Kingwana, Kikongo, Tshiluba

Denmark

Area: 16,640 sq mi (43,098 sq km)
Population: 5,676,000
Capital: Copenhagen, pop. 1,255,000
Currency: Danish krone
Religions: Evangelical Lutheran, other Protestant,
Roman Catholic
Languages: Danish, Faroese, Greenlandic, German,
English as second language

Djibouti

Area: 8,958 sq mi
(23,200 sq km)
Population: 900,000
Capital: Djibouti, pop. 522,000
Currency: Djiboutian franc
Religions: Muslim, Christian
Languages: French, Arabic, Somali, Afar

Dominica

Area: 290 sq mi (751 sq km)
Population: 68,000
Capital: Roseau, pop. 15,000
Currency: East Caribbean
dollar
Religions: Roman Catholic, Seventh-day Adventist,
Pentecostal, Baptist, Methodist, other Christian
Languages: English, French patois

Dominican Republic

Area: 18,704 sq mi
(48,442 sq km)
Population: 10,508,000
Capital: Santo Domingo,
pop. 2,873,000
Currency: Dominican peso
Religion: Roman Catholic
Language: Spanish

Ecuador

Area: 109,483 sq mi (283,560 sq km)
Population: 16,279,000
Capital: Quito, pop. 1,699,000
Currency: U.S. dollar
Religion: Roman Catholic
Languages: Spanish, Quechua, other Amerindian languages

Egypt

Area: 386,874 sq mi (1,002,000 sq km)
Population: 89,074,000
Capital: Cairo, pop. 18,419,000
Currency: Egyptian pound
Religions: Muslim (mostly Sunni), Coptic Christian
Languages: Arabic, English, French

El Salvador

Area: 8,124 sq mi (21,041 sq km)
Population: 6,366,000
Capital: San Salvador, pop. 1,097,000
Currency: U.S. dollar
Religions: Roman Catholic, Protestant
Languages: Spanish, Nahua

5 cool things about EL SALVADOR

1. El Salvador is the smallest country in Central America; at its longest, it is only 88 miles (142 km) long.

2. Known as the Land of Volcanoes, there are over 20 active volcanoes in El Salvador.

3. Green toucans can be found in the cloud forest on Monte Cristo Mountain.

4. In 2005, 13,380 people gathered to brush their teeth together at a world record-setting event in San Salvador.

5. El Salvador's coastlines are popular spots for surfers from around the world.

Equatorial Guinea

Area: 10,831 sq mi (28,051 sq km)
Population: 805,000
Capital: Malabo, pop. 145,000
Currency: Communauté Financière Africaine franc
Religions: Christian (predominantly Roman Catholic), pagan practices
Languages: Spanish, French, Fang, Bubi

Equatorial Guinea is a nesting site FOR ENDANGERED SEA TURTLES.

Eritrea

Area: 45,406 sq mi (117,600 sq km)
Population: 5,200,000
Capital: Asmara, pop. 775,000
Currency: nakfa
Religions: Muslim, Coptic Christian, Roman Catholic
Languages: Afar, Arabic, Tigre, Kunama, Tigrinya, other Cushitic languages

Estonia

Area: 17,462 sq mi (45,227 sq km)
Population: 1,311,000
Capital: Tallinn, pop. 392,000
Currency: euro
Religions: Evangelical Lutheran, Orthodox
Languages: Estonian, Russian

Ethiopia

Area: 426,373 sq mi (1,104,300 sq km)
Population: 98,148,000
Capital: Addis Ababa, pop. 3,168,000
Currency: birr
Religions: Christian, Muslim, traditional
Languages: Amharic, Oromigna, Tigrinya, Guaragigna

Fiji

Area: 7,095 sq mi
(18,376 sq km)
Population: 867,000
Capital: Suva, pop. 176,000
Currency: Fijian dollar
Religions: Christian (Methodist, Roman Catholic, Assembly of God), Hindu (Sanatan), Muslim (Sunni)
Languages: English, Fijian, Hindustani

France

Area: 210,026 sq mi
(543,965 sq km)
Population: 64,347,000
Capital: Paris, pop. 10,764,000
Currency: euro
Religions: Roman Catholic, Muslim
Language: French

Finland

Area: 130,558 sq mi
(338,145 sq km)
Population: 5,476,000
Capital: Helsinki, pop. 1,170,000
Currency: euro
Religion: Lutheran Church of Finland
Languages: Finnish, Swedish

Gabon

Area: 103,347 sq mi (267,667 sq km)
Population: 1,751,000
Capital: Libreville, pop. 695,000
Currency: Communauté Financière Africaine franc
Religions: Christian, animist
Languages: French, Fang, Myene, Nzebi, Bapounou/Eschira, Bandjabi

You Are There!
Fiji Barrier Reef

After slipping on some fins and a snorkel mask, you plunge into the turquoise Pacific Ocean. The water is so clear, you can see straight to the bottom as the sunlight filters down in glittering rays around you. This is what it's like to snorkel in Fiji: a network of some 320 islands all surrounded by about 4,000 square miles (10,360 sq km) of coral reef. Hundreds of species, like turtles, seabirds, and fish, call the "Soft Coral Capital of the World" home. A dip into the waters will welcome you with breathtaking sights, like schools of tropical fish in a rainbow of colors and giant clams that grow as long as a baseball bat. It's like swimming in your very own aquarium!

Gambia

Area: 4,361 sq mi (11,295 sq km)
Population: 2,022,000
Capital: Banjul, pop. 489,000
Currency: dalasi
Religions: Muslim, Christian
Languages: English, Mandinka, Wolof, Fula, other indigenous vernaculars

Georgia

Area: 26,911 sq mi (69,700 sq km)
Population: 3,804,000
Capital: Tbilisi, pop. 1,150,000
Currency: lari
Religions: Orthodox Christian, Muslim, Armenian-Gregorian
Languages: Georgian, Russian, Armenian, Azeri, Abkhaz

Germany

Area: 137,847 sq mi (357,022 sq km)
Population: 81,132,000
Capital: Berlin, pop. 3,547,000
Currency: euro
Religions: Protestant, Roman Catholic, Muslim
Language: German

Ghana

Area: 92,100 sq mi (238,537 sq km)
Population: 27,673,000
Capital: Accra, pop. 2,242,000
Currency: Ghana cedi
Religions: Christian (Pentecostal/Charismatic, Protestant, Roman Catholic, other), Muslim, traditional beliefs
Languages: Asante, Ewe, Fante, Boron (Brong), Dagomba, Dangme, Dagarte (Dagaba), Akyem, Ga, English

Greece

Area: 50,949 sq mi (131,957 sq km)
Population: 11,521,000
Capital: Athens, pop. 3,060,000
Currency: euro
Religion: Greek Orthodox
Languages: Greek, English, French

Grenada

Area: 133 sq mi (344 sq km)
Population: 111,000
Capital: St. George's, pop. 38,000
Currency: East Caribbean dollar
Religions: Roman Catholic, Anglican, other Protestant
Languages: English, French patois

Guatemala

Area: 42,042 sq mi (108,889 sq km)
Population: 16,184,000
Capital: Guatemala City, pop. 2,874,000
Currency: quetzal
Religions: Roman Catholic, Protestant, indigenous Maya beliefs
Languages: Spanish, 23 official Amerindian languages

Guinea

Area: 94,926 sq mi (245,857 sq km)
Population: 10,986,000
Capital: Conakry, pop. 1,886,000
Currency: Guinean franc
Religions: Muslim, Christian, indigenous beliefs
Languages: French, ethnic languages

Guinea-Bissau

Area: 13,948 sq mi (36,125 sq km)
Population: 1,788,000
Capital: Bissau, pop. 473,000
Currency: Communauté Financière Africaine franc
Religions: indigenous beliefs, Muslim, Christian
Languages: Portuguese, Crioulo, African languages

Guyana

Area: 83,000 sq mi (214,969 sq km)
Population: 743,000
Capital: Georgetown, pop. 124,000
Currency: Guyanese dollar
Religions: Christian, Hindu, Muslim
Languages: English, Amerindian dialects, Creole, Hindustani, Urdu

Haiti

Area: 10,714 sq mi (27,750 sq km)
Population: 10,924,000
Capital: Port-au-Prince,
pop. 2,376,000
Currency: gourde
Religions: Roman Catholic, Protestant
(Baptist, Pentecostal, other)
Languages: French, Creole

Honduras

Area: 43,433 sq mi
(112,492 sq km)
Population: 8,340,000
Capital: Tegucigalpa,
pop. 1,101,000
Currency: lempira
Religions: Roman Catholic, Protestant
Languages: Spanish, Amerindian dialects

Hungary

Area: 35,919 sq mi (93,030 sq km)
Population: 9,835,000
Capital: Budapest, pop. 1,717,000
Currency: forint
Religions: Roman Catholic, Calvinist, Lutheran
Language: Hungarian

Iceland

Area: 39,769 sq mi
(103,000 sq km)
Population: 331,000
Capital: Reykjavík, pop. 184,000
Currency: Icelandic krona
Religion: Lutheran Church of Iceland
Languages: Icelandic, English, Nordic
languages, German

India

Area: 1,269,221 sq mi (3,287,270 sq km)
Population: 1,314,098,000
Capital: New Delhi, pop. 24,953,000
(part of Delhi metropolitan area)
Currency: Indian rupee
Religions: Hindu, Muslim
Languages: Hindi, 21 other official languages,
Hindustani (popular Hindi/Urdu variant in the north)

Indonesia

Area: 742,308 sq mi
(1,922,570 sq km)
Population: 255,742,000
Capital: Jakarta, pop. 10,176,000
Currency: Indonesian rupiah
Religions: Muslim, Protestant, Roman Catholic
Languages: Bahasa Indonesia (modified form of Malay),
English, Dutch, Javanese, local dialects

Iran

Area: 636,296 sq mi
(1,648,000 sq km)
Population: 78,483,000
Capital: Tehran, pop. 8,353,000
Currency: Iranian rial
Religions: Shiite Muslim, Sunni Muslim
Languages: Persian, Turkic, Kurdish, Luri,
Baluchi, Arabic

Iraq

Area: 168,754 sq mi
(437,072 sq km)
Population: 37,056,000
Capital: Baghdad, pop. 6,483,000
Currency: Iraqi dinar
Religions: Shiite Muslim, Sunni Muslim
Languages: Arabic, Kurdish, Assyrian, Armenian

Ireland (Éire)

Area: 27,133 sq mi
(70,273 sq km)
Population: 4,630,000
Capital: Dublin, pop. 1,155,000
Currency: euro
Religions: Roman Catholic, Church of Ireland
Languages: Irish (Gaelic), English

Israel

Area: 8,550 sq mi (22,145 sq km)
Population: 8,375,000
Capital: Jerusalem, pop. 829,000
Currency: new Israeli sheqel
Religions: Jewish, Muslim
Languages: Hebrew, Arabic, English

Italy

Area: 116,345 sq mi
(301,333 sq km)
Population: 62,467,000
Capital: Rome, pop. 3,697,000
Currency: euro
Religions: Roman Catholic, Protestant, Jewish, Muslim
Languages: Italian, German, French, Slovene

Japan

Area: 145,902 sq mi (377,887 sq km)
Population: 126,867,000
Capital: Tokyo, pop. 37,833,000
Currency: yen
Religions: Shinto, Buddhist
Language: Japanese

Jamaica

Area: 4,244 sq mi
(10,991 sq km)
Population: 2,727,000
Capital: Kingston, pop. 587,000
Currency: Jamaican dollar
Religions: Protestant (Church of God, Seventh-day Adventist, Pentecostal, Baptist, Anglican, other)
Languages: English, English patois

Jordan

Area: 34,495 sq mi
(89,342 sq km)
Population: 8,118,000
Capital: Amman, pop. 1,148,000
Currency: Jordanian dinar
Religions: Sunni Muslim, Christian
Languages: Arabic, English

You Are There!

Tanjung Puting, Indonesia

There are only two places on the planet where you can spot a wild orangutan—the islands of Borneo and Sumatra. To get a glance of these big orange apes in person, head to Indonesia's Tanjung Puting National Park on the island of Borneo. Here, you can travel with a tour group deep within the forest to ogle orangutans. Tour guides dole out bananas and vitamin-rich milk to lure the animals as visitors stand at a safe distance to watch the apes in action. Don't forget to bring your camera: Orangutans—which share much of the same genetic code as humans—just may strike some funny poses as you snap away!

Asia ● Europe ● North America ● South America

303

Kazakhstan

Area: 1,049,155 sq mi (2,717,300 sq km)
Population: 17,544,000
Capital: Astana, pop. 741,000
Currency: tenge
Religions: Muslim, Russian Orthodox
Languages: Kazakh (Qazaq), Russian

Kiribati

Area: 313 sq mi (811 sq km)
Population: 113,000
Capital: Tarawa, pop. 46,000
Currency: Australian dollar
Religions: Roman Catholic, Protestant (Congregational)
Languages: I-Kiribati, English

Kenya

Area: 224,081 sq mi (580,367 sq km)
Population: 44,306,000
Capital: Nairobi, pop. 3,768,000
Currency: Kenyan shilling
Religions: Protestant, Roman Catholic, Muslim, indigenous beliefs
Languages: English, Kiswahili, many indigenous languages

Kosovo

Area: 4,203 sq mi (10,887 sq km)
Population: 1,802,000
Capital: Prishtina, pop. 207,500
Currency: euro
Religions: Muslim, Serbian Orthodox, Roman Catholic
Languages: Albanian, Serbian, Bosnian, Turkish, Roma

You Are There!
Bokeo Nature Reserve, Laos

Up for an adventure? Head to the Bokeo Nature Reserve, a lush rain forest in northern Laos. There, you can take a three-day tour exploring the depths of this wilderness while looking out for some of the area's most coveted wildlife, including tigers, black bears, clouded leopards, and black-crested gibbons. Shoot down a series of zip lines cutting through the rain forest's canopy, then cool off in a swimming hole found at the base of a rushing waterfall. And when you need a place to rest your head? Spend the night in a tree house nestled 130 feet (40 m) aboveground. No need to set an alarm clock: The gibbons' screeching call will wake you right up.

COLOR KEY ● Africa ● Australia, New Zealand, and Oceania

Kuwait

Area: 6,880 sq mi
(17,818 sq km)
Population: 3,838,000
Capital: Kuwait City,
pop. 2,680,000
Currency: Kuwaiti dinar
Religions: Sunni Muslim, Shiite Muslim
Languages: Arabic, English

Kyrgyzstan

Area: 77,182 sq mi
(199,900 sq km)
Population: 5,951,000
Capital: Bishkek, pop. 858,000
Currency: som
Religions: Muslim, Russian Orthodox
Languages: Kyrgyz, Uzbek, Russian

Laos

Area: 91,429 sq mi
(236,800 sq km)
Population: 6,903,000
Capital: Vientiane, pop. 946,000
Currency: kip
Religions: Buddhist, animist
Languages: Lao, French, English, various ethnic
languages

Latvia

Area: 24,938 sq mi
(64,589 sq km)
Population: 1,978,000
Capital: Riga, pop. 629,000
Currency: Latvian lat
Religions: Lutheran, Roman Catholic,
Russian Orthodox
Languages: Latvian, Russian, Lithuanian

Lebanon

Area: 4,036 sq mi (10,452 sq km)
Population: 6,185,000
Capital: Beirut, pop. 2,179,000
Currency: Lebanese pound
Religions: Muslim, Christian
Languages: Arabic, French, English, Armenian

Lesotho

Area: 11,720 sq mi (30,355 sq km)
Population: 1,924,000
Capital: Maseru, pop. 267,000
Currencies: loti; South African rand
Religions: Christian, indigenous beliefs
Languages: Sesotho, English, Zulu, Xhosa

Liberia

Area: 43,000 sq mi
(111,370 sq km)
Population: 4,503,000
Capital: Monrovia,
pop. 1,224,000
Currency: Liberian dollar
Religions: Christian, indigenous beliefs, Muslim
Languages: English, some 20 ethnic languages

Libya

Area: 679,362 sq mi
(1,759,540 sq km)
Population: 6,317,000
Capital: Tripoli, pop. 1,126,000
Currency: Libyan dinar
Religion: Sunni Muslim
Languages: Arabic, Italian, English

Liechtenstein

Area: 62 sq mi (160 sq km)
Population: 38,000
Capital: Vaduz, pop. 5,000
Currency: Swiss franc
Religions: Roman Catholic, Protestant
Languages: German, Alemannic dialect

Lithuania

Area: 25,212 sq mi
(65,300 sq km)
Population: 2,911,000
Capital: Vilnius, pop. 519,000
Currency: litas
Religions: Roman Catholic, Russian Orthodox
Languages: Lithuanian, Russian, Polish

Luxembourg

Area: 998 sq mi (2,586 sq km)
Population: 569,000
Capital: Luxembourg, pop. 107,000
Currency: euro
Religions: Roman Catholic, Protestant, Jewish, Muslim
Languages: Luxembourgish, German, French

Macedonia

Area: 9,928 sq mi (25,713 sq km)
Population: 2,070,000
Capital: Skopje, pop. 501,000
Currency: Macedonian denar
Religions: Macedonian Orthodox, Muslim
Languages: Macedonian, Albanian, Turkish

Madagascar

Area: 226,658 sq mi (587,041 sq km)
Population: 23,047,000
Capital: Antananarivo, pop. 2,487,000
Currency: Madagascar ariary
Religions: indigenous beliefs, Christian, Muslim
Languages: English, French, Malagasy

Malawi

Area: 45,747 sq mi (118,484 sq km)
Population: 17,174,000
Capital: Lilongwe, pop. 867,000
Currency: Malawian kwacha
Religions: Christian, Muslim
Languages: Chichewa, Chinyanja, Chiyao, Chitumbuka

Malaysia

Area: 127,355 sq mi (329,847 sq km)
Population: 30,789,000
Capital: Kuala Lumpur, pop. 6,629,000
Currency: ringgit
Religions: Muslim, Buddhist, Christian, Hindu
Languages: Bahasa Malaysia, English, Chinese, Tamil, Telugu, Malayalam, Panjabi, Thai, indigenous languages

Maldives

Area: 115 sq mi (298 sq km)
Population: 347,000
Capital: Male, pop. 156,000
Currency: rufiyaa
Religion: Sunni Muslim
Languages: Maldivian Dhivehi, English

Of the 1,190 islands that make up the Maldives, SOME 1,000 ARE UNINHABITED.

Mali

Area: 478,841 sq mi (1,240,192 sq km)
Population: 16,749,000
Capital: Bamako, pop. 2,386,000
Currency: Communauté Financière Africaine franc
Religions: Muslim, indigenous beliefs
Languages: Bambara, French, numerous African languages

Malta

Area: 122 sq mi (316 sq km)
Population: 431,000
Capital: Valletta, pop. 197,000
Currency: euro
Religion: Roman Catholic
Languages: Maltese, English

Marshall Islands

Area: 70 sq mi (181 sq km)
Population: 55,000
Capital: Majuro, pop. 31,000
Currency: U.S. dollar
Religions: Protestant, Assembly of God, Roman Catholic
Language: Marshallese

COLOR KEY ● Africa ● Australia, New Zealand, and Oceania

Mauritania

Area: 397,955 sq mi
(1,030,700 sq km)
Population: 3,641,000
Capital: Nouakchott, pop. 945,000
Currency: ouguiya
Religion: Muslim
Languages: Arabic, Pulaar, Soninke, French,
Hassaniya, Wolof

Mauritius

Area: 788 sq mi (2,040 sq km)
Population: 1,263,000
Capital: Port Louis, pop. 135,000
Currency: Mauritian rupee
Religions: Hindu, Roman Catholic,
Muslim, other Christian
Languages: Creole, Bhojpuri, French

Mexico

Area: 758,449 sq mi
(1,964,375 sq km)
Population: 127,017,000
Capital: Mexico City,
pop. 20,843,000
Currency: Mexican peso
Religions: Roman Catholic, Protestant
Languages: Spanish, Mayan, other indigenous languages

5 cool things about MEXICO

1. Tabasco sauce and Chihuahua dogs share
   their names with two states in Mexico.

2. A Mexican flag larger than an Olympic
   swimming pool is the biggest flag flown
   from a flagpole—so far.

3. Built on a bed of a dried-out lake, Mexico
   City has sunk 26 feet (8 m) in the last
   100 years.

4. The volcano rabbit is found only on the
   slopes of volcanoes in central Mexico.

5. Founded in 1551, Universidad Nacional
   Autónoma de México (UNAM) is North
   America's oldest university.

Micronesia

Area: 271 sq mi (702 sq km)
Population: 103,000
Capital: Palikir, pop. 7,000
Currency: U.S. dollar
Religions: Roman Catholic, Protestant
Languages: English, Trukese, Pohnpeian, Yapese,
other indigenous languages

Moldova

Area: 13,050 sq mi
(33,800 sq km)
Population: 4,109,000
Capital: Chisinau,
pop. 721,000
Currency: Moldovan leu
Religion: Eastern Orthodox
Languages: Moldovan, Russian, Gagauz

Monaco

Area: 0.8 sq mi (2.0 sq km)
Population: 38,000
Capital: Monaco, pop. 38,000
Currency: euro
Religion: Roman Catholic
Languages: French, English, Italian, Monegasque

Mongolia

Area: 603,909 sq mi
(1,564,116 sq km)
Population: 3,029,000
Capital: Ulaanbaatar,
pop. 1,334,000
Currency: togrog/tugrik
Religions: Buddhist Lamaist, Shamanist, Christian
Languages: Khalkha Mongol, Turkic, Russian

Montenegro

Area: 5,333 sq mi
(13,812 sq km)
Population: 622,000
Capital: Podgorica, pop. 165,000
Currency: euro
Religions: Orthodox, Muslim, Roman Catholic
Languages: Serbian (Ijekavian dialect), Bosnian,
Albanian, Croatian

Morocco

Area: 172,414 sq mi
(446,550 sq km)
Population: 34,121,000
Capital: Rabat, pop. 1,932,000
Currency: Moroccan dirham
Religion: Muslim
Languages: Arabic, Berber dialects, French

Myanmar (Burma)

Area: 261,218 sq mi
(676,552 sq km)
Population: 52,147,000
Capitals: Nay Pyi Taw, pop.
1,016,000; Yangon (Rangoon), pop. 4,802,000
Currency: kyat
Religions: Buddhist, Christian, Muslim
Languages: Burmese, minority ethnic languages

Mozambique

Area: 308,642 sq mi
(799,380 sq km)
Population: 25,736,000
Capital: Maputo, pop. 1,174,000
Currency: metical
Religions: Roman Catholic, Muslim, Zionist Christian
Languages: Emakhuwa, Xichangana, Portuguese,
Elomwe, Cisena, Echuwabo, other local languages

Namibia

Area: 318,261 sq mi
(824,292 sq km)
Population: 2,482,000
Capital: Windhoek, pop. 356,000
Currencies: Namibian dollar;
South African rand
Religions: Lutheran, other Christian, indigenous beliefs
Languages: Afrikaans, German, English

You Are There!
Namib-Naukluft National Park, Namibia

Sand dunes as tall as a skyscraper? Only in this national park, where high winds form these star-shaped dunes in the Sossusvlei area. Here they rise from the ground like reddish orange mountains. One of the world's largest national parks, Namib-Naukluft covers an area about the size of Costa Rica and is home to an array of animals such as Hartmann's mountain zebras, leopards, and flamingos. The park's main attraction, of course, is its amazing dunes.

COLOR KEY ● Africa ● Australia, New Zealand, and Oceania

Nauru

Area: 8 sq mi (21 sq km)
Population: 11,000
Capital: Yaren, pop. 10,000
Currency: Australian dollar
Religions: Protestant, Roman Catholic
Languages: Nauruan, English

Nepal

Area: 56,827 sq mi (147,181 sq km)
Population: 28,039,000
Capital: Kathmandu, pop. 1,142,000
Currency: Nepalese rupee
Religions: Hindu, Buddhist, Muslim, Kirant
Languages: Nepali, Maithali, Bhojpuri, Tharu, Tamang, Newar, Magar

Netherlands

Area: 16,034 sq mi (41,528 sq km)
Population: 16,942,000
Capital: Amsterdam, pop. 1,084,000
Currency: euro
Religions: Roman Catholic, Dutch Reformed, Calvinist, Muslim
Languages: Dutch, Frisian

New Zealand

Area: 104,454 sq mi (270,534 sq km)
Population: 4,598,000
Capital: Wellington, pop. 380,000
Currency: New Zealand dollar
Religions: Anglican, Roman Catholic, Presbyterian, other Christian
Languages: English, Maori

Nicaragua

Area: 50,193 sq mi (130,000 sq km)
Population: 6,262,000
Capital: Managua, pop. 951,000
Currency: gold cordoba
Religions: Roman Catholic, Evangelical
Language: Spanish

Niger

Area: 489,191 sq mi (1,267,000 sq km)
Population: 18,884,000
Capital: Niamey, pop. 1,058,000
Currency: Communauté Financière Africaine franc
Religions: Muslim, other (includes indigenous beliefs and Christian)
Languages: French, Hausa, Djerma

Nigeria

Area: 356,669 sq mi (923,768 sq km)
Population: 181,839,000
Capital: Abuja, pop. 2,301,000
Currency: naira
Religions: Muslim, Christian, indigenous beliefs
Languages: English, Hausa, Yoruba, Igbo (Ibo), Fulani

North Korea

Area: 46,540 sq mi (120,538 sq km)
Population: 24,983,000
Capital: Pyongyang, pop. 2,856,000
Currency: North Korean won
Religions: Buddhist, Confucianist, some Christian and syncretic Chondogyo
Language: Korean

Norway

Area: 125,004 sq mi (323,758 sq km)
Population: 5,194,000
Capital: Oslo, pop. 970,000
Currency: Norwegian krone
Religion: Church of Norway (Lutheran)
Languages: Bokmal Norwegian, Nynorsk Norwegian, Sami

Oman

Area: 119,500 sq mi (309,500 sq km)
Population: 4,201,000
Capital: Muscat, pop. 812,000
Currency: Omani rial
Religions: Ibadhi Muslim, Sunni Muslim, Shiite Muslim, Hindu
Languages: Arabic, English, Baluchi, Urdu, Indian dialects

● Asia ● Europe ● North America ● South America

Pakistan

Area: 307,374 sq mi
(796,095 sq km)
Population: 199,047,000
Capital: Islamabad, pop. 1,297,000
Currency: Pakistani rupee
Religions: Sunni Muslim, Shiite Muslim
Languages: Punjabi, Sindhi, Siraiki, Pashto, Urdu, Baluchi, Hindko, English

Palau

Area: 189 sq mi (489 sq km)
Population: 18,000
Capital: Melekeok, pop. 1,000
Currency: U.S. dollar
Religions: Roman Catholic, Protestant, Modekngei, Seventh-day Adventist
Languages: Palauan, Filipino, English, Chinese

Panama

Area: 29,157 sq mi (75,517 sq km)
Population: 3,980,000
Capital: Panama City,
pop. 1,638,000
Currencies: balboa; U.S. dollar
Religions: Roman Catholic, Protestant
Languages: Spanish, English

Papua New Guinea

Area: 178,703 sq mi (462,840 sq km)
Population: 7,745,000
Capital: Port Moresby, pop. 338,000
Currency: kina
Religions: indigenous beliefs, Roman Catholic, Lutheran, other Protestant
Languages: Melanesian Pidgin, 820 indigenous languages

Paraguay

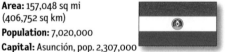

Area: 157,048 sq mi
(406,752 sq km)
Population: 7,020,000
Capital: Asunción, pop. 2,307,000
Currency: guarani
Religions: Roman Catholic, Protestant
Languages: Spanish, Guarani

Peru

Area: 496,224 sq mi
(1,285,216 sq km)
Population: 31,152,000
Capital: Lima, pop. 9,722,000
Currency: nuevo sol
Religion: Roman Catholic
Languages: Spanish, Quechua, Aymara, minor Amazonian languages

Philippines

Area: 115,831 sq mi
(300,000 sq km)
Population: 102,965,000
Capital: Manila,
pop. 12,764,000
Currency: Philippine peso
Religions: Roman Catholic, Muslim, other Christian
Languages: Filipino (based on Tagalog), English

Poland

Area: 120,728 sq mi
(312,685 sq km)
Population: 38,478,000
Capital: Warsaw, pop. 1,718,000
Currency: zloty
Religion: Roman Catholic
Language: Polish

Portugal

Area: 35,655 sq mi
(92,345 sq km)
Population: 10,349,000
Capital: Lisbon, pop. 2,869,000
Currency: euro
Religion: Roman Catholic
Languages: Portuguese, Mirandese

Qatar

Area: 4,448 sq mi
(11,521 sq km)
Population: 2,395,000
Capital: Doha, pop. 699,000
Currency: Qatari rial
Religions: Muslim, Christian
Languages: Arabic; English commonly a second language

Romania

Area: 92,043 sq mi
(238,391 sq km)
Population: 19,839,000
Capital: Bucharest, pop. 1,872,000
Currency: new leu
Religions: Eastern Orthodox, Protestant,
Roman Catholic
Languages: Romanian, Hungarian

Russia

Area: 6,592,850 sq mi
(17,075,400 sq km)
Population: 144,302,000
Capital: Moscow, pop. 12,063,000
Currency: ruble
Religions: Russian Orthodox, Muslim
Languages: Russian, many minority languages
*Note: Russia is in both Europe and Asia, but its capital is in Europe,
so it is classified here as a European country.*

Rwanda

Area: 10,169 sq mi
(26,338 sq km)
Population: 11,331,000
Capital: Kigali, pop. 1,223,000
Currency: Rwandan franc
Religions: Roman Catholic, Protestant,
Adventist, Muslim
Languages: Kinyarwanda, French, English, Kiswahili

Samoa

Area: 1,093 sq mi (2,831 sq km)
Population: 194,000
Capital: Apia, pop. 37,000
Currency: tala
Religions: Congregationalist, Roman Catholic,
Methodist, Church of Jesus Christ of Latter-day
Saints, Assembly of God, Seventh-day Adventist
Languages: Samoan (Polynesian), English

You Are There!
Nazaré, Portugal

Talk about monster waves! The surf's way up in Nazaré—a fishing village along Portugal's Atlantic coast—where one surfer recently caught a 100-foot (30-m) wave, possibly the biggest ever. An underwater canyon produces massive swells farther out to sea, so you can safely splash in much calmer waters closer to Nazaré's coastline. Or, take a funicular, a cliff railway, to the Promontório do Sítio, a clifftop sight offering one of the most famous views of the Portuguese coast. At 360 feet (110 m) above the beach, you can experience the epic waves from above.

● Asia ● Europe ● North America ● South America

San Marino

Area: 24 sq mi (61 sq km)
Population: 33,000
Capital: San Marino, pop. 4,000
Currency: euro
Religion: Roman Catholic
Language: Italian

Sao Tome and Principe

Area: 386 sq mi (1,001 sq km)
Population: 196,000
Capital: São Tomé, pop. 71,000
Currency: dobra
Religions: Roman Catholic, Evangelical
Language: Portuguese

Saudi Arabia

Area: 756,985 sq mi (1,960,582 sq km)
Population: 31,565,000
Capital: Riyadh, pop. 6,195,000
Currency: Saudi riyal
Religion: Muslim
Language: Arabic

Senegal

Area: 75,955 sq mi (196,722 sq km)
Population: 14,690,000
Capital: Dakar, pop. 3,393,000
Currency: Communauté Financière Africaine franc
Religions: Muslim, Christian (mostly Roman Catholic)
Languages: French, Wolof, Pulaar, Jola, Mandinka

Serbia

Area: 29,913 sq mi (77,474 sq km)
Population: 7,097,000
Capital: Belgrade, pop. 1,181,000
Currency: Serbian dinar
Religions: Serbian Orthodox, Roman Catholic, Muslim
Languages: Serbian, Hungarian

Seychelles

Area: 176 sq mi (455 sq km)
Population: 93,000
Capital: Victoria, pop. 26,000
Currency: Seychelles rupee
Religions: Roman Catholic, Anglican, other Christian
Languages: Creole, English

Sierra Leone

Area: 27,699 sq mi (71,740 sq km)
Population: 6,503,000
Capital: Freetown, pop. 986,000
Currency: leone
Religions: Muslim, indigenous beliefs, Christian
Languages: English, Mende, Temne, Krio

Singapore

Area: 255 sq mi (660 sq km)
Population: 5,541,000
Capital: Singapore, pop. 5,500,000
Currency: Singapore dollar
Religions: Buddhist, Muslim, Taoist, Roman Catholic, Hindu, other Christian
Languages: Mandarin, English, Malay, Hokkien, Cantonese, Teochew, Tamil

Slovakia

Area: 18,932 sq mi (49,035 sq km)
Population: 5,424,000
Capital: Bratislava, pop. 403,000
Currency: euro
Religions: Roman Catholic, Protestant, Greek Catholic
Languages: Slovak, Hungarian

Slovenia

Area: 7,827 sq mi (20,273 sq km)
Population: 2,064,000
Capital: Ljubljana, pop. 279,000
Currency: euro
Religions: Roman Catholic, Muslim, Orthodox
Languages: Slovene, Croatian, Serbian

COLOR KEY ● Africa ● Australia, New Zealand, and Oceania

Solomon Islands

Area: 10,954 sq mi
(28,370 sq km)
Population: 642,000
Capital: Honiara, pop. 73,000
Currency: Solomon Islands dollar
Religions: Church of Melanesia, Roman Catholic, South Seas Evangelical, other Christian
Languages: Melanesian pidgin, 120 indigenous languages

Somalia

Area: 246,201 sq mi
(637,657 sq km)
Population: 11,123,000
Capital: Mogadishu, pop. 2,014,000
Currency: Somali shilling
Religion: Sunni Muslim
Languages: Somali, Arabic, Italian, English

South Africa

Area: 470,693 sq mi (1,219,090 sq km)
Population: 55,041,000
Capitals: Pretoria (Tshwane), pop. 1,991,000; Bloemfontein, pop. 496,000; Cape Town, pop. 3,624,000
Currency: rand
Religions: Zion Christian, Pentecostal, Catholic, Methodist, Dutch Reformed, Anglican, other Christian
Languages: IsiZulu, IsiXhosa, Afrikaans, Sepedi, English

5 cool things about SOUTH AFRICA

1. There are over six million trees in the city of Johannesburg, placing it among the world's largest man-made urban forests.

2. South Africa's Namaqua National Park is home to the speckled padloper, believed to be the world's smallest tortoise.

3. June, July, and August are a great time to hit the slopes at a ski resort in South Africa's Drakensberg mountains.

4. You can ride a cable car over 3,500 feet (1,070 m) in five minutes to the top of Cape Town's Table Mountain.

5. South Africa has 11 official languages.

South Korea

Area: 38,321 sq mi
(99,250 sq km)
Population: 50,714,000
Capital: Seoul, pop. 9,775,000
Currency: South Korean won
Religions: Christian, Buddhist
Languages: Korean, English

South Sudan

Area: 248,777 sq mi
(644,329 sq km)
Population: 12,152,000
Capital: Juba, pop. 307,000
Currency: South Sudan pound
Religions: animist, Christian
Languages: English, Arabic, regional languages (Dinke, Nuer, Bari, Zande, Shilluk)

Spain

Area: 195,363 sq mi (505,988 sq km)
Population: 46,368,000
Capital: Madrid, pop. 6,133,000
Currency: euro
Religion: Roman Catholic
Languages: Castilian Spanish, Catalan, Galician, Basque

Sri Lanka

Area: 25,299 sq mi
(65,525 sq km)
Population: 20,869,000
Capitals: Colombo, pop. 704,000; Sri Jayewardenepura Kotte, pop. 128,000
Currency: Sri Lankan rupee
Religions: Buddhist, Muslim, Hindu, Christian
Languages: Sinhala, Tamil

St. Kitts and Nevis

Area: 104 sq mi (269 sq km)
Population: 46,000
Capital: Basseterre, pop. 14,000
Currency: East Caribbean dollar
Religions: Anglican, other Protestant, Roman Catholic
Language: English

St. Lucia

Area: 238 sq mi (616 sq km)
Population: 175,000
Capital: Castries, pop. 22,000
Currency: East Caribbean dollar
Religions: Roman Catholic, Seventh-day Adventist, Pentecostal
Languages: English, French patois

St. Vincent and the Grenadines

Area: 150 sq mi (389 sq km)
Population: 110,000
Capital: Kingstown, pop. 27,000
Currency: East Caribbean dollar
Religions: Anglican, Methodist, Roman Catholic
Languages: English, French patois

Sudan

Area: 718,722 sq mi (1,861,484 sq km)
Population: 40,884,000
Capital: Khartoum, pop. 5,000,000
Currency: Sudanese pound
Religions: Sunni Muslim, indigenous beliefs, Christian
Languages: Arabic, Nubian, Ta Bedawie, many diverse dialects of Nilotic, Nilo-Hamitic, Sudanic languages

Suriname

Area: 63,037 sq mi (163,265 sq km)
Population: 576,000
Capital: Paramaribo, pop. 234,000
Currency: Suriname dollar
Religions: Hindu, Protestant (predominantly Moravian), Roman Catholic, Muslim, indigenous beliefs
Languages: Dutch, English, Sranang Tongo, Hindustani, Javanese

Swaziland

Area: 6,704 sq mi (17,363 sq km)
Population: 1,286,000
Capitals: Mbabane, pop. 66,000; Lobamba, pop. 4,600
Currency: lilangeni
Religions: Zionist, Roman Catholic, Muslim
Languages: English, siSwati

Sweden

Area: 173,732 sq mi (449,964 sq km)
Population: 9,805,000
Capital: Stockholm, pop. 1,464,000
Currency: Swedish krona
Religion: Lutheran
Languages: Swedish, Sami, Finnish

Switzerland

Area: 15,940 sq mi (41,284 sq km)
Population: 8,293,000
Capital: Bern, pop. 358,000
Currency: Swiss franc
Religions: Roman Catholic, Protestant, Muslim
Languages: German, French, Italian, Romansh

Syria

Area: 71,498 sq mi (185,180 sq km)
Population: 17,065,000
Capital: Damascus, pop. 2,574,000
Currency: Syrian pound
Religions: Sunni, other Muslim (includes Alawite, Druze), Christian
Languages: Arabic, Kurdish, Armenian, Aramaic, Circassian

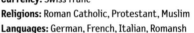

Tajikistan

Area: 55,251 sq mi (143,100 sq km)
Population: 8,452,000
Capital: Dushanbe, pop. 801,000
Currency: somoni
Religions: Sunni Muslim, Shiite Muslim
Languages: Tajik, Russian

Tanzania

Area: 364,900 sq mi (945,087 sq km)
Population: 52,291,000
Capitals: Dar es Salaam, pop. 5,116,000; Dodoma, pop. 228,000
Currency: Tanzanian shilling
Religions: Muslim, indigenous beliefs, Christian
Languages: Kiswahili, Kiunguja, English, Arabic, local languages

COLOR KEY ● Africa ● Australia, New Zealand, and Oceania

Thailand

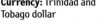

Area: 198,115 sq mi
(513,115 sq km)
Population: 65,121,000
Capital: Bangkok, pop. 9,098,000
Currency: baht
Religions: Buddhist, Muslim
Languages: Thai, English, ethnic dialects

GIANT STINGRAYS that grow to be THE SIZE OF CARS live in Thailand's Mae Klong River.

Timor-Leste (East Timor)

Area: 5,640 sq mi
(14,609 sq km)
Population: 1,245,000
Capital: Díli, pop. 228,000
Currency: U.S. dollar
Religion: Roman Catholic
Languages: Tetum, Portuguese, Indonesian, English,
indigenous languages

Togo

Area: 21,925 sq mi (56,785 sq km)
Population: 7,231,000
Capital: Lomé, pop. 930,000
Currency: Communauté
Financière Africaine franc
Religions: indigenous beliefs, Christian, Muslim
Languages: French, Ewe, Mina, Kabye, Dagomb

Tonga

Area: 289 sq mi (748 sq km)
Population: 103,000
Capital: Nuku'alofa,
pop. 25,000
Currency: pa'anga
Religion: Christian
Languages: Tongan, English

Trinidad and Tobago

Area: 1,980 sq mi (5,128 sq km)
Population: 1,351,000
Capital: Port of Spain, pop. 34,000
Currency: Trinidad and
Tobago dollar
Religions: Roman Catholic, Hindu, Anglican, Baptist
Languages: English, Caribbean Hindustani, French,
Spanish, Chinese

Tunisia

Area: 63,170 sq mi
(163,610 sq km)
Population: 11,026,000
Capital: Tunis, pop. 1,978,000
Currency: Tunisian dinar
Religion: Muslim
Languages: Arabic, French

Turkey

Area: 300,948 sq mi
(779,452 sq km)
Population: 78,215,000
Capital: Ankara, pop. 4,644,000
Currency: new Turkish lira
Religion: Muslim (mostly Sunni)
Languages: Turkish, Kurdish, Dimli (Zaza), Azeri,
Kabardian, Gagauz

Turkmenistan

Area: 188,456 sq mi
(488,100 sq km)
Population: 5,373,000
Capital: Ashgabat, pop. 735,000
Currency: Turkmen manat
Religions: Muslim, Eastern Orthodox
Languages: Turkmen, Russian, Uzbek

Tuvalu

Area: 10 sq mi (26 sq km)
Population: 12,000
Capital: Funafuti, pop. 6,000
Currencies: Australian dollar;
Tuvaluan dollar
Religion: Church of Tuvalu (Congregationalist)
Languages: Tuvaluan, English, Samoan, Kiribati

● Asia ● Europe ● North America ● South America

315

Uganda

Area: 93,104 sq mi
(241,139 sq km)
Population: 40,141,000
Capital: Kampala, pop. 1,863,000
Currency: Ugandan shilling
Religions: Protestant, Roman Catholic, Muslim
Languages: English, Ganda, other local languages, Kiswahili, Arabic

United Arab Emirates

Area: 30,000 sq mi
(77,700 sq km)
Population: 9,577,000
Capital: Abu Dhabi,
pop. 1,114,000
Currency: Emirati dirham
Religion: Muslim
Languages: Arabic, Persian, English, Hindi, Urdu

Ukraine

Area: 233,090 sq mi
(603,700 sq km)
Population: 42,828,000
Capital: Kiev, pop. 2,917,000
Currency: hryvnia
Religions: Ukrainian Orthodox, Orthodox, Ukrainian Greek Catholic
Languages: Ukrainian, Russian

United Kingdom

Area: 93,788 sq mi
(242,910 sq km)
Population: 65,092,000
Capital: London, pop. 10,189,000
Currency: British pound
Religions: Anglican, Roman Catholic, Presbyterian, Methodist
Languages: English, Welsh, Scottish form of Gaelic

You Are There!
Dubai, United Arab Emirates

Can you say dream destination? There's tons to do in Dubai, a city sitting on the coast of the Persian Gulf in the United Arab Emirates. Need a quick itinerary? First, take a lightning-quick elevator ride up to the top of Burj Khalifa, the tallest building in the world. From 148 stories up, watch the cars and people, as tiny as ants, mill below you. Once you're back on the ground, head on over to Ski Dubai, the Middle East's first indoor ski resort. No matter the weather, you can schuss down the slopes on man-made snow at this giant arena, complete with a black diamond run and a chairlift. While you're there, check out the resident king and gentoo penguins—you can even feed and hug one if you'd like. End your day with a fountain and light show on Burj Khalifa Lake in downtown Dubai. With the spray synched up to music and lights, it's literally a can't-miss sight: The water sprays as high as a 50-story building, making it the world's largest dancing fountain.

COLOR KEY   ● Africa   ● Australia, New Zealand, and Oceania

United States

Area: 3,794,083 sq mi
(9,826,630 sq km)
Population: 321,234,000
Capital: Washington, D.C.,
pop. 646,449
Currency: U.S. dollar
Religions: Protestant, Roman Catholic
Languages: English, Spanish

Uruguay

Area: 68,037 sq mi
(176,215 sq km)
Population: 3,562,000
Capital: Montevideo, pop. 1,698,000
Currency: Uruguayan peso
Religion: Roman Catholic
Language: Spanish

Uzbekistan

Area: 172,742 sq mi
(447,400 sq km)
Population: 31,291,000
Capital: Tashkent,
pop. 2,241,000
Currency: Uzbekistani sum
Religions: Muslim (mostly Sunni), Eastern Orthodox
Languages: Uzbek, Russian, Tajik

Vanuatu

Area: 4,707 sq mi (12,190 sq km)
Population: 278,000
Capital: Port Vila, pop. 53,000
Currency: vatu
Religions: Presbyterian, Anglican, Roman Catholic, other Christian, indigenous beliefs
Languages: more than 100 local languages, pidgin (known as Bislama or Bichelama)

Vatican City

Area: 0.2 sq mi (0.4 sq km)
Population: 1,000
Capital: Vatican City, pop. 1,000
Currency: euro
Religion: Roman Catholic
Languages: Italian, Latin, French

Venezuela

Area: 352,144 sq mi
(912,050 sq km)
Population: 30,620,000
Capital: Caracas, pop. 2,912,000
Currency: bolivar
Religion: Roman Catholic
Languages: Spanish, numerous indigenous dialects

Vietnam

Area: 127,844 sq mi
(331,114 sq km)
Population: 91,714,000
Capital: Hanoi, pop. 3,470,000
Currency: dong
Religions: Buddhist, Roman Catholic
Languages: Vietnamese, English, French, Chinese, Khmer

Yemen

Area: 207,286 sq mi
(536,869 sq km)
Population: 26,737,000
Capital: Sanaa, pop. 2,833,000
Currency: Yemeni rial
Religions: Muslim, including Shaf'i (Sunni) and Zaydi (Shiite)
Language: Arabic

Zambia

Area: 290,586 sq mi
(752,614 sq km)
Population: 15,474,000
Capital: Lusaka, pop. 2,078,000
Currency: Zambian kwacha
Religions: Christian, Muslim, Hindu
Languages: English, Bemba, Kaonda, Lozi, Lunda, Luvale, Nyanja, Tonga, about 70 other indigenous languages

Zimbabwe

Area: 150,872 sq mi
(390,757 sq km)
Population: 17,354,000
Capital: Harare, pop. 1,495,000
Currency: Zimbabwean dollar
Religions: Syncretic (part Christian, part indigenous beliefs), Christian, indigenous beliefs
Languages: English, Shona, Sindebele, tribal dialects

EUROPE
A View From Space

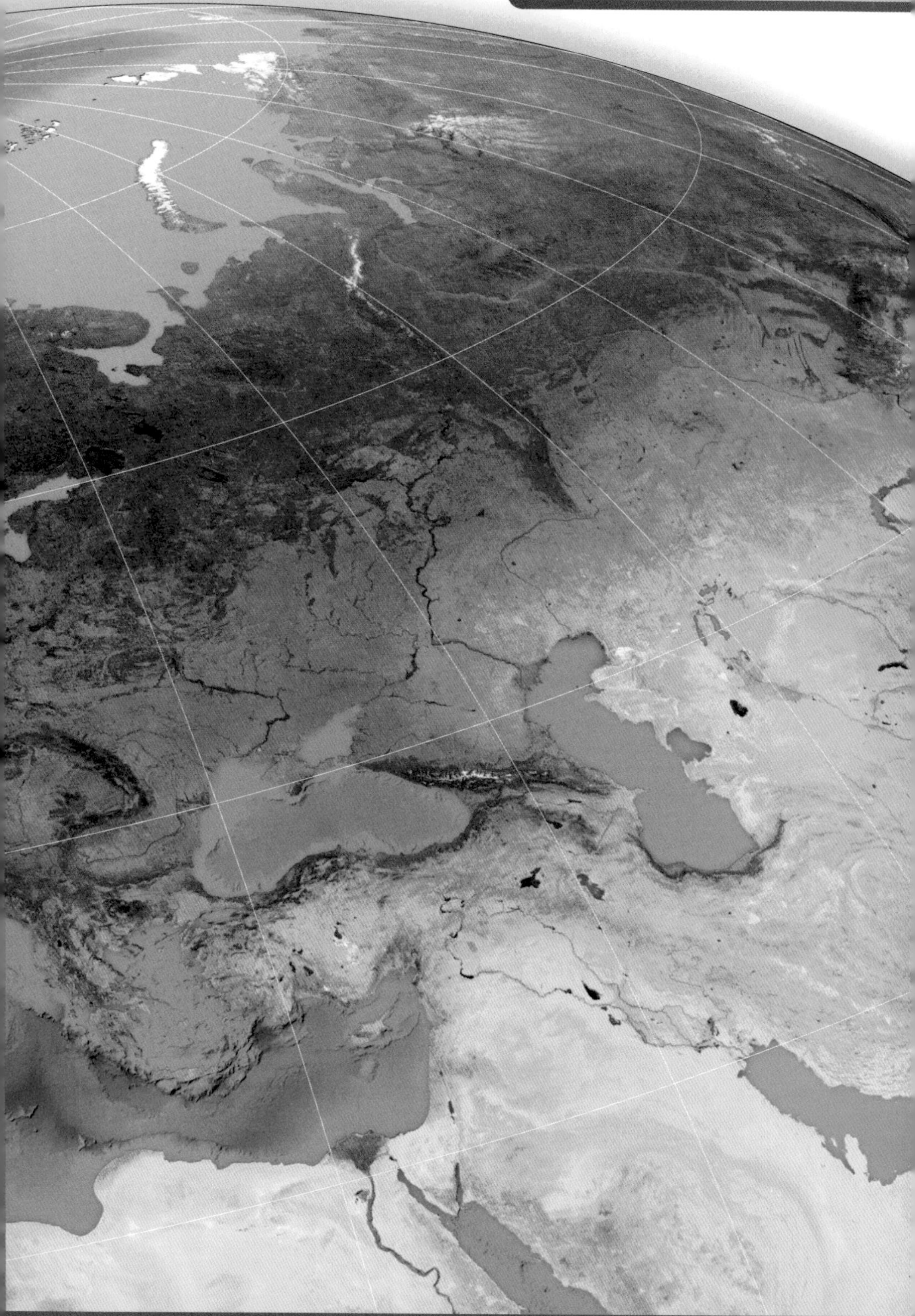

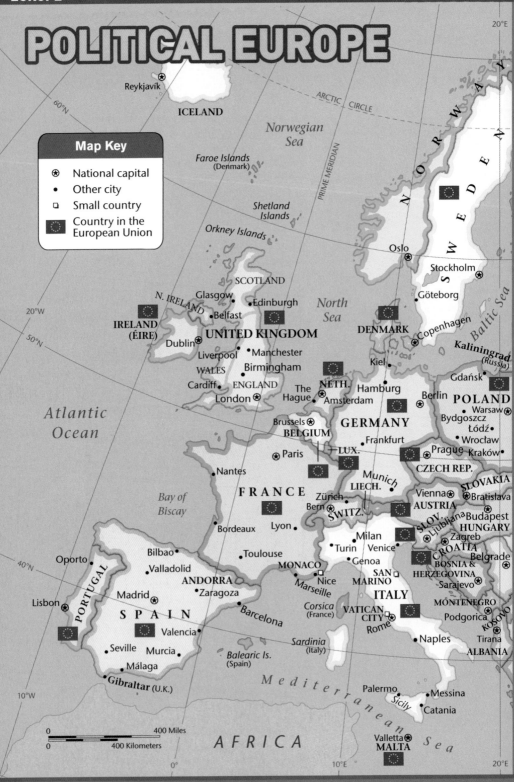

POLITICAL EUROPE

Reykjavík

ICELAND

ARCTIC CIRCLE

Norwegian
Sea

PRIME MERIDIAN

N O R W A Y

S W E D E N

Map Key

⊛ National capital

• Other city

▫ Small country

⊡ Country in the European Union

Faroe Islands
(Denmark)

Shetland
Islands

Orkney Islands

SCOTLAND

Glasgow
Edinburgh
Belfast

N. IRELAND

IRELAND
(ÉIRE)

Dublin

UNITED KINGDOM

Liverpool • Manchester
WALES • Birmingham
Cardiff • ENGLAND
London

North
Sea

DENMARK

Kiel

Hamburg

The
Hague
Amsterdam
NETH.

Oslo

Stockholm

Göteborg

Copenhagen

Baltic Sea

Kaliningrad
(Russia)

Gdańsk

Berlin

POLAND
Warsaw
Bydgoszcz
Łódź
Wrocław

Prague
Kraków

CZECH REP.

Atlantic
Ocean

Brussels
BELGIUM

Paris

LUX.

Frankfurt

GERMANY

Munich

LIECH.

Nantes

FRANCE

Zürich
Bern

SWITZ.

Vienna
AUSTRIA

Bratislava

SLOVAKIA

SLOV.
Ljubljana

Budapest
HUNGARY

Bay of
Biscay

Bordeaux

Lyon

Turin
Milan
Venice
Genoa

Zagreb

CROATIA

Belgrade

BOSNIA &
HERZEGOVINA

Oporto

Bilbao

Valladolid

ANDORRA

Zaragoza

PORTUGAL

Madrid

Lisbon

S P A I N

Valencia

Seville
Murcia
Málaga

Gibraltar (U.K.)

Toulouse

MONACO

Nice
Marseille

SAN
MARINO

ITALY

VATICAN
CITY
Rome

Corsica
(France)

Sardinia
(Italy)

Balearic Is.
(Spain)

Barcelona

M e d i t e r r a n e a n

Sarajevo

MONTENEGRO

Podgorica

KOSOVO

Tirana

ALBANIA

Naples

Palermo

Sicily

Messina

Catania

Valletta
MALTA

AFRICA

S e a

0   400 Miles

0   400 Kilometers

A commonly accepted division between Asia and Europe—marked here by a maroon, dashed line—is formed by the Ural Mountains, Ural River, Caspian Sea, Caucasus Mountains, and the Black Sea with its outlets, the Bosporus and Dardanelles.

PHYSICAL EUROPE

Iceland

Norwegian
Sea

ARCTIC CIRCLE

S C A N D I N A V I A

Gulf of

Faroe Islands

PRIME MERIDIAN

Shetland
Islands

Outer Hebrides

Orkney
Islands

North
Sea

Jutland

Baltic

Highlands

Zealand

Ireland

Great
Britain

N O R T H E R

Irish Sea

British Isles

Vistula

Celtic

Thames

Ruhr Valley

Elbe

Oder

C

Atlantic
Ocean

Sea

English Channel

Rhine

Brittany

Seine

Danube

Bay of
Biscay

Loire

Massif
Central

A L P S

Cantabrian Mts.

Mt. Blanc
15,781 ft
(4,810 m)

Rhône

Po

A p e n n i n e s

Douro

Pyrenees

Riviera

Ligurian
Sea

Adriatic Sea

Iberian

Ebro

Tagus

Corsica

Peninsula

Balearic Sea

Sardinia

Tyrrhenian
Sea

Ionian
Sea

Baetic Mts.

Balearic Is.

Sicily

Strait of Gibraltar

M e d i t e r r a n e a n   S e a

Etna
10,899 ft
(3,322 m)

0   400 Miles

0   400 Kilometers

A F R I C A

30°W

60°N

20°W

50°N

40°N

10°W

0°

10°E

20°E

10°E

20°E

North Cape

Barents Sea

30°E 40°E 50°E 70°E 60°N

LAPLAND

VIAN

Kola Peninsula

White Sea

Pechora

URAL MOUNTAINS

ASIA

Bothnia

Lake Region

Lake Onega

Northern Dvina

Kama

60°N

Lake Ladoga

Gulf of Finland

Western Dvina

EUROPEAN PLAIN

Kama

Central

Russian

Upland

Don

Volga

Europe Asia

Ural

60°N 50°N

Sea

Dnieper

Dniester

arpathian Mts.

Don

-92 ft (-28 m)
Lowest point
in Europe
(at water level)

El'brus
18,510 ft (5,642 m)
Highest point in Europe

Volga

Caspian Sea

Danube

Balkan

Balkan Mts.

Peninsula

Sea of Azov

Crimea

CAUCASUS MOUNTAINS

40°N

Black Sea

Bosporus

Sea of Marmara

Dardanelles

A commonly accepted division
between Asia and Europe—marked
here by a maroon, dashed line—
is formed by the Ural Mountains,
Ural River, Caspian Sea, Caucasus
Mountains, and the Black Sea
with its outlets, the Bosporus
and Dardanelles.

Aegean Sea

Peloponnesus

Crete

Cyprus

30°E 40°E

Map Key

+ Mountain peak

FINLAND

ESTONIA

LATVIA

LITHUANIA

KALININGRAD
(RUSSIA)

POLAND

CZECH
REPUBLIC

SLOVAKIA

Vienna

HUNGARY

AUSTRIA

SLOVENIA

CROATIA

BOSNIA &
HERZEGOVINA

SERBIA

MONTENEGRO

N O R W A Y

S W E D E N

BALTIC SEA

DENMARK

NORTH
SEA

Shetland
Islands

Orkney
Islands

Outer Hebrides
Inner Hebrides

AREA ENLARGED
OPPOSITE PAGE

Inverness

SCOTLAND Aberdeen
Perth   Dundee
Glasgow   Edinburgh
UNITED   Newcastle
Londonderry
(Derry)   NORTHERN   Sunderland
IRELAND
Belfast   Leeds KINGDOM
IRELAND   Isle of Man   Kingston upon Hull
(ÉIRE)   Liverpool
IRISH SEA
Limerick   Dublin   Manchester   ENGLAND   Groningen
Waterford   WALES   Nottingham   NETHERLANDS   Amsterdam
Cork   Birmingham   The Hague   Utrecht
CELTIC   Cardiff   London   Rotterdam
SEA   Bristol   Brugge   Antwerp
Thames   Brussels   Essen
Plymouth   Lille   BELGIUM   Köln

Rockall
(UNITED KINGDOM)

A T L A N T I C   O C E A N

Frisian Islands
Kiel   Rostock
Lübeck
Oldenburg
Bremen   Hamburg   Berlin
Elbe   Oder
Hannover   Magdeburg
Bielefeld   Leipzig
Erfurt   Dresden
GERMANY   Chemnitz
Frankfurt
Rhine   Mannheim   Nürnberg

ENGLISH CHANNEL
Channel
Islands
(U.K.)

Amiens   Charleroi   LUXEMBOURG
Le Havre   Rouen   Luxembourg
Reims   Metz   Mainz
Paris   Nancy
Marne   Strasbourg   Freiburg
Brest   Le Mans   Orléans   Seine   Mulhouse   Stuttgart   Linz
Rennes   Danube   Salzburg
Angers   Tours   Besançon   Basel   Munich   Innsbruck   Graz
Nantes   Loire   Dijon   Zürich
FRANCE   Bern   LIECHTENSTEIN   Bolzano   SLOVENIA   Trieste
Lausanne   SWITZERLAND   Trento   Verona
BAY OF   Limoges   Vichy   Geneva   Milan   Venice
BISCAY   Clermont-Ferrand   Lyon   Mont   Padova
Donostia-San Sebastián   MASSIF   Blanc   Turin   Ferrara   Bologna
Bordeaux   CENTRAL   15,781 ft   Genoa   Modena   SAN MARINO
4,810 m   Florence   Perugia   Ancona
A Coruña   Santander   Bilbao   Toulouse   Nîmes   Pisa   ADRIATIC SEA
Gijón   PYRENEES   Montpellier   Avignon   Nice   Pescara
Oviedo   Santiago de   León   Vitoria-   Pamplona   ANDORRA   Marseille   MONACO   LIGURIAN   ITALY
Compostela   Gasteiz   Andorra   Perpignan   SEA   Terni   Rome
Vigo   Burgos   Lleida   Sabadell   CORSICA   Bastia   VATICAN   Foggia
Braga   Duero   Zaragoza   Tarragona   Barcelona   Ajaccio   CITY   Bari
Bragança   Valladolid   Martaró   Naples   Salerno   Lecce
Oporto   Salamanca   Castelló   Sassari   Vesuvius   Gulf of
Viseu   Madrid   de la Plana   4,203 ft   Taranto   Taranto
Coimbra   Toledo   BALEARIC SEA   1,281 m
PORTUGAL   SPAIN   Valencia   Minorca   SARDINIA   TYRRHENIAN   Cosenza
Lisbon   Tagus   Badajoz   Palma de   Majorca   SEA   Reggio di
Setúbal   Guadiana   Albacete   Mallorca   BALEARIC ISLANDS   Messina   Calabria
SIERRA MORENA   Murcia   Cagliari   Palermo   Taormina
Córdoba   Jaén   Alicante   Marsala   SICILY   Catania
Huelva   Seville   Granada   Cartagena   Syracuse
Jerez   Málaga   M E D I T E R R A N E A N
Algericas   Cádiz   Almería   Valletta   S E A
GIBRALTAR (U.K.)   MALTA
Strait of Gibraltar   Ceuta   ALBORAN   TUNISIA
(SPAIN)   SEA
Melilla
(SPAIN)

A L G E R I A

M O R O C C O

0   200 miles
0   300 kilometers

WESTERN EUROPE

SPOTLIGHT ON THE UNITED KINGDOM AND IRELAND

The **UNITED KINGDOM** is made up of four countries: England, Northern Ireland, Scotland, and Wales. The flag of the United Kingdom, known as the Union Flag, or Union Jack, combines the three crosses of the patron saints of England (St. George), Scotland (St. Andrew), and Ireland (St. Patrick).

First used in 1848, **IRELAND's** tricolor flag was officially adopted when Ireland became independent in 1922. Today, Ireland has a population of more than 4.6 million.

England's flag features the red cross of St. George on a white background. The English have been using it since the 12th century. England, by far the largest country in the United Kingdom, has some 54 million people.

Northern Ireland flies the Union Flag. It has a population of 1.8 million people.

Scotland's flag shows a diagonal white cross on a blue field, known as St. Andrew's Cross. The English and Scottish flags were combined in 1606 as the flag for the union of England and Scotland. Scotland has a population of about 5.3 million people.

Wales was conquered by England in the 13th century. Considered a principality, not a kingdom, its red dragon flag is not part of the United Kingdom flag. Wales is mountainous, and most of its 3.1 million people live along the coast.

SCOTLAND'S national animal is a unicorn.

Mount Everest was named after WELSH surveyor Sir George Everest.

More than 70 million travelers pass through LONDON'S Heathrow Airport every year.

Map labels

Shetland Islands

Orkney Islands

ATLANTIC OCEAN

Rockall (U.K.)

Outer Hebrides

Inner Hebrides

Moray Firth

Inverness

SCOTLAND

Aberdeen

Perth

Dundee

Edinburgh

Londonderry (Derry)

Glasgow

NORTHERN IRELAND

Belfast

GREAT BRITAIN

Newcastle

Sunderland

UNITED

KINGDOM

Isle of Man

Leeds

IRELAND (ÉIRE)

IRISH SEA

Liverpool

Kingston upon Hull

Limerick

Dublin

Manchester

Sheffield

Nottingham

Waterford

Birmingham

Cork

WALES

Cardiff

London

ENGLAND

CELTIC SEA

Bristol

Thames

Plymouth

Southampton

Land's End

ENGLISH CHANNEL

Channel Islands (U.K.)

325

EASTERN EUROPE

Map Key
- ⊛ Country capital
- •••• City or town
- ····· Country boundary

200 miles
300 kilometers

RUSSIA

LATVIA

LITHUANIA

KALININGRAD
(RUSSIA)

Gdynia
Gdańsk
Olsztyn
Szczecin
Bydgoszcz
Toruń
Gorzów
Wielkopolski
Zielona
Góra
Poznań
Kalisz
POLAND
Białystok
Łódź
Radom
Lublin
Kielce
Częstochowa
Wrocław
Opole
Legnica
Wałbrzych
Liberec
**CZECH REP.
(CZECHIA)**
Prague ⊛
Pilsen
Ostrava
Olomouc
Brno
České
Budějovice

GERMANY

Vitsyebsk
Orsha
Mahilyow
Barysaw
Minsk ⊛
BELARUS
Babruysk
Homyel'
Hrodna
Baranavichy
Brest
Pinsk
Mazyr
Prip'yat'
Pinsk Marshes
Western Dvina
Dnieper

Sumy
Chernihiv
Kiev ⊛
Chernobyl'
Dnieper

Kharkiv
Poltava
UKRAINE
Kremenchuk
Cherkasy
Kirovohrad
Oleksandriya
Bila Tserkva
Vinnytsya
Zhytomyr
Rivne
Luts'k
L'viv
Ternopil'
Khmel'nyts'kyy
Ivano-Frankivs'k
Kam'yanets'-Podil's'kyy
Chernivtsi
Uzhhorod

Lublin
Rzeszów
Kraków
Tarnów
Katowice
Tychy
Bytom
Vistula

SLOVAKIA
Košice
Bratislava ⊛
Miskolc
Nyíregyháza
Debrecen

CARPATHIAN MOUNTAINS

HUNGARY
Budapest ⊛
Győr
Székesfehérvár
Szeged
Pécs
Danube
Tisza
Drava

AUSTRIA
SLOVENIA
CROATIA
BOSNIA AND
HERZEGOVINA
SERBIA
ROMANIA

MOLDOVA
Chişinău ⊛
Tiraspol
Bălţi
Dniester
Prut

Slov'yans'k
Kramators'k
Kostyantynivka
Horlivka
Donets'k
Makiyivka
Yenakiyeve
Lysychans'k
Luhans'k
Alchevs'k
Krasnyy Luch
Berdyans'k

Dniprodzerzhyns'k
Dnipropetrovs'k
Zaporizhzhya
Nikopol'
Kryvyy Rih
Melitopol'
Kherson
Mykolayiv
Odesa ⊛

CRIMEA
Yevpatoriya
Sevastopol'
Simferopol'
Yalta
Kerch

SEA OF AZOV

BLACK SEA

Dnieper

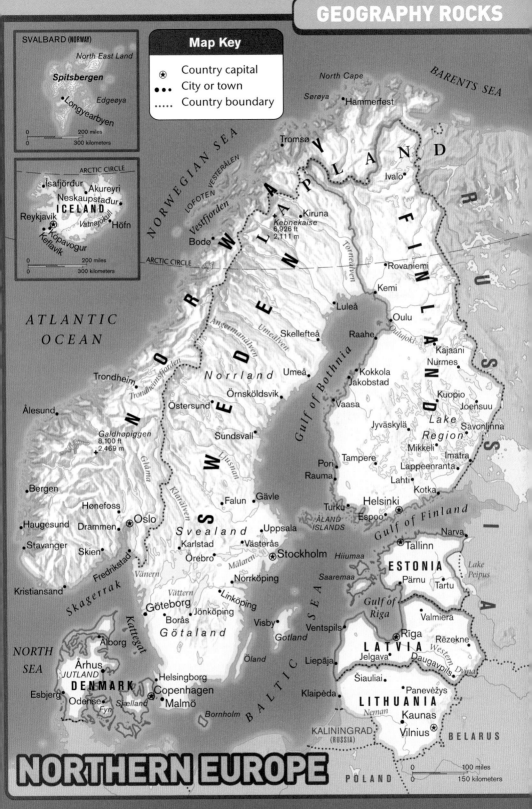

SVALBARD (NORWAY)
North East Land
Spitsbergen
• Longyearbyen
Edgeøya

0 | 200 miles
0 | 300 kilometers

Map Key
⊛ Country capital
••• City or town
····· Country boundary

ARCTIC CIRCLE
Ísafjördur • • Akureyri
Neskaupstadur
Reykjavik • **ICELAND**
⊛ Vatnajökull • Höfn
Kópavogur
Keflavik

0 | 200 miles
0 | 300 kilometers

North Cape
BARENTS SEA
Sørøya • Hammerfest

NORWEGIAN SEA

Tromsø

L A P L A N D

Ivalo

N O R D E N

VESTERÅLEN
LOFOTEN
Vestfjorden
Kiruna
Kebnekaise
6,926 ft
2,111 m
Bodø

F I N L A N D

Torneälven

R U S S I A

ARCTIC CIRCLE
• Rovaniemi

Kemi

ATLANTIC
OCEAN

Luleå

Oulu
Oulujoki

Skellefteå
Raahe
Kajaani
Nurmes

Trondheim
Ångermanälven
Umeälven
Norrland
Umeå
Kokkola
Jakobstad
Kuopio
Joensuu

Trondheimsfjorden
Örnsköldsvik
Vaasa
Jyväskylä
Savonlinna
*Lake
Region*

Ålesund
Östersund
Sundsvall
Galdhøpiggen
8,100 ft
2,469 m
Ljusnan
Mikkeli
Imatra
Lappeenranta
Pori
Tampere
Rauma
Lahti
Kotka

Bergen
Hønefoss
Glåma
Klarälven
Falun
Gävle
Turku
Helsinki
Haugesund
Drammen
Oslo
Svealand
Uppsala
Espoo
ÅLAND
ISLANDS
Gulf of Finland
Narva
Stavanger
Skien
Karlstad
Västerås
Kristiansand
Örebro
Mälaren
Stockholm
Hiiumaa
⊛ Tallinn
Fredrikstad
Vänern
Norrköping
Saaremaa
ESTONIA
Lake
Peipus
Vättern
Linköping
Pärnu
Tartu
Skagerrak
Göteborg
Jönköping
Visby
Gulf of
Riga
Valmiera
Borås
Gotland
Götaland
Ventspils
Rīga
Rēzekne
Kattegat
Öland
Liepāja
LATVIA
Jelgava
Daugavpils
Western Dvina
Ålborg
Šiauliai
Panevėžys
NORTH
SEA
Århus
JUTLAND
Helsingborg
Klaipėda
LITHUANIA
DENMARK
Copenhagen
Kaunas
Esbjerg
Odense
Sjælland
Malmö
Neman
Vilnius
Fyn
Bornholm
KALININGRAD
(RUSSIA)
BELARUS

BALTIC SEA
Gulf of Bothnia

NORTHERN EUROPE

POLAND
0 | 100 miles
0 | 150 kilometers

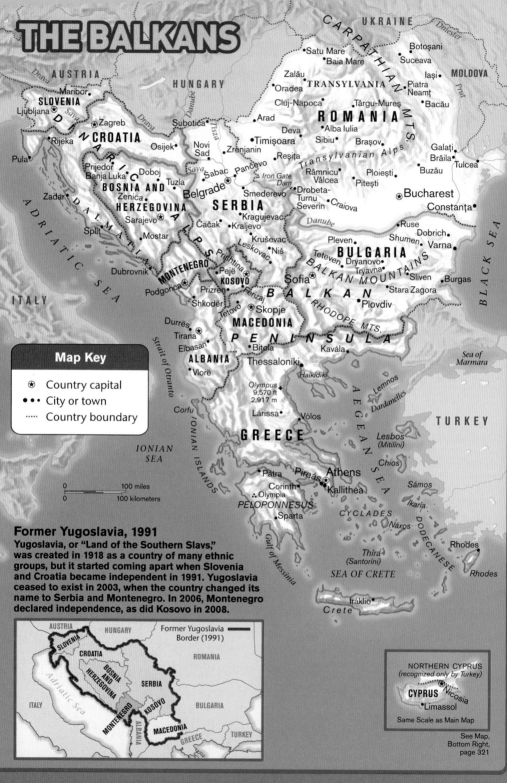

THE BALKANS

Map Key

⊛ Country capital
••• City or town
····· Country boundary

0   100 miles
0   100 kilometers

Former Yugoslavia, 1991

Yugoslavia, or "Land of the Southern Slavs," was created in 1918 as a country of many ethnic groups, but it started coming apart when Slovenia and Croatia became independent in 1991. Yugoslavia ceased to exist in 2003, when the country changed its name to Serbia and Montenegro. In 2006, Montenegro declared independence, as did Kosovo in 2008.

Former Yugoslavia ▬▬▬
Border (1991)

NORTHERN CYPRUS
(recognized only by Turkey)

CYPRUS
⊛Nicosia
•Limassol

Same Scale as Main Map

See Map, Bottom Right, page 321

Map Key

⊛ Country capital
•••• City or town
······ Country boundary

0 ⊢ 200 miles
0 ⊢ 300 kilometers

NORWAY

BARENTS SEA

Kolguyev I.

•Murmansk

Kola
Peninsula

Kanin Peninsula

WHITE SEA

Vorkuta•

Usinsk

ARCTIC CIRCLE

Ob

Pechora•

Sosnogorsk

EUROPE-ASIA
BOUNDARY

SWEDEN

FINLAND

Gulf of Bothnia

•Severodvinsk

•Archangel

Ukhta

Northern Dvina

Zheleznodorozhnyy

Pechora

Petrozavodsk

Syktyvkar

Lake
Ladoga

Lake
Onega

•Kotlas

Berezniki

Gulf of Finland

St. Petersburg

Sukhona

ESTONIA

Lake
Peipus

Cherepovets

Vologda

Kirov

Perm'

NORTHERN EUROPEAN PLAIN

RUSSIA

URAL MOUNTAINS

Velikiy
Novgorod

Rybinsk Reservoir

Kostroma

Izhevsk

Kama

•Pskov

LATVIA

Velikiye
Luki

Rybinsk

Yaroslavl'

Ivanovo

Nizhniy
Novgorod

Kazan'

Naberezhnyye
Chelny

Ufa

KALININGRAD
(RUSSIA) LITHUANIA

Tver'

Vladimir

Cheboksary

Magnitogorsk

Moscow

Smolensk

Oka

Volga

Ul'yanovsk

Sterlitamak

POLAND

BELARUS

Kaluga

Tula

Ryazan'

Saransk

Syzran'

Tol'yatti

Belaya

CENTRAL

Bryansk

Orel

Lipetsk

Oka

Tambov

Penza

Samara

Novotroitsk

RUSSIAN

Kursk

Voronezh

Saratov

Balakovo

Orenburg

Orsk

Dnieper

Belgorod

Engels

UPLAND

Kamyshin

Ural

KAZAKHSTAN

UKRAINE

Don

MOLDOVA

Donets

Volgograd•

Volzhskiy

Volga

CASPIAN DEPRESSION

ROMANIA

Shakhty

Dnieper

Don

Rostov

Astrakhan'

SEA OF
AZOV

Taganrog

CRIMEA

CASPIAN

Krasnodar

Novorossiysk•

Maykop

Stavropol'

Pyatigorsk

BULGARIA

El'brus
18,510 ft
5,642 m

CHECHNYA

Groznyy

SEA

BLACK SEA

Sochi

CAUCASUS MOUNTAINS

Vladikavkaz

Makhachkala

GEORGIA

EUROPEAN
RUSSIA

ARMENIA

AZERBAIJAN

TURKEY

IRAN

Wacky ↓World→

Check out these **bizarre attractions** from around the **UNITED KINGDOM.**

Move over, Big Ben and Parliament: Next time you're cruising around England, make a pit stop at some truly peculiar places found throughout the country. You'll have plenty to write home about after visiting these weird and wacky attractions!

Dog Collar Museum
Where: Kent, England
Why it's wacky: Check out a collection of more than 100 dog collars from five centuries, ranging from spiky iron ones worn by hunting hounds to 21st-century chic neckwear for pampered pooches.

The Gnome Reserve and Wildflower Garden
Where: near West Putford, England
Why it's wacky: More than 2,000 gnome and pixie figurines—the world's largest collection—are scattered amid four acres (1.6 ha) of countryside. Visitors are encouraged to wear pointy hats (provided at the park's entrance) so they don't scare the gnomes.

Dennis Severs' House

Where: London, England
Why it's wacky: Stroll through this "living museum," and you'll get the sense that its 18th-century occupants are still residing there and just left the room. Wait—was that a whisper coming from the next room? Hello? Is anybody home?

The Crooked House

Where: Himley, England
Why it's wacky: Built in 1765, part of this brick house has shifted due to unstable ground, leaving one end four feet (1.2 m) lower than the other. Now a restaurant, the floors have been leveled for safety, but the house's walls remain off-kilter for an unbalanced look.

BANKS'S ALES

BANKS'S ALES

THE CROOKED HOUSE

331

wild Vacation

SLEEP HERE!

COOL THINGS ABOUT TURKEY

Dating from A.D. 537, the famous Hagia Sophia was built as a church, turned into a mosque, and is now a museum.

Early Turkish settlers once lived in the caves of the Cappadocia region.

Yogurt was invented in Turkey and is a main ingredient in local food—from soups to desserts.

King Midas may not have really turned all he touched into gold. But he did rule over the kingdom of Phrygia, in what is now Turkey, in the eighth century B.C.

Cave Hotel
YUNAK EVLERI HOTEL

WHERE Cappadocia region, Turkey

WHY IT'S COOL Here's a hotel that really rocks. The Yunak Evleri is built into caves left by volcanic activity ten million years ago. Follow narrow passageways and stone stairs to rooms that are a cool 57°F (14°C). Spend the day hiking rocky terrain, exploring caverns, or hot air ballooning over "fairy chimneys"—tall rock formations that dot the skyline. At night you won't have to worry about being awakened by eruptions since the Cappadocia volcanoes are now dormant. So they're "sleeping," too!

THINGS TO DO IN TURKEY

Ride a camel to tour the bizarre rock formations around Cappadocia.

Take a boat ride up the Bosporus strait to get from Asia to Europe in 15 minutes.

Haggle with shopkeepers in the bustling market of Istanbul's Grand Bazaar.

EXTREME WEIRDNESS

From AROUND the WORLD

AT EASE, GORILLAS!

GORILLA FOOLS HUMANS

WHAT Ape robot

WHERE Bristol, England

DETAILS Call it *Planet of the Fake Apes.* The Bristol Zoo Gardens' "Wow! Gorillas" exhibit featured an animatronic ape and several five-foot (1.5-m)-tall fiberglass gorilla sculptures. The sculptures were later painted and decorated by local artists. What's next—papier-mâché penguins?

STRAW MAN

WHAT Straw bears

WHERE Heldra, Germany

DETAILS Somebody went overboard with their winter coat. In colder months, some Germans have a tradition of wearing outfits made of straw while attending seasonal festivals. These "straw bears" date back to an old belief that the outfits would scare winter away. All this guy needs is a straw scarf.

MEET STRAW MAN, TIN MAN'S LONG-LOST COUSIN.

BIIIGGG BINOCULARS

WHAT Binocular-shaped entrance

WHERE Venice, California, U.S.A.

DETAILS Did somebody ask for a better view? Sculptors Claes Oldenburg and Coosje van Bruggen designed this 45-foot (14-m)-tall set of binoculars that now serves as an office entrance for Google. So *that's* what they mean by "Internet search."

NOT SURE HOW TO WATCH BIRDS WITH THESE.

1 When building a waterslide, a construction crew follows the manufacturer's directions and puts the slide together piece by piece at the park. It's like assembling a **HUGE TOY RACETRACK!**

2 Riders inside a CLEAR TUNNEL pass through A POOL OF SHARKS on the Leap of Faith waterslide in the Bahamas.

3 WATERSLIDES made out of *STAINLESS STEEL ARE FASTER* than those that are made out of fiberglass.

4 Riders reach speeds of 65 miles an hour (105 kph) on the Insano waterslide at Beach Park in Fortaleza, Brazil.

17 SPLASHY FACTS ABOUT WATER

5 THERE ARE MORE THAN **1,200 water parks** IN NORTH AMERICA.

6 In 2011, more than two million people visited Typhoon Lagoon in Orlando. That's about the same as the entire population of Slovenia, in eastern Europe.

7 A group raft ride in Wisconsin Dells, U.S.A., plunges riders into a 58-foot (18-m)-long tunnel with fake fog and lightning. **It's like riding into a hurricane.**

8 THE 145,000-SQUARE-FOOT (13,471-SQ-M) WAVE PALACE AT SIAM PARK IN SPAIN'S CANARY ISLANDS USES **185,000 gallons** (700,301 L) of salt water TO CREATE HUGE, OCEANLIKE WAVES FOR SURFERS.

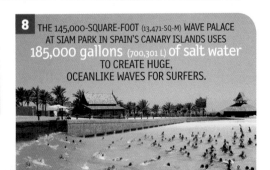

9 New water parks are designed to **CONSERVE WATER.** They generally use less water than people living in a neighborhood of about the same size do.

10  PEOPLE LOVE WATER PARKS. IN 2011, THE TOP 20 IN THE WORLD ATTRACTED A TOTAL OF NEARLY **24 million visitors.**

11  TEN OF THE TOP 20 WATER PARKS IN THE WORLD ARE IN ASIA; 6 ARE IN THE UNITED STATES, AND 4 OF THOSE ARE IN FLORIDA.

12 The tight turns of the Constrictor ride at Wet 'N Wild in Phoenix, Arizona, U.S.A., make riders feel like they are traveling inside a giant snake.

13 The mile- (1.6-km)-long Raging River inner tube ride in Texas's Schlitterbahn (German for "slippery road") takes some 45 minutes to complete.

PARKS

14 Yas Waterworld in Abu Dhabi, in the United Arab Emirates, spreads across 37 acres (15 ha). That's more than 330 NBA-size basketball courts!

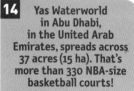

15 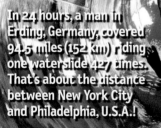 In 24 hours, a man in Erding, Germany, covered 94.5 miles (152 km) riding one waterslide 427 times. That's about the distance between New York City and Philadelphia, U.S.A.!

16 SURFERS TRY TO **GET AIR** ON NINE-FOOT (2.7-M) HIGH WAVES IN THE WAVE POOL AT SUNWAY LAGOON IN MALAYSIA.

17  Wisconsin Dells calls itself the **"Waterpark Capital of the World."** The town boasts more than 20 indoor and outdoor water parks.

335

QUIZ WHIZ

Is your geography knowledge off the map? Quiz yourself to find out!

ANSWERS BELOW

1. Where in the world can you find sand dunes as tall as skyscrapers?
   a. Namibia
   b. Dubai
   c. Croatia
   d. Antarctica

2. Which species of insect makes an annual migration from Canada and the U.S.A. to Mexico?
   a. cricket
   b. monarch butterfly
   c. rhinoceros beetle
   d. banana moth

3. _____ is also known as the "Soft Coral Capital of the World."

4. What are the only ways to get to Bolivia's Isla del Sol?
   a. boat or hike
   b. rocket ship or UFO
   c. car or truck
   d. plane or train

5. **True or false?** There are pink lakes in Australia.

Not **STUMPED** yet? Check out the *NATIONAL GEOGRAPHIC KIDS QUIZ WHIZ* collection for more crazy **GEOGRAPHY** questions!

ANSWERS:
1. a; 2. b; 3. Fiji Barrier Reef; 4. a; 5. True

HOMEWORK HELP

Finding Your Way Around

Every map has a story to tell, but first you have to know how to read one. Maps represent information by using a language of symbols. Knowing how to read these symbols provides access to a wide range of information. Look at the scale and compass rose or arrow to understand distance and direction (see box below).

To find out what each symbol on a map means, you must use the key. It's your secret decoder—identifying information by each symbol on the map.

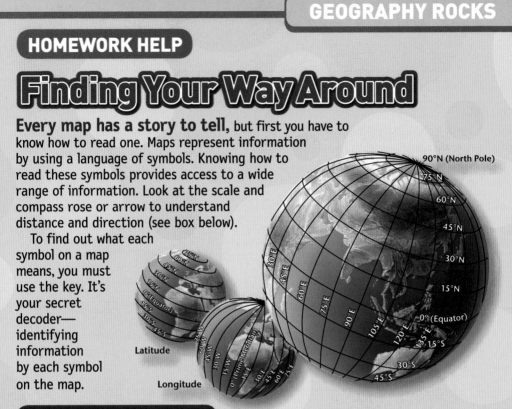

LATITUDE AND LONGITUDE

Latitude and longitude lines (above) help us determine locations on Earth. Every place on Earth has a special address called absolute location. Imaginary lines called lines of latitude run west to east, parallel to the Equator. These lines measure distance in degrees north or south from the Equator (0° latitude) to the North Pole (90°N) or to the South Pole (90°S). One degree of latitude is approximately 70 miles (113 km).

Lines of longitude run north to south, meeting at the Poles. These lines measure distance in degrees east or west from 0° longitude (prime meridian) to 180° longitude. The prime meridian runs through Greenwich, England.

SCALE AND DIRECTION

The scale on a map can be shown as a fraction, as words, or as a line or bar. It relates distance on the map to distance in the real world. Sometimes the scale identifies the type of map projection. Maps may include an arrow or compass rose to indicate north on the map.

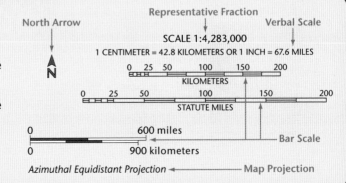

North Arrow

Representative Fraction

Verbal Scale

SCALE 1:4,283,000

1 CENTIMETER = 42.8 KILOMETERS OR 1 INCH = 67.6 MILES

Bar Scale

Azimuthal Equidistant Projection — Map Projection

GAME ANSWERS

Find the Hidden Animals, page 144

1. F, 2. E, 3. D, 4. A, 5. C, 6. B.

What in the World? page 145

Top row: **island, forest, elephant herd.**
Middle row: **flamingos, camels, coral reef.**
Bottom row: **flower fields, icebergs, hot-air balloon.** Bonus: **You crack me up!**

A-MAZE-ing Mind, page 146

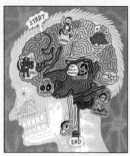

Noun Town, page 148

The 12 compound nouns are: 1. **sleeping bag,** 2. **eggplant,** 3. **catfish,** 4. **bellhop,** 5. **ladybug,** 6. **housework,** 7. **butterfly,** 8. **limelight,** 9. **arrowhead,** 10. **full moon,** 11. **treehouse,** 12. **coffee table.**

Attention on Set, page 149

1. utensils,
2. antennae,
3. stencil,
4. extension cord, 5. tentacle,
6. kitten, 7. tent,
8. Tennessee,
9. tennis ball,
10. mitten.

What in the World? page 150

Top row: **corn, tennis ball, sunflowers.**
Middle row: **snake, canary, banana slug.**
Bottom row: **butterfly, honeycomb, lemon.**
Bonus: **Cut it in half.**

Riddle Me This, page 152

1. *sneak*-ers, 2. zebra, 3. tree, 4. rain, 5. candle, 6. footsteps, 7. clock, 8. goose, 9. bottle, 10. window.

Book Boggle, page 155

The eight book titles are:
Treasure Island (1, 11);
Little House on the Prairie (6, 2);
The Lion, the Witch and the Wardrobe (7, 3);
The Lightning Thief (4, 13);
James and the Giant Peach (10, 5);
Diary of a Wimpy Kid (8, 15);
Harry Potter and the Goblet of Fire (14, 9);
and *Green Eggs and Ham* (16, 12).

Dog Daze, page 157

Your World 2017 (8–17)

p. 13 "Kermit's Twin" by Rose Davidson; p. 15 "Camera Ball" by Crispin Boyer; p. 17 "Pet Smuggler Busted!" by Karen De Seve; all other articles in section by Sarah Wassner Flynn

Amazing Animals (18–79)

pp. 20–25 "17 Cutest Animals of 2017" by Sarah Wassner Flynn; pp. 26–27 "Animal Rascals" by Aline Alexander Newman; p. 28–29 "Sea Otter Shoots Hoops" & "Horse Lives in House" by Kitson Jazynka, "Skateboarding Cat" by Rose Davidson; pp. 30–31 "What Is Taxonomy?" & "Vertebrates"/ "Invertebrates" by Susan K. Donnelly; pp. 32–33 "Mission Animal Rescue: Rhino" by Clare Hodgson Meeker; pp. 34–35 "Wild Hamsters" by Kate Jaimet; pp. 36–37 "Secrets of the Spirit Bear" and "Tough Cats" by Karen De Seve; p. 38 "5 Cool Things About Koalas" by Crispin Boyer; p. 39 "Foxes on Ice" by Karen De Seve; p. 41 "Wolverine!" by Stephanie Warren; pp. 42–43 "Freaky Frogs!" by Ruth A. Musgrave; pp. 44–45 "Goofballs" by Avery Elizabeth Hurt; pp. 46–47 "Big Cats" by Elizabeth Carney; pp. 48–49 "Mission Animal Rescue: Lion" by Scott Elder; p. 50 "Cheetahs: Built for Speed" by Fiona Sunquist; p. 51 "Snow Leopard Secrets" by Karen De Seve; pp. 52–53 "Mission Animal Rescue: Sea Turtle" by Scott Elder; pp. 54–55 "Talking Dolphin" by Ruth A. Musgrave; pp. 56–57 "Parenting, Puffin Style" by Ruth A. Musgrave; pp. 58–59 "Name That Tide Pool Animal" by Nancy Honovich; pp. 60–63 "Awesome Insect Awards" and "Monarchs Hit the Road!" by Sarah Wassner Flynn; p. 64 "What Killed the Dinosaurs?" by Sarah Wassner Flynn; pp. 64–66 "Prehistoric Time Line," "Dino Classification" & "Who Ate What?" by Susan K. Donnelly; pp. 72–73 "How to Speak Cat" by Aline Alexander Newman and Gary Weitzman, D.V.M.; p. 75 "Real Animal Heroes!" by Aline Alexander Newman; pp. 76–77 "Lifestyles of the Rich & Furry" by Patricia J. Murphy

Going Green (80–95)

pp. 82–83 "Saving the Jaguars" by Sarah Wassner Flynn and "Manatee Rescue!" by Scott Elder; pp. 84–87 "17 Cool Things About Going Green," "The Arctic's Disappearing Ice," and "What a Prince!" by Sarah Wassner Flynn; p. 87 "Pollution" by David George Gordon; p. 88 "Food for Thought" by Barton Seaver; pp. 89–90 "Fighting Food Waste" and "6 Tips to Save the Earth" by Sarah Wassner Flynn; pp. 92–93 "Green Extremes" by Sarah Wassner Flynn

Culture Connection (96–121)

pp. 100–101 *Howl-oween Pet Party* by Kay Boatner; p. 102 "What's Your Chinese Horoscope?" by Geoff Williams; pp. 104–105 "Archaeologist Fred Hiebert Digs the Past" by Sarah Wassner Flynn; pp. 106–107 "World's Wackiest Houses" by Zachary Petit; pp. 110–111 "Chew on This" by Kay Boatner; pp. 112–113 "Money Around the World!" by Kristin Baird Rattini; pp. 116–117 "Monster Myths" by Kitson Jazynka; pp. 118–119 "World Religions" by Mark Bockenhauer; p. 119 "Technology Meets Tradition" by Sarah Wassner Flynn

Awesome Adventure (122–141)

pp. 124–127 "Dare to Explore" by C.M. Tomlin; pp. 130–131 "Rhian Waller: Keeping Your Cool!" by Margaret Gurevich; pp. 132–133 "Cave of Secrets" by Scott Elder; p. 135 "Frozen in Time" by Sarah Wassner Flynn; p. 136 "Meerkat Close Encounter" by Kitson Jazynka; p. 137 "How to Survive a K iller Bee Attack!" & "How to Survive a Bee Sting!" by Rachel Buchholz; pp. 138–139 "Getting the Shot" by April Capochino Myers

Fun and Games (142–161)

p. 154 "Funny Fill-In" by Jennifer MacKinnon; p. 159 "Funny Fill-In" by Becky Baines

Super Science (162–197)

pp. 166 "Cool Inventions" by Crispin Boyer; p. 167 "Accidents Happen" by Renee Skelton; p. 169 "The Three Domains of Life" by Susan K. Donnelly; pp. 170–171 "You and Your Cells" & "You Have a Lot of Nerve!" by Christina Wilsdon, Patricia Daniels, and Jen Agresta; p. 172 "Your Amazing Brain" by Douglas E. Richards; p. 173 "Check Your Memory" by Jennifer Swanson; p. 174 "Your Amazing Ears" by Sarah Wassner Flynn; pp. 176–177 "That's Gross!" by Crispin Boyer; pp. 178–179 "Big Bang" by David A. Aguilar; p. 178 "Powerful Particle" by Sarah Wassner Flynn; p. 182 "By the Numbers: Solar System by Julie Beer and Michelle Harris; p. 183 "Dwarf Planets" by Sarah Wassner Flynn; p. 184 "Destination Space: Alien Sea" by Stephanie Warren Drimmer; pp. 186–187 "Constellations" by Sarah Wassner Flynn; p. 189 "Rock Stars" by Steve Tomecek; pp. 190–191 "Name That Rock" by Nancy Honovich; pp. 192–193 "Volcano!" by Renee Skelton; pp. 194–195 "Hot Spot" by Scott Elder

Wonders of Nature (198–221)

p. 200–201 "17 Freaky Facts About Weather" by Thomas M. Kostigen; p. 202 "Weather and Climate" by Mark Bockenhauer; p. 204 "Types of Clouds" by Kathy Furgang; p. 205 "Make a Barometer" by Nancy Honovich; pp. 208–209 "Typhoon!" & "Earthquake!" & "Blizzard!" by Sarah Wassner Flynn; pp. 208–209 "What Is a Tornado?" by Kathy Furgang; p. 210 "How Does Your Garden Grow?" by Susan K. Donnelly; pp. 212–213 "Carnivorous Plants" by Sarah Wassner Flynn; pp. 214–215 "Biomes" by Susan K. Donnelly; pp. 218–219, "Pristine Seas" by Sarah Wassner Flynn

History Happens (222–253)

pp. 224–225 "Jungle of Secrets" by John Micklos, Jr.; pp. 226–227 "Knight Life" by Crispin Boyer; pp. 228–229 "Must-See Sights" by Sarah Wassner Flynn; p. 232 "Mystery of the Stone Giants" by Sean McCollum; p. 233 "Mystery of Atlantis" by John Micklos, Jr.; p. 234 "Treasure!" by Jamie Kiffel-Alech; p. 235 "The Secrets of Stonehenge" by Kristin Baird Rattini

Geography Rocks (254–337)

pp. 256–262 by Mark Bockenhauer; pp. 264–291 by Sarah Wassner Flynn, Mark Bockenhauer, and Susan K. Donnelly; pp. 292–316 "You Are There!" by Sarah Wassner Flynn; pp. 330–331 "Wacky World" by Sarah Wassner Flynn; p. 332 "Wild Vacation" by C.M. Tomlin; p. 333 "Extreme Weirdness From Around the World" by Kay Boatner

All "Homework Help" by Vicki Ariyasu

Want to Learn More?

Find more information about topics in this book in these National Geographic Kids resources.

Brain Games
Jennifer Swanson
2015

Dirtmeister's Nitty Gritty Planet Earth
Steve Tomecek, Fred Harper (illustrator)
2015

Extreme Planet
Carsten Peter, Glen Phelan
2015

How to Speak Cat
Aline Alexander Newman and Gary Weitzman, D.V.M.
2015

National Geographic Kids By the Numbers series

National Geographic Kids Everything series

National Geographic Kids 5,000 Awesome Facts (About Everything!) series

National Geographic Kids Funny Fill-In series

National Geographic Kids Get Outside Guide
Nancy Honovich, Julie Beer, Richard Louv
2014

National Geographic Kids Just Joking series

National Geographic Kids Mission Animal Rescue series
kids.nationalgeographic.com/mission-animal-rescue

National Geographic Kids Ultimate Adventure Atlas of Earth
2015

National Geographic Kids Ultimate Explorer Field Guide series

National Geographic Kids Ultimate Weird But True series

Ultimate Bodypedia
Patricia Daniels, Christina Wilsdon, Jen Agresta
2014

ABBREVIATIONS:

CO: Corbis
GI: Getty Images
IS: iStockphoto
MP: Minden Pictures
NGC: National Geographic Creative
NGS: National Geographic Stock
NPL: Nature Picture Library
SS: Shutterstock

All Maps

By NGS unless otherwise noted

All Illustrations & Charts

By Stuart Armstrong unless otherwise noted

Front Cover/Spine

(penguins), Tim Davis/CO; (chameleon), Life On White/Photodisc/GI; (rock climber), Christopher Kimmel/Flickr RF/GI; (Easter Island statue), Volanthevist/GI; (zebra), Hitoshi Okamato/MP; Spine: (Easter Island statue, up), Timothy Pontrelli/Dreamstime.com; (Easter Island statue, low), Volanthevist/Moment Open/GI; (chameleon), Life On White/Photodisc/GI; (rock climber), Christopher Kimmel/Flickr RF/GI

Back Cover

(Taylor Swift peanut art), Steve Casino; (Earth), Alex Staroseltsev/SS; (chameleon), Thomas Marent/MP; (Easter Island statues), Volanthevist/Moment Open/GI; (lemurs), Pete Oxford/MP; (mountain boarder), Klubovy/E+/GI; (diver and shark), franisekhojdysz/SS; (hat), Steve Collender/SS

Inside Front Cover

(T-Rex), Jim Zuckerman/CO; (giraffe), Roy Toft/NGC; (polar bear cub), Eric Isselee/SS

Front Matter (2–7)

2-3, Suzi Eszterhas/MP; 5 (UP RT), SS; 5 (LO), Nattapol Sritongcom/SS; 5 (UP LE), ESA; 5 (CTR), Thorsten Milse/Robert Harding World Imagery; 6 (UP), Bruno Morandi/Robert Harding World Imagery; 6 (UP CTR), Menno Boermans/Robert Harding World Imagery; 6 (LO CTR), Paul & Paveena Mckenzie/GI; 6 (LO), RAKITA/SIPA/Newscom; 7 (UP), Frans Lanting/Robert Harding World Imagery; 7 (CTR), Danita Delimont/GI; 7 (LO), Angelo Cavalli/Robert Harding World Imagery

Your World 2016 (8–17)

8-9, ESA; 9 (CTR RT), Steve Collender/SS; 10 (UP LE), GI Inc./NGC; 10 (UP RT), Katherine Feng/MP/NGC; 10 (LO LE), Katherine Feng/MP/NGC; 10 (LO RT), Jurgen Otto; 11 (LO LE), AFP/GI; 11 (UP), Gene Blevins/ZUMA Press/CO; 11 (LO LE), Jurgen Otto; 11 (LO RT), Jurgen Otto; 12 (UP), NASA; 12 (UP CTR), NASA; 12 (LO RT), NASA; 12 (LO), LOLIWARE Biodegr(edible)s; 13 (UP LE), Mark Thiessen/NGC; 13 (UP RT), Courtesy NG Studios/NGC; 13 (CTR), Stefan Fichtel/NGC; 13 (LE), Vera Anderson/WireImage/GI; 13 (LO RT), Brian Kubicki/Costa Rican Amphibian Research Center; 14 (UP), Manabu Ogasawara/GI; 14 (CTR LE), © 20th Century-Fox Film Corporation, TM & Copyright/Courtesy Everett Collection; 14 (CTR RT), © Buena Vista Pictures/Courtesy Everett Collection; 14 (LO), © Universal Pictures/Courtesy Everett Collection; 15 (UP), Panono; 15 (UP CTR), Panono; 15 (LO CTR),

AC Manley/SS; 15, Courtesy Kelly Sweet, National Geographic staff; 16 (tiger), Anan Kaewkhammul/SS; 16 (U.S. seal), Joseph Sohm/SS; 16 (garlic), Timmary/SS; 16 (puppet), Opop0/SS; 16 (bird), NH/SS; 16 (Star Wars), © Copyright Twentieth Century-Fox Film Corporation. All rights reserved/Courtesy Everett Collection; 16 (pudding boat), Tony Bartholomew; 16 (pumpkin), topseller/SS; 17 (UP LE), omphoto/SS; 17 (UP RT), Steve Casino; 17 (CTR RT), Steve Casino; 17 (CTR LE), Steve Casino; 17 (LO), Tom Nick Cocotos

Amazing Animals (18–79)

18-19, Thorsten Milse/Robert Harding World Imagery; 20 (UP), Fuse/GI; 20 (LO), iculizard/IS; 21 (UP), Alex Mustard/NPL; 21 (LO LE), Dave Watts/NPL; 21 (LO RT), Molly Prottas; 22 (UP LE), Sebastian Kennerknecht/MP; 22 (UP RT), Shanna Love/Ballarat Wildlife Park; 22 (LO), Willie Davis/SS; 23 (UP), ARCO/NPL; 23 (LO LE), Christophe Lehenaff/Alamy; 23 (LO RT), Pete Oxford/NPL/MP; 24 (UP LE), CO/SuperStock; 24 (UP RT), Masatsugu Ohashi/Rex USA; 24 (LO LE), Robert Harding World Imagery/Alamy; 24 (LO RT), Suzi Eszterhas/MP; 25 (UP), W8 Media/Splash News/CO; 25 (LO), Shedd Aquarium/Brenna Hernandez; 26 (LE), Denise Kappa/SS; 26 (CTR), Courtesy Mavis Knight; 26 (LO), Loisik/Dreamstime; 26 (Dentures), botazsolti/SS; 27 (LO LE), Charlie Summers/NPL; 27 (LO), Barry Mansell/NPL; 27 (UP), Erik Lam/SS; 27 (UP LE), Courtesy Dr. Gary Sloniker; 27 (UP CTR), Uatp1/Dreamstime; 28 (UP), Oregon Zoo/photo by Michael Durham; 28 (LO), Oregon Zoo/photo by Michael Durham; 29, Carsten Rehder/AFP/GI; 29 (LO), CB2/ZOB/Newscom; 30 (LE CTR), Eric Isselee/SS; 30 (LO RT), Joel Sartore/NGC; 30 (UP), Mint Images Limited/Alamy; 31 (UP LE), FloridaStock/SS; 31 (LO RT), Karen Massier/IS.com; 31 (UP RT), cbpix/SS; 31 (LE CTR), mashe/SS; 31 (LO), Eric Isselee/SS; 32 (LE), Beverly Joubert/NGC; 32 (RT), Beverly Joubert/NGC; 33, Beverly Joubert/NGC; 34-35, Eric Baccega/NPL; 34 (LO), Eric Baccega/NPL; 35 (UP LE), Eric Baccega/NPL; 35 (UP CTR), Eric Baccega/NPL; 35 (UP RT), Eric Baccega/NPL; 36 (UP LE), Mark Carwardine/ARDEA; 36 (UP RT), Steven J. Kazlowski/Alamy; 36 (LO LE), Steven J. Kazlowski/Alamy; 37 (UP), Arco Images GmbH/Alamy; 37 (LO), Lisa & Mike Husar/Team Husar; 38 (UP), Jouan & Rius/naturepl.com; 38 (LO), Hotshotsworldwide/Dreamstime.com; 39 (UP), Yva Momatiuk & John Eastcott/MP; 39 (LO), Michio Hoshino/MP; 39 (CTR), Steve Kazloski/NPL; 40, Jean Paul Ferrero/Ardea; 41 (Background), Sergey Gorshkov/MP; 41 (UP), Daniel J. Cox/Oxford Scientific/GI; 41 (RT), A. & J. Visage/Peter Arnold/GI; 42 (UP), Stephen Dalton/naturepl.com; 42 (LO), Andrew Murray/naturepl.com; 42 (LO LE), Pete Oxford/naturepl.com; 43 (UP RT), Stephen Dalton/naturepl.com; 43 (UP LE), Thomas Marent/MP; 44 (UP), Heidi & Hans-Juergen Koch/MP; 44 (LO), M. Watson/Ardea; 45 (UP LE), Bianca Lavies/NGC; 45, Mark Payne-Gill/NPL; 45 (LO LE), Bianca Lavies/NGC; 45 (CTR RT), Claus Meyer/MP; 45 (LO RT), Jason Tharp; 45, Mark Payne-Gill/NPL; 45, Mark Payne-Gill/NPL; 46, Staffan Widstrand/

naturepl.com; 47 (UP LE), worldswildlifewonders/SS; 47 (UP CTR LE), Kesu/SS; 47 (UP CTR RT), WitR/SS; 47 (UP RT), Eric Isselee/SS; 47 (LE CTR), DLILLC/CO; 47 (RT CTR), Eric Isselee/SS; 47 (LO LE), Eric Isselee/SS; 47 (LO RT), Eric Isselee/SS; 48 (LE CTR), BFF; 48 (LO RT), BFF; 49, Pete Oxford/MP; 50 (UP), Andy Rouse/NHPA/Photoshot; 50 (CTR), Stephen Belcher/MP; 50 (LO LE), Martin Harvey/Photolibrary/GI; 50 (LO RT), Suzi Eszterhas/MP; 51 (UP), Steve Winter/NGS; 51 (CTR), Purple Pilchards/Alamy; 51 (LO), NHPA/SuperStock; 52-53, Brian J. Skerry/NGC; 52 (LO), NEAQ Rescue; 53 (UP RT), Terry Dickson/Florida Times-Union; 53 (LO LE), Connie Merigo; 54 (UP), Augusto Leandro Stanzani/ARDEA; 54 (LO), Image Source/Alamy; 54 (CTR), Augusto Leandro Stanzani/ARDEA; 54 (LO RT), Jekyll Island Authority; 55 (UP RT), Arco Images GmbH/Alamy; 55 (LO LE), Eco/UIG/GI; 56 (UP RT), Stefan Huwiler/imagebroker/GI; 56 (CTR), Frans Lanting/CO; 56 (LO), ÊJames Urbach/SuperStock; 57 (LE), age fotostock/SuperStock; 57 (UP RT), Alex Mustard/2020VISION/NPL; 57 (CTR RT), Chris Gomersall/NPL; 57 (LO RT), Jouan & Rius/NPL; 58-59, apsimo1/IS; 59 (UP CTR), Brendan Hunter/IS; 59 (UP RT), Nancy Nehring/IS; 59 (LO LE), Lee Rogers/IS; 59 (LO RT), AtWaG/IS; 59 (UP CTR), Lars Johansson/IS; 60 (UP LE), Stephen Dalton/MP; 60 (UP RT), Nature Production/NPL; 60 (LO), Elio Della Ferrera/MP; 61 (LE), Heidi & Hans-Juergen Koch/MP; 61 (LO RT), Studio Times Ltd/MP; 61 (UP RT), Mitsuhiko Imamori/MP; 61 (LO RT), Bruce Davidson/MP; 62 (UP back), Ingo Arndt/MP; 62 (LO), IS.com/GomezDavid; 63 (LE), Stephen Dalton/NPL; 63 (UP RT), IS.com/Ron Brancato; 63 (CTR RT), IS.com/Sarah Bossert; 63 (LO), Noradoa/SS; 64 (UP), Chris Butler/Science Photo Library/Photo Researchers, Inc.; 64 (CTR), Publiphoto/Photo Researchers, Inc.; 64 (LO), Pixeldust Studios/NGS.com; 65 (B), Laurie O'Keefe/Photo Researchers, Inc.; 65 (C), Chris Butler/Photo Researchers, Inc.; 65 (D), Publiphoto/Photo Researchers, Inc.; 65 (A), Publiphoto/Photo Researchers, Inc.; 65 (E), image Courtesy Project Exploration; 66 (UP), Paul B. Moore/SS; 66 (LO), Andrea Meyer/SS; 67 (UP LE), Gabriel Lio; 67 (UP RT), Courtesy Royal Tyrell Museum of Canada; 67 (LO LE), Lida Xing; 67 (LO RT), Dinostar Co; 68 (UP RT), Franco Tempesta; 68-69 (ALL), Franco Tempesta; 70 (UP LE), Marcio Jose Bastos Silva/SS; 70 (UP RT), ShaneKato/IS; 70 (CTR LE), imv/IS; 70 (LO LE), Eric Isselee/IS; 70 (LO RT), John Cancalosi/Alamy; 70 (CTR RT), Eric Isselee/IS; 71 (LO LE), Peter Mukherjee/IS; 71 (UP CTR), Hornbil Images/Alamy; 71 (UP RT), Oli Scarff/GI; 71 (LO RT), Michael Murphy/National Parks and Wildlife Service; 71 (CTR LE), Eduard Kyslynskyy/SS; 71 (CTR RT), Philip Scalia/Alamy; 71 (LO RT), Vudhikrai/SS; 72 (UP), Damien Richard/SS; 72 (LO), kurhan/SS; 73 (LO LE), Igor Shpilenok/NPL; 73 (UP), SJ Allen/SS; 73 (LO), Hulya Ozkok/GI; 74 (UP LE), SJ Allen/SS; 74 (UP RT), Wegner/ARCO/NPL; 74 (LO), PM Images/GI; 75 (UP), Courtesy Carly Riley; 75 (CTR), Courtesy Patricia Peter; 75 (LO), Courtesy James Jett; 76 (RT), Meredith Parmelee/Stone/GI; 76 (LE), Yoshitsugu Kimura/Fifi & Romeo; 77 (UP), Courtesy La Petite Maison;

77 (CTR LE), Britt Erlanson/The Image Bank/GI; 77 (CTR), James Kegley; 77 (CTR RT), James Kegley; 77 (LO LE), Augustus Butera/Taxi/GI; 77 (LO RT), Courtesy Three Dog Bakery LLC; 78 (UP), Alex Mustard/NPL; 78 (CTR), Jean Paul Ferrero/ARDEA; 78 (LO), Hotshotsworldwide/Dreamstime.com; 79 (UP RT), CampCrazy Photography/SS

Going Green (80-95)
80-81, Nattapol Sritongcom/SS; 82 (UP), Steve Winter/NGC; 82 (LO), SA Team/MP; 83 (LO), James R. D. Scott/GI; 83 (UP), Courtesy FWC/Activities were conducted under the USFWS permit number MA770191; 84 (UP LE), Sathit Plengchawee/Dreamstime.com; 84 (UP RT), Helenbr/Dreamstime; 84 (UP CTR), Johnfoto/Dreamstime; 84 (LO CTR), Raylight3/Dreamstime; 84 (LO LE), Image Source/GI; 84 (LO CTR), Francesco Alessi/Dreamstime; 84 (LO RT), Natthawut Punyosaeng/Dreamstime; 85 (UP LE), AP Photo/Pablo Martinez Monsivais; 85 (UP RT), Hauke Dressler/GI; 85 (up ctr le), Anton Starikov/Dreamstime; 85 (UP CTR RT), Eleni Seitanidou/Dreamstime; 85 (LO CTR LE), Feng Yu/Dreamstime; 85 (LO CTR RT), Burachet/Dreamstime; 85 (LO LE), flashgun/IS Images; 85 (LO RT), Skutvik/Dreamstime; 86 (Background), Mujka Design Inc./IS.com; 87 (CTR), Giorgio Cosulich/GI; 87 (LO), Featureflash/SS; 88 (Back), Brian J. Skerry/NGC; 88 (INSET), CuboImages/Alamy; 89 (LO RT), Adrian Brooks/IMAGEWISE; 90 (LO), Jono Halling; 91 (Back), Walter Zerla/GI; 91 (UP LE), Jiang Hongyan/SS; 91 (UP RT), lucielang/IS; 91 (UP CTR LE), PeJo29/IS; 91 (UP CTR), Imagesbybarbara/IS; 91 (UP CTR RT), toddtaulman/IS; 91 (LO CTR RT), nilsz/IS; 91 (LO CTR LE), talevr/IS; 91 (LO LE), PhotosbyAbby/IS; 91 (LO RT), kedsanee/IS; 92 (UP), Art by Zac Freeman; 92 (LO), Courtesy KWS Infra; 93 (LO), WENN/Newscom; 93 (UP LE), Courtesy Nice Architects; 93 (UP RT), Courtesy Nice Architects; 94 (UP LE), nilsz/IS; 94 (UP RT), SA Team/MP; 94 (LO), Giorgio Cosulich/GI; 95, Alboo03/SS

Culture Connection (96-121)
96-97, Bruno Morandi/Robert Harding World Imagery; 98 (4), Tubol Evgeniya/SS; 98 (1), fotohunter/SS; 98 (7), pattarastock/SS; 98 (10), Shamil Zhumatov/Reuters/CO; 98 (9), Supachita Ae/SS; 98 (6), Maarten Wouters/GI; 99 (11), Dinodia/age fotostock; 99 (14), Zee/Alamy; 99 (15), wacpan/SS; 100-101, James Yamasaki; 100-101 (Back), Lilkar/dreamstime; 100-101 (LO), Lilkar/dreamstime; 100 (UP LE), Heidi Dubourgh Pedersen/GI; 100 (LO LE), Romeo Ranoco/CO; 100 (LO RT), Winnie Au/GI; 101 (UP LE), Philip Carr Photography/Photographers Direct; 101 (UP RT), Maro Hagopian/CO; 103 (RT), Mark Thiessen, NGS; 103 (LE), Mark Thiessen, NGS; 104 (UP), Courtesy Dr. Fred Hiebert; 104 (LE), Rebecca Hale/NGC; 104 (LO), Courtesy Dr. Fred Hiebert; 105 (UP), Courtesy Dr. Fred Hiebert; 105 (CTR LE), Courtesy Dr. Fred Hiebert; 105 (UP RT), Andre Jenny/Alamy; 105 (LO A), Art Directors & TRIP/Alamy; 105 (LO B), Lenscap/Alamy; 105 (LO C), ArtBabii/Alamy; 105 (LO D), Michael Burrell/Alamy; 105 (LO E), Martin Wierink/Alamy; 105 (LO F), razorpix/Alamy; 106, REX USA/Jaime Jacott; 107 (CTR), Reuters/Danish Siddiqui; 107 (LO), Eduardo Longo; 107 (UP), Simon Dale/ZUMAPRESS/Newscom; 108 (UP CTR), Africa Studio/SS; 108 (CTR LE), panda3800/SS; 108 (UP LE), Presselect/Alamy; 108 (LO LE), aa3/SS; 108 (CTR RT), SeanPavonePhoto/SS; 108 (LO RT), Jim1123/IS; 108 (UP RT), Mclein/SS; 109 (UP RT), Charlie Neuman/San Diego Union-Tribune/ZUMA Press/Alamy; 109 (UP CTR), Sethislav/IS; 109 (LO CTR LE), Oliver Arlow/Splash News/CO; 109 (UP CTR RT), bonchan/IS; 109 (LO CTR RT), tenback/IS; 109 (UP CTR RT), holbox/SS; 109 (UP LE), Mikael Andersson/Nordic Photos/GI; 109 (LO RT), Floortje/IS; 109 (UP RT), Catherine Lane/IS; 110 (CTR), Mark Theissen/NGS Staff; 110 (Back), Vertyr/SS; 111, Rebecca Hale/NGS Staff; 112 (CTR RT), Zoonar GmbH/Alamy; 112 (LO RT), Ninette Maumus/Alamy; 112 (UP RT), bullet74/SS; 112 (UP LE), Ivan Vdovin/Alamy; 112 (CTR LE), Fritz Goro/The LIFE Picture Collection/GI; 112 (CTR), PhotoStock-Israel/Alamy; 112 (LO LE), Courtesy The Banknote Book; 113 (LO CTR), D. Hurst/Alamy; 113 (LO LE), Nataliya Evmenenko/dreamstime; 113 (UP RT), Comstock/GI; 113 (UP LE), Ivan Vdovin/Alamy; 113, incamerastock/Alamy; 113, Splash News/NewsCom; 113 (LO RT), Kelley Miller/NGS Staff; 114, Sergey Novikov/SS; 115 (CTR), Gonzalo Ordo–ez; 116 (UP), Dean Macadam; 116 (LO), Dean Macadam; 117 (UP RT), Dean Macadam; 117 (LO RT), Dean Macadam; 117 (LO LE), Dean Macadam; 118 (UP), Randy Olson; 118 (LO LE), Martin Gray/NGS.com; 118 (UP LE), Sam Panthaky/AFP/GI; 119 (LO LE), Reza/NGS.com; 119 (LO RT), Richard Nowitz/NGS.com; 119 (UP), Filippo Monteforte/GI; 120 (UP), Mclein/SS; 120 (CTR), Nataliya Evmenenko/Dreamstime; 120 (LO), Gonzalo Ordo–ez; 121 (UP LE), catwalker/SS; 121 (UP RT), dimitris_k/SS; 121 (UP CTR), oconnelll/SS; 121 (LO), Steve Allen/SS

Awesome Adventure (122-141)
122-123, Menno Boermans/Robert Harding World Imagery; 124 (UP RT), John Catto/Alpenglow Pictures; 124 (CTR), Carsten Peter/NGS; 124 (CTR LE), Carsten Peter/NGS; 125 (UP RT), Charles Trout; 125 (LE), African People & Wildlife Fund; 125 (LO RT), Mitsuaki Iwago/MP; 126 (UP RT), Cory Richards/NGC; 126 (LE), Cory Richards/NGC; 126 (CTR LE), Cory Richards/NGC; 126 (CTR RT), Cory Richards/NGC; 127 (UP RT), Kenneth Garrett/NGS; 127 (LO RT), Robert Campbell; 127 (LOCTR), AP Photo/Kenneth Garrett; 127 (CTR), Scott Bjelland; 128 (7), Charles Brutlag/IS; 128 (UP LE), Sora Devore/NGC; 128 (1), Chokniti Khongchum/SS; 128 (2), Courtesy Jessica Cramp; 128 (3), Snyfer/Dreamstime.com; 128 (4), Sean Macdiarmid/Dreamstime.com; 128 (5), National Geographic Society Cartography Department; 128 (6), Juan Moyano/Dreamstime.com; 128 (8), poomsak suwannasilp/SS; 129 (9), Stuwdamdorp/Alamy; 129 (11), sagir/SS; 129 (12), Helen Sessions/Alamy; 129 (13), Igorp1976/Dreamstime.com; 129 (14), Fixzma/Dreamstime.com; 129 (15), Bloomberg/GI; 129 (16), Kguzel/Dreamstime.com; 129 (17), Image Courtesy Bananagrams; 129 (10), Marco Grob/NGC; 130 (LO), CENGAGE/NGC; 131 (LO CTR), Rhian Waller/NGC; 131 (LO RT), Rhian Waller/NGC; 131 (LO LE), Rhian Waller/National Geographic; 132, Carsten Peter/NGC; 133 (RT), Carsten Peter/NGC; 133 (LE), Carsten Peter/NGC; 134 (CTR), Tyler Stableford/Aurora Photos; 135 (UP), Alasdair Turner/Aurora Photos/CO; 135 (LO LE), Popperfoto/GI; 135 (LO RT), Ashley Cooper pics/Alamy; 136 (UP LE), Will Burrard-Lucas; 136 (UP RT), Will Burrard-Lucas; 136 (CTR), Will Burrard-Lucas; 136 (LO), Will Burrard-Lucas; 137 (UP), Tony Campbell/SS; 137 (CTR RT), PMACD|PHOTOGRAPHY/SS; 138 (CTR), Mattias Klum/NGC; 139 (UP), Brian J. Skerry/NGC; 139 (LO), Michael Nichols/NGC; 140 (UP), Ashley Cooper pics/Alamy; 140 (CTR), Carsten Peter/NGC; 140 (LO), CENGAGE/NGC; 141 (UP RT), Grady Reese/IS.com

Fun and Games (142-161)
142-143, Paul & Paveena Mckenzie/GI; 144 (A), Visuals Unlimited/GI; 144 (B), Donald M. Jones/MP; 144 (C), W. Perry Conway/CO; 144 (D), DLILLC/CO; 144 (E), Thomas Rabeil/NPL; 144 (F), Fred Bavendam/MP; 145 (UP LE), Ira Block/NGC; 145 (UP CTR), Ekaterina Pokrovsky/Dreamstime.com; 145 (UP RT), imageBROKER/Alamy; 145 (CTR LE), Richard du Toit Photography; 145 (CTR), Firefly Productions/CO; 145 (LO LE), Eddie Gerald/Alamy; 145 (LO LE), Frans Lemmens/GI; 145 (LO CTR), Fred Hirschmann/Science Faction/GI; 145 (LO RT), Philip Wallick/CO; 146, C-TON; 147 (Background), Dr. Morley Read/SS; 148, Joren Cull; 149, James Yamasaki; 150 (UP LE), RBP Trust/GI; 150 (UP RT), Stockbyte/GI; 150 (UP RT), Ed Collacott/GI; 150 (CTR LE), George Grall/NGC; 150 (CTR), ARCO/NPL; 150 (CTR RT), Ed Reschke/GI; 150 (LO LE), Charles Smith/CO; 150 (LO CTR), Brian Hagiwara/GI; 150 (LO RT), Francesco Ruggeri/GI; 151 (LO LE), Tom Grill/CO; 151 (UP), Eric Isselee/SS; 151 (LO RT), James Laurie/SS; 151, Tom Grill/CO; 151 (LO CTR), mlorenz/SS; 152, CTON; 153 (UP LE), Chris Ware; 153 (UP RT), Jean Galvao; 153 (CTR RT), Gary Fields; 153 (LO LE), Chris Ware; 154, Art by Jim Paillot; 155, James Yamasaki; 156 (UP), Johan Swanepoel/SS; 156 (CTR LE), s_oleg/SS; 156 (LO LE), Eric Isselee/SS; 156 (CTR RT), Hannamariah/SS; 156 (LO LE), Nick Biemans/SS; 156 (LO RT), Alex Kalmbach/SS; 157, CTON; 158 (CTR LE), Kalmatsuy/SS; 158 (LO), fivespots/SS; 158 (CTR RT), Kris Wiktor/SS; 158 (CTR RT), Chiyacat/SS; 158 (UP), Audrey Snider-Bell/SS; 158 (LO), fivespots/SS; 159, Art by Jason Tharp; 160-161, Strika Entertainment

Super Science (162-197)
162-163, RAKITA/SIPA/Newscom; 164 (4), Neil Fraser/Alamy; 164 (5), Bloomberg/GI; 164 (8), Chris Farina/CO; 164 (1), Everett Collection, Inc.; 164 (6), Rex Features/Rex USA; 165 (10), Joe Raedle/GI; 165 (13), Steve Marcus/Reuters/CO; 165 (17), Matthew Putney/Waterloo Courier/AP Photo; 165 (15), Lightspring/SS; 165 (9), Julie Jacobson/AP Photo; 165 (14), Julie Jacobson/AP Photo; 166 (UP), Georges Gobet/AFP/GI; 166 (UP CTR RT), Carlos Fernández Isoird; 166 (LO LE), 3Doodler; 166 (LO CTR RT), 3Doodler; 166 (LO RT), 3Doodler; 167 (UP), Art By Joe Rocco; 167 (LO), Art By Joe Rocco; 168 (LO), David Aguilar; 169 (E), Marie C. Fields/SS; 169 (D), Fedor A. Sidorov/SS; 169 (F), sgame/SS; 169 (A), Sebastian Kaulitzki/SS; 169 (B), Steve Gschmeissner/Photo Researchers, Inc.; 169 (C), Volker Steger/Christian Bardele/Photo Researchers, Inc.; 169 (G), Benjamin Jessop/IS.com; 170 (UP), Brand X/GI; 170 (LO), SSPL/Science Museum/GI;

342

A WORD FROM THE WISE

To Mum – The Wisest of the Wise

A WORD FROM THE WISE

Rosemarie Jarski

EBURY
PRESS

1 3 5 7 9 10 8 6 4 2

Published in 2006 by Ebury Press, an imprint of Ebury Publishing

Ebury Publishing is a division of the Random House Group

The Random House Group Limited Reg. No. 954009

Addresses for companies within the Random House Group
can be found at www.randomhouse.co.uk

A CIP catalogue record for this book is available from the British Library

Penguin Random House is committed to a sustainable future for
our business, our readers and our planet. This book is made from
Forest Stewardship Council® certified paper.

Printed and bound in Great Britain by Clays Ltd, Elcograf S.p.A.

ISBN 0091909201
ISBN 9780091909208 (from Jan 2007)

CONTENTS

A
1

Ability • Acceptance • Accident • Achievement • Acting
Action • Adolescence • Adult • Adultery • Adventure • Adversity
Advertising • Advice • Afterlife • Age • Agreement • Aims • Alcohol
Ambition • America • Analysis • Angel • Anger • Animal • Apathy
Apology • Appearance • Architecture • Argument • Art • Artist
Assassination • Astrology• Astronomy • Atheist • Attitude
Attraction • Awards and Honours

B
53

Beauty and Ugliness • Begin • Behaviour • Being • Belief • Bird • Birth
Blame • Blessings • Body • Books • Bore • Bureaucracy • Business • Busy

C
71

Capitalism • Capital Punishment • Cat • Category • Censorship
Certainty and Uncertainty • Chance • Change • Chaos • Character
Charity • Charm • Cheerfulness • Childhood • Children • Christianity
Church • Circumstances • City • Civilization • Club • Colour
Commandments • Common Sense • Communication • Communism
Community • Compassion • Compliment • Composer • Compromise
Computer • Confession • Confidence • Conformity and Originality
Conscience • Consequences • Contentment • Conversation
Cosmetic Surgery • Country & Western Music • Courage • Creativity
Crime and Punishment • Critic • Cruelty • Curiosity • Cynic

D
117

Dance • Danger • Dating • Days • Death • Deceiving and Deception
Decision • Democracy • Depression • Design • Desire • Despair • Detail
Devil • Dictator • Diet • Difference and Similarity • Difficult • Disability
Disappointment • Discovery • Divorce and Separation • Doctor
Dog • Doubt • Dreams • Drugs and Addiction

E
155

Education and Learning • Effort • Ego • Emotion • Enemy
Enthusiasm • Environment • Envy • Equality • Euthanasia • Evil
Evolution • Excuse • Exercise • Expectations • Experience • Expert

F
171

Facts • Failure • Faith • Fame • Family • Fanatic • Fashion and Dress
Fate • Father • Faults • Favours • Fear • Feminism • Fight • Film • Fishing
Flattery • Flowers • Food • Fool • Forgive • Freedom • Friend • Future

G
203

Gambling • Games • Garden • Gender and Sexuality • Generosity
Genius • Gentleness • Ghosts • Gifts and Giving • God • Good and Bad
Goodbyes • Gossip • Government • Gratitude • Greatness
Grief • Guest and Host • Guilt

H
227

Habit • Hair • Happiness • Hate • Health and Illness • Heart • Heaven
Hell • Help • Hero • History • Hobbies • Holiday • Home • Honesty
Hope • Humour • Hunting • Hurry • Hypocrisy

I
257

Ideas • Idle • Ignorance • Illusion • Imagination • Immortality
Importance • Impossible and Possible • Improvement • Indifference
Individuality • Information • Innocence • Insect • Inspiration
Instinct • Intellectual • Intelligence • Internet • Invention

J
275

Jazz • Jealousy • Jew • Journalism • Journalist • Joy • Justice

K
283

Kindness • Kiss • Knowledge

L
287

Language • Law • Lawyer • Leader • Letter • Lies and Lying • Life
Light and Dark • Listening • Literature • Little Things • Living
Logic, Reason and Nonsense • Loneliness • Love • Luck
Luxury and Necessity

M
311

Madness • Man • Manners • Marriage • Martyr • Masses and Minorities
Maths • Meaning • Meaning of Life • Memory • Men • Men and Women
Mind • Miracle • Misery • Mistake • Money • Morals • Mother
Murder • Music • Mystery

N
347

Name • Nature • Needs • Neighbour • Neutral • Never...
Noise • Normal • Nostalgia • Nothing

INTRODUCTION

An angel appears at a college faculty meeting and tells the Dean that in return for his exemplary behaviour, the Lord will reward him with his choice of infinite wealth, wisdom or beauty. Without hesitating, the Dean chooses infinite wisdom. 'Done' says the angel, and disappears in a puff of smoke and a bolt of lightning. All heads then turn towards the Dean, who is bathed in a halo of light. At length, one of his colleagues whispers, 'Say something.' The Dean looks at them and says, 'I should have taken the money.'

That's the trouble with wisdom – you don't get it until *after* you need it. If only there was a way to acquire the wisdom without first having to suffer the slings and arrows of outrageous fortune, how much easier would that make our journey through life.

'To know the road ahead ask those coming back,' goes an old Chinese saying. Who better to offer guidance than those who've been there, done that, got the metaphorical long white beard and furrowed brow? 'Better be wise by the misfortunes of others than by your own,' declared Aesop. They suffer the slings and arrows so you don't have to.

A Word from the Wise gathers together hundreds of fellow travellers on life's highway to share their pearls of hard-won wisdom. They cover all the hot-button issues including life, death, war, peace, truth, beauty, and how to test the ripeness of Camembert cheese. Subjects are arranged alphabetically so whatever challenge you're facing, you can speedily locate some nugget of wisdom to inspire, console or amuse.

Traditionally, the oracle of wisdom has been the philosopher. The word itself is Greek, meaning 'lover of wisdom', and there have been philosophers of the past who lived up to that definition. Sages such as Montaigne, Voltaire and La Rochefoucauld had a passion for inquiry which they communicated in a sparklingly witty and engaging style that spoke to everybody; however, over the last century the subject of philosophy has been hijacked by academics. Philosophers, ensconced in their ivory towers, deep in the groves of academe, have lost touch with the lives of ordinary people. For example, here's a thought plucked at random from contemporary French philosopher Jacques Derrida:

> One can expose only that which at a certain moment can
> become present, manifest, that which can be shown, presented
> as something present, a being-present in its truth, in the truth
> of a present or the presence of the present.

Compare that with this from fellow French thinker, Nicolas Chamfort, more than 200 years earlier:

> Swallow a toad every morning to be sure of encountering
> nothing more disgusting the rest of the day.

Whose advice do you prefer? Perhaps more to the point, whose advice do you actually understand? It's no contest. 'Too much perspiration for too little inspiration' is how one commentator summed up Monsieur Derrida and that goes for too many modern professional purveyors of profundity. It's easy to be intimidated by long-winded and abstruse prose, but don't confuse complexity with profundity. Cleverness is not wisdom. Wisdom doesn't depend on how many letters you have after your name. It comes from experience, from those who have, in the words of Mae West, 'been things and seen places'. The wisdom collected here bears the stamp of authenticity because the speakers are all graduates of the University of Life. They come from every imaginable category of humankind – saints and sinners, rebels and reprobates, celebrities and cynics, royals and revolutionaries, and Michael Winner.

Comedians are well represented. Surprising, perhaps, since wisdom is generally considered to be serious and sombre – it wears a sober suit, whereas comedy is shallow and slight – it wears a silly hat ('Comedy sits at the children's table,' Woody Allen once remarked). In fact, wisdom and humour are closely allied. The word 'wise' is related to the Old English word 'witan' meaning 'wit', from which we get words like 'wisecrack' and 'wiseacre'. The eye for absurdity, ear for cant, and built-in bullshit-detector possessed by the best comics are precisely the qualities of wisdom. Wits like Woody Allen, Groucho Marx, Steven Wright and Spike Milligan are true philosophers of our time. You can learn more about the human condition by watching *Manhattan*, *The Simpsons* or *Duck Soup* than reading philosophy books. Plus you get the bonus of a laugh. As Irving Berlin put it: 'The world would not be in such a snarl, had Marx been Groucho instead of Karl.'

The emphasis is on wisdom for everyday life so expect a liberal sprinkling of proverbs. A proverb is a brief sentence based on long experience, an Oxo cube containing the concentrated wisdom of man. The way they work is by converting abstract thought into concrete language, often via a picturesque image or metaphor. Since we discover what something is largely by comparing it to something else that we already understand, this is an ideal way to learn. Chinese thinker Lin Yutang explains the process: 'To say, "How could I perceive his inner mental processes?" is not so intelligible as

"How could I know what is going on in his mind?" and this in turn is decidedly less effective than the Chinese "Am I a tapeworm in his belly?" '

Colourful, memorable and user-friendly, but therein lies the problem: with excess use, proverbs eventually lose their lustre, and turn into clichés. But a cliché is only a cliché if you've heard it before. Reset a worn-out gem in a new setting and suddenly it sparkles anew:

Other people's eggs have two yolks. (Bulgarian)
The grass is always greener on the other side of the fence.

You can't teach an old monkey how to make faces. (French)
You can't teach an old dog new tricks.

He who has a head of butter must not come near the oven. (Dutch)
If you can't stand the heat keep out of the kitchen.

He ate the camel and all it carried. (Arabian)
He ate us out of house and home.

When the sky falls we shall catch larks. (French)
Pigs might fly.

'By a country's proverbs shall ye know its people' isn't a proverb as far as I know – but it ought to be. Vivid idioms and expressions provide a glimpse into a culture, an insight into a nation's foibles and fixations. For example, the German language is littered with sausage-based sayings, the Bulgarians favour hens and eggs, while the Arabs can't resist a camel.

The net to catch words of wisdom has been cast not only across cultures and continents but centuries too. Can ancient wisdom speak to us as clearly as modern musings? Try this for size: 'Children today are tyrants. They have no respect for their elders, flout authority and have appalling manners. What terrible creatures will they grow up into?' This may sound like a letter in the *Daily Mail* but it is in fact the Ancient Greek thinker, Socrates, speaking two and a half thousand years ago. He may be sporting a tunic and have a chariot parked outside, but the sentiments expressed are unmistakably modern.

'Colours fade, temples crumble, empires fall, but wise words endure,' wrote Edward Thorndike. Wise words endure because, in spite of radical changes in society, in spite of technological advances, and in spite of what we ourselves like to think about 'progress', human nature does not change: kids rebel, men cheat, women cry, politicians lie, the rich get richer and the poor get stuffed again. The big questions of life also remain constant: Who are we? Why are we here? Where are we going? And what if the hokey cokey really is what it's all about?

Questioning is the key to wisdom. Look at the world's greatest minds, past or present, and what distinguishes them is an unquenchable curiosity without which any innate intelligence or talent would wither and die. When Nobel Prize-winner for physics, Isidor Isaac Rabi, was asked to account for his extraordinary achievements, he explained: 'When we got out of school, all the mothers would ask their children what they had learned that day. My mother would inquire instead, "What did you ask today in class?"'

'The important thing is not to stop questioning,' urged Albert Einstein. The greatest genius of the twentieth century never lost his child-like ability to ask questions and modestly asserted, 'I have no special gift. I am only passionately curious.' Jacob Bronowski described him as 'a man who could ask immensely simple questions. And what his work showed is that when the answers are simple too, then you can hear God thinking.'

To the great questions in life, even Einstein did not have the answers, because there are no right or wrong solutions. 'There are trivial truths and there are great truths. The opposite of a trivial truth is plainly false. The opposite of a great truth may well be another profound truth,' explained physicist Niels Bohr. For every wise thought there is another equally wise thought expressing precisely the opposite point of view. Contradictory proverbs illustrate the point at its simplest:

Too many cooks spoil the broth.
Many hands make light work.

Better safe than sorry.
Nothing ventured, nothing gained.

The more the merrier.
Two's company, three's a crowd.

Fools rush in where angels fear to tread.
He who hesitates is lost.

The ability to juggle in your mind conflicting attitudes on the same topic may be defined as understanding; the ability to reconcile conflicting attitudes is wisdom in its deepest sense. 'The way of paradoxes is the way of truth,' wrote Oscar Wilde. 'To test Reality we must see it on the tightrope. When the Verities become acrobats we can judge them.'

The irony is that, although we brand ourselves *Homo sapiens* ('wise man'), we are, as a species, resistant to contradictions and ambiguity. Contradictions mean uncertainty and insecurity, which lead to anxiety and fear. What *Homo sapiens* craves most is certainty. Hence the popularity of the 'expert' in his many manifestations – guru, life-coach, inspirational guide, etc. The expert has all the answers. There's never room for doubt in the expert's mind. He knows the 'one true path' to enlightenment/success/wealth/health/happiness, or all of the above.

A Word from the Wise is wise enough to know it does not have all the answers. After all, how can you understand the universe when it's hard enough to find your car in the multi-story car park? Nor does it promise to show you the one true path for the simple reason that the only true path is the one you forge yourself. The best that these words of wisdom can do is to serve as streetlamps, lighting up the road ahead. Then again, 6,000 kindly lights can spread quite a lot of wattage amid the encircling gloom. So, to set you on your way with a spring in your step, chew on this illuminating piece of advice from Yogi Berra: 'If you come to a fork in the road, take it.' With guidance like that, who needs Sat Nav?

Rosemarie Jarski

ABILITY

Life is like a ten-speed bike. Most of us have gears we never use.

Charles M. Schulz

I can levitate birds. No one cares.

Steven Wright

Competence, like truth, beauty and contact lenses, is in the eye of the beholder.

Laurence J. Peter

A human being should be able to change a diaper, plan an invasion, butcher a hog, conn a ship, design a building, write a sonnet, balance accounts, build a wall, set a bone, comfort the dying, take orders, give orders, cooperate, act alone, solve equations, analyze a new problem, pitch manure, programme a computer, cook a tasty meal, fight efficiently, die gallantly. Specialization is for insects.

Robert Heinlein

It is always our inabilities that vex us.

Joseph Joubert

Caution: Cape does not enable user to fly.

Warning label on Batman costume

The girl who can't dance says the band can't play.

Jewish proverb

What one has to do, usually can be done.

Eleanor Roosevelt

Sometimes it is more important to discover what one cannot do, than what one can do.

Lin Yutang

ACCEPTANCE

Welcome death, quoth the rat, when the trap fell.   Thomas Fuller

When a dog runs at you, whistle for him.   Henry David Thoreau

It is so much easier sometimes to sit down and be resigned than to rise up
and be indignant.   Ella Winter

Inaction may be the highest form of action.   Jerry Brown

Lie down and listen to the crabgrass grow, the faucet leak, and learn to
leave them so.   Marya Mannes

The important thing is to know how to take all things quietly.
                Michael Faraday

Wonderful maxim: not to talk of things any more after they are done.
                Baron de Montesquieu

It is so. It cannot be otherwise.
                Inscription on the ruins of a fifteenth-century cathedral in Amsterdam

Let It Be.   John Lennon and Paul McCartney

ACCIDENT

Nothing is accidental in the universe – this is one of my Laws of Physics –
except the entire universe itself, which is Pure Accident, pure divinity.
                Joyce Carol Oates

There are no accidents so unfortunate from which skilful men will not
draw some advantage, nor so fortunate that foolish men will not turn them
to their hurt.   La Rochefoucauld

The most painful household accident is wearing socks and stepping on an upturned plug.

Peter Kay

Accident is veiled necessity.

Marie von Ebner-Eschenbach

ACHIEVEMENT

Some of the best moments in life are not when you have achieved something but when the thought first comes to you to have a go.   Lord Hunt

Three great essentials to achieve anything worthwhile are, first, hard work; second, stick-to-itiveness; third, common sense.

Thomas Edison

My most brilliant achievement was my ability to persuade my wife to marry me.

Winston Churchill

ACTING

Acting is a minor gift; after all, Shirley Temple could do it at the age of four.

Katharine Hepburn

There are five stages in the life of an actor 1) Who's Mary Astor? 2) Get me Mary Astor 3) Get me a Mary Astor type 4) Get me a young Mary Astor 5) Who's Mary Astor?

Mary Astor

Movie actors are just ordinary, mixed-up people – with agents.   Jean Kerr

If there wasn't something called acting, they would probably hospitalize people like me.

Whoopi Goldberg

You can never count anybody out in this business. I've seen actors with careers deader than my mother's brisket come back to life and win Academy Awards.

Rita Rudner

There's a fine line between the Method actor and the schizophrenic.

Nicolas Cage

The question actors most often get asked is how they can bear saying the same things over and over again night after night, but God knows the answer to that is, don't we all anyway; might as well get paid for it.

Elaine Dundy

If there is a streak of ham anywhere in an actor, Shakespeare will bring it out.

Robert Benchley

Even her eyelashes acted.

Virginia Woolf on Ellen Terry

If you give audiences a chance they'll do half your acting for you.

Katharine Hepburn

We are all pretending ... The important thing is to maintain a straight face.

Maurice Valency

Every actor has a natural animosity towards every other actor, present or absent, living or dead.

Louise Brooks

ACTION

We can stand here like the French, or we can do something.

Marge Simpson, *The Simpsons*

All mankind is divided into three classes: those that are immovable, those that are movable, and those that move.

Arabian proverb

Let him that would move the world, first move himself.

Socrates

We are what we do.

Erich Fromm

First do it, then say it.

Russian proverb

The basis of action is lack of imagination. It is the last resource of those who know not how to dream.

Oscar Wilde

It is in human nature to think wisely and to act in an absurd fashion.

Anatole France

Contemplation often makes life miserable. We should act more, think less, and stop watching ourselves live.

Nicolas Chamfort

Action is the antidote to despair.

Joan Baez

What man really wishes to do he will find a means of doing.

George Bernard Shaw

It is not doing the things we like to do, but liking the thing we have to do that makes life blessed.

Johann Wolfgang von Goethe

Either define the moment or the moment will define you.

Walt Whitman

We must scrunch or be scrunched.

Charles Dickens

Be a pianist, not a piano.

A. R. Orage

A peasant must sit in his chair with his mouth open for a very long time before a roast duck will fly in.

Chinese proverb

You'll never plough a field by turning it over in your mind.

Irish proverb

You've got to say, 'I'm a human being, goddammit. My life has value!'
So I want you to get up now. I want all of you to get up out of your chairs.
I want you to get up right now and go to the window, open it, and stick your head out, and yell, 'I'm as mad as hell, and I'm not going to take this anymore!'

Howard Beale, *Network*

There should be less talk … What do you do then? Take a broom and clean someone's house. That says enough.
Mother Teresa

Just do it.
Advertising slogan, Nike sportswear

ADOLESCENCE

Adolescence is just one big walking pimple.
Carol Burnett

We become adolescents when the words that adults exchange with one another become intelligible to us.
Natalia Ginzburg

All Giggle, Blush, half Pertness and half Pout.
Lord Byron

Who would ever think that so much can go on in the soul of a young girl?
Anne Frank

Adolescence is a marketing ploy.
Elaine Miller, *Almost Famous*

Few things are more satisfying than seeing your children have teenagers of their own.
Doug Larson

ADULT

I think adults are just children who owe money.
Andrew Benson, *Peter's Friends*

Another belief of mine: that everyone else my age is an adult, whereas I am merely in disguise.
Margaret Atwood

If this was adulthood, the only improvement she could detect in her situation was that now she could eat dessert without eating her vegetables.
Lisa Alther

We have not passed that subtle line between childhood and adulthood until we move from the passive voice to the active voice – that is, until we have stopped saying, 'It got lost,' and say, 'I lost it.' George Harris

When they tell you to grow up, they mean stop growing. Tom Robbins

We live a protracted adolescence. At some point you must leave the party. Don Henley

But childhood prolonged cannot remain a fairyland. It becomes a hell. Louise A. Bogan

Being a grown-up means assuming responsibility for yourself, for your children, and – here's the big curve – for your parents. Wendy Wasserstein

I'm too old to grow up. Huey Walker, *Flashback*

ADULTERY

I said to the wife, 'Guess what I heard in the pub? They reckon the milkman has made love to every woman in this road except one.' And she said, 'I'll bet it's that stuck-up Phyllis at number 23.' Max Kauffmann

You know the story: I thought I was lonely, and he forgot he was married. Angela Bennett, *The Net*

I know many married men, I even know a few happily married men, but I don't know one who wouldn't fall down the first open coal hole running after the first pretty girl who gave him a wink. George Jean Nathan

A man is only as faithful as his options. Chris Rock

Madame, you must really be more careful. Suppose it had been someone else who found you like this.

Duc de Richelieu on discovering his wife *in flagrante delicto*

—Why did you desert your wife for another woman?
—Because I am a bastard.   Interviewer and Ernest Hemingway

The first thrill of adultery is entering the house. Everything there has been paid for by the other man.   John Updike

Have you ever tried getting dressed quietly in a dark closet with a pocketful of change?   Hawkeye, *M*A*S*H*

As a rule, the person found out in a betrayal of love holds, all the same, the superior position of the two. It is the betrayed one who is humiliated.
                    Ada Leverson

There's nothing in the world like the devotion of a married woman.
It's a thing no married man knows anything about.   Oscar Wilde

Philanderers: avoid the embarrassment of shouting out the wrong name in bed by only having flings with girls who have the same name as your wife.
                    Viz magazine, top tip

It can take a man several marriages to understand the importance of monogamy.   Jason Love

If you marry a man who cheats on his wife, you'll be married to a man who cheats on his wife.   Ann Landers

I could never have a mistress, because I couldn't bear to tell the story of my life all over again.   Oscar Levant

ADVENTURE

One way to get the most out of life is to look upon it as an adventure.
                    William Feather

Life is either a daring adventure or nothing.   Helen Keller

Without adventure all civilization is full of decay. Adventure rarely reaches its predetermined end. Columbus never reached China.

Alfred North Whitehead

The most beautiful adventures are not those we go to seek.

Robert Louis Stevenson

Nobody is ever met at the airport when beginning a new adventure. It's just not done.

Elizabeth Warnock Fernea

People who go to the polar regions are statistically less likely to die than salesmen who drive on motorways in England.

Sir Ranulph Fiennes

But almost any place is Baghdad if you don't know what will happen in it.

Edna Ferber

The real adventure in *Moby Dick* is the one that happens inside Captain Ahab. The rest is a fishing trip.

Salman Rushdie

Adventure is the result of poor planning.

Blatchford Snell

Twenty years from now you will be more disappointed by the things you didn't do than by the ones you did do. So throw off the bowlines. Sail away from the safe harbor. Catch the trade winds in your sails. Explore. Dream. Discover.

Mark Twain

ADVERSITY

By trying we can easily learn to endure adversity. Another man's, I mean.

Mark Twain

There are moments when everything goes well; don't be frightened, it won't last.

Jules Renard

If you're going through hell, keep going.

Winston Churchill

Life for most of us is full of steep stairs to go up and later, shaky stairs to totter down; and very early in the history of stairs must have come the invention of bannisters.
Louis Kronenberg

When you go in search of honey you must expect to be stung by bees.
President Kaunda of Zambia

A clay pot sitting in the sun will always be a clay pot. It has to go through the white heat of the furnace to become porcelain.
Mildred Witte Stouven

The best way out is always through.
Robert Frost

The world is full of cactus, but we don't have to sit on it.
Will Foley

When it is dark enough, you can see the stars.
Ralph Waldo Emerson

Every path hath a puddle.
George Herbert

Men do not stumble over mountains, but over molehills.
Confucius

Kites rise highest against the wind – not with it.
Winston Churchill

Whatever does not kill me makes me stronger.
Friedrich Nietzsche

When any calamity has been suffered, the first thing to be remembered is how much has been escaped.
Samuel Johnson

Lost luggage is just an opportunity to start afresh.
Chris Evans

The woman who has laughed is the same one who will cry, and that is why you can tell from the way a woman is when she is happy how she will be in the face of adversity.
Simone Schwarz-Bart

Let us be of good cheer by remembering that the misfortunes that are hardest to bear are those that never come.
Lord Kitchener

ADVERTISING

I do not read advertisements. I would spend all my time wanting things.

Archbishop of Canterbury

Society drives people crazy with lust and calls it advertising.   *John Lahr*

The art of advertising – untruthfulness combined with repetition.

Freya Stark

Time spent in the advertising business seems to create a permanent deformity like the Chinese habit of foot-binding.   *Dean Acheson*

The deeper problems connected with advertising come less from the unscrupulousness of our 'deceivers' than from our pleasure in being deceived, less from the desire to seduce than from the desire to be seduced.

Daniel J. Boorstin

You can tell the ideals of a nation by its advertisements.   *Norman Douglas*

When someone hands you a flier it's like they're saying, 'Here, you throw this away.'   Mitch Hedberg

Doing business without advertising is like winking at a girl in the dark: you know what you are doing, but nobody else does.   *E. W. Howe*

When the client moans and sighs
Make his logo twice the size.
If he still should prove refractory,
Show a picture of his factory.
Only in the gravest cases
Should you show the clients' faces.

Anon

Is it not clear that a product which must spend fortunes advertising, drawing attention to itself, is probably not one we need?   David Mamet

I think that I shall never see a billboard lovely as a tree.   Ogden Nash

ADVICE

Advice: the suggestions you give someone else which you hope will work for your benefit.   Ambrose Bierce

There is no human problem which could not be solved if people would simply do as I advise.   Gore Vidal

'What would Jesus do?' may be a good philosophy of life for some, but I find that it rarely helps me decide how much to tip a hooker.
          Charles Gulledge

What would Jesus do?   Christian bumper sticker

What would Cher do?   Gay bumper sticker

What would Scooby Doo?   Bumper sticker

What would Lenny Henry say?   David Brent, *The Office*

Advice should always be consumed between two thick slices of doubt.
          Walter Schmidt

Advice is what we ask for when we already know the answer but wish we didn't.   Erica Jong

No one wants advice – only corroboration.   John Steinbeck

A never-failing way to get rid of a fellow is to tell him something for his own good.   Kin Hubbard

I have found the best way to give advice to your children is to find out what they want and then advise them to do it.　　　Harry S. Truman

The art of advice is to make the recipient believe he thought of it himself.
　　　Frank Tyger

The true secret of giving advice is, after you have honestly given it, to be perfectly indifferent whether it is taken or not and never persist in trying to set people right.　　　Hannah Whitall Smith

Strange, when you ask anyone's advice you see yourself what is right.
　　　Selma Lagerlöf

Advice is always a confession.　　　André Maurois

A good scare is worth more to a man than good advice.　　　E. W. Howe

A woman in love never takes advice.　　　Rosamond Marshall

Give help rather than advice.　　　Marquis de Vauvenargues

Don't be troubled if the temptation to give advice is irresistible; the ability to ignore it is universal.　　　Anon

I owe my success to having listened respectfully to the very best advice, and then going away and doing the exact opposite.　　　G. K. Chesterton

Listen, folks, there's no magic formula. I just followed the three Cs: clean living, chewing thoroughly, and a daily dose of vitamin church.
　　　Ned Flanders, *The Simpsons*

Swallow a toad every morning to be sure of encountering nothing more disgusting the rest of the day.　　　Nicolas Chamfort

Beware of long arguments and long beards.　　　George Santayana

Don't squat with yer spurs on.　　　Texas Bix Bender

Pissing in your shoes won't keep your feet warm for long.   **Icelandic proverb**

Don't open a shop unless you know how to smile.   **Jewish proverb**

Do not suck your thumb – or anybody else's, for that matter.   **Forrest Gump**

Do something wonderful, people may imitate it.   **Albert Schweitzer**

Find out what you don't do well, then don't do it.   **Alf, *Alf***

In difficult circumstances always act on first impressions.   **Leo Tolstoy**

If you can't convince them, confuse them.   **Harry S. Truman**

Nothing *risqué*, nothing gained.   **Alexander Woollcott**

Everything is personal.   **Anon**

Remember, no one can make you feel inferior without your consent.

Eleanor Roosevelt

Speak softly and carry a big stick; you will go far.   **Teddy Roosevelt**

Always stay in with the outs.   **David Halberstam**

Don't ever take a fence down until you know why it was put up.   **Robert Frost**

When in doubt, stick your left out.   **Henry Cooper**

Don't ever slam a door; you might want to go back.   **Anon**

Beware of limbo dancers.   **Toilet graffiti**

Always accept a breath mint if offered one.   **M. Jackson Brown**

Most of us would rather risk a catastrophe than read the instructions.

Mignon McLaughlin

If everything seems to be coming your way, you're probably in the wrong lane.

Anon

Distinguish between power and control, delegate, be decisive – and always remember people's first names.

Sir Alex Ferguson

When you're being stalked by an angry mob with raspberries, the first thing to do is to release a tiger.

John Cleese, *Monty Python*

Learn to say no. It will be of more use to you than to be able to read Latin.

Charles Spurgeon

If your boss is getting you down, look at him through the prongs of a fork and imagine him in jail.

David Brent, *The Office*

It is easier for a camel to pass through the eye of a needle if it is lightly greased.

Kehlog Albran

When in charge, ponder. When in trouble, delegate. When in doubt, mumble.

James Boren

If it moves, salute it. If it doesn't move, pick it up. If you can't pick it up, paint it.

British army maxim

Look up and not down; out and not in; forward and not back; and lend a hand.

Edward Everett Hale

See everything, overlook a great deal, correct a little.

Pope John XXIII

Try to be one upon whom nothing is lost.

Henry James

Fear less, hope more, eat less, chew more, whine less, breathe more, talk less, say more, hate less, love more and all good things will be yours.

Swedish proverb

'It can't happen here' is number one on the list of famous last words.

David Crosby

Nothing ever goes away.

Barry Commoner

Three little sentences will get you through life. Number one: Cover for me. Number two: Oh, good idea, boss. Number three: It was like that when I got here.

Homer Simpson

When I was a small boy, my father told me never to recommend a church or a woman to anyone. And I have found it wise never to recommend a restaurant either. Something always goes wrong with the cheese soufflé.

Edmund G. Love

If you drink from a bottle marked 'poison' it is almost certain to disagree with you sooner or later.

Lewis Carroll

When in doubt, play track 4 – it is usually the one you want.

Elvis Costello

The best advice I've ever received is, 'No one else knows what they're doing either.'

Ricky Gervais

Keep your bowels open, your tin hat on and trust to God.

Anon

Ama, et fac quod vis.
Love, and do what you want.

Augustinus, AD 400

AFTERLIFE

George Harrison's passing was really sad, but it does make the afterlife seem much more attractive.

Michael Palin

There is no conclusive evidence of life after death. But there is no evidence of any sort against it. You will know soon enough – why worry about it?

John Marshall

—You could probably convert me because I'm a pushover. And if you make it appealing enough and you promise me some wonderful afterlife with a white robe and wings ... I could go for it.
—I can't promise you wings, but I can promise you a wonderful, exciting life.
—One wing?

Woody Allen and Billy Graham

We do not know what to do with this short life, yet we want another which will be eternal.

Anatole France

I don't believe in an afterlife, so I don't have to spend my whole life fearing hell, or fearing heaven even more. For whatever the tortures of hell, I think the boredom of heaven would be even worse.

Isaac Asimov

If there is a sin against life, it consists perhaps not so much in despairing of life as in hoping for another life and in eluding the implacable grandeur of this life.

Albert Camus

The thought of my sons carrying on after I'm gone is about as close to belief in an afterlife as an ageing pagan like myself is likely to get. But curiously, it's close enough for comfort.

Carey Winfrey

One world at a time.

Ralph Waldo Emerson

AGE

You're sixty-five today – and it's the first day of the rest of your life savings.

Anon

How old would you be if you didn't know how old you was?

Leroy 'Satchel' Paige

It is perhaps life's greatest accomplishment to live to old age, maintaining one's wits, one's sense of humour, one's health, and one's charm.

Yehudi Menuhin

Granny says she was going to grow old gracefully, but she's left it too late.

Christine Kelly

I'm going to Iowa for an award. Then I'm appearing at Carnegie Hall, it's sold out. Then I'm sailing to France to be honored by the French government. I'd give it all up for one erection.

Groucho Marx

How young can you die of old age?

Steven Wright

The first forty years of life give us the text; the last thirty supply the commentary.

Arthur Schopenhauer

If youth knew; if age could.

Henri Etienne

Midlife is when you reach the top of the ladder only to find that it was leaning against the wrong wall.

Joseph Campbell

Middle age is the time when you think that in a week or two you'll feel as good as ever.

Don Marquis

When I was young, I was told: 'You'll see, when you're fifty.' I'm fifty and I haven't seen a thing.

Erik Satie

One of the many things nobody ever tells you about middle age is that it's such a nice change from being young.

William Feather

Old age is the most unexpected of all the things that happen to a man.

Leon Trotsky

By the time a man notices that he is no longer young, his youth has long since left him.

François Mauriac

You know what ages a man – boredom.

Marcello Rubini, *La Dolce Vita*

The problem with being my age is everybody thinks you're a father figure but you're really the same asshole you always were.

Graham Keighley, *The Paper*

Once you get older, people stop listening to what you say. It's very agreeable once you get used to it.

A. S. Byatt

The great secret that all old people share is that you really haven't changed in seventy or eighty years. Your body changes, but you don't change at all. And that, of course, causes great confusion.

Doris Lessing

Our years, our debts, and our enemies are always more numerous than we imagine.

Charles Nodier

'When I was your age—' 'No one,' said Vicki, 'is ever anyone else's age, except physically.'

Faith Baldwin

I don't believe one grows older. I think that what happens early on in life is that at a certain age one stands still and stagnates.

T. S. Eliot

When I was fourteen, I was the oldest I ever was ... I've been getting younger ever since.

Shirley Temple

Age is getting to know all the ways the world turns, so that if you cannot turn the world the way you want, you can at least get out of the way so you won't get run over.

Miriam Makeba

At twenty we worry about what others think of us; at forty we don't care about what others think of us; at sixty we discover they haven't been thinking about us at all.

Anon

It's every woman's tragedy that, after a certain age, she looks like a female impersonator.

Angela Carter

Don't think of it as wrinkles. Think of it as relaxed-fit skin.   Cathy Crimmins

Take care that old age does not wrinkle your spirit even more than
your face.   Michel de Montaigne

Good cheekbones are the brassière of old age.   Barbara de Portago

As a man advances in life he gets what is better than admiration –
judgement to estimate things at their own value.   Samuel Johnson

The longer one lives, the more one realizes that nothing is a dish for
every day.   Norman Douglas

The real sadness of fifty is not that you change so much but that you
change so little.   Max Lerner

Everyone should keep a mental waste-paper basket and the older he grows
the more things he will consign to it – torn up to irrecoverable tatters.
  Samuel Butler

No one is ever old enough to know better.   Holbrook Jackson

I haven't changed much over the years. I use less adjectives now, and
have a kinder heart, perhaps.   Angela Carter

To grow old is to pass from passion to compassion.   Albert Camus

It is not by the grey of the hair that one knows the age of the heart.
  Edward Bulwer-Lytton

The great thing about getting older is that you don't lose all the other
ages you've been.   Madelaine L'Engle

Life is available to anyone no matter what age. All you have to do is
grab it.   Art Carney

After eighty, there are no enemies, only survivors.   David Ben-Gurion

As the evening twilight fades away, the sky is filled with stars invisible by day.
Henry Wadsworth Longfellow

In spite of illness, in spite even of the arch-enemy, sorrow, one can remain alive long past the usual date of disintegration if one is unafraid of change, insatiable in intellectual curiosity, interested in big things, and happy in small ways.
Edith Wharton

If a family has one old person in it, it possesses a jewel.
Chinese proverb

The ageing process has you firmly in its grasp if you never get the urge to throw a snowball.
Doug Larson

I feel I want to be wise with white hair in a tall library in a deep chair by a fireplace.
Gregory Corso, *Writ on the Eve of my 32nd Birthday*

My seventieth year! There is really no comment to make about that except perhaps 'Well, well,' 'Fancy', or 'Oh, fuck'.
Noël Coward

Old places and old persons in their turn, when spirit dwells in them, have an intrinsic vitality of which youth is incapable; precisely the balance and wisdom that comes from long perspectives and broad foundations.
George Santayana

I used to think getting old was about vanity but actually it's about losing people you love.
Joyce Carol Oates

By the time you're eighty years old you've learned everything. You only have to remember it.
George Burns

Of course I'm respectable. I'm old. Politicians, public buildings, and whores all get respectable if they last long enough.
Noah Cross, *Chinatown*

I hope I never get so old I get religious.
Ingmar Bergman

A man of eighty has outlived probably three new schools of painting,
two of architecture and poetry and a hundred in dress.   Joyce Carey

All sorts of allowances are made for the illusion of youth; and none,
or almost none, for the disenchantment of age.   Robert Louis Stevenson

Those who love deeply never grow old; they may die of old age, but they
die young.   Sir Arthur Wing Pinero

When the wires are all down and your heart is covered with the snow
of pessimism and the ice of cynicism, then – and then only – are you
grown old.   Douglas MacArthur

The secret of salvation is this: keep sweet, be useful, and keep busy.
          Elbert Hubbard

Do not grow old, no matter how long you live. Never cease to stand like
curious children before the Great Mystery into which we are born.
          Albert Einstein

When Goya was eighty he drew an ancient man propped up on two sticks,
with a great mass of white hair and beard all over his face, and the
inscription 'I am still learning'.   Simone de Beauvoir

AGREEMENT

One of my favourite philosophical tenets is that people will agree with you
only if they already agree with you. You do not change people's minds.
          Frank Zappa

When people agree with me I always feel that I must be wrong.
          Oscar Wilde

Elinor agreed with it all, for she did not think he deserved the compliment
of rational opposition.   Jane Austen

There is nothing more likely to start disagreement between people or countries than an agreement.

E. B. White

My sad conviction is that people can only agree about what they're not really interested in.

Bertrand Russell

The fellow who agrees with everything you say is either a fool or he is getting ready to skin you.

Kin Hubbard

I don't necessarily agree with everything I say.

Marshall McLuhan

AIMS

The aim of life is self-development. To realize one's nature perfectly – that is what each of us is here for.

Oscar Wilde

There are two things to aim at in life: first, to get what you want; and after that, to enjoy it. Only the wisest of mankind achieve the second.

Logan Pearsall Smith

Most people have never learned that one of the main aims in life is to enjoy it.

Samuel Butler

Many people have the right aims in life. They just never get around to pulling the trigger.

Sunshine magazine

Ours is a world where people don't know what they want and are willing to go through hell to get it.

Don Marquis

In the absence of clearly defined goals, we become strangely loyal to performing daily trivia until ultimately we become enslaved by it.

Robert Heinlein

As you ramble on through life, brother, whatever be your goal: keep your eyes upon the donut, and not upon the hole!

Dr Murray Banks

The ordinary objects of human endeavour – property, outward success, luxury have always seemed to me contemptible ... The ideals which have lighted me on my way and time after time given me new courage to face life cheerfully, have been Truth, Goodness, and Beauty.   Albert Einstein

ALCOHOL

—Pour you a beer, Mr Peterson?
—All right, but stop me at one. Make that one-thirty.
                      Woody Harrelson and Norm Peterson, *Cheers*

Life, Liberty, and Pursuit of Happy Hour.   Hawkeye, *M*A*S*H*

Conversation, like certain portions of the anatomy, always runs more smoothly when lubricated.   Marquis de Sade, *Quills*

One of the most awkward things that can happen in a pub is when your pint-to-toilet cycle gets synchronized with a complete stranger.   Peter Kay

There comes a time in every woman's life when the only thing that helps is a glass of champagne.   Kitty Marlowe, *Old Acquaintance*

No government could survive without champagne. Champagne in the throats of our diplomatic people is like oil in the wheels of an engine.
                                              Joseph Dargent

I'll stick with gin. Champagne is just ginger ale that knows somebody.
                                              Hawkeye, *M*A*S*H*

A cocktail is to a glass of wine as rape is to love.   Paul Claudel

Never refuse wine. It is an odd but universally held opinion that anyone who doesn't drink must be an alcoholic.   P. J. O'Rourke

Always carry a corkscrew and the wine shall provide itself.   Brendan Behan

—Shiraz, Chardonnay and Chablis are all names of what?
—Footballers' wives. **Darren Lee and Contestant, Chiltern FM**

A bottle of wine contains more philosophy than all the books in the world.
Louis Pasteur

Some people tell you you should not drink claret after strawberries.
They are wrong. **William Maginn**

—I can tell by the colour – yes, it's a red. The bouquet – yes, it's wine.
—Would you mind moving on, there's a lot of other people waiting to
take Communion. **Communicant and Priest, *The Samuel Pepys Show***

The nearest my parents came to alcohol was at Holy Communion and they
utterly overestimated its effects. However bad the weather, Dad never
drove to church because Mam thought the sacrament might make him
incapable on the return journey. **Alan Bennett**

Be wary of strong drink. It can make you shoot at tax collectors and miss.
Robert Heinlein

You know you haven't had enough to drink if the dog hasn't been given
a Martini. ***The Preppy* magazine**

Drunkenness is temporary suicide: the happiness it brings is merely negative, a momentary cessation of unhappiness.
Bertrand Russell

—Confidentially, with me, one's too many and a million's not enough.
—I got the same problem with men.
Bartender and Theresa Dunn, *Looking For Mr Goodbar*

Plastered makes perfect. **Tagline, *My Favorite Year***

I am a character. *You* are a loose cannon. *He* is drunk.   Craig Brown

Always do sober what you said you'd do drunk. That will teach you to keep your mouth shut.   Ernest Hemingway

—I have a pounding headache, my mouth tastes like vomit, and I don't remember a thing.
—Welcome to my world.   Ned Flanders and Homer Simpson, *The Simpsons*

The best way to avoid a hangover is to stay drunk.
Dorothy Parker, *Dorothy Parker and the Vicious Circle*

What a man says drunk he has thought sober.   Belgian proverb

I have taken more out of alcohol than alcohol has taken out of me.   Winston Churchill

For a bad hangover take the juice of two quarts of whisky.   Eddie Condon

After I got sober, I achieved so much clarity that I despise myself even more.   Richard Lewis

I distrust camels and anyone else who can go a week without a drink.
Joe E. Lewis

Don Marquis came down after a month on the wagon, ambled over to the bar, and announced, 'I've conquered that goddamn willpower of mine. Gimme a double Scotch.'   E. B. White

To get over the guilt of drinking, take your brandy in milk. This way, it becomes medicinal.   Catherine Cookson

Drink! for you know not whence you came, nor why:
Drink! for you know not why you go, nor where.   Edward Fitzgerald

AMBITION

My mother said to me, 'If you are a soldier, you will become a general. If you are a monk, you will become Pope.' Instead I became a painter, and became Picasso.

Pablo Picasso

We are all in the gutter, but some of us are looking at the stars. **Oscar Wilde**

My grandmother was utterly convinced I'd wind up as the Archbishop of Canterbury. And, to be honest, I've never entirely ruled it out. **Hugh Grant**

If you would be Pope, you must think of nothing else. **Spanish proverb**

You have to think anyway, so why not think big? **Donald Trump**

Every private in the army carries a field marshal's baton in his knapsack.

Napoleon Bonaparte

I used to work at The International House of Pancakes. It was a dream, and I made it happen.

Paula Poundstone

—Is there a chance for advancement in this job?
—No.
—Woo-hoo! No pressure!

Homer Simpson and Manager of Sprawl-Mart, *The Simpsons*

Ah, a man's reach should exceed his grasp or what's a heaven for?

Robert Browning

Mama exhorted her children at every opportunity to 'jump at de sun'. We might not land on the sun but at least we would get off the ground.

Zora Neale Hurston

Reach for the stars, even if you have to stand on a cactus. **Susan Longacre**

Ambition is but avarice on stilts, and masked. **Walter Savage Landor**

Every scarecrow has a secret ambition to terrorize.   Stanislaw J. Lec

I have found some of the best reasons I ever had for remaining at the
bottom simply by looking at the men at the top.   Frank Moore Colby

Always be nice to people on the way up because you'll meet the same
people on the way down.   Wilson Mizner

AMERICA

As an American, I'd like to apologize – for everything.   Rich Hall

We Americans only voted for George Bush to prove to the British that
Americans understand irony. Unfortunately, it kinda backfired. Scott Capuro

America is just a nation of two hundred million used car salesmen with
all the money we need to buy guns and no qualms about killing anybody
else in the world who tries to make us uncomfortable.   Hunter S. Thompson

It's an appropriate coincidence that the word 'American' ends in 'I can'.
Alexander Animator

Americans keep telling us how successful their system is – then they remind
us not to stray too far from our hotel at night.
European official at the G-8 economic summit in Denver, 1997

The youth of America is their oldest tradition. It has been going on now
for three hundred years.   Oscar Wilde

I have never been able to look upon America as young and vital but rather
as prematurely old, as a fruit which rotted before it had a chance to ripen.
Henry Miller

What other culture could have produced someone like Hemingway and
not seen the joke?   Gore Vidal

The Americans are the illegitimate children of the English.   H. L. Mencken

America is a vast conspiracy to make you happy.   John Updike

Americans are optimists. They hope they'll be wealthy someday – and they're positive they can get one more brushful of paint out of an empty can.   Bern Williams

We don't do ambivalence well in America. We do courage of our convictions. We do might makes right. Ambivalence is French. Certainty is American.   Anna Quindlen

There's a big anti-intellectual strain in the American south, and there always has been. We're not big on thought.
Donna Tartt

In the United States there is more space where nobody is than where anybody is. That is what makes America what it is.   Gertrude Stein

America is so vast that almost everything said about it is likely to be true, and the opposite is probably equally true.   James T. Farrell

ANALYSIS

We vivisect the nightingale to probe the secret of his note.
Thomas Bailey Aldrich

Analysis kills spontaneity. The grain one ground into flour springs and germinates no more.   Henri Frédéric Amiel

Search not a wound too deep lest thou make a new one.   Thomas Fuller

ANGEL

I've been on the verge of being an angel all my life, but it's never happened yet.
                                                                    Mark Twain

Imagine them as they were first conceived, part musical instrument and part daisy.
                                                                    P. K. Page

We are each of us angels with only one wing, and we can only fly by embracing one another.
                                                                    Rula Lenska

We are one another's angels.
                                                                    Nevada Barr

ANGER

It takes me a long time to lose my temper, but once lost I could not find it with a dog.
                                                                    Mark Twain

Anger blows out the lamp of the mind.
                                                        Robert G. Ingersoll

I was so mad you could have boiled a pot of water on my head.
                                                        Alice Childress

I'm so mad I could beat your brains in.
                            Mary Richards, *The Mary Tyler Moore Show*

In anger, you look ten years older.
                                                        Hedda Hopper

The worst-tempered people I have ever met were those who knew that they were in the wrong.
                                                        Wilson Mizner

Many people lose their tempers merely from seeing you keep yours.
                                                        Frank Moore Colby

Great fury, like great whiskey, requires long fermentation.   Truman Capote

Never ask a woman why she's angry at you. She will either get angrier at you for not knowing, or she'll tell you. Both ways, you lose. **Ian Shoales**

I know of no more disagreeable situation than to be left feeling generally angry without anybody in particular to be angry at. **Frank Moore Colby**

Anger is a great force. If you control it, it can be transmuted into a power which can move the whole world. **William Shenstone**

Whispering works wonders with an angry child. Simply whisper gently into his ear and he will stop crying to hear what you are saying. This is also 100 per cent effective on husbands. **Lady Dashwood**

I am righteously indignant; *you* are annoyed; *he* is making a fuss about nothing. **Anon**

Act nothing in furious passion; it's putting to sea in a storm. **Thomas Fuller**

Resentment is like taking poison and waiting for the other person to die. **Malachy McCourt**

Speak when you are angry, and you'll make the best speech you'll ever regret. **Ambrose Bierce**

Never forget what a man says to you when he's angry. **Henry Ward Beecher**

Consider, when you are enraged at anyone, what would probably become your sentiments should he die during the dispute. **William Shenstone**

When angry, count four; when very angry, swear. **Mark Twain**

One can't be angry when one looks at a penguin. **John Ruskin**

At least if I can stay mad I can stay alive. **Magdalena Gomez**

ANIMAL

Two kangaroos were talking to each other, and one said, 'I hope it doesn't rain today. I hate it when the children play inside.'   Henny Youngman

On the sixth day, God created the platypus. And God said: 'Let's see the evolutionists try and figure this one out.'   Anon

Animals in different countries have different expressions just as the people in different countries differ in expression.   Gertrude Stein

In the distance, the gestures of animals look human, the gestures of human beings bestial.   Malcolm de Chazal

Whenever you observe an animal closely, you feel as if a human being sitting inside were making fun of you.   Elias Canetti

We watched Saskia jug a hare, once, on television, years ago ... The hare had been half rotted, then cremated, then consumed. If there is a God and she is of the rabbit family, then Saskia will be in deep doo-doo on Judgement Day.   Angela Carter

We can judge the heart of a man by his treatment of animals.   Immanuel Kant

It is inexcusable for scientists to torture animals; let them make their experiments on journalists and politicians.   Henrik Ibsen

How many of those dead animals you see on the highway are suicides?   Dennis Miller

The best thing about animals is that they don't talk much.   Thornton Wilder

Did you ever see a giraffe? It is like something from between the regions of truth and fiction.   Geraldine Jewsbury

I'd hate to be a giraffe with a sore throat.   Mitch Hedberg

Animals have these advantages over man: they never hear the clock strike, they die without any idea of death, they have no theologians to instruct them, their last moments are not disturbed by unwelcome and unpleasant ceremonies, their funerals cost them nothing, and no one starts lawsuits over their wills.

Voltaire

The popularity of an animal is directly correlated with the number of anthropomorphic features it possesses.

Anon

The age of a child is inversely correlated with the size of the animals it prefers.

Desmond Morris

The dinosaur's eloquent lesson is that if some bigness is good, an over-abundance of bigness is not necessarily better.

Eric A. Johnston

If you want to get a pet for your child, I suggest a chicken so that when they get bored of it after a couple of days at least you can have a nice roast dinner.

Jo Brand

That special bond you think you have with your pet is imaginary. As long as it has food and water, you could get hit by a train tomorrow, and your pet wouldn't think anything of it.

Scott Dikker

I tend to be suspicious of people whose love of animals is exaggerated; they are often frustrated in their relationships with humans.

Camilla Koffler

When one loves animals and children *too much*, one loves them against human beings.

Jean-Paul Sartre

If an animal does something, we call it instinct. If we do the same thing for the same reason, we call it intelligence.

Will Cuppy

A zoo is a place where your child asks loud questions about the private parts of large mammals.

Joyce Armor

The camel driver has his thoughts; the camel, he has his.

Arabian proverb

Do not free a camel of the burden of his hump: you may be freeing him from being a camel.   G. K. Chesterton

The hyena is said to laugh: but it is rather in the way in which the MP is said to utter 'an ironical cheer'.   Saki

Monkeys very sensibly refrain from speech, lest they should be set to earn their livings.   Kenneth Grahame

What do you get when you cross an onion with a donkey? Ninety-nine times out of a hundred, you get an onion with long ears, but one time out of a hundred, you get a piece of ass that makes your eyes water.   Anon

A tortoise is, I suppose, a Jewish pet. It knows its place. Out on the lawn. It doesn't bark. It doesn't tear the Dralon.   Maureen Lipman

Never try to teach a pig to sing; it wastes your time and it annoys the pig.
                                                                 Paul Dickson

Even if you feed the cow cocoa you will not get chocolate.   Stanislaw J. Lec

An elephant: a mouse built to government specifications.   Robert Heinlein

If anyone wants to know what elephants are like, they are like people only more so.   Peter Corneille

He who mounts a wild elephant goes where the wild elephant goes.
                                                                 Randolph Bourne

To catch a mouse make a noise like a cheese.   Lewis Kornfeld

Humpback whales sing in different accents. You can tell where they come from by listening to them.   Dr Howard Winn

There are 350 varieties of shark, not counting loan and pool.   L. M. Boyd

Don't catch a leopard by the tail, but if you do, don't let go.   **Ethiopian proverb**

An infallible method of conciliating a tiger is to allow oneself to be
devoured.
                                                                Konrad Adenauer

Do not blame God for having created the tiger, but thank him for not
having given it wings.
                                                                Ethiopian proverb

The fox has many tricks. The hedgehog has but one. But that is the best
of all.
                                                                Desiderius Erasmus

There is something about riding down the street on a prancing horse that
makes you feel like something, even when you ain't a thing.   **Will Rogers**

My experience with horses is that they never throw away a chance to
go lame.
                                                                Mark Twain

The hippopotamus is monogamous. He looks as if he would have to be.
                                                                Will Cuppy

A horse that can count to ten is a remarkable horse, not a remarkable
mathematician.
                                                                Samuel Johnson

APATHY

I don't know. I don't care. And it doesn't make any difference.   **Jack Kerouac**

Most human beings have an almost infinite capacity for taking things for
granted.
                                                                Aldous Huxley

The only thing necessary for the triumph of evil is for good men to do
nothing.
                                                                Edmund Burke

A society of sheep must in time beget a government of wolves.
                                                                Bertrand de Jouvenel

We shall have to repent in this generation not so much for the evil deeds of the wicked people but for the appalling silence of the good people.

Martin Luther King

First they came for the Jews. I didn't speak up. I was not a Jew. Then they came for the communists. I didn't speak up. I was not a communist. Then they came for the trade unionists. I didn't speak up. I was not a trade unionist. Then they came for me and by that time there was nobody left to speak up.

Martin Niemöller, 1945

We know what happens to people who sit in the middle of the road: they get run over.

Aneurin Bevan

APOLOGY

I never apologize, Lisa. I'm sorry, but that's just the way I am. **Homer Simspon**

There are only so many times I can say sorry and still mean it.

Homer Simpson

Apologies are seldom of any use. **Samuel Johnson**

A stiff apology is a second insult. **G. K. Chesterton**

I asked Tom if countries always apologized when they had done wrong, and he says: 'Yes; the little ones does.'

Mark Twain

To apologize is to lay the foundation for a future offence. **Ambrose Bierce**

Never ruin an apology with an excuse. **Benjamin Franklin**

APPEARANCE

I believe a person of any fine feeling scarcely ever sees a new face without a sensation akin to a shock, for the reason that it presents a new and surprising combination of unedifying elements. **Arthur Schopenhauer**

A mask tells us more than a face. **Oscar Wilde**

Let us be grateful to the mirror for revealing to us our appearance only. **Samuel Butler**

Looks are so deceptive that people should be done up like food packages with the ingredients clearly labelled. **Helen Hudson**

It is only shallow people who do not judge by appearances. **Oscar Wilde**

There are people who think that everything one does with a serious face is sensible. **Georg Christoph Lichtenberg**

If the nose of Cleopatra had been a little shorter the whole face of the world would have changed. **Blaise Pascal**

To lose a lover or even a husband or two during the course of one's life can be vexing. But to lose one's teeth is a catastrophe. **Hugh Wheeler**

ARCHITECTURE

Architecture is inhabited sculpture. **Constantin Brancusi**

Architecture approaches nearer than any other art to being irrevocable because it is so difficult to get rid of. **G. K. Chesterton**

The secret of great cathedrals is that their proportions conform to cosmic laws, 'shaping' people who spend time in them. **Theodor Schwenk**

No house should ever be on any hill or anything. It should be of the hill, so hill and house can live together each the happier for the other.

Frank Lloyd Wright

The pyramids of Egypt will not last a moment compared to the daisy.

D. H. Lawrence

Don't just look at buildings ... watch them.

John Ruskin

ARGUMENT

Anyone who thinks there aren't two sides to every argument is probably in one.

Anon

In a recent British survey, most Britons would rather argue than have sex. Actually, arguing is a lot like sex: first you get excited, then you start screaming, and when it's over, the man winds up apologizing.

Jay Leno

The great charm in argument is really finding one's own opinions, not other people's.

Evelyn Waugh

Never argue at the dinner table, for the one who is not hungry always gets the best of the argument.

Richard Whately

I got into an argument with my girlfriend inside a tent. A tent is not a good place for an argument. I tried to walk out on her and had to slam the flap.

Mitch Hedberg

In my home, we've got a system for ending arguments: we just talk and talk until my wife is right.

Jason Love

Sex after a fight is often the best there is, which is why you're never allowed in the locker room right after a prize fight.

Jay Leno

Arguments with furniture are rarely productive.

Kehlog Albran

Never fall out with your bread and butter.   **English proverb**

There is no good in arguing with the inevitable. The only argument available with an east wind is to put on your overcoat.   **James R. Lowell**

I dislike arguments of any kind. They are always vulgar, and often convincing.   **Oscar Wilde**

A long dispute means that both parties are wrong.   **Voltaire**

The most important thing in an argument, next to being right, is to leave an escape hatch for your opponent, so that he can gracefully swing over to your side without too much apparent loss of face.   **Sydney J. Harris**

It is the mark of an educated mind to be able to entertain a thought without accepting it.   **Aristotle**

Every quarrel is a private one. Outsiders are never welcome.   **Texas Bix Bender**

If you feel a row coming on, and the words 'we have to talk' spoken in a certain tone are heard, grab the dogs' leads and head outdoors. Outdoors, feelings can be bellowed to the four winds – the dogs don't mind a bit and generally join in with joyful barking.   **Hugh Palmer**

I've had a few arguments with people, but I never carry a grudge. You know why? While you're carrying a grudge, they're out dancing.

Buddy Hackett

I have won every argument I ever had with myself.   **William Feather**

If you cannot answer a man's argument, all is not lost; you can still call him vile names.   **Elbert Hubbard**

ART

Mmm . . . split peas – with ham!

Homer Simpson, viewing Andy Warhol's Campbell's soup can painting

Life is a shit storm and when it's raining shit, the best umbrella is art.

Pedro Carmichael, *Tune in Tomorrow*

We have art in order not to die of life.

Albert Camus

What makes people the world over stand in line for Van Gogh is not that they will see beautiful pictures but that in an indefinable way they will come away feeling better human beings.

John Russell

Art can excite, titillate, please, entertain, and sometimes shock; but its ultimate function is to ennoble.

Marya Mannes

When I judge art, I take my painting and put it next to a God-made object like a tree or flower. If it clashes, it's not art.

Marc Chagall

Art is the lie that reveals the truth.

Pablo Picasso

Real art has the capacity to make us nervous.

Susan Sontag

Art isn't something you marry, it's something you rape.

Edgar Degas

Every work of art is an uncommitted crime.

Theodor W. Adorno

Art is continually working to take the crust of familiarity off everyday objects.

Rudolf Arnheim

A copy of the universe is not what is required of art; one of the damned things is ample.

Rebecca West

Where the spirit does not work with the hand, there is no art.

Leonardo da Vinci

It's not what you see that is art, art is the gap.   Marcel Duchamp

My feeling about technique in art is that it has about the same value as technique in lovemaking. Heartfelt ineptitude has its appeal and so does heartless skill; but what you want is passionate virtuosity.   John Barth

Great art is cathartic; it is always moral.   Joyce Carol Oates

Great art changes you.   Sister Wendy Beckett

If one does not understand the usefulness of the useless and the uselessness of the useful, one cannot understand art.   Eugene Ionesco

The most important thing in art is The Frame. For painting: literally; for other arts: figuratively – because without this humble appliance, you can't know where The Art stops and The Real World begins.   Frank Zappa

A good legible label is usually worth, for information, a ton of significant attitude and expression in a historical picture.   Mark Twain

We have no art. We try to do everything well.   Balinese villager

—Do you find it hard to paint a picture?
—It's either easy or impossible.   Interviewer and Salvador Dali

When I sit down to make a sketch from nature, the first thing I try to do is *to forget that I have ever seen a picture.*   John Constable

—Why do you place a sofa in the middle of the jungle?
—One has a right to paint one's dreams.   Interviewer and Henri Rousseau

I don't paint things. I only paint the difference between things. Henri Matisse

The celebrated painter Gainsborough got as much pleasure from seeing violins as from hearing them.   Georg Christoph Lichtenberg

—You are asking a fee of 200 guineas for just two days' painting?
—No, I ask it for the knowledge of a lifetime.   Lawyer and James Whistler

Until I saw Chardin's paintings, I never realized how much beauty lay around me in my parents' house, in the half-cleared table, in the corner of a tablecloth left awry, in the knife beside the empty oyster shell.

Marcel Proust

—How do you achieve such lifelike flesh tones in your nudes?
—I just keep painting till I feel like pinching. Then I know it's right.

Interviewer and Pierre Auguste Renoir

No work of art is ever completed, it is only abandoned.

Paul Valéry

With an apple I will astonish Paris.

Paul Cézanne

Picasso only registers the deformities which have not yet penetrated our consciousness. Art is a mirror which goes 'fast' like a watch – sometimes.

Franz Kafka

I murmured to Picasso that I liked his portrait of Gertrude Stein. Yes, he said, everybody said that she does not look like it, but that does not make any difference, she will, he said.

Gertrude Stein

Good art will never match your sofa.

Fred Babb

All great art and literature is propaganda.

George Bernard Shaw

Painting is saying 'Ta' to God.

Stephen Spender

How often my soul visits the National Gallery, and how seldom I go there myself!

Logan Pearsall Smith

I never can pass by the Metropolitan Museum of Art in New York without thinking of it not as a gallery of living portraits but as a cemetery of tax-deductible wealth.

Lewis H. Lapham

The painting showed Brother Barnabas walking through a snowstorm from Baden-Baden to Carlsbad, clad in white pyjamas, followed by a flock of white ponies. Overhead, as if leading the way, is a mystic white guillemot.

The painting looked like this:

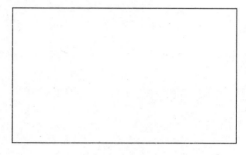

Flann O'Brien

—Why is the Renoir in your apartment hung crooked?
—It's better like that. If you want to kill a picture, all you have to do is to hang it beautifully on a nail and soon you will see nothing of it but the frame. When it's out of place you see it better.

Interviewer and Pablo Picasso

Visiting a popular exhibition or art gallery, start at the end and go backwards – the crowds are always at the beginning. **Dr Alan Borg**

Treat a work of art like a prince: let it speak to you first.

Arthur Schopenhauer

One of the best things about paintings is their silence – which prompts reflection and random reverie. **Mark Stevens**

That which perhaps hears more silly remarks than anything else in the world is a picture in a museum. **Edmond de Goncourt**

It's clever, but is it art? **Rudyard Kipling**

Most people don't do something seminal. I've done it twice: with my tent and my bed. Picasso did it with Cubism. **Tracey Emin**

The history of modern art is also the history of the progressive loss of art's audience. Art has increasingly become the concern of the artists and the bafflement of the public.

Paul Gauguin

The idea is more important than the object.

Damien Hirst

You meet rich people and you hang around with them, and one night they've had a few drinks and they say 'I'll buy it!' Then they tell their friends, 'You must have this person's work, darling,' and that's all you need. That's all it takes. Get it?'

Andy Warhol

A work of art that contains theories is like an object on which the price tag has been left.

Marcel Proust

There's one sure method of making peace. You've only got to take the Tsar, the Emperor William, the King of England, the President of the Republic, the King of Italy, and the other kings of belligerent countries, and put them in front of a bad picture. They'll all promptly unite in adoring it. They'll fall into each other's arms, and peace will reign.

Théodore Duret

Art is anything you can get away with.

Marshall McLuhan

ARTIST

A man who works with his hands is a labourer; a man who works with his hands and his brain is a craftsman; but a man who works with his hands and his brain and his heart is an artist.

Louis Nizer

If you ask me what I have come to do in the world, I who am an artist, I will reply: 'I am here to live aloud.'

Émile Zola

Every artist is an unhappy lover.

Iris Murdoch

An artist is his own fault.

John O'Hara

He will lie even when it is inconvenient; the sign of the true artist. **Gore Vidal**

Every artist dips his brush in his own soul, and paints his own nature into his pictures. **Henry Ward Beecher**

What an artist is for is to tell us what we see but do not know that we see. **Edith Sitwell**

The job of the artist is always to deepen the mystery. **Francis Bacon**

The real artist's work is a surprise to himself. **Robert Henri**

When I was a kid I drew like Michelangelo. It took me years to learn to draw like a kid. **Pablo Picasso**

The great artist is the simplifier. **Henri Frédéric Amiel**

To be first-rate at anything you have to stake your all. Nobody's an artist 'on the side'. **Eleanor Clark**

Only a born artist can endure the labour of becoming one. **Comtesse Diane**

Draw bamboos for ten years, become a bamboo, then forget all about bamboos when you are drawing. **Georges Duthuit**

There is one art, no more, no less; to do all things with artlessness. **Piet Hein**

People think I'm an artist because my films lose money. **Woody Allen**

Artistic temperament is the disease that afflicts amateurs. **G. K. Chesterton**

But we must not forget that only a very few people are artists in life; that the art of life is the most distinguished and rarest of all the arts. **C. G. Jung**

To practice any art, no matter how well or badly, is a way to make your soul grow. So do it. **Kurt Vonnegut**

ASSASSINATION

Do you know the real reason Abraham Lincoln was shot in the theater?
His cell phone kept going off.   Jay Leno

So now he is a legend, when he would have preferred to have been a man.
Jackie Kennedy on John F. Kennedy

Assassination has never changed the history of the world.
Benjamin Disraeli

There's never a dearth of reasons to shoot at the President.   Don DeLillo

ASTROLOGY

You can tell a lot about someone's personality if you know his star sign –
Jesus, born on 25 December, fed the five thousand, walked on water –
typical Capricorn.   Harry Hill

I think I might have a bad psychic advisor. When I asked her to contact
the dead, she gave me Keith Richards' phone number.   David Letterman

I was on a corner the other day when a wild-looking sort of gypsy-
looking lady with a dark veil over her face grabbed me right on Ventura
Boulevard and said, 'Karen Haber! You're never going to find happiness,
and no one is ever going to marry you.' I said, 'Mom, leave me alone.'
Karen Haber

—Do you believe in astrology?
—I don't even believe in astronomy.   Peter De Vries

Astrology is a disease, not a science.   Moses Maimonides

We are all at times unconscious prophets.   Charles Spurgeon

A belief in God and a belief in astrology cannot be reconciled.

Rev. Jerry Falwell

There should be three days a week when no one is allowed to say: 'What's your sign?' Violators would have their copies of Kahlil Gibran confiscated.

Dick Cavett

The fault, dear Brutus, is not in our stars but in ourselves.

William Shakespeare, *Julius Caesar*

You can make a good living from soothsaying but not from truthsaying.

Georg Christoph Lichtenberg

ASTRONOMY

The Mars *Polar Lander* has been quieter than George W. Bush after a foreign policy question.

David Letterman

According to modern astronomers, space is finite. This is a very comforting thought – particularly for people who can never remember where they have left things.

Woody Allen

To go up into space – it's like Chessington World of Adventures times ten thousand.

Sarah-Jane Cass, *Space Cadets*

Astronauts: rotarians in outer space.

Gore Vidal

When man, Apollo man, rockets into space, it isn't in order to find his brother, I'm quite sure of that. It's to confirm that he hasn't any brothers.

Françoise Sagan

Ah, aliens! Don't eat me. I have a wife and kids … eat them! Homer Simpson

What was most significant about the lunar voyage was not that men set foot on the moon but that they set eye on the earth.

Norman Cousins

It suddenly struck me that that tiny pea, pretty and blue, was the earth.
I put up my thumb and shut one eye, and my thumb blotted out the planet
earth. I didn't feel like a giant. I felt very, very small.   Neil Armstrong

I don't know what you could say about a day in which you have seen
four beautiful sunsets.   John Glenn

For those who have seen the earth from space, and for the hundreds and
perhaps thousands more who will, the experience most certainly changes
your perspective. The things that we share in our world are far more
valuable than those which divide us.   Donald Williams

ATHEIST

Why isn't there a book about someone losing their faith and it being a
beautiful experience?   Julia Sweeney

To you I'm an atheist. To God I'm the loyal opposition.   Woody Allen

Perhaps God chose me to be an atheist?   Stanislaw J. Lec

The annoying thing about being an atheist is that you'll never have the
satisfaction of saying to believers, 'I told you so.'   Mark Steel

Among the repulsions of atheism for me has been its drastic
uninterestingness as an intellectual position. Where was the ingenuity,
the ambiguity, the humanity (in the Harvard sense) of saying that the
universe just happened to happen and that when we're dead we're dead?
                                                                            John Updike

In a way, the greatest praise of God is his denial by the atheist who thinks
creation is so perfect it does not need a creator.   Marcel Proust

That is the whole trouble with being a heretic. One usually must think out
everything for oneself.   Aubrey Menan

I once wanted to become an atheist, but I gave up – they have no holidays.

Henny Youngman

By night an Atheist half believes a God.

Edward Young

ATTITUDE

Your attitude, not your aptitude, will determine your altitude.   Zig Ziglar

Ability is what you're capable of doing. Motivation determines what you do. Attitude determines how well you do it.   Lou Holtz

Our attitude towards life determines life's attitude towards us.   John Mitchell

A positive attitude may not solve all your problems, but it will annoy enough people to make it worth the effort.   Herm Albright

ATTRACTION

You had me at 'hello'.   Dorothy Boyd, *Jerry Maguire*

She wore a short skirt and a tight sweater and her figure described a set of parabolas that would cause cardiac arrest in a yak.   Woody Allen

Looking at a cleavage is like looking at the sun. You don't stare at it. It's too risky. You get a sense of it and then you look away.

Jerry Seinfeld, *Seinfeld*

According to a study in *McCall* magazine, the sexiest thing a man can say to a woman is, 'Let me do the dishes.' This is what I hate about these magazines – they set impossible standards.   Jay Leno

No one worth possessing can be quite possessed.   Sara Teasdale

Spencer was searching for a woman interested in gold, inorganic chemistry, outdoor sex and the music of Bach. In short, he was looking for himself, only female.
Woody Allen

You're never going to meet the perfect person. The timing's off. You're married, she's single. You're a Jew, he's Palestinian. One's a Mexican, one's a racoon. One's a black man, one's a black woman. It's always something.
Chris Rock

Saffron is a virgin in a world where men will even turn to soft fruit for pleasure.
Patsy Stone, *Absolutely Fabulous*

Want him to be more of a man? Try being more of a woman! Coty perfume advert

I don't know if I should care for a man who made life easy; I should want someone who made it interesting.
Edith Wharton

My dearest Albert put on my stockings for me. I went in and saw him shave; a great delight for me.
Queen Victoria

Appealingness is inversely proportional to attainability.
John Updike

She has eyes that men adore so and a torso even more so.
E. Y. Harburg

What attracts us in a woman rarely binds us to her.
John Churton Collins

There is no spectacle on earth more appealing than that of a beautiful woman in the act of cooking dinner for someone she loves.
Tom Wolfe

Flo, Flo, I love you so
I love you in your nightie;
When the moonlight flits across your tits –
Oh, Jesus Christ Almighty!
Anon

AWARDS AND HONOURS

The cross of the Legion of Honour has been conferred upon me. However, few escape that distinction.

Mark Twain

Every society honors its live conformists and its dead troublemakers.

Mignon McLaughlin

I was once asked if I wanted to be Pipe Smoker of the Year. I had to tell them I didn't smoke a pipe. They said, 'Oh, that doesn't matter.'   Jack Dee

People with honorary awards are looked upon with disfavor. Would you let an honorary mechanic fix your brand new Mercedes?   Neil Simon

What I like about the Order of the Garter is that there is no damned merit about it.

Lord Melbourne

It is a little awkward kneeling before another human being with whom you have no personal connection.

Sir Ian McKellen about his receiving a knighthood from the Queen

I turned down a knighthood. It would be like having to wear a suit every day of your life.

Alan Bennett

To those of you who received honors, awards and distinctions, I say, 'Well done.' And to the 'C' students, I say, 'You, too, can be President of the United States.'   George W. Bush, address to Yale University

I once had a sparrow alight upon my shoulder for a moment, while I was hoeing in a village garden, and I felt that I was more distinguished by that circumstance than I should have been by any epaulet I could have worn.

Henry David Thoreau

God will not look you over for medals, degrees, or diplomas, but for scars.

Elbert Hubbard

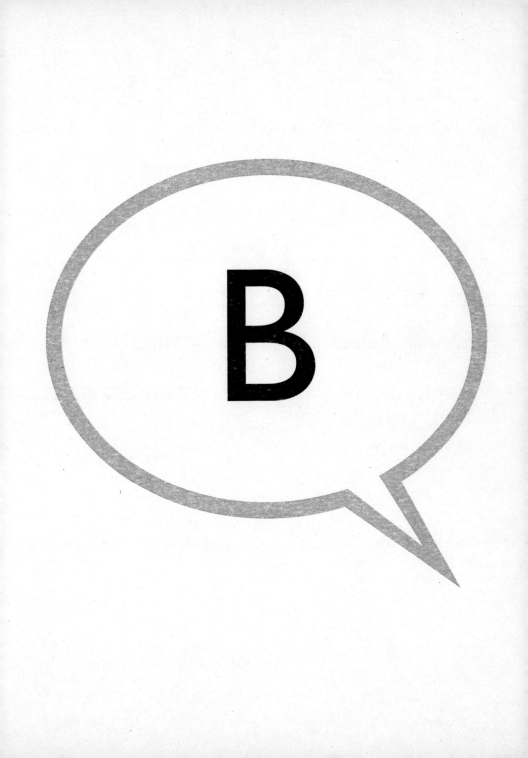

BEAUTY AND UGLINESS

A woman who cannot be ugly is not beautiful.

Karl Kraus

There is no excellent beauty that hath not some strangeness in the proportion.

Francis Bacon

Seldom is a Gothic head more beautiful than when broken.   **André Malraux**

People who are very beautiful make their own laws.

Karen Stone, *The Roman Spring of Mrs Stone*

Every time you see a beautiful woman, just remember, somebody got tired of her.

Kinky Friedman

Plain women know more about men than beautiful ones do.

Katharine Hepburn

Put even the plainest woman into a beautiful dress and unconsciously she will try to live up to it.

Lady Duff-Gordon

All women are not Helen ... but have Helen in their hearts.

William Carlos Williams

A woman is truly beautiful only when she is naked, and she knows it.

André Courrèges

I don't know any woman who is happy with her looks. I certainly wouldn't want to be friends with anyone who was.

Zoe Wanamaker

A beautiful woman with a brain is like a beautiful woman with a club foot.

Bernard Cornfeld

When I am working on a problem, I never think about beauty. I think only how to solve the problem. But when I have finished, if the solution is not beautiful, I know it is wrong.

R. Buckminster Fuller

Beauty is desired in order that it may be befouled; not for its own sake, but for the joy brought by the certainty of profaning it. **Georges Bataille**

The contemplation of beauty causes the soul to grow wings. **Plato**

Love is a great beautifier. **Louisa May Alcott**

The inappropriate cannot be beautiful. **Frank Lloyd Wright**

It is amazing how complete is the delusion that beauty is goodness. **Leo Tolstoy**

Attractive people are assumed to be kinder, more genuine, sincere, warm, sexually responsive, poised, modest, sociable, sensitive, interesting, strong, more exciting, more nurturant, and of better character than the less attractive. **Dr Ellen Berscheid, psychologist**

Nothing is more moving than beauty which is unaware of itself, except for ugliness which is. **Robert Mallet**

The genitals themselves have not undergone the development of the rest of the human form in the direction of beauty. **Sigmund Freud**

There are beautiful flowers that are scentless, and beautiful women that are unlovable. **Anon**

I never saw an ugly thing in my life: for let the form of an object be what it may, light, shade, and perspective will always make it beautiful. **John Constable**

Ugliness is superior to beauty, because ugliness lasts. **Serge Gainsbourg**

BEGIN

Who would venture upon the journey of life, if compelled to begin at the end?
Françoise d'Aubigné Maintenon

I am rather like a mosquito in a nudist camp; I know what I ought to do, but I don't know where to begin.
Stephen Bayne

The time to begin most things is ten years ago.
Mignon McLaughlin

It is a tremendous act of violence to begin anything. I am not able to begin. I simply skip what should be the beginning.
Rainer Maria Rilke

A journey of a thousand miles begins with a single step. Of course, so does falling down a flight of stairs.
Jewish saying

Do one small thing immediately – often this is all you need to do to get started.
Brian Tracy

BEHAVIOUR

You wouldn't be caught wearing cheap perfume, would you? Then why do you want to wear cheap perfume in your conduct?
Margaret Culkin Banning

With a gentleman I am always a gentleman and a half, and with a fraud I try to be a fraud and a half.
Otto von Bismarck

You've got to have something to eat and a little love in your life before you can hold still for any damn body's sermon on how to behave.
Billie Holiday

When people are on their best behaviour they aren't always at their best.
Alan Bennett

Best behaviour means the same thing as the most uncomfortable behaviour.

Lin Yutang

Always act as if you were seen.

Baltasar Gracián

BEING

Today I saw a red-and-yellow sunset and thought, how insignificant I am! Of course, I thought that yesterday, too, and it rained. Woody Allen

Everything in nature is lyrical in its ideal essence, tragic in its fate, and comic in its existence. Being, then, is the dazzle each of us makes as we thread the dance of those three rhythms in our lives. George Santayana

Where there is a stink of shit, there is a smell of being. Antonin Artaud

Once upon a time, there was a woman who discovered she had turned into the wrong person. Anne Tyler

It's never too late to be who you might have been. George Eliot

Don't be yourself – be someone a little nicer. Mignon McLaughlin

We are not trapped by a difficult past life any more than we are by a difficult childhood. Diane Mariechild

We become what we think about all day long. Ralph Waldo Emerson

Tell me who admires and loves you, and I will tell you who you are.

Charles Augustin Sainte-Beuve

'I think, therefore I am' is the statement of an intellectual who underrates toothaches. Milan Kundera

I owe, therefore I am.

Nino Manfredi, *Alberto Express*

Cogito ergo sum.
I think, therefore I am.

René Descartes

Cogito ergo spud.
I think, therefore I yam.

Herb Caen

Cogito ergo dim sum.

Richard Byrne

I think therefore I am. I think.

Anon

I think that I think; therefore, I think that I am.

Ambrose Bierce

I don't think so, therefore I'm probably not.

Alan Smithee

Sexual freedom has become more important than identity. Indeed, it has superseded it. The modern philosophy states 'I ejaculate, therefore I am.'

Quentin Crisp

To be is to do – Descartes
To do is to be – Jean-Paul Sartre
Dobedobedo – Frank Sinatra

Graffiti

BELIEF

The most costly of all follies is to believe passionately in the palpably not true. It is the chief occupation of mankind.

H. L. Mencken

Man prefers to believe what he prefers to be true.

Francis Bacon

A man can believe a considerable deal of rubbish, and yet go about his daily work in a rational and cheerful manner.

Norman Douglas

I am positively against all this crap which is carried on first in the name of this thing, then in the name of that. I believe only in what is active, immediate, and personal.

Henry Miller

Some things are true whether you believe in them or not. Seth, *City of Angels*

We believe that electricity exists, because the electric company keeps
sending us bills for it. Dave Barry

There's nothing that can help you understand your beliefs more than
trying to explain them to an inquisitive child. Frank A. Clark

—How do you feel about reincarnation?
—You know, I don't think it would be any more unusual for me to show
up in another life, than showing up in this one!
  Interviewer and Eleanor Roosevelt

I used to believe in reincarnation, but that was in a past life. Karen Salmansohn

Disbelief in magic can force a poor soul into believing in government
and business. Tom Robbins

Men will believe anything at all provided they are under no obligation
to believe it. Thomas Gray

Though a good deal is too strange to be believed, nothing is too strange
to have happened. Thomas Hardy

You believe easily what you hope for earnestly. Terence

Those who can make you believe absurdities can make you commit
atrocities. Voltaire

Unless we stand for something, we shall fall for anything. Peter Marshall

An agnostic is a cowardly atheist. Studs Terkel

Don't be agnostic – be something. Charles Darwin

The men who really believe in themselves are all in lunatic asylums.
  G. K. Chesterton

My problem is I'm a man of no convictions – at least, I think I am.

Chris Hampton

He who believes in nothing still needs a girl to believe in him.

Eugen Rosenstock-Huessy

I would never die for my beliefs because I might be wrong.   Bertrand Russell

BIRD

I hope you love birds too. It is economical. It saves going to heaven.

Emily Dickinson

If I had to choose, I would rather have birds than airplanes.

Charles A. Lindbergh

I planted some bird seed. A bird came up. Now I don't know what to feed it.

Steven Wright

I had started imitating a parrot, which is unusual, in that a parrot is supposed to imitate you. By taking the initiative you allow the parrot no alternative but to be itself, which proves again that attack is often the best defence.

Peter Ustinov

The ostrich is the only animal officially endowed with political direction.

Pierre Daninos

The love bird is one hundred per cent faithful to his mate, who is locked in the same cage.

Will Cuppy

If you were a pigeon you could fuck forty times a day. It's something to bear in mind when filling out the form for reincarnation.

A. A. Gill

A Zen master stood up to give a lecture. As he was about to speak, a bird sang sweetly outside. He immediately sat down saying, 'The lecture is over. I have nothing more to add.'

Anon

The dodo never had a chance. He seems to have been invented for the sole purpose of becoming extinct and that was all he was good for.   **Will Cuppy**

In order to see birds it is necessary to become a part of the silence. One has to sit still like a mystic and wait.   **Robert Lynd**

One swallow doesn't make an orgy.   *I'm Sorry I Haven't A Clue*

And before Buddha or Jesus spoke the nightingale sang, and long after the words of Jesus and Buddha are gone into oblivion the nightingale still will sing. Because it is neither preaching nor commanding nor urging. It is just singing. And in the beginning was not a Word, but a chirrup.
    D. H. Lawrence

Everyone wants to understand painting. Why is there no attempt to understand the song of the birds?   **Pablo Picasso**

BIRTH

The human comedy begins with a vertical smile.   **Richard Condon**

Inter faeces et urinam nascimur.
We are born between shit and piss.   **St Augustine**

Our birth is nothing but our death begun.   **Edward Young**

Just think. Because certain people aren't getting married, certain people aren't being born. It's a frightening thought.   **Adam Parkinson, *Butterflies***

Human beings are not born once and for all on the day their mothers give birth to them, but that life obliges them over and over again to give birth to themselves.   **Gabriel García Márquez**

Death is much simpler than birth; it is merely a continuation. Birth is the mystery, not death.   **Stewart Edward White**

BLAME

It's not whether you win or lose – it's how you lay the blame.   **Fran Lebowitz**

I couldn't help blaming myself, and, unfortunately, neither could he.
Clive James

She knitted a loud woollen cap of her recriminations and yanked it over
his head.   **Karen Elizabeth Gordon**

When I was a boy, my mother used to say to me, 'Never point your finger
at anyone because when you do, three fingers are pointing back at you.'
Dr John Sentamu, Archbishop of York

When we blame, we give away our power.   **Greg Anderson**

I praise loudly, I blame softly.   **Catherine II of Russiat**

A man can fail many times, but he isn't a failure until he begins to blame
someone else.   **William Burroughs**

The search for someone to blame is always successful.   **Robert Half**

The reason people blame things on the previous generation is that there's
only one other choice.   **Doug Larson**

Our culture peculiarly honours the act of blaming, which it takes as the
sign of virtue and intellect.   **Lionel Trilling**

There is luxury in self-reproach. When we blame ourselves, we feel no one
else has a right to blame us.   **Oscar Wilde**

Take your life in your own hands and what happens? A terrible thing: no
one to blame.   **Erica Jong**

Whose fault is it we have a blame culture?   **William Chapman**

There can be no doubt that the average man blames much more than he praises. His instinct is to blame. If he is satisfied, he says nothing; if he is not, he most illogically kicks up a row.   **Arnold Bennett**

In passing, I would like to say that the first time Adam had a chance he laid the blame on a woman.   **Nancy Astor**

BLESSINGS

Some people are always complaining that roses have thorns; I am thankful that thorns have roses.   **Alphonse Karr**

A Jewish grandmother is watching her grandchild playing on the beach when a huge wave comes and takes him out to sea. She pleads, 'Please God, save my only grandson. I beg of you, bring him back.' And a big wave comes and washes the boy back onto the beach, good as new. She looks up to heaven and says: 'He had a hat!'   **Myron Cohen**

Oh, blessed a thousand times the peasant who is born, eats and dies without anybody bothering about his affairs.   **Guiseppe Verdi**

I am a confirmed believer in blessings in disguise. I prefer them undisguised when I myself happen to be the person blessed; in fact, I can scarcely recognize a blessing in disguise except when it is bestowed upon someone else.   **Robert Lynd**

A thankful person is thankful under all circumstances. A complaining soul complains even if he lives in paradise.   **Baha'u'llah**

May you have warm words on a cold evening, a full moon on a dark night, and the road downhill all the way to your door.   **Irish blessing**

May you live a thousand years, and I, a thousand years less one day, that I might never know the world without you.   **Hungarian saying**

May you have warmth in your igloo, oil in your lamp, and peace in your heart.

Eskimo blessing

BODY

Human beings are divided into mind and body. The mind embraces all the nobler aspirations, like poetry and philosophy, but the body has all the fun.

Woody Allen

I used to think that the brain was the most wonderful organ in my body. Then I realized who was telling me this.

Emo Phillips

Our own physical body possesses a wisdom which we who inhabit the body lack. We give it orders which make no sense.

Henry Miller

There is more wisdom in your body than in your deepest philosophy.

Friedrich Nietzsche

This body is not a home, but an inn; and that only for a short time.

Seneca

The body never lies.

Martha Graham

BOOKS

If you ever go home with somebody and they don't have books in their house, don't sleep with them. I think that's very important.

John Waters

I like a thick book because it will steady a table, a leather volume because it will strop a razor, and a heavy book because it can be thrown at a cat.

Mark Twain

Reading is thinking with someone else's head instead of one's own.

Arthur Schopenhauer

When you read a good book it is like an author is right there. Sitting and talking to you right there. That is why I don't like to read books.

Jack Handey

To want to meet an author because you like his books is as ridiculous as wanting to meet the goose because you like pâté de foie gras.

Arthur Koestler

Reading is like the sex act – done privately, and often in bed. Daniel J. Boorstin

I got news for you, if it wasn't for the toilet, there would be no books.

George Costanza, *Seinfeld*

All my good reading, you might say, was done in the toilet ... There are passages in *Ulysses* which can be read only in the toilet – if one wants to extract the full flavour of their content. Henry Miller

—Homer's *Odyssey*. Is this about that mini-van I rented once?
—No, Dad, it's an epic tale from Ancient Greece. Homer and Lisa Simpson

When a book and a head collide and there is a hollow sound, is it always from the book? Georg Christoph Lichtenberg

There is no mistaking a real book when one meets it. It is like falling in love. Christopher Morley

There are books which take rank in your life with parents and lovers and passionate experiences, so medicinal, so stringent, so revolutionary, so authoritative. Ralph Waldo Emerson

The most invigorating form of reading matter is, of course, a will.

Nancy Banks-Smith

A book is like a garden carried in the pocket. Chinese proverb

A truly great book should be read in youth, again in maturity and once more in old age, as a fine building should be seen by morning light, at noon and by moonlight. **Robertson Davies**

I went to a bookstore and asked the saleswoman, 'Where's the self-help section?' She said if she told me, it would defeat the purpose. **Steven Wright**

—Why do the young die? Why does anybody die? Tell me.
—I don't know.
—What's the use of all your damn books? If they don't tell you that, what the hell do they tell you?
—They tell me about the agony of men who can't answer questions like yours. **Alexis Zorba and Basil, *Zorba the Greek***

A book must be the axe for the frozen sea inside us. **Franz Kafka**

The better the book the more room for the reader. **Holbrook Jackson**

One man, I'm told, asked the bookseller for a packet of condoms because he was too embarrassed to ask for a copy of my autobiography. **Sir Terry Wogan**

—The Ashmolean in Oxford was England's first what?
—Indian restaurant. **Contestant and Graeme Garden, *Beat the Nation***

I hate libraries. I can never tell if the whispering is coming from inside my head or out. **Max Ryan, *The Geena Davis Show***

Buying books would be a good thing if one could also find the time to read them; but as a rule the purchase of books is mistaken for the appropriation of their contents. **Arthur Schopenhauer**

A book is a success when people who haven't read it pretend they have. ***Los Angeles Times***

Just the knowledge that a good book is waiting for one at the end of a long day makes that day happier. **Kathleen Norris**

BORE

A subject for a great poet would be God's boredom after the seventh day of creation.
Friedrich Nietzsche

The effect of boredom on a large scale in history is underestimated. It is a main cause of revolutions.
Dean W. R. Inge

The war between being and nothingness is the underlying illness of the twentieth century. Boredom slays more of existence than war.
Norman Mailer

Is not life a hundred times too short for us to bore ourselves?
Friedrich Nietzsche

It's a sad truth that everyone is a bore to someone.
Llewellyn Miller

Boredom is the fear of self.
Comtesse Diane

Man is bored not only when there is nothing to do, but also when there is too much, or when everything waiting to be done has lost its lustre.
Geoffrey Clive

The cure for boredom is curiosity. There is no cure for curiosity.
Dorothy Parker

One can be bored until boredom becomes a mystical experience.
Logan Pearsall Smith

If something is boring after two minutes, try it for four. If still boring, try it for eight, sixteen, thirty-two, and so on. Eventually, one discovers that it's not boring at all but very interesting.
Zen saying

I wanted to be bored to death, as good a way to go as any.
Peter De Vries

BUREAUCRACY

Although I can accept talking scarecrows, lions, and great wizards of emerald cities, I find it hard to believe there is no paperwork involved when your house lands on a witch.   **Dave James**

In any bureaucracy, paperwork increases as you spend more and more time reporting on the less and less you are doing.   **Anon**

Every revolution evaporates and leaves behind only the slime of a new bureaucracy.   **Franz Kafka**

I do not rule Russia. Ten thousand clerks do.   **Nicholas I, Czar of Russia**

Bureaucracy defends the *status quo* long past the time when the *quo* has lost its *status*.   **Laurence J. Peter**

Britain has invented a new missile. It's called the civil servant – it doesn't work and it can't be fired.   **Walter Walker**

If you are going to sin, sin against God, not the bureaucracy. God will forgive you but the bureaucracy won't.   **Hyman Rickover**

BUSINESS

Business? It's quite simple. It's other people's money.   **Alexandre Dumas**

It very seldom happens to a man that his business is his pleasure.   **Samuel Johnson**

The business man – the man to whom age brings golf instead of wisdom.   **Bernard Shaw**

If two people agree all the time, one of them is unnecessary.   **David Mahoney**

Business is so much lower a thing than learning that a man used to the last cannot easily bring his stomach down to the first.   Lord Halifax

Half the times when men think they are talking business, they are wasting time.   E. W. Howe

It took me years to work out the difference between net and gross. In meetings I just used to say, 'Tell me if it's good or bad news.'

Richard Branson

Meetings are indispensable when you don't want to do anything.
J. K. Galbraith

Meetings are an addictive, highly self-indulgent activity that corporations and other large organizations habitually engage in only because they cannot actually masturbate.   Dave Barry

Having served on various committees, I have drawn up a list of rules: never arrive on time; this stamps you as a beginner. Don't say anything until the meeting is half over; this stamps you as being wise. Be as vague as possible; this avoids irritating the others. When in doubt, suggest that a subcommittee be appointed. Be the first to move for adjournment; this will make you popular; it's what everyone is waiting for.
Harry Chapman

The first thing to decide before you walk into any negotiation is what to do if the other fellow says 'no'.   Ernest Bevin

Marketing is far too important to leave to the marketing department.
David Packard, founder of Hewlett-Packard

Next week, a doctor with a flashlight shows us where sales projections come from.
Scott Adams

Never dump a good idea on a conference table. It will belong to the conference.
Jane Trahey

BUSY

Beware the barrenness of a busy life.
Socrates

Women aren't trying to do too much. Women have too much to do.
Mary Kay Blakely

In a society that judges self-worth on productivity, it's no wonder we fall prey to the misconception that the more we do, the more we're worth.
Ellen Sue Stern

The hardest job of all is trying to look busy when you're not. William Feather

Bees are not as busy as we think they are. They just can't buzz any slower.
Kin Hubbard

I am convinced that there are times in everybody's experience when there is so much to be done, that the only way to do it is to sit down and do nothing.
Fanny Fern

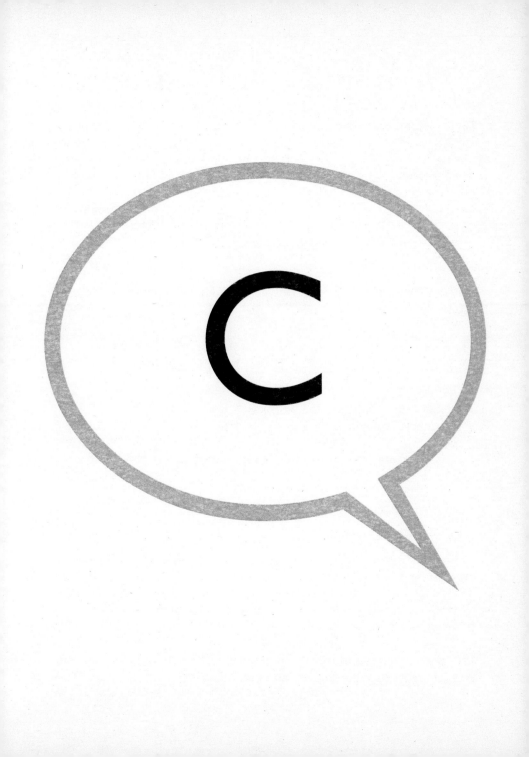

CAPITALISM

Under capitalism man exploits man; under socialism it's the other way round.
Polish saying

The inherent vice of capitalism is the unequal sharing of blessings; the inherent virtue of socialism is the equal sharing of miseries.
Winston Churchill

Capitalism without bankruptcy is like Christianity without hell.
Frank Borman

We have a society based on having and owning; we need a society based around being and giving.
Mike Scott

CAPITAL PUNISHMENT

—I cannot imagine any crime worse than taking a life, can you?
—It'd depend whose life.
Brendan Behan

Capital punishment is society's recognition of the sanctity of human life.
Senator Orrin Hatch

Men are not hanged for stealing horses, but that horses may not be stolen.
Lord Halifax

Capital punishment would be more effective as a deterrent if it were administered prior to the crime.
Woody Allen

Why do we kill people who are killing people to show that killing people is wrong?
Tim Martin

I support capital punishment. Where would Christianity be if Jesus got eight to ten years with time off for good behaviour?
James Donovan

If Jesus had been killed twenty years ago, Catholic school children would be wearing little electric chairs around their necks, instead of crosses.

Lenny Bruce

The compensation for a death sentence is knowledge of the exact hour when one is to die. A great luxury, but one that is well earned.

Vladimir Nabokov

The cure for crime is not the electric chair, but the high chair.

J. Edgar Hoover

Isn't all mankind ultimately executed for a crime it never committed?

Woody Allen

If the Old Testament were a reliable guide in the matter of capital punishment, half the people in the United States would have to be killed tomorrow.

Steve Allen

CAT

When I play with my cat, who knows but that she regards me more as a plaything than I do her?

Michel de Montaigne

A cat is there when you call her – if she has nothing better to do.

Bill Adler

If a man could be crossed with a cat, it would improve man, but deteriorate the cat.

Mark Twain

—If there was a fire, which of your sculptures would you rescue?
—It depends on what is in my house. If there was a cat and my works, I would save the cat. A cat's life is more important than art.

Interviewer and Alberto Giacometti

Cats are intended to teach us that not everything in nature has a purpose.

Garrison Keillor

I myself think to have a cat is more important than to have a Bible.

R. H. Blyth

If cats could talk, they would lie to you.

Rob Kopack

A cat can be trusted to purr when she is pleased, which is more than can be said for human beings.

Dean W. R. Inge

The problem with cats is that they get the exact same look on their face whether they see a moth or an axe-murderer.

Paula Poundstone

The man who carries a cat by the tail learns something that can be learned in no other way.

Mark Twain

Cats are a fairly right-wing group politically. They are lovers of the *status quo*. They don't like anything that might represent change. They hate marriages, divorces, moving days, graduations, bar mitzvahs, bill collectors, rug shampooers, painters, plumbers, electricians, television repairmen, out-call masseuses, Jehovah's Witnesses, and just about everything else, most of which I agree with them about.

Kinky Friedman

Why isn't there mouse-flavored cat food?

Jerry Seinfeld

Do not meddle in the affairs of cats, for they are subtle and will piss on your computer.

Elisabeth Riba

The best things in life are free. So how many kittens do you want?

Nancy Jo Perdue

In order to keep a true perspective of one's importance, everyone should have a dog that will worship him and a cat that will ignore him.

Derek Bruce

CATEGORY

Knowledge is one. Its division into subjects is a concession to human
weakness. **Halford J. Mackinder**

Only the human mind invents categories and tries to force facts into
separated pigeonholes. **Dr Alfred Kinsey**

Probably a crab would be filled with a sense of personal outrage if it could
hear us class it without ado or apology as a crustacean, and thus dispose of
it. 'I am no such thing,' it would say; 'I am MYSELF, MYSELF alone.'
William James

We think that if we can label a thing we have understood it.
Maha Sthavira Sangharakshita

Either people walk round dressed as chickens or they listen to Beethoven.
John Cleese

For most men life is a search for a proper manilla envelope in which to
get themselves filed. **Clifton Fadiman**

CENSORSHIP

We live in far too permissive a society. Never before has pornography been
this rampant. And those films are so badly lit! **Woody Allen**

If they didn't show it on the screen, most people would never know about
oral sex. **Mary Whitehouse**

I hate to think of this sort of book getting into the wrong hands. As soon
as I've finished this, I shall recommend they ban it. **Tony Hancock**

Censorship has been my best press agent my whole life. **John Waters**

People have a right to be shocked; the mention of unmentionable things is a kind of participation in them. Logan Pearsall Smith

You have not converted a man because you have silenced him. John Morley

CERTAINTY AND UNCERTAINTY

The only things that are certain are death and taxes, and that I can buy a penis extension from my inbox. Mark Austen

The only thing that makes life possible is permanent, intolerable uncertainty; not knowing what comes next. Ursula Le Guin

When we are not sure, we are alive. Graham Greene

To be absolutely certain about something, one must know everything or nothing about it. Anatole France

The minute one utters a certainty, the opposite comes to mind. May Sarton

The whole problem with the world is that fools and fanatics are always so certain of themselves, but wiser people so full of doubts. Bertrand Russell

CHANCE

Chance rules my life ... It was chance meeting you. It was chance falling in love; it's chance that we're here, particularly after your driving.
Amanda Prynne, *Private Lives*

So, I never lose a sense of the whimsical and perilous charm of daily life, with its meetings and words and accidents. Logan Pearsall Smith

No victor believes in chance.   Friedrich Nietzsche

He that leaveth little to chance will do few things ill, but he will do very few things.   Lord Halifax

I have written that life is ninety-nine per cent chance. I wish to correct this figure to one hundred per cent.   Samuel Butler, on his deathbed

CHANGE

Philosophers have sought to interpret the world: the point, however, is to change it.   Karl Marx

Change is not made without inconvenience, even from worse to better.
Richard Hooker

It's the most unhappy people who most fear change.   Mignon McLaughlin

Progress is impossible without change, and those who cannot change their minds cannot change anything.   George Bernard Shaw

People change and forget to tell each other.   Lillian Hellman

Any very great and sudden change is death.   Samuel Butler

There was no such thing on this earth as real change. You could change husbands, but not the situation. You could change who, but not what. We're all just spinning here, she thought, and she pictured the world as a little blue teacup, revolving like those rides at Kiddie Land where everyone is pinned to his place by centrifugal force.   Anne Tyler

You change people by delight, by pleasure.   Thomas Aquinas

Why not upset the apple cart? If you don't, the apples will rot anyway.
Frank A. Clark

The only difference between a Rut and a Grave are their dimensions.

Ellen Glasgow

If one changes internally, one should not continue to live with the same objects. They reflect one's mind and psyche of yesterday. I throw away what has no dynamic, living use. I keep nothing to remind me of the passage of time, deterioration, loss, shrivelling.

Anaïs Nin

No man ever steps in the same river twice, for it's not the same river, and he's not the same man.

Heraclitus

It is wonderful how quickly you get used to things, even the most astonishing.

Edith Nesbit

Adaptable as human beings are and have to be, I sometimes sympathize with the chameleon who had a nervous breakdown on a patchwork quilt.

John Stephen Strange

One man can change the world with a bullet in the right place.

Mick Travis, *If*

God grant me the serenity to accept the things I cannot change, courage to change the things I can, and wisdom to know the difference.

Reinhold Niebuhr

One must change one's tactics every ten years if one wishes to maintain one's superiority.

Napoleon Bonaparte

Never doubt that a small group of thoughtful committed citizens can change the world; indeed it's the only thing that ever has.

Margaret Mead

Be the change.

Mahatma Gandhi

CHAOS

All things are contingent, and there is always chaos. In other words, shit happens.
Spalding Gray

I'm a study of a man in chaos in search of frenzy.
Oscar Levant

Chaos often breeds life, when order breeds habit.
Henry Brooks Adams

One must have chaos in oneself in order to give birth to a dancing star.
Friedrich Nietzsche

We adore chaos because we like to restore order.
M. C. Escher

CHARACTER

History is made at night. Character is what you are in the dark.
John Whorfin

Character is doing the right thing when no one is watching.
J. C. Watt

Character may be manifested in the great moments, but it is made in the small ones.
Phillip Brooks

Only a few persons influence the formation of our character; the multitude pass us by like a distant army. One friend, one teacher, one beloved, one club, one dining table, one work table are the means by which his nation and the spirit of his nation affect the individual.
Jean Paul Richter

You've got to learn to survive a defeat. That's when you develop character.
Richard Nixon

A person who is nice to you, but rude to the waiter, is not a nice person.
Dave Barry

The best index to a person's character is a) how he treats people who can't do him any good, and b) how he treats people who can't fight back.

Abigail Van Buren

No man knows his true character until he has run out of gas, purchased something on the instalment plan, and raised an adolescent.   Marcelene Cox

About all you can do in life is be who you are. Some people will love you for you. Most will love you for what you can do for them, and some won't like you at all.

Rita Mae Brown

CHARITY

We make a living by what we get, we make a life by what we give.

Winston Churchill

This homeless guy asked me for money the other day. I was about to give it to him and then I thought he was going to use it on drugs or alcohol. And then I thought, that's what I'm going to use it on. Why am I judging this poor bastard?

Greg Giraldo

The *Big Issue* would sell a lot more copies if they made their vendors smarten up a bit. Most of them look like tramps.

Tim Woods, *Viz*

You have no idea, sir, how difficult it is to be the victim of benevolence.

Zora Neale Hurston

A beggar hates his benefactor as much as he hates himself for begging.

Oscar Wilde

It is only by feeling your love that the poor will forgive you for the gifts of bread.

St Vincent de Paul

The highest exercise of charity is charity towards the uncharitable.

J. S. Buckminster

The fragrance always stays in the hand that gives the rose.   Hadia Bejar

Socially prominent people are very fond of disease, because it gives them a chance to have these really elaborate charity functions, and the newspaper headlines say 'EVENING IN PARIS BALL RAISES MONEY TO FIGHT GOUT' instead of 'RICH PEOPLE AMUSE THEMSELVES'.
Dave Barry

A large part of altruism, even when it is perfectly honest, is grounded upon the fact that it is uncomfortable to have unhappy people about one.
H. L. Mencken

All philanthropy is only a savoury fumigation burning at the mouth of a sewer.   Ellen Key

The man who leaves money to charity in his will is only giving away what no longer belongs to him.   Voltaire

I don't want you to give me your surplus. I want you to give with personal deprivation.   Mother Teresa

Charity is the bone shared with the dog when you are just as hungry as the dog.   Jack London

If you see him riding on a bamboo-cane, say to him, 'Good health to your horse.'   Moroccan proverb

Foreign aid: when the poor people of a rich nation send their money to the rich people of a poor nation.   Anon

The most melancholy of human reflections, perhaps, is that, on the whole, it is a question whether the benevolence of mankind does more good or harm.   Walter Bagehot

You are much surer that you are doing good when you pay money to those who work, as the recompense of their labour, than when you give money merely in charity.

Samuel Johnson

If you see a man approaching with the obvious intent of doing you good, run for your life.

Henry David Thoreau

No people do so much harm as those who go about doing good.

Bishop Mandell Creighton

The compulsion to do good is an innate American trait. Only North Americans seem to believe that they always should, may, and actually can choose somebody with whom to share their blessings. Ultimately this attitude leads to bombing people into the acceptance of gifts.

Ivan Illich

The urge to save humanity is almost always only a false-face for the urge to rule it.

H. L. Mencken

CHARM

I was raised to be charming, not sincere.

Stephen Sondheim

There is a difference between beauty and charm. A beautiful woman is one I notice. A charming woman is one who notices me.

John Erskine

Give me a few minutes to talk away my face and I can seduce the Queen of France.

Voltaire

Charm is a way of getting the answer yes without having asked any clear question.

Albert Camus

Charm is the enchanted dart, light and subtle as a hummingbird. But it is deceptive in one thing: like a sense of humour, if you think you've got it, you probably haven't.

Laurie Lee

A stranger loses half his charm the day he is no longer a stranger.

Geneviève Antoine Dariaux

CHEERFULNESS

My religion of life is always to be cheerful.

George Meredith

The highest wisdom and the highest genius have been invariably accompanied with cheerfulness. We have sufficient proofs on record that Shakespeare and Socrates were the most festive companions.

Thomas Love Peacock

He that is of a merry heart hath a continual feast.

Bible, Proverbs

While there is a chance of the world getting through its troubles, I hold that a reasonable man has to behave as though he were sure of it. If at the end your cheerfulness is not justified, at any rate you will have been cheerful.

H. G. Wells

CHILDHOOD

Every man remembers his childhood as a kind of mythical age, just as every nation's childhood is its mythical age.

Giacomo Leopardi

I suppose we all tend to remember only the happiness from our childhood, as a sundial refuses to tell the time except in fine weather.

Bernard Levin

The illusions of childhood are necessary experiences: a child should not be denied a balloon just because an adult knows that sooner or later it will burst.

Marcelene Cox

Childhood may have periods of great happiness, but it also has times that must simply be endured. Childhood at its best is a form of slavery tempered by affection.

Robertson Davies

As for childhood being carefree, I know from my own experience that black care can sit behind us even on our rocking-horses.

Lord Berners

The dominant expression of a child is gravity. Bret Harte

My childhood was a period of waiting for the moment when I could send everyone and everything connected to it to hell. Igor Stravinsky

A happy childhood can't be cured. Mine'll hang around my neck like a rainbow, that's all, instead of a noose. Hortense Calisher

Childhood shows the man as morning shows the day. John Milton

In the lost boyhood of Judas, Christ was betrayed. G. W. Russell

There is always one moment in childhood when the door opens and lets the future in. Graham Greene

Childhood in large parts of modern Britain, at any rate, has been replaced by premature adulthood, or rather adolescence. Children grow up very fast but not very far. That is why it is possible for fourteen-year-olds now to establish friendships with twenty-six-year-olds – because they know by the age of fourteen all they are ever going to know. Theodore Dalrymple

CHILDREN

I don't have any kids. Well, at least none I know about. Cathy Ladman

I had a dream that all the victims of the Pill came back ... boy, were they mad. Steven Wright

Making the decision to have a child – it's momentous. It is to decide forever to have your heart go walking around outside your body.
Elizabeth Stone

Babies are a nuisance, of course. But so does everything seem to be that is worthwhile – husbands and books and committees and being loved and everything. We have to choose between ease and rich unrest. Vera Brittain

Did you hear about the Irish girl who went home and told her mother she was pregnant – and the mother said, 'Are you sure it's you?'   Dennis Taylor

I didn't know how babies were made until I was pregnant with my fourth child.   Loretta Lynn

Giving away baby clothes and nursery furniture is a major cause of pregnancy.   Esther Selsdon

The reason most people have kids is because they get pregnant.   Barbara Kingsolver

If newborns could remember and speak, they would emerge from the womb carrying tales as wondrous as Homer's.   *Newsweek* magazine

I'm happy to say I lost the weight after the baby. Of course, it took me four years, and we adopted.   Andrea Henry

We have nine children now – half girls and half boys.   Mark Twain

There's a time when you have to explain to your children why they're born, and it's marvellous if you know the reason by then.   Hazel Scott

If you bungle raising your children, I don't think whatever else you do well matters very much.   Jackie Kennedy Onassis

A perfect parent is a person with excellent child-rearing theories and no actual children.   Dave Barry

Who of us is mature enough for offspring before the offspring themselves arrive? The value of marriage is not that adults produce children but that children produce adults.   Peter De Vries

Men worry about childcare with their wallets, women feel it in their wombs.   Allison Pearson

A child's hand in yours – what tenderness and power it arouses. You are instantly the very touchstone of wisdom and strength.   Marjorie Holmes

To show a child what has once delighted you, to find the child's delight added to your own, so that there is now a double delight seen in the glow of trust and affection, this is happiness.   J. B. Priestley

A child's attitude to everything is always an artist's attitude.   Willa Cather

All children alarm their parents, if only because you are forever expecting to encounter yourself.   Gore Vidal

Adults are always asking kids what they want to be when they grow up because they are looking for ideas.   Paula Poundstone

Always take out your watch when a child asks you the time.   J. A. Spender

Never help a child with a task at which he feels he can succeed.   Maria Montessori

One of the things I've discovered in general about raising kids is that they really don't give a damn if you walked five miles to school.   Patty Duke

Teaching a child not to step on a caterpillar is as valuable to the child as it is to the caterpillar.   Bradley Millar

Children in a family are like flowers in a bouquet: there's always one determined to face in an opposite direction from the way the arranger desires.   Marcelene Cox

It's simply wrong to always order kids to stop that fighting. There are times when one child is simply defending his rights and damned well should be fighting.   Erma Bombeck

Parents of young children should realize that few people, and maybe no one, will find their children as enchanting as they do.   Barbara Walters

The child of Themistocles governed his mother; the mother governed her husband; the husband governed Athens; Athens governed Greece; Greece governed the world. Therefore, Themistocles' child governed the world.
Ralph L. Woods

The discontented child cries for toasted snow.   Arabian proverb

The fault that no child ever loses is the one he was most punished for.
Cesare Beccaria

There is no end to the violations committed by children on children, quietly talking alone.   Elizabeth Bowen

Children are apt to live up to what you believe of them.   Lady Bird Johnson

It is not a bad thing that children should occasionally, and politely, put parents in their place.   Colette

If there is anything that we wish to change in the child, we should first examine it and see whether it is not something that could better be changed in ourselves.   Carl Jung

When you are dealing with a child, keep all your wits about you, and sit on the floor.   Austin O'Malley

One of the most obvious facts about grown-ups to a child, is that they have forgotten what it is like to be a child.   Randall Jarrell

It's a waste of time to read books on child psychology written by adults unless we are willing to check every page by what children know about the psychology of parents.   John Erskine

Allow children to be happy in their own way, for what better way will they find?   Samuel Johnson

CHRISTIANITY

There are 108 beads in a Catholic rosary and there are 108 stitches in a baseball. When I heard that, I gave Jesus a chance.

Annie Savoy, *Bull Durham*

The Christian religion is based on the economic policy that dead people don't ask for refunds.

Anon

Two great European narcotics, alcohol and Christianity.   Friedrich Nietzsche

Christian: one who believes that the New Testament is a divinely inspired book admirably suited to the spiritual needs of his neighbor.

Ambrose Bierce

The *Bible* takes much of its colour from whoever is reading it, and it provides a text to support almost every shade of opinion, however preposterous.

Robertson Davies

The total absence of humour from the *Bible* is one of the most singular things in all literature.

Alfred North Whitehead

If Christ were here today, there is one thing he would not be – a Christian.

Mark Twain

We know Jesus wasn't English because he wore sandals – but never with socks.

Linda Smith

The idea of Christ is much older than Christianity.   George Santayana

Christianity has done a great deal for love by making a sin of it.

Anatole France

I was raised as a Catholic and received the body and blood of Jesus Christ every Sunday at communion until I was thirty years of age, when I became a vegetarian.

Joe Queenan

The chief contribution of Protestantism to human thought is its massive proof that God is a bore.

H. L. Mencken

Catholic: confession on Saturday, absolution on Sunday. At it again on Monday.

H. G. Wells

Infidel: in New York, one who does not believe in the Christian religion; in Constantinople, one who does.

Ambrose Bierce

A sparrow fluttering about the church is an antagonist which the most profound theologian in Europe is wholly unable to overcome.

Sydney Smith

The Pope one day told his cardinals that he had good news and bad news. The good news: 'I've just received a phone call from Jesus, who has returned to earth.' The bad news: 'He was calling from Salt Lake City.'

Monsignor Geno Baroni

Any hope that America would finally grow up vanished with the rise of fundamentalist Christianity. Fundamentalism, with its born-again regression, its pink-and-gold concept of heaven, its literal-mindedness, its rambunctious good cheer … its anti-intellectualism … its puerile hymns … and its faith-healing … are made to order for King Kid America.   **Florence E. King**

CHURCH

So she goes to church. It's cheaper than the psychoanalyst and more convenient, being only once a week.

Aubrey Menen

Going to church does not make you a Christian any more than going to the garage makes you a car.

Laurence J. Peter

This is the Gate of Heaven. Enter ye all by this door.
(This door is kept locked because of the draught. Please use side entrance.)

Sign on a church door

A Martian would think that the English worship at supermarkets,
not in churches. **Dr Jonathan Sacks**

Lighthouses are more helpful than churches. **Benjamin Franklin**

An Ohio church committee slips a dollar bill into one hymn book every
Sunday to stimulate attendance. **Anon**

Every day people are straying away from church and going back to God.
Lenny Bruce

Avoid kneeling in unheated stone churches. Ecclesiastical dampness causes
prematurely grey hair. **John Cheever**

CIRCUMSTANCES

Caesar might have married Cleopatra, but he had a wife at home.
There's always something. **Will Cuppy**

Do you know the times when one seems to stick fast in circumstances like
the fly in the jam-pot? It can't be helped, and I suppose the best thing to do
is to lay in a good store of jam! **A. C. Benson**

People are always blaming their circumstances for what they are. I don't
believe in circumstances. The people who get on in this world are the
people who get up and look for the circumstances they want, and, if they
can't find them, they make them. **George Bernard Shaw**

Sometimes you just have to pee in the sink. **Charles Bukowski**

It is easy to say what you would do in given circumstances if you know
perfectly well that those circumstances will never arise. **Henry Cecil**

Most people never have to face the fact that, at the right time, and the
right place, they're capable of anything. **Noah Cross, *Chinatown***

I believe that in every circumstance I have been able to see rather clearly the most advantageous course I could follow, which is very rarely the one I did follow.   André Gide

Do not wait for ideal circumstances; they will never come.   Janet Erskine Stuart

Instead of seeing the rug being pulled from under us, we can learn to dance on a shifting carpet.   Thomas Crum

CITY

Cities have sexes: London is a man, Paris a woman, and New York a well-adjusted transsexual.   Angela Carter

Cities, like cats, will reveal themselves at night.   Rupert Brooke

City life: millions of people being lonesome together.   Henry David Thoreau

I'd rather wake in the middle of nowhere than in any city on earth.
                                                                              Steve McQueen

You cannot see the Milky Way in New York City any more ... We risk the loss of our sensual perception. And if you lose those, naturally, you try to compensate by other stimulations, by very loud noises, or by bright lights or drugs.   René Dubos

CIVILIZATION

The first human being who hurled a curse instead of a weapon ... was the founder of civilization.   Sigmund Freud

Civilization has been thrust upon me ... and it has not added one whit to my love for truth, honesty, and generosity.   Chief Luther Standing Bear

Civilization rests on two things: the discovery that fermentation produces alcohol, and the voluntary ability to inhibit defecation. And I put it to you, where would this splendid civilization be without both?

Robertson Davies

It seems to me the mark of a civilized society that certain privileges should be taken for granted such as education, health care and the safety to walk the streets.

Alan Bennett

The flush toilet is the basis of Western civilization.

Alan Coult

There is precious little in civilization to appeal to a yeti.

Edmund Hillary

We are born princes and the civilizing process makes us frogs.

Eric Berne

The fate of civilization is like needlework. You can take it up and worry about it at odd moments.

Frank Sullivan

Civilization is drugs, alcohol, engines of war, prostitution, machines and machine slaves, low wages, bad food, bad taste, prisons, reformatories, lunatic asylums, divorce, perversion, brutal sports, suicides, infanticide, cinema, quackery, demagogy, strikes, lockouts, revolutions, putsches, colonization, electric chairs, guillotines, sabotage, floods, famine, disease, gangsters, money barons, horse racing, fashion shows, poodle dogs, chow dogs, Siamese cats, condoms, pessaries, syphilis, gonorrhea, insanity, neuroses, etc., etc.

Henry Miller

The military superiority of Europe to Asia is not an eternal law of nature, as we are tempted to think, and our superiority in civilization is a mere delusion.

Bertrand Russell

A decent provision for the poor is the true test of civilization.   Samuel Johnson

To be a man is to feel that one's own stone contributes to building the edifice of the world.   Antoine de Saint-Exupéry

The United States will never be a civilized country until we spend more money for books than we do for chewing gum.   Elbert Hubbard

Civilization is the acceptance and the encouragement of differences.
Mahatma Gandhi

Civilization is hideously fragile ... there's not much between us and the horrors underneath, just about a coat of varnish.   C. P. Snow

The end of the human race will be that it will eventually die of civilization.
Ralph Waldo Emerson

Many clever men like you have trusted to civilization. Many clever Babylonians, clever Egyptians, many clever men at the end of Rome. Can you tell me, in a world that is flagrant with the failures of civilization, what there is particularly immortal about yours?   G. K. Chesterton

CLUB

I don't belong to any organization. I've never been a joiner. The last thing I joined was the Tufty Club.   Linda Smith

Beware membership in a body of persons pledged to only one side of anything.   Henry S. Haskins

Regarding the Boy Scouts, I'm very suspicious of any organization that has a handbook.   George Carlin

Please accept my resignation. I don't care to belong to any club that will accept me as a member.   Groucho Marx

COLOUR

Roses are Red,
Violets are Blue –
So why are they called violets then?   **Anon**

Colours speak all languages.   **Joseph Addison**

Colour in a picture is like enthusiasm in life.   **Vincent Van Gogh**

Artists can color the sky red because they know it's blue. Those of us who
aren't artists must colour things the way they are or people might think
we're stupid.   **Jules Feiffer**

If artists do see fields blue they are deranged, and should go to an asylum.
If they only pretend to see them blue, they are criminals and should go
to prison.   **Adolf Hitler**

The colours that show best by candlelight are white, carnation, and a kind
of sea-water green.   **Francis Bacon**

When painting the faces of young persons ... use the yolk of the egg of a
city hen, because they have lighter yolks than those of country hens.
                    Cennino Cennini

A thimbleful of red is redder than a bucketful.   **Henri Matisse**

If I could find anything blacker than black, I'd use it.   **J. M. W. Turner**

Violet will be a good color for hair at just about the same time that
brunette becomes a good color for flowers.   **Fran Lebowitz**

I'm intrigued that one can recognize different parts of the world solely by
the particular color of the water.   **Leonard Mizerek**

My favourite color? I hate colors.   **Ian Shoales**

COMMANDMENTS

How wise are thy commandments, Lord. Each of them applies to
somebody I know.
Sam Levenson

Most people believe that the Christian commandments, e.g. to love one's
neighbour as oneself, are intentionally a little too severe – like setting a
clock half an hour ahead to make sure of not being late in the morning.
Søren Kierkegaard

I'm glad God gave the Ten Commandments to a man. A woman would
have thought, I know that's what he said, but I don't think that's what
he meant.
Diane Nichols

Say what you like about the Ten Commandments, you must always
come back to the pleasant truth that there are only ten of them.
H. L. Mencken

This is the age of bargain hunters. If it had been this way in biblical times,
we'd probably have been offered another commandment free if we had
accepted the first ten.
Earl Wilson

Hear about the new-wave church in California? It has three
commandments, and six suggestions.
Anon

COMMON SENSE

There are forty kinds of lunacy, but only one kind of common sense.
African proverb

Common sense in an uncommon degree is what the world calls wisdom.
Samuel Taylor Coleridge

Common sense is genius dressed in its working clothes.   Ralph Waldo Emerson

Common sense is the collection of prejudices acquired by age eighteen.

Albert Einstein

Soap and water and common sense are the best disinfectants. **William Osler**

It is a thousand times better to have common sense without education than to have education without common sense. **Robert Green Ingersoll**

Nothing astonishes men so much as common sense and plain dealing.

Ralph Waldo Emerson

Common sense is perhaps the most equally divided, but surely the most underemployed, talent in the world. **Christine Collange**

COMMUNICATION

Hiya, Wall. **Shirley Valentine, *Shirley Valentine***

In our house, the direct statement was seldom used as a vehicle for communication. Innuendo was the order of the day.

Gloria DeVidas Kirchcheimer

Two prisoners whose cells adjoin communicate with each other by knocking on the wall. The wall is the thing which separates them but is also their means of communication. It is the same with us and God. Every separation is a link. **Simone Weil**

Can the cannibal speak in the name of those he ate? **Stanislaw J. Lec**

The two words 'information' and 'communication' are often used interchangeably, but they signify quite different things. Information is giving out; communication is getting through. **Sydney J. Harris**

On Sunday Mr Green paid a visit from Lichfield, and, having nothing to say, said nothing and went away. **Samuel Johnson**

Sometimes a scream is better than a thesis.   Ralph Waldo Emerson

Her tongue knows no Sunday.   African American saying

Every time you open your mouth you let men look into your mind.
Bruce Barton

Nothing can be so clearly and carefully expressed that it cannot be utterly misinterpreted.   Fred W. Householder

Everyone realizes that one can believe little of what people say about each other. But it is not so widely realized that even less can one trust what people say about themselves.   Rebecca West

As I grow older, I pay less attention to what men say. I just watch what they do.   Andrew Carnegie

COMMUNISM

When I give food to the poor they call me a saint. When I ask why the poor have no food they call me a communist.   Helder Camara

Communists are frustrated capitalists.   Eric Hoffer

What a communist he is! He would have equal distribution of sin as well as property.   Oscar Wilde

When the people are beaten with a stick, they are not much happier if it is called 'The People's Stick'.   Mikhail Bakunin

The wonder is that communism lasted so long. But then again, modern poetry lasted a long time, too.   P. J O'Rourke

COMMUNITY

Community is gathering around a fire and listening to someone tell a story.

Bill Moher

An ideal community is one that has a place for every human gift.

Margaret Mead

Human beings will be happier – not when they cure cancer or get to Mars or eliminate racial prejudice or flush Lake Erie but when they find ways to inhabit primitive communities again. That's my utopia.

Kurt Vonnegut

COMPASSION

Compassion is the anti-toxin of the soul: where there is compassion even the most poisonous impulses remain relatively harmless.

Eric Hoffer

Bob Geldof feels the big picture all the time, even in the smallest argument when someone's saying, 'Well, no, you've got to have three staples in the programme, not just two,' Bob feels people dying somewhere.

Richard Curtis

The Asian tsunami resulted in the largest international aid operation in history, driven by what Jan Egeland, head of humanitarian affairs at the UN, described as competitive compassion.

The *Irish Times*

Human compassion is equal to human cruelty, and it is up to each of us to tip the balance.

Alice Walker

I am not interested in picking up crumbs of compassion thrown from the table of someone who considers himself my master. I want the full menu of rights.

Archbishop Desmond Tutu

COMPLIMENT

When a man makes a woman his wife, it's the highest compliment he can pay her – and it's usually the last.   Helen Rowland

Never lose a chance of saying a kind word. As Collingwood never saw a vacant place in his estate but he took an acorn out of his pocket and planted it, so deal with your compliments through life. An acorn costs nothing, but it may spread into a prodigious timber.

William Makepeace Thackeray

Some fellows pay a compliment like they expect a receipt.   Kin Hubbard

I've made this conscious decision to tell people on the street when I think they're wearing something great. If more people did that, the world would be a better place.   Ashley Jensen

Nothing is so silly as the expression of a man who is being complimented.
André Gide

A little boy sent me a charming card with a little drawing. I loved it … I sent him a postcard and I drew a picture of a Wild Thing on it. I wrote, 'Dear Jim, I loved your card.' Then I got a letter back from his mother and she said, 'Jim loved your card so much he ate it.' That to me was one of the highest compliments I've ever received. He didn't care that it was an original drawing or anything. He saw it, he loved it, he ate it.

Maurice Sendak

Everybody knows how to utter a complaint, but few can express a graceful compliment.   William Feather

A compliment is something like a kiss through a veil.

Victor Hugo

COMPOSER

—Why do you compose?
—Because I cannot swim.   Interviewer and Frederick Delius

In order to compose, all you need do is remember a tune that no one else
has thought of.   Robert Schumann

Composers should write tunes that chauffeurs and errand boys can whistle.
                                                   Thomas Beecham

Music is only understood when one goes away singing it and only loved
when one falls asleep with it in one's head, and finds it still there on
waking up the next morning.   Arnold Schoenberg

I don't choose what I compose. It chooses me.   Gustav Mahler

I write songs about things that I'm simultaneously trying not to think about.
                                                   Warren Zevon

Every composer's music reflects in its subject-matter and in its style the
source of the money the composer is living on while writing the music.
                                                   Virgil Thomson

I have always found it difficult to study. I have learnt almost entirely what I
have learnt by trying it out on the dog.   Ralph Vaughan Williams

My music is purposeless play. It is an affirmation of life – not an attempt to
bring order out of chaos, nor to suggest improvements in creation, but
simply to wake up to the very life we are living.   John Cage

Would you have your songs endure? Build on the human heart.
                                                   Robert Browning

When I play Beethoven I always feel as if my soul were at the dry-cleaners.
                                                   Alma Mahler-Werfel

Grieg's music has the odd and pleasant taste of a pink sweet filled with snow. **Claude Debussy**

Puccini – silver macaroni, exquisitely tangled. **H. L. Mencken**

—The Hallelujah Chorus occurs in which oratorio by Handel?
—*The Sound of Music.* **Anne Robinson and Contestant,** *The Weakest Link*

If you don't believe in God, you can suspend it while listening to Bach, and then go back to being an atheist. **Joan Marsh**

Whether the angels play only Bach praising God, I am not quite sure; I am sure, however, that *en famille* they play Mozart. **Karl Barth**

We all drew on the comfort which is given out by the major works of Mozart, which is as real and material as the warmth given up by a glass of brandy. **Rebecca West**

You should never trust anyone who listens to Mahler before they're forty. **Clive James**

My music is best understood by children and animals. **Igor Stravinsky**

COMPROMISE

Do compromises work? Have you ever tasted rosé? **Jeff Green**

My husband and I went to buy a lamp. We couldn't find one that we both liked, so we had to compromise and buy one that we both hated. **Janet Rosen**

A compromise is an agreement between two men to do what they both agree is wrong. **Edward Cecil**

A compromise is the art of dividing a cake in such a way that everyone believes that he has got the bigger piece. **Paul Gauguin**

I would rather play 'Chiquita Banana' and have my swimming pool, than play Bach and starve. Xavier Cougar

Don't compromise yourself. You are all you've got. Janis Joplin

COMPUTER

I shop at a computer store called 'Your Crap's Already Obsolete'. Jeff Cesario

Built by engineers. Used by normal people. Hewlett-Packard slogan

Beware of programmers carrying screwdrivers. Chip Salzenberg

I conclude that there are two ways of constructing a software design: one way is to make it so simple that there are obviously no deficiencies and the other way is to make it so complicated that there are no obvious deficiencies. C. A. R. Hoare

The question of whether a computer can think is no more interesting than the question of whether a submarine can swim. Edsgar Dijkstra

Some people worry that artificial intelligence will make us feel inferior, but then, anybody in his right mind should have an inferiority complex every time he looks at a flower. Alan Kay

The real danger is not that computers will begin to think like men, but that men will begin to think like computers. Sydney J. Harris

CONFESSION

Confession is good for the soul only in the sense that a tweed coat is good for dandruff – it is a palliative rather than a remedy. Peter De Vries

It is not the criminal things which are hardest to confess, but the ridiculous and shameful. Jean Jacques Rousseau

Confession is a kind of pride.   Balfour Browne

It is the confession, not the priest, that gives us absolution.   Oscar Wilde

All the good writers of confessions, from Augustine onwards, are men who
are still a little in love with their sins.   Anatole France

CONFIDENCE

When I went duck hunting with Bear Bryant, he shot at one but it kept
flying. 'John,' he said, 'there flies a dead duck.' Now, that's confidence.
                                                                    John McKay

Putting the World to Rights
                 Margaret Thatcher, chapter title, *The Downing Street Years*

One cannot govern with 'buts'.   Charles de Gaulle

I admire the assurance and confidence everyone has in himself, whereas
there is hardly anything I am sure I know or that I dare give my word I
can do.   Michel de Montaigne

Some days confidence shrinks to the size of a pea, and the backbone feels
like a feather. We want to be somewhere else, and don't know where –
want to be someone else and don't know who.   Jean Hersey

If a dish doesn't turn out right, change the name and don't bat an eyelid.
A fallen soufflé is only a risen omelette. It depends on the self-confidence
with which you present it.   Rabbi Lionel Blue

An important key to self-confidence is preparation.   Arthur Ashe

Be humble, for the worst thing in the world is of the same stuff as you;
be confident, for the stars are of the same stuff as you.   Nicholai Velimirovic

Act as if it were impossible to fail.   Dorothea Brande

CONFORMITY AND ORIGINALITY

We are all born originals – why is it so many of us die copies?   Edward Young

It is better to fail in originality than to succeed in imitation.   Herman Melville

Do not fear to be eccentric in opinion, for every opinion now accepted
was once eccentric.   Bertrand Russell

If one is a greyhound, why try to look like a Pekingese?   Edith Sitwell

He who goes against the fashion is himself its slave.   Logan Pearsall Smith

Why do you have to be a non-conformist like everybody else?   Stan Hunt

He who lives among dogs must learn to pant.   Fred Hoyle

A society made up of individuals who were all capable of original thought
would probably be unendurable.   H. L. Mencken

CONSCIENCE

Conscience is the inner voice which warns us that someone may be looking.
                                                                  H. L. Mencken

I believe I once considerably scandalized her by declaring that clear soup
was a more important factor in life than a clear conscience.   Saki

An uneasy conscience is a hair in the mouth.   Mark Twain

The laws of conscience, though we ascribe them to nature, actually come
from custom.   Michel de Montaigne

Coleridge declares that a man cannot have a good conscience who refuses apple dumplings, and I confess that I am of the same opinion.

Charles Lamb

Most people sell their souls and live with a good conscience on the proceeds.

Logan Pearsall Smith

People with bad consciences always fear the judgement of children.

Mary McCarthy

And what saved her virtue? The voice of her conscience? Oh no. The voice of her neighbour.

Friedrich Nietzsche

CONSEQUENCES

There is no limit to how complicated things can get, on account of one thing leading to another.

E. B. White

Did Bill Clinton actually think that he could get blow jobs from a Jewish woman and there would be no *consequences*?

Larry David

Sooner or later everyone sits down to a banquet of consequences.

Frank Gannon

A man must properly pay the fiddler. In my case it so happened that a whole symphony orchestra had to be subsidized.

John Barrymore

Heard about the guy who fell off a skyscraper? On his way down past each floor, he kept saying to reassure himself: 'So far so good ... so far so good ... so far so good.' How you fall doesn't matter. It's how you land.

Hubert, *La Haine*

You can do anything in this world if you are prepared to take the consequences.

W. Somerset Maugham

Consequences schmonsequences, as long as I'm rich.

Daffy Duck

CONTENTMENT

Cloud nine gets all the publicity, but cloud eight is actually cheaper, less crowded, and has a better view.
George Carlin

We may pass violets looking for roses. We may pass contentment looking for victory.
Bern Williams

I would rather sit on a pumpkin, and have it to myself, than to be crowded on a velvet cushion.
Henry David Thoreau

Better a handful of dry dates and content therewith than to own the Gate of Peacocks and be kicked in the eye by a broody camel.   Arabian proverb

All shall be well, and all shall be well and all manner of things shall be well.
Julian of Norwich

Don't let's ask for the moon. We have the stars.   Charlotte Vale, *Now, Voyager*

When you are unhappy or dissatisfied, is there anything in the world more maddening than to be told that you should be contented with your lot?
Kathleen Norris

CONVERSATION

People say conversation is a lost art; how often I have wished it were.
Edward Murrow

Beware the conversationalist who adds, 'In other words.' He is merely starting afresh.
Robert Morley

No animal should ever jump up on the dining room furniture unless absolutely certain that he can hold his own in the conversation.
Fran Lebowitz

As hills of sand to the feet of the traveller, so is the voice of the incessant talker to the ears of the wise.

Arabian proverb

She was not a woman of many words; for, unlike people in general, she proportioned them to the number of her ideas.

Jane Austen

In a conversation, keep in mind that you're more interested in what you have to say than anyone else is.

Andy Rooney

It appears that even the different parts of the same person do not converse among themselves, do not succeed in learning from each other what are their desires and their intentions.

Rebecca West

One way to prevent conversation from being boring is to say the wrong thing.

Frank Sheed

COSMETIC SURGERY

It's now rare in certain social enclaves to see a woman over the age of thirty-five with the ability to look angry.

Alex Kuczynski

I have a professional acquaintance whose recent eyelid job has left her with a permanent expression of such poleaxed astonishment that she looks at all times as if she had just read one of my books.

Florence King

To maintain our family resemblance, my entire extended family had their noses done by the same doctor.

Janice Heiss

We know more about the lifespan of automobile tyres than we do about breast implants.

Dr David Kessler

What does it profit a 78-year-old woman to sit around the pool in a bikini if she cannot feed herself?   Erma Bombeck

It would have been cheaper to have my DNA changed.   Joan Rivers

Women over fifty should always have at least one pink shirt in their wardrobe. It's much cheaper than a facelift. Anne Dickinson

An unforgiving nature reflects in your face. Holding negative energy drags down the facial muscles, puckers one's frown and causes lines around the mouth. Working daily on forgiveness (forgiving oneself as well as one's enemies) is the cheapest, most effective facelift in the whole wide world. All it requires is love and discipline.   Sarah Miles

When life is too interesting to worry about how my face looks, that's the way I like it.   Jean Vint

A girl's best beauty aid is a near-sighted man.   Yoko Ono

I did not use paint. I made myself up morally.   Eleanora Duse

Taking joy in living is a woman's best cosmetic.   Rosalind Russell

COUNTRY & WESTERN MUSIC

Country music is three chords and the truth.   Harlan Howard

You got to have smelt a lot of mule manure before you can sing like a hillbilly.   Hank Williams

Her Teeth Were Stained But Her Heart Was Pure
She Got The Ring And I Got The Finger
I'd Rather Pass A Kidney Stone Than Another Night With You
How Can I Miss You If You Won't Go Away?
Walk Out Backwards Slowly So I'll Think You're Walking In
I Bought The Shoes That Just Walked Out On Me
My Wife Ran Off With My Best Friend And I Sure Do Miss Him
When Your Phone Don't Ring You'll Know It's Me
I've Been Flushed From The Bathroom Of Your Heart
At The Gas Station Of Love, I Got The Self-Service Pump
The Last Word In Lonesome Is 'Me'
If The Jukebox Took Teardrops I'd Cry All Night Long
I Don't Know Whether To Kill Myself Or Go Bowling
Can't Get Over You, So Why Don't You Get Under Me
If Whiskey Were A Woman I'd Be Married For Sure
I'm Comin' Back To You, One Barstool At A Time

Country music song titles

COURAGE

Courage is being scared to death and saddling up anyway.   John Wayne

The way it works is, you do the thing you're scared shitless of, and you get the courage *after* you do it, not before you do it.   Archie Gates, *Three Kings*

Courage is rightly esteemed the first of human qualities because it is the quality which guarantees all others.   Winston Churchill

Perfect courage means doing unwitnessed what we would be capable of with the world looking on.   La Rochefoucauld

All of us have moments in our lives that test our courage. Taking children into a house with a white carpet is one of them.   Erma Bombeck

It is always brave to say what everyone thinks.   Georges Duhamel

I never thought much of the courage of a lion-tamer. Inside the cage he is at least safe from people.

George Bernard Shaw

Courage doesn't always roar. Sometimes courage is the quiet voice at the end of the day saying, 'I will try again tomorrow.'

Mary Anne Radnacher

Many would be cowards if they had courage enough.

Thomas Fuller

It is curious – curious that physical courage should be so common in the world, and moral courage so rare.

Mark Twain

As to moral courage, I have very rarely met with the *two o'clock in the morning kind*. I mean unprepared courage, that which is necessary on an unexpected occasion, and which, in spite of the most unforeseen events, leaves full freedom of judgement and decision.

Napoleon Bonaparte

A boy doesn't have to go to war to be a hero; he can say he doesn't like pie when he sees there isn't enough to go around.

E. W. Howe

The greatest form of courage is to act as if our lives made a difference.

William Sullivan

If you don't dare say 'no', how will you ever dare say 'yes'?

Paul Tournier

When a resolute young fellow steps up to the great bully, the world, and takes him boldly by the beard, he is often surprised to find it comes off in his hand, and that it was only tied on to scare away the timid adventurers.

Ralph Waldo Emerson

Being brave lets no one off the grave.

Philip Larkin

There is no greater act of courage than to be the one who kisses first.

Paul Buchman, *Mad About You*

CREATIVITY

Creativity can solve almost any problem. The creative act, the defeat of
habit by originality, overcomes everything.   George Lois

Any activity becomes creative when the doer cares about doing it right,
or better.   John Updike

Creativity always dies a quick death in rooms that house conference tables.
                                                          Bruce Hershensohn

Sometimes I think more creativity is put into muffin recipes than into the
rest of society combined.   Jerry Seinfeld

The deepest experience of the creator is feminine, for it is experience of
receiving and bearing.   Rainer Maria Rilke

CRIME AND PUNISHMENT

This woman goes into a gun shop and says, 'I want to buy a gun for my
husband.' The clerk says, 'Did he tell you what kind of gun?' 'No,' she
replied. 'He doesn't even know I'm going to shoot him.'   Phyllis Diller

I haven't committed a crime. What I did was fail to comply with the law.
                                                               David Dinkins

Obviously crime pays, or there'd be no crime.   G. Gordon Liddy

A thief believes everybody steals.   E. W. Howe

He that cries 'Stop, thief' is often he that has stolen the treasure.
                                                          William Congreve

The big thieves hang the little ones.   Czech proverb

To steal from a thief is not theft. It is merely irony.   Johnston McCulley, *Zorro*

I once stole a pornographic book that was printed in Braille. I used to rub the dirty parts.   Woody Allen

Many a man is saved from being a thief by finding everything locked up.   E. W. Howe

What man have you ever seen who was contented with one crime only?   Juvenal

The reason crime doesn't pay is that when it does, it is called by a more respectable name.   Laurence J. Peter

Nothing is illegal if a hundred businessmen decide to do it.   Andrew Young

A man generally judges of the disposition of others by his own. Claude, being himself a deceiver, feared deception.   Regina Maria Roche

Those who are incapable of committing great crime, do not readily suspect them in others.   La Rochefoucauld

Nobody ever commits a crime without doing something stupid.   Oscar Wilde

As a rule, the more bizarre a thing is the less mysterious it proves to be. It is your commonplace, featureless crimes which are really puzzling, just as a commonplace face is the most difficult to identify.   Sherlock Holmes

A face shaped like lotus petals, a voice as cool as sandalwood, a heart like a pair of scissors, and excessive humility; these are the signs of a rogue.   Sanskrit proverb

I prefer rogues to imbeciles, because they sometimes take a rest.   Alexandre Dumas

There is a woman in every case; as soon as they bring me a report, I say, 'Look for the woman.'   Alexandre Dumas

You want to make a guy comfortable enough to confess to murder.

Bill Clark, American detective

—How many did you frame?
—Nobody that wasn't guilty.

Police Sergeant Pete Menzies and Police Captain Hank Quinlan, *Touch of Evil*

Wherever a man commits a crime, God finds a witness. Every secret crime has its reporter. Ralph Waldo Emerson

Dark windows are often a very clear proof. **Stanislaw J. Lec**

Commit a crime and the earth is made of glass. **Ralph Waldo Emerson**

Distrust all those in whom the urge to punish is strong.

Johann Wolfgang von Goethe

Punishment is now unfashionable ... because it creates moral distinctions among men, which, to the democratic mind, are odious. We prefer a meaningless collective guilt to a meaningful individual responsibility.

Thomas Szasz

The common argument that crime is caused by poverty is a kind of slander on the poor. **H. L. Mencken**

Every man is his own law court and punishes himself enough.

Patricia Highsmith

If we could read the secret history of those we would like to punish, we would find in each life enough grief and suffering to make us stop wishing anything more on them. **Anon**

CRITIC

Assassins! Arturo Toscanini to his orchestra

Listen carefully to first criticisms of your work. Note just what it is about your work that critics don't like – then cultivate it. That is the part of your work that's individual and worth keeping. Jean Cocteau

It is advantageous to an author that his book should be attacked as well as praised. Fame is a shuttlecock. If it be struck at only one end of the room, it will soon fall to the ground. To keep it up, it must be struck at both ends. Samuel Johnson

Every actor in his heart believes everything bad that's printed about him.
Orson Welles

Appreciation of art is a moral erection, otherwise mere dilettantism. Jean Cocteau

You're never as good as everyone tells you when you win, and you're never as bad as everyone tells you when you lose. Lou Holtz

The criterion for judging whether a movie is successful or not is time. Peter Bogdanovich

I, along with the critics, have never taken myself very seriously. Elizabeth Taylor

Great critics, of whom there are piteously few, build a home for the truth. Raymond Chandler

Dear Mrs Jones: Thank you for your letter. I shall try to do better. Carl Sandburg, standard letter used for replying to critical letters

Pay no attention to what critics say; no statue has ever been put up to a critic.
                                                                    Jean Sibelius

I'm too rich to care what the critics say.
                                                                    Mel Gibson

CRUELTY

All cruelty springs from weakness.
                                                                    Seneca

A hurtful act is the transference to others of the degradation which we bear in ourselves.
                                                                    Simone Weil

Everyone makes a greater effort to hurt other people than to help himself.
                                                                    Alexis Carrel

CURIOSITY

I think, at a child's birth, if a mother could ask a fairy godmother to endow it with the most useful gift, that gift would be curiosity.   Eleanor Roosevelt

Curiosity is, in great and generous minds, the first passion and the last.
                                                                    Samuel Johnson

The days on which one has been most inquisitive are among the days on which one has been happiest.   Robert Lynd

A man should live if only to satisfy his curiosity.   Yiddish proverb

A sense of curiosity is nature's original school of education.   Dr Smiley Blanton

CYNIC

A cynic is just a man who found out when he was about ten that there wasn't any Santa Claus, and he's still upset.   James Gould Cozzens

A cynic is a man who, when he smells flowers, looks around for a coffin.
                                                              H. L. Mencken

Cynicism is reality with an alternate spelling.   Woody Allen

No matter how cynical you get, it's impossible to keep up.   Lily Tomlin

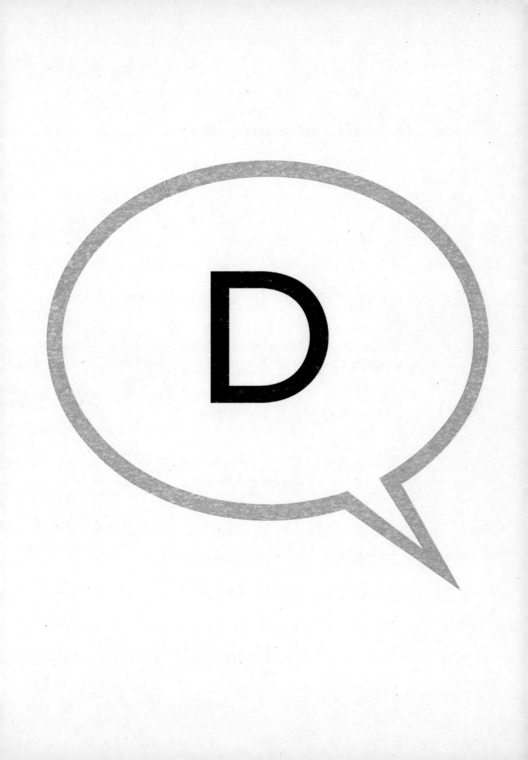

DANCE

Dance is the only art of which we ourselves are the stuff of which it is made.

Ted Shawn

Dancing is the poetry of the foot.

John Dryden

If I could tell you what it meant, there would be no point dancing it.

Isadora Duncan

Dancing is like bank robbery, it takes split-second timing.

Twyla Tharp

A good education is usually harmful to a dancer. A good calf is better than a good head.

Agnes de Mille

If you never want to see the face of hell, when you come home from work every night, dance with your kitchen towel and, if you're worried about waking up your family, take off your shoes.

Rabbi Nachman of Breslov

If you wanna dance, a windshield wiper'll do it – all you need is a beat.

Artie Shaw

Philosophers have argued for centuries about how many angels can dance on the head of a pin, but materialists have always known it depends on whether they are jitterbugging or dancing cheek to cheek.

Tom Robbins

Learn to dance, otherwise the angels in heaven won't know what to do with you.

St Augustine

Dancing is wonderful training for girls. It's the first way you learn to guess what a man is going to do before he does it.

Christopher Morley

DANGER

When you're up to your ass in alligators, it's hard to remember that your purpose is draining the swamp.   George Napper

The trouble with life is, there's no danger music.

Chip Douglas, *The Cable Guy*

Everything that's fun in life is dangerous. Horse races, for instance, are very dangerous. But attempt to design a safe horse and the result is a cow … It is impossible to be alive and safe.   P. J. O'Rourke

Avoiding danger is no safer in the long run than outright exposure. The fearful are caught as often as the bold.

Helen Keller

There is a slippery step at every man's door.   H. W. Thompson

It is the fine rain that soaks us through.   Madame de Sévigné

Danger, the spur of all great minds.   George Chapman

There is no one who does not represent a danger to someone.

Madame de Sévigné

The biggest danger for a politician is to shake hands with a man who is physically stronger, has been drinking and is voting for the other guy.

William Proxmire

There's nothing more dangerous than someone who thinks of himself as a victim. Victims feel it's within their rights to fuck over everyone.

Cynthia Heimel

DATING

If you think there are no new frontiers, watch a boy ring the front
doorbell on his first date.   Olin Miller

On a first date, usually guys take you to a movie where you sit in the
dark staring at a screen, not speaking to each other. Makes perfect sense,
it prepares you for marriage.   Denise Munro Robb

I hate first dates. I made the mistake of telling a date a lie about myself and
she caught me. I didn't think she'd actually demand to see the Bat Cave.
                                                                Alex Reed

How do you know if a guy is really into you? Before the first time you go
over to his apartment, he cleans his bathroom.   Wendy Wilkins

My computer dating bureau came up with a perfect gentleman. Still, I've
got another three goes.   Sally Poplin

Last night I met a guy, and I was wondering, 'What would our kids look
like, where would we live? Would he get along with my mother?' And then
he asked, 'Can I take your order?'   Denise Munro Robb

Dating is like a box of chocolates, sometimes you get something weird.
                                                               Rosie Tran

When a man says he wants to meet a girl with a sense of humor, he
means one who will laugh at everything he says while her breasts jiggle.
                                                              Cheri Oteri

I went out with one girl who said, 'Don't treat me like a date, treat me like
you would your mom.' So I didn't call her for six months.   Zorba Jevon

I had a blind date. I waited two hours on the corner. A girl walked by, and
I said, 'Are you Louise?' She said, 'Are you Rodney?' I said, 'Yeah.' She
said, 'I'm not Louise.'   Rodney Dangerfield

I once had a man break up with me. He said I was using him because right after making love I would weigh myself.   Emily Levine

I would never want to belong to a club that would have someone like me as a member. That's the key joke of my adult life in terms of my relationships with women.   Alvy Singer, *Annie Hall*

I don't think of myself as single. I'm romantically challenged.   Stephanie Piro

I just broke up with my girlfriend, because I caught her lying. Under another man.   Doug Benson

When men break up they want to remain friends. Why? Why can't they just get lost?   Rita Rudner

When I'm not in a relationship, I shave one leg, so when I sleep, it feels like I'm with a woman.   Garry Shandling

Committing is hard for men. I can't even commit to one TV programme. I get this nervous feeling that there's something better on the other channel.
                    Jason Love

She was just a passing fiancée.   Alfred McFote

I'm still going on bad dates, when by now I should be in a bad marriage.

                    Laura Kightlinger

The possibility of a young man meeting a desirable and receptive young female increases by pyramidal progression when he is already in the company of 1) a date, 2) his wife, 3) a better-looking and richer male friend.
                    Ronald Beifield

It's relaxing to go out with my ex-wife because she already knows I'm an idiot.   Warren Thomas

Challenge, and not desire, lies at the heart of seduction. Jean Baudrillard

Faint heart ne'er won fair frog. Miss Piggy

As you get older, the pickings get slimmer, but the people don't. Carrie Fisher

DAYS

Look at me, jerking off in the shower ... This will be the high point of my day – it's all downhill from here. Lester Burnham, *American Beauty*

One day can make your life. One day can ruin your life. All life is, is four or five days that change everything. Beverly Donofrio

How we spend our days is how we spend our lives. Anna Quindlen

Every man has a day in his life when nobody can defeat him. Robert Boswell

TODAY Word carved on a stone on John Ruskin's desk

Yesterday is history. Tomorrow is a mystery. Today is a gift. That's why they call it the present. Anon

Of all the days, the day on which one has not laughed is surely the most wasted. Nicolas Chamfort

The day after tomorrow is the third day of the rest of your life. George Carlin

The morning after always looks grim if you happen to be wearing last night's dress. Grand Duchess Swana, *Ninotchka*

DEATH

If you were going to die soon and had only one phone call you could make, who would you call and what would you say? And why are you waiting?

Stephen Levine

Dust thou art, and unto dust shalt thou return. *Bible*, Genesis

Death is that after which nothing is of interest. V.V. Rozanov

Death is nothing to us, for when we are, death has not come, and when death has come, we are not. Epicurus

Neither death nor the sun can be looked at full in the face. La Rochefoucauld

Death is not an event in life: we do not live to experience death. If we take eternity to mean not infinite temporal duration but timelessness, then eternal life belongs to those who live in the present. Ludwig Wittgenstein

At my age, I'm often asked if I'm frightened of death and my reply is always, I can't remember being frightened of birth. Peter Ustinov

Perhaps the best cure for the fear of death is to reflect that life has a beginning as well as an end. There was a time when you were not: that gives us no concern. Why then should it trouble us that a time will come when we shall cease to be? To die is only to be as we were before we were born. William Hazlitt

Death is no more than passing from one room into another. But there's a difference for me, you know. Because in that other room I shall be able to see. Helen Keller

I knew the facts of death before I knew the facts of life. There never was a time when I didn't see the skull beneath the skin. P. D. James

Death is no different whined at than withstood. Philip Larkin

If some died and others did not die, death would be a terrible affliction.

Jean de La Bruyère

How frighteningly few are the persons whose death would spoil our appetite and make the world seem empty. Eric Hoffer

For life and death are one, even as the river and the sea are one. Kahlil Gibran

A bearer of news of death appears to himself as very important. His feeling – even against all reason – makes him a messenger from the realm of the dead. Walter Benjamin

It is better to tell someone bad news in the morning after they have slept, rather than last thing at night or during the night. It might not always be possible but it is a good guideline. Hugo Vickers

Life and death are but phases of the same thing, the reverse and obverse of the same coin. Death is as necessary for man's growth as life itself.

Mahatma Gandhi

If I had my life to live over again, I would form the habit of nightly composing myself to thoughts of death. I would practice, as it were, the remembrance of death. There is not another practice which so intensifies life. Death, when it approaches, ought not to take one by surprise. It should be part of the full expectancy of life. Muriel Spark

I feel so much the *continual* death of everything and everybody, and have so learned to reconcile myself to it, that the final and official end loses most of its impressiveness. George Santayana

Anderl Heckmair spent his life as a mountaineer and led the first successful ascent of the North Face of the Eiger in 1938. He was told by a fortune teller in the thirties that he would die an unnatural death. 'Oh no!' he exclaimed. 'That means I'll die in bed.' *The Daily Telegraph*

We should all live as if we were never going to die, for it is the deaths of our friends that hurt us, not our own.   Gerald Brenan

Death doesn't affect the living because it has not happened yet. Death doesn't concern the dead because they have ceased to exist.
                                                                                    W. Somerset Maugham

There is nothing terrible in life for the man who realizes there is nothing terrible in death.   Epicurus

No one owns life, but anyone who can pick up a frying pan owns death.
                                                                                    William Burroughs

Fear not that thy life shall come to an end, but rather fear that it shall never have a beginning.   Cardinal Newman

I pray that death may strike me in the middle of a large meal. I wish to be buried under the tablecloth between four large dishes.   Marc Desaugiers

My father was a film-maker. He always said he wanted to go like Humphrey Jennings, the legendary director who stepped backwards over a cliff while framing a better shot.   A. A. Gill

Do not seek death. Death will find you. But seek the road which makes death fulfilment.   Dag Hammarskjöld

My head to be separated from my body immediately after my death, the latter to be buried in a grave; the former, duly macerated and prepared, to be brought to the theatre where I have served all my life, and to be employed to represent the skull of Yorick.
                                                     John Reed, actor, excerpt from his will

Didn't Wake Up This Morning   Epitaph for a blues singer

There Goes the Neighborhood   Rodney Dangerfield, epitaph

It is a tragedy that most of us die before we have begun to live. Erich Fromm

Dying is the most embarrassing thing that can ever happen to you,
because someone's got to take care of all your details.   Andy Warhol

All say 'How hard it is to have to die' – a strange complaint to come from
the mouths of people who have had to live.   Mark Twain

My dear, I'm always nervous about doing something for the first time.
                                        Gwen Ffrangcom-Davies, aged 101

One dies only once and then for such a long time.   Molière

One should always have one's boots on and be ready to leave.
                                            Michel de Montaigne

There is not much difference between a mortal man and a dying man. The
absurdity of making plans is only slightly more obvious in the second case.
                                              E. M. Cioran

I wonder what day I shall die on – one passes year by year over one's death
day, as one might pass over one's grave.   Cardinal Newman

Perhaps passing through the gates of death is like passing quietly through
the gate in a pasture fence. On the other side, you keep walking, without
the need to look back. No shock, no drama, just the lifting of a plank or
two in a simple wooden gate in a clearing. Neither pain, nor floods of light,
not great voices, but just the silent crossing of a meadow.   Mark Helprin

My girlfriend's weird. One day she asked me, 'If you could know how and
when you were going to die, would you want to know?' I said, 'No.' She
said, 'Okay, forget it.'   Steven Wright

Viewing life from the perspective of death, we are made freer. Seeing
something for the last time is nearly as good as seeing it for the first time.
                                              Peter Noll

There are so many little dyings every day, it doesn't matter which one of them is death. Kenneth Patchen

I look upon life as a gift from God. I did nothing to earn it. Now that the time is coming to give it back, I have no right to complain. Joyce Cary

I cheerfully quit from life as if it were an inn, not a home; for Nature has given us a hostelry in which to sojourn, not to abide. Cicero

It's not that I'm afraid to die. I just don't want to be there when it happens. Woody Allen

We sometimes congratulate ourselves at the moment of waking from a troubled dream; it may be so the moment after death. Nathaniel Hawthorne

To die is easy when we are in perfect health. On a fine spring morning, out of doors, on the downs, mind and body sound and exhilarated, it would be nothing to lie down on the turf and pass away. Mark Rutherford

Death used to announce itself in the thick of life but now people drag on so long it sometimes seems that we are reaching the stage when we may have to announce ourselves to death ... It is as though one needs a special strength to die, and not a final weakness. Ronald Blythe

Oh, write of me, not 'Died in bitter pains' but 'Emigrated to another star!' Helen Hunt Jackson

The art of dying graciously is nowhere advertised, in spite of the fact that its market potential is great. Milton Mayer

If death could be seen as a beautiful clear lake, refreshing and buoyant, then when a consciousness moves towards its exit from a body there would be that delightful plunge and it would simply swim away. Pat Rodegast

I never had a dog that showed a human fear of death. Death, to a dog, is the final unavoidable compulsion, the least ineluctable scent on a fearsome trail, but they like to face it alone, going out into the woods, among the leaves, if there are any leaves when their time comes, enduring without sentimental human distraction the Last Loneliness, which they are wise enough to know cannot be shared by anyone.   James Thurber

Your end, which is endless, is as a snowflake dissolving in the pure air.

Buddhist saying

Let life be beautiful like summer flowers and death be like autumn leaves.
Rabindranath Tagore

What a simple thing death is, just as simple as the falling of an autumn leaf.
Vincent Van Gogh

Is that all it is?   **Elinor Wylie, last words**

George Gershwin died yesterday, but I don't have to believe it if I don't want to.   **John O'Hara**

A man's dying is more the survivors' affair than his own.   **Thomas Mann**

His death was the first time that Ed Wynn ever made anyone sad.
Red Skelton

He who had always been larger than life turned out to be smaller than death.   **Burton Bernstein on Leonard Bernstein's death**

Who knows when the end is reached? Death may be the beginning of life. How do I know that love of life is not a delusion after all? How do I know that he who dreads to die is as a child who has lost the way and cannot find his way home? How do I know that the dead repent of having previously clung to life?   **Chuang Tse, 300 BC**

Say not 'Good-night' but in some brighter clime, bid me 'Good-morning.'
Anna Laetitia Barbauld

—Why aren't you attending the funeral of your ex-wife, Marilyn Monroe?
—Why should I? She won't be there.   Reporter and Arthur Miller

Even the best of friends cannot attend each other's funeral.   Kehlog Albran

I'm always relieved when someone is delivering a eulogy and I realize I'm listening to it.   George Carlin

The consumer side of the coffin lid is never ostentatious.   Stanislaw J. Lec

We're all cremated equal.   Jane Ace

He was some kind of a man. What does it matter what you say about people?   Tanya, *Touch of Evil*

DECEIVING AND DECEPTION

A man generally has two reasons for doing a thing. One that sounds good, and a real one.   J. Pierpoint Morgan

You can fool all of the people some of the time, and some of the people all of the time. But you cannot fool all of the people all of the time.
Abraham Lincoln

You can fool too many of the people too much of the time.   James Thurber

You can fool some of the people all of the time, and those are the ones you need to concentrate on.   Robert Strauss

People are deceived in masses, but enlightened one at a time.   Dick Boddie

Any woman can fool a man if she wants to and if he's in love with her.

Pearl S. Buck

When a person cannot deceive himself the chances are against his being able to deceive other people.

Mark Twain

I am always at a loss to know how much to believe my own stories.

Washington Irving

The ability to delude yourself might be an important survival tool ...
Delusions of grandeur make me feel a lot better about myself.

Jane Wagner

Delusion: belief said to be false by someone who does not share it.

Thomas Szasz

We are more often treacherous through weakness than through calculation.

La Rochefoucauld

I give you bitter pills in sugar coating. The pills are harmless, the poison is in the sugar.

Stanislaw J. Lec

To betray, you must first belong.

Harold 'Kim' Philby, spy

Many a man may look respectable, and yet be able to hide at will behind a spiral staircase.

P. G. Wodehouse

We are inclined to believe those whom we do not know because they have never deceived us.

Samuel Johnson

When a man wants to deceive you, he'll find a way of escape through the tiniest of holes.

Colette

One is never so easily fooled as when one thinks one is fooling others.

La Rochefoucauld

One may smile and smile and be a villain. **William Shakespeare**, *Hamlet*

You can't wake a person who is pretending to be asleep. **Navajo proverb**

One of the saddest lessons of history is this: if we've been bamboozled long enough, we tend to reject any evidence of the bamboozle. The bamboozle has captured us. Once you give a charlatan power over you, you almost never get it back. **Carl Sagan**

Everything that deceives can be said to enchant. **Plato**

In football it is widely acknowledged that if both sides agree to cheat, cheating is fair. **C. B. Fry**

One should always play fairly when one has the winning cards. **Oscar Wilde**

Nothing so completely baffles one who is full of trick and duplicity himself, than straightforward and simple integrity in another. **Charles Caleb Colton**

The secret of life is to appreciate the pleasure of being terribly deceived. **Oscar Wilde**

We are never deceived: we deceive ourselves. **Johann Wolfgang von Goethe**

DECISION

Every great leap forward in your life comes after you have made a clear decision of some kind. **Brian Tracy**

No trumpets sound when the important decisions of our life are made. Destiny is made known silently. **Agnes de Mille**

Every decision you make is a mistake. **Edward Dahlberg**

A peacefulness follows any decision, even the wrong one. **Rita Mae Brown**

Whatever course you decide upon, there is always someone to tell you that you are wrong.

Ralph Waldo Emerson

When you are fretting around, worrying about moving house, losing your job, getting married or setting up in business, just tell yourself, 'Big decisions make themselves,' so don't exhaust yourself with 'what if' scenarios.

Louise Botting

DEMOCRACY

Democracy: in which you say what you like and do what you're told.

Dave Barry

Democracy is good. I say this because other systems are worse.

Jawaharlal Nehru

American democracy is the inalienable right to sit on your front porch, in your pyjamas, drinking a can of beer and shouting out 'Where else is this possible?' Which doesn't seem to me to be freedom, really.   Peter Ustinov

Remember one thing about democracy. We can have anything we want and at the same time, we always end up with exactly what we deserve.

Edward Albee

The death of democracy is not likely to be an assassination by ambush. It will be a slow extinction from apathy, indifference and undernourishment.

Robert M. Hutchins

Democracy is the recurrent suspicion that more than half of the people are right more than half the time. E. B. White

DEPRESSION

If life is a bowl of cherries, what am I doing in the pits?   Erma Bombeck

Depression sits on my chest like a sumo wrestler.   Sandra Scoppettone

Depression is a very sensible reaction to just about everything we live
in now.   Chrystos

This is the difference between depression and sorrow – sorrowful, you are
in great trouble because something matters so much; depressed, you are
miserable because nothing really matters.   J. E. Buckrose

Depression is merely anger without enthusiasm.   Steven Wright

When you're depressed, it makes a lot of difference how you stand ...
The worst thing you can do is straighten up and hold your head high
because then you'll start to feel better.   Charles M. Schulz

My depression is the most faithful mistress I have known – no wonder,
then, that I return the love.   Søren Kierkegaard

Depression is the most extreme form of vanity.   Julie Burchill

I think other people's depression is frightfully dreary, don't you?
Julian Fellowes

'Pull yourself together' is seldom said to anyone who can.
Mignon McLaughlin

There's nothing wrong with you that a little Prozac and a polo mallet
can't cure.   Woody Allen

There is no chiropractic treatment, no yoga exercise, no hour of meditation
in a music-throbbing chapel that will leave you emptier of bad thoughts
than the homely ceremony of making bread.   W. F. K. Fisher

Philip Larkin used to cheer himself up by looking in the mirror and saying the line from *Rebecca*, 'I am Mrs de Winter now!'   **Alan Bennett**

A new study shows that licking the sweat off a frog can cure depression. The downside is, the minute you stop licking, the frog gets depressed again.
Jay Leno

Come and take choice of all my library and so beguile thy sorrow.
William Shakespeare, *Titus Andronicus*

The people on the QVC shopping channel convince me that life is worth living. They see the good in everything. People who go to counselling should actually go to a room with a QVC seller for half an hour and let them find the qualities within them. For example, they'd look at me and say, 'To anybody else this looks like a stomach but, actually, his feet never get wet in the rain.'   **Johnny Vegas**

It is impossible to walk rapidly and be unhappy.   **Howard Murray**

Take long walks in stormy weather or through deep snow in the fields and woods, if you would keep your spirits up. Deal with brute nature. Be cold and hungry and weary.   **Henry David Thoreau**

You handle depression in much the same way as you handle a tiger.
Dr R. W. Shepherd

The best remedy for those who are afraid, lonely, or unhappy is to go outside, somewhere where they can be quite alone with the heavens, nature, and God. Because only there does one feel that all is as it should be and that God wishes to see people happy, amidst the simple beauty of nature.   **Anne Frank**

I can't think of any sorrow in the world that a hot bath wouldn't help, just a little bit.   **Susan Glaspell**

There is a certain frame of mind to which a cemetery is, if not an antidote, at least an alleviation. If you are in a fit of the blues, go nowhere else.
Robert Louis Stevenson

If the heart of a man is depressed with cares,
The mist is dispelled when a woman appears.

John Gay

May I make a suggestion, hoping it is not an impertinence? Write it down: write down what you feel. It is sometimes a wonderful help in misery.

Robertson Davies

When the spirits are low, when the day appears dark, when work becomes monotonous, when hope hardly seems worth having, just mount a bicycle and go out for a spin down the road, without thought on anything but the ride you are taking.

Arthur Conan Doyle

If you're on the Underground
and feel a bit depressed,
Stare at the person opposite
and imagine them undressed.

Rosemarie Jarski

There is nothing like employment, active indispensable employment, for relieving sorrow.

Jane Austen

The best thing for being sad is to learn something.

T. H. White

I merely took the energy it takes to pout and wrote some blues.

Duke Ellington

The only way to avoid being miserable is not to have enough leisure to wonder whether you are happy or not.

George Bernard Shaw

Fake feeling good … You may have the most legitimate reason in the world to be unhappy … but when you're with people, don't wear your depression like a badge … learn to fake cheerfulness. Believe it or not, eventually that effort will pay off: you'll actually start feeling happier.

Jean Bach

The best way to cheer yourself up is to try to cheer somebody else up.

Mark Twain

No one's head aches when he is comforting another.

Indian proverb

DESIGN

If you are in a shipwreck and all the boats are gone, a piano-top buoyant enough to keep you afloat that comes along makes a fortuitous life preserver. But this is not to say that the best way to design a life preserver is in the form of a piano-top.
R. Buckminster Fuller

Good design is a lot like clear thinking made visual.
Edward Tufte

Art has to move you and design does not, unless it's a good design for a bus.
David Hockney

Attractive things work better.
Donald Norman

DESIRE

There are two tragedies in life. One is to lose your heart's desire. The other is to gain it.
George Bernard Shaw

Our desires always increase with our possessions. The knowledge that something remains yet unenjoyed impairs our enjoyment of the good before us.
Samuel Johnson

Too much of a good thing can be wonderful.
Mae West

We grow weary of those things (and perhaps soonest) which we most desire.
Samuel Butler

If there is nothing left to desire, there is everything to fear, an unhappy state of happiness.
Baltasar Gracián

DESPAIR

More than any other time in history, mankind faces the crossroads. One path leads to despair and utter hopelessness, the other to total extinction. I pray we have the wisdom to choose wisely. **Woody Allen**

Despair is the price one pays for setting oneself an impossible aim ... It is the sin the corrupt or evil man never practises. He always has hope ... Only the man of goodwill carries always in his heart this capacity for damnation. **Graham Greene**

Don't despair, not even over the fact that you don't despair. **Franz Kafka**

If, every day, I dare to remember that I am here on loan, that this house, this hillside, these minutes are all leased to me, not given, I will never despair. Despair is for those who expect to live for ever. I no longer do. **Erica Jong**

One despairs of others so as not to despair too much of oneself. **Henri Petit**

DETAIL

The moment one gives close attention to anything, even a blade of grass, it becomes a mysterious, awesome, indescribably magnificent world in itself. **Henry Miller**

One should absorb the colour of life, but one should never remember its details. Details are always vulgar. **Oscar Wilde**

There is no one who has cooked but has discovered that each particular dish depends for its rightness upon some little point which he is never told. It is not only so of cooking: it is so of splicing a rope; of painting a surface of wood; of mixing mortar; of almost anything you like to name among the immemorial human arts. **Hilaire Belloc**

We think in generalities, but we live in details.   Alfred North Whitehead

God is in the details.   Ludwig Mies van der Rohe

Anyone nit-picking enough to write a letter of correction to an editor doubtless deserves the error that provokes it.   Alvin Toffler

DEVIL

God created the world, but it is the devil who keeps it going. Tristan Bernard

The devil is a gentleman who never goes where he is not invited.
          John A. Lincoln

Have you ever danced with the devil by the pale moonlight?
          The Joker, *Batman*

I don't suppose God laughs at the people who think He doesn't exist. He's above jokes. But the devil isn't. That's one of his most endearing qualities.
          Robertson Davies

You are permitted in times of great danger to walk with the devil until you have crossed the bridge.   Bulgarian proverb

The devil knows everything except where women sharpen their knives.
          Bulgarian proverb

It must be remembered that we have only heard one side of the case. God has written all the books.   Samuel Butler

DICTATOR

A dictatorship is a country where they have taken the politics out of politics.
Sam Himmell

Genghis Khan wasn't very loveable but he was bloody efficient. Kerry Packer

A dictator must fool all the people all the time and there's only one way to do that, he must also fool himself.
W. Somerset Maugham

Dictators have only become possible through the invention of the microphone.
Thomas Inskip

If I were a dictator I should make it compulsory for every member of the population between the ages of four and eighty to listen to Mozart for at least a quarter of an hour daily for the coming five years.
Thomas Beecham

Hitler is no worse, nay better, in my opinion, than the other lugs. He makes the German mistake of being tactless, that's all.
Henry Miller

The essence of modern dictatorship is the combination of one-dimensional, flat thinking with power and terror.
Theodor Haecker

A man may build himself a throne of bayonets, but he cannot sit on it.
Dean W. R. Inge

There is an interesting resemblance in the speeches of dictators, no matter what country they may hail from or what language they may speak.
Edna Ferber

I'm not a dictator. It's just that I have a grumpy face.
Augusto Pinochet

Dictators ride to and fro upon tigers which they dare not dismount. And the tigers are getting hungry.
Winston Churchill

DIET

The journey of a thousand pounds begins with a single burger.   Chris O'Brien

All fat people are 'outed' by their appearance.   Jennifer A. Coleman

I would rather be called a serial killer than fat.   Dale Winton

When are we going to learn that fat is an adjective, not an epithet?
Denise Rubin

Gluttony is an emotional escape, a sign that something is eating us.
Peter De Vries

Obesity is the result of a loss of self-control. Indeed, loss of self-control might be said to be the defining social (or anti-social) characteristic of our age: public drunkenness, excessive gambling, promiscuity and common-or-garden rudeness are all examples of our collective loss of self-control.
Theodore Dalrymple

More are slain by suppers than the sword.   English proverb

For women, eating has taken on the sinful state once reserved for sex.   Anon

Never eat more than you can lift.   Miss Piggy

I've decided that perhaps I'm bulimic and just keep forgetting to purge.
Paula Poundstone

It is harder to eat sparingly than to fast. Moderation requires awareness. Renunciation requires only the tyranny of will.   Sandor McNab

Do you want to live in a world where a man lies about calories?   Gail Parent

When a man diets, he eats oatmeal in addition to everything else he usually eats.
E. W. Howe

A really busy person never knows how much he weighs. E.W. Howe

The only time to eat diet food is while you're waiting for the steak to cook.
Julia Child

Remember, your body needs six to eight glasses of fluid daily. Straight up or on the rocks. P. J. O'Rourke

It doesn't matter to me that you haven't seen your navel in twenty-five years and that you wear your stomach as a kilt: tell me you're happy.
Edina Monsoon, *Absolutely Fabulous*

DIFFERENCE AND SIMILARITY

Whatever you may be sure of, be sure of this: that you are dreadfully like other people. James Russell Lowell

An unlearned carpenter of my acquaintance once said in my hearing: 'There is very little difference between one man and another, but what there is is *very important.*' William James

I love men, not for what unites them, but for what divides them, and I want to know most of all what gnaws at their hearts. Guillaume Apollinaire

Be daring, be different, be impractical, be anything that will assert integrity of purpose and imaginative vision against the play-it-safers, the creatures of the commonplace, the slaves of the ordinary. Cecil Beaton

Most people can't understand how others can blow their noses differently than they do. Ivan Turgenev

When people are free to do as they choose, they usually imitate each other.
Eric Hoffer

You don't get harmony when everybody sings the same note.   Doug Floyd

In order to be irreplaceable one must always be different.   Coco Chanel

It is the American vice, the democratic disease which expresses its tyranny by reducing everything unique to the level of the herd.   Henry Miller

The problem is not how to wipe out all differences, but how to unite with all differences intact.   Rabindranath Tagore

DIFFICULT

It is not because things are difficult that we do not dare; it is because we do not dare that they are difficult.   Seneca

Settle one difficulty, and you keep a hundred others away.   Chinese proverb

Some men storm imaginary Alps all their lives, and die in the foothills cursing difficulties which do not exist.   E. W. Howe

Not everything that is more difficult is more meritorious.   St Thomas Aquinas

To endure oneself may be the hardest task in the universe.   Frank Herbert

DISABILITY

Some days you see lots of people on crutches.   Peter Kay

I saw a man with a wooden leg, and a real foot.   Steven Wright

When I rang a restaurant to ask if they had wheelchair access I was told that they accepted all major credit cards.   Pat Fitzpatrick

The only disability in life is a bad attitude.   Scott Hamilton

All life's important things take place above the knee.

Richard Leakey, after losing his feet in a plane crash

If you have an artificial leg, make it unnoticeable by wearing long trousers.

O. Craig, *Viz*, top tip

Now she is like all the rest.

Charles de Gaulle on the burial of his mentally disabled daughter

DISAPPOINTMENT

People seldom live up to their baby pictures.　　**Rodney Dangerfield**

Leigh Hunt was probably the only man in the world who, if he saw something yellow in the distance and thought it was a buttercup, would be disappointed if he found it was only a guinea.　　**Anon**

Life is full of its disappointments, and I suppose the art of being happy is to disguise them as illusions.　　**Saki**

The main emotion of the adult American who has had all the advantages of wealth, education, and culture is disappointment.　　**John Cheever**

A pier is a disappointed bridge.　　**James Joyce**

DISCOVERY

The most exciting phrase to hear in science, the one that heralds new discoveries, is not 'Eureka!' (I found it!) but 'That's funny … '　　**Isaac Asimov**

Discovery is seeing what everybody else has seen, and thinking what nobody else has thought.　　**Albert Szent-Gyorgy**

The more original a discovery, the more obvious it seems afterwards.

Arthur Koestler

All great discoveries are made by mistake.   Murphy's Law

We don't know who discovered water, but we're certain it wasn't fish.
                                                              John Culkin

When Thomas Edison worked late into the night on the electric light, he
had to do it by gas lamp or candle. I'm sure it made the work seem that
much more urgent.   George Carlin

The greatest obstacle to discovering the shape of the earth, the continents
and the oceans was not ignorance but the illusion of knowledge.
                                                         Daniel J. Boorstin

I do not know what I may appear to the world, but to myself I seem to
have been only a child playing on the seashore while the great ocean of
truth lay all undiscovered before me.   Isaac Newton

DIVORCE AND SEPARATION

I never even believed in divorce until after I got married.   Diane Ford

—She says she wants a divorce.
—What? Just because she caught him flirting with a couple of nurses?
—She was giving birth at the time.   Ken and Joe, *Early Doors*

Getting divorced just because you don't love a man is almost as silly as
getting married just because you do.   Zsa Zsa Gabor

Why leave the nut you got for one you don't know?   Loretta Lynn

In every marriage more than a week old, there are grounds for divorce.
The trick is to find, and to continue to find, grounds for marriage.
                                                         Robert Anderson

It destroys one's nerves to be amiable every day to the same human being.
Benjamin Disraeli

Having two bathrooms ruined the capacity to co-operate.   Margaret Mead

It is hardly possible to estimate how many marriages fail to prosper or are actually ruined because the man lacks any inkling of the art of love.
Count Hermann Keyserling

Divorce is the one human tragedy that reduces everything to cash.
Rita Mae Brown

To lose the touch of flowers and women's hands is the supreme separation.
Albert Camus

A divorce is like an amputation; you survive, but there's less of you.
Margaret Atwood

Remarrying a husband you've divorced is like having your appendix put back in.
Phyllis Diller

The time you spend grieving over a man should never exceed the amount of time you actually spend with him.
Rita Rudner

DOCTOR

The doctor said, 'I have good news and bad news. The good news is you're not a hypochondriac ... '
Dave Carpenter

The best cure for hypochondria is to forget about your body and get interested in someone else's.
Goodman Ace

Hypochondria, the excessive fear of illness, has now been overtaken by cyberchondria – the same fear made much worse, fuelled by volumes of easily accessible material available on the internet.   *The Daily Record*

The modern sympathy with invalids is morbid. Illness of any kind is
hardly a thing to be encouraged in others.   Oscar Wilde

—Aren't you proud of being a doctor?
—Well, mostly because I can park anywhere.
                    Interviewer and Doc Hollywood, Carl Reiner and Mel Brooks

I have never gone to a doctor in my adult life, feeling instinctively that
doctors meant either cutting or, just as bad, diet.   Carson McCullers

A medical maxim for doctors in diagnosis: when you hear hoofbeats,
think of horses before zebras.   Anon

One finger in the throat and one in the rectum make a good diagnostician.
                                                              William Osler

I finally have a dental plan. I chew on the other side.   Janine Ditullio

My first neurologist had a very holistic approach to my illness. No more
red meat, no more salt, no more alcohol. I said, 'What about sex?' He said,
'I'm seeing someone.'   Jonathan Katz

I've decided to skip 'holistic'. I don't know what it means, and I don't
want to know. That may seem extreme, but I followed the same strategy
toward 'Gestalt' and the 'Twist', and lived to tell the tale.   Calvin Trillin

My acupuncturist said, 'Take two thumbtacks and call me in the morning.'
                                                              Leo Steiner

—Doc, those pills you gave me. I'm not sure that they work.
—Well, I'm not sure either, but you don't hear me complain.
                                    Postman and Doc Wilson, *State and Main*

He bore the stamp of the unforgivable sin in a physician – uncertainty.
                                                              Rae Foley

He's a Fool that makes his Doctor his Heir.   Benjamin Franklin

The doctor will persist in laboring under the delusion that patients want common sense instead of magic.
Rae Foley

Optimistic lies have such immense therapeutic value that a doctor who cannot tell them convincingly has mistaken his profession.
George Bernard Shaw

Formerly, when religion was strong and science weak, men mistook magic for medicine; now, when science is strong and religion weak, men mistake medicine for magic.
Thomas Szasz

The great secret of doctors, known only to their wives, but still hidden from the public, is that most things get better by themselves; most things, in fact, are better in the morning.
Lewis Thomas

The witch doctor succeeds for the same reason all the rest of us succeed. Each patient carries his own doctor inside him. They come to us not knowing that truth. We are at our best when we give the doctor who resides within each patient a chance to go to work.
Dr Albert Schweitzer

Can placebos cause side effects?
If so, are the side effects real?
George Carlin

A really conscientious doctor ought to die with his patient. The captain goes down with his ship.
Eugene Ionesco

—Oh, no, no, I can't eat fifteen gallons of yoghurt.
—Oh, it's not going in that end, Mr Lightbody.
Dr John Harvey Kellogg and William Lightbody, *The Road to Wellville*

Life as we find it is too hard for us … We cannot do without palliative remedies. There are perhaps three of these means: powerful diversions of interest, which lead us to care little about our misery; substitutive gratifications, which lessen it; and intoxicating substances, which make us insensitive to it.
Sigmund Freud

To do nothing is sometimes a good remedy. Hippocrates

When a lot of remedies are suggested for a disease, that means it can't be cured. Anton Chekhov

Of all the home remedies, a good wife is the best. Kin Hubbard

Of one thing I am certain, the body is not the measure of healing, peace is the measure. Phyllis McGinley

Looking out of a hospital window is different from looking out of any other. Somehow you do not see outside. Carol Matthau

It may seem a strange principle to enunciate as the very first requirement in a hospital that it should do the sick no harm. Florence Nightingale

Getting out of hospital is a lot like resigning from a book club. You're not out until the computer says you're out. Erma Bombeck

DOG

—Why do dogs lick their private parts?
—Because they can. Anon

I love a dog. He does nothing for political reasons. Will Rogers

All knowledge, the totality of all questions and answers, is contained in the dog. Franz Kafka

A dog has the soul of a philosopher. Plato

The dog is a Yes-animal, very popular with people who can't afford to keep a Yes-man. Robertson Davies

A wet dog is lovingest. James Thurber

You will find that the woman who is really kind to dogs is always one who has failed to find sympathy in men.   Max Beerbohm

In order to really enjoy a dog, one doesn't merely try to train him to be semi-human. The point of it is to open oneself to the possibility of becoming partly a dog.   Edward Hoagland

Dogs are better than human beings, because they know but do not tell.   Emily Dickinson

Acquiring a dog may be the only opportunity a human ever has to choose a relative.   Mordecai Wyatt Johnson

To sit with a dog on a hillside on a glorious afternoon is to be back in Eden, when doing nothing was not boring – it was peace.   Milan Kundera

The best thing about a man is his dog.   French proverb

DOUBT

I respect faith, but doubt is what gets you an education.   Wilson Mizner

Just think of the tragedy of teaching children not to doubt.   Clarence Darrow

You've gotta be a little sceptical, otherwise you end up believing in everything – UFOs, elves, income tax rebates.   Adrian Monk, *Monk*

The trouble with the world is that the stupid are cocksure and the intelligent are full of doubt.   Bertrand Russell

I am plagued by doubts. What if everything is an illusion and nothing exists? In that case, I definitely overpaid for my carpet. If only God would give me some clear sign! Like making a large deposit in my name at a Swiss bank.   Woody Allen

A proof tells us where to concentrate our doubts.   W. H. Auden

The only thing I don't doubt is my doubt.   Spalding Gray

If a man will begin with certainties he shall end in doubts; but if he will be content to begin with doubts he shall end in certainties.   Francis Bacon

DREAMS

Dreaming permits each and every one of us to be quietly and safely insane every night of our lives.   William Dement

A dream is the mind's way of answering a question it hasn't yet figured out how to ask.   Fox Mulder, *The X-Files*

All the things one has forgotten scream for help in dreams.   Elias Canetti

Dreams are real while they last; can we say more of life?   Havelock Ellis

I did not know whether I was then a man dreaming I was a butterfly, or whether I am now a butterfly, dreaming I am a man.   Chuang Tse

I had a dream about reality. It was such a relief to wake up.   Stanislaw J. Lec

The best way to make your dreams come true is to wake up.   Paul Valéry

How many of our daydreams would darken into nightmares, were there a danger of their coming true.   Logan Pearsall Smith

—Oh, my dreams will go unfulfilled? Oh, no! Marge, make it better, please!
—Homer, when a man's biggest dreams include seconds of dessert, occasional snuggling, and sleeping in 'til noon on weekends, no one man can destroy them.   Homer and Marge Simpson

I have spread my dreams under your feet; tread softly because you tread on my dreams.   W. B. Yeats

DRUGS AND ADDICTION

In the course of history many more people have died for their drink and their dope than have died for their religion or their country.   Aldous Huxley

Every generation finds the drug it needs.   P. J. O'Rourke

Drugs are a bet with the mind.   Jim Morrison

Drugs are a carnival in hell.   Edith Piaf

Drug misuse is not a disease, it is a decision, like the decision to step out in front of a moving car. You would call that not a disease but an error of judgement.   Philip K. Dick

Just say no, no, no, no, no … you'll get a much better price.   Joan Rivers

Why is marijuana not legal? It's a natural plant that grows in the dirt. Do you know what's not natural? Eighty-year-old dudes with hard-ons. That's not natural. But we got pills for that. We're dedicating all our medical resources to keeping the old guys erect, but we're putting people in jail for something that grows in the dirt?   Greg Giraldo

Marijuana is self-punishing. It makes you acutely sensitive, and in this world, what worse punishment could there be?   P. J. O'Rourke

In extreme cases marijuana can so destroy a man's character that he mixes freely with persons of another race.   South African criminology textbook, 1966

Pot is like a gang of Mexican bandits in your brain. They wait for thoughts to come down the road, then tie them up and thrash them.   Kevin Rooney

Heroin may be bad, but it sure as hell hasn't hurt my CD collection.   Bill Maher

Why should Ben Johnson give up his gold medal from Seoul, for example, when the Beatles remain revered for *Sgt Pepper* – an album that owed as much to banned substances as anything the Canadian did.   **Harry Pearson**

LSD is an awfully overrated aspirin and very similar to old people's Disneyland.   **Captain Beefheart**

When it snows in your nose, you catch cold in your brain.   **Allen Ginsberg**

Before you let yourself go, be sure you can get yourself back.   **Roger Allen**

To really enjoy drugs you've got to want to get out of where you are. But there are some wheres that are harder to get out of than others. This is the drug-taking problem for adults. Teenage *Weltschmerz* is easy to escape. But what drug will get a grown-up out of, for instance, debt?
      P. J. O'Rourke

'Just say no' has done as much for drugs and sex as 'Have a nice day' has for depression.   Dr E. Tyson

If we could sniff or swallow something that would, for five or six hours each day, abolish our solitude as individuals, atone us with our fellows in a glowing exaltation of affection and make life in all its aspects seem not only worth living, but divinely beautiful and significant, and if this heavenly, world-transfiguring drug were of such a kind that we could wake up next morning with a clear head and an undamaged constitution – then, it seems to me, all our problems (and not merely the one small problem of discovering a novel pleasure) would be wholly solved and earth would become paradise.   **Aldous Huxley**

The only thing I thought might ever kill me off was clean living. I thought, How am I going to listen to that horrible noise I make without a gram of coke and a couple of double Jack Daniels?   **Iggy Pop**

The basic thing nobody asks is why do people take drugs of any sort? Why do we have these accessories to normal living to live? I mean, is there something wrong with society that's making us so pressurized, that we cannot live without guarding ourselves against it?   John Lennon

It is in the interests of our society to promote those things that take the edge off, keep us busy with our fixes, and keep us slightly outnumbered and zombie-like. In this way our modern consumer society itself functions as an addict.   Anne Schaef

No drug, not even alcohol, causes the fundamental ills of society. If we're looking for the sources of our troubles, we shouldn't test people for drugs, we should test them for stupidity, ignorance, greed and love of power.
                                                                P. J. O'Rourke

Addiction, obesity, starvation (anorexia nervosa) are political problems, not psychiatric: each condenses and expresses a contest between the individual and some other person or persons in his environment over the control of the individual's body.   Thomas Szasz

I called a detox centre – just to see how much it would cost: $13,000 for three and a half weeks! My friends, if you can come up with thirteen grand, you don't have a problem yet!   Sam Kinison

Did you know that the White House drug test is multiple choice?
                                                                Rush Limbaugh

If alcohol were a communicable disease, a national emergency would be declared.   William Menninger

There is more refreshment and stimulation in a nap, even of the briefest, than in all the alcohol ever distilled.   E. V. Lucas

I was into pain reduction and mind expansion, but what I've ended up with is pain expansion and mind reduction.   Carrie Fisher

I tried to give up drugs by drinking.   Lou Reed

The more necessary it becomes to stop drinking, the more impossible it becomes to stop.   Jeffrey Bernard

The public hungers to see talented young people kill themselves.   Paul Simon

Were Moses to go up Mount Sinai today, the two tablets he'd bring down with him would be aspirin and Prozac.   Joseph Califano

What is dangerous about tranquillizers is that whatever peace of mind they bring is a packaged peace of mind. Where you buy a pill and buy peace of mind with it, you get conditioned to cheap solutions instead of deep ones.
                                                                                    Max Lerner

I don't drink or do any drugs. I never have and I never will. I don't need them. I'm a black woman from the land of the free, home of the brave, and I figure I don't need another illusion.   Bertice Berry

There isn't a feeling you can get on drugs that you can't get without drugs.
                                                                          William Burroughs

The human mind is capable of excitement without the application of gross and violent stimulants; and he must have a very faint perception of its beauty and dignity who does not know this.   William Wordsworth

The sun is nature's Prozac.   Astrid Alauda

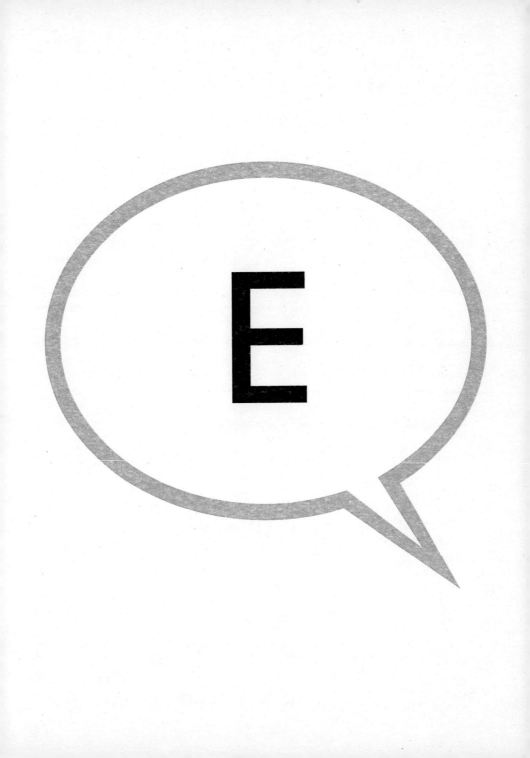

EDUCATION AND LEARNING

Try not to have a good time. This is supposed to be educational.

Charles M. Schulz

And how is education supposed to make me feel smarter? Besides, every time I learn something new, it pushes some old stuff out of my brain. Remember when I took that home wine-making course, and I forgot how to drive?

Homer Simpson

Education's purpose is to replace an empty mind with an open mind.

Malcolm Forbes

A child is not a vase to be filled, but a fire to be lit.

François Rabelais

Spoon-feeding in the long run teaches us nothing but the shape of the spoon.

E. M. Forster

Nine-tenths of education is encouragement.

Anatole France

Curiosity is the very basis of education and if you tell me that curiosity killed the cat, I say only the cat died nobly.

Arnold Edinborough

You're trying to run the school like a factory for turning out money-making machine-made snobs. Modern methods, intensive training – poppycock! Give a boy a sense of humour and a sense of proportion and he'll stand up to anything.

Mr 'Chips' Chipping, *Goodbye, Mr Chips*

Education is worth little if it teaches only how to make a living rather than how to make a life.

Mary Hatwood Fatrell

How essential it is in youth to acquire some intellectual or artistic tastes, in order to furnish the mind, to be able to live inside a mind with attractive and interesting pictures on the walls.

William Lyons Phelps

School doesn't teach you the three most important things in the world: how to have relationships, how to raise children and, most importantly, why on earth you'd want to be in this world in the first place.

Clive Stafford Smith

The great advantage of the sort of education I had was precisely that it made practically no mark upon those subjected to it.　**Malcolm Muggeridge**

Education is the ability to listen to almost anything without losing your temper or your self-confidence.　**Robert Frost**

You know there is a problem with the education system when you realize that out of the 3 Rs, only one begins with an R.　**Dennis Miller**

Education is ... hanging around until you've caught on.　**Robert Frost**

Self-education is, I firmly believe, the only kind of education there is.

Isaac Asimov

The only useful thing I ever learned in school was that if you spit on your eraser it erased ink.　**Dorothy Parker**

Must we always teach our children with books? Let them look at the stars and the mountains above. Let them look at the waters and the trees and flowers on earth. Then they will begin to think, and to think is the beginning of a real education.　**David Polis**

The illiterate of the twenty-first century will not be those who cannot read and write, but those who cannot learn, unlearn and relearn.　**Alvin Toffler**

The effects of infantile instruction are, like those of syphilis, never completely cured.　**Robert Briffault**

I liked being half educated; you were so much more surprised at everything when you were ignorant.　**Gerald Durrell**

I expect I shall be a student to the end of my days.　**Anton Chekhov**

EFFORT

All rising to Great Place is by a winding stair.
Francis Bacon

You have to climb to reach a deep thought.
Stanislaw J. Lec

Parties who want milk should not seat themselves on a stool in the middle of a field in the hope that the cow will back up to them.
Elbert Hubbard

It is not enough to do our best. Sometimes we have to do what is required.
Winston Churchill

A team effort is a lot of people doing as I say.
Michael Winner

You must do the thing you think you cannot do.
Eleanor Roosevelt

Do, or do not. There is no try.
Yoda, *The Empire Strikes Back*

When running up a hill it is all right to give up as many times as you wish as long as you keep your feet moving.
Shoma Morita

Don't be afraid to take a big step. You can't cross a chasm in two small jumps.
David Lloyd George

If there is no wind, row.
Latin proverb

Big shots are only little shots who keep shooting.
Christopher Morley

Pace yourself. An elephant can be swallowed ... one bite at a time.
Anon

Grain by grain, a loaf; stone by stone, a castle.
Serbian proverb

One sad thing about this world is that the acts that take the most out of you are usually the ones that other people will never know about.
Anne Tyler

All it takes is all you got.
Marc Davis

I have always tried to hide my efforts and wished my works to have the light joyousness of springtime which never lets anyone suspect the labours it has cost me.   Henri Matisse

If we'd known we were going to be the Beatles, we'd have tried harder.
                                                          George Harrison

Many things – such as loving, going to sleep or behaving unaffectedly – are done worst when we try hardest to do them.   C. S. Lewis

EGO

Gentlemen, start your egos.   Billy Crystal

The very purpose of existence is to reconcile the glowing opinion we hold of ourselves with the appalling things that other people think about us.
                                                          Quentin Crisp

We are so vain that we even care for the opinion of those we don't care for.
                                              Maria von Ebner-Eschenbach

The ring always believes that the finger lives for it.   Malcolm de Chazal

It was prettily devised of Aesop: The fly sat upon the axle-tree of the chariot-wheel and said, 'What a dust do I raise!'   Francis Bacon

Is a narcissist's suicide a crime of passion?   Howard Ogden

Egotism is the anaesthetic that dulls the pain of stupidity.   Frank Leahy

It's all about self-esteem now. Build the kids' self-esteem, make them feel good about themselves. If everybody grows up with high self-esteem, who's gonna dance in our strip-clubs?   Greg Giraldo

Most people's self-esteem isn't low enough.   Howard Ogden

An inferiority complex would be a blessing if only the right people had it.

Alan Reed

If one is really a superior person, the fact is likely to leak out without too much assistance.　　　　　　　　　　　　　　　　　John Andrew Holmes

What's wrong with this egotism? If a man doesn't delight in himself and the force in him and feel that he and it are wonders, how is all life to become important to him?　　　　　　　　　　　　　　Sherwood Anderson

It would be a colourless world if each individual did not secretly believe himself superior to almost everyone else.　　　　　　　　Don Marquis

He who despises himself esteems himself as a self-despiser.　　Susan Sontag

I occasionally swank a little because people like it; a modest man is such a nuisance.　　　　　　　　　　　　　　　　　George Bernard Shaw

Shyness is just egotism out of its depth.　　　　　　　　Penelope Keith

Humility is like underwear, essential, but indecent if it shows.　Helen Nielsen

Part of me suspects that I'm a loser, and the other part of me thinks I'm God Almighty.　　　　　　　　　　　　　　　　　John Lennon

Every man has a right to be conceited until he is successful.　Benjamin Disraeli

EMOTION

Bobby, if you weren't my son, I'd hug you.　　　Hank Hill, *King of the Hill*

I hate people doing an emotional striptease. It's never genuine or they wouldn't drag outsiders in.　　　　　　　　　　　　　Evelyn Anthony

Spilling your guts is just exactly as charming as it sounds.　　Fran Lebowitz

Centuries of make-up that can be smudged by emotion have taught women to control their feelings.   Arturo Perez-Reverte

Never apologize for showing feeling. When you do so, you apologize for truth.   Benjamin Disraeli

It is always one of the tragedies of any relationship, even between people sensitive to each other's moods, that the moments of emotion so rarely coincide.   Nan Fairbrother

Most often it happens that one attributes to others only the feelings of which one is capable oneself.   André Gide

We feel in one world, we think and name in another. Between the two we can set up a system of references, but we cannot fill the gap.   Marcel Proust

Feeling good and feeling bad are not necessarily opposites. Both at least involve feelings. Any feeling is a reminder of life. The worst 'feeling' evidently is non-feeling.   Willard Gaylin

The world is a comedy to those that think, a tragedy to those that feel.
                    Horace Walpole

I've learned that people will forget what you said, people will forget what you did, but people will never forget how you made them feel.   Anon

ENEMY

I learned early in life that you get places by having the right enemies.
                    Bishop John Spong

One of the most time-consuming things is to have an enemy.   E.B. White

I'd rather have him inside my tent pissing out, than outside my tent pissing in.   Lyndon B. Johnson

A conquered foe should be watched.

E. W. Howe

For a good enemy, choose a friend. He knows where to strike.

Diane de Poitiers

To make an enemy, do someone a favor.

James McLaughry

If you have no enemies, you are apt to be in the same predicament in regard to friends.

Elbert Hubbard

Our enemies' opinion of us comes closer to the truth than our own.

La Rochefoucauld

If we could read the secret history of our enemies, we would find in each man's life a sorrow and a suffering enough to disarm all hostility.

Henry Wadsworth Longfellow

ENTHUSIASM

Zest is the secret of all beauty. There is no beauty that is attractive without zest.

Christian Dior

I am an electric eel in a pool of catfish.

Edith Sitwell

The enthusiastic, to those who are not, are always something of a trial.

Alban Goodier

If you aren't fired with enthusiasm, you'll be fired with enthusiasm.

Vince Lombardi

Men who never get carried away should be.

Malcolm Forbes

ENVIRONMENT

Who will speak for Planet Earth?   Carl Sagan

The sun and the moon and the stars would have disappeared long ago
had they happened to be within reach of predatory human hands.
                                                          Havelock Ellis

Children alive today may live to see the first man on Mars and the last
elm tree in the United States.   *Buffalo News*

Suburbia is where the developers bulldoze out the trees, then name the
streets after them.   Bill Vaughn

Remember when atmospheric contaminants were romantically called
stardust?   Lane Olinghouse

Suicide by carbon monoxide used to be done in the garage. Now, all you
have to do is go to Mexico City and inhale.   Richard Bayan

Bergeron's epitaph for the planet, I remember, which he said should be
carved in big letters in a wall of the Grand Canyon for the flying-saucer
people to find, was this: WE COULD HAVE SAVED IT BUT WE WERE
TOO DOGGONE CHEAP. Only he didn't say 'doggone'.   Kurt Vonnegut

The sun is the source of all the earth's energy. This is important because
one day we're going to get the bill.   Tom Weller

Geologists claim that although the world is running out of oil, there is still
a 200-hundred-year supply of brake fluid.   George Carlin

Since global warming the Eskimos have seventeen different words
for water.   Euan Ferguson

How can the spirit of the earth like the White man? Everywhere the White
man has touched it, it is sore.   **Native American woman of the Wintu tribe**

I confess that when I first read that smog is particularly hazardous to children, senior citizens, and physically active people, for a brief moment I thought, I'm in the clear for at least ten years.   Paula Poundstone

We do not inherit the earth from our fathers; we borrow it from our children.   Native American saying

ENVY

Anybody can sympathize with the sufferings of a friend, but it requires a very fine nature to sympathize with a friend's success.   Oscar Wilde

When yellow wants to become blue, it becomes green.   Russian proverb

Other people's eggs have two yolks.   Bulgarian proverb

To be envious, in Chinese, is 'to guzzle vinegar'.   Maxine Hong Kingston

The man with toothache thinks everyone happy whose teeth are sound.   George Bernard Shaw

He is less upset by his poverty than your wealth.   Yiddish saying

EQUALITY

Before God and the bus driver we are all equal.   German proverb

Kings and philosophers shit; and so do ladies.   Michel de Montaigne

All animals are equal, but some animals are more equal than others.   George Orwell

If your wife is small, stoop down and whisper in her ear.   Jewish proverb

If all were equal, if all were rich, and if all were at table who would lay the cloth?

German proverb

If you've been put in your place long enough you begin to act like the place.

Randall Jarrell

The cry of equality pulls everyone down.

Iris Murdoch

After death all men smell alike.

Italian proverb

EUTHANASIA

The woman who committed suicide in Switzerland ... My God. What dignity. What courage. To have all your marbles and decide that before they are replaced with pain and humiliation, it is better to die. One thing, though. There was some television footage of her going to the clinic and I couldn't help thinking: why is she bothering to wear a seatbelt?

Jeremy Clarkson

Dying well is part of living well and one day our society will surely recognize that. But I suppose we'll only know that we've reached that promised land on the day that the President of the Voluntary Euthanasia Society begins his address to the Annual General Meeting with the words: 'Tremendous news for the society. It's been our most successful year ever. So successful, indeed, that we now have no members at all.'

Victor Lewis-Smith

Euthanasia is a long, smooth-sounding word, and it conceals its danger as long, smooth-sounding words do, but the danger is there, nonetheless.

Pearl S. Buck

Euthanasia is a way of putting old people out of their family's misery.

Mike Barfield

EVIL

—Do you believe in evil?
—Of course I believe in evil – I work in real estate.

Susan Mayer and Edie Britt, *Desperate Housewives*

There is nothing that makes us feel so good as the idea that someone else is an evil-doer.

Robert Lynd

Why does God allow evil in the world? To thicken the plot.

Sri Ramakrishna

Evil is unspectacular and always human, and shares our bed and eats at our own table.

W. H. Auden

It is a sin to believe evil of others, but it is seldom a mistake.

H. L. Mencken

Nobody ever suddenly became depraved.

Juvenal

Boredom and stupidity and patriotism, especially when combined, are three of the greatest evils of the world we live in.

Robertson Davies

There are evils that have the ability to survive identification and go on for ever ... money, for instance, or war.

Saul Bellow

Once we assuage our conscience by calling something a 'necessary evil', it begins to look more and more necessary and less and less evil.

Sydney J. Harris

All that's needed for evil to triumph is that good men do nothing.

Edmund Burke

For good people to do evil things, it takes religion.

Stephen Weinberg

Perhaps everything terrible is in its deepest being something helpless that wants help from us.

Rainer Maria Rilke

Among life's perpetually charming questions is whether the truly evil do more harm than the self-righteous and wrong. Jon Margolis

EVOLUTION

Imagine spending four billion years stocking the oceans with seafood, filling the ground with fossil fuels, and drilling the bees in honey production – only to produce a race of bed-wetters! Barbara Ehrenreich

If evolution was worth its salt, by now it should've evolved something better than survival of the fittest. I think a better idea would be survival of the wittiest. Jane Wagner

My theory of evolution is that Darwin was adopted. Steven Wright

Nevertheless, it is even harder for the average ape to believe that he has descended from man. H. L. Mencken

Evolution has been removed.
Janet Waugh, opposing Kansas Board of Education's vote to drop Darwin's theory of evolution from its curriculum, 1999

EXCUSE

That's your excuse for everything, isn't it – being dead?
David Lister, *Red Dwarf*

'But' is a fence over which few leap. German proverb

The man who cannot dance will blame the drum. African proverb

Remember that in giving any reason at all for refusing, you lay some foundation for a future request. Arthur Helps

EXERCISE

—Are you just looking to lose weight, or do you want increased strength and flexibility too?
—I want to look good naked.

Jim Olmeyer and Lester Burnham, American Beauty

My doctor told me I should get out of breath three times a week, so I took up smoking.

Jo Brand

I ran two miles yesterday. Then the cat let go of my saveloy.

Jo Brand

Walking isn't a lost art – one must, by some means, get to the garage.

Evan Esar

My wife is doing Pilates. I think that's his name.

Peter Sasso

This is how bad I am at working out: I've got a personal trainer and he's getting fat.

Gina Yashere

Exercise is the most *awful* illusion. The secret is a lot of aspiring and *marrons glacés*.

Noël Coward

EXPECTATIONS

There is one illusion that has much to do with most of our happiness, and still more to do with most of our unhappiness. It may be told in a word. We expect too much.

Joseph Farrell

Men have a trick of coming up to what is expected of them, good or bad.

Jacob Riis

Life's under no obligation to give us what we expect.

Margaret Mitchell

We are never prepared for what we expect.

James A. Michener

What a wonderful world this would be if we all did as well today as we
expect to do tomorrow.   **Anon**

When I was a child people simply looked about them and were moderately
happy; today they peer beyond the seven seas, bury themselves waist deep
in tidings, and by and large what they see and hear makes them
unutterably sad.   **E. B. White**

Nothing is so good as it seems beforehand.   **George Eliot**

EXPERIENCE

A fool learns from his experience. A wise person learns from the
experience of others.   **Otto von Bismarck**

To know the road ahead, ask those coming back.   **Chinese proverb**

Experience enables you to recognize a mistake when you make it again.
                                                        Franklin Jones

Education is when you read the fine print; experience is what you get
when you don't.   **Pete Seeger**

We learn geology the day after the earthquake.   **Ralph Waldo Emerson**

The first experience can never be repeated. The first love, the first sunrise,
the first South Sea Island, are memories apart, and touched a virginity
of sense.   **Robert Louis Stevenson**

Nothing ever becomes real until it is experienced – even a proverb is no
proverb to you until your life has illustrated it.   **John Keats**

Experience is not what happens to you; it is what you do with what
happens to you.   **Aldous Huxley**

Only the wearer knows where the shoe pinches.   **English proverb**

Human beings, who are almost unique in having the ability to learn from the experience of others, are also remarkable for their apparent disinclination to do so.   Douglas Adams

We should be careful to get out of an experience only the wisdom that is in it – and stop there; lest we be like the cat that sits down on a hot stove lid. She will never sit on a hot stove lid again – and that is well; but also she will never sit down on a cold one anymore.   Mark Twain

If you can learn from hard knocks, you can also learn from soft touches.
Carolyn Kenmore

I've had very little experience in my life. In fact, I try to avoid experience if I can. Most experience is bad.   E. L. Doctorow

The best substitute for experience is being sixteen.   Raymond Duncan

EXPERT

An expert is a man who knows more and more about less and less until he knows absolutely everything about nothing.   Nicholas Murray Butler

Always listen to experts. They'll tell you what can't be done, and why. Then do it.   Robert Heinlein

If an expert says it can't be done, get another expert.   David Ben-Gurion

You'll always find some Eskimos ready to instruct the Congolese on how to cope with heatwaves.   Stanislaw J. Lec

In the beginner's mind there are many possibilities; in the expert's mind there are few.   Shunryu Suzuki

Even when the experts all agree, they may well be mistaken. Bertrand Russell

If the world should blow itself up, the last audible voice would be that of an expert saying it can't be done.   Peter Ustinov

FACTS

First, get the facts, then you can distort them at your leisure.   Mark Twain

The trouble with facts is that there are so many of them.
                                                    Samuel McChord Crothers

The fewer the facts, the stronger the opinion.   Arnold H. Glascow

We all want to be happy, and we're all going to die … You might say those are the only two unchallengeably true facts that apply to every human being on this planet.   William Boyd

How meagre one's life becomes when it is reduced to its basic facts. And the last, most complete reduction is on one's tombstone: a name, two dates.
                                                    Helen MacInnes

Facts are generally over-esteemed. For most practical purposes, a thing is what men think it is. When they judged the earth flat, it was flat. As long as men thought slavery tolerable, tolerable it was.   John Updike

No facts, however indubitably detected, no effort of reason, however magnificently maintained, can prove that Bach's music is beautiful.   Edith Hamilton

There is no sadder sight in the world than to see a beautiful theory killed by a brutal fact.   Thomas Henry Huxley

Never face facts; if you do you'll never get up in the morning.
                                                    Marlo Thomas

FAILURE

What would you attempt to do if you knew you would not fail?

Robert Schuller

I think the greatest taboos in America are faith and failure.   Michael Malone

A retired teacher from Suffolk has lost her fight to have the word 'fail'
replaced by 'deferred success' in schools. She argued many children were
put off learning for life by being labelled 'failures'.   BBC News website

Failure is unimportant. It takes courage to make a fool of yourself.

Charlie Chaplin

The real loser of our times is the one who is expected to win. Claude Lelouch

I don't know the key to success, but the key to failure is trying to please
everybody.   Bill Cosby

If at first you don't succeed, try to hide your astonishment.   Harry F. Banks

If at first you don't succeed, you may be at your level of incompetence
already.   Laurence J. Peter

If at first you don't succeed, lie, lie again.   Laurence J. Peter

If at first you don't succeed, find out if the loser gets anything.   Bill Lyon

If at first you don't succeed, remove all evidence that you ever tried.

David Brent, *The Office*

When I was young I observed that nine out of ten things I did were failures,
so I did ten times more work.   George Bernard Shaw

Ever tried? Ever failed? No matter. Try again. Fail again. Fail better.

Samuel Beckett

Fall seven times, stand up eight.

Japanese proverb

Many of life's failures are men who did not realize how close they were to success when they gave up.

Thomas Edison

And behind every man who's a failure, there's a woman, too!

John Ruge

If you wish to be a failure in life, offend the chief executive's secretary.

Michael Green

The purpose of life is to be defeated by greater and greater things.

Rainer Maria Rilke

We are all failures – at least, all the best of us are.

J. M. Barrie

FAITH

Faith dares the soul to go further than it can see.

William Clarke

I can't even make a leap of faith to believe in my own existence.

Woody Allen

Religious faith has a lot to do with perspective. One goldfish said to the other goldfish, 'Do you believe in God?' And the other goldfish said, 'Of course I do. Who do you think changes the water?'

Bob Monkhouse

A faith that cannot survive collision with the truth is not worth many regrets.

Arthur C. Clarke

Faith: Not *wanting* to know what is true.

Friedrich Nietzsche

Where there is the necessary technical skill to move mountains, there is no need for the faith that moves mountains.

Eric Hoffer

Absolute faith corrupts as absolutely as absolute power.

Eric Hoffer

Treat the other man's faith gently; it is all he has to believe with. His mind was created for his own thoughts, not yours or mine.　　Henry S. Haskins

Faith is under the left nipple.　　Martin Luther

FAME

Fame has only the span of a day, they say. But to live in the hearts of people – that is something.　　Ouida

I dream that my face appears on a postage stamp.　　John Cheever

They gave me star treatment because I was making a lot of money. But I was just as good when I was poor.　　Bob Marley

If you become a star, *you* don't change, everyone else does.　　Kirk Douglas

A plague on eminence! I hardly dare cross the street anymore without a convoy, and I am stared at wherever I go like an idiot member of a royal family or an animal in a zoo; and zoo animals have been known to die from stares.　　Igor Stravinksy

I don't think humans are meant to be looked at when we're buying pants.　　Ricky Gervais

That so many people respond to me is fabulous. It is like having a kind of Alzheimer's disease, where everyone knows you and you don't know anyone.　　Tony Curtis

I've signed dicks, asses, parole cards, a colostomy bag while it was still pumping. A couple of years ago, I signed a bloody Tampax. That's one you don't forget. I'm not asking for someone to top that!　　John Waters

Here is the autobiography. I would send you a lock of my hair but it's at the barbershop getting washed.　　Groucho Marx

When I went to America I had two secretaries, one for autographs, one for locks of hair. Within six months the one had died of writer's cramp, the other was completely bald.

Oscar Wilde

I can tell you his Who's Who is six inches long.

Minnie Guggenheim, introducing a prominent political figure

With fame I became more and more stupid, which of course is a very common phenomenon.

Albert Einstein

The real trap of fame is its irresistibility.

Ingrid Bengis

I still have my feet on the ground, I just wear better shoes.

Oprah Winfrey

Being on the telly, you're in a funny position – not famous, just current.

Robert Robinson

The nice thing about being a celebrity is that if you bore people, they think it's their fault.

Henry Kissinger

It's too bad I'm not as wonderful as people say I am, because the world could use a few people like that.

Alan Alda

Fame is proof that the people are gullible.

Ralph Waldo Emerson

I never wanted to be famous.
I only wanted to be great.

Ray Charles

Celebrity is a mask that eats into the skin.

John Updike

Once you become famous, there is nothing left but to become infamous.

Don Johnson

Stardom is like making love in a hammock – a happy experience but one of uncertain duration.

David Niven

It's a short walk from the hallelujah to the hoot.   Vladimir Nabokov

In the final analysis, it's true that fame is unimportant. No matter how
great a man is, the size of his funeral usually depends on the weather.
                                                                  Rosemary Clooney

Do not trust to the cheering, for those very persons would shout as much
if you and I were going to be hanged.   Oliver Cromwell

FAMILY

No matter how many communes anybody invents, the family always
creeps back.   Margaret Mead

Family ... the we of me.   Carson McCullers

Family love is messy, clinging, and of an annoying and repetitive pattern,
like bad wallpaper.   P. J. O'Rourke

I think film-makers invented the happy American family and put it into
movies to drive everyone crazy.   Jill Robinson

Families, I hate you! Shut-in living, closed doors, jealous protectors of
happiness.   André Gide

When I can no longer bear to think of the victims of broken homes, I begin
to think of the victims of intact ones.   Peter De Vries

I believe that more unhappiness comes from this source than from any
other – I mean from the attempt to prolong family connections unduly and
to make people hang together artificially who would never naturally do so.
                                                                 Samuel Butler

People talk about dysfunctional families; I've never seen any other kind.
                                                                 Sue Grafton

I'm sure Hitler was great with his family.   George Carlin

—Why is it so easy to love our families but so hard to like them?
—That is one of those questions that makes life so rich – and psychiatrists
even richer.   Daphne Moon and Frasier Crane, *Frasier*

All happy families resemble one another; every unhappy family is unhappy
in its own way.   Leo Tolstoy

To my way of thinking, the American family started to decline when
parents began to communicate with their children.   Erma Bombeck

Family jokes, though rightly cursed by strangers, are the bond that keeps
most families alive.   Stella Benson

Everyone had an uncle who tried to steal their nose.   Peter Kay

Every man sees in his relatives, and especially in his cousins, a series of
grotesque caricatures of himself.   H. L. Mencken

Of all the peoples whom I have studied, from city dwellers to cliff dwellers,
I always find that at least fifty per cent would prefer to have at least one
jungle between themselves and their mothers-in-law.   Margaret Mead

A good horse is a member of the family.   Iranian saying

Everyone has a family tree; the Dawsons have one, it's a weeping willow.
                    Les Dawson

The craze of genealogy is connected with the epidemic for divorce. If we
can't figure out who our living relatives are, then maybe we'll have more
luck with the dead ones.   Jane Howard

If you want to trace your family tree, all you have to do is to run for
public office.   Patricia Vance

The families of our friends are always a disappointment.   Norman Douglas

The most socially subversive institution of our time is the one-parent family.
Paul Johnson

As the family goes, so goes the nation and so goes the whole world in which we live.
Pope John Paul II

FANATIC

A fanatic is a man who does what he thinks the Lord would do, if He knew the facts of the case.
Peter Finley Dunne

Fanaticism is not a state of religion but a state of mind.
Tony Blair

An infallible method of making fanatics is to persuade before you instruct.
Voltaire

A fanatic is one who can't change his mind and won't change the subject.
Winston Churchill

What is objectionable, what is dangerous about extremists is not that they are extreme, but that they are intolerant. The evil is not what they say about their cause, but what they say about their opponents.
Robert F. Kennedy

A fanatic is always the fellow on the other side.
Will Rogers

When people are fanatically dedicated to political or religious faiths or any other kind of dogmas or goals, it's always because these dogmas or goals are in doubt.
Robert M. Pirsig

A fanatic is a man who consciously overcompensates for a secret doubt.
Aldous Huxley

A fanatic is someone who redoubles his effort when he has forgotten his aim.
George Santayana

The worst vice of the fanatic is his sincerity.   Oscar Wilde

Fanatics seldom laugh. They never laugh at themselves.   James M. Gillis

Scratch a fanatic and you find a wound that never healed.
                                                    William North Jayme

One defeats the fanatic precisely by *not* being a fanatic oneself, but on the
contrary by using one's intelligence.   George Orwell

Tolerance and freedom of thought are the veritable antidotes to religious
fanaticism.   Paul-Henri Holbach

FASHION AND DRESS

Fashion: a beautiful thing that becomes ugly. Art: an ugly thing that
becomes beautiful.   Coco Chanel

Does fashion matter? Always – though not quite as much after death.
                                                        Joan Rivers

As soon as a fashion is universal, it is out of date. Marie von Ebner-Eschenbach

A dress has no meaning unless it makes a man want to take it off.
                                                    Françoise Sagan

A dress that zips up the back will bring a husband and wife together.
                                                    James H. Boren

Only men who are not interested in women are interested in women's
clothes. Men who like women never notice what they wear.   Anatole France

Have you noticed when you wear a hat for a long time it feels like it's not
there anymore? And then when you take it off it feels like it's still there?
                                                    George Carlin

To most people a savage nation is one that doesn't wear uncomfortable clothes.   Finley Peter Dunne

In a tuxedo, I'm a star. In regular clothes, I'm a nobody.   Dean Martin

I love Superman. I'm a big fan of anyone who can make his living in his underwear.   David Mamet

Judge not a man by his clothes, but by his wife's clothes.   Thomas R. Dewar

Never try to wear a hat that has more character than you do. Lance Morrow

I never had a hat, never wore one, but recently was given a brown suede duck-hunting hat. The moment I put it on I realized I was starved for a hat. I kept it warm by putting it on my head. I made plans to wear it especially when I was going to do any thinking. Somewhere in Virginia, I lost my hat.
                                                                  John Cage

When in doubt, wear red.   Bill Blass

At Marks and Spencer's I bought a peach-coloured vest and trollies to match with insertions of lace. Disgraceful I know but I can't help choosing my underwear with a view to being seen!
                                          Barbara Pym, diary entry, 8 January 1934

I don't see how an article of clothing can be indecent. A person, yes. Robert Heinlein

I put on a peekaboo blouse, he peeked and booed.   Phyllis Diller

A man's tie should never be louder than his wife.   John Hughes

Never trust anybody who wears a bow tie. A cravat's supposed to point down to accentuate the genitals. Why'd you wanna trust somebody whose tie points out to accentuate his ears?   Doc Wilson, *State and Main*

I lost a buttonhole.   Steven Wright

I wish I had invented blue jeans: the most spectacular, the most practical, the most relaxed and nonchalant. They have expression, modesty, sex appeal, simplicity – all I hope for in my clothes.   Yves Saint Laurent

French pox and a leather vest wear for life.   German proverb

Give a girl the right shoes and she can conquer the world.   Bette Midler

Your socks should never be funnier than you are.   Hal Rubinstein

For a lifetime I had bathed with becoming regularity, and thought the world would come to an end unless I changed my socks every day. But in Africa I sometimes went without a bath for two months, and I went two weeks at a time without even changing my socks. Oddly enough, it didn't seem to make much difference.   Ernie Pyle

When I was young, I found out that the big toe always ends up making a hole in the sock. So I stopped wearing socks.   Albert Einstein

They need a good, stiff, all-purpose dress shoe. Something for church, but also for doctor's appointments, dental checkups, piano recitals, building dedications, visiting elderly relatives, haircuts and shoe shopping.
          Marge Simpson, *The Simpsons*

The high-heeled shoe is a marvellously contradictory item; it brings a woman to a man's height but makes sure she cannot keep up with him.
          Germaine Greer

Not enough attention is paid to the negative side of fashion. Great effort is exerted to make people look smart, but somebody should face the fact that a lot of people never will be smart, and that they should be given some assistance in maintaining their fascinating dowdiness.   Robertson Davies

—What do you call a Frenchman in sandals?
—Philippe Philoppe.   Anon

Be careless in your dress if you must, but keep a tidy soul.   Mark Twain

FATE

We are merely the stars' tennis balls, struck and banded, which way
pleases.   John Webster

It's odd to think we might have been sun, moon and stars to each other –
only I turned down one little street, and you turned up another.
                                                    Fanny Heaslip Lea

There is no such thing as an omen. Destiny does not send us heralds.
She is too wise or too cruel for that.   Oscar Wilde

Fortune loves to give bedroom slippers to people with wooden legs, and
gloves to those with no hands.   Théophile Gautier

Destiny is something we've invented because we can't stand the fact that
everything that happens is accidental.   Annie Reed, *Sleepless in Seattle*

Destiny is the invention of the cowardly and the resigned.   Ignazio Silone

I have noticed even people who claim everything is predestined, and that
we can do nothing to change it, look before they cross the road.
                                                    Stephen Hawking

When Fortune empties her chamberpot on your head, smile and say,
'We are going to have a summer shower.'   John McDonald

We have to believe in free will.
We've got no choice.
                                                    Isaac Bashevis Singer

FATHER

The other night I told my kid, 'Someday you'll have children of your own.'
He said, 'So will you.'
Rodney Dangerfield

This is my father. Try what you can with him! He won't listen to me,
because he remembers what a fool I was when I was a baby.
George Bernard Shaw

When I was ten, my pa told me never to talk to strangers. We haven't
spoken since.
Steven Wright

The most important thing a father can do for his children is to love their
mother.
Theodore Hesburgh

I think the saddest day of my life was when I realized I could beat my
dad at most things, and Bart experienced that at the age of four.
Homer Simpson

It doesn't matter who my father was; it matters who I remember he was.
Anne Sexton

I'd been told of all the things you're meant to feel when your father dies.
Sudden freedom, growing up, the end of dependence, the step into the
sunlight when no one is taller than you and you're in no one's shadow.
I know what I felt. Lonely.
John Mortimer

FAULTS

The camel never sees its own hump, but that of its brother is always
before its eyes.
Persian proverb

We are dismayed when we find that even disaster cannot cure us of our
faults.
Marquis de Vauvenargues

Almost all our faults are more pardonable than the methods we resort to hide them.

La Rochefoucauld

A man's foibles are what makes him lovable.

Johann Wolfgang von Goethe

There is so much good in the worst of us, and so much bad in the best of us, that it ill behoves any of us to find fault with the rest of us.

James Truslow Adams

Think of your own faults the first part of the night when you are awake, and of the faults of others the latter part of the night when you are asleep.

Chinese proverb

Don't find a fault, find a remedy.

Henry Ford

FAVOURS

Learn how to refuse favours. This is a great and very useful art.

Thomas Fuller

Never claim as a right what you can ask as a favour.

John Churton Collins

There's no such thing as a free lunch.

Milton Friedman

Free cheese is found only in mousetraps.

Russian proverb

FEAR

—Are you ever afraid?
—Always.

Interviewer and Alfred Hitchcock

I get goose pimples. Even my goose pimples get goose pimples.

Wally Campbell, *The Cat and the Canary*

Fear has a smell, as love does.   Margaret Atwood

The world is divided into two kinds of people: those who have tattoos,
and those who are afraid of people with tattoos.   Anon

You can discover what your enemy fears most by observing the means he
uses to frighten you.   Eric Hoffer

If I hazarded a guess as to the most endemic, prevalent anxiety among
human beings – including fear of death, abandonment, loneliness –
nothing is more prevalent than the fear of one another.   R. D. Laing

The thing I fear most is fear.   Michel de Montaigne

One of the mistakes the Germans made ... was that they were not brave
enough to be afraid.   Günter Grass

There is no terror in a bang, only in the anticipation of it.   Alfred Hitchcock

As a child, I was more afraid of tetanus shots than, for example, Dracula.
                                                                 Dave Barry

The more you can increase fear of drugs and crime, welfare mothers,
immigrants and aliens, the more you control all the people.   Noam Chomsky

To suffering there is a limit;
to fearing, none.   Francis Bacon

We often pretend to fear what we really despise, and more often despise
what we really fear.   Charles Caleb Colton

Everything is so dangerous that nothing is really very frightening.
                                                              Gertrude Stein

Do the thing you fear, and the death of fear is certain.   Ralph Waldo Emerson

True terror is to wake up one morning and discover that your high-school class is running the country.   Kurt Vonnegut

Fear is the main source of superstition and one of the main sources of cruelty. To conquer fear is the beginning of wisdom.   Bertrand Russell

It's all right to have butterflies in your stomach. Just get them to fly in formation.   Rob Gilbert

FEMINISM

So it's *our* car, *our* flat and *our* money, but I notice it's always *her* tits. There's feminism for you.   Neil, *Viz*

The universal religion – contempt for women.   Andrea Dworkin

I've always said I have nothing against a woman doing anything a man can do as long as she gets home in time to cook dinner.   Barry Goldwater

I wanted to be more than a hole in the mattress that answers to a name.
                                    Eleanor Lightbody, *The Road to Wellville*

There's a new thing called Women's Lib. It means women get whatever they want.   Marcia Brady, *A Very Brady Sequel*

Feminism encourages women to leave their husbands, kill their children, practise witchcraft, destroy capitalism and become lesbians.
                                                    Reverend Pat Robertson

Of course I'm a feminist. You have to be these days – it's the only way to pull the chicks.   Rick, *The Young Ones*

'I hate discussions of feminism that end up with who does the dishes,' she said. So do I. But at the end, there are always the damned dishes.
                                                            Marilyn French

To celebrate 'Take Your Daughter to Work Day', this year we're both cleaning out the toilet.
Helene Siskind Parsons

There are very few jobs that actually require a penis or a vagina. All other jobs should be open to everybody.
Florynce R. Kennedy

Women who seek to be equal with men lack ambition.
Timothy Leary

How do I feel about women's rights? I like either side of them.
Groucho Marx

So what if Columbus discovered America? Queen Isabella gave him the money.
Anon

FIGHT

The man who strikes first admits that his ideas have given out.
Chinese saying

When you go out to fight for freedom and truth it's never a good idea to wear your best trousers.
Henrik Ibsen

Never pick a fight with an ugly person; they've got nothing to lose.
Robin Williams

Whoever fights monsters should see to it that in the process he does not become a monster.
Friedrich Nietzsche

When two elephants fight, it is the grass underneath which suffers.
African proverb

Retreat, hell! We're just fighting in another direction.
Major-General Smith

—I've got to nip this guy in the bud. This sort of behavior is contagious, you know. One guy decides he's not gonna fight anymore, it catches on, and pretty soon you know what we've got?
—Peace?
Colonel Flagg and B.J., M*A*S*H

FILM

Film is a collaborative business: bend over.   **David Mamet**

Not everyone who wants to make a film is crazy, but almost everyone who is crazy wants to make a film.   **Clive James**

There's a standard formula for success in the entertainment medium, and this is: 'Beat it to death if it succeeds.'   **Ernie Kovacs**

If I could change one thing about this industry, I would skip the part where you have to demonstrate to people dumber than you that you are talented and worthy of their time and money.   **Jonathan Katz**

—Which of the Marx brothers remained silent throughout all their movies?
—Karl.   **Anne Robinson and Contestant,** *The Weakest Link*

If you can tune into the fantasy life of an eleven-year-old girl, you can make a fortune in the film business.   **George Lucas**

Screenwriting is an opportunity to fly first class, be treated like a celebrity, sit around the pool and be betrayed.   **Ian McEwan**

Being a writer in Hollywood is like going to Hitler's Eagle Nest with a great idea for a bar mitzvah.   **David Mamet**

Hollywood – it's either people who are unhappy or soon will be.   **Jonathan Ross**

They say the movies should be more like life. I think life should be more like the movies.   **Myrna Loy**

Every year you work in Hollywood takes a year off your soul.

Calista Flockhart

—Ginger Rogers and Fred Astaire first appeared together in the film *Flying Down to ...* where?
—Halifax.   **Anne Robinson and Contestant,** *The Weakest Link*

Film music should have the same relationship to the film drama that somebody's piano-playing in my living room has to the book I'm reading.
Igor Stravinsky

The most beautiful thing I have ever seen in a movie theatre is to go down to the front and turn around, and look at all the uplifted faces, the light from the screen reflected upon them.   **François Truffaut**

Jack Lemmon in ...   **Jack Lemmon, epitaph**

FISHING

In my family, there was no clear division between religion and fly-fishing.
Norman Maclean, *A River Runs Through It*

The charm of fishing is that it is the pursuit of what is elusive but attainable, a perpetual series of occasions for hope.   **John Buchan**

Fishing is boring, unless you catch an actual fish, and then it is disgusting.
Dave Barry

Fishing, with me, has always been an excuse to drink in the daytime.   Jimmy Cannon

It has always been my private conviction that any man who pits his intelligence against a fish and loses has it coming.   **John Steinbeck**

Advice to anglers: don't take advice from people with missing fingers.
Henry Beard

Someone just back of you while you are fishing is as bad as someone looking over your shoulder while you write a letter to your girl.

Ernest Hemingway

Where there's smoke, there's salmon.

Jewish proverb

Whoever came up with ice fishing must have had the worst marriage on the planet.

Jeff Cesario

The gods do not deduct from man's allotted span the hours spent in fishing.

Babylonian proverb

Many men go fishing all of their lives without knowing that it is not fish they are after.

Henry David Thoreau

FLATTERY

What really flatters a man is that you think him worth flattering.

George Bernard Shaw

I hate careless flattery, the kind that exhausts you in your effort to believe it.

Wilson Mizner

Perfumed and gallant words make our ears belch.

Pietro Aretino

They say princes learn no art truly, but the art of horsemanship. The reason is, the brave beast is no flatterer. He will throw a prince as soon as his groom.

Ben Jonson

Flattery, if judiciously administered, is always acceptable, however much we may despise the flatterer.

Lady Marguerite Blessington

Never interrupt when you're being flattered.

Anon

FLOWERS

He was quite eloquent on the subject of flowers, which he loves because 'they're not always borrowing money'.　　　　　　　Woody Allen

Flowers are the sweetest thing God ever made and forgot to put a soul into.
　　　　　　　Henry Ward Beckford

People from a planet without flowers would think we must be mad with joy the whole time to have such things about us.　　　　Iris Murdoch

When you have only two pennies left in the world, buy a loaf of bread with one, and a lily with the other.　　　　　　　Chinese proverb

One of the attractive things about flowers is their magnificent reserve.
　　　　　　　Henry David Thoreau

A morning-glory at my window satisfies me more than the metaphysics of books.　　　　　　　Walt Whitman

The flower in the vase still smiles, but no longer laughs.　　Malcolm de Chazal

Flowers are one of the few things we buy, bring home, watch die, and we don't ask for our money back.　　George Carlin

To be overcome by the fragrance of flowers is a delectable form of defeat.
　　　　　　　Beverley Nichols

The perfumes are the feelings of the flowers.　　　　　Heinrich Heine

The earth laughs in flowers.　　　　　　　Ralph Waldo Emerson

FOOD

I love the Chinese words for greeting: not strictly 'Hello' but 'Have you eaten yet?'

Rick Stein

No man can be wise on an empty stomach.

George Eliot

You become what you think. You are what you eat.

Barbara Cartland

I fancy having a bit of rabbit for my tea tonight. Could anyone tell me if it's cheaper from a butcher's or a pet shop?

J. Picklay, *Viz*

The dinner table is the centre for the teaching and practising not just of table manners but of conversation, consideration, tolerance, family feeling, and just about all the other accomplishments of polite society except the minuet.

Judith Martin

In general, I think, human beings are happiest at table when they are very young, very much in love, or very alone.

M. F. K. Fisher

If I could only have one food for the rest of my life? That's easy. Pez. Cherry-flavor Pez.

Vern Tessio, *Stand By Me*

Licorice is the liver of candy.

Michael O'Donoghue

Donuts. Is there anything they can't do?

Homer Simpson

A bagel is a donut with the sin removed.

George Rosenbaum

Anyhow, the hole in the donut is at least digestible.

H. L. Mencken

I like rice. Rice is great when you're hungry and want 2000 of something.

Mitch Hedberg

It's difficult to think anything but pleasant thoughts while eating a home-grown tomato.

Lewis Grizzard

I like spaghetti because you don't have to take your eyes off the book to pick about among it, it's all the same.   Philip Larkin

It has always pleased me to read while eating if I have no companion; it gives me the society I lack. I devour alternately a page and a mouthful; it is as though my book were dining with me.   Jean Jacques Rousseau

Almost every person has something secret he likes to eat.   M. F. K. Fisher

—What popular chocolate bar was named after the Roman god of war?
—Snickers.   Sonjy Zietlow and Contestant, *The Weakest Link*, Germany

Triangular sandwiches taste better than square ones.   Peter Kay

Canapé – a sandwich cut into twenty-four pieces.   Bill Rose

It is the destiny of mint to be crushed.   Waverley Root

While it is undeniably true that people love a surprise, it is equally true that they are seldom pleased to suddenly and without warning happen upon a series of prunes in what they took to be a normal loin of pork.
          Fran Lebowitz

Sacred cows make the best hamburger.   Abbie Hoffman

Among the classic tastes: bread sauce, Nuits St Georges Les Perdrix 1962, Worcestershire sauce, Toblerone and Bovril.   Kenneth Tynan

If this sauce was a person, I'd get naked and make love to it.
          Sophia Petrillo, *The Golden Girls*

In every plate of chips there is a bad chip.   Peter Kay

A well-made sauce will make even an elephant or a grandfather palatable.
          Alexander Grimod de la Reynière

Appetite is the best sauce.   French proverb

Put Tabasco sauce on everythin' you eat; this way, you can eat very cheap.

Forrest Gump

You're never quite sure whether it's OK to eat green crisps.　　Peter Kay

The noise from good toast should reverberate in the head like the thunder of July.　　E. V. Lucas

Raspberries are best not washed. After all, one must have faith in something.

Ann Batchelder

Cabbage, n: a familiar kitchen-garden vegetable about as large and wise as a man's head.　　Ambrose Bierce

A louse in the cabbage is better than no meat at all.

Pennsylvania Dutch proverb

Please understand the reason why Chinese vegetables taste so good. It is simple. The Chinese do not cook them, they just threaten them.

Jeff Shaw

A man may esteem himself happy when that which is his food is also his medicine.　　Henry David Thoreau

Bread and butter, devoid of charm in the drawing room, is ambrosia eating under a tree.　　Elizabeth Russell

Bread that must be sliced with an axe is bread that is too nourishing.

Fran Lebowitz

Human beings do not eat nutrients, they eat food.　　Mary Catherine Bateson

Lettuce is like conversation: it must be fresh and crisp, and so sparkling that you scarcely notice the bitter in it.　　Charles Dudley Warner

I always wanted to open a delicatessen in Jerusalem and call it 'Cheeses of Nazareth'.

Sandi Toksvig

To test the ripeness of Camembert cheese: put your left index finger on your eye and your right index finger on the cheese … if they sort of feel the same, the cheese is ready.

M. Taittinger

Always serve too much hot fudge sauce on hot fudge sundaes. It makes people overjoyed, and puts them in your debt.

Judith Olney

Maybe you know why a child can reject a hot dog with mustard served on a soft bun at home, yet eat six of them two hours later at fifty cents each.

Erma Bombeck

There are five elements: earth, air, fire, water, and garlic.

Louis Diat

Eat, drink and love; the rest's not worth a fillip.

Lord Byron

FOOL

Some men are wise and some are otherwise.

Tobias Smollett

Ninety-nine per cent of people in the world are fools, and the rest of us are in great danger of contagion.

Thornton Wilder

Though all his life a fool associates with a wise man, he no more comprehends the truth than a spoon tastes the flavour of the soup.

Dhammapada

The wisest thing to do with a fool is to encourage him to hire a hall and discourse to his fellow citizens. Nothing chills nonsense like exposure to the air.

Woodrow Wilson

There are well-dressed foolish ideas just as there are well-dressed fools.

Diane Ackerman

A fool sees not the same tree that a wise man sees. **William Blake**

A fellow who's always declaring he's no fool usually has his suspicions.

Wilson Mizner

If fifty million people say a foolish thing, it is still a foolish thing.

Anatole France

Better to be silent and be thought a fool, than to speak and remove all doubt.

Anon

The greatest lesson in life is to know that even fools are right sometimes.

Winston Churchill

We're fools whether we dance or not, so we might as well dance.

Japanese proverb

Everyone is a damn fool for at least five minutes every day. Wisdom
consists in not exceeding the limit. **Elbert Hubbard**

FORGIVE

Everyone says forgiveness is a lovely idea, until they have something to
forgive. **C. S. Lewis**

There is no revenge as complete as forgiveness. **H. W. Shaw**

Forgiveness is the fragrance the violet sheds on the heel that has crushed it.

Mark Twain

It is easier to forgive an Enemy than to forgive a Friend. **William Blake**

It is easier to get forgiveness than permission. **Grace Hopper**

A God all mercy is a God unjust. **Edward Young**

Other-cheekism is not only a way of purifying the soul, it is also part of every weak person's survival kit. Quentin Crisp

The stupid neither forgive nor forget; the naïve forgive and forget; the wise forgive but do not forget. Thomas Szasz

They buried the hatchet, but in a shallow, well-marked grave. Dorothy Walworth

Children are innocent and love justice, while most adults are wicked and prefer mercy. G. K. Chesterton

The offender never pardons. George Herbert

God will pardon me. It's his job. Heinrich Heine, last words

Be assured that if you knew all, you would pardon all. Thomas à Kempis

FREEDOM

It is by the fortune of God that in our country we have three unspeakably precious things: freedom of speech, freedom of thought, and the prudence never to practise either of them. Mark Twain

People demand freedom of speech to make up for the freedom of thought which they avoid. Søren Kierkegaard

Freedom is the right to tell people what they don't want to hear. George Orwell

My definition of a free society is a society where it is safe to be unpopular. Adlai Stevenson

If we don't believe in freedom of expression for people we despise, we don't believe in it at all. Noam Chomsky

I disapprove of what you say, but I will defend to the death your right to say it.
                                                                    Voltaire, attrib.

Liberty doesn't work as well in practice as it does in speeches.   Will Rogers

If people have to choose between freedom and sandwiches, they will take sandwiches.
                                                                    Lord Boyd-Orr

Liberty means responsibility. That is why most men dread it.
                                                                    George Bernard Shaw

You can only be free if I am free.   Clarence Darrow

The basic test of freedom is perhaps less in what we are free to do than in what we are free not to do.
                                                                    Eric Hoffer

A man's worst difficulties begin when he is able to do as he likes.
                                                                    T. H. Huxley

The moment the slave resolves that he will no longer be a slave, his fetters fall. He frees himself and shows the way to others. Freedom and slavery are mental states.
                                                                    Mahatma Gandhi

No human being, however great, or powerful, was ever so free as a fish.
                                                                    John Ruskin

FRIEND

I was real friendly with a boy named Earl once – well, twice really.
                                                                    Ramona, *Neighbours*

A friend is the only person you will let into the house when you are Turning Out Drawers.
                                                                    Pam Brown

A real friend is one who walks in when the rest of the world walks out.
                                                                    Walter Winchell

However rare true love is, true friendship is rarer. La Rochefoucauld

Good friends offer to help you in a crisis; great friends don't take no for an answer. **Bree Van De Kamp,** *Desperate Housewives*

It's the friends you can call up at 4:00 a.m. that matter. Marlene Dietrich

A single rose can be my garden … a single friend, my world. Leo Buscaglia

Go often to the house of the friend; for weeds soon choke up the unused path.

Scandinavian proverb

Old friends are best, King James used to call for his old shoes; they were easiest on his feet. John Selden

I always felt that the great high privilege, relief and comfort of friendship was that one had to explain nothing. Katherine Mansfield

'Tis the privilege of friendship to talk nonsense, and have her nonsense respected. Charles Lamb

The proper office of a friend is to side with you when you are in the wrong. Nearly anybody will side with you when you are right. Mark Twain

When a friend is in trouble, don't annoy him by asking if there is anything you can do. Think up something appropriate and do it. E. W. Howe

Today, people often make the American mistake of confusing acquaintances with friends. The former are there to share life's pleasures; only the latter should be invited to share one's problems. Julian Fellowes

The holy passion of Friendship is of so sweet and steady and loyal and enduring a nature that it will last through a whole lifetime, if not asked to lend money. Mark Twain

Do not use a hatchet to remove a fly from your friend's forehead.

Chinese proverb

There is no stronger bond of friendship than a mutual enemy.

Frankfort Moore

Everyone ought to be friends with a nun and a whore and while talking with them forget which is which.   Brendan Francis

If we were all given by magic the power to read each other's thoughts, I suppose the first effect would be to dissolve all friendships.

Bertrand Russell

I never had any friends later on like the friends I had at twelve – Jesus, does anyone?   Narrator, *Stand By Me*

You'll have many, many friends, but if your relationship with your mate is one hundred per cent of your heart, you'll never need a friend.   Bill Cosby

To the world you may be one person, but to one person you may be the world.   Brandi Snyder

FUTURE

This is the first age that has paid much attention to the future, which is rather ironic since we may not have one.   Arthur C. Clarke

Our obsession with security is a measure of the power we have granted the future to hold over us.   Wendell Berry

The world is full of people whose notion of a satisfactory future is, in fact, a return to an idealized past.   Robertson Davies

If He has given us one marvellous gift, it is that He does not permit us to know the future. It would be unbearable.   Edward G. Robinson

The future will be exactly like the past, only more expensive.   John Sladek

God made the world round so we could never see too far down the road.

Isak Dinesen

Predicting is very difficult, especially if it's about the future.   Niels Bohr

It is the business of the future to be dangerous.   Alfred North Whitehead

Map out your future, but do it in pencil.   Jon Bon Jovi

I got the blues thinking of the future, so I left off and made some marmalade. It's amazing how it cheers one up to shred oranges and scrub the floor.   D. H. Lawrence

GAMBLING

Money won is twice as sweet as money earned.

Fast Eddie Felson, *The Color of Money*

In the casino, the cardinal rule is to keep them playing and to keep them coming back. The longer they play, the more they lose, and in the end, we get it all.

Ace Rothstein, *Casino*

When we put in fifty more machines, I consider them fifty more mousetraps. You have to have a mousetrap to catch a mouse.

Bob Stupak, former Las Vegas casino owner

The roulette table pays nobody except him who keeps it. Nevertheless, a passion for gaming is common, though a passion for keeping roulette wheels is unknown.

George Bernard Shaw

Time spent in a casino is time given to death, a foretaste of the hour when one's flesh will be diverted to the purposes of the worm and not of the will.

Rebecca West

Buying stock is exactly the same thing as going to a casino, only with no cocktail service.

Ted Allen

If you mind losing more than you enjoy winning, don't bet.

Clement Freud

Betting and gambling would lose half their attractiveness, did they not deceive us with the fancy that there may be an element of personal merit in our winnings. Our reason may protest, but our self-love is credulous.

Robert Lynd

When a man tells me he's going to put all his cards on the table, I always look up his sleeve.

Lord Leslie Hore-Belisha

If you must play, decide upon three things at the start: the rules of the game, the stakes, and the quitting time.   Chinese proverb

My wife made me join a bridge club. I jump off next Tuesday.
                                                    Rodney Dangerfield

Never contend with a man who has nothing to lose.   Baltasar Gracián

GAMES

You can learn more about a person in an hour of play than in a year of conversation.   Plato

Most sorts of diversions in men, children, and other animals are imitation of fighting.   Jonathan Swift

Almost any game with any ball is a good game.   Robert Lynd

The laws of chess are as beautiful as those governing the universe – and as deadly.   Katherine Neville

I like video games but they're really violent. I'd like to play a video game where you help the people who were shot in all the other games. It'd be called 'Really Busy Hospital'.   Demetri Martin

As a family we find great relaxation in jigsaws, but we don't like them to be too easy. We always turn the pieces out onto the lid, so that we can't see the picture, and we make a rule to start in the middle and do the outside last. When we want to make things *really* tricky, we mix a couple of old jigsaws together.   Brian Jenkins

It may be that all games are silly. But then, so are most human beings.
                                                        Robert Lynd

The game of life is worth playing, but the struggle is the prize.   William Inge

GARDEN

God Almighty first planted a garden. And, indeed, it is the purest of
human pleasures.
                                                          Francis Bacon

I think that if ever a mortal heard the voice of God it would be in a garden
at the cool of the day.
                                                     F. Frankfort Moore

A modest garden contains, for those who know how to look and to wait,
more instruction than a library.
                                                 Henri Frédéric Amiel

I have never had so many good ideas day after day as when I worked in
the garden.
                                                          John Erskine

Gardens are a form of autobiography.
                                                       Sydney Eddison

Almost any garden, if you see it at just the right moment, can be confused
with paradise.
                                                      Henry Mitchell

The difference between a good garden and bad garden is a fortnight.
                                                      Bob Flowerdew

We have descended into the garden and caught 300 slugs. How I love the
mixture of the beautiful and the squalid in gardening. It makes it so lifelike.
                                                      Evelyn Underhill

A rule to remember when dealing with garden pests: if it is slow-moving
stamp on it; if it is fast-moving leave it alone – it will probably kill
something else.
                                                        Esme Boughey

Gardening gives one back a sense of proportion about everything –
except itself.
                                                          May Sarton

After his death the gardener does not become a butterfly, intoxicated by
the perfumes of the flowers, but a garden worm tasting all the dark,
nitrogenous, and spicy delights of the soil.
                                                          Karel Čapek

I had never 'taken a cutting' before ... Do you realize that the whole thing is miraculous? It is exactly as though you were to cut off your wife's leg, stick it in the lawn, and be greeted on the following day by an entirely new woman, sprung from the leg, advancing across the lawn to meet you.

Beverley Nichols

Weather means more when you have a garden. There's nothing like listening to a shower and thinking how it is soaking in around your green beans.

Marcelene Cox

Where would the gardener be if there were no more weeds?

Chuang Tse

A weed is no more than a flower in disguise.

James Russell Lowell

One is tempted to say that the most human plants, after all, are the weeds.

John Burroughs

I once saw a botanist most tenderly replace a plant which he had inadvertently uprooted, though we were on a bleak hillside in Tibet, where no human being was likely to see the flower again.

Francis Younghusband

Green fingers are the extension of a verdant heart.

Russell Page

Our vegetable garden is coming along well, with radishes and beans up, and we are less worried about revolution than we used to be.

E. B. White

There is a kind of immortality in every garden.

Gladys Taber

GENDER AND SEXUALITY

—Is it a boy or a girl?
—I think it's a bit early to start imposing roles on it, don't you?

New mother and Obstetrician, *Monty Python's The Meaning of Life*

People are not heterosexual or homosexual, just sexual.

Quentin Crisp

The mind has no sex.

George Sand

What is most beautiful in virile men is something feminine; what is most beautiful in feminine women is something masculine.

Susan Sontag

A bisexual told me I didn't quite coincide with either of her desires.

Woody Allen

I don't consider myself bisexual. I just think of myself as a 'people person'.

Michael Dane

Sometimes I think if there was a third sex men wouldn't get so much as a glance from me.

Amanda Vail

I don't mind straight people as long as they act gay in public.

T-shirt slogan

For those of you who don't know what a friend of Dorothy is: ask a policeman or one in five Tory MPs.

Stephen Fry

Buggery was invented to fill that awkward hour between evensong and cocktails.

Maurice Bowra

The priesthood is in many ways the ultimate closet in Western civilization, where gay people particularly have hidden for the past two thousand years.

Bishop John Spong

There is probably no sensitive heterosexual alive who is not preoccupied with his latent homosexuality.

Normal Mailer

You know, my family always said no man would be good enough for me.

Suzy Berger

I support gay marriages. I believe they have the right to be as miserable as the rest of us.

Kinky Friedman

—Plato was gay.
—Mickey Mouse's dog was *gay*?

Jodie Dallas and Jessica Tate, *Soap*

I have never been attracted to another man, but I like to touch myself around my penis when I masturbate. As a result, I am worried that I may be homosexual.

Viz, reader's letter

The lesbian is one of the least-known members of our culture. Less is known about her – and less accurately – than about the Newfoundland dog.

Sidney Abbott and Barbara Love

I find it sad that by not talking about who I sleep with, that makes me mysterious. There was a time when I would have been called a gentleman.

Kevin Spacey

It always seemed to me a bit pointless to disapprove of homosexuality. It's like disapproving of rain.

Francis Maude

Why is being outed such a big deal? When I find out that someone's gay, my respect for them increases tenfold.

Scott Thompson

I came out to my family on Thanksgiving. I said, 'Mom, please pass the gravy to a homosexual.' She passed it to my father. A terrible scene ensued.

Bob Smith

When asked, 'Shall I tell my mother I'm gay?', I reply, 'Never tell your mother anything.'

Quentin Crisp

I'm in favor of gay marriage. Then at least both people are excited about the wedding.

Jay Leno

I was once involved in a same-sex marriage. There was the same sex over and over and over.

David Letterman

I feel there is something unexplored about a woman that only a woman can explore.

Georgia O'Keeffe

Feminism is the theory and lesbianism is the practice.   Ti-Grace Atkinson

Love is love. Gender is merely spare parts.   Wendy Wasserstein

Black, white, gay, straight, what's the difference? We all finish ourselves off in the end anyway.   Karen Walker, *Will and Grace*

GENEROSITY

To know the value of generosity, it is necessary to have suffered from the cold indifference of others.   Eugene Cloutier

It's easy to be generous with money. Far harder to be generous with your time.   Alan Bleasdale

A candle loses nothing by lighting another candle.   James Keller

Never measure your generosity by what you give, but by what you have left.   Bishop Fulton J. Sheen

All you can hold in your cold dead hand is what you have given away.   Joaquin Miller

What I kept, I lost. What I spent, I had. What I gave, I have.   Persian proverb

GENIUS

To do what others cannot do is talent. To do what talent cannot do is genius.   Henri Frédéric Amiel

Genius is talent exercised with courage.   Ludwig Wittgenstein

A man who is a genius and doesn't know it probably isn't.   Stanislaw J. Lec
You're a genius! And the proof is that both common people and
intellectuals find your work completely incoherent.   Woody Allen

The word 'genius' isn't applicable to football. A genius is a guy like
Norman Einstein.   Joe Theisman

In every work of genius we recognize our own rejected thoughts.
Ralph Waldo Emerson

One of the strongest characteristics of genius is the power of lighting its
own fire.   John Ruskin

Every man is a potential genius until he does something.
Herbert Beerbohm Tree

I don't want to be a genius, I have enough problems just trying to be a man.
Albert Camus

Geniuses are like ocean liners: they should never meet.   Louis Aragon

GENTLENESS

There is nothing in the world stronger than gentleness.   Han Suyin

A gentle word opens an iron gate.   Bulgarian proverb

Even in a time of elephantine vanity and greed, one never has to look far
to see the campfires of gentle people.   Garrison Keillor

Gentleness is everywhere in daily life, a sign that faith rules through
ordinary things: through cooking and small talk, through storytelling,
making love, fishing, tending animals and sweet corn and flowers, through
sports, music, and books, raising kids – all the places where the gravy
soaks in and grace shines through.   Garrison Keillor

Beyond a wholesome discipline, be gentle with yourself. Max Ehrmann

GHOSTS

You want to know whether I believe in ghosts? Of course I do not believe in them. If you had known as many of them as I have, you would not believe in them either. Don Marquis

Behind every man now alive stand thirty ghosts, for that is the ratio by which the dead outnumber the living. Arthur C. Clarke

The more enlightened our houses are, the more their walls ooze ghosts. Italo Calvino

Does one ever see any ghost that is not oneself? Joseph Shearing

GIFTS AND GIVING

One reason people get divorced is that they run out of gift ideas. Robert Byrne

There are few things more subtly distressing than an inappropriate gift from someone close to you. Anatole Broyard

What can you give a friend who has everything? Shelves. Patty Marx

Rings and jewels are not gifts but apologies for gifts. The only true gift is a portion of yourself. Ralph Waldo Emerson

Greeting cards: when you care enough to send the very best, but not enough to actually *write* something. Howard Ogden

Gifts must affect the receiver to the point of shock. Walter Benjamin

You never want to give a man a present when he's feeling good. You want

to do it when he's down.
Lyndon B. Johnson

The joy of giving is indeed a pleasure, especially when you get rid of something you don't want.
Frank Butler

Gifts are like hooks.
Martial

There is sublime thieving in all giving. Someone gives us all he has and we are his.
Eric Hoffer

Surely there must be a better gift God could have given us than life?
Michael O'Donoghue

GOD

Do you believe in God? That's the wrong question. Does God believe in us?
Old man, *La Haine*

I met God. 'What,' he said, 'you already?' 'What,' I said, 'you still?'
Laura Riding

Nice to meet you, God. Nice job on the Grand Canyon and good luck with the Apocalypse.
Bruce, *Bruce Almighty*

God is really only another artist. He invented the giraffe, the elephant, the ant. He has no real style. He just goes on trying other things.
Pablo Picasso

Callum: Is God everywhere?
Mother: Yes, dear.
Callum: Is he in this room?
Mother: Yes, he is.
Callum: Is he in my mug?
Mother (*growing uneasy*): Er – yes.
Callum (*clapping his hands over his mug*): Got him!
(*Callum was four years old at the time of the conversation*)

Margaret Donaldson
God, who winds up our sundials ...   Georg Christoph Lichtenberg

What if God is a woman? Not only am I going to hell, but I'll never
know why.   Adam Ferrara

I've had people say to me, 'Look at the sky, the fields, the ocean, the
beautiful sunset. Isn't that proof positive of God?' Following that line of
thought, look at the magnificent rainbows after a big rainstorm. Isn't that
proof positive that God is gay?   Ray Romano

I have too much respect for the idea of God to make it responsible for
such an absurd world.   Georges Duhamel

Good God, how much reverence can you have for a supreme being who
finds it necessary to include such phenomena as phlegm and tooth decay
in His divine system of creation?   Joseph Heller

It would be very nice if there were a God who created the world and was a
benevolent providence, and if there were a moral order in the universe and
an afterlife; but it is a very striking fact that all this is exactly as we are
bound to wish it to be.   Sigmund Freud

How terrible the need for God.   Theodore Roethke

Many people believe that they are attracted by God, or by nature, when they are only repelled by man. Dean W. R. Inge

With God, what is terrible is that one never knows whether it's not just a
trick of the devil.   Jean Anouilh

Either God exists or He doesn't. Either I believe in God or I don't. Of the
four possibilities, only one is to my disadvantage. To avoid that possibility,

I believe in God.   **Blaise Pascal**

Man is certainly stark mad. He cannot even make a worm, and yet he will be making gods by the dozens.   **Michel de Montaigne**

Even if God exists, he's done such a terrible job, it's a wonder people don't get together and file a class action suit against him.   **Woody Allen**

Whatever you imagine, God is the opposite of that.   **Llewellyn Vaughan-Lee**

I don't believe in God because I don't believe in Mother Goose.   Clarence Darrow

I think if there is a God, he takes a lot of long lunches.

Andrew Benson, *Peter's Friends*

God seems to have left the receiver off the hook, and time is running out.

Arthur Koestler

In the absence of any other proof, the thumb alone would convince me of God's existence.   **Isaac Newton**

You can safely assume you have created God in your own image when it turns out that God hates all the same people you do.   **Anne Landers**

What can you say about a society that says that God is dead and Elvis is alive?   **Irv Kupcinet**

Believing in Santa Claus doesn't do kids any harm for a few years but it isn't smart for them to continue waiting all their lives for him to come down the chimney with something wonderful. Santa Claus and God are cousins.   **Andy Rooney**

If there is no God, who pops up the next Kleenex?   **Art Hoppe**

A day will come when the European god of the nineteenth century will be

classed with the gods of Olympus and the Nile.   **Winwood Reade**
I think of God in much the same way that I think of the Royal Family. If
we didn't live in this toytown with princes and kings then we might make
a better stab at being citizens.   **Linda Smith**

There is not sufficient love and goodness in the world to permit us to give
some of it away to imaginary beings.   **Friedrich Nietzsche**

I do not believe in God, but I am afraid of him.   **Gabriel García Márquez**

A Russian child asked his mother, 'Does God know we don't believe
in Him?'   **E. Y. Harburg**

If God did not exist, we should have to invent him. If God did exist, we
should have to abolish Him.   **Albert Camus**

God has been replaced, as he has been all over the West, with respectability
and air conditioning.   **Imamu Amiri Baraka**

In a city a man may feel second to none. But alone in the immensity of the
universe, among all the creatures that preceded man and built up the
human species, even a most fervent atheist will wonder if Darwin found
the visible road but not the invisible mechanism.   **Thor Heyerdahl**

There is no such thing as an atheist. Everyone believes that he is God.
Alan Ashley Pitt

When did I realize I was God? Well, I was praying and suddenly realized
I was talking to myself.   **Peter O'Toole**

No matter how I probe and prod I cannot quite believe in God. But oh!
I hope to God that he unswervingly believes in me.   **E. Y. Harburg**

Is Google the new God?   *The Times* online

GOOD AND BAD

You're right about there being some good in me. That's what's been
holding me back for years.   Alan Melville

Expecting life to treat you well because you are a good person is like
expecting an angry bull not to charge because you are a vegetarian.
                                                             Shari R. Barr

Goodness does not more certainly make men happy than happiness makes
them good.   Walter Savage Landor

Few things are harder to put up with than the annoyance of a good
example.   Mark Twain

A Native American said this: 'Inside of me there are two dogs. One of the
dogs is mean and evil. The other dog is good. The mean dog fights the
good dog all the time.' When asked which dog wins, he reflected for a
moment and replied, 'The one I feed the most.'   Anon

Working out what it would take to programme goodness into a robot
shows not only how much machinery it takes to be good but how slippery
the concept of goodness is to start with.   Steven Pinker

There is nothing either good or bad but thinking makes it so.
                                             William Shakespeare, *Hamlet*

We are more prone to generalize the bad than the good. We assume that
the bad is more potent and contagious.   Eric Hoffer

The wicked are always surprised to find that the good can be clever.
                                             Marquis de Vauvenargues

Be not simply good; be good for something.   Henry David Thoreau

Pretend to be good always, and even God will be fooled.　　Kurt Vonnegut

A good head and a good heart are always a formidable combination.

Nelson Mandela

I always prefer to believe the best of everybody, it saves so much trouble.

Rudyard Kipling

We can never give up the belief that the good guys always win. And that we are the good guys.　　Faith Popcorn

GOODBYES

Visits always give pleasure – if not the arrival, the departure.

Portuguese proverb

I can generally bear the separation, but I don't like the leave-taking.

Samuel Butler

Every parting gives a foretaste of death; every remeeting a foretaste of the resurrection. That is why even people who are indifferent to each other rejoice so much if they meet again after twenty or thirty years of separation.　　Arthur Schopenhauer

A man never knows how to say goodbye; a woman never knows when to say it.　　Helen Rowland

Hello, I must be going, I cannot stay, I came to say, I must be going.
I'm glad I came, but just the same, I must be going! I'll stay a week or two,
I'll stay the summer through, but I am telling you, I must be going!

Groucho Marx, *Animal Crackers*

GOSSIP

Conversation between Adam and Eve must have been difficult at times because they had nobody to talk about.   **Agnes Repplier**

A woman and a mouse, they carry a tale wherever they go.   **Gelett Burgess**

Gossip is just news running ahead of itself in a red satin dress.   **Liz Smith**

I don't call it gossip, I call it 'emotional speculation'.   **Laurie Colwin**

Each person sweeps the snow before his own door, and never minds the frost on another family's roof.   **Chinese proverb**

Gossip needn't be false to be evil – there's a lot of truth that shouldn't be passed around.   **Frank Clarke**

Whoever gossips *to* you will gossip *about* you.   **Sir Philip Sidney**

Malicious gossip takes the place of creation in non-creative lives.
Nancy Hale

When gossip grows old it becomes myth.   **Stanislaw J. Lec**

GOVERNMENT

In general, the art of government consists in taking as much money as possible from one party of the citizens to give to the other.   **Voltaire**

Life under a good government is rarely dramatic; life under a bad government is always so.   **Oscar Wilde**

Governments tend not to solve problems, only to rearrange them.
Ronald Reagan

It is not impossible to rule Italians, but it would be useless. Benito Mussolini

Let the people think they govern, and they will be governed. William Penn

You can lead a man to Congress, but you can't make him think. Milton Berle

Whenever governments adopt a moral tone as opposed to an ethical one you know something is wrong. John Ralston Saul

It is dangerous to be right when the government is wrong. Voltaire

Whatever happens in a government could have happened differently, and it usually would have been better if it had. Charles Frankel

GRATITUDE

If the only prayer you say in your whole life is 'Thank you', that would suffice. Meister Eckhart

A thankful person is thankful under all circumstances. A complaining soul complains even if he is in paradise. Baha'u'llah

Do not refuse a wing to the persons who gave you the whole chicken. R. G. H. Sui

Gratitude: the meanest and most snivelling attribute in the world. Dorothy Parker

Gratitude is such an unpleasant quality, you know; there is always a grudge behind it. Ouida

Gratitude is merely the secret hope of further favours. La Rochefoucauld

Never thank anybody for anything, except a drink of water in the desert – and then make it brief. Gene Fowler

GREATNESS

I have always been a quarter of an hour before my time, and it has made a man of me.
Lord Nelson

To accomplish great things, we must not only act but also dream, not only plan, but also believe.
Anatole France

To be great is to be misunderstood. Pythagoras was misunderstood, and Socrates, and Jesus, and Luther, and Copernicus, and Galileo, and Newton, and every pure and wise spirit that ever took flesh.
Ralph Waldo Emerson

Before a brilliant person begins something great, they must look foolish in a crowd.
I Ching

Breaking the ice in the pitcher seems to be a feature of the early lives of all great men.
Robert Benchley

A certain excessiveness seems a necessary element in all greatness.
Harvey Cushing

To feel themselves in the presence of true greatness many men find it necessary only to be alone.
Tom Mason

Behind every great man … there's a woman rolling her eyes.
Bruce, *Bruce Almighty*

To see the greatness of a mountain, one must keep one's distance.
Angarika Govinda

Great eaters and great sleepers are incapable of doing anything great.
Henri IV of France

There are no great men, only great challenges that ordinary men are forced by circumstances to meet.
William Halsey, *The Gallant Hours*

I'd rather be a great bad poet than a good bad poet.   Ogden Nash

Keep away from people who try to belittle your ambitions. Small people always do that, but the really great make you feel that you, too, can become great.   Mark Twain

I believe that the first test of a truly great man is his humility. I do not mean by humility, doubt of his own powers. But really great men have a curious feeling that the greatness is not in them, but through them. And they see something divine in every man.   John Ruskin

A great man's greatest good luck is to die at the right time.   Eric Hoffer

GRIEF

Grief is the price we pay for love.   Queen Elizabeth II

Part of getting over it is knowing that you will never get over it.   Anne Finger

You don't get over it because 'it' is the person you loved.   Jeanette Winterson

Nothing on earth can make up for the loss of one who has loved you.   Selma Lagerlof

Those who have lost an infant are never, in any way, without an infant.   Leigh Hunt

Death ends a life, not a relationship.   Robert Benchley

Time is not a great healer. It is an indifferent and perfunctory one. Sometimes it does not heal at all. And sometimes when it seems to, no healing has been necessary.   Ivy Compton-Burnett

Sorrow makes us all children again – destroys all differences of intellect. The wisest know nothing.   Ralph Waldo Emerson

There are griefs which grow with years.   Harriet Beecher Stowe

After a while, the telephone rang. Like a snakebite the thought darted into me, I shall never be rung up by her again. Total grief is like a minefield. No knowing when one will touch the tripwire.   Sylvia Townsend Warner

To everyone else, the death of that being you love for his own sake, for her own sake, is an event that occurs on a certain day. For you, the death only begins that day. It is not an event: it is only the first moment in a process that lives in you, springing up into the present, engulfing you years, decades, later, as though it were the first moment again.   Alice Koller

To mourn is to be extraordinarily vulnerable. It is to be at the mercy of inside feelings and outside events in a way most of us have not been since early childhood.   Christian McEwen

No one ever told me that grief felt so like fear. The same fluttering in the stomach, the same restlessness, the yawning. I keep on swallowing.
C. S. Lewis

Grief is a mute sense of panic.   Marion Roach

Grief can't be shared. Everyone carries it alone. His own burden in his own way.   Anne Morrow Lindbergh

There are some griefs so loud they could bring down the sky, and there are griefs so still none knows how deep they lie.   May Sarton

When someone dies, it is like when your house burns down; it isn't for years that you realize the full extent of your loss.   Mark Twain

People do not die for us immediately, but remain bathed in a sort of aura of life which bears no relation to true immortality but through which they continue to occupy our thoughts in the same way as when they were alive. It is as though they were travelling abroad.   Marcel Proust

In deep sadness there is no place for sentimentality.   William S. Burroughs

Grief remains one of the few things that has the power to silence us.
It is a whisper in the world and a clamor within. More than sex, more
than faith, even more than its usher death, grief is unspoken, publicly
ignored except for those moments at the funeral that are over too quickly,
or the conversations among the cognoscenti, those of us who recognize
in one another a kindred chasm deep in the center of who we are.

Anna Quindlen

How small and selfish is sorrow. But it bangs one about until one is
senseless.   **Queen Elizabeth, the Queen Mother, after the death of George VI**

In any man who dies there dies with him, his first snow and kiss and
fight ... Not people die but worlds die in them.   **John Greenleaf Whittier**

The deep pain that is felt at the death of every friendly soul arises from the
feeling that there is in every individual something which is inexpressible,
peculiar to him alone, and is, therefore, absolutely and *irretrievably* lost.

Arthur Schopenhauer

When a person dies, it's as if a library burns down – all singular
experiences, anchored in unique cells, are extinguished.   **George Koehler**

On hearing of the death of a close friend, go round with a box of delicious
food and strong drink. The family will have forgotten the shopping and
will be distraught.   **Jennifer Paterson**

Honest plain words best pierce the ear of grief.

William Shakespeare, Love's Labour's Lost

When a friend needs consoling, do not give in to the temptation of telling
stories similar to theirs of disaster or bereavement. It is something people
often do to show empathy but nothing is more tiresome than other people's
problems when you want to focus on your own. Listening is by far the best
form of consolation.   **Giles Andreae**

Knowing what to say isn't always necessary; just the presence of a caring
friend can make the world of difference.   **Sheri Curry**

While grief is fresh, every attempt to divert only irritates.   Samuel Johnson

Be as much as you can in the open air without fatigue.   Sydney Smith

Take a short view of human life not farther than dinner or tea. Sydney Smith

Don't order any black things. Rejoice in his memory; and be radiant ...
Be patient with the poor people who will snivel: they don't know; and
they think they will live for ever, which makes death a division instead of
a bond.   George Bernard Shaw

Sorrow you can hold, however desolating, if nobody speaks to you. If they
speak, you break down.   Bede Jarrett

When we lose one we love, our bitterest tears are called forth by the
memory of hours when we loved not enough.   Maurice Maeterlinck

After any major sadness or crisis in life, make a conscious effort to
recapture joy in very small things: be it the first snowdrop, dew on a
spider's web, the song of a bird, the sun on your back – or even something
as simple as feeling just the right temperature at a particular moment.
But it takes practice.   Mary Sheepshanks

In three words I can sum up everything I've learned about life: it goes on.
Robert Frost

GUEST AND HOST

Hospitality: the virtue which induces us to feed and lodge certain persons
who are not in need of food and lodgings.   Ambrose Bierce

Every guest hates the others, and the host hates them all.   Albanian proverb

Treat your guest as a guest for two days; on the third, give them a hoe.
Swahili proverb

A host is like a general: it takes a mishap to reveal his genius.　　Horace

True friendship's laws are by this rule expressed: Welcome the coming, speed the parting guest.　　Alexander Pope

The guest is always right – even if we have to throw him out.
　　Charles Ritz, hotelier

GUILT

Guilt: the Gift that keeps on giving.　　Erma Bombeck

I carry around such a load of non-specific guilt that every time the metal detector beeps, I always have a wild fear that this trip I absent-mindedly packed a Luger.　　Dan Greenburg

I've got enough guilt to start my own religion.　　Tori Amos

Show me a woman who doesn't feel guilty and I'll show you a man.
　　Erica Jong

My mother could make anybody feel guilty. She used to get letters of apology from people she didn't even know.　　Joan Rivers

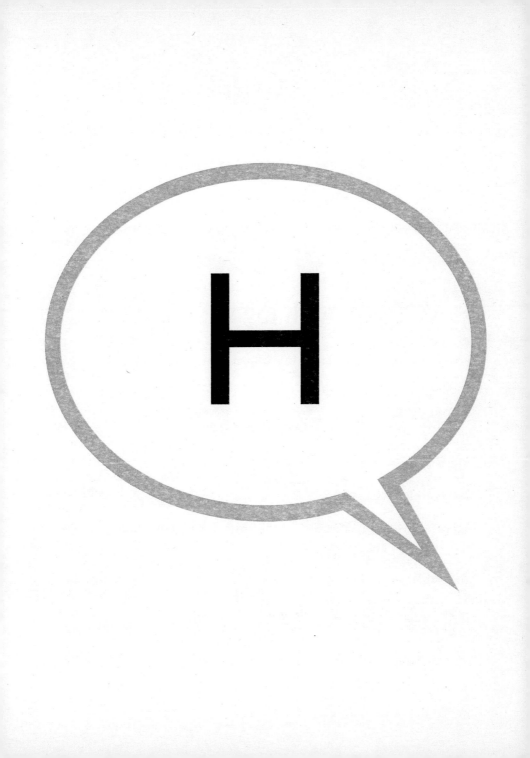

HABIT

In twenty-three years of married life, Mrs Babbit had seen the paper before her husband just sixty-seven times.   **Sinclair Lewis**

Habit is a cable; we weave a thread of it every day, and at last we cannot break it.   **Horace Mann**

If you do what you've always done, you'll get what you've always gotten.
Tony Robbins

My problem lies in reconciling my gross habits with my net income. Errol Flynn

A habit is something you can do without thinking – which is why most of us have so many of them.   **Frank A. Clark**

Curious things, habits. People themselves never know they have them.
Agatha Christie

After you've done a thing the same way for two years look it over carefully. After five years look at it with suspicion and after ten years throw it away and start all over again.   **Alfred Perlman**

Old habits cannot be thrown out the upstairs window. They have to be coaxed downstairs one step at a time.   **Mark Twain**

Laws are never as effective as habits.   **Adlai Stevenson**

It's like magic: when you live by yourself, all your annoying habits are gone.
Merrill Markoe

The long habit of living indisposeth us for dying.   **Thomas Browne**

HAIR

—So, Frank, you have long hair. Does that make you a woman?
—If I had a wooden leg would that make me a table?

Interviewer and Frank Zappa

Hair is another name for sex.

Vidal Sassoon

I have always believed that hair is a very sure index of character.

Katharine Tynan

Hair matters. This is a life lesson Wellesley and Yale Law School failed to instil. Your hair will send significant messages to those around you.

Hillary Clinton

Earlier this year I had my hair feng-shuied.

Jerry Hall

I've discovered over the years that if my hair is all right, then generally speaking, so am I.

Maureen Lipman

That gentlemen prefer blondes is due to the fact that, apparently, pale hair, delicate skin and an infantile expression represent the very apex of frailty which every man longs to violate.

Alexander King

A good hairdresser can express every mood and every passion of the human heart.

W. Somerset Maugham

Most barbers have one haircut they can do, and if they suspect you are asking for something different, they panic.

Hugo Williams

—What would you call that hairstyle you're wearing?
—Arthur.

Reporter and George Harrison, A Hard Day's Night

—Why do people have eyebrows?
—The reason people have eyebrows is so that bald people can remember
what colour their hair was.   **James Cameron and Small Child**

Gorgeous hair is the best revenge.   **Ivana Trump**

HAPPINESS

There is only one inborn error, and that is the notion that we exist in order
to be happy.   **Arthur Schopenhauer**

If life on Planet Earth was really supposed to be a picnic, we would all have
been born clutching gingham tablecloths.   **Jonathan Cainer**

Happiness depends on wisdom.   **Sophocles**

It takes great wit and interest and energy to be happy. The pursuit of
happiness is a great activity. One must be open and alive. It is the greatest
feat man has to accomplish.   **Robert Herrick**

We act as though comfort and luxury were the chief requirements of life,
when all that we need to make us happy is something to be enthusiastic
about.   **Charles Kingsley**

To me there is in happiness an element of self-forgetfulness. You lose
yourself in something outside yourself when you are happy; just as when
you are desperately miserable you are intensely conscious of yourself, are a
solid little lump of ego weighing a ton.   **J. B. Priestley**

If you observe a really happy man you will find him building a boat,
writing a symphony, educating his son, growing double dahlias in his
garden.   **W. Beran Wolfe**

Happiness? A good cigar, a good meal, and a good woman – or a bad
woman. It depends on how much happiness you can handle.   **George Burns**

In order to be utterly happy the only thing necessary is to refrain from comparing this moment with other moments in the past, which I often did not fully enjoy because I was comparing them with the other moments of the future.   André Gide

An echo of music, a face in the street, the wafer of the new moon, a wanton thought – only in the iridescence of things the vagabond soul is happy.
                                                              Logan Pearsall Smith

A table, a chair, a bowl of fruit and a violin; what else does a man need to be happy?   Albert Einstein

Any man should be happy who is allowed the patience of his wife, the tolerance of his children and the affection of waiters.   Michael Arlen

I'm happiest when my wife gets her way, or so she tells me.   Jason Love

The only true happiness comes from squandering ourselves for a purpose.
                                                              William Cowper

In order to be happy oneself it is necessary to make at least one other person happy ... The secret of human happiness is not in self-seeking but in self-forgetting.   Theodore Reik

To be without some of the things you want is an indispensable part of happiness.   Bertrand Russell

The secret to true happiness is low expectations and insensitivity. Olivia Goldsmith

There is only one happiness in life, to love and be loved.   George Sand

Even a happy life cannot be without a measure of darkness and the word 'happiness' would lose its meaning if it were not balanced by sadness.
                                                              Carl Jung

How unbearable at times are people who are happy, people for whom everything works out.
Anton Chekhov

If we only wanted to be happy it would be easy; but we want to be happier than other people, which is almost always difficult, since we think them happier than they are.
Baron de Montesquieu

If you were happy every day of your life, you wouldn't be a human being – you'd be a game-show host.
Veronica Sawyer, *Heathers*

—Are you happy?
—What do you take me for, an idiot?
Reporter and Charles de Gaulle

Ask yourself whether you are happy, and you cease to be so.   John Stuart Mill

Happiness in intelligent people is the rarest thing I know.   Ernest Hemingway

Happiness is a mystery like religion, and should never be rationalized.
G. K. Chesterton

As a child I was told by my parents that I was happy, but I did not believe them.
Mason Cooley

It is an aspect of all happiness to suppose that we deserve it.   Joseph Joubert

It is not easy to find happiness in ourselves, and it is not possible to find it elsewhere.
Agnes Repplier

To be happy is to be able to become aware of oneself without fright.
Walter Benjamin

It is one of the most saddening things in life that, try as we may, we can never be certain of making people happy, whereas we can almost always be certain of making them unhappy.
Thomas Huxley

We have no more right to consume happiness without producing it than to consume wealth without producing it.　　　　　George Bernard Shaw

Let us be grateful to people who make us happy; they are the charming gardeners who make our souls blossom.　　　　　Marcel Proust

The greater part of our happiness depends on our dispositions and not on our circumstances.　　　　　Martha Washington

I never believe much in happiness. I never believe in misery either. Those are things you see on the stage or the screen or the printed page, they never really happen to you in life.　　　　　F. Scott Fitzgerald

Happiness is always a by-product. It is probably a matter of temperament, and for anything I know it may be glandular. But it is not something that can be demanded from life, and if you are not happy you had better stop worrying about it and see what treasures you can pluck from your own brand of unhappiness.　　　　　Robertson Davies

The greatest happiness you can have is knowing that you do not necessarily require happiness.　　　　　William Saroyan

I begin to see that a man's got to be in his own heaven to be happy.
　　　　　Mark Twain

The Constitution only guarantees the American people the right to pursue happiness. You have to catch it yourself.　　　　　Benjamin Franklin

Many in this world run after felicity like an absent-minded man hunting for his hat while all the time it is on his head.　　　　　Sydney Smith

Now and then it's good to pause in our pursuit of happiness and just be happy.　　　　　Guillaume Apollinaire

Happiness is getting a brown gravy stain on a brown dress.　　　　　Totie Fields

Give me a bed and a book and I am happy.　　　　　Logan Pearsall Smith

I do think awful things may happen at any moment, so while they are not
happening, you may as well be pleased.   Nigella Lawson

Do not wait for a reason to be happy.   Mason Cooley

Everyday happiness means you can't wait to come home, because the soup
is hot.   George Burns

The happiness of life is made up of minute fractions – the little soon
forgotten charities of a kiss or smile, a kind look, a heartfelt compliment,
and the countless infinitesimal of pleasurable and genial feeling.
                                                      Samuel Taylor Coleridge

People are about as happy as they make up their minds to be.
                                                            Abraham Lincoln

For the happiest life, days should be rigorously planned, nights left open
to chance.   Mignon McLaughlin

Even if happiness forgets you a little bit, never completely forget about it.
                                                              Jacques Prévert

A lifetime of happiness! No man alive could bear it: it would be hell on
earth.   George Bernard Shaw

Happiness is an imaginary condition, formerly often attributed by the
living to the dead, now usually attributed by adults to children, and by
children to adults.   Thomas Szasz

Happy Hour: a depressing comment on the rest of the day and a victory
for the most limited Dionysian view of human nature.   John Ralston Saul

The grand essentials to happiness in this life are something to do,
something to love, and something to hope for.   Joseph Addison

We are never happy; we can only remember that we were so once.
                                                            Alexander Smith

Cherish all your happy moments, they make a fine cushion for old age.

Christopher Morley

Happiness, whether in business or private life, leaves very little trace in history.

Fernand Braudel

I got rhythm, I got music, I got my man, who could ask for anything more?

George Gershwin

HATE

Why do I hate people? Who else is there to hate?

Florence King

People hate as they love, unreasonably.

William Thackeray

There is nothing in the whole world so painful as feeling that one is not liked. It always seems to me that people who hate me must be suffering from a strange form of lunacy.

Sei Shōnagon

I don't want everyone to like me; I should think less of myself if some people did.

Henry James

I find a fascination, like the fascination for the moth of a star, in those who hold aloof and disdain me.

Logan Pearsall Smith

Everybody hates me because I'm so universally liked.

Peter De Vries

What a man hates, he takes seriously.

Michel de Montaigne

Love makes everything lovely; hate concentrates itself on the one thing hated.

George MacDonald

If you hate a person, you hate something in him that is part of yourself. What isn't part of ourselves doesn't disturb us.

Herman Hesse

You cannot be beautiful and hate.

Bess Myerson

In hatred as in love, we grow like the thing we brood upon. What we loathe, we graft into our very soul.

Mary Renault

He loved me absolutely, that's why he hates me absolutely.

Frieda Lawrence, wife of D. H. Lawrence

Like the greatest virtue and the worst dogs, the fiercest hatred is silent.

Jean Paul Richter

I imagine one reason people cling to their hates so stubbornly is because they sense, once hate is gone, that they will be forced to deal with pain.

James Baldwin

Maybe there are times when an honest hatred serves us better than love corrupted by sentimentality, meretriciousness, sententiousness, cuteness.

Walker Percy

Passionate hatred can give meaning to an empty life.

Eric Hoffer

It is part of human nature to hate the man you have hurt.

Tacitus

I have three phobias which, could I mute them, would make my life as slick as a sonnet, but as dull as ditch water: I hate to go to bed, I hate to get up, and I hate to be alone.

Tallulah Bankhead

I have decided to stick with love. Hate is too great a burden to bear.

Martin Luther King, Jr

None of my 'clients' – not Eichmann, not Stangl, not Mengele, and not even Hitler or Stalin – was born a criminal. Somebody had to teach them to hate: maybe the society, maybe the politics, maybe just a Jewish prostitute.

Simon Wiesenthal, Nazi hunter

The worst sin towards our fellow creatures is not to hate them, but to be indifferent to them: that's the essence of inhumanity.

George Bernard Shaw

HEALTH AND ILLNESS

Next to gold and jewelry, health is the most important thing you can have.
Phyllis Diller

Health! The 'open sesame' to the sucker's purse.
Goodloe Bender, *The Road to Wellville*

We are all ill; but even a universal sickness implies an idea of health.
Lionel Trilling

Health consists of having the same diseases as one's neighbours.
Quentin Crisp

Take care of your health so that you may die young as late as possible.
Anon

I've never met a really healthy person who worried much about his health, or a really good person who worried much about his soul.
J. B. S. Haldane

The preservation of health is a duty. Few seem conscious that there is such a thing as physical morality.
Herbert Spencer

He who has health has hope, and he who has hope has everything.
Arabian proverb

Measure your health by your sympathy with morning and spring.
Henry David Thoreau

Nobody is sicker than the man who is sick on his day off.
E. C. McKenzie

To feel keenly the poetry of a morning's roses, one has to have just escaped from the claws of this vulture which we call sickness.
Henri Frédéric Amiel

When he is sick, every man wants his mother.
Philip Roth

Illness is the most heeded of doctors: to kindness and wisdom we make promises only; pain we obey.

Marcel Proust

There are two kinds of people; those who are always well and those who are always sick. Most of the evils of the world come from the first sort and most of the achievements from the second.

Louis Dudek

It is much more important to know what sort of patient has a disease than what sort of disease a patient has.

William Osler

If you treat a sick child like an adult and a sick adult like a child, everything usually works out pretty well.

Anon

A cough is a symptom, not a disease. Take it to your doctor and he can give you something serious to worry about.

Robert Morley

Asthma doesn't seem to bother me any more unless I'm around cigars or dogs. The thing that would bother me most would be a dog smoking a cigar.

Steve Allen

Much more is known about the stars than about rheumatism.

Henry S. Haskins

—We have a man with a large carrot stuck in his colon coming in.
—How did he ever swallow it whole?

Dr Carter and Lucy Knight, *ER*

Be true to your teeth and they won't be false to you.

Soupy Sales

Fact One: Cataract surgery is simple, painless and (except with implants) risk free ... the whole procedure is common, routine and nothing to worry about. Fact Two: Fact One applies only to cataracts on the eyes in somebody else's head.

Helene Hanff

Be afraid of the cancer, not the mammogram.

Nancy Reagan

There is probably no moment more appalling than that in which the tongue comes suddenly upon the ragged edge of a space from which the old familiar filling has disappeared. Robert Benchley

In middle life, the human back is spoiling for a technical knockout and will use the flimsiest excuse, even a sneeze, to fall apart. E. B. White

Do not show your wounded finger for everything will knock up against it. Baltasar Gracián

The worst time to have a heart attack is during a game of charades. Demetri Martin

Cancer tore through her body as if it were late for an important meeting with a lot of other successful diseases. Will Self

Cancer got me over unimportant fears, like getting old. Olivia Newton-John

An individual doesn't get cancer, a family does. Terry Tempest Williams

When they told me I needed a mastectomy, I thought of the thousands of luncheons and dinners I had attended where they slapped a name tag on my left bosom. I always smiled and said, 'Now, what shall we name the other one?' That would no longer be a problem. Erma Bombeck

A few weeks after my surgery, I went out to play catch with my golden retriever. When I bent over to pick up the ball, my prosthesis fell out. The dog snatched it, and I found myself chasing him down the road yelling, 'Hey, come back here with my breast!' Linda Ellerbee

I'm the only topless octogenarian in Washington. Alice Roosevelt Longworth, after a double mastectomy

I am not going to fight against death but for life. Norbert Segard

We 'need' cancer because, by the very fact of its insurability, it makes all other diseases, however virulent, not cancer. Gilbert Adair

Scientists now say you can get cancer from the radiation thrown off by your electric blanket. I'm so depressed. Here I am, fifty-six years old, and the most dangerous thing I've ever done in bed is turn on the blanket.

Anita Milner

We are all pre-cancerous.

George Carlin

Don't think of organ donations as giving up part of yourself to keep a total stranger alive. It's really a total stranger giving up almost all of themselves to keep part of you alive.

Anon

So I went to the doctor's and he said, 'You've got hypochondria.' I said, 'Not that as well!'

Tim Vine

The incurable ills are the imaginary ills.

Marie von Ebner-Eschenbach

Hope your labial carcinoma clears up soon. Funny, I'd for some time been trying to lick into shape an aphorism along the lines of, 'Every hypochondriac picks a winner in the end.' Kingsley Amis, letter to Philip Larkin

HEART

You know how they say we only use ten per cent of our brains? I think we only use ten per cent of our hearts.

John Beckwith, *Wedding Crashers*

There are no little events with the heart. It magnifies everything; it places in the same scales the fall of an empire and the dropping of a woman's glove, and almost always the glove weighs more than the empire. Honoré de Balzac

We must not always try to plumb the depths of the human heart; the truths it contains are among those that are best seen in half-light or in perspective.

François Chateaubriand

Most things break, including hearts. The lessons of life amount not to wisdom, but to scar tissue and callus.

Wallace Stegner

Don't trust your heart, it wants your blood. Stanislaw J. Lec

A woman's heart always has a burned mark. Louise Labé

People who have never had a broken heart will never understand dead roses, Tolstoy, airport lounges, Albinoni's *Adagio in G Minor*, neat brandy, the moon and drizzle. Wendy Harmer

If you haven't got any charity in your heart, you have the worst kind of heart trouble. Bob Hope

Stories are full of hearts being broken by love, but what really breaks a heart is taking away its dream – whatever the dream might be.
Pearl S. Buck

The best remedy for a bruised heart is not, as so many people seem to think, repose upon a manly bosom. Much more efficacious are honest work, physical activity, and the sudden acquisition of wealth.
Dorothy L. Sayers

The heart has its reasons, which reason does not know. Blaise Pascal

The heart wants what the heart wants. Woody Allen

A lion lurks in everyone's heart; awake him not. Bulgarian proverb

You should do something that will make your heart dance once a day. If you can't do that because you're too depressed, then do something that will make somebody else's heart dance. Yoko Ono

Throw your heart over the fence and the rest will follow.
Norman Vincent Peale

If seed in the black earth can turn into such beautiful roses, what might not the heart of man become in its long journey towards the stars?
G. K. Chesterton

HEAVEN

What a pity that the only way to heaven is in a hearse!   Stanislaw J. Lec

Do not ask God the way to heaven; He will show you the hardest way.
                                                        Stanislaw J. Lec

Probably no invention came more easily to man than heaven.
                                        Georg Christoph Lichtenberg

We may be surprised at the people we find in heaven. God has a soft spot
for sinners. His standards are quite low.   Archbishop Desmond Tutu

If I have any beliefs about immortality, it is that certain dogs I have known
will go to heaven, and very, very few persons.   James Thurber

For me, heaven is likely to be a bit of a come-down.
                Queen Elizabeth II, *A Question of Attribution*, by Alan Bennett

To be excited and at the same time satisfied; to desire and possess –
that has been described somewhere as the wise man's idea of heaven.
                                                        Alec Waugh

If I am not allowed to laugh in heaven, I don't want to go there.   Martin Luther

Heaven is a house with porch lights.   Ray Bradbury

Whatever the theologians might say about heaven being in a state of union
with God, I knew it consisted of an infinite library; and eternity was simply
what enabled one to read uninterruptedly for ever.   Dervla Murphy

Our Father, which art in heaven – stay there – and we will stay on earth –
which is sometimes so pretty.   Jacques Prévert

Most people can't bear to sit in church for an hour on Sundays. How are they supposed to live somewhere very similar to it for eternity?

Mark Twain

HELL

Dear God, I understand that if I fail to believe in you, I'll burn in hell for eternity. Thanks for being such a good sport about it.   Scott Dikker

God so loved the world that He made up his mind to damn a large majority of the human race.   Robert Ingersoll

My mother always said that in hell, you could see God, but He is ignoring you.   Janine Ditullion

In hell, all the messages you ever left on answering machines will be played back to you.   Judy Horacek

In hell they will bore you, in heaven you will bore them.   Katharine Whitehorn

Hell, madame, is to love no longer.   Georges Bernanos

Hell is other people.   Jean-Paul Sartre

We are all deep in a hell each moment of which is a miracle.   E. M. Cioran

Somewhere, and I can't find where, I read about an Eskimo hunter who asked the local missionary priest, 'If I did not know about God and sin, would I go to hell?' 'No,' said the priest, 'not if you did not know.' 'Then why,' asked the Eskimo earnestly, 'did you tell me?'   Annie Dillard

To work hard, to live hard, to die hard, and then go to hell after all would be too damn hard.   Carl Sandburg

There is probably no hell for authors in the next world. They suffer so much from critics and publishers in this.   Christian Bovee

Who will say with confidence that sexual abuse is more permanently
damaging to children than threatening them with the eternal and
unquenchable fires of hell?   Richard Dawkins

There is no hell. There is only France.   Frank Zappa

HELP

'Can I help you?' she enquired, in a manner that said she hoped she
wouldn't have to.   Liza Cody

Never reach out your hand unless you're willing to extend an arm.
                                                          Elizabeth Fuller

Hands that help are holier than lips that pray.   Sai Baba

I think you should use whatever power you have to try to help people who
need your help. Then we'd all be happy. Instead there's this bizarre notion
the government propounds that we should all run around selfishly
acquiring money. I just don't understand that.   Clive Stafford Smith

The best way to get on in the world is to make people believe it's to their
advantage to help you.   Jean de La Bruyère

Caring is a reflex. Someone slips, your arm goes out. A car is in the ditch,
you join the others and push. You live, you help.   Ram Dass

We're not primarily put on this earth to see through one another, but to see
one another through.   Peter De Vries

Great opportunities to help others seldom come, but small ones surround
us every day.   Sally Koch

It is one of the most beautiful compensations of this life that no man can
sincerely try to help another without helping himself.   Ralph Waldo Emerson

People seldom refuse help, if one offers it in the right way.   A. C. Benson

We cannot hold a torch to light another's path without brightening our own.
                                                          Ben Sweetland

Nothing makes one feel so strong as a call for help.   George MacDonald

There's nothing I wouldn't do for Bing, and there's nothing he wouldn't do
for me. And that's the way we go through life – doing nothing for each
other.   Bob Hope on Bing Crosby

HERO

The difference between a hero and a coward is one step sideways.
                                                          Gene Hackman

This, to me, is the ultimately heroic trait of ordinary people; they say no to
the tyrant and they calmly take the consequences of this resistance.
                                                          Philip K. Dick

The high sentiments always win in the end, the leaders who offer blood,
toil, tears and sweat always get more out of their followers than those who
offer safety and a good time. When it comes to the pinch, human beings
are heroic.   George Orwell

A light supper, a good night's sleep and a fine morning have often made a
hero out of the same man who, by indigestion, a restless night and a rainy
morning would have proved a coward.   G. K. Chesterton

The trouble with superheroes is what to do between phone booths.
                                                          Ken Kesey

Anyone can be heroic from time to time, but a gentleman is something you
have to be all the time.   Luigi Pirandello

Why should we honour those that die upon the field of battle? A man may show as reckless a courage in entering into the abyss of himself.

W.B. Yeats

We're all heroes if you catch us at the right moment.   **John Bubber,** *Hero*

HISTORY

All history, of course, is the history of wars.   **Penelope Lively**

The first lesson of history is that evil is good.   **Ralph Waldo Emerson**

History is a vast early warning system.   **Norman Cousins**

The farther backward you can look, the farther forward you are likely to see.   **Winston Churchill**

History is merely a list of surprises. It can only prepare us to be surprised yet again.   **Kurt Vonnegut**

More history is made by secret handshakes than by battles, bills and proclamations.   **John Barth**

For women, history does not exist. Murasaki, Sappho, and Madame Lafayette might be their own contemporaries.   **Cesare Pavese**

Empires rise and fall like the abdomen of God. It's just the universe breathing.   **Scoop Nisker**

Medieval life was artful, exquisite, and short. I think the shortness contributed to their living intensely.   **Madeleine Pelner Cosman**

History never looks like history when you are living through it. It always looks confusing and messy, and it always feels uncomfortable.

John W. Gardner

Perhaps in time the so-called Dark Ages will be thought of as including our own.
Georg Christoph Lichtenberg

If *The Flintstones* has taught us anything, it's that pelicans can be used to mix cement.
Homer Simpson

If I could have dinner with anyone who lived in history, it would depend on the restaurant.
Rodney Dangerfield

History must not be written with bias, and both sides must be given, even if there is only one side.
John Betjeman

History is so indifferently rich that a case for almost any conclusion from it can be made by a selection of instances.
Will Durant

The very ink with which all history is written is merely fluid prejudice.
Mark Twain

Political history is far too criminal a subject to be a fit thing to teach children.
W. H. Auden

In a certain sense, every single human soul has more meaning and value than the whole of history.
Nikolai Berdyaev

This time like all times is a very good one if we but know what to do with it.
Ralph Waldo Emerson

History is that thing you hastily delete as you log off the internet.
Anon

HOBBIES

Life would be tolerable but for its amusements.
George Bernard Shaw

I don't think anyone who has ever counted drinking amongst their hobbies has never kissed a man.
Dave Rowntree

Amusement is the happiness of those who cannot think.   **Alexander Pope**

Some people collect paperweights, or pre-Columbian figures, or old masters, or young mistresses, or tombstone rubbings, or five-minute recipes, or any of a thousand other things ... My own collection is sunrises; and I find that they have their advantages. Sunrises are usually handsome, they can't possibly be dusted, and they take only a little room, so long as it has a window to see them from.   **Peg Bracken**

Collecting interest does not count as a hobby.   **Citibank advert**

Beware the hobby that eats.   **Benjamin Franklin**

I want to make a jigsaw puzzle that's 40,000 pieces. And when you finish it, it says, 'Go outside.'   **Demetri Martin**

The finest amusements are the most pointless ones.   **Jacques Chardonne**

HOLIDAY

A vacation frequently means that the family goes away for a rest, accompanied by Mother, who sees that the others get it.   **Marcelene Cox**

To many people holidays are not voyages of discovery, but a ritual of reassurance.   **Philip Andrew Adams**

The weather is here, I wish you were beautiful.   **Jimmy Buffett**

When properly administered, vacations do not diminish productivity: for every week you're away and get nothing done, there's another when your boss is away and you get twice as much done.   **Daniel B. Luten**

There is probably no more obnoxious class of citizen, taken end for end, than the returning vacationist.   **Robert Benchley**

With me, a change of trouble is as good as a vacation.   **David Lloyd George**

HOME

—And make yourself at home.
—Hear that, Dad? You can lie around in your underwear and scratch
yourself.   **Mr Burns and Bart Simpson,** *The Simpsons*

Home is the best place when life begins to wobble.   **Elizabeth von Arnim**

Home is where you hang your head.   **Groucho Marx**

Home is where the heartache is.   **Kathy Lette**

Home is a great place – after all the other places have closed.   **Texas Guinan**

Home is where you come to when you have nothing better to do.
Margaret Thatcher

In Japan, homeless people are called *johatsu*, meaning wandering spirit or
one who has lost his identity.   **Jennifer Toth**

I do have a home. I just don't have a house to put it in.
Homeless ten-year-old girl

HONESTY

I have no idea what the mind of a low-life scoundrel is like, but I know
what the mind of an honest man is like: it is terrifying.   **Abel Hermant**

The only appropriate response to the question, 'Can I be frank?' is, 'Yes, if
I can be Barbara.'   **Fran Lebowitz**

Don't believe your friends when they ask you to be honest with them.
All they really want is to be maintained in the good opinion they have of
themselves.   **Albert Camus**

The person who is brutally honest enjoys the brutality quite as much as the honesty. Possibly more.
Richard Needham

The great consolation in life is to say what one thinks.
Voltaire

I have always thought that if we began for one moment to say what we thought, society would collapse.
Charles Augustin Sainte-Beuve

Don't call a man honest just because he never had the chance to steal.
Yiddish saying

Whatever else has been said about me is unimportant. When I sing, I believe I am honest.
Frank Sinatra

Solitaire is the only thing in life that demands absolute honesty.
Hugh Wheeler

HOPE

There is one thing which gives radiance to everything. It is the idea of something around the corner.
G. K. Chesterton

Hope is the feeling you have, that the feeling you have, isn't permanent.
Jean Kerr

The natural flights of the human mind are not from pleasure to pleasure, but from hope to hope.
Samuel Johnson

Hope is the thing with feathers that perches in the soul.
Emily Dickinson

If I keep a green bough in my heart, the singing bird will come.
Chinese proverb

In the kingdom of hope there is no winter.
Russian proverb

Extreme hopes are born of extreme misery.
John Milton

Amateurs hope, professionals work.   Garson Kanin

Hope is itself a species of happiness, and perhaps, the chief happiness
which this world affords.   Samuel Johnson

Take hope from the heart of man and you make him a beast of prey.   Ouida

Where there is no hope, we must invent it.   Albert Camus

Very seldom will a person give up on himself. He continues to have hope
because he knows he has the potential for change ... Yet people are very
quick to give up on friends, and especially on their spouses, to declare
them hopeless, and to either walk away or do nothing more than resign
themselves to a bad situation.   Hugh Prather

If one truly has lost hope, one would not be on hand to say so.   Eric Bentley

HUMOUR

Rest and laughter are the most spiritual and subversive acts of all.
                                                            Anne Lamott

Humor is how you change people's opinions, and if you can make
someone laugh, they'll listen, even if they hate you.   John Waters

I once asked Eric Morecambe what funny is. 'Wrong question,' he said.
'Just laugh.'   Simon Bates

Laugh? I nearly bought my own beer.   Anon

Make us laugh and you can pick all pockets.   Clemence Dane

A maid that laughs is half taken.   English proverb

We cannot really love anyone with whom we do not laugh.   Agnes Repplier

He who laughs most, learns best.

John Cleese

If I were to be given the opportunity to present a gift to the next generation, it would be the ability for each individual to learn to laugh at himself.

Charles M. Schulz

Laughter is wine for the soul – laughter soft, or loud and deep, tinged through with seriousness ... the hilarious declaration made by man that life is worth living.

Sean O'Casey

A difference of taste in jokes is a great strain on the affections.

George Eliot

Hearty laughter is a way to jog internally without having to go outdoors.

Norman Cousins

If I had no sense of humour, I would long ago have committed suicide.

Mahatma Gandhi

The love of truth lies at the root of much humor.

Robertson Davies

The secret source of humor itself is not joy, but sorrow. There is no humor in heaven.

Mark Twain

You can't write comedy in California. It's not depressing enough.

Sy Benson, *My Favorite Year*

You can read Kant by yourself, if you wanted to; but you must share a joke with someone else.

Robert Louis Stevenson

It's funny – there's nothing that stops you laughing like the sight of other people laughing about something else.

Michael Frayn

Men will confess to treason, murder, arson, false teeth, or a wig. How many of them will own up to a lack of humor?

Frank Moore Colby

Funny noises are not funny.   *The Simpsons*

Why are men impersonating women funny while women impersonating
men are not? It is a matter of gravity. A heavy thing trying to become
lighter is automatically funnier than a light thing trying to become heavy.
                                                                        Arlene Croce

If only Groucho had written 'Das Kapital'.   **Graffiti**

If you tell a joke in the field, but nobody laughs, was it a joke?   Rod Schmidt

Beware of those who laugh at everything or nothing.   Arnold Glasgow

The people who fear humor – and they are many – are suspicious of its
power to present things in unexpected lights, to question received opinions
and to suggest unforeseen possibilities.   Robertson Davies

A person reveals his character by nothing so clearly as the joke he resents.
                                                          Georg Christoph Lichtenberg

The tragedy of men is that they live in this ghastly wasteland of
secondhand jokes.   Jonathan Miller

A joke isn't yours. It's used and you don't know where it's been.
                                                                     Ricky Gervais

Nobody in love has a sense of humor.
                                                                     S. N. Behrman

The aim of a joke is not to degrade the human being but to remind him
that he is already degraded.   George Orwell

Imagination was given to man to compensate him for what he is not.
A sense of humour was provided to console him for what he is.
                                                                    Horace Walpole

In the end, everything is a gag.   Charlie Chaplin

HUNTING

I ask people why they have deer heads on their walls, and they say, 'Because it's such a beautiful animal.' Well, I think my mother's attractive, but I have photographs of her. Ellen DeGeneres

When I was twelve, I went hunting with my father and we shot a bird. He was laying there and something struck me. Why do we call this fun to kill this creature who was as happy as I was when I woke up this morning? Marv Levy

It is very strange, and very melancholy, that the paucity of human pleasures should persuade us ever to call hunting one of them. Samuel Johnson

Opponents of fox hunting foolishly suggest that drag hunting would be an adequate replacement for our sport. Well, I for one would take no pleasure from hunting foxes dressed in women's clothing. E. B. Poole, *Viz*

He who hunts two hares leaves one and loses the other. Japanese proverb

Until the lions have their historians, tales of hunting will always glorify the hunter. African proverb

My sister has a social conscience now. She still wears her fur coat, but across the back she embroidered a sampler that says 'Rest in Peace'. Julia Willis

I'm against hunting – in fact, I'm a hunt saboteur. I go out the night before and shoot the fox. Peter Kay

HURRY

Along with being forever on the move, one is forever in a hurry, leaving things inadvertently behind – friend or fishing tackle, old raincoat or old allegiance. Louis Kronenberger

What is this life if, full of care, we have no time to stand and stare?

W. H. Davies

In the old days, if a person missed the stagecoach, he was content to wait a day or two for the next one. Nowadays, we feel frustrated if we miss one section of a revolving door.

Anon

Being in a hurry seems so fiercely important when you yourself are the hurrier and so comically ludicrous when it is someone else.

Christopher Morley

One of the great disadvantages of hurry is that it takes such a long time.

G. K. Chesterton

When you want to hurry something, that means you no longer care about it and want to get on to other things.

Robert M. Pirsig

The microwave oven is one of the modern objects that convey the most elemental feeling of power over the passing seconds ... If you suffer from hurry sickness in its most advanced stages, you may find yourself punching 88 seconds instead of 90 because it is faster to tap the same digit twice.

James Gleick

Instant gratification takes too long.

Carrie Fisher

People in a hurry cannot think, cannot grow, nor can they decay. They are preserved in a state of perpetual puerility.

Eric Hoffer

I have discovered that all human evil comes from this: man's being unable to sit still in a room.

Blaise Pascal

It is a great art to saunter.

Henry David Thoreau

Always take time to stop and smell the roses, and sooner or later, you'll inhale a bee.

Anon

HYPOCRISY

A man generally has two reasons for doing a thing. One that sounds good, and a real one.
J. Pierpoint Morgan

I hope you have not been leading a double life, pretending to be wicked and really being good all the time. That would be hypocrisy.
Oscar Wilde

They are not all saints who use holy water.
English proverb

When you see a great deal of religion displayed in his shop window, you may depend on it that he keeps a very small stock of it within.
Charles Spurgeon

All reformers, however strict their social conscience, live in houses just as big as they can pay for.
Logan Pearsall Smith

Never to talk about oneself is a very refined form of hypocrisy.
Friedrich Nietzsche

Most people have seen worse things in private than they pretend to be shocked at in public.
E. W. Howe

Whatever you condemn, you have done yourself.
Georg Groddeck

Spread yourself upon his bosom publicly, whose heart you would eat in private.
Ben Jonson

Hypocrisy is the Vaseline of political intercourse.
Pieter-Dirk Uys

The true hypocrite is the one who ceases to perceive his deception, the one who lies with sincerity.
André Gide

If I were two-faced, would I be wearing this one?
Anon

We are what we pretend to be, so we must be careful what we pretend to be.
Kurt Vonnegut

IDEAS

Every man is wise when attacked by a mad dog; fewer when pursued by a mad woman; only the wisest survive when attacked by a mad notion.

Robertson Davies

Good ideas, like good pickles, are crisp, enduring, and devilishly hard to make.

Rushworth M. Kidder

Don't trust the brilliant idea unless it survives the hangover.

J. Breslin

All the really good ideas I ever had came to me while I was milking a cow.

Grant Wood

No one has ever had an idea in a dress suit.

Frederick G. Banting

Ideas are like rabbits. You get a couple and learn how to handle them, and pretty soon you have a dozen.

John Steinbeck

Don't worry about people stealing your ideas. If your ideas are any good, you'll have to ram them down people's throats.

Howard Aiken

Never invest in an idea you can't illustrate with a crayon.

Peter Lynch

Nothing is more dangerous than an idea, when you have only one idea.

Émile-Auguste Chartier

The clash of ideas is the sound of freedom.

Lady Bird Johnson

In a war of ideas it is people who get killed.

Stanislaw J. Lec

An idea is a greater monument than a cathedral.

Clarence Darrow

No army can withstand the strength of an idea whose time has come.

Victor Hugo

IDLE

There is no pleasure in having nothing to do; the fun is in having lots to do and not doing it.
Mary Wilson Little

—But don't you hate yourself for being so idle?
—Oh yes.
—Why don't you do something about it?
—Because I dislike hating myself slightly less than I dislike effort.
Reporter and Kenneth Tynan

Never do anything standing that you can do sitting, or anything sitting that you can do lying down.
Chinese proverb

Whenever there is a hard job to be done I assign it to a lazy man; he is sure to find an easy way of doing it.
Walter Chrysler

Generally speaking anybody is more interesting doing nothing than doing something.
Gertrude Stein

Of the two smartest creatures on the earth, man and the dolphin, each thought they were smarter than the other. Man thought he was smarter because he built many things and did much work, while the dolphins just played all day. The dolphins thought they were smarter for the same reason.
Gershon Legman

If you can spend a perfectly useless afternoon in a perfectly useless manner, you have learned how to live.
Lin Yutang

Note to self: stop doing anything.
Homer Simpson

Take a rest; a field that has rested gives a bountiful crop.
Ovid

IGNORANCE

We went out on the streets of Los Angeles and asked people, 'How was Mount Rushmore formed?' The most popular answer was, 'Erosion.'

Jay Leno

Ignorance is when you don't know something and somebody finds it out.

Jethro Burns

Nothing is more terrible than to see ignorance in action.

Johann Wolfgang von Goethe

Ignorance is the soil in which belief in miracles grows.   Robert Ingersoll

A great deal of intelligence can be invested in ignorance when the need for illusion is deep.

Saul Bellow

According to a charming law of nature which is evident even in the most sophisticated societies, we live in complete ignorance of whatever we love.

Marcel Proust

It is fortunate that each generation does not comprehend its own ignorance. We are thus enabled to call our ancestors barbarous.

Charles Dudley Warner

ILLUSION

What is actually happening is often less important than what appears to be happening.

William V. Shannon

Anyone who can handle a needle convincingly can make us see a thread which is not there.

E. H. Gombrich

We read the world wrong and say that it deceives us.   Rabindranath Tagore

The more intelligent and cultured a man is, the more subtly he can humbug himself.
Carl Jung

Our greatest illusion is to believe that we are what we think ourselves to be.
Henri Frédéric Amiel

Losing an illusion makes you wiser than finding a truth.
Ludwig Borne

Rob the average man of his life-illusion and you rob him of his happiness at one stroke.
Henrik Ibsen

After an hour or so in the woods looking for mushrooms, Dad said, 'Well, we can always go and buy some real ones.'
John Cage

IMAGINATION

You see things; and you say 'Why?' But I dream things that never were; and say 'Why not?'
George Bernard Shaw

Imagination is the eye of the soul.
Joseph Joubert

Imagination is the voice of daring. If there is anything godlike about God it is that. He dared to imagine everything.
Henry Miller

A rock pile ceases to be a rock pile the moment a single man contemplates it, bearing within him the image of a cathedral.
Antoine de Saint-Exupéry

Imagination is more important than knowledge.
Albert Einstein

Sometimes I feel like a figment of my own imagination.
Lily Tomlin

Let us leave pretty women to men without imagination.
Marcel Proust

Imagination is what sits up with Mum and Dad the first time their teenager stays out late.
Lane Olinghouse

I doubt that the imagination can be suppressed. If you truly eradicated it in a child, he would grow up to be an eggplant.
Ursula Le Guin

IMMORTALITY

All men think all men mortal but themselves.
Edward Young

Melnick says that the soul is immortal and lives on after the body drops away, but if my soul exists without my body, I am convinced all my clothes will be loose-fitting.
Woody Allen

Immortality: a fate worse than death.
Edgar A. Shoaff

The fact of having been born is a bad augury for immortality.
George Santayana

On the neck of a giraffe a flea begins to believe in immortality.
Stanislaw J. Lec

To himself everyone is immortal; he may know that he is going to die, but he can never know that he is dead.
Samuel Butler

I do not believe in personal immortality; it seems so unnecessary. Show me one man who deserves to live for ever.
Edward Abbey

If something comes to life in others because of you, then you have made an approach to immortality.
Norman Cousins

My ambition is to become immortal – and then to die.

Parvulesco, *A Bout de Souffle*

Neither can I believe that the individual survives the death of his body, although feeble souls harbour such thoughts through fear or ridiculous egotism.

Albert Einstein

IMPORTANCE

Life is like a field of newly fallen snow. Where I choose to walk, every step will show.

Denis Waitley

It matters immensely. The slightest sound matters. The most momentary rhythm matters. You can do as you please, yet everything matters.

Wallace Stevens

A toothache will cost a battle, a drizzle cancel an insurrection.

Vladimir Nabokov

The most important things to say are those which often I did not think necessary for me to say – because they seemed to me too obvious.

André Gide

Whatever you think matters – doesn't. Follow this rule, and it will add decades to your life.

Roger Rosenblatt

We all lead more pedestrian lives than we think we do. The boiling of an egg is sometimes more important than the boiling of a love affair in the end.

Lillian Hellman

Everything is worth precisely as much as a belch, the difference being that a belch is more satisfying.

Ingmar Bergman

There are no passengers on spaceship earth. We are all crew.

Marshall McLuhan

IMPOSSIBLE AND POSSIBLE

If someone says 'can't', that shows you what to do.   John Cage

I believe because it is impossible.   Tertullian

The Difficult is that which can be done today. The Impossible is that which takes a little longer.   George Santayana

Start by doing what is necessary, then what's possible, and suddenly you're doing the impossible.   St Francis of Assisi

It is necessary; therefore it is possible.   C. A. Borghese

All things are possible except skiiing through a revolving door.   Murphy's Law

Never tell a young person that something cannot be done. God may have been waiting for centuries for somebody ignorant enough of the impossible to do that thing.   Dr J. A. Holmes

The world is moving so fast these days that the man who says it can't be done is generally interrupted by someone doing it.   Harry Fosdick

Achieving the impossible means only that the boss will add it to your regular duties.   Doug Larson

If a thing can be done, why do it?   Gertrude Stein

All things are possible once enough human beings realize that everything is at stake.   Norman Cousins

IMPROVEMENT

Yesterday I was a dog. Today I'm a dog. Tomorrow I'll probably still be a dog. Sigh! There's so little hope for advancement.   **Charles M. Schulz,** *Snoopy*

Put cream and sugar on a fly and it tastes very much like a raspberry.
E. W. Howe

You don't get anything clean without getting something else dirty.
Cecil Baxter

I've upped my standards. Now, up yours.   **Pat Paulsen**

INDIFFERENCE

The opposite of love is not hate; it's indifference.   **Claire Rayner**

Most of us have no real loves and no real hatreds. Blessed is love, less blessed is hatred, but thrice accursed is that indifference which is neither one nor the other.   **Mark Rutherford**

Impartiality is a pompous name for indifference, which is an elegant name for ignorance.   **G. K. Chesterton**

Indifference may not wreck a man's life at any one turn, but it will destroy him with a kind of dry-rot in the long run.   **Bliss Carmen**

Frankly, my dear, I don't give a damn.   **Rhett Butler,** *Gone With the Wind*

INDIVIDUALITY

But Marge, I'm not like other men! That's why you buy my pants at that special store!
Homer Simpson

Always remember that you are absolutely unique. Just like everyone else.
Margaret Mead

There is no one alive who is Youer than You.
Dr Seuss

Once in a while it really hits people that they don't have to experience the world in the way they have been told to.
Alan Keightley

Read, every day, something no one else is reading. Think, every day, something no one else is thinking. Do, every day, something no one else would be silly enough to do. It is bad for the mind to continually be part of unanimity.
Christopher Morley

Inside my empty bottle I was constructing a lighthouse while all the others were making ships.
Charles Simic

Always be a first-rate version of yourself, instead of a second-rate version of somebody else.
Judy Garland

From now on I'll connect the dots my own way.
Bill Watterson

If a man does not keep pace with his companions, perhaps it is because he hears a different drummer.
Henry David Thoreau

Do not go where the path may lead, go instead where there is no path and leave a trail.
Ralph Waldo Emerson

Oh Charlie Brown, of all the Charlie Browns in the world, you are the Charlie Browniest.
Linus Van Pelt, *A Charlie Brown Christmas*

Each of us must make our own true way, and when we do, that way will express the universal way.
Suzuki Roshi

INFORMATION

Everybody gets so much information all day long that they lose their common sense.
Gertrude Stein

Where is the knowledge we have lost in information?
T. S. Eliot

So much has already been written about everything that you can't find out anything about it.
James Thurber

I find that a great part of the information I have was acquired by looking up something and finding something else on the way.
Franklin P. Adams

Information about money is more important than money itself.
Walter Wriston

Google Announces Plan To Destroy All Information It Can't Index
Spoof headline, *The Onion* online newspaper

INNOCENCE

Until Eve gave him the apple, Adam didn't even know he wasn't wearing underpants.
Paula Yates

It is only rarely that one can see in a little boy the promise of a man, but one can always see in a little girl the threat of a woman.
Alexandre Dumas

The knowingness of little girls is hidden underneath their curls.

Phyllis McGinley

The truly innocent are those who not only are guiltless themselves but who think others are. Josh Billings

Nobody ever was – or ever again will be – as green as I was the day I landed in New York. That shade has been discontinued. Carolyn Kenmore

It is well for the heart to be naïve and for the mind not to be. Anatole France

INSECT

If Noah had been very wise, he would have swatted those two flies. Anon

A fly is as untamable as a hyena. Ralph Waldo Emerson

Worms have played a more important part in the history of the world than humans would at first suppose. Charles Darwin

Nothing seems to please a fly so much as to be taken for a currant; and if it can be baked in a cake and palmed off on the unwary, it dies happy. Mark Twain

Ants are so much like human beings as to be an embarrassment. They farm fungi, raise aphids as livestock, launch armies into war, use chemical sprays to alarm and confuse enemies, capture slaves, engage in child labor, exchange information ceaselessly. They do everything but watch television.

Lewis Thomas

If all mankind were to disappear, the world would regenerate back to the rich state of equilibrium that existed ten thousand years ago. If insects were to vanish, the environment would collapse into chaos.

Edward O. Wilson

The ant is knowing and wise, but he doesn't know enough to take a vacation.

Clarence Day

What the caterpillar calls the end of the world, the master calls a butterfly.

Richard Bach

What would be left of our tragedies if an insect were to present us his?

E. M. Cioran

Butterflies ... not quite birds, as they are not quite flowers, mysterious and fascinating as are all indeterminate creatures.

Elizabeth Goudge

INSPIRATION

—Which comes first, the lyrics or the tune?
—First comes the phone call.

Interviewer and Sammy Cahn, composer

Inspiration is a hoax fabricated by poets for their own self-importance.

Jean Anouilh

Inspiration is the impact of a fact on a well-prepared mind.

Louis Pasteur

You cannot wait for inspiration. You have to go after it with a club.

Jack London

The ultimate inspiration is the deadline.

Nolan Bushnell

Inspirations never go in for long engagements; they demand immediate marriage to action.

Brendan Francis

When you do not know what you are doing and what you are doing is the best – that is inspiration.

Robert Bresson

I could never tell where inspiration begins and impulse leaves off. I suppose the answer is in the outcome. If your hunch proves a good one, you were inspired; if it proves bad, you are guilty of yielding to thoughtless impulse.

Beryl Markham

Here is the secret of inspiration: tell yourself that thousands and tens of thousands of people, not very intelligent and certainly no more intelligent than the rest of us, have mastered problems as difficult as those that now baffle you.

William Feather

INSTINCT

You cannot teach a crab to walk straight.

Aristophanes

The centipede was quite happy until a toad in fun said, 'Pray, which leg goes after which?' That worked her mind to such a pitch, she lay distracted in a ditch considering how to run.

Mrs Edward Craster

Follow your instincts. That's where true wisdom manifests itself.

Oprah Winfrey

Sweet instinct leaps; slow reason feebly climbs.

Edward Young

INTELLECTUAL

The course of every intellectual, if he pursues his journey long and unflinchingly enough, ends in the obvious, from which the non-intellectuals have never stirred.
Aldous Huxley

A good reliable set of bowels is worth more to a man than any quantity of brains.
Henry Wheeler Shaw

An intellectual is a man who doesn't know how to park a bike. **Spiro Agnew**

I've been called many things, but never an intellectual. **Tallulah Bankhead**

Intellectuals can tell themselves anything, sell themselves any bill of goods, which is why they were so often patsies for the ruling classes in 19th-century France and England, or 20th-century Russia and America.
Lillian Hellman

What is a highbrow? It is a man who has found something more interesting than women.
Edgar Wallace

Clever people seem not to feel the natural pleasure of bewilderment, and are always answering questions when the chief relish of a life is to go on asking them.
Frank Moore Colby

I think that those of us who are what are called intellectuals make a terrible mistake in overvaluing the yen we have for the arts, books, etc. There is a sweet, fine quality in life that has nothing to do with this, and more and more I find myself valuing myself with those people.
Sherwood Anderson

An intellectual is someone whose mind watches itself.
Albert Camus

The intellectual is constantly betrayed by his vanity. Godlike he blandly assumes that he can express everything in words; whereas the things one loves, lives, and dies for are not, in the last analysis, completely expressible in words.
Anne Morrow Lindbergh

INTELLIGENCE

We're a planet of nearly six billion ninnies living in a civilization that was designed by a few thousand amazingly smart deviants.   **Scott Adams**

Intelligence is quickness in seeing things as they are.   **George Santayana**

We should take care not to make the intellect our god; it has, of course, powerful muscles, but no personality.   **Albert Einstein**

If the Aborigine drafted an IQ test, all of Western civilization would presumably flunk it.   **Stanley Garn**

So far as I can remember, there is not one word in the Gospels in praise of intelligence.   **Bertrand Russell**

It is not clear that intelligence has any long-term survival value.   **Stephen Hawking**

Intelligence, like fire, is a power that is neither good nor bad in itself but rather takes its virtue, its moral colouring, from its application.   **Roger Kimball**

Life gets harder the smarter you get, the more you know.   **Katharine Hepburn**

Mother is far too clever to understand anything she does not like.

Arnold Bennett

Women are brighter than men, that's true. But it should be kept very quiet or it ruins the whole racket.   **Anita Loos**

No matter how smart you are, you spend much of your day being an idiot.   **Scott Adams**

INTERNET

Oh, they have the internet on computers now.

Homer Simpson

The internet is becoming the town square for the global village of tomorrow.

Bill Gates

There's so much darn porn on the internet, I never get out of the house.

Jack Nicholson

We've all heard that a million monkeys banging on a million typewriters will eventually reproduce the entire works of Shakespeare. Now, thanks to the internet, we know this is not true.

Robert Silensky

The internet is the world's largest library. It's just that all the books are on the floor.

John Allen Paulos

The internet is an elite operation. Most of the population of the world has never even made a phone call.

Noam Chomsky

The net is a waste of time, and that's exactly what's right about it.

William Gibson

For me, the internet is just yet another way of being rejected by women.

George Pappas, *You've Got Mail*

INVENTION

Invention, my dear friends, is ninety-three per cent perspiration, six per cent electricity, four per cent evaporation, and two per cent butterscotch ripple.

Willy Wonka, *Willy Wonka & the Chocolate Factory*

Everything has been thought of before, but the problem is to think of it again.

Johann Wolfgang von Goethe

Name the greatest of all inventors. Accident.   Mark Twain

—What is the use of a new invention?
—What is the use of a newborn child?   Anon and Benjamin Franklin

If the Nobel Prize was awarded by a woman, it would go to the inventor of
the dimmer switch.   Kathy Lette

I doubt whether all mechanical inventions yet made have lightened the
day's toil of any human being.   John Stuart Mill

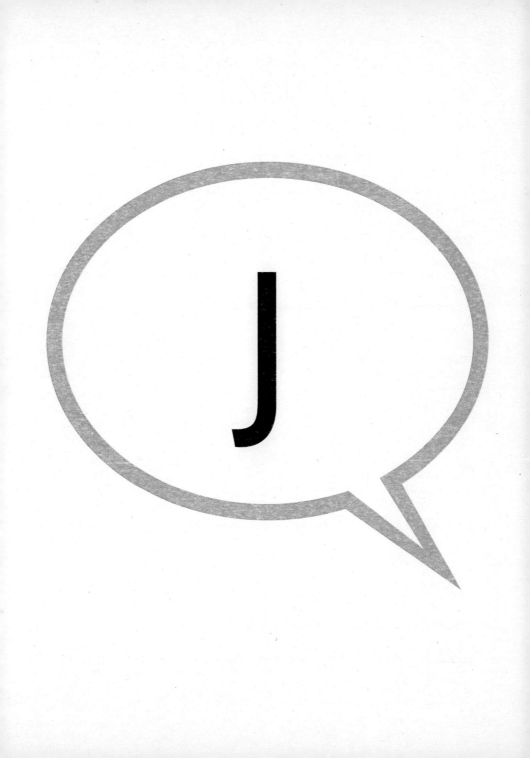

JAZZ

If you have to ask what jazz is, you'll never know.   Louis Armstrong

Jazz and love are the hardest things to describe from rationale.   Mel Torme

Jazz has always been like the kind of man you wouldn't want your daughter to associate with.   Duke Ellington

Jazz music is an intensified feeling of nonchalance.   Françoise Sagan

Jazz is five guys playing different songs.   Steve McGrew

A jazz musician is a juggler who uses harmonies instead of oranges.   Benny Green

First you master your instrument, then you master the music, then you forget all that shit and just play.   Charlie Parker

I'll play it first and tell you what it is later.   Miles Davis

If you don't live it, it won't come out of your horn.   Charlie Parker

There are no wrong notes.   Thelonius Monk

Beiderbecke took out a silver cornet. He put it to his lips and blew a phrase. The sound came out like a girl saying yes.   Eddie Condon

JEALOUSY

Jealousy is all the fun you think they had.   Erica Jong

Jealousy is an ugly thing, Dorothy. And so are you in anything backless.
          Sophia Petrillo, *The Golden Girls*

Jealousy has the 'lousy' built right in. Jason Love

Al Jolson turned the faucets on full in his dressing room when other people in the show he was in were getting applause. Carol Channing

A jealous man always finds more than he is looking for. Madeleine de Scudéry

Jealousy, that dragon which slays love under the pretence of keeping it alive. Havelock Ellis

Jealousy would be far less torturous if we understood that love is a passion entirely unrelated to our merits. Paul Elridge

In jealousy, there is more self-love than love. La Rochefoucauld

It's too big a world to be in competition with everyone. The only person who I have to be better than is myself. Colonel Potter, *M*A*S*H*

JEW

They say we Jews are mean, greedy and all we think about is money. I wish I had five pounds for every time I've heard that. Ivor Dembina

Jesus was a Jew, yes, but only on his mother's side. Archie Bunker, *All in the Family*

If my Catholic boyfriend and I ever have a kid, we'll just be honest with it. We'll say that Mommy is one of God's chosen people, and Daddy believes that Jesus is magic! Sarah Silverman

I know, God, we are your chosen people. But once in a while, can't you choose someone else? Tevye, *Fiddler on the Roof*

The only advantage I have found in being Jewish is that I can be openly anti-Semitic. Kirk Douglas

Like all Jewish girls, I left home in order to eat pork and take birth control pills.

Roseanne

Who hates the Jews more than the Jew?

Henry Miller

As everyone knows, where there are two Jews there are three opinions.

Rabbi Anthony Bayfield

It is a family joke that when I was a tiny child I turned from the window out of which I was watching a snowstorm, and hopefully asked, 'Momma, do we believe in winter?'

Philip Roth

I suppose the nearest equivalent to a bar mitzvah in terms of emotional build-up would probably not even be one's wedding day, but one's coronation.

Maureen Lipman

For me this is the vital litmus test: no intellectual society can flourish where a Jew feels even slightly uneasy.

Paul Johnson

JOURNALISM

In city rooms and in the bars where newspeople drink, you can find out what's going on. You can't find it in the papers.

Molly Irvins

If I'd written all the truth I knew for the past ten years, about 600 people – including me – would be rotting in prison cells from Rio to Seattle today. Absolute truth is a very rare and dangerous commodity in the context of professional journalism.

Hunter S. Thompson

Have you noticed that life, real honest-to-goodness life, with murders and catastrophes and fabulous inheritances, happens almost exclusively in the newspapers?

Jean Anouilh

One of the most valuable philosophical features of journalism is that it realizes that truth is not a solid but a fluid.

Christopher Morley

Never believe in mirrors or newspapers. Tom Stoppard

As independent as our advertisers allow us to be.

Motto of an American newspaper

Once a newspaper touches a story, the facts are lost for ever, even to the protagonists. Norman Mailer

Instead of being arrested, as we stated, for kicking his wife down a flight of stairs and hurling a lighted kerosene lamp after her, the Revd James P. Wellman died unmarried four years ago.

Correction in an American newspaper

Newspapers are unable, seemingly, to discriminate between a bicycle accident and the collapse of civilization. George Bernard Shaw

Newspapers always excite curiosity. No one ever lays one down without a feeling of disappointment. Charles Lamb

A newspaper is not just for reporting the news, it's to get people mad enough to do something about it. Mark Twain

Four hostile newspapers are more to be feared than a thousand bayonets.

Napoleon Bonaparte

How to deal with the press: say nowt, win it, then talk your head off.

Brian Clough, football manager

JOURNALIST

Just because your voice reaches halfway around the world doesn't mean you are wiser than when it reached only to the end of the bar.

Edward R. Murrow

The secret of success is an absolute ungovernable curiosity. Larry King

In the real world, the right thing never happens in the right place and the right time. It is the job of journalists and historians to make it appear that it has.   Mark Twain

The first law of journalism is to confirm existing prejudice, rather than contradict it.   Linda Ellerbee

When you write never get too fancy. Never put one foot on the mantelpiece, and be sure your style is so honest that you can put the word *shit* in any sentence without fear of consequence.

Newspaper Editor to Ben Hecht

Journalists say a thing that they know isn't true, in the hope that if they keep on saying it long enough it will be true.   Arnold Bennett

Being a newspaper columnist is like being married to a nymphomaniac. It's great for the first two weeks.   Lewis Grizzard

I always warn aspiring reporters to observe three basic rules: 1. Never trust an editor. 2. Never trust an editor. 3. Never trust an editor.

Edna Buchanan

Never lose your sense of the superficial.   Lord Northcliffe

Remember, you only have that space because some advertiser wouldn't buy it.   **Herb Caen to newspaper columnists**

A person does feel sheepish picking on journalists, a class already so richly despised that if a planeload of them crashed in flames, most people would smile from pure reflex.   Garrison Keillor

JOY

Yabba-dabba-doo!

Fred Flintstone, *The Flintstones*

When you jump for joy, beware that no one moves the ground from beneath your feet.

Stanislaw J. Lec

Joy and sorrow are inseparable ... together they come and when one sits alone with you ... remember that the other is asleep upon your bed.

Kahlil Gibran

I cannot believe that the inscrutable universe turns on an axis of suffering; surely the strange beauty of the world must somewhere rest on pure joy.

Louise Bogan

Know that joy is rarer, more difficult, and more beautiful than sadness. Once you make this all-important discovery, you must embrace joy as a moral obligation.

André Gide

It is strange what a contempt men have for the joys that are offered them freely.

Georges Duhamel

This is the true joy in life, the being used for a purpose recognized by yourself as a mighty one; the being thoroughly worn out before you are thrown on the scrap heap; the being a force of nature instead of a feverish selfish little clod of ailments and grievances complaining that the world will not devote itself to making you happy.

George Bernard Shaw

Then there's the joy of getting your desk clean, and knowing that all your letters are answered, and you can see the wood on it again. Lady Bird Johnson

I find my joy of living in the fierce and ruthless battles of life, and my pleasure comes from learning something.

August Strindberg

Discover that we are capable of solitary joy and having experienced it, know that we have touched the core of self.

Barbara Lazear Ascher

Grief can take care of itself, but to get the full value of a joy you must have somebody to divide it with.
Mark Twain

Ideology, politics and journalism, which luxuriate in failure, are impotent in the face of hope and joy.
P. J. O'Rourke

We should all do what, in the long run, gives us joy, even if it is only picking grapes or sorting the laundry.
E. B. White

Keep knocking and the joy inside will eventually open a window and look out to see who's there.
Rumi

JUSTICE

I have found men more kind than I expected, and less just.
Samuel Johnson

The world is not a place where good is rewarded and evil is punished.
Colin Semper

Since when do you have to agree with people to defend them from injustice?
Lillian Hellman

Courtroom: a place where Jesus Christ and Judas Iscariot would be equals, with the betting odds in favour of Judas.
H. L. Mencken

Corn can't expect justice from a court composed of chickens.   African proverb

Everyone wants to see justice done, to somebody else.   Bruce Cockburn

KINDNESS

My religion is very simple – my religion is kindness.   **The Dalai Lama**

What wisdom can you find that is greater than kindness?
Jean Jacques Rousseau

If someone were to pay you ten cents for every kind word you ever spoke and collect five cents for every unkind word, would you be rich or poor?
Anon

You have not lived a perfect day, even though you have earned your money, unless you have done something for someone who will never be able to repay you.   **Ruth Smeltzer**

Truth generally is kindness, but where the two diverge and collide, kindness should override truth.   **Samuel Butler**

The best portion of a good man's life – his little, nameless, unremembered acts of kindness and of love.   **William Wordsworth**

Kindness is in our power, even when fondness is not.   **Samuel Johnson**

No act of kindness is ever wasted, no matter how small.   **Aesop**

Kindness isn't sacrifice so much as it is being considerate for the feelings of others, sharing happiness, the unselfish thought, the spontaneous and friendly act, forgetfulness of our own present interests.   **Carl Holmes**

Kindness can become its own motive. We are made kind by being kind.
Eric Hoffer

Men are cruel, but man is kind.   **Rabindranath Tagore**

I think women need kindness more than love. When one human being is kind to another it's a very deep matter.   **Alice Childress**

Men often treat others worse than they treat themselves, but they rarely treat anyone better. It is the height of folly to expect consideration and decency from a person who mistreats himself.   Thomas Szasz

—Do you have any beauty secrets?
—For attractive lips, speak words of kindness.
                                        Interviewer and Audrey Hepburn

Kindness is the golden thread that holds society together.
                                        Johann Wolfgang von Goethe

Be kind, for everyone you meet is fighting a harder battle.   Plato

Let us be kinder to one another.   Aldous Huxley, last words

KISS

Mrs Norton is perhaps the most beautiful, but the Duchess, to my mind, is the more kissable.   Charles Dickens

Never let a fool kiss you or a kiss fool you.   Joey Adams

Were kisses all the joy in bed,
One woman would another wed.
                    William Shakespeare, *Sonnets to Sundry Notes of Music, IV*

Kissing is pretty much an opening act. It's like the stand-up comedian you have to sit through before Pink Floyd comes out.   Chandler Bing, *Friends*

A lawful kiss is never worth a stolen one.   Guy de Maupassant

When you entered a room, you had to kiss Frank Sinatra's ring. I wouldn't have minded, but he kept it in his back pocket.   Don Rickles

KNOWLEDGE

Knowledge is power – if you know it about the right person.

Ethel Watts Mumford

I want to know God's thoughts … the rest are details.　　Albert Einstein

Men are four:
He who knows not and knows not he knows not: he is a fool – shun him;
He who knows not and knows he knows not: he is simple – teach him;
He who knows and knows not he knows: he is asleep – wake him;
He who knows and knows he knows: he is wise – follow him.

Lady Burton

To know is not to be wise. To know how to use knowledge is to have wisdom.　　Charles Spurgeon

Knowledge is the antidote to fear.　　Ralph Waldo Emerson

The afternoon knows what the morning never suspected.　　Swedish proverb

The next best thing to knowing something is knowing where to find it.

Samuel Johnson

It wasn't until late in life that I discovered how easy it was to say, 'I don't know.'　　Somerset Maugham

The public have an insatiable curiosity to know everything, except what is worth knowing.　　Oscar Wilde

We are here and it is now. Further than that, all human knowledge is moonshine.　　H. L. Mencken

I've learned one thing – people who know the least anyways seem to know it the loudest.　　Andy Capp

LANGUAGE

One does not inhabit a country; one inhabits a language. That is our country, our fatherland – and no other. E. M. Cioran

Tell me how much a nation knows about its own language, and I will tell you how much that nation cares about its own identity. John Ciardi

In what language do you think? Question on the Swiss census form, 2001

Language exerts hidden powers, like a moon on the tides. Rita Mae Brown

Language is the pedigree of nations. Samuel Johnson

I personally think we developed language because of our deep inner need to complain. Jane Wagner

Language was only needed when unattractive people were born so they could be commented on. Jack McFarland, *Will and Grace*

To have another language is to possess a second soul. Charlemagne

Life is a foreign language; all men mispronounce it. Christopher Morley

I think the interpreter is the harder to understand of the two. Richard Brinsley Sheridan

The sum of human wisdom is not contained in any one language, and no single language is CAPABLE of expressing all forms and degrees of human comprehension. Ezra Pound

I am French but I like speaking English for a change. You use fewer facial muscles. Marie-France Pisier

The only thing I'd rather own than Windows is English, because then I could charge you $249 for the right to speak it. Scott McNealy

A French politician once wrote that it was a peculiarity of the French language that in it words occur in the order in which one thinks them.

Ludwig Wittgenstein

A language is a dialect that has an army and a navy.   Professor Max Weinreich

It may be that in private moments the language at Buckingham Palace is quite similar to that of a rugby changing room.   Charles Curran

The great thing about human language is that it prevents us from sticking to the matter at hand.   Lewis Thomas

After all, when you come right down to it, how many people speak the same language even when they speak the same language?   Russell Hoban

Even if you do learn to speak correct English, whom are you going to speak it to?   Clarence Darrow

He would only be known to be a foreigner by the correctness of his language.   Anthony Trollope

LAW

You want justice, go to a whorehouse. You wanna get fucked, go to court.   Marty Vail, *Primal Fear*

For certain people, after fifty, litigation takes the place of sex.   Gore Vidal

Our civilization is shifting from science and technology to rhetoric and litigation.   Mason Cooley

Litigation, n. A machine which you go into as a pig and come out as a sausage.   Ambrose Bierce

May you have a lawsuit in which you know you are in the right.   Gypsy curse

I was never ruined but twice: once when I lost a lawsuit, and once when I won one.

Voltaire

Almost without fail, lawsuits are about revenge.

Liz Smith

I decided law was the exact opposite of sex; even when it was good, it was lousy.

Mortimer Zuckerman

An appeal is when you ask one court to show its contempt for another court.

Finley Peter Dunne

People say law but they mean wealth.

Ralph Waldo Emerson

Litigation only makes lawyers fat.

Wilbur Smith

The houses of lawyers are roofed with the skins of litigants.

Welsh proverb

I defy the allegations, and I defy the allegator.

Fred Gardiner

There are defendants whom the judges are afraid of.

Alexander Solzhenitsyn

Never forget that everything Hitler did in Germany was legal.

Martin Luther King, Jr

The more corrupt the state, the more numerous the laws.

Tacitus

Please remember that law and sense are not always the same.

Jawaharlal Nehru

The more laws, the more offenders.

Thomas Fuller

Bad laws are the worst sort of tyranny.

Edmund Burke

No society can ever make a perpetual constitution, or even a perpetual law.

Thomas Jefferson

The best way to get a bad law repealed is to enforce it strictly.   Abraham Lincoln

If you choose to live outside the law, you must obey the law more stringently than anyone.
                                                                                    Bob Dylan

Each man is his own absolute law-giver, the dispenser of glory or gloom to himself; the decreer of his life, his reward, his punishment.   Mabel Collins

Wise people, even though all laws were abolished, would still lead the same life.
                                                                                    Aristophanes

LAWYER

Lawyers are always more ready to get a man into troubles than out of them.
                                                                            Oliver Goldsmith

He is no lawyer who cannot take two sides.   Charles Lamb

A lawyer's relationship to justice and wisdom ... is on a par with a piano tuner's relationship to a concert. He neither composes the music, nor interprets it – he merely keeps the machinery running.   Lucille Kallen

Never shake hands with colleagues in court; the customers think you're making deals.
                                                                            John Mortimer

I get paid for seeing that my clients have every break the law allows. I have knowingly defended a number of guilty men. But the guilty never escape unscathed. My fees are sufficient punishment for anyone.   F. Lee Bailey

I'm not an ambulance chaser. I'm usually there before the ambulance.
                                                                            Melvin Belli, lawyer

One listens to one's lawyer prattle on as long as one can stand it and then signs where indicated.
                                                                            Alexander Woollcott

God save us from a lawyer's et cetera.   French proverb

LEADER

First rule of leadership: everything is your fault.

Hopper, *A Bug's Life*

A leader is one who, out of madness or goodness, volunteers to take upon himself the woe of the people. There are few men so foolish, hence the erratic quality of leadership in the world.

John Updike

A leader is a dealer in hope.

Napoleon Bonaparte

It is very comforting to believe that leaders who do terrible things are, in fact, mad. That way, all we have to do is make sure we don't put psychotics in high places and we've got the problem solved.

Tom Wolfe

I am more afraid of an army of a hundred sheep led by a lion than an army of a hundred lions led by a sheep.

Talleyrand

To lead the people, walk behind them.

Lao Tzu

Look over your shoulder now and then to be sure someone's following you.

Henry Gilmer

Either lead, follow, or get out of the way.

Ted Turner, sign on his desk

Only one man in a thousand is a leader of men – the other 999 follow women.

Groucho Marx

It is an interesting question how far men would retain their relative rank if they were divested of their clothes.

Henry David Thoreau

LETTER

I believe in opening mail once a month, whether it needs it or not.

Bob Considine

Why is it that you can sometimes feel the reality of people more keenly through a letter than face to face?

Anne Morrow Lindbergh

I would have answered your letter sooner, but you didn't send one.

Goodman Ace

A letter always feels to me like immortality because it is the mind alone without corporeal friend.

Emily Dickinson

A woman's best love letters are always written to the man she is betraying.

Lawrence Durrell

I hold that the parentheses are by far the most important parts of a non-business letter.

D. H. Lawrence

When a man sends you an impudent letter, sit right down and give it back to him with interest ten times compounded – and then throw both letters in the wastebasket.

Elbert Hubbard

The email of the species is deadlier than the mail.

Stephen Fry

My dear mother is determined to master the new technology: she typed an email to me on the computer, printed it out, popped it in an envelope and posted it to me.

John O'Farrell

I am a little pencil in the hand of a writing God who is sending a love letter to the world.

Mother Teresa

LIES AND LYING

There are a terrible lot of lies going around the world, and the worst of it is half of them are true.
Winston Churchill

It takes two to lie: one to lie, and one to listen.
Homer Simpson

He led a double life. Did that make him a liar? He did not feel a liar. He was a man of two truths.
Iris Murdoch

It's not a lie. It's a gift for fiction.
Walt Price, *State and Main*

Economical with the *actualité*.
Alan Clark

I was provided with further input that was radically different from the truth. I assisted in furthering that version.
Colonel Oliver North

My interview technique rests on the question: Why is this lying bastard lying to me?
Jeremy Paxman

I've got my own lie detector at home. I call her 'honey'.
Jason Love

Women lie about their age; men lie about their income.
William Feather

Gentlemen are not supposed to tell the truth about their sex lives, nor are ladies, for that matter. Of course Clinton lied – as would anybody in his position.
Gore Vidal

A man who will not lie to a woman has very little consideration for her feelings.
Olin Miller

I wouldn't think of asking you to lie; you haven't the necessary diplomatic training.
John Farrow

There's no need to lie. It's like poker. The truth is best. The others still think you're bluffing, so you win.
Michel Poiccard, *A Bout de Souffle*

Lying is not only excusable; it is not only innocent; it is, above all, necessary and unavoidable. Without the ameliorations that it offers, life would become a mere syllogism and hence too metallic to be borne.

H. L. Mencken

The best liar is he who makes the smallest amount of lying go the longest way.

Samuel Butler

The greater the lie, the more readily it will be believed.

Adolf Hitler

All men can be led to believe the lie they want to believe.

Italo Bombolini

It was a Roman who said it was sweet to die for one's country. The Greeks never said it was sweet to die for anything. They had no vital lies.

Edith Hamilton

Even a lie is a psychic fact.

Carl Jung

One always has the air of someone who is lying when one speaks to a policeman.

Charles-Louis Philippe

The liar's punishment is not in the least that he is not believed, but that he cannot believe anyone else.

George Bernard Shaw

LIFE

There'll be two dates on your tombstone, and all your friends will read 'em. But all that's gonna matter is that little dash between 'em.

Kevin Welch

Someone once sent me a marvellous postcard. It said: 'Knock hard. Life is deaf.'

Arnold Wesker

Life is like a camel: you can make it do anything except back up.

Marcelene Cox

Life is two locked boxes, each containing the other's key.   Piet Hein

Life is like a B-movie. You don't want to leave in the middle of it, but you don't want to see it again.
                                                                    Ted Turner

Sometimes it seemed to him that his life was delicate as a dandelion. One little puff from any direction, and it was blown to bits.
                                                          Katherine Paterson

Life is a shipwreck, but we must not forget to sing in the lifeboats.   Voltaire

Not a shred of evidence exists in favour of the idea that life is serious.
                                                                 Brendan Gill

'Life is very strange,' said Jeremy. 'Compared with what?' said the spider.
                                                                 Norman Moss

You wanna know the secret of life? The saliva of young girls.   Tony Curtis

I have only three rules of life: never do anything underhand, never get your feet wet, go to bed at ten.   Bishop William Stubbs

The tragedy of life is not that man loses but that he almost wins. Heywood Broun

—Jeeves, have you ever pondered on life?
—From time to time, sir, in my leisure moments.
—Grim, isn't it, what?
—Grim, sir?
—I mean, the difference between things as they look and things as they are.
—The trousers perhaps half an inch higher, sir. A very slight adjustment of the braces will effect the necessary alteration. You were saying, sir?
              Bertie Wooster and Jeeves, *Very Good, Jeeves* by P. G. Wodehouse

There are two great rules of life: never tell everything at once.   Ken Venturi

This is the Great Theater of Life. Admission is free but the taxation is mortal. You come when you can, and leave when you must. The show is continuous. Goodnight.

Robertson Davies

LIGHT AND DARK

Our existence is but a brief crack of light between two eternities of darkness.

Vladimir Nabokov

In the evening, I walked sadly along the shore of The Solent, eastwards by Pylewell – returning, brought home a glow-worm and put it in a white lily, through which it shone.

William Allingham

Light, God's eldest daughter.

Thomas Fuller

People are like stained-glass windows. They sparkle and shine when the sun is out, but when the darkness sets in, their true beauty is revealed only if there is a light from within.

Elisabeth Kübler-Ross

To keep a lamp burning we have to keep putting oil in it.

Mother Teresa

The real meaning of enlightenment is to gaze with undimmed eyes on all darkness.

Nikos Kazantzakis

There isn't enough darkness in the world to snuff out the light of one little candle.

Gautama Siddharta

If you want to look at the stars, you will find that darkness is necessary. But the stars neither require nor demand it.

Annie Dilliard

Who must die must die in the dark, even though he sells candles.

Colombian proverb

Turn up the lights. I don't want to go home in the dark.   O. Henry, last words

Lead, kindly light, amid the encircling gloom, lead thou me on.   J. H. Newman

LISTENING

This isn't one of my sermons. I expect you to listen.

Father Mulcahy, *M*A*S*H*

If we were supposed to talk more than we listen, we would have two mouths and one ear.

Mark Twain

—What would you say to the kids responsible for the Columbine School tragedy?
—I wouldn't say a single word to them, I would listen to what they have to say. And that's what no one did.

Michael Moore and Marilyn Manson, *Bowling For Columbine*

Knowledge speaks, but wisdom listens.

Jimi Hendrix

Listening is a magnetic and strange thing, a creative force. When we are listened to, it creates us, makes us unfold and expand.

Karl Menninger

The highest ecstasy is the attention at its fullest.

Simone Weil

Lenin could listen so intently that he exhausted the speaker.

Isaiah Berlin

No one really listens to anyone else, and if you try it for a while you'll see why.

Mignon McLaughlin

If you listen carefully enough to anything, it will talk to you.

George Washington Carver

Course, a guy'll listen to anything if he thinks it's foreplay.

Annie Savoy, *Bull Durham*

No one is listening until you fart.

Anon

There's nothing like eavesdropping to show you that the world outside your head is different from the world inside your head.

Thornton Wilder

It is said in Java that the tiger's hearing is so acute that hunters must keep their nose hairs cut lest the tiger hear the breath whistle through their nostrils.
Peter Matthiessen

LITERATURE

Let's say there was a burning building and you could rush in and you could save only one thing: either the last known copy of Shakespeare's plays or some anonymous human being. What would you do?
Woody Allen

I think if a third of all novelists and maybe two-thirds of all the poets now writing dropped dead suddenly, the loss to literature would not be great.
Charles Osborne

There is a great discovery still to be made in literature, that of paying literary men by the quantity they do not write.
Thomas Carlyle

Only the more rugged mortals should attempt to keep up with current literature.
George Ade

What literature can and should do is change the people who teach the people who don't read the books.
A. S. Byatt

Literature ceases to be literature when it commits itself to moral uplift; it becomes moral philosophy or some such dull thing.
Anthony Burgess

LITTLE THINGS

It is not necessary to have great things to do. I turn my little omelette in the pan for the love of God.
Brother Laurence

Whatever you do will be insignificant, but it is very important that you do it.
Mahatma Gandhi

The most powerful way to change the world is to secretly commit little acts of compassion. You must behave as if your every act, even the smallest, impacted a thousand people for a hundred generations. Because it does.

Thom Hartmann

If you cannot feed a million people, then feed just one.　　**Mother Teresa**

Too often we underestimate the power of a touch, a smile, a kind word, a listening ear, an honest compliment, or the smallest act of caring, all of which have the potential to turn a life around.　　**Leo Buscaglia**

Every little helps – as the old woman said when she pissed into the sea.

English proverb

There was once a Hindu sage, who sat down on the banks of the Ganges and thought for seventy years about the millennium. Just as he arrived at the solution and was putting it into verse, a mosquito stung him and he forgot it again at once.　　**Don Marquis**

What a profound significance small things assume when the woman we love conceals them from us.　　**Marcel Proust**

Sometimes when I consider what tremendous consequences come from little things I am tempted to think there are no little things.　　**Bruce Barton**

A little work, a little sleep, a little love and it is all over.

Mary Roberts Rinehart

LIVING

Everything has been figured out except how to live.　　**Jean-Paul Sartre**

We are always getting ready to live but never living.　　**Ralph Waldo Emerson**

Most of us spend our lives as if we had another one in the bank.　　**Ben Irwin**

To live is the rarest thing in the world. Most people exist, that is all.

Oscar Wilde

Life has a practice of living you, if you don't live it. Philip Larkin

Statistically, the probability of any of us being here is so small that you'd think the mere fact of existing would keep us all in contented dazzlement of surprise. Lewis Thomas

Keep not your roses for my dead, cold brow. The way is lonely, let me feel them now. Arabella Smith

I don't want to get to the end of my life and find that I lived just the length of it. I want to have lived the width of it as well. Diane Ackerman

Life is so short, it seems careless not to use it all. Sir Trevor McDonald

What good are vitamins? Eat a lobster, eat a pound of caviar – live! If you are in love with a beautiful blonde with an empty face and no brains at all, don't be afraid. Marry her! Live! Artur Rubinstein

Try to learn to breathe deeply, really to taste food when you eat, and when you sleep, really to sleep. Try as much as possible to be wholly alive, with all your might, and when you laugh, laugh like hell, and when you get angry, get good and angry. Try to be alive. You will be dead soon enough.

William Saroyan

I went to the woods because I wanted to live deliberately. I wanted to live deep and to suck out all the marrow of life, to put to rout all that was not life, and not, when I had come to die, discover that I had not lived.

Henry David Thoreau

I am cherry alive. Delmore Schwartz

The aim of life is to live, and to live means to be aware, joyously, drunkenly, serenely, divinely aware.

Henry Miller

While I thought I was learning how to live, I have been learning how to die.

Leonardo da Vinci

I believe you should live each day as if it was your last, which is why I don't have any clean laundry, because who wants to wash clothes on the last day of their life?

Jack Handey

LOGIC, REASON AND NONSENSE

If the world were a logical place, men would ride side-saddle. Rita Mae Brown

Since attaining the full use of my reason no one has ever heard me laugh.

Lord Chesterfield

No one is exempt from talking nonsense; the misfortune is to do it solemnly.

Michel de Montaigne

The formula 'two and two make five' is not without its attractions.

Fyodor Dostoevsky

Fish die belly-upward and rise to the surface; it is their way of falling.

André Gide

There's a rule saying I have to ground anyone who's crazy … There's a catch. Catch-22. Anyone who wants to get out of combat duty isn't really crazy.

Joseph Heller

Rational answers seldom do explain.

Patrick White

Few women are dumb enough to listen to reason.

William Feather

Nothing defines humans better than their willingness to do irrational things in the pursuit of phenomenally unlikely payoffs.　Scott Adams

The fact that logic cannot satisfy us awakens an almost insatiable hunger for the irrational.　A. N. Wilson

One of the things to come out of the home computer revolution could be the general and widespread understanding of how severely limited logic really is.　Frank Herbert

It is a far, far better thing to have a firm anchor in nonsense than to put out on the troubled seas of thought.　J. K. Galbraith

A mind all logic is like a knife all blade. It makes the hand bleed that uses it.　Rabindranath Tagore

A little nonsense now and then is cherished by the wisest men.　Willy Wonka

There is as much sense in nonsense as there is nonsense in sense.　Anthony Burgess

The learned fool writes his nonsense in better language than the unlearned, but still 'tis nonsense.　Benjamin Franklin

Heaven knows what seeming nonsense may not tomorrow be demonstrated truth.　Alfred North Whitehead

Conclusions arrived at through reasoning have very little or no influence in altering the course of our lives.

Carlos Castaneda

LONELINESS

The eternal quest of the individual human being is to shatter his loneliness.

Norman Cousins

I live alone and sometimes I wish there were a toothbrush in the holder next to mine. I often eat alone, sleep alone, and go to the movies alone, even on Saturday night. Some of my friends live the same way, and we agree that being alone is a tax we pay for the luxury of our freedom.   **Anon**

I've been so lonely for long periods of my life that if a rat walked in I would have welcomed it.   **Louise Nevelson**

If you are lonely when you are alone, you are in bad company.

Jean-Paul Sartre

It is better to be lonely than to wish to be alone.   **Margaret Deland**

Real loneliness consists not in being alone, but in being with the wrong person, in the suffocating darkness of a room in which no deep communication is possible.   **Sydney J. Harris**

If you think nobody cares if you're alive or dead, try missing a couple of car payments.   Flip Wilson

Oh lonesome's a bad place to get crowded into.   **Kenneth Patchen**

When so many are lonely as seem to be lonely, it would be inexcusably selfish to be lonely alone.   **Tennessee Williams**

LOVE

Love is friendship set on fire.

Jeremy Taylor

Love is a fire. But whether it is going to warm your heart or burn down your house, you can never tell.

Joan Crawford

The first sigh of love is the last of wisdom.

Antoine Bret

Love and a red nose can't be hid.

Thomas Holcraft

'I love you' is really a question.

Meryl Streep

I met a guy who said those three little words girls want to hear: 'You're not fat.'

Joanne Syrigonakis

The only way of knowing a person is to love them without hope.

Walter Benjamin

The important thing is not the object of love, but the emotion itself.

Gore Vidal

People liking you or not liking you is an accident and is to do with them and not you. That goes for love, too, only more so.

Edna O'Brien

No matter what the shrinks, or the pundits, or the self-help books tell you, when it comes to love, it's luck.

Woody Allen

It is something – it can be everything – to have found a fellow bird with whom you can sit among the rafters while the drinking and boasting and reciting and fighting go on below.

Wallace Stegner

The first act of love is always the giving of attention.

Dallas Willard

We looked into each other's eyes. I saw myself, she saw herself.

Stanislaw J. Lec

Love is but the discovery of ourselves in others, and the delight in the recognition.
Alexander Smith

Love is the extremely difficult realization that someone other than yourself is real.
Iris Murdoch

Love is the self-delusion we manufacture to justify the trouble we take to have sex.
Dan Greenburg

People would never fall in love if they had never heard love talked about.
La Rochefoucauld

To fall in love is to create a religion that has a fallible God.   Jorge Luis Borges

The only love that lasts is unrequited love.
Woody Allen

Love is that condition in which the happiness of another person is essential to your own.
Robert Heinlein

One seeks to make the loved one entirely happy, or, if that cannot be, entirely wretched.
Jean de La Bruyère

These are the things I know: you always throw spilled salt over your left shoulder; plant rosemary at your gate; keep lavender for luck; and fall in love whenever possible.
Alice Hoffman

One hour of right-down love is worth an age of dully living on.   Aphra Behn

Everyone has a gripping stranger in their lives, Andy, a stranger who unwittingly possesses a bizarre hold over you. Maybe it's the kid in cut-offs who mows your lawn or the woman wearing white shoulders who stamps your book at the library – a stranger who, if you were to come home and find a message from them on your answering machine saying, 'Drop everything. I love you. Come away with me now to Florida,' you'd follow them.
Douglas Coupland

When you really want love you will find it waiting for you.   Oscar Wilde

Nothing is possible without love ... For love puts one in a mood to risk everything.
Carl Jung

I can understand companionship. I can understand purchased sex in the afternoon. I cannot understand the love affair.
Gore Vidal

Without love, what are we worth? Eighty-nine cents! Eighty-nine cents' worth of chemicals walking around lonely.
Hawkeye, *M*A*S*H*

Love: the effort a man makes to be satisfied with only one woman.
Paul Géraldy

Many who have spent a lifetime in it can tell us less of love than the child that lost a dog yesterday.
Thornton Wilder

In real love you want the other person's good. In romantic love you want the other person.
Margaret Anderson

I met on the street a very poor young man who was in love. His hat was old, his coat was worn, his elbows were in holes; water trickled through his shoes, and the stars through his soul.
Victor Hugo

When you love somebody, your eyelashes go up and down and little stars come out of you.
Karen, aged seven

In love, there is always one who kisses and one who offers the cheek.
French proverb

I have always been the lover – never the beloved – and I have spent much of my life waiting for trains, planes, boats, footsteps, doorbells, letters, telephones, snow, rain, thunder.
John Cheever

Why is it better to love than to be loved? It is surer.
Sacha Guitry

The way to love anything is to realize that it might be lost.
G. K. Chesterton

Perhaps a great love is never returned.
Dag Hammarskjöld

To marry a woman you love and who loves you is to lay a wager with her as to who will stop loving the first. **Alfred Capus**

When you start having lunch and actually eating, it's already over. **Erica Jong**

The beginning and the decline of love are both marked by the embarrassment the lovers feel to be alone together. **Jean de La Bruyère**

How do you know that love is gone? If you said you would be there by seven, you get there by nine, and he or she has not called the police yet – it's gone. **Marlene Dietrich**

You gave me wings to fly, then took away my sky. **Leonora Speyer**

Who knows how to make love stay? Tell love you are going to Junior's Deli on Flatbush Avenue in Brooklyn to pick up a cheesecake, and if love stays, it can have half. It will stay. **Tom Robbins**

Don't think that every sad-eyed woman has loved and lost. She may have got him. **Anon**

Every love's the love before in a duller dress. **Dorothy Parker**

Falling out of love is chiefly a matter of forgetting how charming someone is. **Iris Murdoch**

Falling out of love is very enlightening; for a short while you see the world with new eyes. **Iris Murdoch**

Can one ever remember love? It's like trying to summon up the smell of roses in a cellar. You might see a rose, but never the perfume. **Arthur Miller**

Love that ends is the shadow of love; true love is without beginning or end. **Hazrat Inayat Khan**

So long as we love, we serve; so long as we are loved by others, I would almost say we are indispensable. **Robert Louis Stevenson**

Love is what you've been through with somebody. James Thurber

That love is all there is,
Is all we know of Love. Emily Dickinson

My motto is 'Love and let love' – with the one stipulation that people who love in glass-houses should breathe on the windows. P. G. Wodehouse

LUCK

Some people find oil. Others don't. John Paul Getty

Luck: the success of people you don't like. Hyman Maxwell Berston

Avoid employing unlucky people – throw half of the pile of CVs in the bin without reading them. David Brent, *The Office*

Some days, even my lucky rocketship underpants don't help. Bill Watterson

Be prepared for luck. Robin Williams

Luck is not something you can mention in the presence of a self-made man. E. B. White

Luck's a chance, but trouble's sure. A. E. Housman

Throw a lucky man in the sea, and he will come up with a fish in his mouth. Arabian proverb

Depend on the rabbit's foot if you must but remember, it didn't work for the rabbit. R. E. Shay

Luck never gives; it only lends. Swedish proverb

If a man who cannot count finds a four-leaf clover, is he entitled to happiness? Stanislaw J. Lec

If I travelled to the end of the rainbow, as Dame Fortune did intend,
Murphy would be there to tell me the pot's at the other end.   Bert Whitney

LUXURY AND NECESSITY

Just living is not enough. One must have sunshine, freedom, and a little
flower.   Hans Christian Andersen

The superfluous is the most necessary.   Voltaire

Give me all the luxuries of life, and I will willingly do without the
necessities.   Frank Lloyd Wright

Luxury is an ancient notion. There was once a Chinese mandarin who
had himself wakened three times every morning simply for the pleasure
of being told it was not yet time to get up.   *Argosy* magazine

His life was one long extravagance, like living inside a Fabergé egg.
                                                            John Lahr

Souls are more often sold for luxuries than necessities.   John King

In an affluent society no useful distinction can be made between
luxuries and necessaries.   J. K. Galbraith

It takes less than a decade for today's luxury to become a universal
necessity.   Paul Johnson

The price of tapping water into every house is that no one values water
any more.   John Fowles

Luxury, today, is solitude and silence.   Paul-Henri Spaak

Every luxury must be paid for, and everything is a luxury, starting with
being in the world.   Cesare Pavese

MADNESS

—Lady, don't take this the wrong way, but you're nuts.
—Oh, you sound just like the toaster.

Jay Sherman and Old Lady, *The Critic*

I am here but not all there.

Alan Bennett

I have not lost my mind – it's backed up on disk somewhere.

Steven Wright

The discovery of phobias by psychiatrists has done much to clear the atmosphere. Whereas in the old days a person would say: 'Let's get the heck out of here!' today she says: 'Let's get the heck out of here! I've got claustrophobia.'

Robert Benchley

Everyone is more or less mad on one point.

Rudyard Kipling

I doubt if a single individual could be found from the whole of mankind free from some form of insanity. The only difference is one of degree. A man who sees a gourd and takes it for his wife is called insane because this happens to very few people.

Erasmus

The Man Who Mistook His Wife For A Hat

Dr Oliver Sachs, book title

Why don't you have a right to say you are Jesus? And why isn't the proper response to that 'Congratulations'?

Thomas Szasz

Anyone, provided that he can be amusing, has the right to talk to himself.

Charles Baudelaire

Insanity: a perfectly natural adjustment to an insane world.

R. D. Laing

It is more comfortable to be mad and not know it than to be sane and have one's doubts.

G. B. Burgin

I read somewhere that seventy per cent of all the mentally ill live in poverty. Actually, I'm more intrigued by the twenty-three per cent who are apparently doing quite well for themselves.

Jerry Garcia

Howard Hughes was able to afford the luxury of madness, like a man who not only thinks he is Napoleon, but hires an army to prove it.

Ted Morgan

A man who is 'of sound mind' is one who keeps the inner madman under lock and key.

Paul Valéry

To be mad is not necessarily to be creative, or there'd be a Shelley on every corner.

The New York Times

In individuals, insanity is rare; but in groups, parties, nations and epochs it is the rule.

Friedrich Nietzsche

Men will always be mad and those who think they can cure them are maddest of all.

Voltaire

When dealing with the insane, the best method is to pretend to be sane.

Herman Hesse

In the West, the insane are so many that they are put in an asylum, in China the insane are so unusual that we worship them.

Lin Yutang

The first step towards madness is to think oneself wise.

Fernando de Rojas

Madness is no madness when shared.

Zygmunt Bauman

Some people never go crazy. What truly horrible lives they must live.

Charles Bukowski

MAN

Man is Creation's masterpiece. But who says so?   Elbert Hubbard

From the point of view of a tapeworm, man was created by God to serve the appetite of the tapeworm.   William Abbey

All we are is a lot of talking nitrogen.   Arthur Miller

It is a fact that seventy-five per cent of our make-up is the same as a pumpkin. Although we like to think we are special, our genes bring us down to earth.   Monise Durrani

I believe the best definition of man is the ungrateful biped. Fyodor Dostoevsky

Man is the only animal that laughs and weeps; for he is the only animal that is struck by the difference between what things are and what they might have been.   William Hazlitt

—Love is what separates us from animals.
—No. What separates us from animals is that we don't use our tongues to clean our own genitals.   Lister and Rimmer, *Red Dwarf*

I know at last what distinguishes man from animals: financial worry.   Jules Renard

If I could get my membership fee back, I'd resign from the human race.
                Fred Allen

There are times when one would like to hang the whole human race, and finish the farce.   Mark Twain

Weaseling out of things is important to learn. It's what separates us from the animals. Except the weasels.   Homer Simpson

Man is vile, I know, but people are wonderful.   Peter De Vries

Man is a sad mammal that combs its hair.   Cees Nooteboom

MANNERS

A car is useless in New York, essential everywhere else. The same with
good manners.   Mignon McLaughlin

Good manners are like traffic rules for society.   Michael Levine

That man is loud, ill-mannered, and the last time he stayed here, he killed a
Ficus tree on the downstairs neighbor's balcony by which means are best
left to the imagination.   Frasier Crane, *Frasier*

A gentleman always gets out of his bath before peeing.   Scottie Hird

It is the first duty of a gentleman to remember in the morning who he
went to bed with the night before.   Dorothy L. Sayers

The single essential ingredient of good manners is a sensitive awareness of
the feelings of others.   Emily Post

The most difficult thing in the world is to know how to do a thing and
to watch someone else doing it wrong, without commenting.
                                                            Theodore H. White

Treat everyone with politeness, even those who are rude to you – not
because they are nice, but because you are.   Anon

The best thing to do is to behave in a manner befitting one's age. If you are
sixteen or under, try not to go bald.   Woody Allen

Our lives are fed by kind words and gracious behavior. We are nourished
by expressions like 'excuse me', and other such simple courtesies.   Ed Hays

Rudeness is the weak man's imitation of strength. Eric Hoffer

Politeness is fictitious benevolence. Samuel Johnson

Formal courtesy between husband and wife is even more important than it is between strangers. Robert Heinlein

You can't be truly rude until you understand good manners. Rita Mae Brown

Bad table manners have broken up more households than infidelity.
Aunt Alicia, *Gigi*

Cleanse not your teeth with the tablecloth, napkin, fork or knife.
George Washington

The Chinese remark on meeting you unexpectedly: 'The sun has risen twice today.' Geoffrey Madan

Use a sweet tongue, courtesy, and gentleness, and thou wilt manage to guide an elephant with a hair. Sa'di

MARRIAGE

I'm not married. I hope to be someday so I can stop exercising. Jeff Stilson

By all means marry. If you get a good wife you'll be happy, if you get a bad one, you'll become a philosopher. Socrates

And at home by the fire, whenever you look up, there shall I be – and whenever I look up, there will you be.
Gabriel Oak proposes to Bathsheba Everdene,
Far From the Madding Crowd by Thomas Hardy

It is always incomprehensible to a man that a woman should ever refuse an offer of marriage. Jane Austen

Why couldn't we have arranged marriages in America? At least you could spend the rest of your life blaming your parents instead of yourself.

Faith Corvatch, *Only You*

Mr Hardy was making big preparations to get married. Mr Laurel was taking a bath too.

Title card, *Come Clean*

After the chills and fever of love, how nice is the 98.6 degrees of marriage!

Mignon McLaughlin

What is fascinating about marriage is why anyone wants to get married.

Alain de Botton

Many a man in love with a dimple makes the mistake of marrying the whole girl.

Stephen Leacock

Marriage is like twirling a baton, turning handsprings, or eating with chopsticks; it looks so easy till you try it.

Helen Rowland

The trouble with marriage is that it's relentless. Every morning when you wake up, it's still there.

George Schneider, *Chapter Two*

Do not choose your wife at a dance, but in the field among the harvesters.

Czech proverb

Never marry a girl named 'Marie' who used to be known as 'Murray'.

Johnny Carson

If you cannot catch a bird of paradise, better take a wet hen.

Nikita Khrushchev

It is the woman who chooses the man who will choose her.   **Paul Geraldy**

Get married, but never to a man who is home all day.   **George Bernard Shaw**

Whenever you want to marry someone, go have lunch with his ex-wife.

Shelley Winters

It was a marriage of convenience, as my father had a blister on his big toe and couldn't travel far to find a girl.

W.C. Fields

Never marry a man who hates his mother, because he'll end up hating you.

Jill Bennett

Given the expectations of society at large, men are generally correct in their assumption that it is important for a woman to have a man. What they do not understand is how pathetically little difference it makes what man.

Gloria Steinem

It doesn't much signify whom one marries, for one is sure to find next morning that it was someone else.

Samuel Rogers

I'm interested in the modern suggestion that you can have a combination of love and sex in a marriage – which no previous society has ever believed.

Alain de Botton

In a society which really supported marriage the wife would be encouraged to go to the office and make love to her husband on the company's time and with its blessing.

Brendan Francis

A marriage is likely to be called happy if neither party ever expected to get much happiness out of it.

Bertrand Russell

More belongs to marriage than four legs in a bed.

Rainer Maria Rilke

Even the God of Calvin never judged anyone as harshly as married couples judge each other.

Wilfred Sheed

Love is the coldest of critics.

George William Curtis

The real marriage of true minds is for any two people to possess a sense of humor or irony pitched in exactly the same key, so that their joint glances at any subject cross like interarching searchlights. Edith Wharton

I've been married so long I'm on my third bottle of Tabasco. Susan Vass

The only thing my husband and I have in common is that we were married on the same day. Phyllis Diller

Making love within a marriage means that if the phone goes you sometimes answer it. Mavis Cheek

If my wife has taught me anything, it's this: no matter what in the world I am doing, I should be doing it differently. Jason Love

In every marriage the wife has to keep her mouth shut about at least one small thing her husband does that disgusts her. John O'Hara

One doesn't have to get anywhere in marriage. It is not a public conveyance. Iris Murdoch

Marriage is an alliance entered into by a man who can't sleep with the window shut, and a woman who can't sleep with the window open.
George Bernard Shaw

A married couple are well suited when both partners feel the need for a quarrel at the same time. Jean Rostand

I've never won an argument with my wife; and the only time I thought I had I found out the argument wasn't over yet. Jimmy Carter

It helps in a pinch to be able to remind your bride that you gave up a throne for her. The Duke of Windsor

Never question your wife's judgement. Look at who she married. Anon

Marriage is a covered dish. Swiss proverb

Marriage – that thing where you button each other's hard-to-reach buttons.

David Larrabee, *Sabrina*

Impossible for anyone to conceive the torments of his nights in bed with his beloved one and estranged from her. That turning of backs, that cold space between their two unhappy bodies. Elizabeth von Arnim

I used to believe that marriage would diminish me, reduce my options. That you had to be someone less to live with someone else when, of course, you have to be someone more. Candice Bergen

In almost every marriage there is a selfish and an unselfish partner. A pattern is set up and soon becomes inflexible, of one person always making the demands and one person always giving way. Iris Murdoch

A happy marriage is the union of two good forgivers. Robert Quillen

When one cries, the other tastes salt. Hebrew saying

Let there be spaces in your togetherness. Kahlil Gibran

Sometimes I wonder if men and women really suit each other. Perhaps they should just live next door and just visit now and then. Katharine Hepburn

The happiest marriages are full of alternative lives, lived in the head, unknown to the partner. John Bayley

One should never know too precisely whom one has married.

Friedrich Nietzsche

Intelligent discussion of practically everything is what is breaking up modern marriage, if anything is. E. B. White

Your soul-mate is the person that pushes all your buttons – pisses you off on a regular basis. It's not easy having a good marriage but I don't want easy. I thank God every day that I married a man who made me think. That's my definition of true love. Madonna

A successful marriage requires falling in love many times, always with the same person.   Mignon McLaughlin

It is not a lack of love, but a lack of friendship that makes unhappy marriages.   Friedrich Nietzsche

You stay married by being, and by marrying, the sort of person who stays married.   Phyl Amison

The secret of marriage is: separate bedrooms and separate bathrooms.
                                                                              Bette Davis

Before marriage, a man declares that he would lay down his life to serve you; after marriage, he won't even lay down his newspaper to talk to you.
                                                                              Helen Rowland

The husband who wants a happy marriage should learn to keep his mouth shut and his check book open.   Groucho Marx

My husband believed that all women who want to should be free, equal, independent, creative, well informed, and lead stimulating, interesting lives. Except me.   Lucille Kallen

Every marriage tends to consist of an aristocrat and a peasant. Of a teacher and a learner.   John Updike

One advantage of marriage is that, when you fall out of love with him or he falls out of love with you, it keeps you together until you fall in again.
                                                                              Judith Viorst

There is no lonelier man in death, except the suicide, than that man who has lived many years with a good wife and then outlived her. If two people love each other there can be no happy end to it.   Ernest Hemingway

A woman seldom comes out of a sullen spell until she's sure her husband has suffered as much as she thinks he should. William Feather

Eat, Drink, and Remarry. Anon

He first deceased; she for a little tried
To live without him, liked it not and died. Sir Henry Wotton

There is so little difference between husbands. You might as well keep the first. Adela Rogers St John

MARTYR

It is easier to die for a cause than to live for it. Diane de Poitiers

Martyrdom covers a multitude of sins. Mark Twain

The tyrant dies and his rule is over; the martyr dies and his rule begins. Søren Kierkegaard

No human beings are more dangerous than those who have suffered for a belief: the great persecutors are recruited from the martyrs not quite beheaded. Far from diminishing the appetite for power, suffering exasperates it. E. M. Cioran

MASSES AND MINORITIES

There is not a more mean, stupid, dastardly, pitiful, selfish, spiteful, envious, ungrateful animal than the public. It is the greatest of cowards, for it is afraid of itself. William Hazlitt

All the world over, I will back the masses against the classes. William Gladstone

The only one who is wiser than anyone is everyone.   Napoleon Bonaparte

Whenever you find yourself on the side of the majority, it's time to pause
and reflect.   Mark Twain

My hatred of crowds, the obviousness of crowds, of anything en masse.
Is this why I like little-known books? A general desire to escape the main
world.   John Fowles

The public! The public! How many fools does it take to make up a public?   Nicolas Chamfort

There is an accumulative cruelty in a number of men, though none in particular are ill natured.   Lord Halifax

A man has his distinctive personal scent which his wife, his children and
his dog can recognize. A crowd has a generalized stink. The public is
odourless.   W. H. Auden

Public opinion, a vulgar, impertinent, anonymous tyrant who deliberately
makes life unpleasant for anyone who is not content to be the average man.   Dean W. R. Inge

When a hundred men stand together, each of them loses his mind and gets
another one.   Friedrich Nietzsche

No snowflake in the avalanche ever feels responsible.   Stanislaw J. Lec

When the multitude detests a man, inquiry is necessary; when the multitude
likes a man, inquiry is equally necessary.   Confucius

If forty million people say a foolish thing it does not become a wise one,
but the wise man is foolish to give them the lie.   W. Somerset Maugham

The hope of the world is still in dedicated minorities. The trail-blazers in human, scientific and religious freedom have always been in a minority.

Martin Luther King

To succeed in chaining the crowd you must seem to wear the same fetters.

Voltaire

A thousand men can't undress a naked man.

Greek proverb

MATHS

The creator of the universe works in mysterious ways. But he uses a base ten counting system and likes round numbers.

Scott Adams

The subject I most disliked was mathematics. I have thought about it. I think the reason was that mathematics leaves no room for argument. If you made a mistake, that was all there was to it.

Malcolm X

Mathematics, rightly viewed, possesses not only truth, but supreme beauty.

Bertrand Russell

It is impossible to be a mathematician without being a poet in soul.

Sophia Kovalevskaya

In mathematics you don't understand things, you just get used to them.

John von Neumann

Describe a circle, stroke its back, and it turns vicious.

Eugene Ionesco

I don't agree with mathematics: the sum total of zeros is a frightening number.

Stanislaw J. Lec

MEANING

I saw somebody peeing in Jermyn Street the other day. I thought, is this the end of civilization as we know it? Or is it simply somebody peeing in Jermyn Street?   Alan Bennett

It depends on what the meaning of the word 'is' is.   President Bill Clinton

That must be wonderful; I have no idea what it means.   Albert Camus

Some people can read *War and Peace* and come away thinking it's a simple adventure story. Others can read the ingredients on a chewing gum wrapper and unlock the secrets of the universe.   Lex Luthor, *Superman*

Be sure you go to the author to get at his meaning, not to find yours.
                                                                     John Ruskin

Things are entirely what they appear to be and behind them ... there is nothing.   Jean-Paul Sartre

'If there's no meaning in it,' said the King, 'that saves a world of trouble, you know, as we needn't try to find any.'
                              Lewis Carroll, *Alice's Adventures in Wonderland*

Sometimes a cigar is just a cigar.   Sigmund Freud

MEANING OF LIFE

Decent clothes ... a car, but what's it all about?   Alfie, *Alfie*, 1966

The essence of life is the smile of round female bottoms, under the shadow of cosmic boredom.   Guy de Maupassant

What would life be without coffee? But then, what is it even with coffee?
                                                                       Louis XV

Why is life worth living? Well, there are certain things that make it worthwhile ... Groucho Marx, Willie Mays, the second movement of the 'Jupiter Symphony', and ... Louis Armstrong's recording of 'Potato Head Blues' ... Swedish movies, naturally ... *Sentimental Education* by Flaubert ... and Marlon Brando, Frank Sinatra ... those incredible apples and pears by Cézanne.
Woody Allen

That life is worth living is the most necessary of assumptions, and were it not assumed, the most impossible of conclusions.
George Santayana

Life has to be given a meaning because of the obvious fact that it has no meaning.
Henry Miller

He who has a why to live can bear almost any how.
Friedrich Nietzsche

I tell you, we are here on earth to fart around, and don't let anybody tell you different.
Kurt Vonnegut

The fact that life has no meaning is a reason to live – moreover, the only one.
E. M. Cioran

Man is the only animal for whom his existence is a problem that he has to solve.
Erich Fromm

Life is not that complicated. You go to work, you eat three meals, you take one good shit, and you go back to bed. What's the fuckin' mystery?
George Carlin

The meaning of life cannot be told; it has to happen to a person ...
To speak as though it were an objective knowledge, like the date of the war of 1812, misses the point altogether.
Ira Progoff

The meaning of life is that it stops.
Franz Kafka

Anyone can carry his burden, however hard, until nightfall. Anyone can do his work, however hard, for one day. Anyone can live sweetly, patiently, lovingly, purely, till the sun goes down. And this is all life really means.

Robert Louis Stevenson

'What is the meaning of life?' is a stupid question. Life just exists. You say to yourself, 'I can't accept that I mean nothing so I have to find the meaning of life so that I shouldn't mean as little as I know I do.' Subconsciously you know you're full of shit. I see life as a dance. Does a dance have to have a meaning? You're dancing because you enjoy it.

Jackie Mason

Here we are, trapped in the amber of the moment. There is no why.

Kurt Vonnegut

That it will never come again
Is what makes life so sweet.

Emily Dickinson

You will never live if you are looking for the meaning of life.   Albert Camus

I don't believe people are looking for the meaning of life as much as they are looking for the experience of being alive.   Joseph Campbell

We are here to laugh at the odds and live our lives so well that death will tremble to take us.   Charles Bukowski

Life and love are life and love, a bunch of violets is a bunch of violets, and to drag in the idea of a point is to ruin everything. Live and let live, love and let love, flower and fade, and follow the natural curve, which flows on, pointless.   D. H. Lawrence

We're here because we're here because we're here because we're here.   Anon

MEMORY

Am in Market Harborough. Where ought I to be?

G. K. Chesterton, telegram to his wife

I forget more and more, and even when it comes to what I used to be able to do – change a fuse or send a fax – something goes wrong. But these are just the inevitable punishments for having lived a long time and also a hedonistic life. I don't regret that at all. I feel pretty good. I've a rich memory bank to draw on and I don't care too much what happened yesterday afternoon.

George Melly

About four years ago … No, it was yesterday.

Steven Wright

I don't think I remember my first memory.

Ellen DeGeneres

Everybody needs his memories. They keep the wolf of insignificance from the door.

Saul Bellow

We do not know the true value of our moments until they have undergone the test of memory.

Georges Duhamel

We do not remember days, we remember moments.

Cesare Pavese

We forget all too soon the things we thought we could never forget.

Joan Didion

The existence of forgetting has never been proved: we only know that some things do not come to our mind when we want them to.

Friedrich Nietzsche

Nothing fixes a thing so intensely in the memory as the wish to forget it.

Michel de Montaigne

You can close your eyes to reality but not to memories.

Stanislaw J. Lec

In memory, everything seems to happen to music.   Tennessee Williams

There is no greater sorrow than to recall a happy time in the midst of wretchedness.   Dante Alighieri

If you are going to be able to look back on something and laugh about it, you might as well laugh about it now.   Marie Osmond

A man is a fool to remember anything that happened more than a week ago unless it was pleasant.   Samuel Butler

MEN

Like most men, I'm a life support system for a phallus.   Tibor Fischer

Men and melons are hard to know.   Benjamin Franklin

As long as you know that most men are like children, you know everything.   Coco Chanel

When you meet a man, don't you always idly wonder what he'd be like in bed? I do.   Helen Gurley Brown

Perhaps men could be divided into two kinds – those who take their watches off, and those who leave them on.   Charlotte Chandler

Men are like pay phones. Some of them take your money. Most of them don't work, and when you find one that does, someone else is on it.   Catherine Franco

Beware of men who cry. It's true that men who cry are sensitive to and in touch with feelings, but the feelings they tend to be sensitive to and in touch with are their own.   Nora Ephron

What do men want? Men want a mattress that cooks.   Judy Tenuta

Men have hidden agendas. For instance, every time a man holds the door open for me, I think he's just doing it to check out my ass. Or at least I hope he is.

Stacey Prussman

To define a man: he must be a creature who makes me feel that I am a woman.

Elinor Glyn

Men won't stop and ask for directions because driving is too much like sex: they can't stop until they get where they're going.

Diana Jordan

On the one hand, we'll never experience childbirth. On the other hand, we can open all our own jars.

Bruce Willis

Men will always opt for things that get finished and stay that way – putting up screens, but not planning menus.

Jane O'Reilly

When two men fight over a woman it's the fight they want, not the woman.

Brendan Francis

Men build bridges and throw railroads across deserts, and yet they contend successfully that the job of sewing on a button is beyond them.

Heywood Broun

Men are more conventional than women and much slower to change their ideas.

Kathleen Norris

Makes of men date, like makes of car.

Elizabeth Bowen

If there were no women in the world, men would be naked, driving trucks, living in dirt. Women came along and gave us a reason to comb our hair.

Sinbad

MEN AND WOMEN

Men and women, women and men. It will never work.   Erica Jong

Women always worry about the things men forget; men always worry about the things women remember.   Robert Bloch

One of my theories is that men love with their eyes; women love with their ears.   Zsa Zsa Gabor

When a man gives his opinion he's a man. When a woman gives her opinion she's a bitch.   Bette Davis

—Why are all rich men such jerks?
—The same reason why all beautiful women are bitches.
        Gabrielle and Carlos Solis, *Desperate Housewives*

If a man does something silly, people say, 'Isn't he silly?' If a woman does something silly, people say, 'Aren't women silly?'   Doris Day

When a man says, 'We've got to talk,' the woman hears, 'We're going to have a nice conversation.' When a woman says, 'We've got to talk,' a man hears, 'Will the defendant please rise?'   Peter Sasso

A foolish man tells a woman to stop talking, but a wise man tells her that her mouth is extremely beautiful when her lips are closed.   Robert Bloch

No matter how long he lives, no man ever becomes as wise as the average woman of forty-eight.   H. L. Mencken

A man's gotta do what a man's gotta do. A woman must do what he can't.
        Rhonda Hansome

Women have served all these centuries as looking-glasses possessing the magic and delicious power of reflecting the figure of man at twice its natural size.   Virginia Woolf

A woman wants a man to make her happy, and doesn't a man dare each new woman to make him good?
Irma Kurtz

Love which is only an episode in the life of men, is the entire history of the life of women.
Madame de Staël

Like most men, my father is interested in action. And this is why he disappoints my mother when she tells him she doesn't feel well and he offers to take her to the doctor. He is focused on what he can do, whereas she wants sympathy.
Deborah Tannen

In the duel of sex, woman fights from a dreadnought and man from an open raft.
H. L. Mencken

There are poems about the internet and about the shipping forecast but very few by women celebrating men.
Germaine Greer

But most men regard their life as a poem that women threaten. They may not have two spondees to rub together but they still want to pen their saga untrammelled by life-threatening activities like trailing round Sainsbury's, emptying the dishwasher or going to the nativity play.
Alan Bennett

I asked a Burmese man why women, after centuries of following their men, now walk in front. He said there were many unexploded landmines since the war.
Anon

From my experience of life I believe my personal motto should be: 'Beware of any man bringing flowers.'
Muriel Spark

At the end of one millennium and nine centuries of Christianity, it remains an unshakable assumption of the law in all Christian countries and of the moral judgement of Christians everywhere that if a man and a woman, entering a room together, close the door behind them, the man will come out sadder and the woman wiser.
H. L. Mencken

MIND

You live your life between your ears.

Bebe Moore Campbell

The mind of man is capable of anything because everything is in it, all the past as well as all the future.

Joseph Conrad

The mind itself is an art object ... The mind is a blue guitar on which we improvise the song of the world.

Annie Dillard

The more refined and subtle our minds, the more vulnerable they are.

Paul Tournier

The most merciful thing in the world, I think, is the inability of the human mind to correlate all its contents.

H. P. Lovecraft

By all means let's be open-minded, but not so open-minded that our brains drop out.

Richard Dawkins

The mind is its own place, and in itself can make a heaven of hell, a hell of heaven.

John Milton

In my sex fantasy, nobody ever loves me for my mind.

Nora Ephron

Minds, like bodies, will often fall into a pimpled, ill-conditioned state from mere excess of comfort.

Charles Dickens

God designed the stomach to eject what is bad for it, but not the human brain.

Konrad Adenauer

It is good to rub and polish our brain against that of others.

Michel de Montaigne

Use it or lose it.

Anon

MIRACLE

If frogs could fly – well, we'd still be in this mess, but wouldn't it be neat?
Drew Carey

A miracle is an event described by those to whom it was told by people who did not see it.
Elbert Hubbard

When a donkey flies, you don't blame him for not staying up that long.
Murray Slaughter, *The Mary Tyler Moore Show*

I went to a convent in New York and was fired finally for my insistence that the Immaculate Conception was a spontaneous combustion.
Dorothy Parker

Miracles happen to those who believe in them. Otherwise, why does not the Virgin Mary appear to Lamaists, Mohammedans or Hindus who have never heard of her?
Bernard Berenson

A belief in miracles has been the difference between living and dying as often as any surgeon's scalpel.
Doctor Noah Praetorius, *People Will Talk*

All the biblical miracles will at last disappear with the progress of science.
Matthew Arnold

Do not stand in a place of danger trusting in miracles.
Arabian proverb

Miracles are made in the heart.
Pinnochio, *Adventures of Pinnochio*

The miracle is not to walk on water, but to walk on land.
Thich Nhat Hanh

There are only two ways to live your life. One is as though nothing is a miracle. The other is as though everything is a miracle.
Albert Einstein

MISERY

Misery is when you heard on the radio that the neighborhood you live in is a slum but you always thought it was home. **Langston Hughes**

Most people would rather be certain they're miserable than risk being happy. **Robert Anthony**

The trick is in what one emphasizes ... We either make ourselves miserable, or we make ourselves strong. The amount of work is the same.
Carlos Castaneda

Nobody really cares if you are miserable, so you might as well be happy.
Cynthia Nelms

It is seldom that the miserable can help regarding their misery as a wrong inflicted by those who are less miserable. **George Eliot**

MISTAKE

All men make mistakes, but married men find out about them sooner.
Red Skelton

I beseech you, in the bowels of Christ, think it possible you may be mistaken. **Oliver Cromwell**

I make mistakes; I'll be the second to admit it. **Jean Kerr**

Even monkeys fall out of trees. **Japanese proverb**

About mistakes it's funny. You got to make your own; and not only that, if you try to keep people from making theirs they get mad. **Edna Ferber**

Make only big mistakes. **Byron L. Johnson**

Never interrupt your enemy when he is making a mistake.

Napoleon Bonaparte

The difference between greatness and mediocrity is often how an individual views a mistake.

Nelson Boswell

I am humble enough to recognize that I have made mistakes, but politically astute enough to know that I have forgotten what they are.

Michael Heseltine

If you board the wrong train, it is no use running along the corridor in the other direction.

Dietrich Bonhoeffer

An error doesn't become a mistake until you refuse to correct it. Orlando A. Battista

Give me a fruitful error any time, full of seeds, bursting with its own corrections. You can keep your sterile truth for yourself.

Vilfredo Pareto

One day when I was studying with Schoenberg, he pointed out the eraser on his pencil and said, 'This end is more important than the other.' After twenty years I learned to write directly in ink.

John Cage

Allowing an unimportant mistake to pass without comment is a wonderful social grace.

Judith Martin

One makes mistakes: that is life. But it is never quite a mistake to have loved.

Romain Rolland

We do not err because truth is difficult to see. It is visible at a glance. We err because this is more comfortable.

Alexander Solzhenitsyn

Most of the major mistakes I made in my life, I made when I was too tired to know what I was doing – both personally and professionally.

President Bill Clinton

Some of the worst mistakes of my life have been haircuts.   Jim Morrison

It was worse than a crime, it was a blunder.   Marquis de Talleyrand

Every great mistake has a halfway moment, a split second when it can be recalled and perhaps remedied.   Pearl S. Buck

By the time you reach my age, you've made plenty of mistakes if you've lived your life properly.   Ronald Reagan

If I had to live my life again I'd make all the same mistakes – only sooner.   Tallulah Bankhead

You must learn from the mistakes of others. You can't possibly live long enough to make them all yourself.   Sam Levenson

MONEY

—Money can't buy happiness.
—Sure it can. That's just a lie we tell poor people to stop them from rioting.
          Sister Mary and Gabrielle Solis, *Desperate Housewives*

Money brings some happiness but after a certain point it just brings more money.   Neil Simon

With money in your pocket you are wise, you are handsome, and you sing well, too.   Yiddish proverb

A fool and his money are soon married.   Carolyn Wells

Money makes even bastards legitimate.   Billy Wilder

It's often been said that money won't make you happy, and this is undeniably true, but everything else being equal, it's a lovely thing to have around the home.   Groucho Marx

The only reason to have money is to tell any sonovabitch to go to hell.

Humphrey Bogart

I don't even like money. It just quiets my nerves.

Joe Louis

The chief value of money lies in the fact that one lives in a world in which it is overestimated.

H. L. Mencken

Money isn't everything as long as you have enough.

Malcolm Forbes

When it is a question of money, everybody is of the same religion.

Voltaire

To money, the finest linguist in the world!

Minna Thomas Antrim

Money is something you got to make in case you don't die.

Max Asnas

Having money isn't the important thing. The most important thing is having friends – especially friends with money.

Phyllis Nefler, *Troop Beverly Hills*

I'm not interested in money. I only want to be wonderful.

Marilyn Monroe

It's not that it's so good with money, but that it's so bad without it.

George Sanders

There is nothing more demoralizing than a small but adequate income.

Edmund Wilson

The love of money is the source of an enormous amount of good; the fact that the good is a by-product of the selfish pursuit of riches has nothing to do with its indisputable value.

Leo Rosten

Budget: a mathematical confirmation of your suspicions.

A.A. Latimer

No one would remember the Good Samaritan if he only had good
intentions. He had money as well. Margaret Thatcher

My mother said, 'No matter how hard you hug your money, it never hugs
you back.' H. Jackson Brown

To be extravagant you need money. True. But you do not need your own
money. George Mikes

Banking establishments are more dangerous than standing armies.
Thomas Jefferson

I don't have a bank account because I don't know my mother's maiden
name. Paula Poundstone

Never in the history of human credit has so much been owed.
Margaret Thatcher

There are several ways to apportion the family income, all of them
unsatisfactory. Robert Benchley

Annual income twenty pounds, annual expenditure nineteen nineteen six,
result happiness. Annual income twenty pounds, annual expenditure twenty
pounds ought and six, result misery. Charles Dickens, *David Copperfield*

If you want to steal some money, don't rob a bank – open one. Bertolt Brecht

Keeping accounts, sir, is of no use when a man is spending his own money,
and has nobody to whom he is to account. You won't eat less beef today
because you have written down what it cost yesterday. Samuel Johnson

Jesus saves! But wouldn't it be better if he had invested? Anon

Never put your money in anything that eats or needs repairing. Billy Rose

Before you borrow money from a friend, decide which you need more.

Anon

Mr Potts said that lending money always made him feel as if he were rubbing velvet up the wrong way.

P. G. Wodehouse

He is rich who owes nothing.

Polish proverb

My worst fault is my belief that if you put bills unopened behind a picture frame, there is no need to pay them.

Hermione Gingold

If economists were doctors, they would today be mired in malpractice suits.

John Ralston Saul

Bankruptcy is like losing your virginity. It doesn't hurt the next time.

Clarissa Dickson Wright

The darkest hour in any man's life is when he sits down to plan how to get money without earning it.

Horace Greeley

What's the use of money if you have to earn it?

George Bernard Shaw

Spare no expense to save money on this one.

Sam Goldwyn

Money is only useful when you get rid of it. It is like the odd card in 'Old Maid'; the player who is finally left with it has lost.

Evelyn Waugh

They say you can't take it with you when you go. Well, if I can't take it with me, I won't go!

Louis B. Mayer

Money doesn't buy happiness. But happiness isn't everything.

Jean Seberg

MORALS

There is a moral, of course, and like all morals it is better not pursued.
Sylvia Townsend Warner

Morality is simply the attitude we adopt towards people whom we personally dislike. **Oscar Wilde**

Morality is the theory that every human act must be either right or wrong, and that 99 per cent of them are wrong. **H.L. Mencken**

The essence of immorality is the tendency to make an exception of one's self. **Jane Addams**

Morality turns on whether the pleasure precedes the pain or follows it ... Thus, it is immoral to get drunk because the headache comes after the drinking, but if the headache came first, and the drunkenness afterwards, it would be moral to get drunk. **Samuel Butler**

As soon as one is unhappy one becomes moral. **Marcel Proust**

Moral indignation is jealousy with a halo. **H.G. Wells**

I never came across anyone in whom the moral sense was dominant who was not heartless, cruel, vindictive, log-stupid, and entirely lacking in the smallest sense of humanity. Moral people, as they are termed, are simple beasts. **Oscar Wilde**

I now believe in nothing, but I do not the less believe in morality. I mean to live and die like a gentleman, if possible.
Reverend Leslie Stephen, after reading Darwin

The so-called new morality is too often the old immorality condoned.
Lord Shawcross

When the sun comes up, I have morals again. **Elizabeth Taylor**

—Have you no morals, man?
—Can't afford them, Governor.

Colonel Pickering and Alfred Doolittle, *Pygmalion* by George Bernard Shaw

The highest possible stage in moral culture is when we recognize that we ought to control our thoughts.

Charles Darwin

Moral certainty is always a sign of cultural inferiority. The more uncivilized the man, the surer he is that he knows precisely what is right and what is wrong.

H. L. Mencken

MOTHER

A female salmon lays three thousand eggs a year – and has yet to receive a Mother's Day card from one of them.

Joan Rivers

Marge, listen to me … you're the backbone of this family. You're like the electrical tape that holds the two halves of my car together.

Homer Simpson

Whenever my mother sees me she says, 'Jenny, Jenny, why aren't you wearing a petticoat?' 'Mother, it's because I've got jeans on.'

Jenny Eclair

I told my mother I was going to have a natural childbirth. She said to me, 'Linda, you've been taking drugs all your life. Why stop now?'

Linda Maldonada

The moment a child is born, the mother is also born. She never existed before. The woman existed, but the mother, never. A mother is something absolutely new.

Bhagwan Shree Rajneesh

When you are a mother, you are never really alone in your thoughts. A mother always has to think twice, once for herself and once for her child.

Sophia Loren

There's no way to repay a mother's love, or lack of it.   Mignon McLaughlin

Things a mother should know: how to construct a packed lunch, a shepherd's costume and a plausible Off Games note in ten minutes flat, usually while cooking breakfast.   Katharine Whitehorn

Things a mother should know: how to comfort a son without exactly saying Daddy was wrong.   Katharine Whitehorn

I know how to do anything – I'm a mom.   Roseanne

Mothers are the most instinctive philosophers.   Harriet Beecher Stowe

An ounce of mother is worth a pound of priests.   Spanish proverb

What the mother sings to the cradle goes all the way down to the coffin.
                    Henry Ward Beecher

Mama always had a way of explaining things so I could understand them.
                    Forrest Gump

All mothers think their children are oaks, but the world never lacks for cabbages.   Robertson Davies

In the eyes of its mother every beetle is a gazelle.   Moroccan proverb

No matter how old a mother is, she watches her middle-aged children for signs of improvement.   Florida Scott-Maxwell

If you begin to think you're changing the culture of the world, just ask your mom what she thinks you do for a living.

Jürgen Stringenz

MURDER

Kill a man and you are a murderer. Kill millions of men, and you are a conqueror. Kill everyone, and you are a god.   **Jean Rostand**

If the desire to kill and the opportunity to kill came always together, who would escape hanging?   **Mark Twain**

As a test of the closeness of your relationship with the world, sex could never be a patch on being murdered. (That's when someone really does risk his life for you.)   **Quentin Crisp**

It takes two to make a murder. There are born victims, born to have their throats cut, as the cut-throats are born to be hanged.   **Aldous Huxley**

A person is more likely to be hit or killed in his or her own home by another family member than anywhere else or by anyone else.   **R. J. Gelles**

Murder is unique in that it abolishes the party it injures, so that society has to take the place of the victim and on his behalf demand atonement or grant forgiveness; it is the one crime in which society has a direct interest.

W. H . Auden

Death by drink driving is the only socially acceptable form of homicide.

Candy Lightner

For some strange reason murder has always seemed more respectable than fornication. Few people are shocked when they hear God described as the God of Battles; but what an outcry there would be if anyone spoke of him as the God of Brothels.   **Aldous Huxley**

—Hell of a thing, killin' a man. Takes away all he's got and all he's ever gonna have.
—Yeah, well, I guess he had it comin'.
—We all got it comin', kid.   **Bill Munny and The Schofield Kid, *Unforgiven***

MUSIC

Music is the eye of the ear.   Thomas Draxe

Music is only love looking for words.   Lawrence Durrell

Music washes away from the soul the dust of everyday life.   Berthold Auerbach

Music is essentially useless, as life is.   George Santayana

Music is the best means we have of digesting time.   W. H. Auden

Music is too idealistic a thing to permit itself to be bound to concrete
references. You cannot have a white horse in music.   Paul Rosenfield

—Your violin concerto will require a soloist with six fingers.
—Very well, I can wait.   Conductor and Arnold Schoenberg

There are two golden rules for an orchestra: start together and finish
together. The public doesn't give a damn what goes on in between.
                                                                Thomas Beecham

Never look at the brass – it only encourages them.   Richard Strauss

People who make music together cannot be enemies, at least not while the
music lasts.   Paul Hindemith

All music jars when the soul's out of tune.   Miguel de Cervantes

The notes I handle no better than many pianists. But the pauses between
the notes – ah, that is where the art resides!   Artur Schnabel

Second violins can play a concerto perfectly if they're in their own home
and nobody's there.   Garrison Keillor

A guitar has moonlight in it.   James M. Cain

Cello players, like other great athletes, must keep their fingers exercised.
Julian Lloyd Webber

Singing is near miraculous because it is the mastering of what is
otherwise a pure instrument of egotism: the human voice.
Hugo von Hofmannsthal

Truly to sing, that is a different breath. **Rainer Maria Rilke**

There's only one way to sum up music: either it's good or it's bad. If it's
good you don't mess about with it; you just enjoy it. **Louis Armstrong**

You might say everyone of us is a fiddler on the roof trying to scratch out a
pleasant, simple tune without breaking his neck.
Tevye, *Fiddler on the Roof*

MYSTERY

It began in mystery, and it will end in mystery, but what a savage and
beautiful country lies in between. **Diane Ackerman**

The most beautiful experience we can have is the most mysterious …
He to whom the emotion is a stranger, who can no longer pause and stand
wrapped in awe, is as good as dead; his eyes are closed. **Albert Einstein**

As we acquire more knowledge, things do not become more
comprehensible, but more mysterious. **Will Durant**

Let mystery have a place in you … leave a little fallow corner in your heart
ready for any seed the wind may bring, and reserve a nook of shadow for
the passing bird; keep a place in your heart for the unexpected guest, an
altar for an unknown God. **Henri Frédéric Amiel**

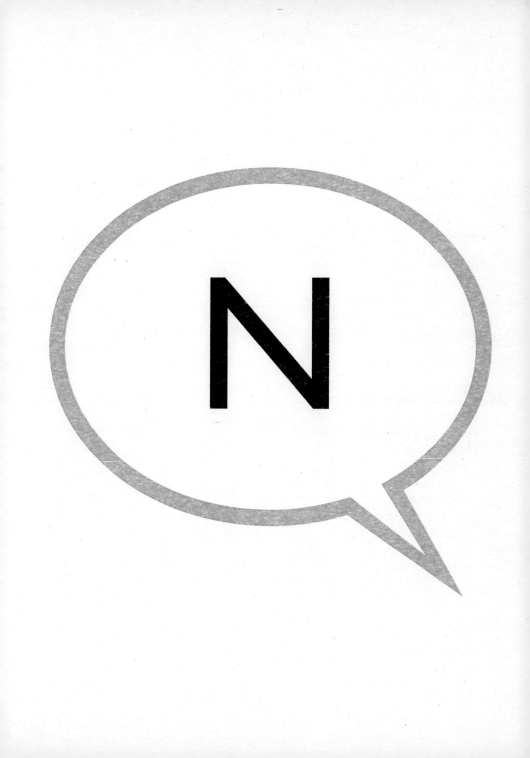

NAME

—There's even a rose named after Margaret Thatcher.
—Oh, what's it called?   **Gardening Expert and Steve Jones**

I sometimes think I was born to live up to my name. How could I be
anything else but what I am, having been named Madonna? I would either
have ended up a nun or this.   **Madonna**

Our names are labels, printed clearly on the bottled essence of our past
behavior.   **Logan Pearsall Smith**

I don't like your miserable, lonely single 'front name'. It is so limited, so
meagre … It is worn threadbare with much use. It is as bad as having only
one jacket and one hat … Never set a child afloat on the flat sea of
life with only one sail to catch the wind.   **D. H. Lawrence**

Any child can tell you that the sole purpose of a middle name is so he can
tell when he's really in trouble.   **Dennis Frakes**

How many legs does a dog have if you call the tail a leg? Four. Calling a
tail a leg doesn't make it a leg.   **Abraham Lincoln**

To give a name to a thing is as gratifying as giving a name to an island, but
it is also dangerous: the danger consists in one's becoming convinced that
all is taken care of and that once named, the phenomenon has also been
explained.   **Primo Levi**

Names, once they are in common use, quickly become mere sounds, their
etymology being buried, like so many of the earth's marvels, beneath the
dust of habit.   **Salman Rushdie**

To name oneself is the first act of both the poet and the revolutionary.
When we take away the right to an individual name, we symbolically take
away the right to be an individual. Immigration officials did this to
refugees; husbands routinely do it to wives.   **Erica Jong**

When Charlotte really liked a guy, she said his whole name – it helped her to imagine their future monogrammed towels.

Carrie Bradshaw, *Sex and the City*

When someone loves you, the way they say your name is different. You just know it is safe in their mouth.

Anon

Readers called Stephen, save time by calling yourself 'Steve'.

Viz magazine, top tip

What signifies knowing the Names, if you know not the Natures of things.

Benjamin Franklin

Never allow your child to call you by your first name. He hasn't known you long enough.

Fran Lebowitz

It ain't what they call you, it's what you answer to.

W. C. Fields

—Which island in the Indian Ocean was named after the date of its discovery, the 25th December 1643?
—Guam?

Anne Robinson and Contestant, *The Weakest Link*

NATURE

I would feel more optimistic about a bright future for man if he spent less time proving that he can outwit Nature and more time tasting her sweetness and respecting her seniority.

E. B. White

The sun, with all those planets revolving around it and dependent on it, can still ripen a bunch of grapes as if it had nothing else in the universe to do.

Galileo

We need nature more than nature needs us.

Sadruddin Aga Khan

Nature will tell you a direct lie if she can.

Charles Darwin

There seems to be a feeling that anything that is natural is good. Strychnine is natural.   Isaac Asimov

Nature abhors a lot of things, including vacuums, ships called the *Marie Celeste*, and the chuck keys for electric drills.   Terry Pratchett

Everybody wants to go back to nature – but not on foot.
                                                                    Werner Mitsch

There is nothing like walking to get the feel of a country. A fine landscape is like a piece of music; it must be taken at the right tempo. Even a bicycle goes too fast.   Paul Scott Mowrer

Take nothing but pictures. Leave nothing but footsteps. Kill nothing but time.   The Countryside Code

Look, Mummy, God painted a rainbow!   Jennie Clinton, aged five

The earth is mankind's ultimate haven, our blessed terra firma. When it trembles and gives way beneath our feet, it's as though one of God's cheques has bounced.   Gilbert Adair

I believe that if one always looked at the skies, one would end up with wings.   Gustave Flaubert

For real company and friendship, there is nothing outside the animal kingdom that is comparable to a river.   Henry Van Dyke

I think that I shall never see
A poem lovely as a tree ...
Poems are made by fools like me,
But only God can make a tree.   Joyce Kilmer

Nature composes some of her loveliest poems for the microscope and telescope.   Theodore Roszak

The sky is the ultimate art gallery just above us.   Ralph Waldo Emerson

If you look at eggs, you will see that each one is almost round but not quite … Nature's way of distinguishing eggs from large golf balls.
                                                          Robert Benchley

Whenever I look at a mountain I always expect it to turn into a volcano.
                                                          Italo Svevo

Human judges can show mercy. But against the laws of nature, there is no appeal.   Arthur C. Clarke

When one tugs at a single thing in nature, he finds it hitched to the rest of the universe.   John Muir

I am part of the sun as my eye is part of me. That I am part of the earth my feet know perfectly, and my blood is part of the sea. There is not any of me that is alone and absolute except my mind, and we shall find that the mind has no existence by itself, it is only the glitter of the sun on the surfaces of the water.   D. H. Lawrence

NEEDS

If you have a garden and a library, you have everything you need.   Cicero

Having someone wonder where you are when you don't come home at night is a very old human need.   Margaret Mead

Make yourself necessary to somebody.   Ralph Waldo Emerson

At the heart of personality is the need to feel a sense of being lovable without having to qualify for that acceptance.   Paul Tournier

There comes a time in every man's life when he needs his own toilet.
                                                          Patrick Süskind

If you've got a video player, always make sure you've got a TV. **Forrest Gump**

Four be the things I'd be better without: love, curiosity, freckles and doubt.
Dorothy Parker

Don't go around saying the world owes you a living; the world owes you nothing; it was here first. **Mark Twain**

I'm a firm believer in anxiety and the power of negative thinking.
Gertrude Berg

NEIGHBOUR

Of course we don't know her, she's a neighbour. **Morris Panych**

Neighbours: the strangers who live next door. **Richard Bayan**

We make our friends; we make our enemies; but God makes our next door neighbour. **G. K. Chesterton**

It is easier to love humanity as a whole than to love one's neighbour.
Eric Hoffer

Choose your neighbour before your house and your companion before the road. **Arabian proverb**

Welcome thy neighbor into thy fallout shelter. He'll come in handy if you run out of food. **Dean McLaughlin**

I am happy to find you are on good terms with your neighbors. It is almost the most important circumstance in life, since nothing is so corroding as frequently to meet persons with whom one has any difference.
Thomas Jefferson

Your own safety is at stake when your neighbor's wall is ablaze. **Horace**

In the field of world policy I would dedicate this nation to the policy of the good neighbor.   F. D. Roosevelt

My neighbor does not want to be loved as much as he wants to be envied.
                                                          Irving Layton

Love thy neighbour as thyself, but choose your neighborhood.   Louise Beal

NEUTRAL

The hottest places in hell are reserved for those who, in time of great moral crisis, maintain their neutrality.   Dante Alighieri

It is not the neutrals or the lukewarm who make history.   Adolf Hitler

If you are neutral in situations of injustice, you have chosen the side of the oppressor. If an elephant has its foot on the tail of a mouse and you say that you are neutral, the mouse will not appreciate your neutrality.
                                              Archbishop Desmond Tutu

The heart is never neutral.   Lord Shaftesbury

NEVER ...

Never ask a barber if you need a haircut.   Daniel Greenberg

Never buy a fur from a veterinarian.   Joan Rivers

Never hire anybody whose CV rhymes.   Rita Rudner

Never advise anyone to go to war or to marry.   Spanish proverb

Never say 'bite me' to a vampire.   Anon

Never moon a werewolf.   Mike Binders

Never throw a punch at a redwood.   Tom Selleck

Never ask a man where he has been.   Mae West

Never rub another man's rhubarb.   The Joker, *Batman*

Never lick a steak knife.   Dave Barry

Never play leapfrog with a unicorn.   Anon

Never buy tights off a mermaid.   Anon

Never co-sign.   Al McGuire

Never say 'oops' in the operating room.   Dr Leo Troy

Never cut what you can untie.   Joseph Joubert

Never interrupt one's desire to defecate.
                Dr John Harvey Kellogg, *The Road to Wellville*

Never take the antidote before the poison.   Latin proverb

Never think you've seen the last of anything.   Eudora Welty

Never answer an anonymous letter.   Yogi Berra

Never rub bottoms with a porcupine.
                                               Akan proverb

Never kick a fresh turd on a hot day.   Harry S. Truman

Never have your wife in the morning – the day may have something
better to offer.   P. V. Taylor

Never go to bed quite sober. — Hilary Hook

Never mistake asthma for passion, and vice versa. — A. J. Cromer

Never underestimate the hypocrisy of politicians. — James Herbert

Never whisper to the deaf or wink at the blind.
Slovenian proverb

Never miss a chance to have sex or appear on television. — Gore Vidal

Never eat a heavily sugared doughnut before you go on TV. — John Cheever

Never play cat and mouse games if you're a mouse. — Don Addis

Never request that *he* sleep in the wet spot. — C. E. Crimmins

Never use a long word when a diminutive one will do. — William Safire

Never make a defence or apology before you are accused. — King Charles I

Never take a solemn oath. People think you mean it. — Norman Douglas

Never appeal to a man's 'better nature'. He might not have one.
Robert Heinlein

Never say something remarkable. It is sure to be wrong. — Mark Rutherford

Never get a mime talking. He won't stop. — Marcel Marceau

Never under any circumstances take a sleeping pill and a laxative on the same night. — Dave Barry

Never trust a woman whose father calls her 'Princess'. Chances are she believes it. — Wes Smith

Never cry over spilt milk. It could've been whiskey.   'Pappy Maverick', *Maverick*

Never assume that the guy understands that you and he have a
relationship.   Dave Barry

Never date a man who has a freshly used fly swatter as his only
living-room decoration.   Vicki Christian

Never approach a bull from the front, a horse from the rear or a fool from
any direction.   Ken Alstad

Never eat anything whose listed ingredients cover more than one-third of
the package.   Joseph Leonard

Never drink black coffee at lunch; it will keep you awake all afternoon.
                                                          Jilly Cooper

Never say anything on the phone that you wouldn't want your mother to
hear at your trial.   Sydney Biddle Barrows

Never do anything to a clitoris with your teeth that you wouldn't do to an
expensive waterproof wristwatch.   P. J. O'Rourke

Never play cards with a man named Doc. Never eat at a place called
Mom's. Never sleep with a woman who's got more troubles than you.
                                                         Nelson Algren

Never let people see the bottom of your purse or your mind.
                                                         Italian proverb

Never settle with words what you can accomplish with a flame-thrower.
                                                        Bruce Fierstein

Never give in! Never, never, never, never! Except to convictions of honour
or good sense!   Winston Churchill

NOISE

Nowadays, most men lead lives of noisy desperation.

James Thurber

Noise, n: A stench in the ear ... the chief product and authenticating sound of civilization.

Ambrose Bierce

Noise is the most impertinent of all forms of interruption. It is not only an interruption, but a disruption of thought. Of course, where there is nothing to interrupt, noise will not be so particularly painful.

Arthur Schopenhauer

What a blessing it would be if we could open and shut our ears as easily as we open and shut our mouths.

Georg Christoph Lichtenberg

It might be a good thing if people's ears would bleed. Then people might get aroused.

Symposium on noise pollution

Noise pollution is a relative thing. In a city, it's a jet plane taking off. In a monastery, it's a pen that scratches.

Robert Orben

He who sleeps in continual noise is awakened by silence.

William Dean Howells

But ice-crunching and loud gum-chewing, together with drumming on tables, and whistling the same tune 70 times in succession, because they indicate an indifference on the part of the perpetrator to the rest of the world in general, are not only registered on the delicate surfaces of the brain but eat little holes in it until it finally collapses or blows up.

Robert Benchley

For children is there any happiness which is not also noise?

Frederick W. Faber

When asked what he thought the future would be like he said, 'The same, but louder.'

Anon

We like no noise unless we make it ourselves.   Marie de Rabutin-Chantal

If we don't sit down and shut up once in a while we'll lose our minds even earlier than we had expected. Noise is an imposition on sanity, and we live in very noisy times.   Joan Baez

NORMAL

I told the doctor I was overtired, anxiety-ridden, compulsively active, constantly depressed, with recurring fits of paranoia. Turns out I'm normal.
Jules Feiffer

I can't cure normal.   Dr Debbie

There are four types: the cretin, the imbecile, the stupid and the mad. Normality is a balanced mixture of all four.   Umberto Eco

Nobody realizes that some people expend tremendous energy merely to be normal.   Albert Camus

The only normal people are the ones you don't know very well.   Joe Ancis

An abnormal reaction to an abnormal situation is normal behavior.
Viktor E. Frankl

Sanity is madness put to good uses.   George Santayana

NOSTALGIA

They spend their time mostly looking forward to the past.   John Osborne

The people who are always hankering loudest for some golden yesteryear usually drive new cars.   Russell Baker

—What is the name given to the condition where the sufferer can fall asleep at any time?
—Nostalgia.   **Melanie Sykes and Contestant,** *The Vault*

Nostalgia, the vice of the aged.   **Angela Carter**

Every generation believes that there was a golden age that ended about forty years previously.   **Anon**

The people who live in a Golden Age usually go around complaining how yellow everything looks.   **Randall Jarrell**

Don't look back. Something may be gaining on you.   **Leroy 'Satchel' Paige**

NOTHING

God created the world out of nothing. But the nothingness still shows through.   **Paul Valéry**

People have the illusion that all over the world, all the time, all kinds of fantastic things are happening. When in fact, over most of the world, most of the time, nothing is happening.   **David Brinkley**

Nothing, like something, happens anywhere.   **Philip Larkin**

Nothing is more real than nothing.   **Samuel Beckett**

Sometimes nothin' can be a real cool hand.   **Luke Jackson,** *Cool Hand Luke*

A hole is nothing at all, but you can break your neck in it.   **Austin O'Malley**

Nothing is often a good thing to do and always a good thing to say.
                                    Will Durant

Even a good thing isn't as good as nothing.   **Zen saying**

I have spent my life laboriously doing nothing.   Hugo Grotius

It is nothing – they are only thrashing my husband.   Portuguese proverb

If nothing works faster than Anadin, take nothing.   Anon

'I am a human nothing' should have read 'I am assuming nothing'.
                    Correction in The *Guardian* in a letter from Tom Stoppard

Sitting quietly, doing nothing, spring comes, and the grass grows by itself.
                                                          Zen saying

OBVIOUS

It is the familiar that usually eludes us in life. What is before our nose is what we see last.

William Barrett

The obvious is that which is never seen until someone expresses it simply.

Kahlil Gibran

Sometimes the first duty of intelligent men is the restatement of the obvious.

George Orwell

Ignore the obvious at your peril.

Huw Wheldon

OPINION

When anyone says they often think something, it means they've just thought of it now.

Michael Frayn

Too often we enjoy the comfort of opinion, without the discomfort of thought.

John F. Kennedy

The fact that an opinion is widely held is no evidence whatever that it is not utterly absurd.

Bertrand Russell

I would like to be able to admire a person's opinions as I would their dog – without being expected to take it home with me.

Frank A. Clark

If you want to discover your true opinion of anybody, observe the impression made on you by the first sight of a letter from him.

Arthur Schopenhauer

What others think of us would be of little moment did it not, when known, so deeply tinge what we think of ourselves.

George Santayana

I think everyone is entitled to my opinion.   Victor Borge

If one person calls you a donkey, ignore him; if two people call you a donkey, buy a saddle.   Yiddish saying

In view of the stupidity of the majority of people, a widely held opinion is more likely to be foolish than sensible.   Bertrand Russell

OPPORTUNITY

If you are looking for a big opportunity, find a big problem.   Anon

The reason so many people never get anywhere in life is because when opportunity knocks, they are out in the backyard looking for four-leaf clovers.   Walter Chrysler

If opportunity came disguised as temptation, one knock would be enough.   Lane Olinghouse

If a window of opportunity appears, don't pull down the shade.   Tom Peters

My place is in the sunlight of opportunity.   Martin Luther King Jr

Opportunity is missed by most people because it is dressed in overalls and looks like work.   Thomas Alva Edison

If opportunity doesn't knock, build a door.
Milton Berle

Every exit is an entrance somewhere else.   Tom Stoppard

Once you have missed the first buttonhole, you'll never manage to button up.
Johann Wolfgang von Goethe

Opportunity is a bird that does not perch.   Claude McDonald

Next to knowing when to seize an opportunity, the most important thing in life is to know when to forgo an advantage.   Benjamin Disraeli

OPTIMIST AND PESSIMIST

Your bladder's either half full or half empty depending on your world view.
Anon

An optimist stays up until midnight to see the new year in. A pessimist stays up to make sure the old year leaves.   Bill Vaughan

Rosiness is not a worse windowpane than gloomy grey when viewing the world.   Grace Paley

I am a pessimist because of intelligence, but an optimist because of will.
Antonio Gramsci

I find nothing more depressing than optimism.   Paul Fussell

The basis of optimism is sheer terror.   Oscar Wilde

Optimist, n. A proponent of the doctrine that black is white.   Ambrose Bierce

I'm a recovering optimist.   Larry Gelbart

A pessimist is someone who has had to listen to too many optimists.
Don Marquis

I've always expected the worst, and it's always worse than I expected.
Henry James

I don't consider myself a pessimist. I think of a pessimist as someone who is waiting for it to rain. And I feel soaked to the skin.   Leonard Cohen

The most prolific period of pessimism comes at twenty-one, or thereabouts, when the first attempt is made to translate dreams into reality.

Heywood Broun

Even when I put my Sunray lamp on, it rains on me.   Woody Allen

Getting out of bed in the morning is an act of false confidence.   Jules Feiffer

Pessimism, when you get used to it, is just as agreeable as optimism.

Arnold Bennett

Situation hopeless ... but not serious.   Southern German proverb

No one really knows enough to be a pessimist.   Norman Cousins

Keep your face to the sunshine and you cannot see the shadow. It's what sunflowers do.   Helen Keller

A pessimist is correct oftener than an optimist, but an optimist has more fun – and neither can stop the march of events.   Robert Heinlein

This country cherishes the belief that the sounding alarm is only the dinner gong signalling second helpings.   John Peyton

I always feel an optimist when I emerge from a tunnel.   Robert Lynd

A lament in one ear, maybe, but always a song in the other.   Sean O'Casey

An optimist is a person who sees a green light everywhere, while the pessimist sees only the red stop light. The truly wise person is colour-blind.

Albert Schweitzer

I wish I could think of a positive point to leave you with. Will you take two negative points?   Woody Allen

—Is the glass half full or half empty?
—Depends on whether you're pouring or drinking.

Bill Cosby and his Grandmother

One day, someone showed me a glass of water that was half full. And he said, 'Is it half full or half empty?' So I drank the water. No more problem.

Alexander Jodorowsky

PAIN

Laugh and the world laughs with you. Stub your toe and the world laughs whether you do or not.
Linda Perret

Life is pain, Highness. Anyone who says differently is selling something.
Westley, *The Princess Bride*

The stabbing horror of life is not contained in calamities and disasters, because these things wake one up and one gets very familiar and intimate with them and finally they become tame again … No, it is more like being in a hotel room in Hoboken, let us say, and just enough money in one's pocket for another meal.
Henry Miller

Is there any stab as deep as wondering where and how much you failed those you loved?
Florida Scott-Maxwell

Behind joy and laughter there may be a temperament, coarse, hard, and callous. But behind sorrow there is always sorrow. Pain, unlike pleasure, wears no mask.
Oscar Wilde

You need bruises to know blessings and I have known both.
Frances Shand Kydd

Pain is life – the sharper, the more evidence of life.
Charles Lamb

PARADISE

I should have no use for a paradise in which I should be deprived of the right to prefer hell.
Jean Rostand

The earth is a Paradise, the only one we will ever know. We will realize it the moment we open our eyes. We don't have to make it a Paradise – it is one. We have only to make ourselves fit to inhabit it.
Henry Miller

The only paradise is a lost paradise.

Marcel Proust

The longing for paradise is paradise itself.

Kahlil Gibran

PARANOIA

Sometimes I get the feeling that the whole world is against me, but deep down I know that's not true. Some of the smaller countries are neutral.

Robert Orben

I moved to New York for health reasons. I'm paranoid and New York is the only place where my fears are justified.

Anita Weiss

Paranoia is knowing all the facts.

Woody Allen

I'm a tad paranoid. I think the person in front of me is following me the long way round.

Dennis Miller

Those are the kind of windows faces look in at.

Withnail, *Withnail and I*

If you see in your wine the reflection of a person not in your range of vision, don't drink it.

Chinese proverb

To the man who is afraid everything rustles.

Sophocles

A paranoid is someone who knows a little of what's going on.

William Burroughs

I envy paranoids; they actually feel people are paying attention to them.

Susan Sontag

I am a kind of paranoiac in reverse. I suspect people of plotting to make me happy.

J. D. Salinger

PASSION

You know the Greeks didn't write obituaries. They only asked one question after a man died: did he have passion?   Dean Kansky, *Serendipidity*

A man may be short and dumpy and getting bald, but if he has fire, women will like him.   Mae West

Nobody notices postmen, yet they have passions like other men.

G. K. Chesterton

Passion in a dromedary doesn't go so deep; a camel when it's mating never sobs itself to sleep.   Noël Coward

Live passionately, even if it kills you, because something is going to kill you anyway.   T. E. Lawrence

Follow your bliss.   Joseph Campbell

PAST

The past is a foreign country; they do things differently there.   L. P. Hartley

Doesn't one always think of the past, in a garden with men and women lying under the trees? Aren't they one's past, all that remains of it, those men and women, those ghosts lying under the trees … one's happiness, one's reality?   Virginia Woolf

The past is the only dead thing that smells sweet.   Cyril Connolly

The past is always attractive because it is drained of fear.   Thomas Carlyle

The past is almost as much a work of the imagination as the future.

Jessamyn West

He who believes the past cannot be changed has not yet written his memoirs.
David Ben-Gurion

Those who cannot remember the past are condemned to repeat it.
George Santayana

The past must be a springboard, not a sofa.
Harold Macmillan

PATIENCE

Perhaps there is only one cardinal sin: impatience. Because of impatience we were driven out of Paradise, because of impatience we cannot return.
W. H Auden

No man is impatient with his creditors.
Talmud

Patience and the mulberry leaf become a silk robe.
Chinese proverb

The real secret of patience is to find something to do in the meantime.
Doug Larson

Beware the fury of a patient man.
John Dryden

Things may come to those who wait, but only the things left by those who hustle.
Anon

All human wisdom is summed up in two words – wait and hope.
Alexandre Dumas

Everything comes to him who waits, except a loaned book.
Kin Hubbard

PATRIOT

—What I did was for the good of the country.
—Fortunately our country always manages to survive patriots like you.

Fred Van Ackerman and Bob Munson, Advise & Consent

Patriotism is often an arbitrary veneration of real estate above principles.

George Jean Nathan

What is patriotism but a love of the food one ate as a child?   Lin Yutang

A healthy nation is as unconscious of its nationality as a healthy man of his bones. But if you break a nation's nationality it will think of nothing else but getting it set again.

George Bernard Shaw

A patriot must always be ready to defend his country against his government.

Edward Abbey

A real patriot is the fellow who gets a parking ticket and rejoices that the system works.

Bill Vaughan

The proper means of increasing the love we bear our native country is to reside some time in a foreign one.

William Shenstone

Talking of patriotism, what humbug it is; it is a word which always commemorates a robbery. There isn't a foot of land in the world which doesn't represent the ousting and re-ousting of a long line of successive owners.

Mark Twain

The politicians were talking themselves red, white and blue in the face.

Clare Booth Luce

Soak the American flag in heroin and I'll suck it.   William Burroughs

Don't burn the flag, wash it.   Norman Thomas

PEACE

Man's greatest blunder has been in trying to make peace with the skies instead of with his neighbors.
Kin Hubbard

If we have no peace, it is because we have forgotten that we belong to each other.
Mother Teresa

Peace is not an absence of war, it is a virtue, a state of mind, a disposition of benevolence, confidence, justice.
Baruch Spinoza

I hope for peace and sanity – it's the same thing.
Studs Terkel

Almost all of us long for peace and freedom; but very few of us have much enthusiasm for the thoughts, feelings and actions that make for peace and freedom.
Aldous Huxley

You cannot shake hands with a clenched fist.
Indira Gandhi

People who talk about peace are very often the most quarrelsome.
Nancy Astor

Don't tell me peace has broken out?
Bertolt Brecht

PEACE OF MIND

All fortune belongs to him who has a contented mind. Is not the whole earth covered with leather for him whose feet are encased in shoes?
Panchatantra

Peace of mind produces right values, right values produce right thoughts. Right thoughts produce right actions and right actions produce work which will be a material reflection for others to see of the serenity at the center of it all.
Robert M. Pirsig

There is no need to go to India or anywhere else to find peace. You will find that deep place of silence right in your room, your garden or even your bathtub.

Elisabeth Kübler-Ross

Everywhere I have sought rest and not found it, except sitting in a corner by myself with a little book.

Thomas à Kempis

Arranging a bowl of flowers in the morning can give a sense of quiet in a crowded day – like writing a poem, or saying a prayer.

Anne Morrow Lindbergh

There is no such thing as inner peace. There is only nervousness and death.

Fran Lebowitz

You are the first person who has been perfect rest to me.

Olive Schreiner, letter to Havelock Ellis

PERCEPTION

There is nothing wrong with the world. What's wrong is our way of looking at it.

Henry Miller

They tell you that a tree is only a combination of chemical elements. I prefer to believe that God created it, and that it is inhabited by a nymph.

Pierre Auguste Renoir

The tree which moves some to tears of joy is in the eyes of others only a green thing which stands in the way. As a man is, so he sees.   William Blake

People only see what they are prepared to see.   Ralph Waldo Emerson

To a worm in horseradish, the whole world is horseradish.   Yiddish proverb

We don't see things as they are; we see them as we are.   Anaïs Nin

I shut my eyes in order to see.   Paul Gauguin

It is only with the heart that one can see rightly; what is essential is invisible to the eye.   Antoine de Saint-Exupéry

It was too late to unsee.   Hannah Green

PERFECT

Perfection is such a nuisance that I often regret having cured myself of using tobacco.   Émile Zola

It's not evil that's ruining the earth, but mediocrity. The crime is not that Nero played while Rome burned, but that he played badly.   Ned Rorem

I never realized how mediocre the world was until I got involved with some of its supposedly top people.   Mason Williams

Sometimes I worry about being a success in a mediocre world.   Lily Tomlin

We aren't here to make things perfect. The snowflake is perfect. The stars are perfect. Not us. Not us! We are here to ruin ourselves and to break our hearts and love the wrong people and die.   Ronny Cammareri, *Moonstruck*

The indefatigable pursuit of an unattainable perfection, even though it consists in nothing more than the pounding of an old piano, is alone what gives meaning to our life on this unavailing star.   Logan Pearsall Smith

It is only imperfection that complains of what is imperfect. The more perfect we are the more gentle and quiet we become towards the defects of others.   Joseph Addison

In our corrupted state, common weaknesses and defects contribute more towards the reconciling us to one another than all the precepts of the philosophers and divines.   Lord Halifax

There is a crack in everything God has made.   Ralph Waldo Emerson

PERSISTENCE

Knowing trees, I understand the meaning of patience. Knowing grass, I can appreciate persistence.
Hal Borland

Persistence is the hard work that you do after you are tired of doing the hard work you already did.
Newt Gingrich

It is no good getting furious if you get stuck. What I do is keep thinking about the problem but work on something else. Sometimes it is years before I see the way forward. In the case of information loss and black holes, it was twenty-nine years.
Stephen Hawking

Two little mice fell in a bucket of cream. The first mouse quickly gave up and drowned. The second mouse wouldn't quit. He struggled so hard that eventually he churned that cream into butter and crawled out.
Frank Abagnale, Catch Me If You Can

The game isn't over till it's over.
Yogi Berra

My mum used to say to me, 'Spit on yer 'ands and take a fresh 'old.' Keep going even if you have setbacks.
Leslie Garrett

The question isn't who's going to let me; it's who's going to stop me.
Ayn Rand

PHILOSOPHY

Philosophy asks the simple question: What is it all about?
Alfred North Whitehead

Some people see things that are and ask, Why? Some people dream of things that never were and ask, Why not? Some people have to go to work and don't have time for all that shit.
George Carlin

When I want philosophy, I'll turn on *Oprah*.　　Jake Metzner, *Jack Frost*

There is no religion in which everyday life is not considered a prison; there is no philosophy or ideology that does not think that we live in alienation.
Eugene Ionesco

The only difference between graffiti and philosophy is the word fuck.
Graffiti

Philosophy is questions that may never be answered. Religion is answers that may never be questioned.　　Adam L. Carley

Philosophy: a route of many roads leading from nowhere to nothing.
Ambrose Bierce

Beware when the great God lets loose a thinker on this planet.
Ralph Waldo Emerson

Philosophers are adults who persist in asking childish questions.　Isaiah Berlin

To be a real philosopher all that is necessary is to hate someone else's type of thinking.　　William James

Why are philosophers intent on forcing others to believe things? Is that a nice way to behave towards someone?　　Robert Nozick

I have tried in my time to be a philosopher, but cheerfulness was always breaking in.　　Oliver Edwards

Everyone should study at least enough philosophy and *belles-lettres* to make his sexual experience more delectable.　Georg Christoph Lichtenberg

If everybody contemplates the infinite instead of fixing the drains, many of us will die of cholera.　　John Rich

When I study philosophical works I feel I am swallowing something which I don't have in my mouth. **Albert Einstein**

Philosophy is common sense in a dress suit. **Oliver S. Braston**

My philosophy is as simple as ever – smoking, drinking, moderate sexual intercourse on a diminishing scale, reading and writing (not arithmetic). I have a selfish absorption in the well-being and achievement of Noël Coward. **Noël Coward**

My philosophy? Have a laugh for as long as you can and don't get run over. Or stabbed. **Ricky Gervais**

I've tried Buddhism, Scientology, Numerology, Transcendental Meditation, Qabbala, t'ai chi, feng shui and Deepak Chopra but I find straight gin works best. **Phyllis Diller**

My advice to you is not inquire why or whither, but just enjoy your ice cream while it's on your plate – that's my philosophy. **Thornton Wilder**

PHOTOGRAPH

I really believe there are things nobody would see if I didn't photograph them. **Diane Arbus**

The magic of photography is metaphysical. What you see in the photograph isn't what you saw at the time. **Terence Donovan**

A photograph is a secret about a secret. The more it tells you, the less you know. **Diane Arbus**

There are always two people in every picture: the photographer and the viewer. **Ansel Adams**

Not everybody trusts paintings but people believe photographs. **Ansel Adams**

People believe that photographs are true and therefore cannot be art.

Mason Cooley

Photography is the 'art form' of the untalented ... Where is credit due?
To the designer of the camera? To the finger on the button? To the law of
averages?

Gore Vidal

The rarest thing in the world is a woman who is pleased with photographs of herself.

Elizabeth Metcalf

Using a camera appeases the anxiety which the work-driven feel about not
working when they are on vacation and supposed to be having fun. They
have something to do that is like a friendly imitation of work: they can
take pictures.

Susan Sontag

What most of us are after, when we have a picture taken, is a good
natural-looking picture that doesn't resemble us.

Peg Bracken

Today, everything exists to end in a photograph.

Susan Sontag

PITY

Ah, sweet pity. Where would my love life have been without it?

Homer Simpson

More helpful than all wisdom is one draft of simple human pity that will
not forsake us.

George Eliot

There is always an element of pity in love.

John Stephen Strange

A tear dries quickly when it is shed for the troubles of others.

Cicero

Cosmic upheaval is not so moving as a little child pondering the death of a sparrow in the corner of a barn. **Thomas Savage**

Pity is not natural to man. Children and savages are always cruel. Pity is acquired and improved by the cultivation of reason. We may have uneasy sensations from seeing a creature in distress, without pity; but we have not pity unless we wish to relieve him. **Samuel Johnson**

How much better a thing it is to be envied than to be pitied. **Herodotus**

Pity is exhaustible. What a terrible discovery! **Enid Bagnold**

People in distress never think that you feel enough. **Samuel Johnson**

In our world, pity implies a degrading act of condescension, a patronizing good deed performed by someone in a superior position for the sake of someone presumably inferior. **Ralph C. Wood**

The response man has the greatest difficulty in tolerating is pity, especially when he wants it. Hatred is a tonic, it makes one live, it inspires vengeance, but pity kills, it makes our weakness weaker. **Honoré de Balzac**

Pity costs nothin' and ain't worth nothin'. **Josh Billings**

Pity is often a reflection of our own evils in the ills of others. It is a delicate foresight of the troubles into which we may fall. **La Rochefoucauld**

I seem to be the only person in the world who doesn't mind being pitied. If you love me, pity me. The human state is pitiable: born to die, capable of so much, accomplishing so little; killing instead of creating, destroying instead of building, hating instead of loving. Pitiful, pitiful. **Jessamyn West**

Those who do not complain are never pitied. **Jane Austen**

PLACES

You can fall in love at first sight with a place as with a person.   Alec Waugh

Some places speak distinctly. Certain dank gardens cry aloud for a murder; certain old houses demand to be haunted; certain coasts are set apart for shipwrecks.   Robert Louis Stevenson

Some other places were not so good but maybe we were not so good when we were in them.   Jeff Greenwald

One always begins to forgive a place as soon as it's left behind.
                                                                   Charles Dickens

How hard it is to escape from places. However carefully one goes they hold you – you leave little bits of yourself fluttering on the fences – little rags and shreds of your very life.   Katherine Mansfield

The spot of ground on which a man has stood is forever interesting to him.
                                                                  Alexander Smith

One does not love a place the less for having suffered in it, unless it has been all suffering, nothing but suffering.
                                                                       Jane Austen

There is nothing like returning to a place that remains unchanged to find the ways in which you yourself have altered.   Nelson Mandela

Places remember events.   James Joyce

It's not on any map; true places never are.   Herman Melville

PLEASURE

Ooh, laundry ... hot off the dryer.   Bobby Hill, *King of the Hill*

To wash one's hair, make one's toilet, and put on scented robes; even if not a soul sees one, these preparations still produce an inner pleasure.

Sei Shōnagon

Everybody knows how to weep, but it takes a fine texture of mind to know thoroughly how to enjoy the bright and happy things of life.

Oliver Bell Bunce

To sit in the shade on a fine day and look upon verdure is the most perfect refreshment.   Jane Austen

Take delight in a thing, or rather in anything, not as a means to some other end, but just because it is what it is. A child in the full health of his mind will put his hand flat on the summer lawn, feel it, and give a little shiver of private glee at the elastic firmness of the globe.   Charles E. Montague

Perhaps it's a good time to reconsider pleasure at its roots. Changing out of wet shoes and socks, for instance.   Barbara Holland

I have never yet met anyone who did not think it was an agreeable sensation to cut tinfoil with scissors.   Georg Christoph Lichtenberg

To poke a wood fire is more solid enjoyment than almost anything else in the world.   Charles Dudley Warner

A hot bath! How exquisite a vespertine pleasure, how luxurious, fervid and flagrant a consolation for the rigours, the austerities, the renunciations of the day.   Rose Macaulay

Nobody who looks as though he enjoyed life is ever called distinguished, though he is a man in a million.   Robertson Davies

To torture a man, you have to know his pleasures.   Stanislaw J. Lec

POET

I was too slow a mover to be a boxer. It was much easier to be a poet.

T. S. Eliot

That man is either crazy or he is a poet.

Horace

Everywhere I go, I find a poet has been there before me.

Sigmund Freud

It is the role of the poet to look at what is happening in the world and to know that quite other things are happening.

V. S. Pritchett

A poet looks at the world as a man looks at a woman.

Wallace Stevens

Everybody has their own idea of what's a poet ... I like to think of myself as the one who carries the light bulb.

Bob Dylan

POETRY

Poetry is what makes my toenails twinkle.

Dylan Thomas

I've written some poetry I don't understand myself.

Carl Sandburg

Genuine poetry can communicate before it is understood.

T. S. Eliot

Someone says: 'Whom do you write for?' I reply: 'Do you read me?' If they say, 'Yes,' I say, 'Do you like it?' If they say 'No,' then I say, 'I don't write for you.'

W. H. Auden

Then he asked the question that you are all itching to ask me: 'How can you tell good poetry from bad?' I answered, 'How does one tell good fish from bad? Surely by the smell? Use your nose.'

Robert Graves

A poem is a form of refrigeration that stops language going bad. **Peter Porter**

—Miss Moore, your poetry is very difficult to read.
—It is very difficult to write. **Reader and Marianne Moore**

A poem is never a put-up job so to speak. It begins as a lump in the throat, a sense of wrong, a homesickness, a love sickness. It is never a thought to begin with. **Robert Frost**

The reader who is illuminated is, in a real sense, the poem. **H. M. Tomlinson**

POLITICAL CORRECTNESS

Being politically correct means always having to say you're sorry.
Charles Osgood

At its grandest, political correctness is an attempt to accelerate evolution.
Martin Amis

Political correctness is the natural continuum from the party line. What we are seeing once again is a self-appointed group of vigilantes imposing their views on others. It is a heritage of communism, but they don't seem to see this. **Doris Lessing**

Open discussion of many major public questions has for some time now been taboo. We can't open our mouths without being denounced as racists, misogynists, supremacists, imperialists or fascists. As for the media, they stand ready to trash anyone so designated. **Saul Bellow**

POLITICS

When we got into office, the thing that surprised me most was to find that things were just as bad as we'd been saying they were. **John F. Kennedy**

Political solutions work as long as the situation is hopeless. **J. R. Slaughter**

Politics is not the art of the possible. It consists of choosing between the disastrous and the unpalatable.   J. K. Galbraith

Modern politics is civil war carried on by other means.   Alasdair MacIntyre

Political advice is a bit like your average Christmas fruitcake: something everyone gives and no one wants.   Bob Dole

The end move in politics is always to pick up a gun.   R. Buckminster Fuller

It would be a great reform in politics if wisdom could be made to spread as easily and as rapidly as folly.   Winston Churchill

I don't know why they call the House of Commons the 'Westminster village' because most villages usually have only one idiot.   Andy Hamilton

The Greek word for *idiot*, literally translated, means one who does not participate in politics. That sums up my conviction on the subject.
                                                                Gladys Pyle

The whole reason we have elected officials is so we don't have to think all the time.   Homer Simpson

Just because you don't take an interest in politics doesn't mean politics won't take an interest in you.   Pericles

The penalty that good men pay for not being interested in politics is to be governed by men worse than themselves.   Plato

Take our politicians: they're a bunch of yo-yos. The presidency is now a cross between a popularity contest and a high school debate, with an encyclopedia of clichés the first prize.   Saul Bellow

In politics stupidity is not a handicap.   Napoleon Bonaparte

The vice presidency is a spare tyre on the automobile of government.
                              John Nance Garner, former US Vice President

You better take advantage of the good cigars. You don't get much else in that job.   **Thomas 'Tip' O'Neill to Vice President Walter Mondale**

Political language is designed to make lies sound truthful and murder respectable, and to give an appearance of solidity to pure wind.

George Orwell

The most successful politician is he who says what the people are thinking most often and in the loudest voice.   Theodore Roosevelt

I have always liked the Kennedys as politicians. They had such great hair.

Pamela Anderson

You have to give the electorate a tune they can whistle.   **Enoch Powell**

It's dangerous for a national candidate to say things people might remember.   **Senator Eugene McCarthy**

Sometimes people mistake the way I talk for what I am thinking.   **Idi Amin**

Since a politician never believes what he says, he is quite surprised to be taken at his word.   Charles de Gaulle

Nothing corrupts a politician quite as much as friendship. Good politicians don't bribe; they make us like them.   **Matthew Parris**

Political promises are much like marriage vows. They are made at the beginning of the relationship between candidate and voter, but are quickly forgotten.   Dick Gregory

There are some politicians who, if their constituents were cannibals, would promise them missionaries for dinner.   H. L. Mencken

A liberal is a man who leaves the room before the fight starts. **Dorothy Parker**

When things haven't gone well for you, call in a secretary or staff man and chew him out. You will sleep better and they will appreciate the attention.

Lyndon B. Johnson

Politics will eventually be replaced by imagery. The politician will be only too happy to abdicate in favor of his image, because the image will be much more powerful than he could ever be.   Marshall McLuhan, 1971

Probably the most distinctive characteristic of the successful politician is selective cowardice.   Richard Harris

The public man needs but one patron, namely, the lucky moment.

Edward Bulwer-Lytton

I don't believe in the hereditary principle in the House of Lords. Imagine going to the dentist, sitting in the chair and he says, 'I'm not a dentist myself, but my father was a dentist and his father before him. Now, open wide!'   Tony Benn

Never murder a man when he's busy committing suicide.   Woodrow Wilson

A Conservative is a man who wants the rules changed so no one can make a pile the way he did.   Gregory Nunn

Nothing is so abject and pathetic as a politician who has lost his job, save only a retired stud-horse.   H. L. Mencken

I am a Tory anarchist. I should like everyone to go about doing just as he pleased – short of altering any of the things to which I have grown accustomed.   Sir Max Beerbohm

All isms end in fascism.   Gilbert Adair

To grasp the true meaning of socialism, imagine a world where everything is designed by the post office, even the sleaze.　　　　P. J. O'Rourke

Politics is not a bad profession. If you succeed there are many rewards, if you disgrace yourself you can always write a book.　　　Ronald Reagan

POPULAR MUSIC

Pop music is about stealing pocket money from children.　　Ian Anderson

Youth has many glories, but judgement is not one of them, and no amount of electronic amplification can turn a belch into an aria.
　　　　Alan Jay Lerner

Keith Richards is the only man who can make the Osbournes look Amish.
　　　　Robin Williams

Rock is a corruption of rhythm and blues which was a dilution of the blues, so that today's mass-marketed noise is a vulgarization of a vulgarization.　　　　Benny Green

I don't think anyone can really explain rock 'n' roll. Except Pete Townshend.　　　　Jeff Bebe, *Almost Famous*

Advice to rock gods: drugwise, stick to Ibuprofen, decaf lattes, and pale Pilsners ... If your stomach is not a flat slab, please leave your shirt on while performing ... If your girlfriend asks you to choose between her and your music, sell your instruments immediately – especially if you're a drummer ... Finally, go easy on the supermodels, don't forget to tune, and remember: a tiny bit of dry ice and lasers goes a long way. Ditto with tattoos.　　　　Ian Shoales

I remember when I was very young, I read an article by Fats Domino which has really influenced me. He said, 'You should never sing the lyrics out very clearly.'　　　　Mick Jagger

—What's it like being in the Rolling Stones for the last twenty-five years?
—Five years of work and twenty years of hanging around.

Interviewer and Charlie Watts

What is soul? It's like electricity – we don't really know what it is, but it's a force that can light a room.

Ray Charles

PORNOGRAPHY

If pornography releases sexual tension, why don't we send recipe books to the starving?

Andrea Dworkin

Pornography is rather like trying to find out about a Beethoven symphony by having someone tell you about it and perhaps hum a few bars.

Robertson Davies

Pornography tells lies about women. But pornography tells the truth about men.

John Stoltenberg

Women reading *Vogue* magazine about the latest fashions to come off the Paris runway, is the same as men looking at naked women in *Playboy*. We're both looking at places we're never going to visit.

Andi Rhoads

The difference between pornography and erotica is lighting.

Gloria Leonard

POWER

I am the Emperor, and I want dumplings.

Ferdinand I, Emperor of Austria

Nearly all men can stand adversity, but if you want to test a man's character, give him power.

Abraham Lincoln

With great power comes great responsibility.

Peter Parker, *Spider-Man*

Power is delightful and absolute power is absolutely delightful.

Lord Lester of Herne Hill

Power always thinks it has a great soul and vast views beyond the comprehension of the weak.

John Adams

We thought, because we had power, we had wisdom.   **Stephen Vincent Benét**

Power is not only what you have but what the enemy thinks you have.

Saul Alinksy

The less the power, the greater the desire to exercise it.   **Bernard Levin**

Nobody is as powerful as we make them out to be.   **Alice Walker**

Upon the highest throne in the world, we are seated, still, on our arses.

Michel de Montaigne

Why are stamps adorned with kings and presidents? That we may lick their hinder parts and thump their heads.   **Howard Nemerov**

The higher a monkey climbs, the more you see of his behind.

General Joe Stillwell

You don't have power if you surrender all your principles – you have office.

Ron Toddon

Next to power without honor, the most dangerous thing in the world is power without humor.   **Eric Sevareid**

There are few things more dangerous than a mixture of power, arrogance and incompetence.   **Bob Herbert**

Uneasy lies the head that wears a crown.   **William Shakespeare, *Henry IV, Part II***

We are most deeply asleep at the switch when we fancy we control any switches at all.
Annie Dillard

Authority without wisdom is like a heavy axe without an edge, fitter to bruise than polish.
Anne Bradstreet

What connects two thousand years of genocide? Too much power in too few hands.
Simon Wiesenthal

I have a fantasy where Ted Turner is elected president but refuses because he doesn't want to give up power.
Arthur C. Clarke

Nowhere does power give itself up willingly.
Nan Levinson

All the Caesars have not the staying power of a lily in a cottage border.
Reginald Farrer

Ironically, women who acquire power are more likely to be criticized for it than are the men who have always had it.
Carolyn Heilbrun

The thing women have got to learn is that nobody gives you power. You just take it.
Roseanne

The most common way people give up their power is by thinking they don't have any.
Alice Walker

The one power a man has that cannot be stripped from him is the power to do nothing.
Morgan Llywelyn

Power tends to corrupt, but absolute power corrupts absolutely. Great men are almost always bad men.
Lord Acton

If absolute power corrupts absolutely, does absolute powerlessness make you pure?
Harry Shearer

When you sweep stairs, start at the top.   German proverb

If absolute power corrupts absolutely, where does that leave God?
                                                            George Deacon

The most powerful people on earth are focus groups.   President Bill Clinton

PRACTICE

Champions keep playing until they get it right.   Billie Jean King

If you don't practise, you don't deserve to dream.   Andre Agassi

To be number one, you must train like you are number two.   Maurice Green

You don't run twenty-six miles at five minutes a mile on good looks and
a secret recipe.   Frank Shorter, US marathon runner

For every pass I caught in a game, I caught a thousand passes in practice.
                                        Don Hutson, American football player

James Green's trainer used to blow bubbles and make the fighter punch
them.   Miguel Diaz

If I don't practise for one day, I know it; if I don't practise for two days, the
critics knows it; if I don't practise for three days, the audience knows it.
                                            Ignacy Paderewski, pianist

I never practise; I always play.   Wanda Landowska, harpsichordist

Cab drivers are living proof that practice does not make perfect.
                                                            Howard Ogden

PRAISE

People ask for criticism but they only want praise.   **Somerset Maugham**

Praise is a powerful people-builder. Catch individuals doing something right.   **Brian Tracy**

We refuse praise in a desire to be praised twice.   **La Rochefoucauld**

Praise out of season, or tactlessly bestowed, can freeze the heart as much as blame.   **Pearl S. Buck**

I would have praised you more if you had praised me less.
          Louis XIV, having been given a flattering poem by Nicolas Boileau

Praise is warming and desirable. But it is an earned thing. It has to be deserved, like a hug from a child.   **Phyllis McGinley**

The meanest, most contemptible kind of praise is that which first speaks well of a man, and then qualifies it with a 'but'.   **Henry Ward Beecher**

PRAYER

I'm not normally a praying man, but if you're up there, please save me, Superman!   **Homer Simpson**

Pray, n. To ask that the laws of the Universe be annulled on behalf of a single petitioner, confessedly unworthy.   **Ambrose Bierce**

Whatever man prays for, he prays for a miracle. Every prayer reduces itself to this – Great God, grant that twice two be not four.   **Ivan Turgenev**

If a dog's prayers were answered, bones would rain from the sky.

          Turkish proverb

Most people like short prayers and long sausages.   German proverb

More tears are shed over answered prayers than unanswered ones.
                                                         St Teresa of Avila

—Do you pray for the senators, Dr Hale?
—No, I look at the senators and I pray for the country.
                                   Van Wyck Brooks and Edward Everett Hale

Might never prays.   Bulgarian proverb

All I ask of Thee, Lord, is to be a drinker and a fornicator, an unbeliever
and a sodomite, and then to die.   Claude de Chauvigny

When I marched with Martin Luther King in Selma, I felt my legs were
praying.   Abraham Joshua Heschel

When I get down on my knees, it is not to pray.   Madonna

PREJUDICE

Prejudice is an unwillingness to be confused with facts.   H. L. Mencken

One may no more live in the world without picking up the moral
prejudices of the world than one will be able to go to hell without
perspiring.   H. L. Mencken

We are all tattooed in our cradles with the beliefs of our tribe; the record
may seem superficial but it is indelible.   Oliver Wendell Holmes Sr

Our prejudices are our mistresses; reason is at best our wife, very often
needed, but seldom minded.   Lord Chesterfield

An unbiased person is someone who has the same bias as we have.
                                              Mason City Globe Gazette

What in me is pure conviction is simple prejudice in you.   Phyllis McGinley

Intolerance of groups is often, strangely enough, exhibited more strongly against small differences than against fundamental ones.   Sigmund Freud

The people who are most bigoted are those who have no conviction at all.
G. K. Chesterton

I hang onto my prejudices, they are the testicles of my mind.   Eric Hoffer

PREPARATION

It wasn't raining when Noah built the ark.   Howard Ruff

If I had eight hours to cut down a tree, I'd spend six sharpening my axe.
Abraham Lincoln

Before filling your wheelbarrow, point it in the direction you intend to go.
B. A. Mello

Talking about straws and camels' backs is just one way of approaching things. If you have enough camels, no backs need be broken.   Idries Shah

Once you start buying first aid kits you start having accidents. George Mikes

Coming, ready or not!   Refrain to childhood game of Hide and Seek

PRIDE

Honey, I'm so proud of you. I watched you very closely and you didn't screw up once!   Carolyn Burnham, *American Beauty*

Swallow your pride occasionally. It's not fattening.   Frank Tyger

Pride – that's a luxury a woman in love can't afford.

Mary Haines, The Women

The little stations are very proud because the expresses have to pass them by.

Karl Kraus

This sad little lizard told me that he was a brontosaurus on his mother's side. I did not laugh; people who boast of ancestry often have little else to sustain them.

Robert Heinlein

PRISON

Wow! Look at these toilets! And just inches from your bed – talk about luxury!

Bart Simpson looking at cells in a penitentiary, The Simpsons

Prison is a Socialist paradise where equality prevails, everything is supplied, and competition is eliminated.

Elbert Hubbard

It is often safer to be in chains than to be free.

Franz Kafka

In my country, we go to prison first and then become president.

Nelson Mandela

The most anxious man in a prison is the governor.

George Bernard Shaw

We think caged birds sing, when indeed they cry.

James Webster

Stone walls do not a prison make nor iron bars a cage.

Richard Lovelace

A man will be imprisoned in a room with a door that's unlocked and opens inwards; as long as it does not occur to him to pull rather than push.

Ludwig Wittgenstein

The worst evil of being in prison is that one can never bar one's door.

Stendhal

All my life I had feared imprisonment, the nun's cell, the hospital bed, the places where one faced the self without distraction, without the crutches of other people.

Edna O'Brien

We are all serving a life sentence in the dungeon of the self.   Cyril Connolly

PRIVACY

I considered it desirable that he should know nothing about me but it was even better if he knew several things which were quite wrong.

Flann O'Brien

The human animal needs a freedom seldom mentioned, freedom from intrusion. He needs a little privacy as much as he wants understanding or vitamins or exercise or praise.

Phyllis McGinley

Civilization is the progress toward a society of privacy. The savage's whole existence is public, ruled by the laws of his tribe. Civilization is the process of setting man free from men.

Ayn Rand

Privacy exists only when others let you have it – privacy is an accorded right.

Alida Brill

What is privacy if not for invading?

Quentin Crisp

Privacy is a privilege not granted to the aged or the young.   Margaret Laurence

The thing that is most interesting about people is the way they are when no one is looking at them or the way they are when they are in private.

Suzanne Vega

Probably one of the most private things in the world is an egg until it is broken.

M. F. K. Fisher

PROBLEM

Nothing is a matter of life and death except life and death. **Angela Carter**

If you break your neck, if you have nothing to eat, if your house burns down, then you got a problem. Everything else is inconvenience.
Robert Fulghum

The two real problems in life are boredom and death. **Saul Bellow**

The problem is not that there are problems. The problem is expecting otherwise and thinking that having problems is a problem. **Theodore Rubin**

If you only have a hammer, you tend to see every problem as a nail.
Abraham H. Maslow

I'm no good at being noble, but it doesn't take much to see that the problems of three little people don't amount to a hill of beans in this crazy world. Someday you'll understand that. **Rick Blaine, *Casablanca***

That's part of your problem: you haven't seen enough movies. All of life's riddles are answered in the movies. **Davis, *Grand Canyon***

What a pity human beings can't exchange problems. Everyone knows exactly how to solve the other fellow's. **Olin Miller**

When one finds oneself in a hole of one's own making, it is a good time to examine the quality of the workmanship. **John Renmerde**

It often happens that I wake at night and begin to think about a serious problem and decide I must talk to the Pope about it. Then I wake up completely and remember that I am the Pope. **Pope John XXIII**

When confronted by a difficult problem, you can solve it more easily by reducing it to the question, 'How would the Lone Ranger have handled this?' **Brady's First Law of Problem Solving**

The most pleasant and useful persons are those who leave some of the problems of the universe for God to worry about.　　　**Don Marquis**

For every problem there is one solution which is simple, neat and wrong.
H. L. Mencken

It is often wonderful how putting down on paper a clear statement of a case helps one to see, not perhaps the way out, but the way in.　　**A. C. Benson**

I think the next best thing to solving a problem is finding some humor in it.
Frank A. Clark

Most problems are caused by solutions.　　　**Eric Sevareid**

There are very few problems that cannot be solved by orders ending with 'or die'.　　　**Alistair Young**

PROCRASTINATE

My friend Winnie is a procrastinator. He didn't get his birthmark until he was eight years old.　　　**Steven Wright**

My mother said, 'You won't amount to anything because you procrastinate.' I said, 'Just wait.'　　　**Judy Tenuta**

The Great Arizona Desert is full of the bleaching bones of people who waited for me to start something.　　　**Robert Benchley**

Procrastination is like a credit card – it's a lot of fun until you get the bill.
Christopher Parker

By the streets of 'by and by' one arrives at the house of 'never'.　　**Spanish proverb**

Never do today that which will become someone else's responsibility tomorrow.　　　**David Brent,** *The Office*

Don't put off for tomorrow what you can do today, because if you enjoy it today you can do it again tomorrow.   James Michener

A motto: Do it tomorrow; you've made enough mistakes today.
                                                          Dawn Powell

The only thing that has to be finished by next Tuesday is next Monday.
                                                     Jennifer Unlimited

You must have been warned against letting the golden hours slip by; but some of them are golden only because we let them slip by.   James M. Barrie

PROGRESS

It's 2003. Why can't I teleport?   Lewis Black

Humanity has advanced, when it has advanced, not because it has been sober, responsible, and cautious, but because it has been playful, rebellious, and immature.   Tom Robbins

The reason the Romans built their great paved highways was because they had such inconvenient footwear.   Baron de Montesquieu

Reasonable people adapt themselves to the world. Unreasonable people attempt to adapt the world to themselves. All progress, therefore, depends on unreasonable people.   George Bernard Shaw

Belief in progress is the Prozac of the thinking classes.   John Gray

Is it progress if a cannibal uses a knife and fork?   Stanislaw J. Lec

We have not crawled so very far up our individual grass blade toward an individual star.   Hilda Doolittle

The only real progress lies in learning to be wrong all alone.   Albert Camus

Usually, terrible things that are done with the excuse that progress requires them are not really progress at all, but just terrible things.   Russell Baker

A man learns to skate by staggering about making a fool of himself; indeed, he progresses in all things by making a fool of himself.

George Bernard Shaw

If I have seen further it is by standing on the shoulders of giants.

Isaac Newton

All this progress is marvellous ... now if only it would stop!   Allan Lamport

PROMISE

I am the child of an alcoholic. I know about promises.   Sandra Scoppettone

Don't let your mouth write no check your tail can't cash.   Bo Diddley

The Christian always swears a bloody oath that he will never do it again. The civilized man simply resolves to be a bit more careful next time.

H. L. Mencken

The best way to keep one's word is not to give it.   Napoleon Bonaparte

PROPERTY

Well! Some people talk of morality, and some of religion, but give me a little snug property.   Maria Edgeworth

No man but feels more of a man in the world if he have a bit of ground that he can call his own. However small it is on the surface, it is four thousand miles deep; and that is a very handsome property.

Charles Dudley Warner

My father owned a small piece of land. He carried it with him wherever he went.

Woody Allen

I said to my mother-in-law, 'My house is your house.' She said, 'Get the hell off my property.'

Joan Rivers

PROSTITUTE

—I've never paid for sex in my life.
—You just think you haven't.

Kleinman and Prostitute, *Shadows and Fog*

It's always a business doing pleasure with you.

Mona Stangley, *The Best Little Whorehouse in Texas*

Coquettes know how to please, not love, and that is why men love them so much.

Pierre Marivaux

When a guy goes to a hooker, he's not paying her for sex, he's paying her to leave.

Anon

A hooker told me, 'Not on the first date.'

Rodney Dangerfield

The man who rings the bell at the brothel is unconsciously looking for God.

Bruce Marshall

On some level, almost every client wanted to believe that the girl was spending time with him not for money but because she found him irresistible.

Sydney Biddle Barrows

I may be good for nothing, but I'm never bad for nothing.

Sydney Biddle Barrows

A perfect whore should, like the fabled Proteus of old, be able to assume every form, and to vary the attitudes of pleasure according to the times, circumstances, and temperaments.

The Whore's Catechism, c. 1900

I like prostitution. My heart has never failed to pound at the sight of one of those provocatively dressed women walking in the rain under the gaslamps, just as the sight of monks in their robes and girdles touches some ascetic, hidden corner of my soul.

Gustave Flaubert

Prostitutes, more than any other profession, help keep American marriages together.

Brendan Francis

I have only hated men at those moments when I realized that I was doing all the giving and they the taking. At least when I was a prostitute, it was all honest and upfront.

Xaviera Hollander

I never once went to a prostitute, maybe because so many enthusiastic amateurs were around.

A. S. Neil

She was a 'honeychile' in New Orleans,
The hottest of the bunch;
But on the old expense account,
She was gas, cigars and lunch.

Anon

PROVERBS

The grass is always greener over the septic tank.

Erma Bombeck

A nose that can see is worth two that sniff.

Eugene Ionesco

If there's no lead in your pencil you don't need a rubber.

J. A. Smith

One does not moisten a stamp with the Niagara Falls.

P. W. R. Foot

Eagles may soar high, but weasels don't get sucked into jet engines.

David Brent, *The Office*

You can lead a herring to water, but you have to walk really fast or he'll die.

Rose Nylund, *The Golden Girls*

You've buttered your bread, now sleep in it.

Gracie Allen

We'll jump off that bridge when we come to it.

Leslie Blumberg

A new dishwasher can't mend a broken heart, but it will do the washing up.

Adam Khan

Love, smoke and a man on a camel cannot be hid.

Persian proverb

Many hands make a tall horse.

Michael Russell

You can make few friends by driving northwards on a southbound carriageway.

W. F. N. Watson

A knowledge of Sanskrit is of little use to a man trapped in a sewer.

C. H. R. Roll

Quietly, quietly, with your horns in your pocket.

Maltese saying

PSYCHIATRY AND PSYCHOANALYSIS

There once was a man who cried every time it snowed. He went to a psychotherapist. Now when the snow falls, he weeps for his mother, who died in the winter.

Joe Riener

The man who once cursed his fate, now curses himself – and pays his psychoanalyst.

John W. Gardner

Mental illness is a myth, whose function is to disguise and thus render more palatable the bitter pill of moral conflicts in human relations.

Thomas Szasz

Psychoanalysis is the illness whose cure it considers itself to be.   Karl Kraus

Why should I tolerate a perfect stranger at the bedside of my mind?

Vladimir Nabokov

Freud is the father of pyschoanalysis. It has no mother.   Germaine Greer

Psychiatry enables us to correct our faults by confessing our parents' shortcomings.   Laurence J. Peter

Psychoanalysis pretends to investigate the Unconscious. The Unconscious by definition is what you are not conscious of. But the Analysts already know what's in it – they should, because they put it all in beforehand.

Saul Bellow

The Five Myths of Pop Psychology: 1. Human beings are basically good. 2. We need more self-esteem and self-worth. 3. You can't love others until you love yourself. 4. You shouldn't judge anyone. 5. All guilt is bad.

Chris Thurman

Psychiatric expert testimony: mendacity masquerading as medicine.

Thomas Szasz

Psychoanalysis and Zen, in my private psychic geometry, are equal to nicotine. They are anti-existential. Nicotine quarantines one out of existence.   Norman Mailer

If my devils are to leave me, I fear my angels will take flight as well.

Rainer Maria Rilke

There are now electrical appliances with the main unit so sealed in that it cannot be got at for repair. There have always been human beings like that.

Mignon McLaughlin

The poor need jobs and money, not psychoanalysis. The uneducated need knowledge and skills, not psychoanalysis.   Thomas Szasz

Why waste money on psychoanalysis when you can listen to the B Minor Mass?   Michael Torke

When I went to the analyst for a kind of preliminary meeting, he said,
'I'll be able to fix you so that you'll write much more music than you do
now.' I said, 'Good heavens! I already write too much, it seems to me.'
That promise of his put me off. John Cage

There is no psychiatrist in the world like a puppy licking your face.
Ben Williams

It is often more beneficial to jog around the psychiatrist's building than to
enter – and cheaper than a couch. Anon

PUNCTUAL

I've been on a calendar, but never on time. Marilyn Monroe

Unfaithfulness in the keeping of an appointment is an act of clear
dishonesty. You may as well borrow a person's money as his time.
Horace Mann

People count up the faults of those who keep them waiting. French proverb

We may assume that we keep people waiting symbolically because we do
not wish to see them and that our anxiety is due not to being late, but to
having to see them at all. Cyril Connolly

A man who has to be punctually at a certain place at five o'clock has the
whole afternoon ruined for him already. Lin Yutang

The surest way to be late is to have plenty of time. Leon Kennedy

I knew I was going to take the wrong train so I left early. Yogi Berra

The trouble with being punctual is that there's nobody there to
appreciate it. Franklin P. Jones

QUESTIONS AND ANSWERS

Ah! What is man? Wherefore does he why? Whence did he whence?
Whither is he dithering?
Dan Leno

Who am I? How did I come into the world? Why was I not consulted?
Søren Kierkegaard

If a tree falls in the forest and no one is there to hear it, does it make a
sound?
Philosophical conundrum

Where does my fist go when I open up my hand? Where does my lap go
when I stand up?
Alan Watts

If blind people wear sunglasses, why don't deaf people wear earmuffs?
Bob Monkhouse

When a book and a head collide and there is a hollow sound, is it always
in the book?
Georg Christoph Lichtenberg

Why, in a country of free speech, are there phone bills?   Steven Wright

What happens to the hole when the cheese is gone?   Bertolt Brecht

When you can do nothing, what can you do?   Zen koan

What is the colour of the wind?   Zen koan

What is the sound of one hand?   Zen koan

Reason can answer questions, but imagination has to ask them. Ralph Gerard

Millions saw the apple fall, but Newton was the one who asked why.
Bernard Baruch

Isn't it sad to go to your grave without ever wondering why you were born? Who, with such a thought, would not spring from bed, eager to resume discovering the world and rejoicing to be part of it? **Richard Dawkins**

Homework, root canals and deadlines are the important things in life, and only when we have these major dramas taken care of can we presume to look at the larger questions. **Cynthia Heimel**

She was the kind of woman who liked to ask questions to which she already knew the answers. It gave her a sense of security. **Margaret Millar**

There's nothing people like better than being asked an easy question. For some reason, we're flattered when a stranger asks us where Maple Street is in our hometown and we can tell him. **Andrew A. Rooney**

My rule in making up examination questions is to ask questions which I can't myself answer. It astounds me to see how some of my students answer questions which would play the deuce with me. **Henry Brooks Adams**

In politics there is no right answer – and no final answer. **Ann Widdecombe**

Curiosity is one of the most certain and permanent characteristics of a vigorous intellect. Samuel Johnson

My favorite question that is asked only of women is, 'What do you do with yourself all day?' The only possible answer is, 'Make nuclear bombs in my bathroom. Just little ones, though.' **Lois Gould**

It's the little questions from women about tappets that finally push men over the edge. **Philip Roth**

In politics, the rule is, 'Never answer a question until you're asked it.' **Robert Williams**

—Opposition's about asking awkward questions.
—And government is about not answering them.

Jim Hacker and Sir Humphrey Appleby, *Yes, Prime Minister*

Never, never, never on cross-examination ask a witness a question you don't already know the answer to, was a tenet I absorbed with my baby food. Do it, and you'll often get an answer you don't want.   **Harper Lee**

We have learned the answers, all the answers: it is the question that we do not know.   **Archibald MacLeish**

If they can get you asking the wrong questions, they don't have to worry about the answers.   **Thomas Pynchon**

He was trying to frame a question that would take in all the questions and elicit an answer that would be all the answers, but it kept coming out so simple that he distrusted it.   **Tom Stoppard**

I have six honest serving men. They taught me all I know. Their names are What and Why and When and How and Where and Who.

Rudyard Kipling

Questions are creative acts of intelligence.   **Frank Kingdon**

He who asks is a fool for five minutes, but he who does not remains a fool forever.   Chinese proverb

Perhaps the most important word in success and happiness is 'ask'.

Brian Tracy

It is not the answer that enlightens, but the question.   **Eugene Ionesco**

A wise man's question contains half the answer.   **Solomon Ibn Gabirol**

The 'silly question' is the first intimation of some totally new development.
Alfred North Whitehead

The power to question is the basis of all human progress. **Indira Gandhi**

Don't ask questions you don't want answers to. **Captain Schroeder**

Literature is the question minus the answer. **Roland Barthes**

I should like to insist that nearly all the important questions, the things we ponder in our profoundest moments, have no answers. **Jacquetta Hawkes**

In the book of life, the answers aren't in the back. **Charlie Brown**

The important thing is not to stop questioning. **Albert Einstein**

Computers are useless. They can only give you answers. **Pablo Picasso**

A sign in the yard of a church next door said CHRIST IS THE ANSWER. (The question, of course, is: What do you say when you strike your thumb with a hammer?) **Bill Bryson**

Sleep with a question, and you often get up with the answer. **Anon**

An answer is always a form of death. **John Fowles**

There ain't no answer. There ain't going to be any answer. There never has been an answer. That's the answer. **Gertrude Stein**

A bird does not sing because it has an answer. It sings because it has a song.
Chinese proverb

If the rose puzzled its mind over the question of how it grew, it would not have been the miracle that it is. **W. B. Yeats**

The answer is in the plural and they bounce. **Edwin Lutyens**

QUOTATIONS

The wisdom of the wise and the experience of the ages are perpetuated by quotations.

Benjamin Disraeli

Any stupid remark, quoted often enough, becomes gospel.

Leslie Charteris

I pick my favourite quotations and store them in my mind as ready armour, offensive or defensive, amid the struggle of this turbulent existence.

Robert Burns

A quotation at the right moment is like bread in a famine.

Talmud

The quotations when engraved upon the memory give you good thoughts. They also make you anxious to read the authors and look for more.

Winston Churchill

All my best thoughts were stolen by the ancients.

Ralph Waldo Emerson

What a good thing Adam had – when he said a good thing, he knew nobody had said it before.

Mark Twain

I always like to quote Albert Einstein because nobody dares contradict him.

Studs Terkel

Life itself is a quotation.

Jorge Luis Borges

Sooner or later we all quote our mothers.

Bern Williams

RACE AND DISCRIMINATION

I went in this restaurant and the woman told me, 'I'm sorry, but we don't serve Negroes.' I said, 'And I don't eat 'em.' **African American joke**

Give me your tired, your poor, your huddled masses yearning to be free, provided they have satisfactorily filled out forms 3584-A through 3597-Q. **Dwight Macdonald**

Diversity might be the hardest thing for a society to live with, and perhaps the most dangerous thing for a society to be without. **William Sloane Coffin**

The world is built on discrimination of the most horrible kind. The problem with South Africans is they admit it. **P. J. O'Rourke, 1989**

A foreigner is an individual who is considered either comic or sinister. When the victim of a disaster – preferably natural but sometimes political – the foreigner may also be pitied from a distance for a short period of time. **John Ralston Saul**

Racism is the snobbery of the poor. **Raymond Aron**

It is very difficult now in South Africa to find anyone who ever supported apartheid. **Archbishop Desmond Tutu**

Racism is man's gravest threat to man – the maximum of hatred for the minimum of reason. **Abraham Joshua Heschel**

The most certain test by which we judge whether a country is really free is the amount of security enjoyed by minorities. **Lord Acton**

In America, black is a country.

Amira Baraka

America is not a melting pot. It is a sizzling cauldron.   Barbara Ann Mikulski
I don't care if you think I'm racist. I just want you to think I'm thin.

Sarah Silverman

It is a great shock at the age of five or six to find that in a world of Gary
Coopers you are the Indian.

James Baldwin

I'm racist? How can that even be possible? I was a friend of Michael Jackson's back when he was black.

Joan Rivers

When we're unemployed, we're called lazy; when the whites are
unemployed, it's called a depression.

Reverend Jesse Jackson

Blacks can get into medical school with a lower grade ... If that's true,
a Jew should be able to play basketball with a lower net.

Jackie Mason

We ask for nothing that is not right, and herein lies the great power of our
demand.

Paul Robeson

I'm a white male, aged 18 to 49. Everyone listens to me – no matter how
dumb my suggestions are.

Homer Simpson

Everyone's colored, or you wouldn't be able to see 'em.

Captain Beefheart

White, black and yellow men – they all cry salt tears.

Claude Aveline

It's not that easy being green.

Kermit the Frog

The mind of the bigot is like the pupil of the eye; the more light you pour
upon it, the more it will contract.

Oliver Wendell Holmes Jr

Never look down on anybody unless you're helping him up.

Reverend Jesse Jackson

Look back, to slavery, to suffrage, to integration, and one thing is clear. Fashions in bigotry come and go. The right thing lasts.　　Anna Quindlen

REALITY

I believe in looking reality straight in the eye and denying it.　　Garrison Keillor

You have been told that Real Life is not like college, and you have been correctly informed. Real Life is more like high school.

Meryl Streep, speech to graduates

Reality is whatever refuses to go away when I stop believing in it.

Philip K. Dick

Reality is the leading cause of stress amongst those in touch with it.

Jane Wagner

Humankind cannot bear very much reality.　　T. S. Eliot

Cloquet hated reality but he realized it was still the only place to get a good steak.　　Woody Allen

What I'm above all primarily concerned with is the substance of life, the pith of reality. If I had to sum up my work, I suppose that's it really: I'm taking the pith out of reality.　　Alan Bennett

Since we cannot change reality, let us change the eyes with which we see reality.　　Nikos Kazantzakis

Reality leaves a lot to the imagination.　　John Lennon

One's real life is so often the life that one does not lead.　　Oscar Wilde

REGRETS

It's the things I might have said that fester.   Clemence Dane

Maybe all one can do is hope to end up with the right regrets.   Arthur Miller

The only things one never regrets are one's mistakes.   Oscar Wilde

I started with the firm conviction that when I came to the end, I wanted to be regretting the things I had done, not the things I hadn't.   Michael Caine

You can't turn back the clock, but you can wind it up again.   Bonnie Pruden

—But isn't there something you would do if you had your life to live all over again?
—I'd try more positions.   Interviewer and Groucho Marx

RELATIONSHIP

On the whole I prefer cats to women because cats seldom if ever use the word 'relationship'.   Kinky Friedman

Relationship is a cold word. It has no vibrancy like, for instance, kinship, which immediately stirs something in one's blood, or like love with its infinity of overtones.   Irene Claremont de Castillejo

Now the whole dizzying and delirious range of sexual possibilities has been boiled down to that one big, boring, bulimic word: relationship.
                    Julie Burchill

'Never' and 'always' are the two most inflammable words in human relationships.   Diane Rehm

I am part of all that I have met.   Alfred Lord Tennyson

How far we travel in life matters far less than those we meet along the way.
John Barth

A fella ain't got a soul of his own, just a piece of a big soul, the one that belongs to everybody.
John Steinbeck, *The Grapes of Wrath*

Someone to tell it to is one of the fundamental needs of human beings.
Miles Franklin

The ultimate test of a relationship is to disagree but hold hands.
Alexander Penney

We are all islands – in a common sea.
Anne Morrow Lindbergh

RELIGION

Religion is the masterpiece of the art of animal training, for it trains people as to how they shall think.
Arthur Schopenhauer

We are circumcized or baptised – Jews or Moslems or Christians – before we know we are human beings.
Pierre Charon

The various modes of worship which prevailed in the Roman world were all considered by the people as equally true; by the philosopher as equally false; and by the magistrate as equally useful.
Edward Gibbon

Religion is excellent stuff for keeping common people quiet.
Napoleon Bonaparte

Religion is not merely the opium of the masses, it is the cyanide.
Tom Robbins

It's an incredible con job when you think of it, to believe something now in exchange for life after death. Even corporations with all their reward systems don't try to make it posthumous.
Gloria Steinem

Religion is a monumental chapter in the history of human egotism.

William James

The religion of one age is, as a rule, the literary entertainment of the next.

Fridtjof Nansen

One man's theology is another man's belly laugh.　　Robert Heinlein

This so-called new religion is nothing but a pack of weird rituals and chants designed to take away the money of fools. Let us say the Lord's Prayer forty times, but first, let's pass the collection plate.

Reverend Lovejoy, *The Simpsons*

The preponderance of pain over pleasure is the cause of our fictitious morality and religion.　　Friedrich Nietzsche

Religion has always been the wound, not the bandage.　　Dennis Potter

No man with any sense of humor ever founded a religion.

Robert Green Ingersoll

A cult is a religion with no political power.　　Tom Wolfe

It's hard to be religious when certain people are never incinerated by bolts of lightning.　　Bill Watterson

My principal objections to orthodox religion are two: slavery here and hell hereafter.　Robert Green Ingersoll

Religion is a crutch for people not strong enough to stand up to the unknown without help. But, like dandruff, most people do have a religion and spend time and money on it and seem to derive considerable pleasure from fiddling with it.　　Robert Heinlein

I am against religion because it teaches us to be satisfied with not
understanding the world.   Richard Dawkins

You never see animals going through the absurd and often horrible
fooleries of magic and religion ... Only man behaves with such gratuitous
folly. It is the price he has to pay for being intelligent but not, as yet, quite
intelligent enough.   Aldous Huxley

We have just enough religion to make us hate, but not enough to make us
love one another.   Jonathan Swift

Your religion is what you do when the sermon is over.   H. Jackson Brown Jr

There is not the least use preaching to anyone unless you chance to catch them ill.

Sydney Smith

It is usually when men are at their most religious that they behave with the
least sense and the greatest cruelty.   Ilka Chase

People who want to share their religious views with you almost never want
you to share yours with them.   Dave Barry

If your religion does not work at home, don't export it.   Howard Hendricks

We must respect the other fellow's religion, but only in the sense and to the
extent that we respect his theory that his wife is beautiful and his children
are smart.   H. L. Mencken

It is the test of a good religion whether you can joke about it.
G. K. Chesterton

All religions will pass, but this will remain: simply sitting in a chair and
looking in the distance.   V. V. Rozanov

RETIREMENT

Retirement? You're talking about death, right?

Robert Altman

Retirement: statutory senility.

Emmett O'Donnell

Most people perform essentially meaningless work. When they retire, that truth is borne upon them.

Brendan Francis

I married him for better or worse, but not for lunch.

Hazel Weiss on her husband's retirement

The important thing about women today is, as they get older, they still keep house. It's one reason why they don't die, but men die when they retire. Women just polish the teacups.

Margaret Mead

Don't simply retire from something; have something to retire to.

Harry Emerson Fosdick

Dismiss the old horse in good time, lest he fail in the lists and the spectators laugh.

Horace

Retire? I'm not going to ease up, let up, shut up or give up until I'm taken up. In fact I'm just getting warmed up.

Zig Zigler

REVENGE

Life being what it is, one dreams of revenge.

Paul Gauguin

Revenge is a kind of wild justice, which the more a man's nature runs to, the more ought law to weed it out.

Francis Bacon

The best revenge you can have on intellectuals is to be madly happy.

Albert Camus

—According to the common saying, revenge is a dish best served ... what? Cold or on toast?
—On toast.   **Anne Robinson and Contestant,** *The Weakest Link*

Like vichyssoise, revenge is a dish best served cold.   **Stephen Fry**

The person who pursues revenge should dig two graves.   **English proverb**

One must be a woman to know how to revenge.   **Madame de Rieux**

An eye for an eye and the world would be blind.   **Mahatma Gandhi**

Do unto others, then run.   **Benny Hill**

REVOLUTION

Revolution is the festival of the oppressed.   **Vladimir Ilyich Lenin**

—Come the revolution, everyone will eat ice cream.
—But, comrade, I don't like ice cream.
—Come the revolution, *everyone* will eat ice cream.   **Willis Hall**

The first duty of a revolutionary is to get away with it.   **Abbie Hoffman**

It is only the religious mind that is a truly revolutionary mind.
                    Jiddu Krishnamurti

Revolutions are not made from trifles, but spring from trifles.   **Aristotle**

Revolutionaries do not make revolutions! The revolutionaries are those who know when power is lying in the street and when they can pick it up.
                    Hannah Arendt

A modern revolutionary group heads for the television station.
                    Abbie Hoffman

Every revolutionary becomes a conservative the day after the revolution.

Hannah Arendt

Mercy, it's the revolution and I'm in my bathrobe!   Nicole Hollander

When smashing monuments, save the pedestals; they always come in handy.

Stanislaw J. Lec

One revolution is like one cocktail, it just gets you ready for the next.

Will Rogers

In America the word revolutionary is used to sell pantyhose.   Rita Mae Brown

The great revolution of the future will be Nature's revolt against man.

Holbrook Jackson

RICH AND POOR

If you can count your money, you don't have a billion dollars.

John Paul Getty

She was born with an entire silver dinner service in her mouth.

Clive James on Grace Kelly

The way to make money is to buy when blood is running in the streets.

John D. Rockerfeller Jr

Behind every great fortune there is a crime.   Honoré de Balzac

I make myself rich by making my wants few.   Henry David Thoreau

I live way below my means.   Oprah Winfrey

I made my first million dollars the old-fashioned way: I made a hundred million for somebody else.
Roseanne

The have and the have-nots can often be traced back to the dids and the did-nots.
Bob Goddard

The difference between old veau and nouveau is that one dies, and the other buys.
Beauregard Houston-Montgomery

Sudden money is going from zero to two hundred dollars a week. The rest doesn't count.
Neil Simon

The rich are the scum of the earth in every country.
G. K. Chesterton

People are fascinated by the rich: Shakespeare wrote plays about kings, not beggars.
Dominick Dunne

The rich, you know why they're so odd? Because they can afford to be.
The Joker, *Batman*

Every man thinks God is on his side. The rich and powerful know he is.
Jean Anouilh

The very rich and the very social are, often, the very stuffy.
Edna Ferber

One is not rich by what one owns, but more by what one is able to do without with dignity.
Immanuel Kant

How often the rich like to play at being poor. A rather nasty game, I've always thought.
Lillian Hellman

Think what stupid things the people must have done with their money who say they're 'happier without'.
Edith Wharton

It's no disgrace to be poor, but it might as well be.　　　Kin Hubbard

He was always ready to pick a halfpenny out of the dirt with his teeth.
　　　　　　　　　　　　　　　　　　　　　　　Petronius

The petty economies of the rich are just as amazing as the silly
extravagances of the poor.　　　　　　　　　　　　William Feather

Most idealistic people are skint. I have discovered that people with money have no imagination, and people with imagination have no money.

　　　　　　　　　　　　　　　　　　　　　　　George Weiss

He was one of those born clever enough at gaining a fortune, but incapable
of keeping one; for the qualities and energies which lead a man to achieve
the first, are often the very cause of his ruin in the latter case.
　　　　　　　　　　　　　　William Makepeace Thackery

The slimming of an elephant and the losses of a rich man are not
noticeable.　　　　　　　　　　　　　　　　　Ethiopian saying

If all men were rich, all men would be poor.　　　　　Mark Twain

If you aren't rich, you should always look useful.　　Louis-Ferdinand Céline

Eat with the rich, but go to the play with the poor, who are capable of joy.
　　　　　　　　　　　　　　　　　　　　Logan Pearsall Smith

The greatest crime of welfare isn't that it's a waste of money, but that it's a
waste of people.　　　　　　　　　　　　　　　　Mark Steyn

Compared to us, poor was already rich.　　　　　　Walter Matthau

I've never been poor, only broke. Being poor is a frame of mind. Being broke is a temporary situation.   Mike Todd

We were poor when I was young but the difference was that the government didn't come around telling you you were poor.   Ronald Reagan

The poor on the borderline of starvation live purposeful lives. To be snagged in a desperate struggle for food and shelter is to be wholly free from a sense of futility.   Eric Hoffer

I'm so broke I'm actually considering getting a second boyfriend.
                                                    Christina Walkinshaw

The Great Depression, 1931 – that was the year when our family ate the piano.   James C. Wright

'Poor but happy' is not a phrase invented by a poor person.   Mason Cooley

Boredom is the keynote of poverty … it's dark brown sameness.   Moss Hart

I used to think I was poor. Then they told me I wasn't poor, I was needy. They told me it was self-defeating to think of myself as needy, I was deprived. Then they told me underprivileged was overused. I was disadvantaged. I still don't have a dime. But I have a great vocabulary.
                                                    Jules Feiffer

If you've ever really been poor you remain poor at heart all your life. I've often walked when I could very well afford to take a taxi because I simply couldn't bring myself to waste the shilling it would cost.   Arnold Bennett

It would be nice if the poor were to get even half of the money that is spent in studying them.   Bill Vaughan

It is not economical to go to bed early to save the candles if the result is twins.   Benjamin Franklin

No matter how bad it gets, I'm rich at the dollar store.   Jason Love

RIGHT AND WRONG

—You're playing all the wrong notes.
—I'm playing all the right notes, but not necessarily in the right order, I'll give you that, sunshine.   André Previn and Eric Morecambe

—You don't think there's anything wrong with what you're doing, do you?
—I don't think anything I've done is wrong.   Marge and Homer Simpson

When everyone is against you, it means that you are absolutely wrong – or absolutely right.   Albert Guinon

My father, to whom I owe so much, never told me the difference between right and wrong; now I think that's why I remain so greatly in his debt.

John Mortimer

Human beings are perhaps never more frightening than when they are convinced beyond doubt that they are right.   Laurens van der Post

It is dangerous to be right in matters on which the established authorities are wrong.   Voltaire

It infuriates me to be wrong when I know I'm right.   Molière

The need to be right – the sign of a vulgar mind.   Albert Camus

Some people are worried about the difference between right and wrong. I'm worried about the difference between wrong and fun.
P. J. O'Rourke

A long habit of thinking a thing wrong gives it a superficial appearance of being right.   Thomas Paine

Too far east is west.   English proverb

If you're going to do something wrong, at least enjoy it.   Leo Rosten

H. L. Mencken told me once that he answered all his mail, pleasant and unpleasant, with just one line, 'You may be right.' That's the way I feel now. It is in the realm of possibility, just barely, that I could be the one who's wrong.   Clare Booth Luce

RIGHTS

A right is not what someone gives you; it's what no one can take away from you.   Ramsey Clark

Give to every other human being every right that you claim for yourself.
Robert Green Ingersoll

What men value in this world is not rights but privileges.   H. L. Mencken

The right to be let alone is the most comprehensive of rights and the right most valued in civilized man.   Louis D. Brandeis

The right to be heard does not automatically include the right to be taken seriously.   Hubert H. Humphrey

The right to bear arms is only slightly less idiotic than the right to arm bears.   Chris Addison

To have a right to do a thing is not at all the same as to be right in doing it.
                                                                 G. K. Chesterton

The right to kill: supposing the life of X ... were linked with our own so that the two deaths had to be simultaneous, should we still wish him to die? If with our whole body and soul we desire life and if nevertheless without lying, we can reply 'yes', then we have the right to kill.   Simone Weil

RISK

He who has a head of butter must not come near the oven.   Dutch proverb

'Why not' is a slogan for an interesting life.   Mason Cooley

Come to the edge
He said. They said:
We are afraid.
Come to the edge
He said. They came.
He pushed them, and
they flew ...   Guillaume Apollinaire

I take my share of risks. I don't always floss.   Angela Bennett, *The Net*

He who is afraid of every nettle should not piss in the grass.   Thomas Fuller

Look twice before you leap.   Charlotte Brontë

If no one ever took risks, Michelangelo would have painted the Sistine floor.
                                                           Neil Simon

Being on the tightrope is living; everything else is waiting.   Karl Wallenda

And the trouble is, if you don't risk anything, you risk even more.   Erica Jong

SADNESS

Janet rang up – and wept. To weep in a public call-box. There's desolation.
Sylvia Townsend Warner

I think if we all acted the way we felt, four out of eight people at a dinner table would be sitting there sobbing.
Jim Carrey

People are ashamed of being unhappy.
Avi

Unhappiness is best described as the difference between our talents and our expectations.
Edward de Bono

I have the true feeling of myself only when I am unbearably unhappy.
Franz Kafka

There is no unhappier creature on earth than a fetishist who yearns for a woman's shoe and has to embrace the whole woman.
Karl Kraus

Sadness is a vice.
Gustave Flaubert

Sadness is very close to hate.
Michael Ondaatje

The usual pretext of those who make others unhappy is that they do it for their own good.
Marquis de Vauvenargues

I think writing about unhappiness is probably the source of my popularity, if I have any – after all, most people are unhappy, don't you think?
Philip Larkin

There are times when sorrow seems the only truth.
Oscar Wilde

I saw sorrow turning into clarity.
Yoko Ono

As I've gotten older, I find I am able to be nourished more by sorrow and to distinguish it from depression.
Robert Bly

Sad soul, take comfort, nor forget that sunset never failed us yet.

Celia Laighton Thaxter

You cannot prevent the birds of sorrow from flying over your head, but you can prevent them from building nests in your hair.　Persian proverb

Everyone is a moon and has a dark side which he never shows to anybody.

Mark Twain

SAFETY

We could easily have evolved eyelids thick enough to keep out the light, but we still need to see the shadows fall across them. We're not yet safe.

Don Paterson

Life is like a cow pasture. If you walk through it with your head down, you'll avoid the crap but never find the gate.　The Lesbitarian

Everybody know that if you're too careful you are so occupied in being careful that you are sure to stumble over something.　Gertrude Stein

Don't play for safety – it's the most dangerous thing in the world.

Hugh Walpole

The streets are safe in Philadelphia; it's only the people who make them unsafe.　Frank Rizzo

Never leave hold of what you've got until you've got hold of something else.

Donald Herzberg

The fly that doesn't want to be swatted is most secure when it lights on the fly-swatter.　Georg Christoph Lichtenberg

Only the most foolish of mice would hide in a cat's ear, but only the wisest of cats would think to look there.　Scott Love

A hole in the ice is dangerous only to those who go skating.　Rex Stout

SAINT

—What do you call a dead person who has been canonized?
—A bishop. **Steve Wright and Contestant,** *The Big Quiz,* **BBC Radio 2**

I don't believe in God, but I do believe in His saints. **Edith Wharton**

Don't call me a saint. I don't want to be dismissed that easily. **Dorothy Day**

Many of the insights of the saint stem from his experience as a sinner. **Eric Hoffer**

Every saint has a bee in his halo. **E. V. Lucas**

What, after all, is a halo? It's only one more thing to keep clean. **Christopher Fry**

Living with a saint is more gruelling than being one. **Robert Neville**

Sainthood is when you can listen to someone's tale of woe and not respond with a description of your own. **Andrew Mason**

SATISFACTION

Life is a hospital where every patient is dominated by a wish to change his bed. One would prefer to suffer near the fire, and another feels sure he would get well if he were near the window. **Charles Baudelaire**

If we are suffering illness, poverty, or misfortune, we think we shall be satisfied on the day it ceases. But there, too, we know it is false; as soon as one has got used to not suffering one wants something else. **Simone Weil**

There are some days when I think I'm going to die from an overdose of satisfaction. **Salvador Dali**

Odd, the years it took to learn one simple fact: that the prize just ahead, the next job, publication, love affair, marriage, always seemed to hold the key to satisfaction but never, in the longer run, sufficed.   Carolyn Heilbrun

Whoever is capable of knowing when they have had enough will always be satisfied.   Lao Tzu

We can never have enough of that which we do not want.   Eric Hoffer

God was satisfied with his own work, and that is fatal.   Samuel Butler

To live content with small means; to seek elegance rather than luxury, and refinement rather than fashion; to be worthy, not respectable, and wealthy, not rich; to listen to stars and birds, babes and sages, with open heart; to study hard; to think quietly, act frankly, talk gently, await occasions, hurry never; in a word, to let the spiritual, unbidden and unconscious grow up through the common – this is my symphony.   William Henry Channing

Some people have food, but no appetite; others have an appetite, but no food. I have both. The Lord be praised.   Oliver Cromwell

SCIENCE

How does gravity work? And if it were to cease suddenly, would certain restaurants still require a jacket?   Woody Allen

This is the essence of science: ask an impertinent question, and you are on your way to a pertinent answer.   Jacob Bronowski

Art is I; science is we.   Claude Bernard

The telescope sweeps the sky without finding God.   Pierre Laplace

As soon as questions of will or decision or reason or choice of action arise, human science is at a loss.   Noam Chomsky

When you tell people you know what is good for them especially if you are a doctor, they will believe you. Having no beliefs of their own they believe. It's a truism that as faith in God has declined belief in science, especially medical science, has increased. Yet most people know even less about science than they did about God. Science is now incomprehensible to the layman but the layman accepts it, even though one of the arguments against God is that He doesn't make sense.   Jeanette Winterson, *Art and Lies*

But as a skeptic I am dubious about science as about everything else, unless the scientist is himself a skeptic, and few of them are. The stench of formaldehyde may be as potent as the whiff of incense in stimulating a naturally idolatrous understanding.   Robertson Davies

I am sorry to say that there is too much point to the wisecrack that life is extinct on other planets because their scientists were more advanced than ours.   John F. Kennedy

Our scientific power has outrun our spiritual power. We have guided missiles and misguided men.   Martin Luther King Jr

What scientists have in their briefcases is terrifying.   Nikita Kruschchev

I almost think it is the ultimate destiny of science to exterminate the human race.   Thomas Love Peacock

Science should be on tap, not on top.   Winston Churchill

Concern for man and his fate must always form the chief interest of all technical endeavours. Never forget this in the midst of your diagrams and equations.   Albert Einstein

Science is a first-rate piece of furniture for a man's upper chamber if he has common sense on the ground floor.   Oliver Wendell Holmes

We have not the reverent feeling for the rainbow that a savage has, because we know how it is made. We have lost as much as we gained by prying into that matter.   Mark Twain

When you sit with a nice girl for two hours you think it's only a minute. But when you sit on a hot stove for a minute you think it's two hours. That's relativity.   Albert Einstein

When does Zurich stop at this train?
                          Albert Einstein, 'Theory of Relativity for Laymen'

Science can only state what is, not what should be.   Albert Einstein

Put off your imagination, as you put off your overcoat, when you enter the laboratory. But put it on again, as you put on your overcoat, when you leave.   Claude Bernard

The true scientist never loses the faculty of amazement.   Hans Selye

With all your science can you tell how it is, and whence it is, that light comes into the soul?   Henry David Thoreau

SCIENCE FICTION

Welcome futurists, cyberphiles, and the rest of you dateless wonders ...
             Mayor Quimby greeting the Bi-Mon-Sci-Fi-Con, *The Simpsons*

Science Fiction: fairy tales for nerds.   Richard Bayan

Science fiction is never about the future, in the same way history is rarely about the past: they're both parable formats for examining or commenting on the present.   A. A. Gill

Once I thought I saw a UFO but it turned out I just rubbed my eyes too hard.   Midge Pinciotti, *That '70s Show*

I wish outer space guys would conquer the earth and make people their pets, because I'd like to have one of those little beds with my name on it.
                                                                Jack Handey

Isn't it interesting that the same people who laugh at science fiction listen to weather forecasts and economists?   Kelvin Throop III

Politicians should read science fiction, not westerns and detective stories.
                                                                Arthur C. Clarke

SEA

There is nothing so desperately monotonous as the sea, and I no longer wonder at the cruelty of pirates.   James Russell Lowell

The thing itself is dirty, wobbly and wet.   Wallace Stevens

I hate to be near the sea, and to hear it raging and roaring like a wild beast in its den. It puts me in mind of the everlasting efforts of the human mind, struggling to be free and ending just where it began.   William Hazlitt

It's hard to bullshit the ocean. It's not listening, you know what I mean.
                                                                David Crosby

The sea makes no promises and breaks none.   Lillian Beckworth

Ocean people are very different from land people. The ocean never stops saying and asking into ears, which don't sleep like eyes.
                                                        Maxine Hong Kingston

In the biting honesty of salt, the sea makes her secrets known to those who care to listen.   Sandra Benitez

I discovered the secret of the sea in meditation upon the dew drop.
                                                                Kahlil Gibran

Dear God, be good to me;
The sea is so wide,
And my boat is so small.   Breton fisherman's prayer

SEASONS

To every thing there is a season, and a time to every purpose under the heaven.

Bible, **Ecclesiastes**

Spring is a virgin; Summer a mother; Autumn a widow; Winter a stepmother.

Russian proverb

To be interested in the changing seasons is a happier state of mind than to be always in love with spring.

George Santayana

Spring has returned. The Earth is like a child that knows poems.

Rainer Maria Rilke

The trees are coming into leaf like something almost being said. **Philip Larkin**

Spring has come when you can put your foot on three daisies. **English proverb**

Summer is the time when one sheds one's tensions with one's clothes, and the right kind of day is jewelled balm for the battered spirit. A few of those days and you can become drunk with the belief that all's right with the world.

Ada Louise Huxtable

It's a sign of summer if the chair gets up when you do. **Walter Winchell**

I like best of all autumn, because its tone is mellower, its colours are richer, and it is tinged with a little sorrow. Its golden richness speaks not of the innocence of spring, nor the power of summer, but of the mellowness and kindly wisdom of approaching age. It knows the limitations of life and it is content.

Lin Yutang

Everyone must take time to sit and watch the leaves turn. **Elizabeth Lawrence**

I prefer winter and fall, when you feel the bone structure in the landscape – the loneliness of it – the dead feeling of winter. Something waits beneath it – the whole story doesn't show.

Andrew Wyeth

Regarding winter: there is a privacy about it which no other season gives you ... In spring, summer and fall people sort of have an open season on each other; only in the winter, in the country, can you have longer, quiet stretches when you can savour belonging to yourself.   Ruth Stout

To shorten winter, borrow some money due in spring.   W. J. Vogel

SECRETS

Everybody has something to conceal.   Dashiell Hammett, *The Maltese Falcon*

People are very secretive – secret even from themselves.   John Le Carré

Secrets are the blood of life. Every big thing is a secret, even when you know it, because you never know all of it. If you can know everything about anything, it is not worth knowing.   Robertson Davies

As soon as you cannot keep anything from a woman, you love her.
                                                                      Paul Géraldy

The vanity of being known to be trusted with a secret is generally one of the chief motives to disclose it.   Samuel Johnson

Three may keep a secret if two of them are dead.   Benjamin Franklin

There is no secret so close as that between a rider and his horse.   R. S. Surtees

The cat which isn't let out of the bag often becomes a skeleton in the cupboard.   Geoffrey Madan

Ninety-two per cent of the stuff told you in confidence you couldn't get anyone else to listen to.   Franklin P. Adams

When a man dies, his secrets bond like crystals, like frost on a window. His last breath obscures the glass.   Anne Michaels

An empty envelope that is sealed contains a secret. Stanislaw J. Lec

I shall tell you a great secret, my friend. Do not wait for the last judgement. It takes place every day. Albert Camus

SECURITY

The mouse that hath but one hole is quickly taken. George Herbert

Security is mostly a superstition. It does not exist in nature. Helen Keller

Some people are making such thorough preparation for rainy days that they aren't enjoying today's sunshine. William Feather

The doghouse is no place to keep a sausage. American proverb

Insurance policies never cover what is happening. Lee Adler

The only security is courage. La Rochefoucauld

But who guards the guardians? Juvenal

SEIZE THE DAY

Life is full of misery, loneliness, and suffering; and it's all over much too soon. Woody Allen

For every person who has ever lived there has come, at last, a spring he will never see. Glory then in the springs that are yours. Pam Brown

It seems to me madness to wake up in the morning and do something other than paint, considering that one may not wake up the following morning.
Frank Auerbach

Too often man handles life as he does bad weather: he whiles away the time as he waits for it to stop.
                                                                    Alfred Polgar

Every moment is a golden one for him who has the vision to recognize it as such. Life is now, every moment, no matter if the world be full of death.
                                                                    Henry Miller

Lost, yesterday, somewhere between sunrise and sunset, two golden hours, each set with sixty diamond minutes. No reward is offered for they are gone forever.
                                                                    Horace Mann

Yesterday is a cancelled check: forget it. Tomorrow is a promissory note: don't count on it. Today is ready cash: use it!
                                                                    Edwin C. Bliss

Make your life a mission – not an intermission.
                                                                    Arnold Glasgow

I have a 'carpe diem' mug and, truthfully, at six in the morning the words do not make me want to seize the day. They make me want to slap a dead poet.
                                                                    Joanne Sherman

Tomorrow we'll not only seize the day, we'll throttle it.
                                                                    Bill Watterson

SELFISH

Every nation makes decisions based on self-interest and defends them on the basis of morality.
                                                                    William Sloane Coffin

Human history is the sad result of each one looking out for himself.
                                                                    Julio Cortázar

The small share of happiness attainable by man exists only insofar as he is able to cease to think of himself.
                                                                    Theodore Reik

Selfishness is not living as one wishes to live, it is asking others to live as one wishes to live.
                                                                    Oscar Wilde

The ruin of the human heart is self-interest, which the American merchant calls self-service. We have become a self-service populace, and all our specious comforts – the automatic elevator, the escalator, the cafeteria – are depriving us of volition and moral and physical energy.   Edward Dahlberg

I have often noticed that when chickens quit quarrelling over their food, they often find that there is enough for all of them. I wonder if it might not be the same with the human race.   Don Marquis

If I am not for myself, who will be?   Pirke Avoth

The greatest productive force is human selfishness.   Robert Heinlein

If we were not all so excessively interested in ourselves, life would be so uninteresting that none of us would be able to endure it.   Arthur Schopenhauer

Every major horror of history was committed in the name of an altruistic motive. Has any act of selfishness ever equalled the carnage perpetrated by disciples of altruism?   Ayn Rand

If you live only for yourself, you are always in immediate danger of being bored to death with the repetition of your own views and interests.   W. Beran Wolfe

If people knew how much ill-feeling unselfishness occasions, it would not be so often recommended from the pulpit.   C. S. Lewis

SELF-KNOWLEDGE

Where is your Self to be found? Always in the deepest enchantment that you have experienced.   Hugo von Hofmannsthal

It doesn't happen all at once. You become. It takes a long time.   Margery Williams

Men go abroad to wonder at the heights of mountains, at the huge waves of the sea, at the long courses of rivers, at the vast compass of the ocean, at the circular motion of the stars; and they pass by themselves without wondering.

St Augustine

He who knows others is learned; he who knows himself is wise.   Lao Tzu

Who looks outside dreams; who looks inside wakes.   Carl Jung

—Dr Crane has tunnelled his way into the very depths of my psyche.
—Well, let's hope he sent a canary down first.

Bebe Glazer and Niles Crane, *Frasier*

Most of us do not like to look inside ourselves for the same reason we don't like to open a letter that has bad news.   Fulton J. Sheen

It is as hard to see one's self as to look backwards without turning round.

Henry David Thoreau

There comes a time in each life like a point of fulcrum. At that time you must accept yourself. It is not any more what you will become. It is what you are and always will be.   John Fowles

I think somehow, we learn who we really are and then live with that decision.   Eleanor Roosevelt

How shall I grasp it? Do not grasp it. That which remains when there is no more grasping is the Self.   Swami Panchadasi

Life isn't about finding yourself. Life is about creating yourself.

George Bernard Shaw

Be who you are and say what you feel, because those who mind don't matter, and those who matter don't mind.   Dr Seuss

The majority of people are subjective toward themselves and objective toward all others, terribly objective sometimes, but the real task is, in fact, to be objective toward oneself and subjective toward all others.

Søren Kierkegaard

Know thyself? If I knew myself, I'd run away.　　　Johann Wolfgang von Goethe

Actualization of self cannot be sought as a goal in its own right ... Rather, it seems to be a by-product of active commitment of one's talents to some cause, outside the self, such as the quest for beauty, truth, or justice.

Sidney Jourard

And this is the simple truth: that to live is to feel oneself lost. He who accepts it has already begun to find himself, to be on firm ground.

José Ortega y Gasset

'Know thyself' – a maxim as pernicious as it is odious. A person who observes himself arrests his own development. A caterpillar that tried to 'know itself' would never become a butterfly.　　　André Gide

SELF-PITY

Self-pity – it's the only pity that counts.　　　Oscar Levant

Life, I fancy, would very often be insupportable but for the luxury of self-compassion; in cases numberless, this it must be that saves from suicide.

George Gissing

Self-pity is the simplest luxury.　　　Rita Mae Brown

Never feel self-pity, the most destructive emotion there is. How awful to be caught up in the terrible squirrel-cage of self.　　　Millicent Fenwick

I never saw a wild thing sorry for itself. A small bird will drop frozen dead from a bough without ever having felt sorry for itself.　　　D. H. Lawrence

Self-pity is in its early stage as snug as a feather mattress. Only when it hardens does it become uncomfortable.   Maya Angelou

Oh, for goodness sake, get down off that crucifix, someone needs the wood.
                        Felicia Jollygoodfellow, *Priscilla, Queen of the Desert*

SENSES

Always make the most of every sense; glory in all the pleasure and beauty which the world reveals to you.   Helen Keller

I see several animals that live so entire and perfect a life, some without sight, others without hearing: who knows whether to us also one, two, or three, or many other senses, may not be wanting?   Michel de Montaigne

The eyes have one language everywhere.   George Herbert

Sight is a promiscuous sense. The avid gaze always wants more. Susan Sontag

As soon as you know a man to be blind, you imagine that you can see it from his back.   Georg Christoph Lichtenberg

The same battle in the clouds will be known to the deaf only as lightning and to the blind only as thunder.   George Santayana

Knock on the sky and listen to the sound.   Zen saying

Her hearing was keener than his, and she heard silences he was unaware of.
                                        D. M. Thomas

Children, savages and true believers remember far less what they have seen than what they have heard.   Eric Hoffer

Smell is the closest thing human beings have to a time machine. Caryl Rivers

The first condition of understanding a foreign country is to smell it.

Rudyard Kipling

Hay smells different to lovers and horses.

Stanislaw J. Lec

The fabled musk deer searches the world over for the source of the scent which comes from itself.

Ramakrishna

You have to ask children and birds how cherries and strawberries taste.

Johann Wolfgang von Goethe

Now join your hands, and with your hands your hearts.

William Shakespeare, *King Henry VI, Part III*

SENTIMENTAL

Sentimentality – that's what we call the sentiment we don't share.

Graham Greene

Sentimentality is the only sentiment that rubs you up the wrong way.

W. Somerset Maugham

Sentimentality is the emotional promiscuity of those who have no sentiment.

Norman Mailer

Hatred of humanity and love of animals make a very bad combination.

Konrad Lorenz

Never trust a sentimentalist. They are all alike, pretenders to virtue, at heart selfish frauds and sensualists.

J. B. Yeats

Cruel men cry easily at the cinema.

Graham Greene

Sentimentality comes from an inability, for whatever reason, to look reality in the face.

Marilyn Sewell

I revolted from sentimentality, less because it was false than because it was cruel.
Ellen Glasgow

To show compassion for an individual without showing concern for the structures of society that make him an object of compassion is to be sentimental rather than loving.
William Sloane Coffin

SEX

Do you wanna see something swell?
Jon Lovitz

What's the matter, you can't think of anybody either?
Rodney Dangerfield

I think sex education in schools is a wonderful idea, but I don't think the kids should be given homework.
Patty Duke

Roses are red and ready for plucking,
You're sixteen and ready for high school.
Kurt Vonnegut

What men desire is a virgin who is a whore.
Edward Dahlberg

He moved his lips about her ears and neck as though in thirsting search of an erogenous zone. A waste of time, he knew from experience. Erogenous zones were either everywhere or nowhere.
Joseph Heller

Sleeping with the help are you? Well, as I say, 'What the hell, they're bending over anyway.'
Andy Richter

My sister was so promiscuous she broke her ankle in the glove compartment of a car.
Phyllis Diller

Sex hasn't been the same since women started enjoying it.
Lewis Grizzard

Just how responsible am I for my partner's orgasm? Well, I guess that depends on whether or not you're there.
Lea Delaria

Germaine Greer once gave a lecture at Oxford, arguing that the female orgasm was not only a facet of gender tyranny but was also vastly overrated. A male student raised his hand. 'About that overrated orgasm,' he drawled. 'Won't you give a Southern boy another chance?' The speaker was a young Rhodes scholar called Bill Clinton.
Caitlin Moran

Why do girls fake orgasms? Because they think we care.
Anon

If the bedroom were a kitchen, women would be crockpots and men would be microwaves.
Diana Jordan

Is it wrong to fake orgasm during masturbation?
Lotus Weinstock

I don't know whether you've ever had a woman eat an apple while you were doing it. Well, you can imagine how that affects you.
Henry Miller

The only unnatural sex act is one which you cannot perform.
Alfred Kinsey

Men perform oral sex like they drive. When they get there they refuse to ask for directions.
Catherine Franco

The closest I ever came to a ménage à trois was when I dated a schizophrenic.
Rita Rudner

Love does not make itself felt in the desire for copulation (a desire that extends to an infinite number of women) but in the desire for shared sleep (a desire limited to one woman).
Milan Kundera

There are things that happen in the dark between two people that make everything that happens in the light seem all right.
Erica Jong

I have tried a little kinky stuff. A woman called me and said, 'I have mirrors all over my bedroom. Bring a bottle.' I brought Windex.
Rodney Dangerfield

All animals are sad after coitus except the female human and the rooster.
Claudius Galen

There is nothing safe about sex. There never will be. Norman Mailer

When it comes to sex, and everything else, the male's great fear is of failure, and the female's is of not being loved.
Irma Kurtz

You use sex to express every emotion except love. Woody Allen

What motivated man to walk upright? To free his hands for masturbation.
Jane Wagner

The closest I ever came to death was masturbating with a 104-degree temperature. Larry David

The nicest thing about masturbation is the cuddling afterwards. Woody Allen

No hanky, no panky. At my age, foreplay is brushing my teeth – when I can remember where I put 'em. Rita Rudner

Man can go seventy years without a piece of ass, but he can die in a week without a bowel movement. Charles Bukowski

The best contraceptive for old people is nudity. Phyllis Diller

To me, Viagra is the same as Disneyland. You wait an hour for a two-minute ride. Rodney Dangerfield

After ecstasy, the laundry. Zen saying

SHARE

I hate sharing. It's what people do when they can't afford one each of something.   **Gary Strang, *Men Behaving Badly***

When two men share an umbrella, both of them get wet.   **Michael Isenberg**

I never share credit or desserts.   **Beverly Sills**

Unshared joy is an unlit candle.   **Spanish proverb**

A bottle of wine begs to be shared. I have never met a miserly wine-lover.   **Clifton Fadiman**

It is easier to halve the potato where there's love.   **Irish proverb**

He who divides gets the worst share.   **Spanish proverb**

Take what you can use and let the rest go by.   **Ken Kesey**

SHOPPING AND CONSUMERISM

Oh, I just love it here. So many things and so many things of each thing.   **Homer Simpson in Sprawl-Mart, *The Simpsons***

Veni, vidi, Visa: I came, I saw, I bought.   **Anon**

In a consumer society there are inevitably two kinds of slaves: the prisoners of addiction and the prisoners of envy.   **Ivan Illich**

Like so many Americans, she was trying to construct a life that made sense from things she found in gift shops.   **Kurt Vonnegut**

The only reason a great many American families don't own an elephant is that they have never been offered an elephant for a dollar down and easy weekly payments.

Mad magazine

The human animal is a beast that eventually has to die. And if he's got money he buys and he buys and he buys. The reason why he buys everything he can is because his crazy hope is that one of the things he buys will be life everlasting, which never can be.

Big Daddy, *Cat on a Hot Tin Roof*

Every time we buy something we deepen our emotional deprivation and hence our need to buy something.

Philip Slater

The sign said 'Eight Items or Less' so I changed my name to Less.

Rod Schmidt

The quickest way to stop noticing something may be to buy it, just as the quickest way to stop appreciating a person may be to marry them.

Allison Pearson

Though the worship of riches is an old religion, there has never been a danger that it might become the sole religion. And yet that is what is surely going to happen in the world.

J.E. Buckrose

Only the rich can achieve enlightenment because the poor are too busy looking for fridge freezers.

Bhagwan Shree Rajneesh

He who buys what he does not want, will soon want what he cannot buy.

Anne Mathews

We need objects to remind us of the commitments we've made. That carpet from Morocco reminds us of the impulsive, freedom-loving side of ourselves we're in danger of losing touch with. Beautiful furniture gives us something to live up to. All designed objects are propaganda for a way of life.

Alain de Botton

There must be more to life than having everything!

Maurice Sendak

Fewer and fewer Americans possess objects that have a patina, old furniture, grandparents' pots and pans – the used things, warm with generations of human touch, essential to a human landscape. Instead, we have our paper phantoms, transistorized landscapes. A featherweight portable museum.

Susan Sontag

—In a natural disaster, which one possession would you rescue from your home?
—If it was a flood, obviously the dinghy. If it was a hurricane … well, it wouldn't be hairspray. And if it was a fire, I'd rescue the smoke alarm so I could get my money back.

Interviewer and Lee Hurst

A woman is always buying something.

Ovid, first century AD

People will buy anything that is one to a customer.

Sinclair Lewis

Put two things together which have never been put together before, and some schmuck will buy it.

George Carlin

One of the most difficult tasks in this world is to convince a woman that even a bargain costs money.

E. W. Howe

Every increased possession loads us with a new weariness.

John Ruskin

You can't have everything. Where would you put it?

Steven Wright

One cannot build life from refrigerators, politics, credit statements and crossword puzzles. That is impossible. Nor can one exist for any length of time without poetry, without colour, without love.

Antoine de Saint-Exupéry

Every spirit passing through the world fingers the tangible and mars the mutable, and finally has come to look and not to buy.

Marilynne Robinson

If you would make a man happy, do not add to his possessions but subtract from the sum of his desires.　　　　　　　　　　Seneca

If there is any peace it will come through being, not having.　　　Henry Miller

Complete possession is proved only by giving. All you are unable to give possesses you.　　　　　　　　　　André Gide

I like to walk down Bond Street, thinking of all the things I don't desire.
　　　　　　　　　　Logan Pearsall Smith

Those who want the fewest things are nearest to the gods.　　　Socrates

The best things in life aren't things.　　　　　　　　　Art Buchwald

Let no one use anything as if it were his private possession.　St Ignatius Loyola

I leave no property behind me of which it is necessary to dispose. As for the everyday objects that were of use to me, I ask they be distributed as seems appropriate.　　　　　Pope John Paul II, from his Last Will and Testament

SILENCE

A friend of mine took a Zen Buddhist monk to hear the Boston Symphony perform Beethoven's Fifth Symphony. His comment was, 'Not enough silence!'　　　　　　　　　　Winthrop Sargent

Nothing in all creation is so like God as silence.　　　Meister Eckhart

I like the silent church before the service begins better than any preaching.
　　　　　　　　　　Ralph Waldo Emerson

Silence is exhilarating at first – as noise is – but there is a sweetness to silence outlasting exhilaration, akin to the sweetness of listening and the velvet of sleep.　　　　　　　　　　Edward Hoagland

There are very few people who do not become more interesting when they stop talking.   Mary Lowry

My personal hobbies are reading, listening to music and silence.
                                                                      Dame Edith Sitwell

Silence is the sleep that nourishes wisdom.   Francis Bacon

True silence is the rest of the mind; it is to the spirit what sleep is to the body, nourishment and refreshment.
                                                                      William Penn

Keep your mouth shut and you won't get any flies in it.   Argentinian proverb

I believe in the discipline of silence and could talk for hours about it.
                                                                      George Bernard Shaw

Accustomed to the veneer of noise, to the shibboleths of promotion, public relations, and market research, society is suspicious of those who value silence.   John Lahr

Born in elevators and supermarkets, Muzak has spread to restaurants, hotels, airplanes, telephone hold services, and waiting rooms. The public-relations experts believe that human beings fear silence – that is, the absence of constantly imposed direction. It is further believed that if we can be relieved of our fears, we will gain enough self-confidence to buy, eat, vote, fly, or simply go on living.   John Ralston Saul

The more evolved someone becomes, the greater his need for silence.
                                                                      Omraam Mikaël Aïvanhov

Men do not mirror themselves in running water; they mirror themselves in still water.   Chuang Tse

Soon silence will have passed into legend. Man has turned his back on silence. Day after day he invents machines and devices that increase noise and distract humanity from the essence of life, contemplation, meditation.

Jean Arp

Many people confuse silence with solitude. That is why they are afraid of silence: they are afraid of loneliness. The truth is, though, that silence is inhabited.

Omraam Mikaël Aïvanhov

Much silence has a mighty noise.

Swahili proverb

Silence is as full of wisdom and wit as the unhewn marble of great sculpture.

Aldous Huxley

Speech is silver, silence golden; speech sows, silence reaps.

Persian saying

SIMPLE AND COMPLEX

Like all magnificent things, it's very simple.

Natalie Babbitt

The greatest thing a human being ever does is to see something and tell what he sees in a plain way.

John Ruskin

Stained glass, engraved glass, frosted glass; give me plain glass.

John Fowles

Everything deep is also simple and can be reproduced simply as long as its reference to the whole truth is maintained.

Albert Schweitzer

Everything should be as simple as it is, but not simpler.

Albert Einstein

Everything is simpler than you think and at the same time more complex than you imagine.

Johann Wolfgang von Goethe

Out of intense complexities intense simplicities emerge.

Winston Churchill

SIN

Bless me, Father, for I have sinned, it's been a minute since my last
confession.   **Frank McCourt,** *Angela's Ashes*

There is no original sin. It's all been done before.   **Louis Dudek**

We don't call it sin today, we call it self-expression.   **Baroness Stocks**

Sin has been made not only ugly but *passé*. People are no longer sinful,
they are only immature or underprivileged or frightened or, more
particularly, sick.   **Phyllis McGinley**

Everything that used to be a sin is now a disease.   **Bill Maher**

The seven deadly sins are: Politics without principle; Wealth without work;
Commerce without morality; Pleasure without conscience; Education
without character; Science without humanity; Worship without sacrifice.
                                                      Mahatma Gandhi

I try to commit at least one deadly sin each day. If I don't get round to it,
I can always chalk it up to sloth.   **Robert Ragno**

How extraordinary it is that one feels most guilt about the sins one is
unable to commit.   **V. S. Pritchett**

Sins look much more terrible to those who look at it than to those who
do it.   **Ralph Iron**

Many are saved from sin by being so inept at it.   **Mignon McLaughlin**

Those who have more power are liable to sin more; no theorem in
geometry is more certain than this.   **Lord Acton**

A sense of humour keen enough to show a man his own absurdities as well
as those of other people will keep a man from the commission of all sins,
or nearly all, save those that are worth committing.   **Samuel Butler**

No fury more righteous than that of a sinner accused of the wrong sin.

Don Paterson

Women keep a special corner of their hearts for sins they have never committed.

Cornelia Otis Skinner

If there is a sin against life, it consists perhaps not so much in despairing of life as in hoping for another life and in eluding the implacable grandeur of this life.

Albert Camus

We are all Christ and Hitler. Yoko and I want Christ to win.

John Lennon

SLAVERY

We fight for men and women whose poetry is not yet written.

Robert Gould Shaw, abolitionist

To relive the relationship between owner and slave we can consider how we treat our cars and dogs – a dog exercising a somewhat similar leverage on our mercies and an automobile being comparable in value to a slave in those days.

Edward Hoagland

I freed a thousand slaves. I could have freed a thousand more if only they knew they were slaves.

Harriet Tubman

You can be up to your boobies in white satin, with gardenias in your hair and no sugar cane for miles, but you can still be working on a plantation.

Billie Holiday

The worst thing about slavery is that the slaves eventually get to like it.

Aristotle

Today the large organization is lord and master, and most of its employees have been desensitized much as were the medieval peasants who never knew they were serfs.

Ralph Nader

Slaves lose everything in their chains, even the desire of escaping from them.

Jean Jacques Rousseau

Oppressed people are frequently very oppressive when first liberated. They know but two positions: somebody's foot on their neck or their foot on somebody's neck.   Florence Kennedy

SLEEP

Sleep is the best of all worlds: you get to be alive and unconscious.

Rita Rudner

Is sleep a mating with oneself?   Novalis

Sleep came slower than a frigid woman.   Kinky Friedman

Sleep is still most perfect ... when it is shared with a beloved.   D. H. Lawrence

If you are living with a snorer it is important that you learn to 'tune out', otherwise you may find it puts you off your orgasm.   Jeff Green

Sometimes I wake up grumpy; other times I let him sleep.   Car bumper sticker

SMALL PLEASURES

One of the secrets of a happy life is continuous small treats.   Iris Murdoch

Most of us miss out on life's big prizes. The Pulitzer. The Nobel. Oscars. Tonys. Emmys. But we're all eligible for life's small pleasures. A pat on the back. A kiss behind the ear. A four-pound bass. A full moon. An empty parking space. A crackling fire. A great meal. A glorious sunset. Hot soup. Cold beer. Don't fret about copping life's grand awards. Enjoy its tiny delights.   *The Wall Street Journal*

A mere trifle consoles us, for a mere trifle distresses us. Blaise Pascal

One can get just as much exultation in losing oneself in a little thing as in a big thing. It is nice to think how one can be recklessly lost in a daisy.
Anne Morrow Lindbergh

Sun lighting a child's hair. A friend's embrace. Slow dancing in a safe and quiet place. The pleasures of an ordinary life. Judith Viorst

A glass of wine, a roast chestnut, a wretched little brazier, the sound of the sea … All that is required to feel that here and now is a simple, frugal heart. Nikos Kazantzakis

I have a friend who has developed a special ritual for getting up in the morning. She wakes up a few minutes before daybreak and makes herself a special cup of tea … She knew that even if the rest of the day turns hectic, she'll have one memory of something beginning exactly the way she likes it.
Elaine St James

One ought, every day at least, to hear a little song, read a good poem, see a fine picture, and, if it were possible, to speak a few reasonable words.
Johann Wolfgang von Goethe

A book of verses underneath the bough,
A jug of wine, a loaf of bread, and thou … Edward Fitzgerald

A bed, a nice fresh bed with smoothly drawn sheets and a hot water bottle at the end of it, soft to the feet like a live animal's tummy. Colette

SMOKING

Quit puffing that hell fume in God's clean air. Carry Nation

Smoking is the great romance of my lifetime. If I could find someone I wanted forty-five times a day, perhaps I could stop. Fran Lebowitz

You have to work at it if you want to be a good smoker. Especially today with all the non-smoking world constantly harassing you.

Kinky Friedman

It is bad enough stopping people doing something you don't like. But it is far worse to stop them doing it *for their own sake*. This is the first symptom of the totalitarian mind, and there is a lot of it about. Hilary Spurling

But when I don't smoke I scarcely feel as if I'm living. I don't feel as if I'm living unless I'm killing myself.

Russell Hoban

I would rather smoke one cigar than hear two sermons. Robert Green Ingersoll

If I could smoke from more than one orifice, I most certainly would.

Graham Parker

I offered Dawn a cigarette. She refused. 'No thanks, I've already got cancer.'

Elaine Dundy

I'm eighty-three and I've been smoking since I was eleven. I'm suing the cigarette company because it promised to kill me and it hasn't.

Kurt Vonnegut

Smoking cigars is like falling in love; first you are attracted to its shape; you stay with it for its flavour; and you must always remember never, never let the flame go out. Winston Churchill

A good cigar is like a beautiful chick with a great body who also knows the American League box scores. Sgt Max Klinger, *M*A*S*H*

People think there's a choice between smoking and immortality, but we've all got to die of something.

Tom Stoppard

The only thing that bothers me is if I'm in a restaurant and I'm eating and someone says, 'Hey, mind if I smoke?' I always say, 'No. Mind if I fart?'

Steve Martin

I'd much rather sit next to a smoker in a restaurant than a nose-blower.

Lewis Grizzard

SOLITUDE

Solitude can be frightening because it invites us to meet a stranger we think we may not want to know – ourselves.

Melvyn Kinder

One of the advantages of living alone is that you don't have to wake up in the arms of a loved one.

Marion Smith

When you live alone, you can be sure that the person who squeezed the toothpaste tube in the middle wasn't committing a hostile act.

Ellen Goodman

No man should go through life without once experiencing healthy, even bored solitude in the wilderness, finding himself depending solely on himself and thereby learning his true and hidden strength.

Jack Kerouac

I never found the companion that was so companionable as solitude.

Henry David Thoreau

True solitude is a din of birdsong, seething leaves, whirling colors, or a clamor of tracks in the snow.

Edward Hoagland

Man is never alone. Acknowledged or unacknowledged, that which dreams through him is always there to support him from within.

Laurens van der Post

Being alone and liking it is, for a woman, an act of treachery, an infidelity far more threatening than adultery.

Molly Haskell

One's need for loneliness is not satisfied if one sits at a table alone. There must be empty chairs as well.

Karl Kraus

We're all in this alone.

Lily Tomlin

SPEECH

Before I speak, I have something important to say.

Groucho Marx

There are two kinds of speeches: the Mother Hubbard speech, which, like the garment, covers everything but touches nothing, and the French bathing suit speech, which covers only the essential points.

Lyndon Johnson

There is all the difference in the world between having something to say and having to say something.

John Dewey

Neil Kinnock's speeches go on for so long because he has nothing to say and so he has no way of knowing when he's finished saying it.

John Major

Some speakers electrify their listeners, others only gas them.

Anon

Speeches are like steer horns – a point here, a point there, and a lot of bull in between.

Evelyn Anderson

It is with words as with sunbeams – the more they are condensed, the deeper they burn.

Robert Southey

As man is now constituted, to be brief is almost a condition of being inspired.

George Santayana

Always be shorter than anyone dared to hope.

Lord Reading

Be sincere ... be brief ... be seated.

James Roosevelt

SPEED

Men travel faster now, but I do not know if they go to better things.

Willa Cather

It is an ironic habit of human beings to run faster when we have lost our way.

Rollo May

You don't have to be faster than the lion. You only have to be faster than the slowest guy.

Zimbabwean saying

Tortoises can tell you more about the road than hares.

Kahlil Gibran

In skating over thin ice it is our speed that saves us.

Ralph Waldo Emerson

I foresee the time when human beings, having ceased to regard speed as a novelty, will lose much of their taste for it.

Robert Lynd

Nothing travels faster than light, with the possible exception of bad news.

Douglas Adams

The fastest way to travel is to be already there.

Terry Pratchett

SPORT

I used to think the only use for sport was to give small boys something else to kick besides me.

Katharine Whitehorn

I have never willingly chased a ball.

Robert Morley

Sports do not build character. They reveal it.

Haywood Hale Broun

Always play a game with somebody, never against them. Always win a game, never beat an opponent.

Andrew Bailey

In sports, as in love, one can never pretend. Rita Mae Brown

Show me a good sportsman and I'll show you a player I'm looking to trade.
Leo Durocher, US baseball manager

We are inclined to think that if we watch a football game or a baseball game, we have taken part in it. John F. Kennedy

Sports play a societal role in engendering jingoist and chauvinist attitudes. They're designed to organize a community to be committed to their gladiators. Noam Chomsky

The more violent the body contact of the sports you watch, the lower the class.
Paul Fussell

Bullfights are hugely popular because you can sit comfortably with a hot dog and possibly watch a man die. Albert Brooks

Serious sport has nothing to do with fair play. It is bound up with hatred, jealousy, boastfulness, disregard of all rules and sadistic pleasure in witnessing violence. In other words, it is war minus the shooting.
George Orwell

You have to play American football like somebody just hit your mother with a two-by-four. Dan Birdwell

What makes a good manager? Good players! Yogi Berra

Baseball and cricket are beautiful and highly stylized medieval war substitutes, chess made flesh, a mixture of proud chivalry and base – in both senses – greed. John Fowles

The stronger women get, the more men love football. Mariah Burton Nelson

We've all been blessed with God-given talents. Mine just happens to be
beating people up.   Sugar Ray Leonard

Boxing is a celebration of the lost religion of masculinity all the more
trenchant for its being lost.   Joyce Carol Oates

Don Quixote would understand golf. It is the impossible dream. Jim Murray

There are fools, bloody fools, and men who remount in a steeplechase.
                                                              John Oaksey

All that I know most surely about morality and obligations I owe to
football.   Albert Camus

They say football is a game of two halves. Not for me it isn't. I regularly
down eight or nine pints whilst watching a live game on Sky TV in my
local.   Adrian Bond, *Viz*

We Germans are so good at penalties because we have had to rebuild our
country twice.   Jürgen Klinsmann

Boxing is the only sport in the world where two guys get paid for doing something they'd be arrested for if they got drunk and did it for nothing.

Michael Kelly, *Champion*

If you see a tennis player who looks as if he is working hard, that means he
isn't very good.   Helen Wills Moody

I'm learning to use others' weaknesses. I don't hammer a man's soft spot
constantly, because he may strengthen it. I just save it as a trump up my
sleeve for moments when I really need a point.   Arthur Ashe

If you're up against a girl with big boobs, bring her to the net and make her play backhand volleys.   Billie Jean King

To play mixed doubles: hit the girl whenever possible.   Bill Tilden

In the human race today, you came last.   Spike Milligan

Running a marathon is just like reading a good book. After a while you're just not conscious of the physical act of reading.

Frank Shorter

Reggie's was a troubled spirit these days. He was in love, and he developed a bad slice with his mid-iron. He was practically a soul in torment.

P. G. Wodehouse

The golf swing is like sex: you can't be thinking of the mechanics of the act while you're doing it.   Dave Hill

A typical round of golf: one minute you're bleeding. The next minute you're haemorrhaging. The next minute you're painting the *Mona Lisa*.

Mac O'Grady

The real test of golf – like life – is not keeping out of the rough, but getting out after we are in.   Henry Lash

One of the advantages bowling has over golf is that you seldom lose a bowling ball.   Don Carter

I pulled a hamstring during the New York City Marathon – an hour into the race I jumped up off the couch.   David Letterman

STATISTICS

A single death is a tragedy, a million deaths is a statistic.

Joseph Stalin

—Why do you always assume the worst about people?
—Statistics.

Matt and Gwyn, *Miami Rhapsody*

Like dreams, statistics are a form of wish-fulfilment.

Jean Baudrillard

I could prove God statistically.

George Gallup

Statistics are like a bikini. What they reveal is suggestive, but what they conceal is vital.

Aaron Levenstein

I always find that statistics are hard to swallow and impossible to digest. The only one I can ever remember is that if all the people who go to sleep in church were laid end to end they would be a lot more comfortable.

Mrs Robert A. Taft

43.7 per cent of all statistics are made up on the spot.

Steven Wright

STRENGTH

Top cats often begin as underdogs.

Bernard Meltzer

Ants can carry twenty times their own body weight, which is useful information if you're moving out and you need help getting a potato chip across town.

Ron Darian

The weakest link in a chain is the strongest because it can break it.

Stanislaw J. Lec

The human spirit is stronger than anything that can happen to it.

George C. Scott

There is nothing stronger in the world than tenderness. Hans Suyin

Nobody roots for Goliath. Wilt Chamberlain

Our deepest fear is not that we are inadequate. Our deepest fear is that we are powerful beyond measure. It is our Light, not our Darkness, that most frightens us. Maryanne Williamson

Anyone can give up, it's the easiest thing in the world to do. But to hold it together when everyone else would understand if you fell apart, that's true strength. Douglas Bader

Our strength is often composed of the weakness we're damned if we're going to show. Mignon McLaughlin

Some think it's holding on that makes one strong; sometimes it's letting go. Sylvia Robinson

STRESS

I read this article. It said the typical symptoms of stress are eating too much, smoking too much, impulse buying, and driving too fast. Are they kidding? This is my idea of a great day! Monica Piper

The chief cause of stress is reality. Lily Tomlin

They say that moving is one of the most stressful things in life. Death in the family is the second most stressful, and moving your dead spouse is the third. Kevin Nealon

—How do you bear up so calmly under the strain and stress of a wartime presidency?
—I have a fox-hole in my mind. When I need to I can retire there and allow nothing to bother me. Reporter and President Harry Truman

No pressure, no diamonds. Mary Case

STUPIDITY

One man alone can be pretty dumb sometimes, but for real bona fide stupidity, there ain't nothin' can beat teamwork.   **Edward Abbey**

It's too bad that stupidity isn't painful.   **Anton LaVey**

Have you ever heard more drivel coming from someone who's not even the president?   **Deke, *Hero***

The two most common elements in the universe are hydrogen and stupidity.   **Harlan Ellison**

Think of how stupid the average person is, and realize half of them are stupider than that.   **George Carlin**

Men never sound more stupid than when they're telling you they're a very complex personality.   **Clive James**

He was endowed with a stupidity which by the least stretch would go around the globe four times and tie.   **Mark Twain**

I have always noticed that people only think you are stupid if you do things differently from them.   **Liza Cody**

Stupidity is without anxiety.   **Johann Wolfgang von Goethe**

You should be more afraid of a stupid man than of an evil one.   **Christina of Sweden**

We never really know what stupidity is until we have experimented on ourselves.   **Paul Gauguin**

I see the happy moron,
He doesn't give a damn,
I wish I were a moron,
My God! Perhaps I am!   **Anon**

STYLE

Style is knowing who you are, what you want to say, and not giving a damn.

Gore Vidal

It is the beginning of the end when you discover you have style.

Dashiell Hammett

Never offend people with style when you can offend them with substance.

Sam Brown

It's impossible to look cool whilst picking up a Frisbee. Peter Kay

A hairstyle's not a lifestyle. Jello Biafra

SUCCESS

Quit now, you'll never make it. If you disregard this advice, you'll be halfway there. David Zucker

Success is simply a matter of luck. Ask any failure. Earl Wilson

There is never any magic. We earn our spurs by getting everything right.

Adrian Bellamy

The difference between ordinary and extraordinary is that little extra.

Jimmy Johnson

The biggest trouble with success is that its formula is just about the same as that for a nervous breakdown. John Holmes

Formula for success: underpromise and overdeliver. Tom Peters

Is it possible to succeed without any act of betrayal? Jean Renoir

The secret of success is to know something nobody else knows.

Aristotle Onassis

The secret of success is to offend the greatest number of people.

George Bernard Shaw

The secret of success is to do the common things uncommonly well.

John D. Rockerfeller Jr

To be successful you have to be lucky, or a little mad, or very talented, or to find yourself in a rapid-growth field.

Edward de Bono

Sometimes you have to suffer a little bit in your youth to motivate yourself to succeed in later life. If Bill Gates had got laid in high school, do you think there'd be a Microsoft?

Greg Giraldo

Most success springs from an obstacle or failure. I became a cartoonist largely because I failed in my goal of becoming a successful executive.

Scott Adams

Eighty per cent of success is showing up.

Woody Allen

There's no secret about success. Did you ever meet a successful man that didn't tell you all about it?   Kin Hubbard

The measure of success is not whether you have a tough problem to deal with, but whether it is the same problem you had last year.

John Dulles

Success can make you go one of two ways – it can make you a prima donna, or it can smooth the edges, take away the insecurities, let the nice things come out.

Barbara Walters

On every summit you are on the brink of an abyss.

Stanislaw J. Lec

The common idea that success spoils people by making them vain, egotistic and self-complacent is erroneous; on the contrary it makes them, for the most part, humble, tolerant and kind. **W. Somerset Maugham**

The worst part of success is to try to find someone who's happy for you.
Bette Midler

In Washington, success is just a training course for failure. **Simon Hoggart**

A man is a success if he gets up in the morning and goes to bed at night and in between does what he wants to do.

Bob Dylan

Success is more dangerous than failure, the ripples break over a wider coastline. **Graham Greene**

Success is a lousy teacher. It seduces smart people into thinking they can't lose. **Bill Gates**

Despite the success-cult, men are most deeply moved not by the reaching of the goal but by the grandness of the effort involved in getting there – or failing to get there. **Max Lerner**

What is success? To laugh often and much; to win the respect of intelligent people and the affection of children; to earn the appreciation of honest critics and to endure the betrayal of false friends; to appreciate beauty and find the best in others; to leave the world a bit better whether by a healthy child, a garden patch or a redeemed social condition; to know even one life has breathed easier because you have lived – this is to have succeeded. **Ralph Waldo Emerson**

When you reach the top, keep climbing. **Zen proverb**

SUFFERING

You desire to know the art of living, my friend? It is contained in one phrase: make use of suffering.
Henri Frédéric Amiel

Pain hardens, and great pain hardens greatly, whatever the comforters say, and suffering does not ennoble, though it may occasionally lend a certain rigid dignity of manner to the suffering frame.
A. S. Byatt

If suffering brings wisdom, I would wish to be less wise.
W. B. Yeats

I believe there are more urgent and honourable occupations than the incomparable waste of time we call suffering.
Colette

To love is to suffer. To avoid suffering one must not love. But then one suffers from not loving. Therefore, to love is to suffer; not to love is to suffer; to suffer is to suffer. To be happy is to love. To be happy, then, is to suffer, but suffering makes one unhappy. Therefore, to be unhappy, one must love or love to suffer or suffer from too much happiness. I hope you're getting this down.
Woody Allen

It is a glorious thing to be indifferent to suffering, but only to one's own suffering.
Robert Lynd

One often learns more from ten days of agony than from ten years of contentment.
Harold Coffin

The same suffering is much harder to bear for a high motive than for a base one. The people [during World War II] who stood motionless, from one to eight in the morning, for the sake of having an egg, would have found it very difficult to do in order to save a human life.
Simone Weil

As you look at many people's lives, you see that their suffering is in a way gratifying, for they are comfortable in it. They make their lives a living hell, but a familiar one.
Ram Dass

Misfortunes one can endure – they come from outside, they are accidents. But to suffer for one's own faults – Ah! there is the sting of life.

Oscar Wilde

The only antidote to mental suffering is physical pain.

Karl Marx

SUICIDE

Hemingway shot himself. I don't like a man that takes the short way home.

William Faulkner

Suicide is the only perfect crime that remains unpunished.

Warren Manzi

I don't think suicide is so terrible. Some rainy winter Sundays when there's a little boredom, you should always carry a gun. Not to shoot yourself, but to know exactly that you're always making a choice.

Lina Wertmuller

Suicide is man's way of telling God, 'You can't fire me, I quit.'

Bill Maher

Doesn't suicide seem a little like going where you haven't been invited?

Richard Eberhart

I couldn't commit suicide if my life depended on it.

George Carlin

Suicide is no more than a trick played on the calendar.

Tom Stoppard

Sometimes I wonder if suicides are not sad guardians of the meaning of life.

Václav Havel

To be or not to be, that is the question.

William Shakespeare, *Hamlet*

There is no way of proving it is preferable to be than not to be. E. M. Cioran

Would Hamlet have felt the delicious fascination of suicide if he hadn't had an audience, and lines to speak?

Jean Genet

No one is promiscuous in his way of dying. A man who has decided to hang himself will never jump in front of a train.　　　　　A. Alvarez

The calm, cool face of the river asked me for a kiss.　　　Langston Hughes

If they tell you that she died of sleeping pills you must know that she died of a wasting grief, of a slow bleeding at the soul.
Clifford Odets on the death of Marilyn Monroe

I have always thought the suicide should bump off at least one swine before taking off for parts unknown.　　　　Ezra Pound

A suicide kills two people ... that's what it's for.　　　Arthur Miller

No one ever lacks a good reason for suicide.　　　Cesare Pavese

The thought of suicide is a great comfort; it helps one through many a bad night.　　　　Friedrich Nietzsche

No matter how much a woman loved a man, it would still give her a glow to see him commit suicide for her.　　　　H. L. Mencken

Indecisive about committing suicide? Then hang yourself with a bungee rope.
Viz magazine

I was going to commit suicide the other day, but I must not have been serious because I bought a beach towel.　　　Steven Wright

If you wish to drown, do not torture yourself with shallow water.
Bulgarian proverb

In New York City, one suicide in ten is attributed to a lack of storage space.　　　　Judith Stone

Many a man has decided to stay alive not because of the will to live but because of the determination not to give assorted surviving bastards the satisfaction of his death.　　　　Brendan Francis

If someone with multiple personalities threatens to kill himself, is it considered a hostage situation?

George Carlin

The best way to commit suicide is Russian roulette: that way you make an enjoyable game of it.

Simon Nye

You want to go easy on the suicide stuff – first thing you know, you'll ruin your health.

Robert Benchley

I always think the same thing when I read about someone committing suicide. I think, 'There, but for the grace of God, go I.' I hope that I can give someone else a reason to live through today so that he or she will give me a reason to live through tomorrow.

Dahven White

—I used to be in the Samaritans … But I couldn't take any more.
—I don't blame you. You spoke to five people, and they all committed suicide. I wouldn't mind, but one was a wrong number. He only phoned up for the cricket scores.

Rimmer and Lister, Red Dwarf

There is no suicide for which all society is not responsible.

Cyril Connolly

It is not worth the bother of killing yourself, since you always kill yourself too late.

E. M. Cioran

Life is better than death, I believe, if only because it is less boring, and because it has fresh peaches in it.

Alice Walker

SUPERSTITION

It's bad luck to be superstitious.

Andrew W. Mathis

Superstition is the religion of feeble minds.

Edmund Burke

Let me make the superstitions of a nation and I care not who makes its laws, or its songs either.

Mark Twain

The general root of superstition is that men observe when things hit,
and not when they miss, and commit to memory the one, and pass over
the other.   Francis Bacon

A black cat crossing your path signifies that the animal is going
somewhere.   Groucho Marx

Men will fight for a superstition quite as quickly as for a living truth –
often more so, since a superstition is so intangible you cannot get at it to
refute it, but truth is a point of view, and so is changeable.   Elbert Hubbard

There is superstition in avoiding superstition.   Francis Bacon

Men are probably nearer the central truth in their superstitions than in
their science.   Henry David Thoreau

SURVIVAL

Never saw off the branch you are on, unless you are being hanged from it.
                                                         Stanislaw J. Lec

When you get to the end of your rope – tie a knot in it and hang on.
                                                        Eleanor Roosevelt

Rupert Grayson manifested a talent for survival: it was said of him that
even if – unlikely contingency – he had tried to drown himself in the
Thames he would have been washed up alive in the Grill Room of the
Savoy.   Hugh Massingberd

There is often in people in whom 'the worst' has happened an almost
transcendent freedom, for they have faced 'the worst' and survived it.
                                                           Carol Pearson

As only New Yorkers know, if you can get through the twilight, you'll live
through the night.   Dorothy Parker

SUSPICION

There is nothing makes a man suspect much, more than to know little.
Francis Bacon

When we say we are certain so-and-so can't possibly have done it, what we mean is that we think he very likely did. **Logan Pearsall Smith**

Suspicions amongst thoughts are like bats amongst birds, they ever fly by twilight. **Francis Bacon**

When a husband's story is believed, he begins to suspect his wife.
H. L. Mencken

I know of no rule which holds so true as that we are always paid for our suspicion by finding what we suspect. **Henry David Thoreau**

SYMPATHY

A sympathizer is a fellow that's for you as long as it doesn't cost anything.
Kin Hubbard

We all have strength enough to endure the troubles of others.
La Rochefoucauld

It is very odd how completely unable so many men are to put themselves in the place of their own audience – so very unlike the old Duke of Devonshire, who yawned during his own maiden speech because, as he told somebody, 'It was so damned dull.' **George Lyttleton**

It has always been my temptation to put myself in other people's shoes: even into a horse's shoes as he strains before the heavy dray; into a ballerina's points as she feels age weigh upon her spring. With experience of age I have learned to control this habit of sympathy which deforms truth. **Lady Diana Cooper**

Men are not against you; they are merely for themselves. Gene Fowler

Wisdom must go with sympathy, else the emotions will become maudlin and pity may be wasted on a poodle instead of a child – on a fieldmouse instead of a human soul. Elbert Hubbard

A boil is no big deal. On someone else's neck. Jewish saying

When you are in trouble, people who call to sympathize are really looking for the particulars. E. W. Howe

Never let anyone even catch a glimpse of your sorrow; inquisitive people drink tears as flies drink the blood of a wounded deer. Alexandre Dumas

Don't tell people your troubles: one half don't care, and the other half are glad. English proverb

I think I feel rather differently about sympathy to what seems the normal view. I like just to feel it is there, but not always expressed. A. C. Benson

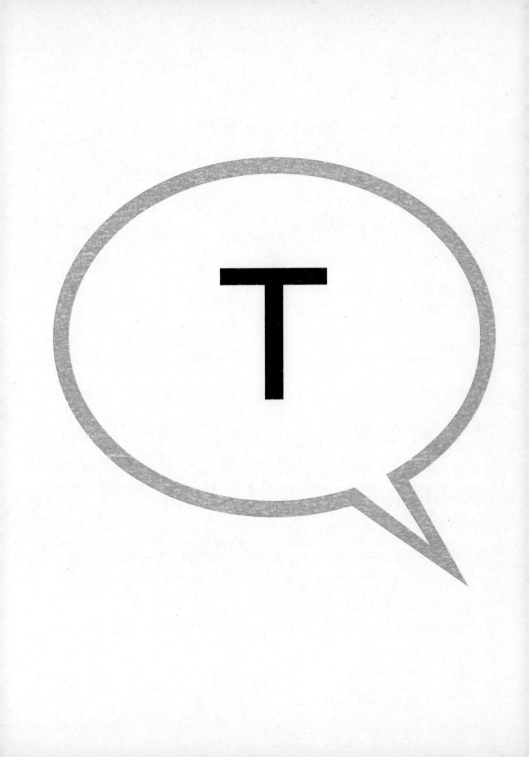

TALENT

I've got a God-given talent. I get it from my dad.

Julian Wakefield, basketball player

Any talent that we are born with eventually surfaces as a need.

Marsha Sinetar

Talent is often a defect in character.

Karl Kraus

There are some bad qualities which make great talents.

La Rochefoucauld

Even with talent, it's who you meet at the right time that tips the scales.

Richard Briers

The only thing that happens overnight is recognition. Not talent.

Carol Haney

No man can discover his own talents.

Brendan Francis

Everyone has talent. What is rare is the courage to follow that 'talent' to the dark place where it leads.

Erica Jong

An actress without talent, forty years old, ate a partridge for dinner, and I felt sorry for the partridge, for it occurred to me that in its life it had been more talented, more sensible, and more honest than the actress.

Anton Chekhov

Talent is forgiven only in the dead; those who are still standing cast shadows.

Comtesse Diane

I have no special gift. I am only passionately curious.

Albert Einstein

TASTE AND VULGARITY

I have the simplest tastes. I am always satisfied with the best.   Oscar Wilde

Bad taste creates many more millionaires than good taste.   Charles Bukowski

She's a very charming and delightful creature ... and has only one fault that
I know of. It happens, unfortunately, that that single blemish is a want
of taste. She don't like me.   Charles Dickens, *The Pickwick Papers*

The essence of taste is suitability. Divest the word of its prim and priggish
implications, and see how it expresses the mysterious demand of the eye
and mind for symmetry, harmony and order.   Edith Wharton

Ah, vulgarity, the cane upon which a cripple wit hobbles.
    Charles, *The In-Laws*

It is only with great vulgarity that you can achieve real refinement, only out
of bawdy that you can get tenderness.   Lawrence Durrell

What is exhilarating in bad taste is the aristocratic pleasure of giving
offence.   Charles Baudelaire

Nothing is more vulgar than haste.   Ralph Waldo Emerson

TAX

The reward of energy, enterprise and thrift is taxes.   William Feather

To tax and to please, no more than to love and to be wise, is not given
to men.   Edmund Burke

The avoidance of taxes is the only intellectual pursuit that still carries any
reward.   John Maynard Keynes

Intaxication: euphoria at getting a tax rebate until you realize it was your
money to start with.   *The Washington Post*

TEACHER

I owe a lot to my teachers and mean to pay them back some day.
                                                        Stephen Leacock

Life is amazing, and the teacher had better prepare himself to be a medium
for that amazement.   Edward Blishen

A teacher should have an atmosphere of awe, and walk wonderingly, as if
he was amazed at being himself.   Walter Bagehot

The reason teaching has to go on is that children are not born human; they
are made so.   Jacques Barzun

I am not a teacher, I am an awakener.   Robert Frost

The secret of teaching is to appear to have known all your life what you
learned only yesterday.   John Burns

To teach is to learn twice.   Joseph Joubert

One might as well say he has sold when no one has bought as to say he has
taught when no one has learned.   John Dewey

One looks back with appreciation to the brilliant teachers, but with
gratitude to those who touched our human feeling. Curriculum is necessary
raw material, but warmth is the vital element for the growing plant and for
the soul of the child.   Carl Jung

Of all the excellent teachers of college English whom I have known I have
never discovered one who knew precisely what he was doing. Therein have
lain their power and their charm.   Mary Ellen Chase

A very wise old teacher once said: 'I consider a day's teaching is wasted if we do not all have one hearty laugh.' He meant that when people laugh together, they cease to be young and old, master and pupils, workers and driver, jailer and prisoners, they become a single group of human beings enjoying its existence. Gilbert Highet

Everything I learn about teaching I learn from bad students. John Holt

A teacher is one who makes himself progressively unnecessary.
Thomas Carruthers

In time even a bear can be taught to dance. Yiddish proverb

Teachers open the door, but you must enter by yourself. Chinese proverb

TEARS

It is such a secret place, the land of tears. Antoine de Saint-Exupéry

Tears are just the soul on location. Charlotte Mitchell

Those who don't know how to weep with their whole heart don't know how to laugh either. Golda Meir

A hearty laugh gives one a dry cleaning, while a good cry is a wet wash.
Puzant Kevork Thomajan

Women are never landlocked; they're always mere minutes away from the briny deep of tears. Mignon McLaughlin

The world's greatest water power is women's tears. J. K. Morley

Be careful not to make a woman weep. God counts her tears. *Talmud*

The soul would have no rainbow had the eyes no tears. John Vance Cheney

Time engraves our faces with all the tears we have not shed.

Natalie Clifford Barnes

Both tears and sweat are salty, but they render a different result. Tears will get you sympathy; sweat will get you change. Reverend Jesse Jackson

TECHNOLOGY

Technology ... is a queer thing. It brings you great gifts with one hand, and it stabs you in the back with the other. C. P. Snow

Technology is the knack of so organizing the world that we don't have to experience it. Max Frisch

There are three roads to ruin – women, gambling and technicians. The most pleasant is with women, the quickest is with gambling, but the surest is with technicians. Georges Pompidou

Never send a human to do a machine's job. Agent Smith, *The Matrix*

Nothing increases the number of jobs so rapidly as labor-saving machinery, because it releases wants theretofore unknown, by permitting leisure. Isabel Paterson

Man will never be enslaved by machinery if the man tending the machine be paid enough. Karel Čapek

The difference between machines and human beings is that human beings can be reproduced by unskilled labour. Arthur C. Clarke

I have no skills with machines. I fear them, and because I cannot help attributing human qualities to them, I suspect that they hate me and will kill me if they can. Robertson Davies

Automatic simply means that you can't repair it yourself. Frank Capra

A refrigerator runs by converting the dust behind it into a peculiar mutant, reptilian substance.

Colin McEnroe

A machine is as distinctively and brilliantly and expressively human as a violin sonata or a theorem in Euclid.

Gregory Vlastos

The pencil sharpener is about as far as I have ever got in operating a complicated piece of machinery with any success.

Robert Benchley

Bill Gates is not necessarily so different from the rest of us. I went into his den and his VCR is still flashing 12:00.

Jay Leno

My VCR flashes 01:35, 01:35, 01:35 ...

Steven Wright

By the year 2000, all Americans must be able to set the clocks on their VCRs.

George Bush

It is only when they go wrong that machines remind you how powerful they are.

Clive James

My dream appliance circa 2050 has one big dial on it, and when I twist it to the right, my IQ goes up to 450.

Bruce Sterling

Electronic calculators can solve problems which the man who made them cannot solve; but no government-subsidized commission of engineers and physicists could create a worm.

Joseph Wood Krutch

We cannot get grace from gadgets.

J. B. Priestley

More and more I come to value charity and love of one's fellow beings above everything else ... All our lauded technological progress – our very civilization – is like the axe in the hand of the pathological criminal.

Albert Einstein

The trouble with machinery is that charm doesn't work.   Hawkeye, *M*A*S*H*

A steam engine has always got character. It's the most human of all man-made machines.   Reverend W. V. Awdry

TELEPHONE

Thank you for calling.
To be placed on hold and listen to a tinny version of 'Greensleeves', press 1.
To speak to a customer service representative who has no interest in your problem, press 2.
To speak to someone who is very friendly and understanding, but no help whatsoever, press 3.
To be plunged into a telephonic abyss of silence, press 4.
To be disconnected for no apparent reason, pre—   Anon

Many are called but few are called back.
Mary Tricky

The telephone is the greatest nuisance among conveniences, the greatest convenience among nuisances.   Norman Douglas

She had to have a telephone. There was no one to whom she wanted to talk but she had to have a telephone.   Joan Didion

The more we elaborate our means of communication, the less we communicate.   J. B. Priestley

I don't answer the phone. I get the feeling whenever I do that there will be someone on the other end.   Fred Couples

There are huge creative advantages in having huge chunks of time when no one can find you. Emails and phones have diluted the experience of travel.
Pete McCarthy

Today the telephone takes precedence over everything. It reaches a point of terrorism, particularly at dinnertime.   **Niels Diffrient**

'Here are your phone messages: "You have thirty minutes to move your car." "You have ten minutes to move your car." "Your car has been impounded." "Your car has been crushed into a cube." "You have thirty minutes to move your cube." '

Ansaphone message for Homer Simpson, *The Simpsons*

Whoever says that mobile phones will one day completely replace the telephone is talking utter nonsense. Have they ever tried to piss into a Nokia 8210, or smear an unwanted kebab on the inside of an Ericsson T65?

A. Tern, *Viz*

The real motive behind the popularity of cell phones is not convenience, but a base desire to be self-important. Cell-phone babblers are never really able to be present 'in the moment', since they are constantly trying to impress an audience with the implication that behind these mysterious phone calls very important things are taking place.   **Natalie Silvers**

In heaven, when the blessed use the telephone they will say what they have to say and not a word besides.

W. Somerset Maugham

Sometimes I think with the telephone that if I concentrate enough I could pour myself into it and I'd be turned into a mist and I would rematerialize in the room of the person I'm talking to. Is that too odd for you?

Nicholson Baker

Electric communication will never be a substitute for the face of someone who with their soul encourages another person to be brave and true.

Anon

TELEVISION

Television! Teacher, mother, secret lover.

Homer Simpson

They say that ninety per cent of TV is junk. But ninety per cent of everything is junk.

Gene Rodenberry

Television is the menace that everyone loves to hate but can't seem to live without.

Paddy Chayevsky

Disparagement of television is second only to watching television as an American pastime.

George F. Will

Imagine what it would be like if TV actually were good. It would be the end of everything we know.

Marvin Minsky

I'm glad cave people didn't invent television because they would have just sat around and watched talk shows all day instead of creating tools.

Dave James

I don't know how long a child will remain utterly static in front of the television, but my guess is that it could be well into their thirties.   **A. A. Gill**

We love television because television brings us a world in which television does not exist. In fact, deep in their hearts, this is what the spuds crave most: a rich, new, participatory life.

Barbara Ehrenreich

Today's audience knows more about what's on television than what's in life.

Larry Gelbart

Perhaps the crime situation would be improved if we could get more cops off television and onto the streets.

Bill Vaughan

We've all been raised on television to believe that one day we'd all be millionaires, and movie gods, and rock stars. But we won't. And we're slowly learning that fact. And we're very, very pissed off.

Tyler Durden, *Fight Club*

The great thing about television is that if something important happens anywhere in the world, night or day, you can always change the channel.

'Reverend' Jim Ignatowski, *Taxi*

The programmes constantly repeat themselves and one another. No one has yet had the nerve to say, 'As we have nothing sensible to tell you between now and 8:30, please tune in again then.'

Quentin Crisp

Television is becoming a collage – there are so many channels that you move through them making a collage yourself. In that sense, everyone sees something a bit different.

David Hockney

For those wretched souls unable to watch *Big Brother* all day, here's what you missed: Maggot's fry-up, live coverage of which was so extensive I had time to count ninety-four beans on his plate.

John Perry

There are times when any electrical appliance in the house, including the vacuum cleaner, seems to offer more entertainment possibilities than the TV set.

Harriet Van Horne

I made a pact with myself a long time ago: never watch anything stupider than you. It's helped me a lot.

Bette Midler

It occurs to me that with all the television people watch, most of their acquaintances are actors.

Arthur Miller

One of television's mysterious powers is to give us the illusion of immediate presence, but, in fact, it gives us the world through a lens darkly.

Richard W. Fox

You're beginning to think that the tube is reality and that your own lives are unreal ... In God's name, you people are the real thing; we're the illusion.

Howard Beale, *Network*

Anyone afraid of what he thinks television does to the world is probably just afraid of the world.   Clive James

Whether or not you love television, you've got to admit that it certainly loves itself.   Mignon McLaughlin

There is nothing more mysterious than a TV set left on in an empty room. It is even stranger than a man talking to himself or a woman standing dreaming at her stove. It is as if another planet is communicating with you.
                                                    Jean Baudrillard

Nothing is really real unless it happens on television.   Daniel J. Boorstin

TEMPTATION

Mmm … forbidden doughnut.   Homer Simpson

Naughty … but nice.   Dennis Potter, advertising slogan for cream cakes

Fancy cream puffs so soon after breakfast. The very idea made one shudder. All the same, two minutes later Jose and Laura were licking their fingers with that absorbed inward look that comes only from whipped cream.
                                                    Katherine Mansfield

Terrible is the temptation to be good.   Bertolt Brecht

Adam was but human – this explains it all. He did not want the apple for the apple's sake, he wanted it only because it was forbidden. The mistake was in not forbidding the serpent – then he would have eaten the serpent.
                                                    Mark Twain

Sometimes the devil tempts me to believe in God.   Stanislaw J. Lec

Opportunity may knock only once, but temptation leans on the doorbell.
                                                    Anon

I find I always have to write something on a steamed-up mirror.

Elaine Dundy

Always yield to temptation. It may not pass your way again. Robert Heinlein

Those who flee temptation generally leave a forwarding address.

Lane Olinghouse

While forbidden fruit is said to taste sweeter, it usually spoils faster.

Abigail Van Buren

The biggest human temptation is to settle for too little. Thomas Merton

It may also be a question whether such wisdom as many of us have in our mature years has not come from the dying out of our power of temptation, rather than as the results of thought and resolution. Anthony Trollope

There is not any memory with less satisfaction than the memory of some temptation resisted. James Branch Cabell

TERRORISM

Terrorism is the tactic of demanding the impossible, and demanding it at gunpoint. Christopher Hitchens

Terrorism is armed propaganda. Major-General Sir Frank Kitson

Terror depends on who's wearing the hood. Roger Woodis

The terrorist and the policeman both come from the same basket.

Joseph Conrad

If we like them, they're freedom fighters, she thought. If we don't like them, they're terrorists. In the unlikely case we can't make up our minds, they're temporarily only guerrillas. Carl Sagan

Everybody's worried about stopping terrorism. Well, there's a really easy way: stop participating in it.   Noam Chomsky

The truth is that there is no terror untempered by some great moral idea.
                                                                                    Jean-Luc Godard

That the quiz show *Deal or No Deal* has been a hit in thirty-five nations, reveals that there are more international threats than terrorism and global warming.   *The Hollywood Reporter*

THEATRE

In New York people don't go to the theatre -- they go to see hits.
                                                                                    Louis Jourdan

The New York audience, the night I went, gave the play a standing ovation. A cynical friend maintains that Broadway audiences always do this to justify to themselves the mountainous cost of the evening out.
                                                                                    William Goldman

A good many inconveniences attend playgoing in any large city, but the greatest of them is usually the play itself.   Kenneth Tynan

You can tell how bad a musical is by how many times the chorus yells, 'Hooray.'   John Crosby

If your job is to leaven ordinary lives with elevating spectacle, be elevating or be gone.   George F. Will

In the theatre, people want to be surprised – but by things they expect.
                                                                                    Tristan Bernard

My favorite stage performance is the show I'm in at the moment. It's like being in love – you can't remember being in love with anybody else.
                                                                                    Carol Channing

I don't go to see sad plays. There are enough sad endings in life without
buying a ticket to one.   Joe Rauh

Love – and a bit with a dog. That's what they want.
                                      Philip Henslowe, *Shakespeare in Love*

One begins with two people on a stage, and one of them had better say
something pretty damn quick.   Moss Hart

Sometimes we go to a play and after the curtain has been up five minutes
we have a sense of being able to settle back in the arms of the playwright.
Instinctively we know that the playwright knows his business.
                                                          Anton Chekhov

Every now and then, when you're on stage, you hear the best sound a
player can hear. It's a sound you can't get in movies or in television. It is
the sound of a wonderful, deep silence that means you've hit them where
they live.   Shelley Winters

At last it was over, and the theatre rang and rang with the grateful applause
of the released.   Edith Wharton

Best performance of the year: Aston Villa v. Milan, September 1994
                                                          Alec Guinness

I think theatre should always be somewhat suspect.   Václav Havel

THEORY

The first time I came to the Comedy Festival some nutcase shot a bunch of
people in Tasmania. I thought, 'Oh, that's just Tasmania.' The second time
I came, some nut shot up Columbine High School. Now I'm here again,
and another nut just shot up a high school in Minnesota. If you can't see
the connection between me playing the Comedy Festival and mass murder,
you're no good at conspiracy theories.   Rich Hall

Ten geographers who think the world is flat will tend to reinforce each other's errors ... Only a sailor can set them straight. John Ralston Saul

Your theory is crazy, but it's not crazy enough to be true. Niels Bohr

No matter what occurs, there's always someone who believes it happened according to his pet theory. J. M. Martin

Generally, the theories we believe we call facts and the facts we disbelieve we call theories. Felix Cohen

Never worry about theory as long as the machinery does what it's supposed to do. Robert Heinlein

Whether or not you can observe a thing depends upon the theory you use. It is the theory which decides what can be observed. Albert Einstein

THINKING

—You know, Ollie, I was just thinking.
—About what?
—Nothing. I was just thinking. Oliver Hardy and Stan Laurel, *Jitterbugs*

If everybody thought before they spoke, the silence would be deafening. Gerald Barzen

If God had intended politicians to think, he would have given them brains. Sir Humphrey Appleby, *Yes, Minister*

A great many people think they are thinking when they are merely rearranging their prejudices. William James

Many highly intelligent people are poor thinkers. Many people of average intelligence are skilled thinkers. The power of a car is separate from the way the car is driven. Edward de Bono

You think too much! Clever people and grocers, they weigh everything!
Alexis Zorba, *Zorba the Greek*

Clear thinking requires courage rather than intelligence. **Thomas Szasz**

To think is to differ. **Clarence Darrow**

Men fear thought as they fear nothing else on earth – more than ruin, more even than death. Bertrand Russell

The trouble is that thinking looks like loafing. Who wants to pay people for daydreaming? **W. Somerset Maugham**

Thinking is harder work than hard work. **Leo Rosten**

I like to think of thoughts as living blossoms borne by the human tree.
James Douglas

If you make people think they're thinking they'll love you: but if you really make them think, they'll hate you. **Don Marquis**

It's much easier to do and die than it is to reason why. **G. A. Studdert-Kennedy**

The most difficult thing in the world is to say thinkingly what everybody says without thinking. **Émile-Auguste Chartier**

If everybody is thinking alike, then somebody isn't thinking.
General George S. Patton

Sometimes I sits and thinks, and sometimes I just sits. **Leroy 'Satchel' Paige**

An Untitled Book About Things to Think About When You Think You've Thought Enough **Leonard M. Foley, book title**

Man is not what he thinks he is, but what he thinks, he is.   Elbert Hubbard

A man is what he thinks about all day long.   Ralph Waldo Emerson

It is always good to spend part of each day writing down your thoughts. That way you will not have to bother others with them.
Sir Randolph Nettleby, *The Shooting Party*

Could it think, the heart would stop beating.   Fernando Pessoa

Think like a man of action, act like a man of thought.   Henri Bergson

Think before you think!   Stanislaw J. Lec

You can think as much as you like but you will invent nothing better than bread and salt.   Russian proverb

TIME

—What time is it?
—You mean now?   Tom Seaver and Yogi Berra

It's later than it's ever been.   Lotus Weinstock

Time doesn't necessarily happen in chronological order.   Douglas Adams

Time is not a road – it is a room.   John Fowles

Once upon a time when there was no time.   John D. Barrow

Time is what death needs to grow people in.   William Burroughs

Time sneaks up on you like a windshield on a bug.   John Lithgow

In the dark, time feels different than when it is light.   Friedrich Nietzsche

Half our life is spent trying to find something to do with the time we have rushed through life trying to save.   Will Rogers

No wonder they execute people at dawn. Who wants to live at 6 a.m.?
                                                        Hawkeye, *M*A*S*H*

Nothing puzzles me more than time and space; and yet nothing puzzles me less, for I never think about them.   Charles Lamb

Nothing very very good and nothing very very bad lasts for very very long.
                                                        Douglas Coupland

Time is a great teacher, unfortunately it kills all its pupils.   Hector Berlioz

It's actually tomorrow in Tokyo. Do you realize that there are people alive here in Minneapolis who are already dead in Tokyo?
                                        Ted Baxter, *The Mary Tyler Moore Show*

There is a time to live, a time to die, a time to laugh, and at no time are the three of them very far apart.   Spike Milligan

TOLERANCE

The highest result of education is tolerance.   Helen Keller

I used to think anyone doing anything weird was weird. Now I know that it is the people that call others weird that are weird.   Paul McCartney

To go through life without ever being converted to anything seems a mark of insensitiveness. The ideal world would be a world in which everybody was capable of conversion and in which at the same time the converts would admit the possibility that they might be mistaken.   Robert Lynd

Persecution was at least a sign of personal interest. Tolerance is composed of nine parts of apathy to one of brotherly love.   Frank Moore Colby

If you would have a hen lay, you must bear with her cackling.   **Thomas Fuller**

Tolerance is only another name for indifference.   **W. Somerset Maugham**

People tolerate those they fear further than those they love.   **E. W. Howe**

So long as a man rides his hobbyhorse peaceably and quietly along the king's highway, and neither compels you or me to get up behind him – pray, sir, what have either you or I to do with it?   **Laurence Sterne**

TRAGEDY

Tragedy is what happens to me; comedy is what happens to you.   **Mel Brooks**

A broken heart is never a tragedy. Only untimely death is a tragedy.

Angela Carter

At fourteen, you don't need sickness or death for tragedy.   **Jessamyn West**

The tragedy of life is what dies inside a man while he lives.   **Albert Schweitzer**

The actual tragedies of life bear no relation to one's preconceived ideas. In the event, one is always bewildered by their simplicity, their grandeur of design, and by that element of the bizarre which seems inherent in them.

Jean Cocteau

It's not the tragedies that kill us, it's the messes.   **Dorothy Parker**

TRANSPORT

The one thing that unites all human beings, regardless of age, gender, religion, economic status or ethnic background, is that, deep down inside, we all believe that we are above-average drivers.   **Dave Barry**

Our motor car is our supreme form of privacy when we are away from
home.   Marshall McLuhan

Everything in life is somewhere else and you get there in a car.   E. B. White

Is fuel efficiency really what we need most desperately? I say what we
really need is a car that can be shot when it breaks down.   Russell Baker

My aunt, thirty years a feminist, says, 'A car is just an extension of your penis.' Oh, I wish.

Tim Allen

If you elect me the first Jewish justice of the peace, I'll reduce the speed
limit to 54.95.   Kinky Friedman

The stop sign reminds us to slow our pace, take a moment's rest, and look
around. Therein lies a whole philosophy of life.   Philip Toshio Sudo

Don't Even Think of Parking Here   Police sign at a bus stop in New York

In the Third World, honk your horn only under the following
circumstances: 1. When anything blocks the road. 2. When anything
doesn't. 3. When anything might. 4. At red lights. 5. At green lights.
6. At all other times.   P. J. O'Rourke

I know that experts say you're more likely to get hurt crossing the street
than you are flying, but that doesn't make me any less frightened of
flying. If anything, it makes me more afraid of crossing the street.
                                                          Ellen DeGeneres

A pedestrian ought to be legally allowed to toss at least one hand grenade
at a motorist every day.   Brendan Francis

YES, this is my van. NO, I will not help you move.   Bumper sticker

I was hitchhiking the other day and a hearse stopped. I said, 'No thanks, I'm not going that far.'
Steven Wright

I'd rather have a goddamn horse. A horse is at least human, for God's sake.
J. D. Salinger

There isn't a train I wouldn't take, no matter where it's going.
Edna St Vincent Millay

The next train's gone.
William Porter, *Oh, Mr Porter*

Why do 'They' retain absurd distinctions between first and second class? Far more helpful if 'They' divided us into, say, talkers and non-talkers, or farters and non-farters.
Anon

I can never think of the time I spend idling in railway stations as lost; it's a waiting liberated from the three temporal vices of regret, anticipation or boredom, the weak echo of that bliss spent between lifetimes.
Don Paterson

He won't fly on the Balinese airline, Garunda, because he won't fly on any airline where the pilots believe in reincarnation.
Spalding Gray

I get airsick just licking an airmail stamp.
Eric Morecambe

Public transportation is for jerks and lesbians.
Homer Simpson

If God had intended us to fly, he wouldn't have invented Spanish air traffic control.
David Lister, *Red Dwarf*

If the airport is overcrowded with long delays, seek peace and calm in the airport chapel, which is usually an oasis of quiet and has plenty of space.
Carol Wright

Cruising – if you thought you didn't like people on dry land ... Carol Leifer

A child on a farm sees a plane fly overhead and dreams of a faraway place. A traveller on the plane sees the farmhouse and dreams of home.

Carl Burns

A luxury liner is really just a bad play surrounded by water. **Clive James**

You feel mighty free and easy and comfortable on a raft. **Mark Twain**

Bicycles have no walls. **Paul Cornish**

Bicycles are almost as good as guitars for meeting girls. **Bob Weir**

The fresh air, the exercise, the pleasure of a leather saddle between one's thighs. 'Bicycle smile' I believe they call it.

Virginia Craneville, *The Road to Wellville*

Progress should have stopped when man invented the bicycle. **Elizabeth West**

TRAVEL

My favorite thing is to go where I've never been. **Diane Arbus**

What's the point of going out? We're just going to end up back here anyway. **Homer Simpson**

The use of travelling is to regulate imagination by reality, and instead of thinking how things may be, to see them as they are. **Samuel Johnson**

If you look like your passport photo, then in all probability you need the journey. **Earl Wilson**

Is there anything as horrible as starting on a trip? Once you're off, that's all right, but the last moments are earthquake and convulsion, and the feeling that you are a snail being pulled off your rock.

Anne Morrow Lindbergh

Whenever I prepare for a journey I prepare as though for death. Should I never return, all is in order. Katherine Mansfield

A journey is like a marriage. The certain way to be wrong is to think you control it. John Steinbeck

All journeys have secret destinations of which the traveller is unaware. Martin Buber

We don't go anywhere. Going somewhere is for squares. We just go!
Marlon Brando, *The Wild One*

If you don't know where you're going, you wind up somewhere else.
Yogi Berra

There is a peculiar pleasure in riding out into the unknown. A pleasure which no second journey on the same trail ever affords. Edith Durham

Why is it the place you want to go to is always under the staple of the road atlas? Advertisement, Prudential Insurance

All roads lead to Rome, or so they say. Not the A57. I drove along it the other day and ended up in Worksop. Chas Newman, *Viz*

You've got to be very careful if you don't know where you're going, because you might not get there. Yogi Berra

It is easiest to lose your way in the forest after it is cut. Stanislaw J. Lec

The true traveller is he who goes on foot, and even then, he sits down a lot of the time. Colette

Everywhere is walking distance if you have the time. Steven Wright

He travelled in order to come home. William Trevor

The man who goes alone can start today; but he who travels with another must wait till that other is ready.　　　　　Henry David Thoreau

—Why do you always travel third class?
—Because there's no fourth class.　　　Interviewer and George Santayana

When you travel, remember that a foreign country is not designed to make you comfortable. It is designed to make its own people comfortable.
　　　　　　　　　　　　　　　　　　　　　Clifton Fadiman

No one realizes how beautiful it is to travel until he comes home and rests his head on his old, familiar pillow.　　　　　Lin Yutang

Sometimes a person has to go a very long distance out of his way to come back a short distance correctly.　　　　　Edward Albee

Most of us have to be transplanted before we blossom.　　Louise Nevelson

You can't see the whole sky through a bamboo tube.　　Japanese proverb

The real voyage of discovery consists not in seeking new landscapes but in having new eyes.　　　Marcel Proust

The end of all our exploring will be to arrive where we started and know the place for the first time.　　　　　T. S. Eliot

The road is better than the inn.　　　　　Cervantes

Every moment is travel – if understood.　　　Benjamin Disraeli

If you go only once round the room, you are wiser than he who sits still.
　　　　　　　　　　　　　　　　　　　　　Estonian proverb

TREES

I said to the almond tree, 'Friend, speak to me of God,' and the almond tree blossomed.

Nikos Kazantzakis

Trees are the earth's endless effort to speak to the listening heaven.

Rabindranath Tagore

If I thought the world were to end tomorrow, I would still plant an apple tree today.

Martin Luther King

I like trees because they seem more resigned to the way they have to live than other things do.

Willa Cather

We complain and complain, but we have lived and seen the blossom – apple, pear, cherry, plum, almond blossom – in the sun; and the best among us cannot pretend they deserve – or could contrive – anything better.

J. B. Priestley

The planting of trees is the least self-centered of all that we can do. It is a purer act of faith than the procreation of children.

Thornton Wilder

TROUBLES

The mass of men live lives of quiet exasperation.

Phyllis McGinley

There will always be something to ruin our lives, it all depends on what or which finds us first. We are always ripe and ready to be taken.

Charles Bukowski

There are three intolerable things in life – cold coffee, lukewarm champagne, and overexcited women.

Orson Welles

To great evils we submit; we resent little provocations.

William Hazlitt

How little it takes to make life unbearable … a pebble in the shoe, a cockroach in the spaghetti, a woman's laugh.   H. L. Mencken

No tyranny is so irksome as petty tyranny: the officious demands of policemen, government clerks, and electromechanical gadgets.   Edward Abbey

It's not true that life is one damn thing after another; it is one damn thing over and over.   Edna St Vincent Millay

When the tide of misfortune moves over you, even jelly will break your teeth.   Persian proverb

Treat all disasters as if they were trivialities but never treat a triviality as if it were a disaster.   Quentin Crisp

Men often bear little grievances with less courage than they do large misfortunes.   Aesop

Be master of your petty annoyances and conserve your energies for the big, worthwhile things. It isn't the mountain ahead that wears you out – it's the grain of sand in your shoe.   Robert Service

I think there is this about the great troubles. They teach us the art of cheerfulness; whereas the small ones cultivate the industry of discontent.
                                                                Mary Adams

If pleasures are greatest in anticipation, just remember that this is also true of trouble.   Elbert Hubbard

Troubles are like babies – they only grow by nursing.   Douglas Jerrold

There is nothing so consoling as to find one's neighbour's troubles are at least as great as one's own.   George Moore

Never trouble trouble till trouble troubles you.   English proverb

If you want to forget all your troubles, wear tight shoes.   *The Houghton Line*

When we are chafed and fretted by small cares, a look at the stars will show us the littleness of our own interests. Maria Mitchell

From troubles of the world I turn to ducks, beautiful comical things. F. W. Harvey

When a man laughs at his troubles he loses a good many friends. They never forgive the loss of their prerogative. H. L. Mencken

Bad is called good when worse happens. Norwegian proverb

Trouble is just the bits in between. *Doctor Who*

That which does not kill us makes us stronger. Friedrich Nietzsche

We say that we cannot bear our troubles but when we get to them we bear them. Ning Lao T'ai-t'ai

A youth was questioning a lonely old man, 'What is life's heaviest burden?' he asked. The old fellow answered sadly, 'To have nothing to carry.' Anon

Nothing lasts for ever – not even your troubles. Arnold Glasgow

TRUST

To be trusted is a far greater compliment than to be loved. Ramsay MacDonald

There is no substitute for the comfort supplied by the utterly taken-for-granted relationship. Iris Murdoch

It is sublime to think and say of another, I need never meet, or speak, or write to him: we need not reinforce ourselves, or send tokens of remembrance; I rely on him as on myself: if he did thus and thus, I know it was right. Ralph Waldo Emerson

You're my parents, for God's sake. Stop trusting me.

Berke Landers, *Get Over It*

I know God will not give me anything I can't handle. I just wish that He
didn't trust me so much.   Mother Teresa

Trust is for lovers. In politics there are only converging interests.

Jalal Talabani

My favourite quote is by Seneca: 'It goes a long way towards making
someone trustworthy if you trust them.'   Clive Stafford Smith

Distrust of authority should be the first civic duty.   Norman Douglas

Where large sums of money are concerned, it is advisable to trust nobody.

Agatha Christie

Once the trust goes out of a relationship, it's no fun lying to them anymore.

Sam Malone, *Cheers*

On one issue at least, men and women agree: they both distrust women.

H. L. Mencken

History is more full of examples of the fidelity of dogs than of friends.

Alexander Pope

One thing you can rely on about him: he can't be relied on.

Rachel Flax, *Mermaids*

We dare not trust our wit for making our house pleasant for our friend, so
we buy ice cream.   Ralph Waldo Emerson

Never trust anybody who says, 'Trust me.' Except just this once, of course.

John Varley

Trust in Allah, but tie up your camel.   Arabian proverb

TRUTH

The truth is like sunlight. People used to think it was good for you.

Nancy Gribble, *King of the Hill*

The real question is: How much truth can I stand?   Friedrich Nietzsche

The young man turned to him with a disarming candour which instantly put him on his guard.   Saki

A world of vested interests is not a world which welcomes the disruptive force of candor.   Agnes Repplier

All people know the same truth; our lives consist of how we choose to distort it.   Woody Allen

The truth has never been of any real value to any human being – it is a symbol for mathematicians and philosophers to pursue. In human relations kindness and lies are worth a thousand truths.   Graham Greene

Truth does not consist in never lying but in knowing when to lie and when not to do so.   Samuel Butler

The pure and simple truth is rarely pure and never simple.   Oscar Wilde

There ain't no truth. All there is is bullshit. Layers of it. One layer of bullshit on top of another. And what you do in life when you get older is, you pick the layer of bullshit that you prefer and that's *your* bullshit, so to speak.   Bernie LaPlante, *Hero*

Believing ourselves to be possessors of absolute truth degrades us: we regard every person whose way of thinking is different from ours as a monster and a threat and by so doing turn our own selves into monsters and threats to our fellows.   Octavio Paz

Anything more than the truth would be too much.   Robert Frost

No blame should be attached when telling the truth. But it does, it does.

Anita Brookner

There are few nudities so shocking as the naked truth.   Agnes Repplier

How awful to reflect that what people say of us is true.   Logan Pearsall Smith

Too much truth is uncouth.   Franklin P. Adams

The truth is often a terrible weapon of aggression. It is possible to lie, and even to murder with the truth.   Alfred Adler

The most important truths are likely to be those which society at that time least wants to hear.   W. H. Auden

It takes two to speak the truth – one to speak and the other to hear.

Henry David Thoreau

I never give them hell. I just tell the truth and they think it's hell.

Harry S. Truman

A thing is not necessarily true because a man dies for it.   Oscar Wilde

Believe those who are seeking the truth. Doubt those who find it.   André Gide

There are trivial truths and there are great truths. The opposite of a trivial truth is plainly false. The opposite of a great truth may well be another profound truth.   Niels Bohr

How often have I said to you that when you have eliminated the impossible, whatever remains, *however improbable*, must be the truth.

Sherlock Holmes

Never tell the truth to people who are not worthy of it.   Mark Twain

The road to truth is long and lined the entire way with annoying bastards.

Alexander Jablokov

It is hard to believe that a man is telling the truth when you know that you would lie if you were in his place. H. L. Mencken

I have a theory that the truth is never told between the nine-to-five hours.

Hunter S. Thompson

If it's not true, it ought to be. Italian saying

All great truths begin as blasphemies. Bertrand Russell

Things are not untrue just because they never happened.

Dennis Hamley

The course of true anything never does run smooth. Samuel Butler

Look, if you absolutely have to tell her the truth, at least wait until the timing's right. And that's what deathbeds are for. Chandler Bing, *Friends*

UNDERSTANDING

How the hell do I know why there were Nazis? I don't know how the can-opener works.

Woody Allen

I do not want the peace which passeth understanding. I want the understanding which bringeth peace.

Helen Keller

A student who parked her car on the University of Toronto campus found this note on it from the Great Communicator, Marshall McLuhan: 'You are parking in my spot. Please find another for yourself elsewhere.' The following day she replied to this note: 'Dear Professor, as you will realize, I moved. I am most grateful to you. Your note is the first of your writings I have fully understood.'

Sam Witchel

These are the moments of revelation which compensate for the chaos, the discomfort, the toil of living.

Virginia Woolf

—Some people say they can't understand your writing even after they read it two or three times. What approach would you suggest for them?
—Read it four times.

Interviewer and William Faulkner

You cannot speak of the ocean to a frog that lives in a well.

Chuang Tse

One should never condemn what one cannot understand.

Hans Suyin

That is what learning is. You suddenly understand something you've understood all your life, but in a new way … I want to take words as ordinary as bread. Or life. Or death. Clichés. I want to have my nose rubbed in clichés.

Doris Lessing

If you truly want to understand something, try to change it.

Kurt Lewin

If one is a master of one thing and understands one thing well, one has at the same time insight into and understanding of many things.

Vincent Van Gogh

You do not really understand something unless you can explain it to your
grandmother.
Albert Einstein

Anyone who has ever 'gotten it' by following some so-called method, has
gotten it in spite of the method, not because of it.
Lee Lozowick

Nobody can develop freely in this world and find a full life without feeling
understood by at least one person.
Paul Tournier

We sometimes feel that we have been really understood, but it was always
long ago, by someone now dead.
Mignon McLaughlin

It is difficult to get a man to understand something when his salary
depends upon his not understanding it.
Upton Sinclair

If you understand, things are just as they are. If you do not understand,
things are just as they are.
Zen proverb

One has not understood until one has forgotten it.
Suzuki Daisetz

Our brains are not capable of comprehending the infinite so, instead, we
ignore it and eat cheese on toast.
Jonathan Cainer

UNIVERSAL LAWS

If anything can go wrong, it will.
Murphy's Law

Most things get steadily worse.
Charles Issawi

If an article is attractive, or useful, or inexpensive, they'll stop making it
tomorrow; if it's all three, they stopped making it yesterday.
Mignon McLaughlin

The length of a country's national anthem is inversely proportional to the
importance of the country.
Alan L. Otten

Things are always getting better and worse in India at the same time.

Purushottam Lal

If there isn't a law, there will be.

Harold Faber

The more irrevocably something is discarded, the more urgently it will be needed after it is discarded.

James Caulfeld

A falling body always rolls to the most inaccessible place.

Theodore Bernstein

Anything you lose automatically doubles in value.

Mignon McLaughlin

No matter what happens there's always somebody who knew it would.

Lonny Starr

The easiest way to find something lost around the house is to buy a replacement.

Jack Rosenbaum

I never had a piece of toast
particularly long and wide,
but fell upon the sanded floor,
and always landed on the buttered side.

James Payn

If you drop a piece of buttered bread on the carpet, the chances of its falling with the buttered side down is directly proportional to the cost of the carpet.

Jennings' Corollary

Work expands to fill the time available for its completion.

C. Northcote Parkinson

Bombeck's Rug Rule: an ugly carpet will last for ever.

Erma Bombeck

Any liquid accidentally spilled doubles in volume.

Lady Curzon Cooper

No matter how radical a group may be, it will soon run into a more radical opposition once it assumes power.

The New York Times

Coles' Law: thinly sliced cabbage.   **Anon**

Every other driver is either stupid or crazy.   **Harold Faber**

A shortcut is the longest distance between two points.   **Charles Issawi**

Good parking spaces are always on the other side of the street.   **Claude Frazier**

Wood burns faster when you personally cut and chop it yourself.

Apple's Law

All tour buses arrive at the same time.   **Robert S. Crandall**

A late train gets later.   **William Dewan**

Vance's Rule of 2½: any military project will take twice as long as planned, cost twice as much and produce only half of what is needed.

Cyrus Vance

The more equally attractive two alternatives seem, the harder it can be to choose between them – no matter that, to the same degree, the choice can only matter less.   **Edward Fredkin's Paradox**

The tendency of an event to occur varies inversely with one's preparation for it.   **David Searls**

If the shoe fits, it's ugly.   **Anon**

The frequency of the occurrence of an event is inversely proportional to its desirability.   **Gumperson's Law**

No matter how many rooms there are in the motel, the fellow who starts up his car at five o'clock in the morning is always parked under your window.   **Anon**

The first pull on the cord always sends the curtains in the wrong direction.

Anon

If a thing is done wrong often enough, it becomes right.   **Leahy's Law**

The only dependable law of life – everything is always worse than you thought it was going to be.   **Dorothy Parker**

Daughters can spend ten per cent more than a man can make in any usual occupation.   **Jubal Harshaw**

Anybody who gets away with something will come back to get away with a little bit more.   **Harold Schonberg**

If you try hard enough, you can always manage to boot yourself in the posterior.   **A. J. Liebling**

A memo is written not to inform the reader but to protect the writer.

Dean Acheson

Fig Newton's Law: when you have been thinking all day about that box of cookies on the kitchen shelf, someone will finish the last cookie minutes before you get home.   **G. O. B. Drews**

Any money left over will be needed tomorrow to pay an unexpected bill.

Anon

Most people do not go to the dentist until they have a toothache; most societies do not reform abuses until the victims begin to make life uncomfortable for others.   **Charles Issawi**

People will accept your idea much more readily if you tell them Benjamin Franklin said it first.   **David H. Comins**

There is a major scandal in American political life every 50 years: Grant's in 1873, Teapot Dome in 1923, Watergate in 1973. Nail down your seats for 2023.   **Richard Strout**

UNIVERSE

The universe is merely a fleeting idea in God's mind – a pretty uncomfortable thought, particularly if you've just made a down payment on a house.
                                                                    Woody Allen

The universe may have a purpose, but nothing we know suggests that, if so, this purpose has any similarity to ours.
                                                            Bertrand Russell

Had I been present at the creation, I would have given some useful hints for the better ordering of the universe.
                                            King Alfonso the Wise of Castile

The more comprehensible the universe becomes the more pointless it seems.
                                                            Steven Weinburg

In answer to the question of why it happened, I offer the modest proposal that our Universe is simply one of those things which happen from time to time.
                                                            Edward P. Tryon

The universe was a vast machine yesterday, it is a hologram today. Who knows what intellectual rattle we'll be shaking tomorrow.
                                                                R. D. Laing

The universe isn't run on the point system. And survival isn't what it's all about. Do what you're going to do; and with humor be aware that you might as well be doing the opposite.
                                                                R. K. Welsh

Listen, there's a hell of a good universe next door: let's go.
                                                            E.E. Cummings

UNIVERSITY

The only result my father got for his money was the certainty that his son had laid faultlessly the foundation of a system of heavy drinking and could be always relied upon to make a break of at least twenty-five even with a bad cue.
                                                            Flann O'Brien

I sincerely believe that if university education were universally available and availed of, the country would collapse in one generation.

Flann O'Brien

The greatest gift that Oxford gives her sons is, I truly believe, a genial irreverence toward learning, and from that irreverence love may spring.

Robertson Davies

Colleges hate geniuses, just as convents hate saints.   Ralph Waldo Emerson

Grad school is the snooze button on the alarm clock of life.   John Rogers

I learned three important things in college: to use a library, to memorize quickly and visually, to drop asleep any time given a horizontal surface and fifteen minutes. What I could not learn was to think creatively on schedule.

Agnes de Mille

Young people at universities study to achieve knowledge and not to learn a trade. We must all learn how to support ourselves, but we must also learn how to live. We need a lot of engineers in the modern world, but we do not want a world of modern engineers.   Winston Churchill

Going to college offered me the chance to play football for four more years.

Ronald Reagan

There was an old cannibal whose stomach suffered from so many disorders that he could only digest animals that had no spines. Thus, for years, he subsisted only upon university professors.   Louis Phillips

You are educated. Your certification is in your degree. You may think of it as the ticket to the good life. Let me ask you to think of an alternative. Think of it as your ticket to change the world.   Tom Brokaw

I went to the University of Life and was chucked out.   Peter Cook

VEGETARIAN

Why we ourselves are the living graves of murdered beasts, how can we expect any ideal conditions on this earth? George Bernard Shaw

Nothing will benefit human health and increase the chances for survival of life on earth as much as the evolution to a vegetarian diet. Albert Einstein

Vegetarian: a person who eats only side dishes. Gerald Lieberman

I don't myself believe that ... we have the right to kill animals. I know I would not have the right to kill you, however painlessly, just because I liked your flavour, and I am not in a position to judge that your life is worth more to you than the animal's to it. Brigid Brophy

You have just dined, and however scrupulously the slaughterhouse is concealed in the graceful distance of miles, there is complicity.
Ralph Waldo Emerson

Animals are my friends ... and I don't eat my friends. George Bernard Shaw

I'm a level five vegan. I don't eat anything that casts a shadow.
Jesse Grass, *The Simpsons*

I am not a *complete* vegetarian. I eat only animals that have died in their sleep. George Carlin

Are there any vegetarians among cannibals? Stanislaw J. Lec

VICE AND VIRTUE

—You no longer smoke, drink or do drugs – are you happier?
—I'm miserable as sin. Jonathan Ross and Ozzy Osbourne

You bet I did. And I enjoyed it. Michael Bloomberg

Vice is its own reward. **Quentin Crisp**

Vice is nice, but liquor is quicker. **Dorothy Parker**

Lust is the craving for salt of a man who is dying of thirst. **Friedrich Buechner**

Virtue consists in avoiding scandal and venereal disease. **Robert Cecil**

Virtue is praised but hated. People run away from it, for it is ice cold and in this world you must keep your feet warm. **Denis Diderot**

A vice is merely a pleasure to which somebody has objected. **Robin Skelton**

Virtue has its own reward but no sale at the box office. **Mae West**

Often devotion to virtue arises from sated desire. **Laurence Hope**

All the Christian virtues rolled into one make a ball that won't bounce.
Nigel Nicolson

It is good to be without vices, but it is not good to be without temptations.
Walter Bagehot

The extremes of vice and virtue are alike detestable; absolute virtue is as sure to kill a man as absolute vice is. **Samuel Butler**

VIOLENCE

Sometimes it seems like this is the choice – either kick ass or kiss ass.
James Caan

When I was a kid my father told me, 'Never hit anyone in anger – unless you're absolutely sure you can get away with it.' **Russell Ziskey, *Stripes***

Violence is the last refuge of the incompetent. **Isaac Asimov**

Nothing is so dangerous as that of violence employed by well-meaning people for beneficial objects.

Alexis de Tocqueville

Violence is the repartee of the illiterate.

George Bernard Shaw

Violence is as American as cherry pie.

H. Rap Brown

Whipping and abuse are like laudanum; you have to double the dose as the sensibilities decline.

Harriet Beecher Stowe

Poverty is the worst form of violence.

Mahatma Gandhi

Never strike your wife – even with a flower.

Hindu proverb

VOTE

Vote Quimby. If you were running for mayor, he'd vote for you.

Campaign slogan for Mayor Quimby, *The Simpsons*

If one man offers you democracy and another offers you a bag of grain, at what stage of starvation will you prefer the grain to the vote?

Bertrand Russell

Voting is a civic sacrament.

Theodore Hesburgh

Bad officials are elected by good citizens who do not vote.   George J. Nathan

What a Woman may be, and yet not have the Vote: mayor, nurse, mother, doctor, teacher, factory hand. What a Man may have been and yet not lose the Vote: convict, lunatic, proprietor of white slaves, unfit for service, drunkard.

Poster, British Women's Suffrage Campaign, c. 1901

WAR

Never think that war, no matter how necessary, nor how justified, is not a crime.   Ernest Hemingway

How is the world ruled and how do wars start? Diplomats tell lies to journalists and then believe what they read.   Karl Kraus

What a country calls its vital economic interests are not the things which enable its citizens to live, but the things which enable it to make war. Petrol is more likely than wheat to be a cause of international conflict.
                                                            Simone Weil, 1949

CNN said that after the war, there is a plan to divide Iraq into three parts: regular, premium and unleaded.   Jay Leno

We have war when at least one of the parties to a conflict wants something more than it wants peace.   Jeane Kirkpatrick

No matter what rallying cries the orators give to the idiots who fight, no matter what noble purposes they assign to wars, there is never but one reason for a war. And that is money. All wars are in reality money squabbles.   Margaret Mitchell

If we fix it so's you can't make money on war, we'll all forget what we're killing folks for.   Woody Guthrie

When the rich make war, it's the poor that die.   Jean-Paul Sartre

I don't believe that the big men, the politicians and capitalists alone, are guilty of war. Oh no, the little man is just as guilty, otherwise the peoples of the world would have risen in revolt long ago!   Anne Frank

It is impossible to give a soldier a good education without making him a deserter. His natural foe is the government that drills him.
                                                        Henry David Thoreau

Naturally the common people don't want war ... But after all it is the leaders of a country who determine policy, and it is always a simple matter to drag the people along ... All you have to do is tell them they are being attacked, and denounce the pacifists for lack of patriotism and exposing the country to danger. Hermann Goering, 1936

Jaw-jaw is better than war-war. Harold Macmillan

The belief in the possibility of a short decisive war appears to be one of the most ancient and dangerous of human illusions. Robert Lynd

If there is a God, the phrase that must disgust him is – holy war. Steve Allen

Who would Jesus bomb? American bumper sticker

Wouldn't it be great if wars could be fought by the same assholes who started them? The Postman, *The Postman*

There are certain rules about a war and rule number one is that young men die.
Henry Blake, *M*A*S*H*

I would no more teach children military training than teach them arson, robbery, or assassination. Eugene Victor Dabs

The professional military mind is by necessity an inferior and unimaginative mind; no man of high intellectual quality would willingly imprison his gifts in such a calling. H. G. Wells

When you join the Parachute Regiment they send you on training and initiation exercises. One of the tasks is to accept and care for a pet white rabbit. The young squaddie has to feed, brush, stroke and comfort his rabbit for a week, and become attached to it. Then he has to shoot it.
Matthew Parris

The aim of military training is not just to prepare men for battle, but to make them long for it. Louis Simpson

Those who fought know a secret about themselves, and it is not very nice. They have experienced secretly and privately their natural human impulse towards sadism and brutality ... Not only did I learn to kill with a noose of piano wire put around someone's neck from behind, but I learned to enjoy the prospect of killing that way. Paul Fussell

I love the smell of napalm in the morning.

Lt Colonel Bill Kilgore, *Apocalypse Now*

It is well that war is so terrible, else we should grow too fond of it. General Robert E. Lee, *Gods and Generals*

Seems nothing draws men together like killing other men. Susan Glaspell

Men love war because it allows them to look serious. Because it is the one thing that stops women laughing at them. John Fowles

Men do not fight for flag or country, for the Marine Corps or glory or any other abstraction. They fight for one another. William Manchester

Everything you do in a war is crime in peace. Helen McCloy

We hear war called murder. It is not: it is suicide. Ramsay MacDonald

Death has a tendency to encourage a depressing view of war. Donald Rumsfeld

I just don't know why they're shooting at us. All we want to do is bring them democracy and white bread. Transplant the American dream. Freedom. Achievement. Hyperacidity. Affluence. Flatulence. Technology. Tension. The inalienable right to an early coronary sitting at your desk while plotting to stab your boss in the back. Hawkeye, *M*A*S*H*

—By the way, what war is this?
—The latest war to end all wars.   Col Sherman T. Potter and Hawkeye, *M*A*S*H*

Only the dead have seen the end of war.   George Santayana

In the long run all battles are lost, and so are all wars.   H. L. Mencken

You can no more win a war than you can win an earthquake.   Jeannette Rankin

The only way to win a war is to prevent it.   George Marshall

Victory is a word to describe who is left alive in the ruins.   Lyndon B. Johnson

In war, there are no unwounded soldiers.   José Narosky

War creates peace like hate creates love.   David L. Wilson

The nuclear bomb took all the fun out of war.   Edward Abbey

A great war leaves the country with three armies – an army of cripples, an army of mourners, and an army of thieves.   German proverb

In the nuclear war, the true enemy is war itself.   Ron Hunter, *Crimson Tide*

A Pentagon official once said the people who would actually push the button probably have never seen a person die. He said the only hope – and it's a strange thought – is if they put the button to launch the nuclear war behind a man's heart. The President, then, with a rusty knife, would have to cut out the man's heart, kill the man, to get to the button.   Robin Williams

Cogito ergo boom. Susan Sontag

If any question why we died
Tell them, because our fathers lied. Rudyard Kipling

WEAPON

—I'd like to buy your deadliest gun, please.
—Aisle six, next to the sympathy cards.
Homer Simpson and Gun Shop Owner, *The Simpsons*

I want you to hold the gun like you're holding a beautiful white dove. Hold it firmly enough that it can't get away, but not so firmly that you can kill it.
Bree Van De Kamp, *Desperate Housewives*

I will not carry a gun … I'll carry your books, I'll carry a torch, I'll carry a tune, I'll carry on, carry over, carry forward, Cary Grant, cash and carry, carry me back to Old Virginia, I'll even hari-kari if you show me how, but I will not carry a gun! **Hawkeye,** *M*A*S*H*

The interesting thing about staring down a gun barrel is how small the hole is where the bullet comes out, yet what a big difference it would make in your social schedule. P. J. O'Rourke

—Sorry, the law requires a five-day waiting period. We've got to run a background check.
—Five days? But I'm mad now!
Gun Shop Owner and Homer Simpson, *The Simpsons*

When French surrealist dramatist, Alfred Jarry, was reprimanded by a woman for firing his pistol close to her child, who might have been killed, he calmly replied, 'Madame, I would have given you another.' Frank Stone

Remember, guns don't kill people. Dangerous minorities do.
Gun Safety Instructor, *Family Guy*

I like a girl in a bikini. No concealed weapons.

Scaramanga, *The Man With the Golden Gun*

Praise the Lord and pass the ammunition! Howell Maurcie Forgy

Even an inaccurate missile is quite a deterrent. Caspar Weinberger

The most potent weapon in the hands of the oppressor is the mind of the oppressed. Steve Biko

The most powerful weapon on earth is the human soul on fire.

Ferdinand Foch

I'm all in favor of keeping dangerous weapons out of the hands of fools. Let's start with typewriters. Frank Lloyd Wright

Sometimes laughter is the only weapon we have.

Roger Rabbit, *Who Framed Roger Rabbit*

I know not with what weapons World War III will be fought, but World War IV will be fought with sticks and stones. Albert Einstein

WEATHER

We will never be an advanced civilization as long as rain showers can delay the launching of a space rocket. George Carlin

Washing your car and polishing it all up is a never failing sign of rain.

Kin Hubbard

It always seems to be raining harder than it really is when you look at the weather through the window. John Lubbock

I think rain is as necessary to my mind as to vegetation. My very thoughts become thirsty, and crave moisture. John Burroughs

Timing has a lot to do with the outcome of a rain dance. Texas Bix Bender

It is one of the secrets of Nature in its mood of mockery that fine weather lays heavier weight on the mind and hearts of the depressed and the inwardly tormented than does a really bad day with dark rain snivelling continuously and sympathetically from a dirty sky. Muriel Spark

There is also an insulting speech about 'one grey day just like another'. You might as well talk about one green tree like another. G. K. Chesterton

It shone on everyone, whether they had a contract or not. The most democratic thing I'd ever seen, that California sunshine. Angela Carter

No umbrella, getting soaked, I'll just use the rain as my raincoat. Daito Kokushi

The wisdom of a single snowflake outweighs the wisdom of a million meteorologists. Francis Bacon

A day without sunshine is like, you know, night. Steve Martin

WIN AND LOSE

I've distilled everything to one simple principle: win or die. Marquise de Merteuil, *Dangerous Liaisons*

There's nothing to winning, really. That is, if you happen to be blessed with a keen eye, and agile mind, and no scruples whatsoever. Alfred Hitchcock

If you can play as if it means nothing when it means everything, then you are hard to beat. Steve Davis

Winning doesn't really matter as long as you win. Vinnie Jones

Winning is a habit. Unfortunately, so is losing. Vince Lombardi

Losses are always a relief. They take a great burden off me, make me feel more normal. If I win several tournaments in a row I get so confident I'm in a cloud. A loss gets me eager again.   Chris Evert

Finish last in your league and they call you idiot. Finish last in medical school and they call you doctor.   Abe Lemons

Win as if you were used to it, lose as if you enjoyed it for a change.
                                                        Ralph Waldo Emerson

Winning is overrated. The only time it is really important is in surgery and war.   Al McGuire

Supporting the English cricket team is like supporting a second division football team. I support Norwich City football team and when they lose I really don't mind because I expect them to; but when we win I'm *so* happy – much happier than any Arsenal supporter could ever be.   Stephen Fry

A gold medal is a wonderful thing, but if you're not enough without one, you'll never be enough with one.   Irv Blitzer, *Cool Runnings*

WISDOM

Who is wise? One who learns from all.   Rabbi Ben Zoma

Wisdom is the principal thing; therefore get wisdom; and with thy getting get understanding.   *Bible*, Proverbs

Better a drop of wisdom than an ocean of gold.   Greek proverb

Never mistake knowledge for wisdom. One helps you make a living; the other helps you make a life.   Sandra Carey

Wisdom is knowledge which has become a part of one's being.
                                                        Orison Swett Marden

The sublimity of wisdom is to do those things living, which are to be desired when dying.   Norman Douglas

Raphael paints wisdom, Handel sings it, Phidias carves it, Shakespeare writes it, Wren builds it, Columbus sails it, Luther preaches it, Washington arms it, Watt mechanizes it.   Ralph Waldo Emerson

There often seems to be a playfulness to wise people, as if either their equanimity has as its source this playfulness or the playfulness flows from the equanimity; and they can persuade other people who are in a state of agitation to calm down and manage a smile.   Edward Hoagland

Wisdom is a life that knows it is living.   Moravian prayer book

Wisdom is to the soul what health is to the body.   La Rochefoucauld

Wisdom is the quality that keeps you from getting into situations where you need it.   Doug Larson

If there's one thing I can't bear, it's people who are wise during the event.
                    Kenneth Tynan

It's so simple to be wise. Just think of something stupid to say and say the opposite.   Sam Levenson

The day the child realizes that all adults are imperfect, he becomes an adolescent; the day he forgives them, he becomes an adult; the day he forgives himself, he becomes wise.   Alden Nowlan

Three things it is best to avoid: a strange dog, a flood, and a man who thinks he is wise.   Welsh proverb

Be happy. It's one way of being wise.   Colette

The well bred contradict other people. The wise contradict themselves.

Oscar Wilde

The wise man can pick up a grain of sand and envision a whole universe. But the stupid man will just lay down on some seaweed and roll around in it until he's completely draped in it. Then he'll stand up and go, 'Hey, I'm Vine Man.'

Jack Handey

The obscure man's reflections may be as wise as the rich cheese-maker's, on everything but cheese.

Henry S. Haskins

It is unwise to be too sure of one's own wisdom. It is healthy to be reminded that the strongest might weaken and the wisest might err.

Mahatma Gandhi

In seeking wisdom the first step is silence, the second: listening, the third: remembering, the fourth: practising, the fifth: teaching others.

Solomon Ibn Gabirol

He swallowed a lot of wisdom, but all of it seems to have gone down the wrong way.

Georg Christoph Lichtenberg

When an ordinary man attains knowledge, he is a sage; when a sage attains understanding, he is an ordinary man.

Zen saying

The only true wisdom is knowing you know nothing.

Socrates

One's first step in wisdom is to question everything and one's last is to come to terms with everything.

Georg Christoph Lichtenberg

WISH

A wish is a desire without an attempt.
Farmer's Digest

If wishes were horses, beggars would ride and all the world be drowned in pride.
Scottish proverb

Never grow a wishbone where your backbone ought to be.
Anon

Mine is a most peaceable disposition. My wishes are a humble cottage with a thatched roof, but a good bed, good food, the freshest milk and butter, flowers before my window, and a few fine trees before my door; and if God wants to make my happiness complete, He will grant me the joy of seeing some six or seven of my enemies hanging from those trees.
Heinrich Heine

Few people know so clearly what they want. Most people can't even think what to hope for when they throw a penny in the fountain.
Barbara Kingsolver

WOMEN

Sure God created man before woman, but then again you always make a rough draft before creating the final masterpiece.
Robert Bloch

Ah, women. They make the highs higher and the lows more frequent.
Friedrich Nietzsche

There are only two types of women: goddesses and doormats.
Pablo Picasso

We are thinking of a woman when we generalize about women.
Roman Doubleday

Women have very little idea how much men hate them.
Germaine Greer

I hate women because they always know where things are.
Voltaire

There is only one woman in the world. One woman, with many faces.

Nikos Kazantzakis

Husbands think we should know where everything is – like the uterus is a tracking device. He asks me, 'Roseanne, do we have any Cheerios left?' Like he can't go over to the sofa cushion and lift it himself.   Roseanne

Feminine intuition, a quality perhaps even rarer in women than in men.

Ada Leverson

My wife has a black belt in body language.   Daren King

You can never get a woman to sit down and listen to a drum solo.

Clive James

Most women who have done something with their lives have been disliked by almost everyone.   Françoise Gilot

Why are we still afraid of being *other* than men? Women are still in hiding.

Lucy Lippard

The especial genius of women I believe to be electrical in movement, intuitive in function, spiritual in tendency.   Margaret Fuller

It is a marvellous thing to be physically a woman if only to know the marvels of a man.   Marya Mannes

Does giving birth make me a real woman? No, earning less than a man makes me a real woman.   Suzy Berger

In spite of my thirty years of research into the feminine soul, I have not been able to answer the question, 'What does a woman want?'   Sigmund Freud

What does a woman want? More.   Chris Evans

I am interested to see how many young women share the illusion that
a woman goes any faster when she runs than she does walking.

George Lyttleton

—The panel discussion is about The Ordeal of Modern Woman.
—You mean those two cars, automatic dishwasher, beautiful house in the
suburbs but Something's Missing? That Ordeal?   Peter De Vries

I've discovered what women want most in life, and it's fruit-scented,
sparkly lotion.   Jeff Scott

What do women want? Shoes.   Mimi Pond

What Women Want: to be loved, to be listened to, to be desired, to be
respected, to be needed, to be trusted, and sometimes, just to be held.
What Men Want: tickets for the World Series.   Dave Barry

Even if you understood women, you'd never believe it.   Frank Dane

Women are repeatedly accused of taking things personally. I cannot see any
other honest way of taking them.   Marya Mannes

My biggest fear is that there is no such thing as PMS and this is who I really am.

Carol Weston, *Empty Nest*

What I learned constructive about women is that no matter how old they
get, always think of them the way they were on the best day they ever had.

Ernest Hemingway

We love women in proportion to their degree of strangeness to us.

Charles Baudelaire

Every woman is a science.   John Donne

The more a woman is admired by a man for her achievements, the less easy it is for him to desire her physically, or to have her at all, without fantasizing about someone else.   Irma Kurtz

If a woman hasn't got a tiny streak of the harlot in her, she's a dry stick as a rule.   D. H. Lawrence

The trouble with women? Elbows.   Michael Caine

There is no female Mozart because there is no female Jack the Ripper.   Camille Paglia

Nature has given women so much power that the law has very wisely given them little.   Samuel Johnson

What, Sir, would the people of the earth be without women? They would be scarce, Sir, almighty scarce.   Mark Twain

Women are the survival kit of the human race.   Councillor Mandizvidza

A woman wouldn't make a bomb that kills you. A woman would make a bomb that makes you feel bad for a while. That's why there should be a woman President. There'd never be any wars, just every twenty-eight days there'd be very intense negotiations.   Robin Williams

Women always excel men in that sort of wisdom which comes from experience. To be a woman is in itself a terrible experience.   H. L. Mencken

Premenstrual syndrome: just before their periods women behave the way men do all the time.   Robert Heinlein

The myth of the strong black woman is the other side of the coin of the myth of the beautiful dumb blonde.   Eldridge Cleaver

You can have it all. You just can't have it all at once.   Oprah Winfrey

WONDER

Life isn't measured by the number of breaths you take, but by the moments that take your breath away.   Chinese proverb

There are certain scenes that would awe an atheist into belief without the help of any other argument.   Thomas Gray

If the stars should appear one night in a thousand years, how would men believe and adore!   Ralph Waldo Emerson

All wonder is the effect of novelty on ignorance.   Samuel Johnson

Our brains are no longer conditioned for reverence and awe. We cannot imagine a Second Coming that would not be cut down to size by the televised evening news, or a Last Judgment not subject to pages of holier-than-thou second-guessing in *The New York Review of Books*.
                                                John Updike

After fifteen minutes nobody looks at a rainbow.   Johann Wolfgang von Goethe

The process of scientific discovery is, in effect, a continual flight from wonder.
                                                Albert Einstein

The world will never starve for want of wonders; but only for want of wonder.   G. K. Chesterton

Every scene, even the commonest, is wonderful, if only one can detach oneself, casting off all memory of use and custom and behold it, as it were, for the first time.   Arnold Bennett

The universe is full of magical things patiently waiting for our wits to grow sharper.   Eden Phillpotts

If I had influence with the good fairy who is supposed to preside over the christening of all children, I would ask that her gift to each child in the world be a sense of wonder so indestructible that it would last throughout life, as an unfailing antidote against the boredom and disenchantment of later years, the sterile preoccupation with things that are artificial, the alienation from the sources of our strength.   Rachel Carson

I do not ask to see the reason for it all: I only ask to see the wonder of it all.
                              Rabbi Joshua Abraham Heschel

—Which of the Seven Wonders of the Ancient World would you have found in Babylon?
—The Hanging Baskets.   Nigel Lythgoe and Contestant, *The Enemy Within*

WORDS

My father still reads the dictionary every day. He says your life depends on your power to master words.   Arthur Scargill

If you have a big enough dictionary, just about everything is a word.
                                          Dave Barry

Words are, of course, the most powerful drug used by mankind.
                                        Rudyard Kipling

A word in a dictionary is very much like a car in a mammoth motor show – full of potential but temporarily inactive.   Anthony Burgess

Excuse me, but 'proactive' and 'paradigm' – aren't these just words dumb people use to sound important?   Conan O'Brien

If the English language made any sense, lackadaisical would have something to do with a shortage of flowers.   Doug Larson

Remember, the plural of 'moron' is 'focus group'.   James A. Wolf

The word 'now' is like a bomb through the window, and it ticks.

Arthur Miller

Saying 'I'm sorry' is the same as saying 'I apologize'. Except at a funeral.

Demitri Martin

Of all the words in all languages I know, the greatest concentration is in the English word I.

Elias Canetti

I wondered whether any woman could be happy with a man who says 'folderol'.

Peter De Vries

Footballer even more pleased than usual.

Crossword puzzle clue (Answer: Overmars)

There were nine buttons on her nightgown but she could only fascinate.

Homer Haynes

If Shakespeare required a word and had not met it in civilized discourse, he unhesitatingly made it up.

Amy Koppelman

The history of a culture can be determined by its untranslatable words.

Salman Rushdie

The right word may be effective, but no word was ever as effective as a rightly timed pause.

Mark Twain

A foreign swear-word is practically inoffensive except to the person who has learnt it early in life and knows its social limits.

Paul Theroux

WORK

This little box will be your home for sixty hours a week. It comes with an obsolete computer and a binder about safety hazards. Your challenge is to look busy until someone gives you a meaningful assignment.

Scott Adams

Noël Coward said work is more fun than fun, but then he didn't work in the Bird's Eye factory packing frozen fish fingers nine hours a day, did he?
Lily Savage

My job consists of basically masking my contempt for the assholes in charge, and, at least once a day, retiring to the men's room so I can jerk off while I fantasize about a life that doesn't so closely resemble hell.
Brad Dupree, *American Beauty*

You get a job. You become the job.
Wizard, *Taxi Driver*

The trouble with the rat race is that if you win, you're still a rat.
Lily Tomlin

Most of us have jobs that are too small for our spirit. Our real imaginations have not been challenged.
Nora Watson, *Working*

When people go to work, they shouldn't have to leave their hearts at home.
Betty Bender

I believe you are your work. Don't trade this stuff of your life, time, for nothing more than dollars. That's a rotten bargain.
Rita Mae Brown

Men for the sake of getting a living forget to live.
Margaret Fuller

The secret of success is making your vocation your vacation.
Mark Twain

School visits are something I do fairly often: I always say to the students that somebody has got to end up with the interesting careers, so why not them?
Julian Fellowes

The best career advice to give to the young is, 'Find out what you like doing best and get someone to pay you for doing it.'
Katharine Whitehorn

Hard work never kills anybody who supervises it.
Harry Bauer

Hard work is as damn near overrated as monogamy. Huey Long

Whoever looks for easy work, goes to bed very tired. Yiddish proverb

How do I work? I grope. Albert Einstein

My grandfather once told me that there are two kinds of people: those who do the work and those who take the credit. He told me to try to be in the first group; there was less competition there. Indira Gandhi

There's no end to what you can accomplish if you don't care who gets the credit. Florence Luscomb

The best labour-saving scheme I discovered is to have a file marked 'Too Difficult', dealing with matters which, in the nature of things, could never be solved or would solve themselves without human contrivance. It saves a lot of meaningless effort and unnecessary qualms of conscience. Stuart Blanch

A career is wonderful, but you can't curl up with a career on a cold night. Marilyn Monroe

Chanel was a workaholic. She must have had a lot to forget. Marlene Dietrich

I have so much to do that I am going to bed. Savoyard proverb

WORLD

I sometimes think that God will ask us, 'That wonderful world of mine, why didn't you enjoy it more?' Ronald Blythe

Any world that can produce the Taj Mahal, William Shakespeare, and striped toothpaste can't be all bad. C. R. McNamara, *One, Two, Three*

Great mother of big apples, it is a pretty world. Kenneth Patchen

Poets, painters and puddings; these three make up the world as it ought
to be. Richard Hughes

There are books in which the footnotes or comments scrawled by some
reader's hand in the margin are more interesting than the text. The world is
one of these books. George Santayana

The world is a rose; smell it and pass it to your friends. Persian proverb

The world began without man, and it will complete itself without him.
Claude Lévi-Strauss

It is not necessary to imagine the world ending in fire or ice. There are two
other possibilities: one is paperwork and the other is nostalgia. Frank Zappa

It happened that a fire broke out backstage in a theatre. A clown came
out to inform the public about it. They thought it was a joke and
applauded. He repeated it; people laughed even more. This is the way
I think the world will end – with general giggling by all the witty heads,
who think it is a joke. Søren Kierkegaard

The world is always ending; the exact date depends on when you came
into it. Arthur Miller

Do not expect too much of the end of the world. Stanislaw J. Lec

WORRY

A man gets on a train with his little boy, and gives the conductor only one
ticket. 'How old's your kid?' the conductor says, and the father says, 'He's
four years old.' 'He looks at least twelve to me,' says the conductor. And
the father says, 'Can I help it if he worries?' Robert Benchley

I highly recommend worrying. It is much more effective than dieting.
William Powell

Worry is interest paid on trouble before it falls due. Dean W. R. Inge

It ain't no use putting up your umbrella till it rains. Alice Caldwell Rice

Worrying is the most natural and spontaneous of all human functions.
It is time to acknowledge this, perhaps even to learn to do it better.
Lewis Thomas

A person must try to worry about things that aren't important so he won't
worry too much about things that are. Jack Smith

Niche worrying is a means of conveniently organizing one's paranoia.
It's concentrating on a specific fear or phobia at an appropriate time, like
focusing on getting legionnaires' disease from inhaling steam containing
Legionella pneumophilia bacteria while taking a shower at the gym.
Cameron Tuttle

People get so in the habit of worry that if you save them from drowning
and put them on a bank to dry in the sun with hot chocolate and muffins,
they wonder whether they are catching cold. John Jay Chapman

Rule number one is, don't sweat the small stuff. Rule number two is, it's all
small stuff. Robert Eliot

I sometimes suspect that half our difficulties are imaginary and that if we kept quiet about them they would disappear.
Robert Lynd

Gentiles don't know how to worry. Stanley Kubrick

Funny, the moment you get someone else worrying, you stop worrying
yourself. Stanley T. Banks, *Father of the Bride*

There are only two things to worry about. You are either sick or you are well. If you are well you have nothing to worry about. If you are sick you have two things to worry about. Either you get well or you will die. If you get well there is nothing to worry about. If you die there are two things to worry about. Either you will go to heaven or hell. If you go to heaven you have nothing to worry about. If you go to hell you will be so busy shaking hands with all your friends, you won't have time to worry.

Mrs Richard Malone

I won't worry about that today. I'll worry about it tomorrow.

Scarlett O'Hara, *Gone With the Wind*

Worries go down better with soup than without.

Jewish proverb

WRITER

Seventeen publishers rejected the manuscript, at which time we knew we had something pretty hot.

Kinky Friedman

If you want to write ... you must lurk in libraries and climb the stacks like ladders to sniff books like perfumes and wear books like hats upon your crazy heads.

Ray Bradbury

My ideal job? Landlord of a bordello! The company's good and the mornings are quiet, which is the best time to write.

William Faulkner

If you asked someone, 'Can you play the violin?' and he says, 'I don't know, I have not tried, perhaps I can,' you laugh at him. Whereas about writing, people always say: 'I don't know, I have not tried,' as though one had only to try and one would become a writer.

Leo Tolstoy

Most people who seek attention and regard by announcing that they're writing a novel are actually so devoid of narrative talent that they can't hold the attention of a dinner table for thirty seconds, even with a dirty joke.

Paul Fussell

Writing is the hardest way of earning a living, with the possible exception of wrestling alligators.

Olin Miller

I always start a book for money. If you're married five times you have to.

Norman Mailer

A man's got to take a lot of punishment to write a really funny book.

Ernest Hemingway

The only advice I have to give a young novelist is to fuck a really good agent.

John Cheever

At the drabber moments of my life (swilling some excrement from the steps, for instance, or rooting with a bent coat-hanger down a blocked sink) thoughts occur like 'I bet Tom Stoppard doesn't have to do this' or 'There is no doubt David Hare would have deputed this to an underling'.

Alan Bennett

The only reason I didn't kill myself after I read the reviews of my first book was because we have two rivers in New York and I couldn't decide which one to jump into.

Wilfrid Sheed

I'm A Writer But Then Nobody's Perfect

Billy Wilder, epitaph

YOUTH

I'm not young enough to know everything.   J. M. Barrie

How ruthless and vile and hard and right the young are.   Hal Porter

The denunciation of the young is a necessary part of the hygiene of
older people, and greatly assists the circulation of the blood.
                                            Logan Pearsall Smith

—Did you experiment with drugs?
—When I was young and irresponsible, I was young and irresponsible.
                                        Reporter and George W. Bush

It is better to waste one's youth than to do nothing with it at all.
                                            Georges Courteline

It takes a long time to become young.   Pablo Picasso

Old and young, we are all on our last cruise.   Robert Louis Stevenson

ZEN

Zen is like looking for the spectacles that are sitting on your nose.

Zen saying

Zen is the unsymbolization of the world.

R. H. Blyth

Zen is to have the heart and soul of a little child.

Takuan

Zen does not confuse spirituality with thinking about God while one is peeling potatoes. Zen spirituality is just to peel the potatoes.

Alan W. Watts

INDEX